FRANCE

A Modern History

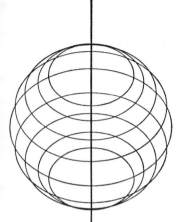

The University of Michigan History of the Modern World

Edited by Allan Nevins and Howard M. Ehrmann

FRANCE

A Modern History

BY ALBERT Léon GUÉRARD

NEW EDITION
REVISED AND ENLARGED BY PAUL A. GAGNON

Ann Arbor : The University of Michigan Press

A WILHELMINA
CE LIVRE
QUE NOUS AVONS PENSÉ
ET VÉCU ENSEMBLE
1905–1959

DC
38
G85
1969

The Biography of a Nation

France as part of Western culture.—History is the conscious, methodi-
cal, critical memory of mankind. It preserves, and often has to recapture,
the life of former days. Now, the life of our ancestors was made up,
like our own, of sickness and health, of labor, repose, and pleasure, of
ambitions and frustrations, of love and quarrels, and, in a degree singularly difficult to measure, of wonder, awe, and worship. These are the
essentials, under the changing pageant of customs; and in all this, governments play but a secondary part. Even today, educated as we deem
ourselves to our civic responsibilities, most of us give little time and
less thought to public affairs. We vote every two years on national issues,
we glance at a few items of political news, we listen for a few minutes
to a radio reporter, and feel that we have done our share. Man's chief
concern never was to support or overthrow governments. When he called
man a political animal, Aristotle meant gregarious or sociable. So political history, which for ages held undisputed sway, records but a small
part of our collective experience; certainly not the highest and best.

Even that small part, closely examined, is not sufficient unto itself.
The strivings and rivalries of individuals and groups would be of little
significance if back of their speeches, votes, intrigues, revolutions, and
wars, we could not discern great issues. It is the presence of such issues
that transmutes the crank, the busybody, the troublemaker, the bandit,
into a historical character. These issues become political; but they arise
from the very life of the people; they are problems of religion or economics, of human dignity, social status, collective security and welfare.
Political events have their roots in civilization and culture, the sum
total of a people's activities. Detached from these realities, the annals
of courts, armies, and parliaments would be futile. Two centuries ago,
Voltaire saw with his matchless clarity that if history is to be intelligent,
it must be all-embracing.

Today, the battle is won. We seldom mention the history of civilization as a special branch: it is taken for granted that all history is the history of civilization. The history of France is the history of the French people; and the history of the French people is the picture of French life in the past: how, through the centuries, men of all classes have worked, thought, felt, and prayed.[1] Such a record seldom emphasizes particular events; for the weft of generations is unbroken, and collective change is multifarious and slow. Events count only in so far as they affect the general course of life. By such a test, religious movements, inventions, discoveries, and even the masterpieces of art deserve our attention far more than, for example, the fall of the Molé Cabinet in 1839, the halfhearted War of the Polish Succession in 1735, or the shadowy figure of King Louis X, the Quarrelsome.

But if we accept such a view, the history of France dissolves altogether. For no great influence shaping the life of the French was special to France. Roman rule, the barbaric migrations, Christianity, feudalism, the growth of the cities and the guilds, the Renaissance, the Reformation, the classical age, the Enlightenment, the conquest of power by the middle class, the industrial revolution—all may be presented from the French point of view; but, although they may offer French features and a French coloring, they are not exclusively and specifically French. If we attempt to depict a "way of life," we shall find that both the period and the social class have far greater reality than the nation. Six hundred years ago there was a medieval mind rather than a French mind; there is a European mind today, sadly bewildered; and the confusion is at bottom the same in England, France, Italy, and Germany. At all times, a soldier, a monk, a scholar, a merchant, a peasant, each had a "way of life" imposed by his status, with differences sharper than territorial frontiers. In my youth it was easier, in Europe, to cross the boundaries of states than those of classes. When I wrote my first book on French civilization in 1913, I was aware that the title was a fallacy. I fully agreed, for once, with Houston Stewart Chamberlain, who had written: "There is a Chinese civilization, but there is no such thing as a French or German civilization." This idea was to become the center of Arnold Toynbee's monumental *Study of History:* the proper unit for our investigation is not the political state, but the civilization, in our case the western European.[2]

The nation grew with the dynasty.—Yet there is a reality called France: what fact is more solid than an ideal for which men are ready to die? That reality is not coextensive with a government: France has known many regimes in the long drama of her national existence, and only a cynic would dare to say that she invariably had the ruler she deserved. France is not identical with her territory, which has grown and at times shrunk in the course of ages. Nature never commanded that the Rhone, the Moselle, the Meuse, the Scheldt, should flow under two or more flags. Some of France's most patriotic provinces were late and reluctant comers into the great family. France never was a race: from remotest antiquity to the present day, many types are found among her sons. France, like all nations, is an increasing consciousness. She exists in the minds of men, because men have faith in her existence.

That faith, like all faiths, cannot be reduced to a single dogma. It is a complex, at times a confused, assembly of memories, interests, aspirations. To borrow the expression of her most inspired historian, Michelet, France is a person: but not even the simplest individual can be defined by a rigid formula.

Like all persons, France exists, not in the abstract, the absolute, the eternal, but in time. Eleven hundred years ago—a minute in the eyes of geologists, a second in the thought of astronomers—there was a Frankish Empire, but there was no France. It may be said that the birth certificate of the France we know bears the date 842. Then, at Strasbourg, two grandsons of Charlemagne pledged their aid to each other against their elder, Lothair. Charles the Bald, King of the Western Franks, spoke in German so as to be understood by the soldiers of his brother and ally; and Louis the German, for the same reason, spoke in Romance, which was to become French. The cleavage thus formally recognized proved irreparable. For two brief seasons (875–877 and 884–887) the unity of the Frankish Empire was precariously restored; thereafter, the two "nations" went their several ways. By that time Robert the Strong had already brought into prominence the line whose descendant claims the kingly title today.

But France did not spring into existence fully formed, clear-eyed, resolute. In the tenth century, she was but an infant, puny and of problematic future. Power and awareness grew together with many a setback. As late as the thirteenth century the South had a civilization of its own, more brilliant than that of the North; as late as the fifteenth it was still uncertain whether France would be linked with England under a common crown, and whether Burgundy would emerge as a separate realm between France and the empire.

It is the story of this increasing purpose called France that I propose to relate, how France grew, in territory, in organization, but above all in consciousness. This will be our sole guiding thread in the maze of events. The forces which affected France as an integral part of Europe will be taken for granted. My appointed task is to write the biography of a nation.

In the main, I accept the thesis of the modern Royalist historians: [3] undeniably, France grew with the Capetian dynasty. There was no pre-existing French people conscious of its destiny, and deliberately choosing or supporting its leaders in fulfillment of a collective ambition. The title of Julien Benda's book, *Sketch of a History of the French in Their Will To Be a Nation,*[4] is misleading. Such a will did not appear for long centuries, except in dubious flashes that posterity interpreted in its own terms: can the expression *doulce France* in the old epic, or the rejoicing over the victory of Bouvines (1214) be accepted as proofs of genuine national feeling? Even after its first manifestations, that will remained uncertain for ages. There was no will to become part of the French nation among the Flemings, the Bretons, the Basques, the Alsatians, the Corsicans, or even the people of Aquitania and Provence. It was the dynasty that made France; the dynasty was France; in Shakespeare's histories, France properly refers not to a country, but to a house and to a man. The words ascribed to Louis XIV were justified: the king was the state. He was not a figurehead, a living symbol; he was the legitimate master, the owner; land and people were his appurtenances. "Monarchy is integral nationalism."

So, in a very literal sense, the growth of France was the increase of the royal domain. On the other hand, France, ever since the close of the Middle Ages, has been more than a chance aggregation of provinces, like the sprawling possessions of the Emperor Charles V, or, until 1918, the ill-assorted dominions of the Hapsburgs. With the king as indispensable center, the sense of unity grew among the heterogeneous populations which are now France. Curiously, that feeling became if not clearer at any rate more massive, with a more irresistable momentum among the people than with the kings themselves.

Here I must differ from the Royalist historians who claim that the Capetians, however unworthy some individual rulers might prove, possessed as a race an obscure but infallible sense of their national mission. For generations, the kings gave away provinces as appanages to younger branches of their family, thus retarding and even endangering the process of national integration. The greatest threat to French unity came from the House of Burgundy, which had been endowed with land and power by the kings themselves. Many sovereigns squandered their efforts on enterprises which were purely dynastic and not national, such as the Italian wars or the War of the Spanish Succession. In their purely European aspect at least (and it was the only one of which the contemporaries took notice), the long wars of Louis XV were nothing but princely games. The French, as detached spectators, could jeer at the futility of the king's generals, such as Soubise; they had to pay the bill, but they felt free to hiss the show.

The king was surrounded by two classes, the feudal nobility, which had so long stood for disruption and placed its own privileges above any feeling of unity with commoners; and the solid body of public servants, mostly of bourgeois origin. The ruler could never quite make up his mind whether he was the first of the nobles or the first of the magistrates and administrators. Louis XIV kept a fair balance between the two elements: to the nobles, empty honors and the delights of court life; to the bourgeois officials, the reality of power. But when it came to a sharp decision, Louis XVI hesitated and, with faltering steps, took the wrong turn. No doubt France and the dynasty grew together until the glorious central years of Louis XIV; but, in the next century, the French people outgrew the dynasty.

The people as collective king.—By the time of the Revolution the monarchy was found wanting. If it was preserved for three uneasy years (1789–1792) and revived from 1814 to 1848, it was with a totally different character. The immemorial sacred glamour had paled: who could believe in Louis XV as the Lord's Anointed? The king was no longer the master, but the servant of the state, a servant who could be dismissed for incompetence. Mirabeau had uttered the decisive words which sum up democracy: "We the people . . ." [5] Then and then only the will of the French to be a nation appeared with full force. At that time "revolution" and "patriotism" were synonymous. It was not the creation but the emancipation of national consciousness. France had attained her majority.

The fact that the monarchical cause was supported by foreign armies could only intensify that feeling; kingless France had to fight for survival. But it also perverted the passionate assertion of collective personality. It made war, for the salvation of the country and the Revolution, the highest duty of the state. It turned France into a beleaguered fortress. For a moment it had seemed as though European unity, destroyed by dynastic conflicts, could be restored on a democratic basis. The French had turned their backs upon a past of pride and violence, renounced conquest, proclaimed the fraternity of all peoples. Even when war came, it was to be waged against tyrants only: the French armies were to bring liberty to the victims of oppression. But victory is an even worse teacher than defeat. By 1795—Napoleon Bonaparte, then a fledgling brigadier general, was not responsible for the change— the fraternal dream had faded. The nation accepted the heavy heritage of the kings, including the craving for expansion, prestige, hegemony. In the Middle Ages a city became a collective feudal lord, with moat and battlements, seal and pennon; in the same way, through the Revolution, the French became a collective Louis XIV.

For the last century and a half France has lived under a hybrid dispensation: the principles and traditions are still those of the monarchy, but the sovereign is, theoretically, Demos. For good republicans the state (*"We* are the State!"*) became more absolute than it had been under the Bourbons. Blind loyalty was transferred from a living symbol, the dynasty, to an abstraction, the Nation. France, a warrior queen, was ready to advance her interests, to defend her honor, to unsheathe the sword according to the code of princes. The diplomats of the stodgy Third Republic, such as Gabriel Hanotaux, sought their inspiration in the example of Richelieu. In his fierce assertion of nationalism, Clemenceau, like his Jacobin ancestors, was a better Royalist than the king, and that spirit survives no doubt in General Charles de Gaulle.[6]

But by the side of this monarchical tradition, Royalist or Jacobin, there lived through the centuries another one which had never forgotten the unity of Europe and the unity of mankind. The two often were strangely blended in the same heart. For the kings themselves, their fellow kings were "brothers," and in many cases actual kinsmen; the people were mere subjects. Joan of Arc's ultimate hope was that France and England, composing their quarrels, would unite against the infidels. Gallicans, eager to maintain the traditional liberties of the French Church, never ceased to be "Catholics," i.e., to raise their eyes above nations. The Revolution proclaimed the rights of Man, not the franchises and immunities of Frenchmen. Michelet and Hugo, ardent patriots, were also good Europeans, and world citizens. The fraternity of mankind appeared to them as the fulfillment, not the destruction, of national loyalty. In 1849, Hugo hailed the United States of Europe; in 1867, he wrote: "O France, farewell! Thou art too great to remain a nation." And Clemenceau told Pershing: "Above Paris, there is France; above France, there is civilization."

Thus, by a process far less mechanical than Hegelian dialectics, we see the national feeling growing out of the long habit of monarchical allegiance; and the world-wide view, implicit in all philosophies and religions, gradually superseding the tribal. Patriotism does not degenerate: it is both transcended and transfigured. England honors Edith Cavell as a great patriot, Edith Cavell, whose message was, "Patriotism is not enough."

We spoke of a birth certificate of the entity called France and suggested the date 842. Future historians will undoubtedly record the time when that glorious myth was buried by the wayside, while the people proceeded on its never-ending pilgrimage. Perhaps the date chosen will be 1946, when the Constitution of the Fourth Republic was adopted. For in the Preamble, France declared herself ready to accept limitations of her sovereignty for the maintenance of world peace: "Above France, there is civilization." The era of absolute nationalism, dynastic or democratic, is closing.

Eleven centuries: 842–1946! by the puny scale of man's life, a mighty aeon. And what a tale it unfolds! Gauls, Romans, barbarians; knights, crusaders, Schoolmen, master builders, and Louis IX, the holy king; Joan of Arc breathing the same air as Gilles de Rais; Louis XI, the cunning spider; Francis I in the glow of the young Renaissance; the bell tolling on the night of St. Bartholomew's; Henry of Navarre, the shrewd and gay, the Huguenot swordsman with a touch of Rabelais and Montaigne; Richelieu, steel under the red robe; Louis XIV in the fresh magnificence of Versailles; the era of Voltaire and Madame de Pompadour, that of Rousseau and Lafayette, the storming of the Bastille echoing throughout Europe, Louis XVI and Marie-Antoinette on the scaffold, Robespierre dedicating France to Virtue and the Supreme Being; Napoleon in Italy, Egypt, Moscow, St. Helena; the sphinx Napoleon III, better than his gaudy empire, between a glimpse of the millennium in 1848 and a vision of the apocalypse in 1871; the Marne and Verdun, Foch and Clemenceau; army and regime tumbling like a house of cards in 1940, the Underground, the Fighting French, liberation. . . . If such a saga is to end, as it must, let us close the book with reverence.

Personalities and myths as protagonists.—The definition of the subject —the growth of France as a nation—will determine the method of the work. I am not attempting integral history, the balanced picture of a whole civilization. I am deliberately reverting to the traditional kind, the chronicles of kings, the annals of those governments which, even though democratic in name, are still the blurred shadows of kings. To be sure, our concern will be with kings and governments only as symbols and instruments of national consciousness: we shall forego the merely picturesque and anecdotal. But in such a sharply defined field, incidents can be decisive, and individual traits should not be overlooked. Even the private virtues of Louis IX are relevant to our theme, for they enhanced the prestige of the monarchy, while the private immorality of Louis XV damaged it. Power and prestige play into each other's hands.

So mere episodes will have their place in these pages, even though unofficial and of small intrinsic importance, if they have significance in the development of our subject. We shall ignore Copernicus, Galileo, and Newton; but we shall relate how Louis XIV, at Marly, stooped to flattering the financier Samuel Bernard, to the consternation of an old-school aristocrat like Saint-Simon. The significance of events in the public mind does not depend upon a reasoned, scientific appreciation. It might be shown that the storming of the Bastille was but an empty gesture; yet the crashing of the old fortress resounded in Koenigsberg and in St. Petersburg. We have been told there was nothing decisive about the battle of Valmy: yet the French have endorsed the words of Goethe, "On this day, at this place, a new era begins in the history of the world."

It may even happen that the facts which shape the growing consciousness of a people are not material facts at all. Those grand myths, the monarchy, the nation, throve not merely on solid food like wealth and armies, but on delusions, legends, and lesser myths. Bishop Hincmar of Rheims, in the ninth century, gave a somewhat imaginative account of the baptism and anointing of Clovis by St. Remigius in 496. This romantic story inspired Joan of Arc in the fifteenth century; it lingered as late as 1825, when Charles X was crowned at Rheims according to the ancient rites. The Charlemagne and the Napoleon who live in the popular mind are very different from those of sober history, but they are of far greater importance in the traditions which form the core of national consciousness. For the life of a nation is an epic; and, as in the *Iliad,* gods or spirits appear and fight among men. The "Marseillaise" carved by Rude on a pillar of the Arc de Triomphe, the Spirit of 1792, is no less real to the French than the figure of Napoleon on the other pillar.

Reality and complexity of history.—This study of growth is founded on two assumptions: the reality of history and its complexity.

By the reality of history, I mean that change is not a delusion. Ecclesiastes wearily affirms: "The thing that has been, it is that which shall be." The historian's point of view is exactly the reverse: everything is new under the sun, for the flow of time is irreversible. History is not philosophy, which dwells among the eternal verities. I earnestly believe that, on a certain plane, the Preacher is right: if human nature changes at all, it is by a process so slow that it is imperceptible to man. The everlasting duel between the Angel and the Beast began with the first creatures conscious of their humanity; and, from the record, we cannot predict the victory of either. History, modestly, is concerned with more superficial problems. Customs and costumes do alter; so do vocabularies and techniques, and all the systems which strive to embrace the universe in their pathetic little arms.

This truism should help us ward off two delusions. The first is that of the medieval writers, and even of some classical historians, who seemed wholly unconscious of change. For Mézeray in the seventeenth century, for Anquetil late in the eighteenth, the court of Pharamond, the dimly known Frankish chieftain, was not essentially different from that of Louis XIV. The second delusion is that of the conservative theorists who, in their love of the good old ways, wish to dam the stream of life at a chosen point—1250, 1661, 1789. Paradoxically, some consider this refusal to admit change a triumph of the historical mind; in very truth, it is the negation of history.

By complexity, I do not mean simply multiplicity. Of course more events occur on any given day than could be recorded in all the books of men. Even the most exacting scholar must select a few samples from that loose mass, according to some rule or standard of his own. What I want to convey is that events never form simple and single sequences. They move on innumerable lines, which remain independent, coalesce, interfere, or even clash. We shall attempt to tell the story of France with the Capetian dynasty as a guiding thread. But even the most fanatical Royalist historians know that the kings did not work, could not have worked, alone. Geography helped them, or put obstacles in their path: rivers and mountains are among the dramatis personae. The predominance of France, the duchy between Seine and Loire, was if not dictated by Nature at least indicated and made possible by her. Royal history is quite different from ecclesiastical history; but we cannot forget that from its very beginning, the French monarchy was closely associated with the Church. The great University of Paris in the Middle Ages was not French, it was Catholic. But it developed there because of the wealth and charm for which the capital was already noted, while the schools of Chartres and Rheims withered. It conferred prestige in return on the city, the kingdom, and the ruler. Paris is as inseparable from the concept of French unity as kingship is. It might be said that there were in France two sovereigns, not always in perfect accord, the king and the capital. In the eighteenth century, Parisian society eclipsed the royal court. From 1789 to 1871 Paris was repeatedly a despotic leader, imposing fashions in dress and thought, sending revolutions ready-made to the provinces. When they rounded off their domains, the kings were satisfied with their personal overlordship and respected local customs; but the king's men, by a slow, barely conscious, invincible process, introduced into all parts of the land that standardization, that centralization, which ultimately were to triumph with the Revolution and the Empire. Arts and literature were fostered by the court, but they never were wholly dependent upon the court. The lines ascribed to Charles IX addressing Ronsard expressed a profound truth: the poet imparts, rather than borrows, greatness.[7]

Our story, therefore, has five or six protagonists, not one: the monarchy in the center, but also the Church, the cities, the writers, building up the nation against the disruptive forces, feudal nobles and foreign foes. History is an elaborate "point-counterpoint." The main theme—in this case, the growth of the national feeling—may be taken up in many keys and by various instruments. At times, the personality of the ruler is predominant: Philip Augustus, St. Louis, Louis XI, Francis I, Louis XIV, Napoleon imposed themselves upon their contemporaries and upon posterity; but Charles VI was mad, and Louis XV shunned the center of the stage. At times foreign relations, military or diplomatic, absorb our attention. At times the religious notes soar above the rest; at times it is the harsh voice of economics, as under Louis Philippe, the only regime in France that was frankly plutocratic. ("If you want a vote, get rich!") [8] At times the cultural elements assume the lead, as under King Voltaire.

The irreversibility of time and the infinite complexity of human affairs drive us to a conclusion which few of us are ready to welcome: there can be no law in history. At best, we may accept those vague recurrent patterns projected upon the events by such thinkers as Oswald Spengler and Arnold Toynbee. But a rule cannot be called a law until it has been checked experimentally, and experiment is impossible in history: the conditions can never be exactly repeated, a Second Empire cannot be the exact reproduction of the first. A purely mechanistic conception of the universe might lead us to accept an infinite series of identical repetitions, as in Nietzsche's nightmare. But this is neither science nor history: it is a metaphysical romance of the most dismal kind.

We work for causes today because we believe that several paths are open; so did our ancestors. Nothing proves that what did happen was alone possible. The thinker who asserts his belief in inevitability destroys the living, the dramatic, character of history. What we haughtily dismiss as a mere might-have-been was at one time a hypothesis which seemed worth testing. The defenders of doomed causes were not invariably blind fools. The men who died in opposing Hitler pitted themselves against the inevitable, since they died; it does not prove that their suicidal choice has no legitimate standing in history. The sole rule of the deterministic historian is *Vae Victis!,* woe to the defeated. That rule is not simply immoral, it is crude and unrealistic. Our sole task is to relate "what actually happened." But, if we do not want to mutilate history beyond recognition, we must never forget that, for the actors themselves, it might have happened otherwise. This quivering indeterminacy is the very essence of life.

It must be admitted that the grand historical symphony called France is full of discords. The moments of perfect harmony are rare and fleeting —a few years under Francis I and Louis XIV, a few months under the Consulate, a few weeks of "Sacred Union" in 1914. National unity never was an objective fact, but an act of faith: the substance of things hoped for and striven for.

It will be seen that the present study is not a compromise between the old-fashioned chronicle of rulers and the Voltairian history of civilization. It has a single theme: the biography of a nation, that is to say of a sentiment. But to bring that theme out every instrument is needed. The theme is definite, yet elusive. We cannot expect it to close with a grand triumphant chord. It ends only by being woven into a richer symphony.

Contents

MAPS

BOOK I

THE ORIGINS

CHAPTER I

The Foundations of French Nationality: Land, Race, Language

✍ FRANCE IN QUEST OF HER PAST

The France we know as a historical entity came into existence in the ninth century, with the disruption of Charlemagne's empire. The event, of such magnitude in retrospect, passed unnoticed at the time. The treaty of Verdun (843) which separated France from Germany and Lotharingia was not a new departure: it was the rule with the Franks to divide the royal dominions among the heirs. It took nearly half a century (843–887) for the partition to become final; both Charles the Bald and Charles the Fat restored the unity of the empire. It took another hundred years (887–987) for a new dynasty finally to supersede the enfeebled Carolingians. When, in 987, Hugh Capet was elected to the throne, no one could have prophesied that his descendants would rule for eight hundred years, and keep up their claims to the French crown for two centuries longer. Heredity was not then an established principle; and it was still possible either for the Western Empire to be restored, or for the French kingdom to be split up into independent principalities. The Capetian line endured, the domain increased, and France became a reality: a dynasty at first, then a nation.

With the growth of French consciousness came a desire to extend the life of the country into an ever-deepening antiquity. France attempted, at the same time and by the same process, to forge her future and reconstruct her past: roots grew as well as branches. The Capetians enhanced their dignity by considering themselves as the legitimate heirs of the Carolingians: so the first Louis in the new line chose to call himself Louis VI, and the first Charles, Charles IV. The Carolingians themselves had gradually supplanted the Merovingians; they had changed the person of the monarch, not the principles and traditions of the monarchy. Thus "French" history was extended retrospectively to the reign of Clovis, who conquered the whole land and was the first Catholic king.

Clovis himself was not a mere invader; if he had imposed his rule, it was by defeating the other barbarians with the aid of the Church and of the Gallo-Roman population. He accepted a Roman title, and was vaguely felt to be the heir of the Roman emperors. So "French" history stretched back another half millennium, to the days when mighty Caesar made Gaul a part of the Roman world.

By the end of the eighteenth century the French believed that they had formed a nation before the Franks swept over the land. The Revolution was interpreted as a movement of liberation from their "Gothic" oppressors, the feudal nobility. "Let us hurl them back into the marshes of Germany, whence they came!"

In quest of their past, the French did not stop at Roman Gaul. Not the Gallo-Romans, but the independent Celts were considered in their turn as the true ancestors of the French. Vercingetorix, the hero of Gallic resistance, became the first great figure in "French" history, instead of Caesar: in the same manner, modern Mexico erects monuments to Cuauhtémoc, not to Hernando Cortés. The Romantic movement, averse to the classic discipline of Rome and eager for the primitive, exalted the misty traditions of the Celts. This "Celtomania" was a sign of the state of mind which had caused the tremendous and prolonged success, in continental Europe, of McPherson's Ossianic poems. For a long while, the Celtic vogue was poetic rather than critical; but it was to inspire, in the last quarter of the nineteenth century, the scholarly work of D'Arbois de Jubainville. Only yesterday, noted historians like Camille Jullian and Frantz Funck-Brentano affected to consider pre-Roman Gaul as an incipient nation, whose promising development was arrested or warped by her brutal Roman masters. Here, for the present, this backward extension of the French nation must pause. No one so far has taken up the cause of the Iberians and Ligurians, subdued by a minority of fierce invading Gauls. Only poets dared to venture into pre-Gallic darkness: Ronsard, in the sixteenth century, traced back the origin of the French monarchy to Francus, son of Hector; just as Geoffrey of Monmouth, Wace, and Layamon had turned to the same fabulous past for the first rulers of Britain.

DID GEOGRAPHY CREATE FRANCE?

It was, however, possible to go beyond prehistory, and claim that Nature herself had fashioned France to be a nation: the figure of France on the map is a familiar and a harmonious one, while the outlines of Germany or Poland remain shifting and blurred. For those who indulge in that pleasing fiction, the opinion of the Greek geographer Strabo, who wrote under Augustus, comes as a godsend; for he detected in the territory of Gaul a balance and a unity so miraculous that they seemed to indicate a design. Centuries later, this conception was to harden into the doctrine of France's "natural" frontiers. The sophisticated age which believed so hard in "natural" law, "natural" rights and "natural" religion would welcome such an idea. It was the historical task of the French to restore the shattered masterpiece, to reconstitute the organic whole described by Strabo. The people (i.e., a few publicists) came to imagine that for a thousand years the nation never had any other thought: it was her manifest destiny. By the treaty of Basel in 1795, the goal was attained at last: it was the myth of the "natural frontiers" that caused the moderate plans of Lazare Carnot to be swept aside. The Republic had abjured all conquests; but in reaching her ancient limits, she was not annexing alien territory, she was only recovering what by right had never ceased to be her own. The treaties of Vienna (1815) which reduced France to her pre-Revolutionary boundaries, were resented as tearing apart the living flesh of the nation. As late as 1842, Victor Hugo, in the resounding political epilogue to his travel book *The Rhine,* urged Germany not to withhold from France what God Himself had given her, the left bank of the Rhine. Perhaps there was still a flicker of that romantic delusion, after World War I, even in as keen a mind as that of Maurice Barrés.

Strabo's happy dictum, with many variations, has become a commonplace, and not exclusively in books penned by Frenchmen. To an unprejudiced observer, it seems evident that the present figure of France was determined, not by the unerring hand of Nature, but by the fumbling hand of History. A country smaller than Texas, lying midway between the North Pole and the Equator, France belongs wholly to the temperate zone and is free from arctic or tropical extremes: within this very general and very fortunate character, she offers the widest range of aspects and climates. For hasty tourists, "France" evokes the lush valleys of Normandy, the delicate wooded hills which encircle the Parisian region, the parklike, quiet beauty of the Loire country, studded with castles which are gracious even in their mass and friendly even in their magnificence. But all France is not a lovely estate. There are rough-hewn parts, as impressive as any in Europe: the sheer unbroken wall of the Pyrenees, the Alps, no less wild and grand in Savoy or Dauphiny than they are in Switzerland, the weird volcanic landscapes found in Auvergne, the granitic bastion of the Breton coast assailed by Atlantic winds and waves, the still untamed Rhône [1] rushing to the sea, between jutting spurs crowned with ruined feudal fortresses. And there are parts of France too which are neither smiling nor majestic: marshy districts such as Sologne and the Dombes, gravel wastes in Provence, dreary treeless plateaus in Champagne, rich but monotonous industrial plains in Flanders. As with the land, so with the skies. There is nothing in common between the cool moist atmosphere of Brittany, and that of the Riviera or Corsica, under the sharp Mediterranean sun. Winters are mild along the whole Atlantic coast, but they are harsh in Alsace and the mountains. Our soldiers, in both world wars, used to smile bitterly when repeating the hackneyed words, "Sunny France!"

Everyone of the great river basins in France could have formed, and actually at some period did form, a sizable separate country, with at least as clear a right to national existence as Belgium or Holland. All that we can assert with safety (after the event) is that Nature opposed no insuperable obstacle to French unity. While the mountains between France and Spain or Italy were indeed formidable barriers, easy communications could be maintained between basin and basin. The Romans, after extending their rule along the Mediterranean shore, found no difficulty in reaching the valley of the Garonne: the Naurouze pass is so low (just over six hundred feet) that, as early as the days of Louis XIV, it could be used for a canal from sea to sea.[2] The Rhône and the Saône valleys provided convenient access into central Gaul. There, in what was to become Burgundy, a rich hilly province afforded not one but many alternative routes into the valley of the Seine. A fact of capital importance in French history is the existence of a commodious gateway, the wide corridor of Poitou, between the northern regions of the Loire and the Seine, and the Aquitanian plain. Had this "threshold" (*seuil*) been less inviting, the face of France would have been changed.

A mere glance at a relief map brings out a few essential facts which, however obvious, are apt to be overlooked. In the first place, France is not predominantly a southern country. She received her culture from Greece, Rome, and Judaea; and, for the last five hundred years at least, she has remained in close touch with the Mediterranean. But Provence and even Languedoc, attractive as they may be, offer only a constricted band of fertility between mountain and sea; and the Rhône valley is but a narrow corridor. The rich plains of France lie mostly in the Atlantic and northern watersheds. There, economically as well as politically, is her center of gravity. The dream of a Latin union, which flitted through the minds of Napoleon III and Marshal Pétain, is in contradiction to the geographic data.

That center of gravity is now Paris, and so it has been for perhaps fourteen hundred years. But here again, Nature did not impose a solution. Had the Mediterranean retained its primacy, Marseilles might have become the capital. Lyons was the official center of Roman Gaul, and remains the religious metropolis of France. If Bordeaux, Nantes, or Rouen had been chosen, at the farthest inland point that sea vessels could reach, they would not have been more eccentric than London, or Washington. There are no outstanding natural resources in the Parisian region; and, although the Seine is in the main a full-flowing, equable river, only small ships can use it above Rouen. But Paris is the actual center of a vast basin; converging rivers provide easy communications in all directions. Between the Seine at Paris and the Loire at Orleans, there is barely a ridge. This gave Paris, even in Merovingian times, a unique strategic and commercial importance, which increased with the centuries. Paris was an incomparable asset to the dynasty; but the benefits were mutual. The king's court might flit from castle to castle, or establish itself ten miles away from the city, but Paris remained the economic, administrative, intellectual center of the kingdom. France has manifestly outgrown her dynasty, but few are the Frenchmen who entertain the possibility that she might outgrow her capital.[3] In many ways, Paris is France: it is the Parisian stamp, superimposed upon local differences, that makes provincial cities truly French.

Finally, geography brings out the fact that a whole side of the French hexagon, the northeastern, is completely artificial. The present frontier, with minor adjustments, is the one that was reached in 1766, when Lorraine was "reunited" with France. There seems no reason to believe that it will be greatly altered. Had the ancient regime continued, the kings, in their oddly fitful yet persistent way, might have acquired here and there a few bits of territory: Luxembourg perhaps, or the Bishopric of Liège, or even the bulk of the Austrian Netherlands. From 1795 to 1814 the whole left bank of the Rhine seemed at least resigned to French rule. But it was late in the day for extensive conquests; national consciousness had already grown to such a degree that the miracle of Alsace could hardly have been repeated on a larger scale. The Rhineland in French hands would have become "unredeemed Germany," *Germania irredenta.*

As it stands, the northeastern boundary respects neither physical geography nor economic interests nor culture. It cuts across the Sarre, the Moselle, the Meuse, the Scheldt (Escaut). It keeps asunder iron and its natural complement, coal. It leaves with France Alsace, which unquestionably had a solid Teutonic substratum, and separates from

France the Walloon parts of Belgium. It is an indefensible compromise reached through sheer lassitude, and it will probably endure until all frontiers within western Europe have lost their tragic significance.

Indefensible in every sense, and especially the strategic. So the thought came to the French that Nature could be corrected, that a system of fortifications could be created, as impassable as the Alps or the Pyrenees: a modern Great Wall of China. But the Maginot Line had loopholes, and it did not extend clear to the sea. Even if it had been perfected from end to end, it would have been anachronistic against the new methods of warfare: it was a 1914 solution to a 1940 problem.

The plain fact is that, throughout the ages, the road to Paris could be barred against invaders only by a wall of human breasts. The valley of the Oise leads straight into the great northern plains, which extend indefinitely across the vast Eurasian continent. Isolation, splendid or sullen, could never be the goal of the French. Geography made it impossible for them to turn their backs at will upon the rest of Europe, and say, as the Spaniards, the English, and the Irish were repeatedly tempted to say, "ourselves alone!"

⬧ MODERN FRANCE NOT SELF-SUFFICIENT

Diversity, not unity, is the key word of French geography: France is the epitome of Europe. This variety enabled her to recuperate swiftly after the most tragic ordeals. Not, however, because she formed an integrated whole, in which the parts were harmoniously balanced; but because, until the nineteenth century, she was a mosaic of regions which, in a large measure, had remained independent and self-sufficient. It must be borne in mind that until the Revolution there were tariff barriers between the various units of the kingdom; some of the richest provinces, such as Alsace, were from the economic point of view considered foreign. In the nineteenth century political centralization, heavy industry, and the railroads conspired to knit France more firmly together. But just as France was achieving unity within her boundaries, she found herself no longer self-sufficient. Since the full impact of the Industrial Revolution, France passed in a single generation (1840–1870) from a local to a continental and even to a world economy. National *autarky,* the Utopia of the protectionists, never was more than a forlorn hope.

Legend will have it that France possesses inexhaustible wealth. This mistaken idea results from a confusion between the gifts of nature and the cumulative achievements of man. For many centuries, France had resources which were moderate, yet ample. She produced wheat and wine, fine breeds of horses and cattle, wool, flax, and hemp for her textile mills. Good building stone, timber, slate, or tile were not lacking for castle and cathedral, manor or farmhouse, and dignified city dwelling. Pockets of iron ore were found in many parts, of tolerable quality and easy to work. The vast forests, which once had covered most of the land, provided all the fuel needed for this simple metallurgy. So, in the course of ages, the well-tilled land acquired a modest but very solid affluence. Only yesterday, in remote districts, the homes of bourgeois and substantial peasants were well stocked with utensils and furniture that collectors would covet. But this is the flattering picture of a fast-vanishing era. In the last hundred years France has actually grown richer, if less secure in her taste; but it was at the cost of her boasted balance.

In the industrial world of today France has only two vital assets: rich reserves of iron ore and of water power. She is practically destitute of precious metals, of the main nonferrous metals except aluminum (bauxite), and of petroleum.[4] Her resources in coal are pitifully inadequate: in the most favorable years, she extracts some fifty million metric tons, not of the best quality or under the easiest conditions, not one-fourth of the normal yield of England or Germany, not one-tenth of coal production in the United States. That she managed to remain among the leading industrial powers in the world is a high tribute to her "know-how," a scientific and technical skill deeply rooted in the past and venturing boldly into new realms. But in order to survive at all, France must buy enormously and sell on the same scale. So France's organic self-sufficiency was but a fleeting vision: before 1789, she did not form a whole; after 1840, she could not longer afford to exist in economic isolation. In this harsh domain also the words of Edith Cavell remain true, "Patriotism is not enough."

THE RACIAL COMPONENTS OF THE FRENCH PEOPLE

If Nature did not make France, neither did she create or evolve a sub-species of *Homo sapiens* called the French. There never was a French race: even in prehistory various breeds, tall or short, long-headed or round-headed, lived side by side. Today, there is not even a French type; there are French manners, ranging from the exquisite to the atrocious. A blond Frenchman is no less authentic than a dark one; Frenchmen of high stature like Generals Giraud and de Gaulle may be as patriotic as diminutive Frenchmen like Adolphe Thiers. It has been aptly said that of two eminently French intellects, Voltaire and Renan, one was a bag of bones, the other a ball of fat. The stage Frenchman, small, dark, gesticulating, is a caricature of the southerner which amuses even the South: Daudet's *Tartarin de Tarascon,* or Pagnol's *Marius.* But provincial types themselves are misleading: Paul Valéry, with his masterly reticence, Marshal Joffre, with his massive calm, were both southerners. Renan was a Breton, but with a dash of Gascon blood; Barrès was of Auvergnat origin, but chose to be rooted in Lorraine; many Alsatians, like the Siegfrieds and the Herzogs, became Normans. It has been repeatedly noted that among prominent and "typical" Frenchmen, we come across such names as Archdeacon, Thomson, Hennessey, Clarke, Macdonald, Mac-Mahon, Wilson; or Kleber, Rapp, Schlumberger, Baldensperger, Koenig; or Gambetta, Zola, Brazza, Galliéni; or Heredia, Fernandez, Bernanos, Zamacois; or Zyromski, Strowski, Stryienski, Kostrowitzky; or, to close the symphony with a crash of cymbals, Papadiamantopoulos.[5]

Centuries before there was a France, the melting pot was already at work. But it never imposed a rigid unity, or established a dead level of indifference: it created a richer scale of values. At all times there were in France idlers and hard workers, aristocrats of the spirit and coarser minds (with no reference to social distinctions), lovers of peace and swashbucklers, timid souls clinging to their village, their class, their habits, their little hoard of gold, and adventurers in every field. If the bourgeois common sense of Boileau be adduced as typically French, the names of St. Bernard, Pascal, Chateaubriand, Lamennais, and Baudelaire might be recalled; if Racine's classic restraint be adopted as the French norm, what about Rabelais, Balzac, Hugo, Michelet, Léon Bloy, Claudel, Sartre? If Voltaire's sardonic smile be the French hallmark, shall we expunge as "unFrench" Calvin, Descartes, Bossuet, Buffon, Guizot, Auguste Comte, Bergson? If it be true that "whatever is not clear is not French," must Rimbaud, Mallarmé, Valéry be cast into outer darkness? Lucidity is a form of courtesy among strangers; it was imposed upon many French writers just because they were so radically different. Other peoples [6] may have a special store of unuttered thoughts and feelings which they tacitly share, and from which foreigners are excluded: the French cannot commune among themselves except through the universal. Paul Claudel could not understand Hugo and Renan (whom he rejects with horror) unless he embraced the whole world.

THE LINGUISTIC BASIS OF FRENCH NATIONALITY

Nature, therefore, did not create the land of France, the French people, the French mind, as we know them: all three are infinitely complex and constantly in flux. Can we hope to define the nationality in terms of language? "Whoever speaks French as his mother tongue is French, or ought to be; whoever lives under the French flag ought to speak French." For the last hundred years, nationalism and linguistics have gone hand in hand. Language groups tended to assert themselves as nationalities: Germany, Italy. Conversely, national sentiment sought to recover and magnify its language: Ireland learns Gaelic anew, and Israel resurrects Hebrew from a sleep of two thousand years.

"One flag, one speech," however, is not a natural law; it is a historic development, recent, and not universally successful. In spite of H. L. Mencken's efforts, we still share English with the members of the British Commonwealth; while Welsh, French and Dutch (Afrikaans) are officially used under British flags. Switzerland, Belgium, Finland refuse to fall apart on linguistic lines. In 1920 even the Polish-speaking population of Allenstein and Marienwerder voted to remain united with Germany, because they were Lutherans, and the Poles Catholics.

France offers a perfect example of a determined, accelerated effort to create linguistic unity. The process is the reverse of the one that prevailed in Germany or Italy: national culture followed, and did not create, the flag. In the Middle Ages, the whole South of France had a language of its own, *Langue d'Oc* (inaccurately called Provençal), as distinguished from *Langue d'Oil* [7] used in the North. That language, which in the twelfth and thirteenth centuries had a most flourishing literature, never disappeared. There were troubadours who wrote in the southern dialect even during the classical age. The revival of "Provençal" by Frederic Mistral, not a hundred years ago, was not an individual miracle; Mistral was only the first among his peers, and he has left successors. As a boy, I was taught that anything spoken in France that differed from standard French was but a debased peasant *patois:* I was surprised to discover later that even in the twentieth century educated southerners preferred to use, among themselves, the sonorous local dialect. Corsican, of course, belongs to the Italian group, as does *Niçois,* now a very minor element in the cosmopolitan Riviera. Catalan is spoken in Roussillon, at the Mediterranean end of the Pyrenees. Even in central and northern France, the village idioms, as old and as legitimate as the French of the kings, have not yet been wholly rooted out.

But in addition to these kindred languages, there are others in France which do not belong to the Romanic family: Flemish in the Hazebrouk district of Flanders, German in the northeastern tip of Lorraine, Alsatian (manifestly Teutonic, but very different from academic High German) in the greater part of Alsace; the mysterious Basque (Euskara) astride of the western Pyrenees, and Celtic dialects in nearly one-third of Brittany.

The Bourbons, like their predecessors, were very tolerant in this matter: Versailles cared little what vernacular was spoken in any province, provided the people feared God, honored the king, and paid their taxes like true Frenchmen. All learned men knew Latin; and all members of good society, within the boundaries of France and beyond, spoke French. It was the Revolution which insisted upon making "the king's language" that of the whole sovereign people. For the last hundred and fifty years, relentless war has been waged on the dialects. Political and economic centralization, compulsory popular education, the daily press, universal military service, all worked in support of this ruthless policy. Even stubborn Alsace will not indefinitely resist the "nationalizing" process. Force was not used with such crudeness as by the Prussians in their portion of Poland: children were not flogged for praying in their mother tongue. But gentle persuasion spoke with unswerving firmness and would not be gainsaid. Linguistic unity is to a large extent in France the result of natural growth: the convenience and prestige of the official language were arguments hard to refute. But it is also the fruit of very deliberate efforts. Our French friends would be greatly shocked if they were told that there is anything illiberal or antidemocratic in such a policy.[8]

On the other hand, the political frontiers of France never reached the elusive limits of the French language. There are still some French-speaking communities under the Italian flag in the valley of Aosta. Savoy was not finally annexed until 1860, and one of the greatest writers in French, Joseph de Maistre, never was a French subject at all. (He would have scorned the title of citizen.) There is a thriving literature in *la Suisse Romande,* French Switzerland; some names are of local importance, some have reached European fame (Amiel, Cherbuliez, Ramuz, Denis de Rougemont), one at least is universal, Jean-Jacques Rousseau. Walloon Belgium, with Liège, Louvain, and a proper share of Brussels, has given to the world notable critics and historians (this book owes much to Henri Pirenne), as well as novelists and poets. Fifty years ago, it was claimed that the two greatest writers in French were Belgians, both of them with Flemish names, Émile Verhaeren and Maurice Maeterlinck.

Apart from this immediate extension, French radiated, not once but twice, far beyond the political domain of the French crown. In the Middle Ages there was for two centuries a vigorous Norman literature in England; even when English came fully into its own, Gower and Chaucer were still bilingual. The prevalent language of the crusaders' kingdom in Jerusalem was French, and so was that of the Latin Empire in Constantinople. Brunetto Latini, one of Dante's masters, wrote in French his *Treasury of Wisdom,* "because that language is the most delectable and the most common among all people." Marco Polo dictated his travels in rough and somewhat peculiar French. In the eighteenth century, "the well-born, the wealthy, and the wise" spoke French from Lisbon to Stockholm and St. Petersburg. Gibbon wrote in French his first work, *Essai sur l'étude de la littérature,* and Beckford, his *Vathek.* Frederick the Great spoke bad German to his servants, and sprightly French to his friends. Rivarol won a prize from the Academy of Berlin (1784) for a *Discourse on the Universality of the French Language.* Even thirty and fifty years later, Prince de Ligne and Metternich, as good European aristocrats, used by choice the tongue of Voltaire. French was current in Constantinople and Salonika under the sultans, and at one time more popular than Romanian in the drawing rooms of Bucarest.

All this proves—and it needs proving—that there is no strict correspondence between language preference and national or dynastic feeling. Frederick II, a Frenchman by culture, felt no qualms at beating the armies of the French king. To be sure, he trounced as vigorously those of Maria Theresa, while the French were led to victory by a German prince, Maurice of Saxony. Nor did Metternich, even when he pretended to be the ally of France, ever work for French interests. It was not the military prestige of Louis XIV that made French the favorite language of aristocrats and men of letters, but the power and charm of French culture. It was, on the contrary, the victories of the Revolution and the empire that killed the supremacy of French: in Tolstoy's *War and Peace* the hero, Pierre Bezúkhov, makes a valiant effort to unlearn French, and, haltingly at first, to speak Russian.[9]

This rapid survey of land, race, and language illustrates our basic hypothesis: France is a slowly elaborated tradition, not the inevitable result of material factors. Nature did not compel, but simply permitted, the unity of France between the Channel and the Pyrenees. On the other hand, she frowned on an Anglo-French empire, the goal of the Plantagenets. The Alps frustrated all dreams of permanent French conquests in Italy. Louis XIV said, "The Pyrenees are no more," when his grandson became king of Spain; but the Pyrenees refused to melt away, as Louis XIV's successor soon discovered, and, a century later, Napoleon.

In the northeast the obstacle, an elastic one, yet no less stubborn than mountain or sea, was language. Southern France could accept northern French as a second language, because the two dialects were closely akin. The Basque and Breton minorities could be subdued and slowly absorbed, because they were of small numerical and economic importance and lacked the support of a powerful community beyond the border. Alsace offered a tougher problem; there France nearly reached the limit of her assimilating power. And it is infinitely probable that the left bank of the Rhine could never have been fully Frenchified, although the people were very much of the same stock and of the same faith as their western neighbors. The safest definition of France as a national unit is this: France is a comradeship grown through the centuries, a comradeship which rises to the noblest heights of loyalty, but which does not preclude differences, constant squabbles, and even tragic feuds.

CHAPTER II

The Dawn: Prehistory and Protohistory

⤧ THE SIGNIFICANCE OF PREHISTORY

In a study of national consciousness, prehistory would seem to have no place. The Neanderthal men and the Cro-Magnons have not yet been retroactively promoted to the dignity of Frenchmen. But modern psychology has taught us to delve into the subconscious. Perhaps the cave dwellers were potential Frenchmen without knowing it. More probably, many Frenchmen of today are cave dwellers in modern garb, unaware, or ashamed, of their ancestry.

This is not so fanciful as it may sound. It is agreed that in historical times no great invasion or migration completely changed the nature of the French population. The earlier inhabitants survived; the invaders remained a minority, and it was they who were absorbed. This is definitely known of the Northmen, even in the duchy of Normandy, and of the Romans, even in the Mediterranean province, *Narbonensis*. It is probably true, not only of the Franks, but of the Teutonic invaders as a whole, and of the Gauls before them. Not even the roughest statistical data are available; but both Teutons and Gauls were described as blonds, and the blonds are a minority in the France we know. There must be in the country today a preponderance of pre-Gallic blood.

The one essential service of history is to restore to man, absorbed in his little concerns of the moment, a sense of due proportion, of the vastness of time, of the slowness of progress, of the transitoriness of so much that is eternal in its own conceit:

> My name is Ozymandias, king of kings:
> Look on my works, ye mighty, and despair!

Prehistory is even better fitted to teach the same lesson. The major part of the history of civilization should by right be what we call prehistory. How a Pithecanthropus assumed the habitual erect position;

how he turned grunts and yelps into articulate speech; how he learned
to wield some rude natural tool, club, or stone, to aid the work of fang,
fist, or claw; the invention of fire, a revelation so momentous that many
races have held it divine; the dawn of religion, as evidenced by ceremonial burial, and of government, as revealed by huge collective works;
the birth of art; the domestication of animals; the beginning of agriculture; the discovery of metallurgy: these indeed are the essential facts
in the growth of mankind. All subsequent progress had been but an
elaboration of these primeval conquests, until the new era of scientific
industry, which bids fair to transform the world.

In this enormous perspective, the patient striving of the Capetians
to extend their acres, to make their rule more effective, and to keep
abreast of their neighbors appears not negligible by any means but significant on a limited scale only. And the growth of French consciousness
which resulted from these efforts must be considered also as a very subordinate phenomenon. Before we study this process from within and
become absorbed in it, we should for a moment view it from without, so
as never to forget that nationalism is not an absolute or an ultimate.

France possesses entrancing remains of prehistoric times, chief among
them the strangely vital art of the Old Stone Age, and the huge blocks
(megaliths) in mysterious monumental array. What is most impressive
about them is not their remote and alien character, but on the contrary
the sense of continuity they convey: we feel that, across the chasm of
myriads of years, there is a connection between these primitive artists
and ourselves. In one case at any rate, actual blood filiation can be
traced: the strongly individualized Cro-Magnon type is found among
peasants of the Dordogne region, in the very parts where the skeletons,
implements, and works of art of their paleolithic ancestors were discovered. More elusively, folklore traditions which have not yet wholly
disappeared have their origin in prehistoric darkness.[1] It has been shown
that demons, saints, sprites, and fairies, dreaded or invoked in the villages, were the heirs of local deities older than Roman or Gallic rule. St.
Michael takes his place in the long line of dragon-slayers—light overwhelming darkness; he inherited on the hilltops the fanes of Teutates,
the Gallic Mercury, who in his turn had dispossessed elder gods. The
bonfires celebrating the summer solstice on Midsummer's Eve survived
into our times, made respectable by being renamed after St. John.

Two fine works in modern literature convey that sense of unfathom-
able depth in the French past, of living ancestral forces in the French
present. One is *Cromedeyre-le-Vieil,* a poetic drama by Jules Romains
(1920). It presents a primitive village in the central mountains, ob-

scurely and tenaciously conscious of its being part of the very soil. Races and regimes pass away; but if Cromedeyre alters at all, it is like the mountains themselves, in aeons, not in generations. In *The Inspired Hill* (1913), Maurice Barrès tells the true story of a small schismatic group in Lorraine nearly a hundred years ago. Barrès will have it that there are high places where the spirit seems to dwell, and which call for worship, whatever be the name invoked on the altar. The hill of Sion-Vaudémont is one of these; it bears a famous Christian abbey, yet it tempts the Baillard Brothers into schism, because the sacred character of the place is older than Christianity. Nationalism in the mystic sense is a tribal faith: it can never fully accept universal religions imported from afar. Barrès himself believed in *la terre et les morts,* the earth and the dead; the Nazis, in *Blut und Boden,* the blood and the soil.

✍ THE PALEOLITHIC AGE: THE CRO-MAGNONS

No European equivalent has been found for the famous ape man of Trinil (Java), the *Pithecanthropus erectus,* supposed to have lived five thousand centuries ago. The oldest inhabitant we can trace is the Heidelberg man, whose powerful jaw was still apelike, but whose teeth present certain human characteristics. He may have flourished—or vegetated—as early as the second interglacial period.[2] This *Eoanthropus* or Dawn man, as he was for a time called, may have used flint instruments which he found ready to his hand, broken by accident into a helpful shape. But since it is impossible in such a case to discriminate between accident and design, the Eolithic period of human industry, the dawn of the Stone Age, is not established with scientific certainty.

We are on safer ground when we reach the finds of flint instruments unmistakably chipped and flaked so as to produce a cutting edge. These characterize the Paleolithic or Old Stone Age. The most primitive types are known as Chellean, from the station of Chelles-sur-Marne, near Paris. The main product of Chellean industry is an omnibus tool, offering as a handle the unbroken natural roundness of the stone, and used as a hatchet, a knife, and a scraper. In Acheulean and Mousterian [3] times, over a period of perhaps fifty thousand years, the technique of chipping flint progressed considerably. To the earlier "hand-stone" or *coup-de-poing* of Chelles were added scrapers, planing tools, drills, and borers.

What kind of human beings were they who left these traces of their rude industry? These men of the lower Paleolithic belonged to races unmistakably human, yet still apelike in some of their traits, and best represented by the Neanderthal type.[4] An enormous head over a short, thickset body; a receding forehead and practically no chin; a powerful jaw and a bony ridge over the brows; arms curiously short in proportion to the legs; knees constantly bent forward; back and neck also curved: such were the Neanderthals, and we are grateful that anthropologists consider them as wholly extinct. No trace of agriculture or pastoral life: these men lived mainly by the chase, and we wonder at the inadequacy of their small stone weapons to cope with the tremendous fauna of those days—southern mammoth, hippopotamus, straight-tusked elephant, rhinoceros, saber-toothed tiger. Their chief method of capture must have been the pitfall. Even though the Neanderthals were barely human in appearance, they had already taken a few decisive steps. There are evidences, in late Acheulean times, of the use of fire; and the arrangement of the bones seems to bear testimony to some kind of ceremonial burial.

This Lower Paleolithic age began during a period of warm climate, probably during the third interglacial stage. Gradually, an arid, steppe climate prevailed, driving away the hippopotamus and the southern mammoth, while the elephant and the rhinoceros persisted. Then the full tundra regime set in, cold and moist, and brought about the disappearance of these animals also. The reindeer, the woolly mammoth, the woolly rhinoceros were the kings of this arctic fauna. The increasing severity of the climate may have caused the degeneracy of the Neanderthals. Perhaps the last of them were driven into barren regions by a stronger race, or killed in battle by invaders who may have known the use of bow and arrow. With their disappearance, during the fourth and last great period of glaciation, the Lower Paleolithic Age comes to a close.

Then came upon the stage men not essentially different from ourselves, erect, taller than the average Frenchman of today, with finely developed heads and a cranial capacity that would meet our modern standard. They are known as the Cro-Magnons, from the cavern in Dordogne where their remains were first identified. Their skulls offer some striking peculiarities: seen from the top, they are elongated (dolichocephalic), but the faces, which normally should be long also, are broad. The cheekbones are prominent; the chin well formed; the brow rugged, but not repulsively so. Their appearance, as reconstituted, is not only absolutely human, but far from displeasing. I have already mentioned that, in the very same region of Dordogne, there dwell at present groups of French peasants offering the same unusual traits; the identity of this type with the prehistoric Cro-Magnon is generally accepted. These living fossils, rooted in the soil for myriads of years, are found sporadically in other parts of Europe and among the Berbers of North Africa. This last fact is of great significance. It seems difficult to admit that the Cro-Magnon type was evolved in the West out of the Neanderthal, and the hypothesis of a migration from the mother continent, Asia, is more tempting. In that case, this migration must have taken place along the southern shore of the Mediterranean and through Spain.

The Cro-Magnons arrived during the postglacial age, when the climate was still subarctic. The reindeer remained the most typical representative of the tundra fauna, and its name is sometimes given to the whole period. The Upper Paleolithic stage of culture is itself divided into subperiods, named after the stations of Aurignac, Solutré, la Madeleine, Mas-d'Azil, and La Fère-en-Tardenois.[5] No sign as yet of domestication, or agriculture. The chipping and flaking of flint reached a high degree of perfection; in Magdalenian times, bone was worked into needles, borers, scrapers, fishhooks with remarkable skill.

Most wonderful of all are the first steps in art, already found in the Aurignacian and early Solutrean periods. Drawing, carving, and even polychrome painting were practiced. The human figure was seldom attempted, and when it was, the result was grotesque, perhaps intentionally so. Little statuettes of the female figure may have been idols; decorated staffs out of reindeer horn are supposed to be emblems of command—scepters, or marshals' batons. But the depicting of animals reveals extraordinary powers of observation, a dexterity which most modern craftsmen might envy, a sense of life in motion rare among the most gifted artists of our days. The fleeing reindeer, the charging bison are not crude and stiff symbols, but creatures animated by fear or rage. If Cro-Magnons could visit our Museum of Modern Art, they would vote many of the exhibits primitive.[6]

It is strange that these men should have crawled into the most inaccessible recesses of their caves, and there, by the light of some animal grease burning in a stone cup, drawn their elaborate representation of animal life with a realism and sureness of touch indicative of long practice. This can hardly be explained except through the association of art with some sort of religious worship. Unless the Cro-Magnons were believers in Art for Art's Sake: then the darkest cavern would be their Ivory Tower.

This strange Upper Paleolithic culture went the way of all flesh. Art faded away among the Cro-Magnons, and the stock itself seems to have become stunted. At the close of the period, several new races appeared in western Europe: one roundheaded, another longheaded, but different from the Cro-Magnon, and possibly the prototype of the present Mediterranean. For the first time do we find that coexistence of various breeds, which was to become one of the dominant traits of European, and particularly of French, history.

⚔ THE NEOLITHIC, BRONZE, AND IRON AGES

The next step is known as the Neolithic, or New Stone Age, characterized by the introduction of the polished stone and its gradual substitution for the older method of chipping. This comparatively small difference is but the inadequate symbol of a radical change in civilization —so radical as to suggest a gap between the passing of the old and the coming of the new.

Europe emerged from the last postglacial period, still subarctic in character, into climatic conditions very similar to those of the present day. The tundra fauna emigrated northward, or vanished altogether; the Alpine species, like the ibex or wild goat and the chamois, were confined within their present habitat; the lion receded into Africa. The bison, the long-horned urus, the stag, the moose, the wild boar, the forest horse, the Celtic horse were still plentiful. The rude beginning of agriculture can be traced; sedentary life gradually superseded nomadism; the dog, and later the horse, the ox, the pig were domesticated. Pottery was known, and the weaving of flax. The burial customs leave no doubt as to the existence of religious ideas. Art is no continuation of the Cro-Magnon forms. Frescoes representing hunting scenes have been dated back to the early Neolithic period. There is some attempt at composition, and the human figure is both more frequent and more successful. But the animals are not treated with the spirited naturalism of the Aurignacian artists: a glory has departed.

France has kitchen-middens (prehistoric refuse heaps) like those of Denmark, lake cities in Savoy, like those of neighboring Switzerland, and mound-graves or *tumuli* like all the rest of Europe. But the most interesting of the remains that belong to the Neolithic or to the Bronze Age are the huge stones long supposed to be associated with the religious life of the Celts, and for that reason called Druidical. It is now certain that they antedate the Celtic invasion of western Europe. Since they were found in large number and in a fair state of preservation in Brittany, they are still known under their local Celtic names: a menhir is a standing stone, a cromlech a circle of menhirs, a dolmen consists of flat stones lying on top of standing ones. The menhir was probably a memorial, a remote forerunner of our Washington Monument: the one at Locqmariaker (Morbihan), now fallen and broken into five pieces, was seventy feet high. A dolmen was the cyclopean masonry of an artificial cave: the sides were filled with smaller stones, and the whole covered with earth, no doubt the elaborate tomb of a ruler, like the great Pyramids. The largest assemblage of great stones is found at Carnac in Morbihan, the French Stonehenge.

But they can be seen in small groups or singly in all parts of the land; place names like Gros-Caillou and Pierrefitte [7] would indicate that at one time they were even more numerous. These enormous blocks— some weighed hundreds of tons—were in some instances transported miles away, and to a point higher than their original location. Such an achievement, beyond the capacity of the most rugged individualist, implies a high degree of organization, probably not of the liberal type. Traces of specialized workshops are found manufacturing in quantities one particular kind of tool or weapon: this supposes a system of barter. Skeletons show the signs of compound fractures which have been healed: this proves a degree of medical skill and of solidarity among the members of the tribe, for the wounded man must have been fed and nursed back to health.

The next step, and perhaps the most decisive, was the discovery of metallurgy. It remains veiled in mystery. Copper and bronze implements did not come as a sudden revelation or importation: the transition from polished stone to metal was a gradual one. The earliest bronze objects reproduce pretty faithfully the shape of their stone models, just as the first automobiles were patterned after horse-drawn carriages. On the other hand, since iron is more abundant than copper or tin in western and central Europe, it seems strange that the Iron Age should have come last. The designs of the bronze tools and ornaments reveal oriental influences; and the bronze culture seems to have been accompanied by the custom of cremating the dead, which is of Eastern origin.

Some twenty centuries before Christ, iron came into its own, although bronze remained in use for artistic purposes. Here again, there was an intermediate stage: iron was first used for the edge of cutting instruments, then for the imitation of bronze objects, as bronze itself had copied polished stone. This transitional period has been named the Hallstatt culture, from a secluded valley in Upper Austria, near Salzburg. The finds at Hallstatt reveal a culture immeasurably superior to that of the Neolithic age and not unlike that of the pre-Etruscan period in Italy, or the Mycenean in Greece. Traces of this culture are particularly abundant in the parts of Europe now occupied by the Alpine or Celto-Slavic race, the stocky, roundheaded population that separates, like an enormous wedge, the blond, longheaded Nordics from the dark, longheaded Mediterraneans. So the race and culture of the Bronze and Early Iron Ages are often referred to as Celtic—one of the loosest meanings of that long-suffering or insufferable term. Because the practice of incineration is part of that culture, we have no way of ascertaining the type of the people who had brought it into Europe. The few skulls found at Hallstatt are long, but it may be argued that their not being cremated proves that they belonged to strangers.

In the La Tène (Lake of Neuchatel) stage, iron had become the dominant material, although bronze was not discarded; and its quality was greatly improved. This type of civilization ranges in date between 500 B.C. and A.D. 100. It appears in the Celtic domain; its center may have been southern France or Switzerland, and it spread from that point to all those parts of Europe that were not under the direct influence of Greece or Rome. The Germans, still in the Bronze Age, eagerly received from the Celts this La Tène culture, the diffusion of which coincided with the greatest extension of the Celtic Empire. "It was the great iron sword of La Tène," says G. Bloch, "which in the fourth century B.C. carried through the ancient world the terror of the Celtic name." The weapon was formidable and uncertain, like the race that wielded it; both failed to pierce the armor of Rome.

PROTOHISTORY: LIGURIANS, IBERIANS, GREEKS

Out of the misty dawn we call protohistory, two names have come down to us: the Ligurians and the Iberians. Both are little more than names. Liguria is at present restricted to the Genoese Riviera; how far it reached in pre-Celtic, pre-Roman times we do not know. Place names ending in *asco, usco*, like Manosque in Provence and Mantoche in the Jura, are supposed to be of Ligurian origin. On this very slender basis, some scholars have stretched the limits of a shadowy Ligurian "Empire" as far as the Channel.

The Iberians are more mysterious still, and more tantalizing. The term is applied today to the great peninsula south of the Pyrenees, but the Iberians may at one time have covered the greater part of Gaul and the British Isles. This would account for the dark substratum still traceable in Scotland ("the old black breed") and in Wales. By the time of Caesar, only "Aquitania," the southwest portion of Gaul, was believed to be Iberian. For a hypothetical mixture of the Gauls with that earlier race, the term "Celtiberian" was coined. In later centuries, Gascony arose out of ancient Aquitania. Now Gascon, or Vascon, is another form of Basque; so Humboldt suggested that the Basques, with their peculiar physical type and their isolated language, were the last remnants of lost Iberia. A plausible hypothesis; of decisive proof there is none.

It is a relief to turn from this palpable darkness to the most articulate and sharply defined people in history, the Greeks. We know that Massalia (Massilia, Marseilles) was established about 600 B.C. by Asiatic Greeks, the Phocaeans. Legend will have it that the king's daughter, Gyptis, a Ligurian Pocahontas, chose the captain of the wanderers as her bridegroom. Marseilles, founded on romance, throve on commerce. It became a prosperous Greek city, the ally, not the subject of Rome, and a center of Hellenic culture. There were Massaliote explorers, geographers, and scientists as well as merchants. Conservative Roman families sent their sons to study Greek there, in preference to Athens, whose moral reputation was dubious. The Phoenicians too, those great rivals of the Greeks in maritime trade, settled on the French coast: the whole Riviera is dotted with Greek and Phoenician place names, and, more doubtfully, with types of classic Grecian purity.

The influence of the Greeks did not spread far inland, but it reached beyond the Mediterranean. Bold navigators venturing beyond the Pillars of Hercules (Straits of Gibraltar), went as far as Cornwall and the Scilly Islands in quest of tin, and gathered amber on the shore of the Baltic. As a result of these extensive voyages, Greek coins and inscriptions in Greek characters are found in many parts of Gaul. Greek was, even under Roman rule, the language of commerce as well as that of philosophy and of the early Church. It was through the ubiquitous colonies of Greeks or Hellenized Jews that Christianity was diffused in Gaul: the early martyrs, at Lyons, bore Greek names. The connection has never been severed. The "Syrians" who in Frankish times had such a hold of Gallic trade were Byzantine Greeks, and there is still a large and active Greek element in the seething population of Marseilles. The great names to which we shall now turn, Gauls, Romans, Franks, do not tell the whole story.

CHAPTER III

Celtic Gaul

✑ WHO WERE THE GAULS?

We still frequently use "Gallic" for "French." The Gauls cannot lodge a protest; the French might. For in sober truth, they owe very little to the Gauls, neither blood nor language, neither faith nor institutions. And what little they owe is singularly hard to define; for everything relating to the Celts and Gauls is hidden under a triple veil: lack of direct evidence, faulty reporting by the Romans, and, twenty centuries later, Romantic distortions. The last is easily the worst.

Ancient writers used the words Gauls and Celts interchangeably. The same confusion has persisted to our own days, growing worse confounded with the rise of new sciences. The word "Celtic" is used in at least three connections, which should be kept clearly separate in our minds.

In philology, Celtic denotes a family of languages, a receding group, one member of which, Cornish, died only a few generations ago, while the rest cling for dear life to the extreme western coast of Europe, the western Highlands and isles of Scotland, Ireland, Wales, Brittany. The ancient Gallic tongue was a member of this family; but the whole country called Gallia, including its western outpost Armorica (Brittany) [1] adopted the Latin language, and at present, the bulk of the French people belong to the Romance-speaking group.

Celtic is also the name of a race, presumably different from the Nordic and the Mediterranean. But what is this race? The term Celtic has been applied, with extreme looseness, to the roundheaded, stocky, darkish breed whose domain extends from Russia, through Austria, Switzerland, southern Germany, and northern Italy, to the central mountains of France and to Brittany. This race, also called Celto-Slavic, Alpine or Cévenole, is supposed to have come from Asia (some Auvergnats, like Pierre Laval, are definitely mongoloid in appearance), and to be associated with the culture of the Bronze Age. It is the most numerous element in Europe; yet but a trifling proportion of it—barely one-third of the Bretons—speaks a Celtic language. The other populations of Celtic speech—Welsh, Gaelic Scot, and Irish—are not round-headed and, from the anthropological point of view, do not belong to the Celtic race.

Then, in history, the word is used as a loose synonym for the ancient Gauls, the people who at one time roamed as far as Great Britain and Asia Minor, and whom Caesar finally subjugated. Caesar tells us, however, that in Gaul only one of the three parts was definitely "Celtic." The Gauls proper were distinct from their neighbors in the Southwest, the Aquitanians; in a more obscure fashion (language? stage of culture?) they differed from the Belgae in the Northeast.

The Gauls were described by all ancient historians as tall, in some cases even huge, with blond or reddish hair and blue eyes: the "blond beasts" of Nietzsche. Now these are the traits which we generally associate with the Teutonic race; and, as a matter of fact, the ancient writers were wholly unable to distinguish these northern barbarian tribes from one another. A superficial kinship in the names might induce us to believe that the *Teutones* defeated by Marius were Teutonic, while the Cimbri were Kymric or Celtic; but it might be exactly the reverse.[2] Tribes in their wanderings did not preserve the purity of their blood, as some of the Jews have done, and still less the integrity of their language, as most of the Jews have not. In spite of linguistic differences, it seems that the Celts and the Teutons, if not identical, were at any rate closely related. This theory, by the way, was adopted by the Teutomaniac philosopher of history, the prophet of Hitlerism, Houston Stewart Chamberlain: it enabled him to claim for the Teutonic genius all the achievements of the French, as well as those of all other European nationalities.

It is curious to note the moral portrait that Caesar has left us of the Gauls. Brave to the point of temerity, with a quick mind, sociable, communicative, fond of oratory, for which they showed a peculiar gift; boastful as well as brave, "fearing nought save that the heavens should fall"; unsteady, impatient, quick to discouragement and despair, with no sense of orderly rule and discipline: such were the Gauls about 50 B.C., and so, a few morose observers would say, are the French of the present time. Lamartine, abandoned by the fickle mob in 1848, exclaimed in disgust: "They are Gauls still!" It might be well to remember that the "fickle Gauls" lived for eight hundred years under the same dynasty and continued, with unexampled tenacity, the same nibbling process of territorial expansion. "Sons of the Gauls" were those poilus of World War I, who obstinately stood their ground for fifteen hundred days even when no ray of hope could be discerned in the threatening east; "sons of the Gauls," a generation later, the tenacious anonymous heroes of the Underground. The so-called Celtic elements in France—Celtic in race or language, or both, like the Auvergnats and the Bretons—are noted, not for capricious versatility, but for stolid conservatism.

Did Caesar's description apply exclusively to those tall blond warriors whom he calls Celts and who must have been first cousins to the Teutons? But if this character sketch has any degree of accuracy today, it would be true chiefly of the South, the basins of the Garonne and the lower Rhône, peopled by the Mediterranean race and showing few traces of any Celtic influence. This is a striking instance of the caution with which the brilliant generalizations of national psychology should be used, especially after an interval of two thousand years.

GALLIC MIGRATIONS

Whence came those Celts who conquered Gaul? From the "hyperborean regions"—the Gauls who sacked Rome in 390 B.C. were still referred to as "Hyperboreans"—"between the Ligurians and the Scythians." In less poetic language, we surmise that they reached as far as the North Sea. At one time the Elbe separated them from the Teutons, who were then inhabiting Jutland and the coast of the Baltic. More advanced than the Teutons, they exercised a vague suzerainty over them; at any rate, a few Gallic words relating to war and government have passed into the Germanic tongues. The barbaric peoples of the ancient world, without being strictly nomadic, were but loosely attached to the soil. We find the Celts wandering over the whole of Europe. As early as the ninth century they had occupied Britain. In the fifth they spread between the central mountains of France and the Atlantic; some found their way as far as Portugal.

Half a century later, they swept southward, over Etruria, and reached Rome, which they burned in 390 B.C., in spite of the watchful and patriotic sacred geese of the Capitol. It was then that their Brennus cast his heavy sword into the scale where the price of defeat was weighed, with the long-echoing words: *Vae victis!*—Woe to the conquered! They withdrew, and settled in the valley of the Po, which became known as Cisalpine Gaul. About the same time another movement was taking place toward the east, and the Celts had their share of the spoils in the downfall of the Scythians. By the fourth century B.C., their spasmodic domination spread from Spain and Britain, over northern and central Gaul, northern Italy and southern Germany, to the middle and lower Danube. The word Bohemia comes from the name of a Celtic tribe, the Boii. But nothing could be more misleading than the term "Celtic

Empire." Restlessness and plunder were not accompanied by any trace
of organization.

The next great movement was the result of pressure from the Germans, whose turn was coming to stalk upon the world's stage. Celtic
tribes migrated to the southeast, defeated the Macedonians, and besieged Delphos. About 240 B.C., a band of Celtic [3] adventurers founded
Galatia in Asia Minor, a state which long retained its independence.
On their own account or as mercenaries, the Gauls were found on all the
battlefields. But the decadence of the turbulent Celtic world was already well under way. In the south they had been checked and driven
back by Rome. In the north they were pressed by the Teutons, who had
already passed the Elbe and were reaching the Rhine. Gaul had thus
to face Romanization as an alternative to Germanization: Caesar or
Ariovistus.

⚔ CONDITIONS IN PRE-ROMAN GAUL

Gaul might have victoriously faced this double danger had she presented a united front to her foes. But Gaul was a geographical expression, not a nation. Not only did the Aquitanians and the Belgians feel
themselves different from the other Gauls, but even among the Celts
there was no semblance of unity. Arriving by waves at long intervals
and mingling in various proportions with the aborigines, the Celts formed
in Gaul a certain number of local states, which Caesar most improperly
called "cities." Between these there was no permanent bond. Some, as
the result of conquest, were held in subjection by others; some were
placed under a sort of protectorate. There were indeed loose con-
federacies or leagues, often extensive, but ever shifting and never
national in spirit or scope. The Arverni, the Aedui, the Sequani were
at the head of such temporary combinations; but these fought against
each other and did not scruple to call in Germans or Romans. It was the
Aedui who, in 121 B.C., brought in the Romans to help them against
the Arverni, and thus won the title, "friends of the Roman people." It
was the Sequani who later summoned Ariovistus against the Aedui. The
Arverni, it is true, united for a while almost all the Celtic tribes under
the leadership of Vercingetorix; and it has been surmised that under
their hegemony, there might be traced the lineaments of a Gallic nation
in the making. But this remains the merest might-have-been.

Within these "cities" we find sharply defined classes. The aristocracy
or knights (*equites:* another of Caesar's rough approximations), with
exclusive control of the extensive public domain, owners of slaves, surrounded by numerous clients, enjoyed all privileges, political as well

as economic. The origin of such inequality is probably to be found in invasion and conquest, but other forces were at work. The caste distinction did not run strictly along ethnic lines: there is no sign that the Gauls kept themselves rigidly apart from the original population. Among the clients of a noble warrior some were his boon companions and brothers-in-arms, his *ambacti,* feasting at his table, fighting his battles, dying over his corpse: an institution as old and as widely spread as the human race, and which we shall find prevailing among the Franks. This powerful oligarchy formed a council or Senate, which was bitterly opposed to monarchy as well as to democracy. In Caesar's time few Gallic cities had a king; the father of Vercingetorix had been burned for aspiring to the royal title. In Gaul as elsewhere Rome took advantage of these dissensions and found supporters among the aristocracy, a familiar policy with imperialist powers. The movement of resistance which almost fused Celtic Gaul into a nation under Vercingetorix was at the same time a popular movement, and Caesar brands the supporters of the young Arvernian chief as "the rabble."

Little is known with certainty about the primitive religion of the Gauls. We possess no firsthand document: the Druidical traditions, not committed to writing, have perished utterly or dissolved into alien forms. Their temples were natural places marked off only by ritual—lonely glades or rocky wildernesses. Whatever buildings may have existed were wooden structures which have left no trace. We find mention of simulacra, which may have been the menhirs; but the Gauls do not seem to have reached the stage when men want to give their deities the form of animate beings. The Gallic statues that survive belong to Roman times, and are the embodiment of Greco-Roman ideas.

Thus we are thrown back entirely upon the testimony of the classical writers; and this testimony is not only vague and scanty, but even what little information it provides is unreliable. Caesar tells us for instance that the Gauls were "the most religious [i.e., superstitious] of men." But he belonged to a cultured age that would naturally scoff at the practices of a backward people. There is no reason to suppose that the Gauls were more superstitious than the Romans, whose every act was presided over by some god or goddess. Then the Romans, and Caesar in particular, had a ruthless way of assimilating foreign deities with their own. In so doing, they showed both the bluntness of their feelings and the soundness of their political instinct. They Romanized the gods as they Romanized the upper class. When Rome came across a god who spurned a niche in her Pantheon, her doom was at hand. But these rough-and-ready equivalents have cast a thick veil over the true facts of the case.

Among the different tribes of Gaul we find in common the worship of geographic deities, the spirits of forest, stream, and mountain. Springs and rivers, in particular, the center of community life, the visible arteries of the land, were "the mothers of cities and of gods." Divona in Bordeaux, Nemausus at Nîmes were famous among fountains; no thermal or mineral spring without its god or goddess.[4] There was a Dea Sequana, and Father Rhine was one of the high gods. The majesty of isolated mountains, Puy-de-Dôme, Ventoux, Donon, gave them a religious character: there is some warrant for the thesis of Maurice Barrès in *The Inspired Hill*. Primitive reverence for the forest found expression in the deification of the wooded uplands of Ardennes and of the Vosges: Dea Arduena, Deus Vosegus.

According to Caesar, the great Celtic god was Mercury; and in Roman times, until the disastrous flood of barbarians in 257, the sanctuary of the Arvernian Mercury remained the most famous and the richest in Gaul. But that Mercury, or Teutates, had little in common with the Roman god of commerce and the useful arts. He was the champion of light, the conqueror of Cernunnos, god of the earth, of night and of death, one of those dark "chthonic" deities so dear to German Romanticism. The Ogmios mentioned by Lucian, the Gallic Hercules from whose mouth golden chains came forth, was probably a form of Teutates.

THE ENIGMA OF THE DRUIDS

The most interesting feature in the religious life of the Gauls was the existence of the Druidical order. Few peoples in antiquity have thus possessed an organized clergy. The Druids were a corporation, not a caste, although they probably were recruited, mostly if not exclusively, from the patricians. They formed a federation, we might almost say a church. They had a Grand Druid, elected for life, sometimes not without bloody strife. Once a year they met in solemn assembly in the land of the Carnutes (Chartres), which was roughly the geographical center of Celtic Gaul. There were also colleges of priestesses, like the half-legendary virgins of the Isle of Sein, revered and dreaded by Greek navigators. There were bards (poets and soothsayers), who, however, were held to be inferior to the Druids. The center of Druidical teaching was not in Gaul, but in Britain, whither the novices repaired to complete their education. Their sacerdotal initiation demanded several years.

What were the rites and doctrines of the Druidical religion? We know that the Druids, with their golden sickles, gathered from the oaks the sacred mistletoe, a symbol of immortality and a panacea. Human sacrifice was practiced: victims, enclosed in wicker hampers, were offered in holocaust to a Gallic Moloch. Even in Paris under Louis XIV, and later in the provinces, basketfuls of live animals were thrown into the "fire of St. John," an attenuated survival of a barbarous tradition. These cruel rites were in all probability pre-Druidic, and the Druids, as we are told by their defenders, may have done their best to mitigate them.

For the Druids have become the heroes of a legend. Already Posidonius of Rhodes, "the most learned man of his time," believed that they taught a secret doctrine of lofty idealism: it is not uncommon for a sophisticated age to praise the purity of primitive cultures. Thus Tacitus' Germany is a satire on Rome at least as much as an objective study; thus the eighteenth century waxed quaintly enthusiastic over the virtues of the Hurons. The Celtic School in the nineteenth century, particularly Edgar Quinet and Jean Reynaud, revived the mysterious glamour of the Druids. There are few facts to support this romantic myth. The belief in immortality evinced by the burial customs of the Gauls seems to have been of the most ordinary kind: a shadowy continuation of the dead warrior's material life. The Druids were the learned men: they were entrusted with the education of the young, they kept the memory of the successive invasions of the land, and they may have taught of an Elysium beyond the western seas. But their lore—magic, astronomy, and the poetic annals of the race—was in all probability not above the childish level of other primitives.

Their authority, or at any rate their influence, went beyond the domain of religion. Civil differences among the nobles were submitted to them, and even conflicts between cities. It is obvious, however, that their arbitration, even supported by the terrible weapon of excommunication, failed to prevent the perpetual clash of arms among the Gallic tribes: there is no trace of a potential unity of Gaul on a theocratic basis. The Druids seem to have played no part in the resistance to Caesar; on the contrary, one of them, Diviciacus,[5] was a trusted auxiliary of the Romans. They may have inspired some of the later rebellions (Sacrovir). The Druids gradually merged with the Gallo-Roman *sacerdotes*. Their once aristocratic title was finally applied to rustic soothsayers who kept up some of the old rites for the benefit of the Celtic peasantry.

The classic terms "city," "aristocracy," "senate," might evoke in our minds a stage of civilization not essentially different from that of Greece and Rome. As a matter of fact, the four or five million people who dwelt between the Rhine and the Roman dominions were, if not savages, at any rate barbarians. Gaul was clad with thick and tangled forests, still haunted by the aurochs and the bear. The "towns," such as Bibracte, were mere *oppida,* that is to say, rude enclosures on elevated places used as a refuge in case of war; or else they were temporary market centers. Even the Avaricum that the Gauls refused to sacrifice in their scorched-earth policy must have been little more than a conglomeration of primitive wooden cabins.

Such was Gaul on the eve of its conquest by Caesar: a region inhabited from time immemorial and covered by layer upon layer of ethnic alluvions. Of these successive invaders the Gauls were then the latest. They had by no means Gallicized the whole country; they formed but a minority even in Celtic Gaul, and that minority offered no political or social unity.

Caesar thus found himself in the presence of a complex population still primitive and fierce, but alert, inventive, open to foreign influences: a people not inferior in aptitude to the classical nations, although far behind them in development. The government, religion, and material progress of the Gauls, incomplete as they were, make us feel that the race was ready and eagerly groping for a fuller civilization. It is idle therefore to regret that the Roman conquest should have checked the growth of an original Gallic culture: absorption by the Latin world meant to Gaul not death, but an accelerated evolution. Rome fulfilled the desires of the Gauls; she led them whither they wanted to go. And that is why, in less than a century, they caught up with their masters, and worshipped the Eternal City.

CHAPTER IV

Roman Gaul

✍ THE CONQUEST

Rome's first steps into Gaul were cautious and natural enough. Massalia, her Greek ally, invoked her aid against Ligurian or Celtic tribes which were proving troublesome neighbors: the honeymoon of Princess Gyptis could not last forever. Rome made good use of the opportunity. It enabled her to bring under her influence the whole Mediterranean shore of Gaul and to secure a land route between Italy and Spain, which had already come under her sway. After defeating the Allobroges and the Arverni, she could create in 121 B.C. "Trousered Gaul," *Gallia Braccata.* This picturesque title was soon changed to *Narbonensis,* from the colony of Narbo Martius (Narbonne). Roman control extended up the Rhône as far as Vienna (Vienne, some twenty miles south of Lyons) and reached the upper valley of the Garonne at Tolosa (Toulouse). Veterans were settled on the land; so Roman names of cities, Roman ruins, and even Roman types still abound in Languedoc and Provence. Triumphal arches, baths, stadia, temples, theaters are found at Aix, Arles, Nîmes, Orange; and the Pont-du-Gard, a great aqueduct, with its three tiers of arches remains a model of good engineering, elegance, and majesty.

We are tempted to think of the Great Invasions as a sudden flood which engulfed the civilized world in the fifth century A.D. In fact, from earliest times, the barbarians never ceased to be a threat to Rome. We have seen that in 390 B.C. the Gauls had swooped down and plundered the city. From 113 to 101 B.C. vast hordes from the wild north, Germanic as well as Celtic, the Teutones and the Cimbri, ravaged southern Gaul and began pouring into Italy over the Brenner Pass. At Aqua Sextiae (Aix in Provence) and Vercellae (in the Po Valley) they were annihilated by Marius. But Rome had shuddered, and the rough soldier who had saved her became the idol of the people.

Forty years later, ominous stirrings were felt among the dimly known populations of the north. The Celtic tribes of Gaul, irremediably divided, could not have checked their advance. Harshly treated by the Aedui, the Sequani called to their help a German chieftain, Ariovistus. The Aedui in their turn sought the support of their "friends," the Romans. The Senate, distracted by civil confusion, hesitated. Meanwhile, the Helvetii, hard pressed by their German neighbors, decided to seek a new abode on the shore of the Atlantic. Burning their old homes, they started on their long trek, devastating as they went. All this seemed to portend another avalanche.

Then appeared the "Providential Man," Julius Caesar.[1] At forty, he was notorious for his vices, his debts, his unscrupulous ambition. He had at last reached the summit; but he had to share it with Pompey, the greatest general of the time, and Crassus, the wealthiest citizen. He meant to rule alone: to achieve his purpose, he needed an army. As his share of the spoils, he had received the government of Cisalpine Gaul and Illyria; the Senate was browbeaten into adding Transalpine Gaul, with extraordinary powers (59 B.C.).

He first checked the wandering Helvetii and drove back Ariovistus. Thus he appeared in Gaul not as a harsh invader, but as an arbiter and a liberator. Like the conquests of Mexico, India, and Morocco, that of Gaul was not purely military. Caesar took advantage of the dissensions between tribe and tribe and of the feud, in every city, between the aristocracy and the plebeians.

The divisions among the Gauls gave the small Roman armies their chance, but they also made their work ubiquitous and indecisive. Hardly had rebellion been quenched in one part of the vast trackless country than it flared up a hundred leagues farther. For eight successive years Caesar or his lieutenants, Labienus and Crassus, had to scour the land from Aquitania to Armorica or Belgium. Twice Caesar found it necessary to cross the Rhine and twice the Channel without effecting permanent conquests. In these campaigns, he displayed a pertinacity and a resourcefulness to be matched only by his cruelty: whole populations were mutilated, massacred, or sold into slavery.

At last, under the leadership of a young Arvernian chief, Vercingetorix, there was in Gaul a movement of resistance widespread enough to have almost a national character. This movement found its strength among the masses, the "rabble," as Caesar contemptuously called them. It is not wholly fanciful to trace a resemblance between that brief flaring up of the Gallic spirit, the mission of Joan of Arc, and the mighty surge of the French people in 1792: in all three cases, the depths were stirred. The campaign of 52 B.C. was stubbornly fought out. Caesar captured Avaricum (Bourges), the only city the Gauls had been unwilling to sacrifice; he suffered a check before Gergovia (Clermont); but he succeeded in besieging Vercingetorix in Alesia (Mont-Auxois, near Alise-Sainte-Reine, Côte-d'Or). All attempts to break the elaborate investing lines failed; an enormous army of relief, horde rather than host, was driven off; Vercingetorix had to surrender. He did so with a dramatic sense, a flourish, a panache worthy of Cyrano. He appeared in his gold-studded armor, mounted on his best steed, as for a last festival; then, without a word, he threw down arms and ornaments at the victor's feet. There was no romanticism in Caesar's soul, and no pity. He kept the young hero imprisoned for five years, dragged him ignominiously to grace his triumph, and, in cold revenge had him put to death.

RAPID ASSIMILATION

The year 51 saw the final and ruthless subjugation of Transalpine Gaul. The work so cruelly but so efficiently done proved lasting. Already under Caesar, a Gallic legion, under the sign of the Lark (*Alauda*) served in the ranks of the conquerors. This Romanization proceeded almost without a setback. There were partial insurrections like that of Florus and Sacrovir (21 A.D.), in which the Druidic order, so curiously apathetic during the struggle for independence, seems to have played a part. Half a century later, the obscene tyranny of Nero and the anarchy that followed his death gave the discontented a chance. First a Gallic noble, then a Batavian chief, Civilis, and a few leaders from northern Gaul, Classicus, Sabinus, Tutor, shook for a while the yoke of Rome. But there was no union among the cities: a congress held at Rheims refused to endorse the movement. So deep had Roman civilization already penetrated that the rebels dreamt of a Gallic empire on Roman lines, not of a return to the ancient regime; Sabinus claimed that the blood of Caesar was flowing in his veins. As soon as Vespasian's power was secure, his general Cerealis found little difficulty in subduing the revolt.

This rapid Romanization was not due to any abundant influx of Roman blood. Only Narbonensis received, as we have seen, a fair number of Roman settlers: there were in that province no less than six Roman and twelve Latin colonies. In the rest of Gaul there were at the beginning of the empire only three colonies, Lyons being the most important by far; Cologne was added under Claudius, then Trêves. Their number grew slowly, and it is uncertain whether any except Lyons were Roman or merely Latin.[2] It may be said that military colonization introduced into Gaul far more barbarians than Romans: many place names reveal the spots where foreign mercenaries or prisoners-of-war were once quartered. The few higher officials sent from Rome did not form a permanent element; they plundered and went home. The trading class was cosmopolitan, and less Roman than Greek.

The true secret of assimilation is twofold. On the one hand, the Gauls had reached a stage of development which enabled them to appreciate the superiority of Greco-Roman culture. On the other, Rome's policy was a model of sane, cautious liberalism. Roman citizenship was neither imposed as a yoke, nor thrown open to raw tribesmen. It was held out to cities and individuals as a privilege and a reward. Each city retained a great deal of self-government, even those called subject, which had to pay tribute and submit to control. The free cities had full jurisdiction over their home affairs. Those which were known as free and federated, such as Massalia, were considered as the voluntary allies of Rome. Latin colonies enjoyed the economic, and sometimes the civil, rights of Roman citizenship, but not the political. Roman colonies were fully privileged daughters of the imperial city. Apart from the status of the cities, there was a personal status: a Roman citizen like St. Paul remained a citizen wherever he went and could appeal to Caesar. When an edict of Caracalla extended Roman citizenship to all the inhabitants of the empire (212), this momentous act attracted little notice, perhaps because, by that time, it meant very little. On the whole, the trend of Roman policy is unmistakable and its success beyond doubt. It was in the nineteenth century, not in the middle of the twentieth, that the colonial powers should have profited by its example.

Material civilization no doubt contributed to this moral conquest. The cities, unworthy of the name under Gallic anarchy, became veritable urban centers. Even a small and remote provincial town such as Lutetia (Paris) had public baths and a *circus* for gladiatorial games. Admirable roads were built, paved with heavy slabs on a thick bed of mortar, lined with ornamental milestones, time-defying in their useful magnificence.

Nowhere is this process of assimilation so strikingly marked as in religion: for religion is as a rule the last stronghold of national conservatism. The Romans, thanks to their political rather than mystic turn of mind, were able to meet the Gauls halfway. As we have seen, they established between the gods of the two races a rough-and-ready correspondence. Thus it was taken for granted that the great national god of the Gauls, Teutates, was Mercury. An altar erected by the guild of Seine bargemen was found in Paris under the chancel of Notre-Dame; on one side it represents Esus, on the other, Jupiter. In the minds of the faithful it was the same god under the Gallic *sagum* or the Roman toga.

This religious approximation went one step further: Romans and Gauls, living under the same wise and strong rule, worshipped in common the Eternal City, the goddess Rome, and her divine ruler on earth, the emperor. In Lyons, the capital of Celtic Gaul, an altar was erected to Rome and Augustus, surrounded by the statues of the sixty Gallic cities. The native nobles considered it an honor to become flamines, or priests of Augustus. With the purpose of associating more closely the lower classes with this civic religion, an order of *Augustales* was created which, in each city, combined the priesthood with municipal duties. Thus heaven and earth united to cement the Roman order.

The most complete victory of Rome was that of the Latin language. Celtic died slowly in the remoter regions, but it died leaving hardly any trace. Out of some ten thousand Gallo-Roman inscriptions barely twenty are in Celtic. About four hundred and fifty words of ancient Celtic have reached us; not more than thirty survive in modern French. The upper classes learned the purest classical Latin. The schools of Gaul, Autun, Rheims, and especially the universities of Aquitania, Toulouse, and Bordeaux, became famous. Professors were richly paid and could be called to the highest functions: Eumenius of Autun, Ausonius of Bordeaux ranked among the greatest personages of their time.

It was a very different Latin that spread among the common people: the rough, ungrammatical, slangy jargon of soldiers, slaves, and traders, further clipped and twisted by the Celtic brogue. Under this form, altered almost beyond recognition, Latin is alive in France today. Not in the Latin countries alone, but throughout Europe, even classical Latin had a prolonged, and at times a magnificent, twilight. It was not until 1539 that French became the language of royal justice and administration. We have to wait until 1541 for a theological treatise in French, Calvin's momentous *Institution chrétienne;* and nearly a century longer for the first work of philosophy in the vulgar tongue, Descartes's *Discours de la méthode* (1637). Half a century ago one of the two theses required in France for the doctor's degree had to be in Latin, so that Jean Jaurès and Romain Rolland quaintly appear among the ultimate Latin writers. It is still the language of the Catholic Church in ritual, administration, and teaching. Thus has the speech of a rude pastoral village imposed itself upon distant nations for nearly two thousand years.[3]

CAUSES OF DECAY. FIRST WAVE OF INVASIONS

Peace, prosperity, culture, such were the benefits that Roman rule conferred upon Gaul. The peace was precarious, the prosperity ill-distributed, the culture lifeless and imitative: still, with all its faults—and they were glaring enough, even under Augustus and Trajan—this regime was infinitely better than the old anarchy. Three dangers, however, had threatened Rome ever since the days of Marius; to a combination of the three she finally succumbed.

The most ineradicable evil was the selfish greed of the Roman people, and particularly of the governing class. Their guiding principle was exploitation, which at times turned into downright plunder. Never was the world governed by such thorough realists: although they kept tame philosophers, the strong men of imperial Rome tolerated no sentimental or theoretical nonsense. The result was a rake's progress: land after land, class after class, were robbed of their vital resources until the whole Roman world was exhausted. The process spread over centuries, for there were merits in Roman administration and above all in Roman peace which almost counterbalanced the causes of decay. Still, from the failure of the Gracchi, it was a losing fight.

The second danger was the rape of power by the soldiery. It began with Marius, and, although veiled under the best emperors, it never ceased. Even the cautious and moderate autocracy of Augustus was born of the army, and the substance of power was bound to pass into the hands of the army. There were times when every general thought of heading his legions Romewards in order to assume the purple; when the Praetorians massacred their newly elected chief for no reason but their desire for another *donativum;* and when the emperors, out of jealous dread, had their best generals assassinated, like Stilicho and Aetius. In early times the legions had been the citizenry in arms; with the enormous extension of the empire men of all races and stations were pressed into service, and an irresponsible horde held the fate of the world.

The third danger is the most dramatic and the most obvious: the onslaught of the barbarians. From that point of view, civilization appears as a besieged fortress: after more than five hundred years of valiant resistance, it succumbed. Like many things that are obvious—the "rising" of the sun, for instance—this convenient explanation is simply not true. The downfall of Rome was due to impoverishment, anarchy, demoralization, not to military defeat: defeat was but a symptom. Up to the very last the long-perfected fighting machine was more than a match for countless hordes. It retained its superiority even when many of the soldiers under the eagles, and some of the generals themselves, were half-assimilated barbarians. In 356 Julian, with thirteen thousand soldiers, few of whom were veterans, defeated an enormous multitude of Alamans. Stilicho, with thirty thousand, routed the two hundred thousand of Radagaisus. For twenty-five years Aetius, in Gaul, was victorious wherever he turned. The barbarians had no sense of unity among themselves and felt no reluctance in serving the empire. A well-organized government could have held the Germans at bay with the help of German troops. Rome perished from within, not from without.

Already in the third century the majestic edifice had rocked on its foundations. While Senate and army made and unmade emperors— shadowy adventurers who flitted across the stage, paid their *donativum,* and were soon killed by their own men—the Franks and the Alamans harried Gaul from the Rhine to the Pyrenees (257). Treasures were hastily buried or cast into lakes; the monuments of two centuries of peace were destroyed; the sanctuary of the Arvernian Mercury, the pride of Gaul, was plundered and burned down. Rome, distracted by civil strife, could barely defend herself; Gaul had to work out her own salvation.

For sixteen years there was a separate Gallic Empire, extending over the old Celtiberian West: Gaul, Britain, and Spain. An energetic leader, Postumus, drove back the barbarians, restored regular government, repaired the roads; the fine gold coins minted under his reign, equal to those of the best emperors, are a sign of returning prosperity. He maintained himself on the Gallic throne for ten years, but the evils of the local empire were the same as those of Rome herself. In 267 Postumus and his son were massacred by their soldiers; murdered too, a few months later, his successor Laelianus; murdered, Marius, after a few weeks; murdered, in 268, the vigorous Victorinus and his son. A last effort was made with a civilian emperor, Tetricus: it was his army that ruined Autun, the academic center of Gaul. Tetricus, discouraged, betrayed his own troops into disaster and made his peace with the restorer of Roman unity, Aurelianus (273). Two years later, Aurelianus himself was assassinated, and a new invasion flooded Gaul, worse than that of 257. The barbarians roamed at will, entering, pillaging, destroying almost every city. Yet they were driven out once more, by Tacitus and Probus, to whom was meted out the usual reward: they were killed by their own men.

⚔ TWILIGHT OF THE ROMAN WORLD

The cataclysms of the third century rank among the great forgotten revolutions. The Roman historians, while duly reporting the tragic details, failed to be impressed by their unique and ominous virulence. Archaeology enables us to measure their terrible character. They actually herald the Dark Ages. When the cities of Gaul were rebuilt, they were smaller than the old; and they were surrounded by high walls of defense into which the fire-scarred fragments of ancient splendor had hastily been thrown. At the same period we hear of the *Bagaudae,* bands of peasants goaded into rebellion and brigandage, an evil which could never be completely suppressed, and which finally merged into the universal chaos of the fifth century.

Yet the recuperative power of the empire was not absolutely exhausted. The reforms of Diocletian served their purpose for a season; Constantine and Theodosius received, and to some extent deserved, the title of Great. Rome, wounded to death, was carried forward by the momentum of five hundred years.

In the angry twilight of the classic world there were still, miraculously, islands of culture and peace. Ausonius (*ca.* 310–394), professor, poet, state dignitary, could compose pleasing sketches of his Bordeaux colleagues or a graceful description of the Moselle countryside. A scholar, a gentleman, and, in a cool and quiet manner, a Christian: of many a man who deserves these titles today, we are tempted to say, "What if he were an Ausonius?" Bishop Apollinaris Sidonius, two generations later, still wrote panegyrics of the emperors, able pastiches of ancient eloquence, at the very moment when the empire was crumbling. He kept his Arvernian bishopric (Clermont) under the Goths; and his letters reveal a man of genial temper, fond of good living and pleasure. Between the two came Rutilius Namatianus, the last, the most passionate, of the Gallo-Roman poets. For him, the dying Pagan religion and the doomed imperial city were still the light and hope of the world:

She alone has received the conquered into her bosom,
She alone has tended all mankind under a common name;
Mother rather than queen, she has turned subjects into citizens;
She binds together the remotest lands by ties of pious reverence.
Thanks to her yoke of peace, the stranger believes himself in his own country;
We have all become one people.

These words echo, after four centuries, Vergil's great call: "Remember, O Roman, these shall be thy arts: to rule the nations with thy sway, to crown peace with law, to spare the conquered, and to humble the proud." Thanks to Rutilius Namatianus, Rome went down with words of noble pride. Through some inner flaw the great Roman experiment failed, but it did not wholly deserve to fail.

CHAPTER V

The Dark Ages:
The Church and the Franks

⚰ THE GROWTH OF CHRISTIANITY

"I have described the triumph of barbarism and religion." In this famous phrase Gibbon summed up his verdict on the Dark Ages. The undertone of Voltairian sarcasm is audible to the dullest ear; but if the matter be considered purely on the basis of chronology, Gibbon's association of terms ceases to be a sneer and becomes a truism. In the fourth and fifth centuries, paganism was finally overthrown by Christianity, and the empire by the barbarians. Gibbon's implicit fallacy lies in the suggestion of a causal relation between the two fateful events: that if the world had not been barbarized, it would not have received Christianity; or that Christianity opened the gates of the empire to the barbarians. It is evident that the barbarians did not impose their religion upon conquered Rome: on the contrary, they adopted Christianity because it was part of that Roman world which they still revered while they precipitated its ruin. But was the decline of the empire due to a new faith, a religion of meekness, submission, and hopes not of this world? The coincidence in time was too striking to escape the contemporaries. St. Augustine and Orosius felt it necessary to answer the charge.

Our concern in this book is not the general philosophy of history, but the biography of a nation. We have already expressed our belief that the evils of the Roman world had their roots in its very core; that they were manifest at a time when the barbarians were still easily held at bay, and a hundred years before Christ was born. All that we have a right to affirm—the facts are patent—is that neither the new faith nor the new blood was able to arrest Roman decay. For our purpose the essential point is the close association between the two powers which were first the foes, then the heirs, of imperial Rome: the Frankish monarchy and the Catholic Church. This association, struck by the first Merovingians, renewed by the Carolingians, continued by the Capetians, found its perfect expression in St. Louis. After his death it survived, although no longer so intimate, for another five hundred years, until the French Revolution; it has left unmistakable traces even in our own days; it is one of the essential keys to French history.

We have already noted three steps in the religious history of Gaul. The first was Druidism. The second was the assimilation of the Celtic gods with those of the Greco-Roman Olympus. Then came the purely civil worship of Rome and the emperor. The last two forms of religion were closely associated with culture and with civic consciousness; this gave them a persistent hold upon large and influential elements. Thus Symmachus, in the latter part of the fourth century, was at the same time and consistently enough an old-fashioned senatorial aristocrat, a purist in style, and a scrupulous pagan. These traditional cults were not incompatible with philosophy: Marcus Aurelius performed his duties to the religion of the state with the same conscientiousness that he showed in all things. They implied the careful observance of a ritual, but no ardent belief and no moral transformation.

Now there was, throughout the vast empire, a yearning to escape from the limitations of its frigid, material, rational civilization, from the unutterable ennui that its splendid mediocrity was spreading over the earth. This desire explains the vogue of the Neo-Platonic philosophies and of the oriental cults. A sharper distinction was drawn between matter and spirit, between the individual body and the soul, between the world and the Deity. The soul was clamoring for deliverance from the body, for a return to God, its home. Such salvation could not be effected by the unaided efforts of human reason and human will. Direct contact must be established with the Divine Power through some act of penitence, cleansing, and consecration: a new birth that would open "the Path of Return." This path the restless society of Rome, especially after the second century, sought with eagerness in all the "mysteries" that were offered to its credulity: in the Greek traditions of Eleusis and Dionysos, in the Phrygian, Syrian, Egyptian, and Persian cults of Magna Mater (Cybele), Dea Syra, Isis and Serapis, Mithra.

Christianity appeared upon the scene as one of these Oriental cults. It sprang from the same region, in response to the same yearning. Neither in its miracles, mysteries, or ritual was it original and unique. In common with the other Oriental cults, it offered the attraction of its close-knit, voluntary associations of fellow believers, oases of brotherly love in the boundless spiritual aridity of the empire. In rivalry with the other Oriental cults, Christianity satisfied the longing for mystic union with a redeeming power. It would be rash to assert, however, that its survival was merely the chance result of a struggle for existence with Mithraism or Isis worship. These religions have not left us their full secret, and we must speak with diffidence; but it seems clear that Christianity offered over them three decisive points of superiority.

In the first place, the Christian faith and its parent stem, Judaism, were unique in their refusal to compromise with pagan superstition. Other national gods had their statues in the Roman Pantheon; the best emperors erected temples to Sol Invictus, Magna Mater, Isis: Jehovah and Christ alone stood apart. The easy syncretism of religious butterflies may seem more liberal: in Judaism and Christianity there was unmistakable earnestness, which made them defy persecution and court martyrdom. By thus standing against the official religion of Rome, Christianity was better able to denounce the evils of the Roman world: its cancer of unchastity, the debasing cruelty revealed in its treatment of slaves and in the gladiatorial games, the hypocrisy of its formal worship.

Radical in its condemnation, Christianity was also radical in its promises. It held forth the prospect of a new heaven and a new earth near at hand. This was just what a nervous and jaded world desired and did not dare to hope for. Mere progress, even when there is undeniable progress, is too uncertain, and at best despairingly slow: mankind wants apocalyptic changes and splendid rewards. The hourly expectation of the Second Coming has been disappointed through nineteen centuries, yet it is alive today. It has been the myth, the "vital lie," which has helped millions to bear more patiently the hardships, the mediocrity, the tedium of their earthly lot.

Lastly, while the idea of redemption through love was not absent from Oriental philosophies and religions, Christianity alone possessed a human, historical, tangible Savior, a Friend to be personally cherished and followed. The legend of the thaumaturgist Apollonius of Tyana challenges, but cannot bear comparison with the simple Gospel story.

CHRISTIANITY IN ROMAN GAUL

The Christian Church in Gaul goes back to very early times, for the country was in close touch with the rest of the Mediterranean world. But for a long while, it remained confined to the Greek and Jewish communities which were found in every center of commerce. In 177, under Marcus Aurelius, a cruel persecution brought the church of Lyons into the full light of history: it was then still predominantly Greek, and, true to the subtle Hellenic spirit, it was already torn by heresies.

French tradition cherishes the venerable or touching figures of the first martyrs: Pothinus, the aged bishop, Irenaeus, his learned successor, and especially the humble and heroic girl slave, Blandina.

There were other martyrs in the Gallo-Roman roll of fame, in particular St. Denis, who picked up his severed head, and became centuries later the patron and ally of the Capetian dynasty. But Gaul suffered less than the Eastern world from the last and most cruel of the persecutions, the one inspired by Galerius and named after Diocletian. Constantius Chlorus, then Caesar in Gaul, Britain, and Spain, preserved an attitude of tolerance. His son Constantine was destined to open a new era in the growth of the Christian religion: in 312 he became its official protector, and under his reign took place, at Nicea, the first ecumenical council of the Church.

A last effort to check the growth of Christianity, more insidious than any persecution, was made by Julian the Apostate.[1] His paganism was something deeper than the formal civic worship and the effete mythology that are generally connoted by that name. He wanted to retain their cultural and patriotic associations, but also to infuse into them a new ethical and mystic spirit borrowed from the philosophies of Greece and the religions of the Orient. The sun was to be the symbol of the one divine essence. Stoicism, Neo-Platonism, and Mithraism were to be fused into a single doctrine, "Hellenism," for the preaching and service of which a clergy was to be created. But a wilful synthesis of old fictions and new mysticism cannot be decreed by a single man, even though he be the Emperor of Rome. Julian would have wasted in the struggle his energy and his undoubted nobility of soul. He perished in a campaign against the Parthians, and "the Galilean conquered."

Soon a soldier, Martin, later bishop of Tours and founder of monasteries, was waging effective warfare against paganism. Numerous monuments of the old faith fell at his command, and he found enthusiastic imitators. His prodigious fame, with a rich embroidery of legends, became one of the traditions which were to create the figure of France. Four hundred towns or villages are named after him, more than three thousand churches are dedicated to him, and for ages his shrine at Tours attracted hosts of pilgrims. When he died about 400, the urban centers of Gaul and the landed aristocracy were, to a large extent, Christianized.

How deep was this rapid and wholesale conversion? On the part of the cultured classes it was no doubt sincere, but these new believers clung fondly to their now meaningless mythology. Ausonius and Apollinaris Sidonius were still pagans in literature—hardly more so, however, than was Boileau in the seventeenth century. Fourteen hundred years after St. Martin had broken their altars of stone, Chateaubriand still had to dethrone the heathen gods from the temples of French poetry. As for the peasants, they remained attached much longer to their ancient worship: thus did the word *paganus* assume its present meaning. Perhaps Celtic, and pre-Celtic, paganism never was fully eradicated. We have seen how immemorial local deities were whitewashed into saints, or degraded to the position of demons. The Golden Legend of Brittany, in particular, under a Christian veneer, is in reality a treasury of Celtic folklore.

The conversion of the imperial power itself was something of a give-and-take. From the ever closer alliance between the state and Christianity the Church of Rome was born. Through her the language, the geographical divisions, the costumes, the very claims and methods of the empire are alive in our twentieth century. Each of the sixty-four Gallic cities became the seat of a bishop; each of the seventeen provinces,[2] the seat of an archbishop or metropolitan. If the unimportant town of Auch still possesses an archbishop, it is because *Auscii,* fourteen centuries ago, had become the capital of Novempopulana. From the empire the Church received many exemptions and privileges. Clerics were free from military service, and also from those curial (municipal) functions which had been first an honor, then a burden, and finally a form of servitude. For many offenses, the bishop, not the civil magistrate, was their sole judge. A great part of Church property escaped taxation altogether.

These material benefits were offset by spiritual liabilities. The Church found it hard to remain unworldly, when the pomp and power of this world were at her feet. For two centuries the Christians had been denounced as the enemies of society; in return, they had branded the emperor as Antichrist. Their religion remained, in spirit, that of the poor and lowly; the empire, as it declined, became more autocratic in principle, more elaborately gorgeous in its vain ceremonial. The alliance between such antagonists was a scandal, or, at any rate, a paradox.

Yet this strange fusion of incompatible elements endured, perhaps because it never was clearly defined: ambiguities outlast clear-cut solutions. In return for his protection the emperor was granted, in Church affairs, the position of an adviser and supervisor. But he felt entitled to more. He never fully relinquished the divine character that paganism had attached to his office; he merely translated it into terms of the new faith. He considered himself as the religious head of the state, an authority inseparable from his sovereign power in the civil and military fields. The bishops were his ecclesiastical ministers; he could convene councils and influence their decisions. The Church never fully admitted this supremacy of the secular arm: she alone remained the judge of what things were Caesar's, but she never was able to enforce her own absolute, theocratic rule. The sovereign, even when he humbled himself as an individual sinner, would not be reduced to the position of a mere soldier and administrator in the service of the hierarchy.

This unresolved conflict explains much of French history. It first explains why there is any French history at all. Had pope and emperor harmonized their claims, the empire, at the same time Holy and Roman, would have provided a firm structure for Europe as a whole, and France would have been merely a province of United Christendom. It is in France that the clashing pretensions of the two powers were most successfully adjusted. Even the most pious kings never abdicated in the hands of the Visible Head of the Church; neither were the most proud rulers tempted into schism, as happened in England and the northern countries. But the balance was precarious at all times. The problem remained as delicate, and theoretically as insoluble, under the two Napoleons as under Louis the Pious in the ninth century, St. Louis in the thirteenth, Louis the Great in the seventeenth.

⚜ THE BARBARIC INVASIONS

In the beginning of the fifth century, the collapse of the Roman world was impending. In 410 Rome herself was desecrated by the Goths of Alaric; in 455, by the Vandals of Genseric; in 476 the Western Empire came to an end with the deposition of Romulus Augustulus; in 481, with Clovis, the new Frankish monarchy began.

The prime movers in the series of tidal waves that swept over the empire were the Huns. Celts and Teutons had been candidates for civilization: the Huns, from deepest Asia, seemed unhuman in their weirdness and ferocity. The milder barbarians, unnerved and awed, sought refuge in the empire, which, unable to protect them, became their prey. It took three quarters of a century (*ca.* 372–451) for the Huns to reach Gaul; they were then under the command of Etzel or Attila. Here the devastating flood was stemmed at last. A religious, Genevieve, in great repute for her piety and her care of the poor, heartened the Parisians and predicted that Attila would not reach the city: her trust was justified, and she has remained the patron saint of the French capital. Anianus (Aignan), Bishop of Orleans, organized the inhabitants for defense, and Attila withdrew. Aetius, the Roman general who had long maintained himself against all comers, directed the joint resistance of Gallo-Romans, Goths, Burgunds, and Franks. An immense and confused battle took place in the "Catalaunian Fields" or Mauriac Plain.[3] The Huns were not annihilated, but they retired. The whole story, amplified and distorted by legend, is full of vague horror:

Attila looms hideously, a figure out of an Apocalypse, the "Scourge of God."

By the end of this tragic fifth century, the Visigoths held Spain and southwestern France (Aquitania), with the Loire as their northern boundary. The Burgunds were established in the valleys of the Saône and of the Rhône, down to the Durance. The Alamans had settled across the middle Rhine and reached beyond the Vosges. North of the Loire, Syagrius, a Roman, ruled an uncertain kingdom. North of his domain and of the Alamans, on the lower Rhine and as far as the Somme, were the Franks.

The Franks, who had ravaged Gaul in the third century, were at first neither a single nation, nor a formal confederacy, but an ill-defined group of tribes. They may even have been a chance agglomeration of warriors, united for conquest and plunder. By the time they played an important part in history, they had, however, become definitely constituted peoples, with their dynasties, their traditions, and their laws. The Ripuarian ("river bank") Franks remained on the lower Rhine. The Salian ("sal," the salt sea) Franks had advanced into the region of the lower Meuse and of the Scheldt. Defeated by Julian, then accepted as allies, they had remained loyal to the empire as long as there was an empire to defend. Their semifabulous King Merovech (Meroveus), son of a sea monster, had fought Attila under Aetius; his son Childeric had helped Aegidius, the successor of Aetius, against the Visigoths.

⚜ THE MEROVINGIANS: CLOVIS ADOPTED BY THE CHURCH

In 486, Cholodovech (Clovis), King of the Salian Franks—he was then twenty years old—defeated Syagrius, "King of the Romans," near the latter's capital, Soissons. The bishop of the city asked for the return of a sacred vase which was part of the booty; and Clovis would have complied with his request, had not an unruly warrior smashed the vessel with his battle-axe. This deference to the wishes of a priest is the first indication of what was to become a settled and a fruitful policy, the alliance of the Frankish monarchs with the Catholic Church.

As the civil government of Roman Gaul declined, the ecclesiastical, by a natural process, had drawn to itself the substance of power. The giving of alms was an important function in a pauperized world; the privilege of sanctuary had passed from the temples to the churches; the bishop had become indeed the *defensor civitatis,* the leader and protector of the people. When the barbarians appeared before a city, it was as a rule the bishop who negotiated with them, like St. Lupus at Troyes, or who was the soul of resistance, like St. Anianus (Aignan) at Orleans. The bishops, in those days, were elected by the community: in the confusion of the age we can discern the elusive lineaments of a democratic and Christian commonwealth.

It was not to be: the Church needed a secular sword, and power was in the hands of the barbarians. The most numerous and most developed among those who had settled in Gaul, the Burgunds and the Visigoths, seemed well prepared to lend her their strength. They were Christians, and they respected the Roman heritage. The law of the Burgund King Gundebad shows a desire to promote equality between the native population and the new settlers. The Visigoth ruler Euric had a court at Toulouse attended by a number of Roman officials, and which was not lacking in brilliancy. His successor, Alaric II, for the use of his Gallo-Roman subjects, ordered a compendium of Roman law to be made, which is known as *Breviarum Alarici*. We have seen that Apollinaris Sidonius was not disturbed in his bishopric by the new masters. Beyond the Alps, their contemporary Theodoric was pursuing at Ravenna the same policy of tolerance, reconciliation, recuperation, and deserved to be called the Great. But in the eyes of the Church, Burgunds and Visigoths offered a fatal flaw: they were heretics.

Chance would have it that, when they entered the empire and were converted, they were taught Arianism instead of Trinitarian orthodoxy. Untrained barbarians failed to appreciate the vital difference between a Divine Son not coequal and coeternal with the Father, and the Eternal Son as one of the Persons of the Triune Deity. These theological disagreements, however, created a gulf between them and the Gallo-Romans. Clovis and his Franks presented a great advantage: they were heathens still and could be won over to the orthodox side.

So Clovis was adopted, not through any deep conscious design, as the sword of the true faith. He was married to the only Catholic princess in Gaul, Clotilda, a Burgund (493). Thenceforth, miracles helped his career. The God of Clotilda gave him victory over the Alamans (near Strasbourg, 496); thereupon, in fulfillment of a vow, he received baptism at the hands of St. Remigius (Rémi), "bowed his proud head, and burned that which he had adored." Tradition has it that a dove brought down from Heaven the vial of holy chrism with which he was then anointed: this ceremony gave the Frankish king a sacred, almost a sacerdotal, character.[4] A mysterious light shone on the cathedral of Poitiers to guide his army; a white doe revealed to him a ford of the river Vienne. Burgundy and Toulouse, his Arian rivals, were honeycombed with Catholic disloyalty. So these two great kingdoms, populous and comparatively civilized, were, the first, held in check, the second, subjugated (Vouillé, near Poitiers, 507) by a chieftain who, at the outset, had led a band of only six thousand warriors.

"He fought: the bishops conquered." On his way back from the Visigothic campaign, Clovis received at Tours the insignia of consular rank from the emperor of the East, Anastasius. He presided over a council at Orleans. Not that he had shed barbarism like a garment: his career was one of cruelty and deceit; his rivals were systematically murdered. But the Church was committed, and he was, though unworthy, revered as a "Man of God." Later, good Gregory of Tours could write with unconscious blasphemy: "Thus day by day God brought low his enemies before him, so that they submitted to him and increased his kingdom, because he walked before Him with an upright heart, and did that which was pleasing in His sight."

The conquest of Gaul was all but completed by the sons of Clovis: they added Burgundy and Provence to their domains. Only Septimania (Languedoc, Narbonne) remained in the hands of the Visigoths, and later of the Arabs, until the reign of Pepin. In the east, the Frankish dominions extended far into what is now Germany, embracing the whole valley of the Rhine with that of its great tributary the Main. This immense empire retained its unity in theory: in practice, it was parceled out, without any regard for physical geography or racial affinities, among the four sons of Clovis (511) and again among the four sons of Chloter (Clotaire) I (561). Gradually more natural and more permanent divisions began to appear: the eastern Frankish kingdom, or Austrasia, in the valleys of the Rhine and the Meuse; the "Newest" Frankish kingdom, or Neustria, in the northwest; Burgundy, in shifting alliance with one or the other of these constant rivals; and, under the joint overlordship of the three, the semi-independent duchy of Aquitania.

We need not dwell upon the dull tale of atrocities recorded by the Merovingian chroniclers, Gregory of Tours and Pseudo-Fredegar. Out of this bloody chaos there stands out one commanding figure, Brunhild or Brunehaut. This Visigothic princess, of great beauty and learning, married Sigebert, King of Metz (Austrasia). Her sister and her husband were both murdered by command of Fredegund, the slave-born concubine of Chilperic, King of Soissons; and the feud between the two families assumed a character of ferocity unexampled even in that dark period. Under the name of her son and of her grandson Brunehaut ruled Austrasia, and even Burgundy. She attempted to curb the lawless aristocracy, and to restore the power and splendor of the kingly office. She was friendly to the Church without subserviency; she corresponded with Gregory the Great, and banished the monk

Columbanus. Such was the impression she made that the works of Rome came to be ascribed to her: in some places the ancient roads are still known as "Brunehaut's Causeway." After the most romantic adventures, the aged and indomitable queen fell into the hands of her enemies. She was tortured for three days and attached naked to the tail of a wild horse.

The only other royal figure that survives is that of Dagobert (628–638): not for the French nursery song which presents him in a ludicrous light, but for the (comparative) power and magnificence that won for him the title of "the Merovingian Solomon." By his side tradition remembers Eligius (Eloi), goldsmith and saint. After him the decadence of the reigning family became irremediable. The kings gave themselves up to gluttony and debauchery in earliest youth; at twenty, they were senile ghosts, preserving no attribute of kingship except their unshorn locks. Under these fainéants, or do-nothing kings, there rose to power a new official, the mayor of the palace, or manager of the royal estates. In Neustria a great mayor, Ebroin, attempted to strengthen the monarchy against the aristocracy. But he was murdered in 681, and his successor, Berthar, was defeated by the Austrasians at Tertry (or Testry) in 687.

RISE OF THE CAROLINGIANS: CHARLEMAGNE

Pepin of Heristal, the victor of Tertry, established at a single stroke the supremacy of Austrasia and that of his own house. After a short period of anarchy, his illegitimate son, Charles Martel, "the Hammer," [5] crushed all opposition in Neustria, Burgundy, and Aquitania as well as in Austrasia, defeated the Arabs between Tours and Poitiers (732), led expeditions into Saxony, and was in all but name the sole king of the Franks.

It is one of history's little ironies that Charles Martel, champion of the Cross against the Crescent, without whose victory "Oxford might be teaching Islamism today," should have been consigned to hell fire: he rewarded his lieutenants too liberally with ecclesiastical benefices. His son on the contrary, Pepin the Short, renewed and strengthened the pact of Clovis: he protected the pope against Byzantines and Lombards and began a much needed reform of the Frankish Church. It was only with the assent of the pope that he discarded the fiction of Merovingian rule: he had King Childeric deposed and shorn (751), was recognized in his place by the liegemen, and finally was crowned by the pope himself at Saint-Denis (754). Thus was solemnly reaffirmed the sacred character of the monarchy, inherited from the "divine" emperors and the miraculous King Clovis, and all but obliterated through generations of Merovingian impotence.

In 768 Pepin died. According to Frankish custom, his domains were divided between his two sons, Charles and Carloman. The latter, however, survived his father by three years only; and Charles, brushing aside the claims of his nephews, became sole ruler. He completed and extended magnificently the work of his two predecessors. He had to subdue Aquitania once more; but, by respecting its traditions, he secured at last its loyalty. He reduced Bavaria to stricter vassalage. He finally destroyed the power of the Lombards. Redeeming the pledge of his father, he gave the pope the Exarchate of Ravenna, which belonged to the Eastern Empire. He made repeated but rather ineffectual incursions into northern Spain, and established a new march or frontier province beyond the Pyrenees.[6] For thirty-two years, moved by religious as well as political motives, he waged war against the heathen Saxons. Their idol Irminsul was destroyed; forty-five hundred men were beheaded in a single day at Verden; their national hero Witikind had to accept Christianity and the rule of Charles; one-third of the population was dragged away and settled in Franconia and Alemannia. Bishops were sent out to organize the Church in Saxon land. It remains doubtful whether a people thus converted by the grace of the sword could ever fully grasp the message of the Prince of Peace. Beyond the limits of the German world, Charles defeated the Avars and held in check the Slavs and the Danes. In the Christian West, the kingdoms of the Asturias and of the British Isles, though unconquered, acknowledged his leadership; the Eastern Empire finally recognized him; and friendly embassies proved that his fame had reached the Caliph of Bagdad.

On Christmas Day, 800, in Rome Pope Leo III set the imperial crown on the head of Charles, while the assembled Romans and Franks burst into the cry, "Long life and victory to Charles, most pious, Augustus, crowned of God, great and pacific Emperor of the Romans!" The details and the full meaning of this transaction are not perfectly clear. Eginhard tells us that Charles was taken by surprise and felt annoyance rather than elation at the pope's initiative. His reluctance, if we accept it as proven and unfeigned, was not due to any Germanic contempt for a Roman title. As *Patricius* and Protector of the Roman Republic, he believed himself to be the temporal head of the Christian commonwealth, and the overlord of the pope. This overlordship he had but recently exercised to the full: to his protection alone did Leo III owe his restoration to the papal throne; and only two days before, the pontiff, accused of adultery and perjury, had cleared himself by an oath in the presence of the Frankish king acting as judge. The title expressed most fittingly the two principal characteristics of Charles's rule: the hegemony of the Franks in the West and the theocratic ideal. But it was the emperor, "crowned of God," who was the theocrat.

The new title, which Charles seems for a while to have ignored, brought no change in his government. The years of conquest were over, and the emperor enjoyed in peace the respect of the whole Christian world. The majesty of his old age was sullied by the licentiousness of his own court, of his own family, and of his own life; and a telling anecdote represents the aged monarch assailed with forebodings at the news of Northmen's raids. He passed away at Aix-la-Chapelle (Aachen), long his favorite residence, in 814.

There is hardly any more impressive personality in history than that of Charlemagne. When we think of Frankish barbarism and chaos, of the ruined conditions of the roads in Gaul, of their total absence in Saxony, his victories, his administration, and even the flickering renaissance of learning that he encouraged assume an almost fabulous grandeur.

As a hero of legend he is unsurpassed except by Caesar and Napoleon. Within three hundred years, he had become the center of an epic cycle— rather, it must be noted, among the French than among the Germans. He was "the Emperor with the Flowery Beard," gigantic, two hundred years old, whose power kept the East as well as the West in awe. In 1165, by an even bolder transformation, he received the halo of a saint: to be sure, it was at the hands of an antipope, Paschal III, and it was Louis XI, a dubious sponsor, who insisted that his feast day (January 28) be properly celebrated. From 1661 at least, and almost to the present day, "St. Charlemagne's" was a holiday for French schoolboys: for another legend made him the founder of modern education. His example was constantly before the eyes of Napoleon, whose empire was almost coextensive with the Carolingian dominions, and who once threatened the pope "to cancel the donation of *my predecessor* Charlemagne." He dominates the whole history of Germany, and his shade has flitted through the morbidly gigantic dreams of modern Teutonic leaders.

The greatness of Charles lies in his personality, which is the surest foundation for his legend. But personality is not transmitted with the blood, and his work perished with him. He had attempted to weld the Western Christian world into a single whole: thirty years after his death, the nations separated, never to be permanently united again. He had stood for a strong central government with his emissaries, the *Missi Dominici,* carrying his will into the remotest provinces; and disintegration proceeded so fast that under kings of his line, in the tenth century, there were in his former domains thousands of independent principalities. The Carolingian renaissance, creditable though it be, was but a false dawn: there were still two hundred years of darkness to go through. His reform of the Church had to be done over again. His capital remained a minor city.

✍ DECLINE OF THE CAROLINGIANS

Charlemagne's successor, whom contemporaries called Louis the Pious, and posterity, Louis the Weak, showed a strange blend of Frankish cruelty and Christian meekness. He ordered the eyes of his rebellious nephew Bernard to be put out (death resulted), and did public penance (Attigny, 822) for this and other crimes. He still considered himself as the temporal head of Western Christendom, and Church administration was his chief concern, as church services were his only delight. He supported the efforts of Benedict of Aniane to federate all the monasteries of the empire, a conception which proved abortive but was later partly realized by Cluny. This imperial monk was also a King Lear: he divided and redivided his domains among his sons without ever satisfying their jealous greed. They constantly revolted. The eldest once captured and deposed him (833–834), but could not come to terms with his grasping brothers. Louis died in 840 in a campaign against his son Louis of Germany. Michelet had a strange fondness for this pathetic figure and called him "the first Saint Louis."

At his death, Lothair, his eldest son, became emperor; but the younger brothers, Louis and Charles, defeated him, bound themselves together against him by the bilingual Oaths of Strasbourg (842), and imposed upon him the Treaty of Verdun (843). This treaty was but a family compact for the division of the Frankish domains: like all previous partitions of the kind, it was drawn without any regard for linguistic differences or natural boundaries. Yet, as we have seen, it may be said to mark the faint beginnings of modern nationalities. For to the share of Louis fell *Francia Orientalis,* where the Teutonic element prevailed; Charles the Bald received *Francia Occidentalis,* almost completely Romanized. Between the two was carved for Lothair *Francia Media,* a long and loose strip of territory in the valleys of the Meuse, the Rhine, the Saône, and the Rhône, with those parts of Italy then under Frankish influence. A variable and ever-dwindling part of this preposterous empire came to be known as Lotharingia, Lothringen, Lorraine. For six hundred years it struggled to be born; it almost reached the definiteness of a hope under the last great dukes of Burgundy. It may be said that Belgium and the Netherlands are a remnant of that elusive middle kingdom, and that for over a thousand years France and Germany have been fighting for the heritage of Lothair.

Throughout the ninth century the incursions of the Northmen were increasing in fierceness and frequency. Their "dragon boats" boldly ascended the Seine and the Loire, spreading terror. In the hope of securing a strong leader, the lords of West Francia elected to the throne Charles the Fat of Germany, under whom the empire was united for the last time. Paris was valiantly defended by Count Odo (Eudes), the son of another vigorous fighter, Robert the Strong. When Charles the Fat appeared with an "immense" army, he simply bribed the invaders off with treasures and the spoils of Burgundy. Indignant at his cowardice, the French liegemen deposed him in 887 and elected in his stead the hero of Paris, Eudes. For a whole century the last Carolingians and the members of the new race occupied the throne, either alternately or in armed rivalry; at times the "Robertinians" were satisfied with the title of "Dukes of the Franks," and a position akin to that of the mayors of the palace. The lowest depths of humiliation were reached by the Carolingian Charles the Simple, by whom Rollo, the Norse pirate, was granted the fair duchy of Normandy (911). This pitiful kinglet, although abler than the Merovingian fainéants, lost his last strongholds to rebellious nobles and died a prisoner at Péronne. Finally, in 987, the direct line of Charles the Great came to an end with Louis V; and Hugh Capet, a descendant of Robert the Strong, was chosen king. No one was conscious of any great revolution; yet with the accession of this national line the history of France, properly so called, may be said to have begun.[7]

BOOK II
MEDIEVAL FRANCE

CHAPTER VI

The Church and Medieval France: 987-1270

⚑ THE FORGOTTEN REFORMATION AND RENAISSANCE OF THE ELEVENTH CENTURY

In the first decades of the tenth century the Dark Ages were at their darkest. The empire, so impressive under Charles the Great, had crumbled into dust. No one cared overmuch if an Italian princeling, such as Guy of Spoleto, chose to assume the phantom title. After Berengar I (924) even the name vanished altogether and remained in abeyance for nearly forty years. Rome was ruled by a corrupt local oligarchy against which the popes were powerless: this moment has been described as "the Pornocracy," and "the nadir of the Papacy." For the French Carolingian Charles the Simple, the throne meant a prison. No new order showed any sign of emerging out of that chaos. We were taught in my childhood that "the feudal regime" had been "created" and "organized" by the capitularies (edicts) of Mersen in 847 and Kiersy-sur-Oise in 877. But there was no organization and no regime. The only law was *Faustrecht,* strong-arm methods; the only system was anarchy. The French crown itself—one of seven that had proliferated out of Carolingian decay—came near disappearing in the universal confusion. In 987 it was a churchman, Adalberon, Archbishop of Rheims, who barely managed to save it for his ally or protégé, Hugh Capet.

By the middle of the eleventh century Europe appears in a new light; the impenetrable darkness had been dispelled; a civilization, far from barbaric and no longer the feeble shadow of Rome, was assuming definiteness. Trade was reviving; the cities were stirring, and would soon demand their communal rights. Even the expeditions of the French Normans were no longer wild forays like those of their Norse ancestors: they were carefully planned wars of conquest to be followed by organization. The first masterpiece of French literature, *The Song of Roland,* was soon to be composed. Clearest symbol of all: Romanesque architecture, long crude and imitative, became articulate; the increasing boldness of its pillars and vaulting anticipated the masterly structural achievements of the Gothic.

This eleventh century, still confused and violent but full of energy and hope, was a worthy prelude to the glorious civilization of the twelfth and thirteenth. It was in very truth a Renaissance. Its freshness and power were long concealed from our sight by the prejudices we inherited from the sixteenth-century humanists. In the eyes of Rabelais, for instance, everything between the fall of Rome and the dawn of his own day was abhorred as "the tenebrous and calamitous night of the Goths." The admirable architecture of the cathedrals was likewise spurned as "Gothic," i.e., barbaric. The enormous effort of the Schoolmen to open a path between revelation and reason was dismissed as a perversely intricate and futile game. The whole millennium, 500–1500, was called the Dark Ages. Even today, we find it difficult to break an inveterate habit of thought and to realize the miraculous change that came at the end of the tenth century.

Because the change was unnoticed, it remained unexplained. One thing is certain: this Renaissance was not due to the leadership of the Capetians. The first four, at any rate, were modest figures, renowned for piety rather than for far-reaching designs. Their one merit—and it was to bear splendid fruit—was to endure, and to have sons. No Clovis, no Charlemagne among them. It was not the genius of the new dynasty, but the increased vitality of the times that, two centuries later, made possible a reign like that of Philip Augustus. The Capetians were carried by a force not of their own devising and not limited to their own country. This vast anonymous Renaissance was marked by the rise of the cities in Italy, by the reconquest of Spain from the Mohammedans, by the vigorous Germanic revival under the Franconians. It was more brilliant in southern France, the *langue d'oc* country, than in the royal domain.

No great revolution can ever be ascribed to a single factor, but the forgotten Renaissance of the eleventh century is more baffling than most. One explanation may easily be dismissed. Mankind had feared that the world would end in the year 1000. Catastrophes and portents deepened the feeling of dread and despair. The year of doom came, and passed; man, reprieved, started hoping and working again. An ingenious, a picturesque, explanation. But it seems that the terrors of the year 1000 were unduly dramatized by romantic historians: lamentations on the wickedness and misery of the age are a perennial commonplace in re-

ENGLAND

London
Thames
Dover · Canterbury
Hastings Calais
Plymouth
PONTHIEU
FLANDERS
Bruges · Antwerp
Brussels
Schelde Liège
Cambrai
Utrecht
Rhine
Moselle
Meuse

English Channel

Amiens
Seine
Bayeaux Caen Bec Rouen
NORMANDY
Mortain
Noyon Laon
Beaumont Rheims
Châlons Verdun
Paris
Marne CHAMPAGNE

St. Pol-de-Léon
BRITTANY
Vannes
Alençon Chartres
Rennes MAINE
Le Mans
Angers ANJOU Tours
Loire
Nantes TOURAINE
Sens Troyes
Orleans Langres
Blois
Cher Sancerre BURGUNDY
Dijon
Autun Saône Doubs

ATLANTIC OCEAN

F R A N C E
Poitiers
POITOU
Chateauroux
LA MARCHE
Bourbon
BOURBONNAIS
BERRY BOURGES Nevers
Loire
Châlon
L. Geneva
Geneva

Clermont
Angoulême
AQUITAINE
(GUYENNE)
AUVERGNE
Allier
Lyon
FOREZ
Vienne
Valence

Bordeaux
La Teste-de-Buch
Dordogne
QUERCY
Lot
Albret Cahors Agen
GASCONY
Bayonne Adour
VELAY
Mende VIVARAIS
Rodez
Uzès
Viviers

NAVARRE BÉARN
BIGORRE
COMMINGES
Albi
Toulouse Montpellier
TOULOUSE
Béziers
Carcassonne Narbonne
Nîmes
Arles
Avignon
PROVENCE

THE EMPIRE

Rhône

ARAGON

MEDITERRANEAN SEA

FRANCE
in 11th to 13th Centuries

|||||| Possessions of William the Conqueror
▓▓▓▓ Possessions of Henry II, about 1180
░░░░ Possessions of Henry III, 1272
▒▒▒▒ French Crown Lands, 1180
∘∘∘∘ Boundary of France in the 12th Century

ligious literature. The first signs of revival certainly came before the fateful date.

For anyone not blindly committed to the economic interpretation of history, the most tempting, the most natural, hypothesis is that salvation came through the Church. As an organization she had been inevitably affected by the decadence of Rome and the surge of barbarism: Church historians do not attempt to conceal the sorry condition of the clergy during the Dark Ages. The Church had wealth, and wealth attracted the worldly, who were also the violent. Benefices were treated as legitimate booty: there were Frankish bishops who could fight, but who could not read. Clerics did not observe celibacy: as a result, Church dignities became family possessions, and Church properties could be inherited by children. Simony, or trafficking with the things that are God's, was rife; the profit motive was brazenly extended into the religious field. The very light of the world was dimmed.

Fortunately, the spirit of Christianity survived in the monasteries. From earliest times a few men had sought perfection in solitude, but these anchorites were too completely withdrawn from the world to help others. It was the greatness of St. Benedict of Nursia to reconcile asceticism with normal activity. His rule (Monte Cassino, *ca.* 529), at the same time austere and humane, combined private meditation with community life and provided a healthy balance of labor and prayer. The Benedictines cleared wildernesses; although they spurned wealth, their estates grew; although they went into "the desert," towns in many cases sprang into existence under the protection of their wise governance. Already Gregory the Great (590–604) had shown what spiritual power a monk could wield when elected to the Papacy. Yet even the monasteries could not fully cope with Frankish barbarism. The thriving abbeys, like the bishoprics, became tempting prey for the war lords. The essential step was to free the monastic establishments from the rapacity of the fighting caste.

The first great reformed abbey was Cluny (founded in 910). With its fame for purity of life, its influence radiated. Branches were created, older houses became affiliated, as "priories," forming a veritable order under the rule of a single abbot. This centralization gave the Cluniacs a power that isolated monasteries had lacked. In conjunction with the Papacy they could carry on their program of Church reform: to enforce the celibacy of the clergy, to eliminate simony, to reject lay control.

Thus purified from within and liberated from wordly bondage, the Church was able to make her influence felt. Her own courts were scrupulous and enlightened, compared with the rough justice meted out by the barons. Her vast and ever-increasing domains were governed with less brutality than those of the secular lords: "it was good to live under the crosier." She attempted, not wholly in vain, to mitigate the great feudal curse of incessant and ubiquitous warfare through the "Peace of God" and the "Truce of God," declaring a closed season against human slaughter. With excommunication and interdict as bloodless but deadly weapons, she enforced upon the rulers some degree of moral discipline. She attempted to turn even those who took the sword into servants of God by making chivalry an order with a moral code and a religious ideal. We shall see that this battle with feudal anarchy was dubious at best; but, however precarious, it was a victory of the spirit. The marked strengthening of moral order led to the improvement of material order, and with order came confidence and prosperity.

The words of the Burgundian monk Raoul Glaber,[1] quoted by Michelet and often repeated, express admirably that sense of a great revival; "It seemed as though the earth were shaking off the rags of its antiquity and clothing itself anew with a white mantle of churches." The first visible efforts, the first visible results, of the movement were undoubtedly ecclesiastical. For three hundred years the Catholic Church, in spite of harrowing struggles within and without, was to dominate the Western world. The paths of the pilgrims turned into trade routes; the guilds were closely associated with brotherhoods under the patronage of a saint; the one great collective enterprise of Europe was the crusade; the supreme cultural achievements—Scholastic philosophy and church architecture—were inseparable from Christianity. It was the age that produced St. Bernard, St. Dominic, St. Francis, St. Thomas, St. Louis, and whose magnificent afterglow was *The Divine Comedy*. The inner harmony of that age, its unity of faith and discipline, was by no means so absolute as Henry Adams,[2] among others, would have us believe: a living culture is made up of conflicts and tensions, not of perfect repose. The Catholic way of life was affected by many antagonistic elements. Still, for three centuries, its supremacy could not be challenged.

So, in studying the growth of France in this period, we cannot take the Capetian house as our center. The dynasty might almost be called a by-product of the Church. We have noted that it was the archbishop of Rheims who secured the crown for Hugh Capet; and the king was later advised by Gerbert of Aurillac, the future Sylvester II, a shrewd politician as well as an earnest reformer. Hugh Capet himself was a quasi-ecclesiastical character, proud of being the lay abbot of the great shrine St. Martin of Tours.[3] His successor Robert, although he ran afoul of the clergy for having married a relative, was a priest in spirit, pious to the core, deeply and, at times, quaintly charitable, a forerunner of the sainted Monseigneur Myriel in *Les Misérables*. To the alliance with

Rheims and Tours was added that with Saint-Denis. The powerful abbey was the mainstay of the Capetians. By acquiring the county of Vexin, they had become the vassals of Saint-Denis: they proudly carried its pennon, the *oriflamme*, and adopted *Montjoie St. Denis!* as their war cry. The abbots were the treasurers and the advisers of the monarchy: Suger governed in the name of Louis VII.

Divine right was not a doctrine in those days but a confused sentiment. The lilies in the king's arms were credited with a mystic significance. The modest Capetians had miraculous powers: their touch healed "the king's evil," a kind of scrofula.[4] The people, led by the clergy, thronged to catch a glimpse of the Lord's Anointed, as though his presence brought a benison. It was thanks to the Church that an almost obliterated Frankish title became endowed with sacred majesty. All this is essential to understand Joan of Arc, and Joan of Arc is the key to French national feeling. France was created by the victory of order, championed by the Church, over chaos, represented by the feudal fighting caste. In this contest, the king was but a chosen instrument, and the bourgeois were later allies. It was the monarchy that made France; but it was the Church that made the monarchy.[5]

⚜ FRANCE'S PRE-EMINENCE IN CHRISTENDOM: CRUSADES, CLUNY, UNIVERSITY OF PARIS, GOTHIC ARCHITECTURE

If our subject were the history of Western civilization, our main task then would be the study of the Church. Monks, friars, crusaders, master builders, Schoolmen are undeniably the most significant characters of the period. But the manifold activities of the Church were not limited to France: nationalism was yet unborn. We cannot think of St. Bernard as a Frenchman, of St. Dominic as a Spaniard, of St. Francis and St. Thomas as Italians. In that immense and fascinating field, we must select only that which pertains to our definite purpose, the biography of France as a nation.

Now the French kings, and that still unformed entity the French people, derived peculiar advantages from their close association with the Catholic faith. The ancient title given to France, "the eldest daughter of the Church," is not a meaningless boast. Ultimately Germany and Italy were to suffer from being the seats of the empire and the Papacy; their national consciousness was retarded; they wore out their strength, and even their faith, in endless strife. Spain was long absorbed in a crusade of her own, the reconquest of the peninsula from the Moors. The sovereigns of England for three centuries remained conscious of their French origin; the larger part of their domains was in France and nominally under the suzerainty of the French kings. This left a free field for

France and gave her not, indeed, a full political and spiritual hegemony, but undoubted prestige; and the collective pride which resulted was to be a basic element in national consciousness. The clever Nazi journalist Friedrich Sieburg asked ironically: "Is God a Frenchman?" [6] The query is but the distant echo of the old chronicles: *Gesta Dei per Francos,* the Deeds of God through the French.

It was in France that the First Crusade was preached, at Clermont, by a pope of French birth. The king abstained; but there were enough French lords in the expedition, including Frenchified Normans and Flemings, to turn the principalities of the Holy Land into curious little bits of feudal France. The main charter, the *Assizes of Jerusalem,* was drawn up in French. Louis VII took part in the Second Crusade, Philip Augustus, in the third—neither of them with brilliant credit. The fourth, diverted by the Venetians against Constantinople, resulted in a brief Latin Empire of the East, which, like Palestine, was French in its institutions, manners, and speech; the story of the epic and sordid adventure was told with great vigor and restraint by Geoffroy de Villehardouin, from Champagne. The last two full-fledged crusades, the seventh and the eighth, were the personal enterprises of St. Louis. The ill-fated mandate of France over Syria and Lebanon, between the two world wars, was the last link in a tradition that began in 1099.

The great orders were of course "Catholic," i.e., universal, and not French. Still, it was not indifferent that the powerful reforming centers, Cluny, Citeaux, Clairvaux, should be located in France. It may be said that the Cluniac order, with two thousand affiliated monasteries, was the chief ecclesiastical power in Christendom: Hildebrand (Gregory VII), who did so much to restore discipline in the Church and to repress abuses, who asserted so boldly the independence, nay, the supremacy, of the spiritual power, sought his inspiration and found his mainstay in that great organization. The abbey church of Cluny, sold and pulled down at the time of Napoleon I, was the largest in Christendom. Cluny could entertain at the same time and in befitting style pope, emperor, and king, with their several retinues. The head of the order, called the Abbot of Abbots, was a magnificent personage.[7]

The University of Paris likewise was a Catholic, not a national, institution. It became and remained for two centuries the great center of theological studies, next to the Papacy, "the second light of the world," *altera lux mundi.* But before it was formally organized, it was the fame of a Frenchman, Abelard, and the attraction of the royal city that drew thousands of students into the Latin Quarter on the slopes of St. Genevieve's Hill. As the kings increased, not in virtue but in power, and as the popes declined, the university was later captured by the city and the nation. With regrettable results; its thought became desiccated; the "other light of the world" turned into a political factor, not invariably on the right side. But before those dismal days, the university served harmoniously the Catholic faith and the spirit of France. Its degrees were valid throughout the Catholic world; and many a cleric carried with him, in remote parts of Europe, the nostalgic memory of his ardent youth in the Latin Quarter.

Finally, the splendid architecture which was to be called in derision "Gothic" was known, when it arose, as *Opus Francigenum,* French-born art. It grew in the royal domain, at Saint-Denis, and in the many cathedrals of that region. Some of the more modest and lesser known, Noyon, Laon, have in their robust austerity an appeal hardly matched by their more magnificent sisters, Paris, Chartres, Rheims, Amiens. That art soon reached the utmost borders of Catholic Europe, from Sweden to Spain. Everywhere the builders who gave the impetus were French; few of their foreign pupils have equalled, none have surpassed, their masters. Because of these achievements, it was a source of pride, even in the darkest hours, to be a subject of His Most Christian Majesty.

COMPLEXITY OF MEDIEVAL FAITH: SAINTS, VIRGIN, SCHOLASTICISM

It is essential, however, that we should not turn the age of the crusades and chivalry into a Utopia. Had this great period been one of perfect harmony under the firm guidance of the Church, we could scarcely understand why it offered so many glaring evils, and why it came to an inglorious end; for in the two centuries after the death of St. Louis (1270), we shall find divisions even within the Holy See, three popes hurling anathemas at one another, the great University of Paris babling in senile decay, the Turks in Constantinople and threatening the whole Danubian basin, a frankly pagan Renaissance, a virulent Reformation, and a schism unhealed to this day.

The fact is that Catholicism never offered in that age of faith the monolithic unity which is a totalitarian dream. Its vitality was proved by its diversity. And Christianity never was the sole ruler of the commonwealth. There were other elements at work, some of barbaric origin, some Greco-Roman, some born of the new conditions; and with these the Church had to establish an ever-shifting *modus vivendi.*

If we attempt to define the faith of the Middle Ages, we find not a single well-ordered system but a tumultuous array. The essential dogmas of orthodoxy were hardly challenged at all: the Oriental heresy of the Cathars, Manichean and mystic, remained an enigmatic exception.[8] But within the Trinitarian framework, we find tendencies so diverse that they

might belong to different civilizations. There is no denying that superstition was rife. Much of it, as we have seen, was of pre-Christian,
and perhaps of pre-Gallic origin. Much was added by the eager credulity
of the time. For in those days, the miraculous was not a scandal: it
was the norm. By definition, anyone noted for holiness was credited
with supernatural powers. St. Bernard, who fled the world and was constantly dragged back into the world, performed miracles wherever he
went; the wondrous healing touch was ascribed even to the commonplace
Capetians. Just as the Bestiaries, gravely mixing natural history with
spiritual instruction, taught the magic virtues and mystic significance
of animals, real or imaginary, so saints of questionable authenticity
proved hardly less potent than their better-established compeers: an
abstraction like St. Sofia, a picture turned into a person like St. Veronica,
a misreading like the Eleven Thousand Virgins of Cologne, or St. Guin-
efort, a greyhound who wrought miracles in his own right.

This magnetic field of the spirit was most active in the places hallowed by the sacred personages, the scenes of their labors and of their
martyrdom. These attracted great throngs of pilgrims. The pilgrimage
was an essential feature of medieval life: a panacea for sickness, grief,
or guilt, the glorious adventure of a lifetime, full of perils and of spiritual
rewards. In France Sainte-Geneviève, Saint-Denis, Mont-Saint-Michel,
the Black Virgin of Chartres, Le Puy-en-Velay were the principal resorts; in Spain, Santiago (St. James) of Compostella; in Italy, the tomb
of St. Nicholas at Bari, later the Santa Casa of Loretto; above all Rome
and the Holy Land. And the power dwelt in the relics of the saints;
these treasures were preserved in jeweled shrines, themselves housed in
churches of surpassing beauty like the Sainte-Chapelle in Paris. When
the Latins took Constantinople, they considered relics, not Greek manuscripts, the richest part of their booty.

Above this multitudinous quasi-pantheon, but apart from the severe
simplicity of Trinitarianism, there was the special veneration (*hyper-
dulia*) accorded to the Virgin. It satisfied the need for an intercessor
all-powerful in Heaven, yet in close touch with humanity. The human
side of Jesus the Mediator had been overshadowed by His Godhead:
His Mother remained the universal maternal friend, not bound by inflexible rules of justice but ever ready with her bountiful grace. The
most touching stories of her benefactions were told in sacred song, narrative, or drama; the finest of the churches were placed under her in-
vocation, so that in our minds "Notre-Dame" and "cathedral" have become almost synonymous.

The rich fantastic garland of the Golden Legend does not give us the
essentials of medieval faith. This faith had two poles, the sense of sin

and mystic union with God. The imagination of the time, at once boldly allegorical and vigorously realistic, pictured, dreaded, and fought sin as a personal enemy, the Devil. He was lurking everywhere, even in the cell of the studious monk, and most of all in the smiles of woman— *janua diaboli*. Life thus became a long struggle with the Prince of Darkness in which man would inevitably succumb but for the somewhat capricious assistance of the Virgin and the saints. So great was the Devil, and so real, that short-sighted, ambitious men would sign a pact with him: the priest Theophilus was the first on record in a long series, which, through Dr. Faustus, reaches Melmoth the Wanderer and Adrian Leverkühn.[9] Hundreds of deluded women confessed to witchcraft and commerce with Satan; devil-worship came to be a recognized and infectious mental disease. But the medieval mind was not forever oppressed by morbid fancies. It was felt that good humor was the best weapon against the Arch-Enemy. Familiarity had bred contempt: the redoubtable tempter was made to cut a sorry figure for the amusement of the populace. The Devil was the fool as well as the villain in the drama of life. Many popular tales relate with gusto the tricks that Devil and saints play upon each other, like village neighbors with a rough sense of fun.

There is hardly any instance of medieval credulity or fanaticism that cannot be matched in our enlightened era; on the other hand, there is hardly an essential problem debated by present-day philosophers that was not anticipated by the Schoolmen. We are apt to think of Scholasticism only in its decadent aspect—an enormous logical mill grinding dead truths into impalpable dust: it has taken the outstanding merit of such scholars as Etienne Gilson and Jacques Maritain to make the lay mind realize the greatness not of Thomism alone but of medieval thought as a whole. Scholasticism did not spend dreary centuries arguing how many angels could stand on the point of a needle. Its problems are the essential problems which are the despair and the glory of the human mind: the nature and validity of general ideas, the conflict between eternal law and that freedom of will which is the condition of spiritual life, the apparent abyss between reason and faith.

That tremendous effort cannot be reduced to a single formula. Scholasticism was not the serene expounding of one majestic doctrine: it was a battlefield. Aristotle, the guide of St. Thomas, was formally condemned before he was enthroned. There was throughout the Scholastic age a mystic strain, notable already in John the Scot (Scotus Erigena), whose genius shines so strangely in the murk of Carolingian decadence. Neither St. Bernard, nor St. Francis, nor St. Bonaventura was a logician first of all. We cannot forget that Joachim of Floris with his promise of a third dispensation, an "Eternal Gospel" of the Holy

Spirit, had a vast and prolonged influence even upon the strictest of Franciscans. There was no unity either among those who attempted to bridge the gap between revelation and the human intellect. If St. Thomas achieved a miraculous balance, others went far in the direction of pure rationalism. In Jean de Jandun, for instance, there are traces of ironic agnosticism worthy of Montaigne, Voltaire, and Renan. And Roger Bacon gave a very definite statement of the experimental method. The idea that "all men, everywhere, at all times" held the same unchangeable faith cannot resist the most cursory examination.

Medieval Christianity was not exclusively a philosophy: it was a way of life, and no ideals could be more sharply contrasted than those of worthy men who called themselves Christians. Some harped on organization and power; some, like the Waldensians and the Franciscans, thought first of holy poverty and the gospel preached to the poor. There were contemplative orders, utterly withdrawn from the world; fighting orders, Templars, Hospitallers, Teutonic Knights; Friars who preached and worked among the common people. These contrasting aims were not merely facets of a single truth: they bred conflicts. The medieval Church was constantly rent by quarrels: between theologians of different schools—*odium theologicum* has remained a byword—between the partisans of Roman autocracy and those of a wide autonomy for the local churches.

To these conflicts within the Church must be added those against antagonistic elements without. Christianity had succeeded in coloring them but had not been able to overcome them. The Church anointed the king: but the origin of royal power was Frankish and Roman, that is to say heathenish and pagan. The Church sought to direct economic life: but her espousal of poverty, her condemnation of interest were doomed to failure. Insidiously, the pursuit of wealth reasserted its power; Jews, Templars, "Lombards," practiced the banking outlawed by the canons. The Church sanctified the fighting man into a knight: but the very existence of the feudal caste was based on violence and pride, while Christianity should have heralded the reign of the meek.

Hence the brutal opposition of light and darkness and the sudden flights from one to the other that bewilder us in medieval history. A lord sets fire to a monastery, but will touch no meat on a Friday; a city, seeking its franchise, kills its bishop; an excommunicated emperor starts on a crusade, but turns the crusade into a friendly visit to the Saracens. A "devil" like Robert of Normandy, or later Gilles de Rais, remains capable of abrupt repentance. The miracle, physical or spiritual, is always at hand. The plays which depict the erring nun, the priest trafficking with Satan, the bandit, the murderer redeemed in a flash, had good psychological justification. It was the age when wonder was commonplace.

So we must be steeled to expect the incredible. A rough familiarity with holy things which to our less robust faith would appear sacrilegious: mock ceremonies right in the sanctuary, the Boy Bishop, the Feast of the Donkey, the Pope of Fools. "Goliards," or wandering scholars, noted for gluttony and gambling, singing lustily in praise of their riotous life—and for all their sinfulness clerics still, whom the pope found it hard to disbar from taking part in services, preaching, selling indulgences. Monks exposed to ridicule not only in merry tales but in the stone carvings of their own churches. Strangest of all, a very early poem, *The Pilgrimage of Charlemagne,* a fantastic medley of epic, satire, and bawdy tale about the great emperor and how he brought back the relics of the Passion worshipped at Saint-Denis. The young hero of the delightful romance *Aucassin and Nicolette* airily proclaiming, "No heaven for me, with the snivelling monks; let me go with the noble knights and fair ladies."

Perhaps the most striking example of medieval contrasts is found in the story of the Children's Crusade. In 1212, Etienne (Stephen), a young shepherd from Cloyes near Vendôme, offered to lead a crusade: where the worldly wise had failed, unspoilt souls, beloved of Christ, would succeed. He claimed miraculous powers; it is said that as many as thirty thousand children responded to his call; the movement was praised by Innocent III. The juvenile host reached Marseilles. Two shipowners, Hugh Ferry and Guillem Porc, offered to transport them. Of the seven ships, two were wrecked. The other five were safely taken to Bougie and Alexandria, where the young crusaders were coolly sold into slavery. Seventeen years later seven hundred survivors were liberated by agreement. A masterly stroke of business: the age of faith was not so naive after all.

CHAPTER VII

Lay Society in the Middle Ages: Nobles, Peasants, Bourgeois

⚔ FEUDALISM: A CONDITION, NOT A SYSTEM

France was created by her kings in their age-long struggle against feudal anarchy. This simple formula agrees with the trend of events over seven centuries, but in the tangle of daily life the vast overall pattern is apt to become obscured. The duel between feudalism and royal power never reached perfect definiteness. Just as Christianity colored all other elements without absorbing them, so did feudalism affect both the monarchy and the Church. Bishops and abbots were feudal lords as well as spiritual leaders. The king belonged to that very feudal order that he combated. The sovereign whose virtues gave unrivalled prestige to his office, St. Louis, was also the one most respectful of feudal rights. Repeatedly the kings gave feudalism a new vigor by creating rich *apanages*—feudal holdings on the grandest scale—for the junior branches of their family. This ambiguity lasted as long as the ancient regime: on the eve of the Revolution Louis XVI could not make up his mind whether he was the apex of the feudal pyramid, that is to say, the born leader of the privileged classes, or the head of the whole nation, bent upon imposing upon all his subjects a single law without distinction of classes.

History is haunted with enormous phantoms which dissolve before the realistic eye, and yet direct imperiously the action of practical men. Feudalism is one of them. At the start it was neither an ideal nor a system but a condition. People did not become conscious of its existence until it had ceased to fit the times. Its "laws" were formulated late in its development, and only in order to limit its abuses: every attempt to define and organize feudalism was intended not to promote but to check its growth.

Three different conceptions are evoked by the term feudalism. They overlap, but they do not coincide. The first is the division of society into classes, each with a sharply different status. In the simplest and roughest form we find a dominant class enjoying every liberty and a subordinate, or even servile, class entirely at the mercy of its masters. Such a condition did prevail in the Dark Ages: the common herd had no rights. This brutal relationship became softened in the Middle Ages: still, the serfs remained *taillables et corvéables à merci*—taxes and forced labor could be exacted from them at their lord's pleasure. The lower classes obtained a status of their own, but the notion of privilege survived until the fourth of August, 1789. Some would say that, faint but distinct, it has endured to the present day.

Such a condition is frequently the result of conquest. A feudal class of this kind was imported into England by William of Normandy. The *adelantados* of Spanish America were examples of such a feudal type. Of course this feature is more strongly marked when the difference in status corresponds to an indelible difference in race: the aristocracy of the Old South liked to think of its privileges as feudal.

This simple explanation of feudalism was implicitly accepted for centuries. The nobles were manifestly the fighting caste: it was reasonable to believe that they had conquered by the sword the position they still held by the sword. This theory was formulated by Boulainvilliers early in the eighteenth century in defense of nobiliary privileges; it was accepted, but as a reason for challenging those very privileges, by Abbé Siéyès, the champion of the Third Estate in 1789.[1] In the case of France the hypothesis, propounded some twelve hundred years after the event, fails to work. Conquest of the most brutal kind is an undeniable fact, but the barbaric invaders did not long remain a separate element. From the first they sought to insert themselves into the framework of Gallo-Roman society, which still enjoyed great prestige in their eyes. The winning of Gaul by Clovis was, as we have seen, mostly a victory of Gallo-Roman Catholicism over Gothic and Burgund Arianism. The Frankish chieftain was proud to accept a Roman title, and he had Gallo-Romans among his advisers and lieutenants. When race and religion create no insuperable obstacle, assimilation may be extremely rapid. In Capetian France, half a millennium after Clovis, conquest had long ceased to be the sole title of the landed nobility. Holdings had been transferred, divided, merged, through inheritance and marriage in such a way as to have little in common with the original grants. When the kings assumed the right to issue patents of nobility to commoners, the last trace of racial difference had long vanished. Feudalism is not "in the blood."

The second conception of feudalism is that of personal allegiance, the fealty of man to man, more binding than any written law. This was supposed to have been introduced by the Franks, although it had existed among the Gauls. In the nineteenth century, the "Teutomaniac" school of history, finding the source of all heroism, faith, chivalry, and freedom in the forests of primitive Germany, was very partial to that conception. It lends itself to romantic idealization, for loyalty is a magic word. And it can be used to construct a Utopian fabric of most impressive symmetry. Every man—every free man, that is, for there is no feudal relationship between lord and villein—acknowledges a liege and holds his estate from him in exchange for definite obligations. No mere sordid cash nexus; no possession without duties; no allegiance that is not reciprocal, for if the vassal owes service, the suzerain owes protection. From step to step, the apex of the feudal pyramid is reached: there stands the king, lord over all, who holds his power from God.

Of all Utopias, this is perhaps the one of greatest appeal; but a glance at the chronicles of the Dark Ages and the Middle Ages suffices to prove that it is but a Utopia. Not merely because sinful men were unworthy of the ideal system, but because the alleged system presented a fatal flaw. In the early stages, and perhaps from the very beginning of feudalism, rights and duties ceased to be attached exclusively to the personal relationships of men: they became merged with the possession of land, which, in practice if not in theory, had become hereditary. This shattered the perfect pyramid of feudal Utopia. It was possible for a man to own several estates and, therefore, to owe allegiance to different masters. With the divisions and reunions of property through marriage, inheritance, or purchase, the situation became inextricable. A lord might find himself the vassal of his own vassal: the king held Vexin from the Abbey of Saint-Denis. The count of Champagne did homage to the king of France for part of his domain but also, for other parts, to the emperor, to the duke of Burgundy, to two archbishops, four bishops, and the abbot of Saint-Denis. The vicinity of Domremy, the village where Joan of Arc was born, was divided between the crown of France, the duchies of Lorraine, Bar, and Burgundy, the county of Champagne. In such a tangle, personal loyalty was bewildered. When a quarrel arose, a man could not keep his faith to one of his overlords without felony to the others.

Finally, the feudal condition (a more adequate term than "regime" or "system") has been defined by Guizot, a profound historian of civilization, as "the confusion of authority and property." It must be noted that such a confusion always exists at the summit. If a government is truly sovereign, even in democratic countries, it can lawfully exercise the right of eminent domain: ultimately, authority *is* property, and private ownership is subordinated to the general interests of the commonwealth. But, on a lower level, the modern state attempts to keep authority and property separate. When property openly wields power, we have plutocracy, which we call an evil; when power is used to command wealth, we have *concussio,* or, in the vernacular, graft.

The "feudal" confusion defined by Guizot arises whenever the central government is so weakened that it cannot control distant parts or powerful individuals. Before the complete collapse of the state there is a twilight stage. The theoretical authority of the sovereign remains unimpaired, but his delegates usurp proprietary rights over their functions and over the territory which they were appointed to rule. Conversely, those men who through their wealth or valor have made themselves paramount in a city or province are acknowledged by the central power as its representatives, an effective face-saving device. The two processes, starting from opposite ends, reach the same stage.[2] A *de facto* situation: the strong man rules. A justification *de jure:* the actual leader is given official recognition by the waning authority still nominally supreme. In the chaotic Morocco of the early twentieth century Raisuli was considered at times as a delegate of the sultan, at times as a bandit. His methods were scrupulously—or unscrupulously—the same under both titles. But in times of trouble, the stark facts count for more than the shadowy legitimacy. It has been said that feudalism of this type is "not a solution, but a dissolution."

This malignant form of decay may appear anywhere in the world and in any age: it is not the sad privilege of any race, creed, or period. It was manifest in the decay of the Roman Empire; it was accelerated when the mighty hand of Charlemagne was removed; it prevailed in old Japan; it was rife in Morocco before the French lent substance to the empty title of the Maghzen. It is virulent wherever there is ubiquitous civil war: the various leaders of armies in the Chinese, Mexican, and Russian crises were for a time incipient feudal lords.

This view is not cynical, but realistic. The Roman generals who conquered the imperial dignity in order to plunder the treasury, the Gothic, Burgund, Frankish, Norse bands which looted Gaul for hundreds of years served as patterns for the later robber barons. Note that the feudal virtues, personal loyalty and physical courage, were eminent, even though spasmodic, among those rough warriors. Note also that among the feudal chiefs some, at any rate, were not bandits: in many of the cities the head of the community was the bishop. (But we must not forget that even the Church, in Frankish times, came near being engulfed in barbaric chaos.) Finally the gang leader, if we care to give him that opprobrious name, did create some degree of rough order within the territory that he controlled. Feudalism is anarchy arrested very near the bottom, but not quite at the bottom. "In those days, there was no king in Israel: every man did that which was right in his own eyes." Conditions in France were a little better: there was a king, although at first there was little royal power; and not "every man," but only the warrior chief, could enjoy the full privilege of the rugged individualist and be a law unto himself.

Even apart from the very real influence of the Church, the barons discovered that in the long run it was more profitable to levy toll on wandering merchants than to plunder them. The local ruler, with his stronghold on the hill and his trained band ready for action, justified his existence by putting down lesser bandits and by directing resistance when the land was harried by still wilder forces, Norsemen, Hungarians, or Saracens. The fighting caste thus foreshadowed the police and the army of less turbulent days. Lord Acton said, and his dictum is profoundly true, that power corrupts; but, in a different light, it may be said also that power educates.

THE FIGHTING CASTE GROWS ORNAMENTAL

The first sign of returning order was the concentration of power into fewer hands. There were innumerable petty sovereigns, but a few great lords stood out: the dukes of Burgundy, Normandy, Aquitaine; the counts of Flanders, Toulouse, Champagne. This process was slow: for two centuries after Hugh Capet, the master of a castle was practically independent. The Sire de Coucy could defy counts, dukes, and kings: he had no title but a stout fortress.[3] The tower of Montlhéry, on the high road between royal cities, remained a thorn in the all-too-solid flesh of Louis the Fat. These miniature potentates who survived in Germany until the Napoleonic era became a rarity in Capetian France. Still, the kinglet of Yvetot, a small town in Normandy, retained his "royal" dignity until the sixteenth century.[4]

Conquerors or bandits, the dominant class was then the fighting caste; no other definition will serve. Fighting was its only warrant to honors and profits, and fighting remained its business. Amending Guizot's formula, we might define feudalism as "the confusion of property and war." *Qui terre a, guerre a,* ran the proverb: land is the guerdon of war, and he who owns land must expect war. So the feudal lord's habitation was not a palace but a fortress; his followers were a garrison. He was educated for war, and for little else: proudly he proclaimed that he could neither read nor write, "being a gentleman." His pleasures were images of war, like the hunt, or training for war, like the tourney. His notion of justice was a challenge and a fight. Of any "chivalrous" reverence for woman there was, in this purely feudal age, hardly any trace. *The Song of Roland* presents the warrior in the most favorable light: rough-hewn, but ennobled by the crusading spirit. Other epics offer a less flattering picture: they are long tales of unrelieved brutality and treachery, as dark as the *Nibelungen*.

In the twelfth and thirteenth centuries there was a softening, almost a transformation, in the manners of the fighting caste. The battling lords were held in check by the Church, by their suzerains, by the king, and even by the newly organized cities. Many of the most turbulent perished in the crusades: it is amusing to find a conservative historian like Jacques Bainville considering this as a distinct benefit to civilization. In the South of France as well as in Italy the nobles frequently dwelt in the cities, not in forbidding fastnesses: as a result they were, in the etymological sense of the terms, more "urbane," more "polite" than their northern congeners.

It was the southern troubadours, some of them of aristocratic birth, who served as models for the northern trouvères. Southern princesses introduced into the uncouth North the refinements of their native land. Notable among them was the countess of Champagne. The court of Champagne was wealthy in those days; for the count protected—not without profit—the thriving fairs of European importance, Troyes, Provins, Lagny, Bar-sur-Aube, held in his rather bleak domains. Thibaut of Champagne was one of the earliest of courtly poets. Chrétien de Troyes gave a sophisticated version of the Breton romances which focused the ideal of the ruling class far beyond the boundaries of Champagne and of France: courtesy as an essential attribute of the noble life, chivalry not merely as rude valor, but as deference for women, love as a liberal education and a virtue. It has been said that romantic love, and perhaps finely shaded sentiment, were inventions of the twelfth century.[5]

These refinements, however, did not spring from the inner principle of old feudalism: they were imposed from without. So, as the feudal caste increased in elegance, it declined in simple integrity. We might say—inevitably forcing the note—that the gorgeous trappings, the intricate ritual, the over-delicate feelings of late medieval society were flowers growing on ruins. While the fighting caste lost some of its offensiveness, it acquired no useful function. From a curse, it turned into a nuisance; from a nuisance, into a museum piece. It is freely admitted that museum pieces, and even nuisances, may be singularly attractive.

In the anxious twilight between the great Middle Ages and the Renaissance, in the fourteenth and fifteenth centuries, feudalism became increasingly ornate as it ceased to be functional. Froissart, indifferent to all lofty causes, took delight in the brilliant show of aristocratic life: for him, fighting had become a pageant. Never were suits of armor so beautiful as when artillery had made them useless. "When Knighthood was in Flower," it had long ceased bearing fruit.

It is a profitable lesson in history to watch the slow fading away of barbaric customs. Much of the feudal spirit has survived into our democratic and business-minded world. Titles still exist, and armorial bearings. Only yesterday, the nobility, English, French, and particularly Prussian, obstinately believed that the career of arms should be their privilege. They ranked horsemanship far above scholarship: it takes but a pedant to understand a book, it takes a gentleman to know horseflesh. A generation ago, a cavalry officer ("dashing" by definition) still commanded a higher price in the matrimonial market than a mere engineer of corresponding rank. And above all, the true aristocrat clung to his right of private warfare, in the form of the duel. No court was competent to safeguard the honor of a nobleman. If you offended a member of your caste (commoners did not count) and killed him in loyal combat, honor was satisfied. German students used to inflict upon each other horrific but perfectly safe wounds: the scars served as a patent of nobility. The French courteously drew a drop of blood, or exchanged bullets without results. Within the memory of living men, dueling was not wholly extinct in our own feudal South. When we read of this aristocratic code, it seems as though Christianity, humanism, the Enlightenment, and the Industrial Revolution had never occurred.[6]

HARSHNESS OF THE PEASANTS' FATE

In the Dark Ages the peasant was not merely plundered, he was despised. He was accused of being filthy, cowardly, evil-minded, subhuman. *Villanus,* the villager, is the origin of the French word *vilain,* which means ugly of countenance and disposition, and of our English word "villain." If people are to be oppressed, it is a comfort to know that they deserve their misery. This feeling of distrust and distaste lasted interminably: it survived not only the Dark Ages, but the Middle Ages as well. Serfhood, however, was not so hopeless a state as ancient slavery; and serfhood itself began to wane with the Renaissance of the eleventh century. The Church encouraged the freeing of serfs, except her own, who, since they belonged to God, had no cause to complain: the last serfs in 1789 were those of the Abbey of Saint-Claude. By 1270 serfhood had been greatly reduced in the royal domain. An edict of Louis X in 1315, declaring that all Frenchmen were "free according to the law of nature," was little more than a rhetorical flourish; at any rate, it was not denounced as an absurdity.

But the lot of the free peasant was hard, even under a gentle lord. His thatched hut was unfloored and windowless; his garments were of coarse hempen cloth, wool being reserved for his betters. A crude rotation of crops condemned one-third of the land to lie fallow every year. Famines were endemic: in the eleventh century, they recurred forty-eight times. Yet, as La Bruyère was to discover five hundred years later, that ill-tended herd was made up of men. They asserted their manhood through desperate revolts: castles were burned, and noble families murdered. If Wace in his *Roman de Rou* is to be trusted, the Norman rebels sang a rustic "Marseillaise" which sounds strangely modern: prophetic of the Lollards, the Chartists, and the agrarian revolutionists in Latin America and China. The *Pastoureaux* or Shepherds, learning that Louis IX was a prisoner in Egypt, assembled in 1251 for the avowed purpose of delivering him; but they accused barons and clerics of having betrayed the king, and their crusade assumed a menacing revolutionary tinge. They were hunted like wild beasts, and massacred without mercy. So were the *Jacques*[7] of a later age; so were the German peasants in the days of Martin Luther. Massacre and again massacre: a tragic refrain in the annals of the poor.

All nobles, quarrel as they might among themselves, united for preserving the privileges of their order. The Church taught that servitude was but condign punishment. So the sole earthly hope of the oppressed was royal justice: and how faint, remote, delusive a hope! Nothing is so obscure as the birth of a feeling: still, because the peasants suffered most from feudal anarchy, it was fitting that they should embrace the alternative, monarchical unity. A treasure of vague mystic faith in the king was thus slowly gathered. As the "Shepherds" had risen in 1251 to deliver the saintly ruler, so did a shepherdess arise in 1429 to save the kingdom.

⚔ TEEMING LIFE OF THE CITIES

Of the one hundred and twelve cities of Roman Gaul, many had disappeared during the Dark Ages. Those which survived, contracted, impoverished, did not preserve their municipal institutions: no great loss, for the Roman regime had become grossly oppressive. The Renaissance of the eleventh century fostered urban growth. The cities ceased to be merely places of refuge and became centers of industry and trade. Order brought increasing wealth, and economic progress resulted in emancipation. If sheer revolt proves nothing but despair, a constructive revolution is a sign of vitality. It was in the richest trading and manufacturing communities, in Italy, on the Rhine, in Flanders, that the communal movement first broke out and achieved its most complete and lasting success.

In southern France, the communes secured their liberties with little violence: a number of noble families lived in the cities and were both more intelligent and more vulnerable than the northern lords. In the North blood was freely shed. The proud bishop of Laon, forced to hide himself in a barrel, was hacked to death by the mob (1112). Chateauneuf, near Tours, rebelled twelve times in a century against its master, the abbot of Saint-Martin; each time it was defeated.

The crusades were a godsend to the burghers. The nobles needed money to set out on their quest: many found it expedient to sell a charter. Or they wanted to secure peace and a steady revenue for their wives and children at home while they were battling the Saracens. Some saw the cool economic light: a charter might make the lord's income larger and safer. There were even "real estate developments," of the most approved modern type: enterprising lords opened new cities and made them attractive with liberal franchises. These deliberate creations may be known by their chessboard plan and by their names, advertising the proffered freedom: Villefranche, La Sauve, Sauveté, Sauveterre.

There was nothing systematic about the communal movement. If certain types of charters served as models, no bond was created between the communities which adopted them: just as, in America, cities under a commission or a manager do not form a federation. In northern France there were no unions to be compared with the Lombard leagues or the Hansa. The kings followed an opportunistic, or perhaps a haphazard, course. They favored communes in territory not their own, and discouraged them in the royal domain. However, they did grant a fair degree of self-government to towns known as *villes de bourgeoisie*. The chief difference between these and the full-fledged communes was that, as a rule, these royal boroughs did not elect their own mayor. Louis VI was called "the Father of the Communes"; but this title was perhaps less deserved than his other nicknames, the Wide-Awake and the Fat. We shall see that the militias of the communes fought for Philip Augustus at Bouvines in 1214: the wide rejoicing that followed that victory made it perhaps the first of "national" events.

The cities, while rebelling against feudal abuses, did not challenge the feudal order—or disorder. Their ambition was to secure a place therein: a commune could become a collective barony, with shield, motto, banner, with fortified walls and moat, with men-at-arms (its militia) and, at times, with vassals as well as suzerains. The belfry of the town hall soared as proudly as the baronial keep.

Cramped within their battlements, the cities were woefully unsanitary and constantly exposed to devastating fires; but their narrow, twisting lanes teemed with colorful life. Shop and workshop were one, and freely open to the gaze of the passer-by. The upper stories jutted out leaving but a jagged slit of sky. Suddenly, out of the gloom, there sprang the miracle of a Gothic spire.

The churches, and particularly the cathedrals, were not only gateways to the mystic world, they were intimately associated with the vigorous and joyous life of the burghers. They were built, no doubt, at the instigation and under the guidance of the clergy; their rich decoration was a Bible of stained glass and chiseled stone inspired by learned treatises such as the *Speculum Mundi* by Vincent of Beauvais. But if the Church maintained leadership, the whole people labored and rejoiced in the common work. The cathedral was a source of earthly civic pride; the tremendous towers were erected to the glory of God, but also as a sign of municipal wealth and power. The splendid edifice was not grimy then, but gleaming white; the ornate windows were gloriously clear; pillars and vaults were gaily painted; somberness, and the haunting thought of death, were later developments. The church served as the backdrop and as wings for the mystery and miracle plays. It was used also as a public hall for festivities, and even for political assemblies not of an ecclesiastical character. It was at Notre-Dame in Paris that the States-General were gathered which supported the antipapal policy of Philip the Fair. The house of God, in those days, rejoiced in being the house of the people.

The trades, reviving after half a millennium of decay, organized themselves into guilds or crafts governed by strict rules for the prevention of unfair practices. After a long apprenticeship the companion or journeyman could become a master, "if he knew the trade and had the wherewithal." As a religious shadow of the craft we find the Brotherhood (*Confrérie*), uniting masters, men, and apprentices to honor the patron saint, their representative in heaven. Since men of the same trade usually lived in the same district, the brotherhood was something of a neighborhood club; it had, if not its own church, at least its own chapel, the goal, on festival days, of its elaborate procession. The *Compagnonnage* was a union among journeymen: frowned upon by the masters, it was at times compelled to turn into a secret order. Traces of the *Compagnonnages* survived quaintly right to the end of the nineteenth century by the side of the modern *syndicats* or unions.

✍ DECAY OF THE CITY SPIRIT

Here we have a third Utopia that failed, like the Christian commonwealth and the feudal regime. The medieval city-state, with its regulation of trade in the common interest, is an ideal which delighted William Morris and still appeals to many. But both from the political point of view and from the economic, the system degenerated. Conservatism and privilege usurped the place of justice. Few cities in France ever were true democracies; even those in which rights of citizenship had been liberally extended became oligarchies in their turn. Only house-holders "possessing a gable on the street" could be burgesses: and among them a few powerful families secured a monopoly of honors, perquisites, and emoluments: a process which might be considered as quasi-feudal, Guizot's "confusion of authority and property."

A similar evolution took place in the crafts. The masters came to be not a natural elite but a caste. The "masterpieces" required to prove that the journeyman knew his trade were made so expensive, and the banquets to celebrate his promotion so elaborate, that only a master's son could afford them: already vested interests could protect themselves, to use Edouard Herriot's famous phrase, with a wall of moneybags. Selfishness is contentious: the crafts were engaged in constant legal fights to maintain their rights, bakers *vs.* pastry cooks, bootmakers *vs.* cobblers. Some of their lawsuits lasted for centuries.

Like the feudal caste the crafts, before the end of the Middle Ages, had become a hindrance. But, like the feudal caste, they could have their redeeming sense of *noblesse oblige.* Up to the Industrial Revolution there were found among craftsmen a respect for sound tradition, a love of work thoroughly done which gave the artisan the dignity of an artist: we can but envy the living, the human, perfection of much handiwork done in ancient France. But these achievements were not due to the abuses of the system. It is necessary to remember the cumbrous, anti-quated policy, the selfish, restrictive spirit of the crafts to understand the liberalism, verging on anarchy, of the eighteenth-century reformers. Not an oppressive tradition alone was condemned, but the very idea of regulation; the sole remedy appeared to be *laissez faire, laissez passer.*

Out of these cities arose a culture with a racy, pungent savor. The bourgeois, no doubt, enjoyed the miraculous stories, in narrative or dramatic form, about the Virgin and the saints, the epics which sang the deeds of the fighting caste, and later, the refined romances of chiv-alry. But they had also a literature of their own: mocking tales with a touch of the bawdy, uproarious farces, satirical songs, the vast animal cycle of *Renart the Fox.* Their tone was frankly antifeudal, at times even anticlerical. Guillaume de Lorris, about 1230, had all but completed a delicate allegory of love, *The Romance of the Rose*. Some forty years later Jean Clopinel, of Meung-sur-Loire, tagged on to the frail and graceful poem an enormous sequel into which he poured his vast store of knowledge, his prejudices, his surprisingly definite and bold opinions about institutions and men. Such a good judge as Gaston Paris called him the Voltaire of the Middle Ages. This monstrosity—two unequal, ill-assorted poems under the same title—achieved instant success, and remained a European classic for over two hundred years.

It would be idle to deny that the bourgeois spirit, at its best in Jean de Meung, had robust qualities: common sense, first of all, and a firm grasp of immediate realities. Polite literature escapes from the close atmosphere of the ladies' court only to lose itself in the haze of a childish fairyland: it is a relief to be on solid earth again. Rabelais, La Fontaine, Molière, Balzac, Maupassant: all show traces of the bourgeois tradition. But that spirit lacks poetry, and most of all generosity. Tough, cynical, often foul, it sullies every great subject it touches. It sees but the seamy side of life: not religion but the avarice, hypocrisy, and licentiousness of clerics; not love but lust, and the deceitfulness and shrewishness of women; not the people struggling and suffering but the villein, dirty, grasping, and stupid. The legend of Charlemagne, refracted through the petty bourgeois mind, becomes a parody freely sprinkled with obscenities. It was said even of Jean de Meung, "The Rose wilts at his touch." Bourgeois fun is cruel: an eternal *Vae Victis!*, a paean to successful cunning: its hero is Renart the Fox, duping everyone, and grinning at his victims. It is a commonplace that in every nation there is a Don Quixote and a Sancho Panza; the aristocracy could be quixotic at times, even the common people had flashes of the crusading or the national fire, the medieval bourgeois hardly ever. Political history, economic history, literary history come to the same verdict.

Yet these petty bourgeois worshipped in the Gothic churches which seem to us permeated with other-worldliness. No civilization is homogeneous, whether its symbol be the Virgin or the Dynamo; and it is vain to attempt any rational reconciliation between its extremes.

CHAPTER VIII

The Rise of the Capetians: 987-1270

⚔ THE CAPETIAN DYNASTY, NUCLEUS OF THE NATION

What did it mean, in 987, to be the king of France? In theory, a great deal. The king was the successor of Clovis and Charlemagne. If he did not aspire to the whole of their heritage, he had at any rate elusive claims to *Francia Occidentalis,* all Frankish land west of the empire. Hugh Capet's kingdom extended even beyond the present limits of France: Flanders was part of it, and so was Catalonia. And the king was the Lord's Anointed, a spiritual prerogative which was to prove more potent than much territory. But the majestic title was a shadow. It conferred no actual power and provided no revenue. The most definite of the privileges attached to it was that, in a vast, ill-defined area, sundry documents bore as a date the year of the king's reign, an honor as empty of significance as our expression *Anno Domini.*

The Frankish crown was supposed to be elective. As a rule, the choice was limited to members of the same family. The change from Merovingians to Carolingians was a bold departure which had to be sanctioned by the Church; and churchmen, Adalberon and Gerbert, stood back of Hugh Capet. There never was a definite electoral body to be compared with the Sacred College or with the later organization of the Holy Roman Empire. In vague tradition all fighting men were entitled to take part in the selection of their war chief, the king. But even in early Frankish times the approval of the armed horde, with vociferations and thumping of shields, was but a pseudodemocratic form akin to the plebiscites of dictators. A small group of leaders, ecclesiastical as well as temporal, assumed the right of nominating the ruler. In France that group never became hardened into an institution. Its membership fluctuated with the circumstances. The "twelve peers," who have

survived in popular imagination, have little more than a mythical existence, like those of Charlemagne and King Arthur.[1] The title Peer of the
Realm, of which the duke of Saint-Simon under Louis XIV was so
intensely proud, carried but a few ceremonial privileges. These became
definite only after they had lost all meaning.

The Capetians, being human, followed a universal tendency: to keep
a good thing within the family. This is exactly what the feudal lords
had done, and what the bourgeois oligarchs were to do. The masters
in the guilds and crafts followed the same pattern; so did, centuries
later, the king's officials, and particularly the judges. This tendency was
checked in the Church when celibacy was enforced; but it reappeared
in the form of "nepotism," and up to the French Revolution, bishoprics
"belonged" to certain noble families: the Rohans owned the see of Strasbourg. The family feeling, at odds with every system, theocracy or
democracy, feudalism or capitalism, invincibly reasserts itself.

Thus a family served as the nucleus of the nation. It was the good
fortune of the Capetians that for eight generations they had male heirs
who could be associated with their fathers' power, so that the election
became a form; Louis IX was the first king too young to rule by himself
at his accession. When, after fourteen generations, there was no male
heir in direct line of descent, an interminable war was the result; but
even in that crisis, the hereditary principle was no longer in dispute.
It had taken nearly three centuries to turn a series of precedents into a
fundamental law. It is strange that no democratic historian should have
deplored this waning and final atrophy of the elective process: perhaps
it was felt that one central usurpation was needed to curb many local
tyrannies. The path of progress is not invariably straight and plain.

In the eleventh century, "France" could mean three things: histori-
cally, the Frankish kingdom, vaguely associated with earlier Roman
Gaul; geographically, a region on the middle Seine, which, with altered
boundaries, was to become the province of Île-de-France;[2] in substantial reality, the domains of the duke of France. These holdings, at
the time of Hugh Capet, covered less than three thousand square miles,
about one-seventieth of the France we know. For a private landlord,
it would have been a handsome estate; but it was not of a different order
from those of other feudal sovereigns, Normandy, Champagne, Aquitania, Toulouse. Furthermore, it did not form a solid territory; the bulk
of it was found between the middle Seine and the middle Loire, with
many enclaves; there were odd detached parcels, Montreuil in the north,
Attigny in the east. The king did not even own Paris outright, although
he had a palace in the island of the city and a castle, the embryo of
the world-famous Louvre, on its western outskirts. He had no fixed

capital: he and his retainers moved from one fortified residence to another, generally in the Orleans region.

The first four Capetians survived and were good sons of the Church, even when they drew upon themselves her severest rebukes. They were not fainéants, like the last Merovingians; but on the national plane, their reigns are practically blank. The fifth in line, Louis VI (1108–1137), was a personage of a different stamp. Supported by the powerful abbot of Saint-Denis, by the archbishop of Rheims and the bishop of Orleans, he asserted himself as more than a mere feudal lord. He waged incessant miniature warfare against the petty barons who made the roads unsafe between two royal cities: the sires of Puiset, Montmorency, Coucy, Montlhéry. He fought with his own hand and was called the Bruiser and the Wide-Awake, although history chooses to remember him by his later and less flattering name, the Fat. He was the first to destroy the lairs of noble bandits; Richelieu completed the work, leaving little work to do for the Revolution, for, by 1789, the châteaux had turned into pleasant and inoffensive country houses. He supported the Communes, somewhat equivocally; he was more interested in weakening the lords than in enfranchising the people. Still, the charter he granted to his township of Lorris was widely imitated. He was vastly popular: not a lifeless symbol but a reality in mail cloth, swift with the sword.

Two great events before the accession of Louis VI were destined to influence his reign: the conquest of England by the Normans, and the First Crusade. The crusade was a boon to him: it had drawn many nobles into the fabulous and deceptive East. "The Eldest Son of the Church"—for he was the first formally to win that title—chose to stay at home and strengthen his position. The king, even though not the direct ruler, appeared as the redresser of wrongs, "the hand of justice"; on the request of the clergy he intervened as far away as Auvergne and the county of Toulouse.

The conquest of England had created a paradoxical situation. A French vassal, the duke of Normandy, found himself richer and more powerful than his suzerain. Unwilling to acknowledge the king's supremacy, he would be even more reluctant to give up his rich ancestral holdings south of the Channel. The inevitable stress was to bring about what Seeley called the first and the second Hundred Years' Wars.[3] Louis VI had repeated and inconclusive quarrels with the Normans. At Brenneville (1119), both he and Henry I (Beauclerc) showed their royal mettle; but it was a gentlemanly encounter, and, according to Orderic Vital, only three men were killed.

In the latter years of his reign, Louis VI was advised by Suger, Abbot of Saint-Denis, whose sagacity has remained proverbial. It was Suger who called the king "the supreme magistrate," a pregnant formula which many of the Capetians, Valois, and Bourbons failed to understand.

The royal heir, Louis the Young, now seventh of the name, had been brought up by clerics, almost in the cloister. He was intensely pious; yet at his first step, he clashed with the pope, Innocent II. The pontiff, over the protest of St. Bernard and Peter the Venerable, had given to his own nephew the important see of Bourges. The bishop-elect, rejected by the king, took refuge in Champagne. Louis VII, who had other grievances against the count, attacked him, undeterred by the pope's anathemas. The royal forces set fire to the town of Vitry; thirteen hundred of the inhabitants, trapped in the church, were burned to death. Their cries unhinged the young king, helpless to rescue them. From that time he was a crowned penitent.

Some realists, including wise Abbot Suger, regretted that the king had such a tender conscience. For an oppressive sense of guilt the approved remedy was a pilgrimage, best of all, that pilgrimage with the sword, the crusade. Louis VII resorted to that font of healing. The Christian colonies in the Holy Land had not been faring well: the whole population of Edessa had been massacred in one night. St. Bernard, the outstanding spiritual force of the age, preached a crusade, in France and in Germany. Both the emperor, Conrad III, and the French king decided to take up the cross. But their ability was not commensurate with their faith: exhausted before they reached their goal, they failed ignominiously. France had not suffered from the king's absence, for the realm was left in the hands of Abbot Suger.

The crusade proved disastrous also to Louis' married life. In the sharp contest for power between Henry I of England and Louis VI, brides were used as pawns. Henry gave his daughter Matilda to Geoffrey of Anjou (Plantagenet), a shrewd move. Louis countered by securing for his son the hand of Eleanor, heiress of Aquitania, an enormous extension of the royal domain. Young Louis fell in love—"immoderately," we are told—with his handsome and brilliant southern wife. He took her with him on his ill-starred crusade. She found the northern barons crude and preferred the company of her own countrymen. At Antioch she met her uncle, Raymond of Aquitania, whom she found more congenial than her royal husband. The rift deepened. Eleanor and Louis discovered after fifteen years that they were cousins and that their bond was not valid in the eyes of the Church. Abbot Suger did his best to save the rich dowry; but after his death a court of bishops and barons decided that the marriage should be annulled (1152).

Two months after recovering her freedom, Eleanor married Henry

Plantagenet, Count of Anjou, Maine, and Touraine, Duke of Normandy. Louis VII objected, as suzerain; but his protest was disregarded, and in 1154 he gave his formal and belated acquiescence. Four months later, on the death of King Stephen, Henry became king of England. The Angevin Empire, dwarfing the Capetian domains, reached from the Tweed to the Pyrenees.[4]

Louis VII was not a strong king; but he was compelled to take action in an even larger theater than his more vigorous father. In 1159, for instance, he came to the aid of Toulouse, threatened by Henry II Plantagenet: the Capetians had reached out a long way from the suburban castles of Montlhéry and Montmorency. He sheltered Thomas à Becket and sincerely attempted to reconcile the prelate with his king. He helped, none too efficiently, the rebellious sons of his rival. He supported Pope Alexander III against the emperor, Frederick I. Thanks to his close alliance with the clergy, he could establish direct connection with distant feudatories; so royal power did not suffer irremediably from his weakness. When he died in 1180, his fifteen-year-old son by a third marriage, Philip, had already been crowned at Rheims, and the Capetian line was secure.

THE FIRST STATESMAN: PHILIP AUGUSTUS

Secure, but not on easy terms, the adolescent ruler was faced with a coalition of his great vassals—chief among them, the counts of Champagne, Blois, and Flanders, and the duke of Burgundy. All were his near relations and were encouraged by his mother. He played them off one against the other, for they had no program but their greed; and he secured the neutrality of the English king, who had troubles of his own. In five years Philip had triumphed over them all.

Philip II (1180–1223) was to be called Augustus. The title is fulsome, but not absurd. For if we judge by results, his reign must be accounted one of the most brilliant in the annals of France. But he recalled Augustus in another respect: both the nephew of Caesar and the great Capetian were wily rather than heroic. Philip lived in the romantic era of chivalry and the crusades; yet no ruler could be more thoroughly realistic, in the usual sense of unscrupulous.

His vassals curbed but not tamed, he could address himself to his lifelong task, to break up the threatening might of the Angevins. Dissensions in his rival's family gave him his opportunity. He first supported Richard against Henry II. The aging choleric Plantagenet, assailed by both his surviving sons, had to come to terms at Azay-le-Rideau, and soon afterwards died at Chinon (1189).

So Richard, now king, and Philip were friends, and as friends they started on the Third Crusade with the mighty Frederick Barbarossa. The glamour of the names, however, covers a dismal story of squabbles, inefficiency, failure. Before reaching the Holy Land, Philip and Richard had quarreled. After the siege of Acre (1191), Philip hastened to return. Richard Coeur-de-Lion fought to his heart's content (and also offered his sister's hand to Saladin's brother). On the road back, Frederick was drowned, Richard captured by the duke of Austria and turned over to the new emperor, who held him for a staggering ransom. He finally managed to buy his freedom, receiving as a sop to his pride the illusory kingdom of Arles.

His brother John and his bosom friend Philip had done their best to keep him away; so he returned athirst for revenge and for five years waged fierce war against the Capetian. He was undoubtedly the better fighter; and, in his continental domains at least, he was worshipped as a hero. Yet unsteady as well as headstrong, "Richard Yea-and-Nay" as well as the Lion-Hearted, he could defeat but never crush the tenacious and resilient Philip. His building a great fortress on the Seine, Château-Gaillard near Les Andelys, was a purely defensive measure. Philip, on his part, although no coward and by far the shrewder statesman, lived through difficult days. He had to encounter a constant coalition of the feudal lords, still unresigned to royal supremacy; and he was at odds with his best ally, the Church, over a matrimonial imbroglio. He was compelled to sign peace with Richard at Vernon, with the rebellious barons at Péronne. But a few weeks later, Richard, disputing a treasure-trove with the viscount of Limoges, besieged him in Chalus and was hit in the shoulder by a bolt from a crossbow. The wound, ill-attended, festered, and the wayward hero died, leaving a free field to his more solid competitor.

To Richard succeeded his brother John (1199), although Arthur, son of an elder brother Geoffrey, may have had the better title. Philip played a cautious game, at first supporting Arthur then deserting him for a bribe. Some high-handed act of John's—he had snatched the fiancée of a southern noble, Hugh of Lusignan—enabled Philip to summon him before a court of his peers. John refused to stand trial. He was declared *félon,* and his holdings in France forfeited to the crown (1203). John, who held Arthur a prisoner, had him murdered. This caused a general revulsion against him; Philip was able to reduce Château-Gaillard, and master Anjou, Brittany, Maine, Normandy, Touraine. But the lands south of the Loire remained loyal to John, deeming the more distant suzerain the less dangerous to their liberties.

For nearly a decade the duel between Angevin and Capetian, although unabated, receded into the background. These years were filled with more spectacular struggles: the capture of Constantinople by the Latin crusaders, the fierce war on the Manichean heretics (Albigensians) in southern France. John was absorbed in his conflict with the Papacy and with his own barons; Philip was organizing his vastly increased domains and biding his time.

John, a byword in history, derisively known as Lackland and Soft-sword, was yet fertile in ambitious schemes and not devoid of energy. In 1213, reconciled with pope and barons, he wove a grand coalition with his nephew the Emperor Otto IV and with the count of Flanders in the hope of regaining possession of his lands in northwestern France. This seems to denote a contest on a European scale: the three mightiest powers of the time were involved. Reality is more modest. John him-self drew but halfhearted support from England. Otto, a Welf, was not secure on the throne but contending for it with Frederick II of Hohens-taufen, who now enjoyed the support of the Papacy. The armies were not tremendous even by medieval standards, some twenty thousand men on either side. They met almost by chance at Bouvines, between Lille and Tournai (1214). The battle was stubbornly fought; Philip was in peril of his life. It ended in the utter defeat of the king's enemies; several counts, including Ferrand of Flanders, were captured.

Like Valmy in 1792, Bouvines is remembered chiefly for its immense echoes in public opinion. The communes had done well in the battle; the king, against a faithless vassal, was standing for a righteous cause. So there were great rejoicings throughout the land. Bouvines is often recorded as the first "national" victory. It did not formally end the first Hundred Years' War: the official close came under St. Louis in 1259. It made England more conscious of a separate existence: hitherto the Anglo-Norman nobles had felt themselves part of the French com-munity; England was their conquest, not their homeland. Now, assert-ing themselves against the king with the support of the lesser nobility and the commons, they took their stand as Englishmen. Magna Charta (1215), is no less important an event than the Battle of Hastings.

John was still snarling defiance. Some Anglo-Norman barons called Louis, son of Philip, to the English throne. The Angevin dream bade fair to be realized, but with a Capetian wearing both crowns. The pope, however, who considered himself as the feudal suzerain of England, rallied to the support of John, and declared Magna Charta null and void: he had no desire to increase the power of the French king be-yond measure. A bitter civil war would have ensued had not John died in 1216. His son, Henry III, a child of nine, was acceptable to all parties. Louis, defeated at Lincoln, had to withdraw to France and soon relinquished his claims (1217).

Philip Augustus more than doubled the domain of the Capetians. But this does not give the full measure of his increased power. He asserted himself far afield, well into the Rhône Valley so long alien to northern France. He held his vassals so strictly accountable that he became in fact their sovereign rather than their suzerain. Feudalism and monarchy were still blended, as in dissolving pictures; but the trend was unmistakably in favor of the central power. He kept by his side no longer mere household servants but state officials. Out of the old *Curia Regis,* the inorganic assembly of bishops and barons, three separate institutions were in process of evolving: a Grand Council or Council of State, a tribunal—the future "Parliament"—and a Court of Accounts. Technicians of bourgeois origin were called into these assemblies, and were ultimately to outweigh the influence of nobles and prelates. Provosts were representing the king in the various parts of his domains; but since they were contaminated with the feudal spirit, he established above them the *baillis* or *sénéchaux,* appointed, salaried, recalled by him alone, the first clear-cut example of a royal, and royalist, bureaucracy, the distant ancestors of Richelieu's intendants and of Napoleon's *préfets.* He moved them about so that they could not take root in the feudal soil: they were the king's men, *les royaux.* He knew as well as any modern government the paramount importance of money; he used every legitimate means of replenishing his coffers, devised a few more, and, in a pinch, took what he needed. He favored the commutation for cash of feudal dues, and he imposed on the clergy contributions which were voluntary only in name. Like most rulers in medieval Europe he allowed the Jews to gather wealth and then virtuously squeezed it into his own treasury. He was not above tampering with the currency; and yet his coinage, the most convenient in the realm, was used even beyond the area of his political rule.

He was truly the founder of the Capetian monarchy, and he may be called also the founder of Paris as a permanent capital. The Louvre, which he grandly rebuilt, and the Palace of the City became in truth centers of royal life. Under his reign, although through no effort of his, Notre-Dame arose in its full majesty.[5] In 1200 Philip granted immunities to the students of Paris; the university, already thriving at the end of the twelfth century, was fully organized by 1215. Philip gave Paris its central market,[6] an aqueduct, new hospitals, new fortifications. Offended by the stench of the streets, he had the first pavement laid in two main thoroughfares, east and west, north and south. No other reign had seen, and none was to see, such decisive changes. Everything that came before Philip Augustus now seems prehistoric. But the stones of his days are still the pride of the city, and his institutions are still alive.

The civilization which had budded out in the early eleventh century was now in full fruition. To be sure, it was not the king who had originated those great forces, guilds, communes, universities, Scholastic philosophy, Gothic art, courtly literature. It is not even certain that he fully understood them. But he was bold and vigorous enough in his dynamic ambition to keep pace with them. This power of synchronization is rare. Francis I had it for a few brilliant years, Louis XIV in his early manhood, even Napoleon III for less than a decade. On the contrary, the first two Valois, Philip VI and John the Good, and Louis XV, three centuries later, did not possess it. When leaders lag too far behind, the result is tragedy.

Louis VIII (1223–1226) was well prepared for the throne: thirty-six years of age, with the looks and temper of a scholar, the reputation of a saint, and the record of a good fighter. He was called the Lion, perhaps a courtesy title. He was the first Capetian not to have been crowned in his father's lifetime: heredity was now an accepted principle. He kept up the work of Philip Augustus, and conquered Poitou and Saintonge from the Plantagenets, if only for a season. He took a leading part in the interminable crusade against the Albigensians, now in its eighteenth year. On his way back from the South, he died of dysentery in Auvergne without having given his full measure. He remains half-forgotten between his "august" father and his "saintly" son.

In one respect, this brief and pallid reign was ominous. The Franks had the custom of dividing the kingdom among the heirs; the Capetians, on the contrary, started building up an ever-increasing domain. No doubt they granted parcels of it as *apanages* or sources of revenue to members of their family, but with enough restraint not to endanger the growth of the kingdom. Louis VIII, on the contrary, gave away whole provinces: Artois to one of his sons, Anjou and Maine to another, Poitou and Auvergne to a third. In theory the unity of the realm was not abridged; in fact a new feudalism was constituted at the very moment when the old one was at last waning. Louis acted as a father rather than as a king. His Valois successors followed his example with results which, in the fifteenth century, were disastrous.

THE CHRISTIAN KNIGHT: ST. LOUIS

On the death of Louis VIII, his eldest son, now Louis IX, was only twelve. His mother, Blanche of Castile, had been appointed regent by her husband. The great nobles did not challenge the right of succession; but they opposed Blanche, because she was a woman, because she was a foreigner, because they had not been consulted, and above all, because, in the French phrase, they were hoping for "good fishing out of turbid waters": feudalism thrives when the central power weakens.

Blanche, devout, imperious, but a good diplomat, was able to cope with the loose and fitful conspiracy of the feudal lords. Their nominal head was the king's uncle, Philip Hurepel (the Coarse); the actual leader was Peter, Count of Brittany, an able man, called *Mauclerc* for his combination of learning and cunning. The duke of Burgundy, the count of Toulouse, Henry III of England, and many others were all seeking some increase in power. Blanche found a faithful ally in Thibaut (Theobald) IV of Champagne, *le Chansonnier,* the Song-Maker, one of the most graceful poets of the age. Rumor, duly recorded in the *Grandes chroniques,* would have it that he had conceived a passion for the queen, "white as a lily," and that she listened with pleasure to his songs. Historians dismiss the pretty tale as out of keeping with the queen's character; but after all, there were romances in the Middle Ages. With little fighting and many negotiations she dissolved the coalition. Far from paying bribes to the malcontents, she managed to add a few choice bits to the royal domain.[7]

Blanche ruled the kingdom and her family with a firm hand, so hard and heavy at times that the students of Paris rebelled against her and went on strike. Yet she had neither broken nor embittered the spirit of her son: his character is her monument. The place of Louis IX is almost unique in history. There had been piety on the throne before—Louis the Pious, Robert the Pious, Louis VII—and the results had been disappointing: in Louis IX virtue turned into a source of strength. He was the crowned saint as Marcus Aurelius had been the crowned philosopher. Both had to fight and fought well, although they were men of peace; both permitted cruel persecutions in spite of their gentleness; neither was invariably successful in his worldly enterprises; yet they did not fail altogether, and remain the honor of mankind.

The interminable contest with the Plantagenets still plagued Louis IX. In 1242 Henry III, in alliance with the rebellious South, invaded France. Louis defeated him sharply at Taillebourg and Saintes. Aquitania and Toulouse submitted. With England no final agreement was reached: Louis was eager to leave for the crusade, and did not press his advantage.

He took up the cross in 1244 but did not start until 1248. His plan, strategically not unsound, was to make Egypt his base as John of Brienne had done thirty years before. Damietta was captured, and the army moved slowly toward Cairo. But, bogged in the delta, it fell a prey to disease—the king was not spared. Greatly weakened, it was checked before Mansourah and, on its retreat to the coast, was hacked to pieces by the Mamelukes. Louis himself was captured and held for ransom (1249). When he was freed, he spent four years in the Holy Land, unable to strike a blow, helping fortify the pitiful remnants of the Christian colonies.

On his return his desire was to establish peace based on the scrupulous recognition of all valid rights. So at Corbeil (1258) he settled the various claims and counterclaims of France and Aragon in no haggling spirit. In 1259, by the Treaty of Paris, he closed the long quarrel with England. Of his own accord he gave back Limousin and Perigord, receiving in return a quit-claim to Normandy, Maine, and Poitou. In theory he was losing nothing, for the king of England acknowledged his suzerainty in the returned provinces. We must remember that Louis represented the perfection of an ideal already on the decline. His aim was not to alter the law but scrupulously to fulfill it. He believed implicitly in feudal custom as he believed in the Church: only abuses were to be resisted and corrected. He was not consciously working for the "France, one and indivisible" of the Jacobins.

As a perfect knight, as a feudal liege, as a crusader, Louis was a lovable anachronism, and his contemporaries were not blind to the fact. Renouncing his father's conquests caused indignation among his followers, and particularly in the provinces concerned: when he was canonized in 1297, they showed their resentment by refusing to observe his *fête* day. His mother, devout as she was, deplored his taking the cross when the kingdom needed his presence. His courtiers, *sotto voce,* ironically called him *Frater Ludovicus,* for his rule of life was of monastic rigor.

Yet the holy man was a good administrator, and his thirst for equity paid unexpected dividends. France remembers him under the oak at Vincennes dispensing justice to the humblest, a wise and fearless ruler. Not to magnify his office but because he desired justice, he intervened directly throughout the kingdom, offering his protection (*la quarantaine-le-roi,* or the king's forty days, and *asseurement*), increasing the number of "royal" cases reserved to his jurisdiction, inviting appeals from lesser authorities. Moral power made conquests more durable than those of the sword; if the king later came to be known as "the living law," it was to a large extent because the halo of St. Louis softened such equivocal figures as Philip the Fair and Louis XI. His renown extended beyond the realm. Since pope and emperor, in bitter quarrel, were sapping each other's authority, the virtues of the good Capetian made him the moral head of Christendom. Even Henry III and his barons chose him as an arbiter in 1264.

But the thought of the crusade would give him no peace: was he not the knight of Christ? Against his more practical advisers, he set out again. His brother, Charles of Anjou, had become king of Sicily in 1265, a move which foreshadowed the senseless and costly expeditions of a later age. Charles had grandiose dreams of restoring for his own benefit the Eastern Empire, and that plan demanded the control of the Mediterranean: it was probably he who suggested Tunis as the first step. Landing near Carthage, Louis was soon stricken with the plague; nothing was achieved but a martyr's death.

The piety of Louis IX had somber aspects. He had himself scourged with wire thongs, he persecuted the Jews, he encouraged the Inquisition, he had heretics blinded and burned. Yet there was no sadism in his rigor: ascetic and fanatical as he proved himself to be, he impressed the world with his gentleness. He was equable in temper, humane, capable of kindly mirth. Perhaps posterity has been unduly influenced by the charming memoirs written by Jean, Sire of Joinville, Seneschal of Champagne, who was his companion on his first crusade. Joinville draws a sharply humorous line between his own worldliness and the king's exacting and exalted piety: *he* would rather have any number of deadly sins on his conscience than be a leper, and let no crowned saint tell him otherwise! Still, Joinville, a garrulous old man when he wrote this *History*, remembered St. Louis as a better Joinville: the harsher sides of his model escaped him. The fame of Louis among the common people is probably a better warrant. We have seen that the *Pastoureaux* (Shepherds) gathered to deliver him, whom they loved, while they distrusted lords and clerics. There was a touching dirge at his death—perhaps the finest epitaph written for a king: "To whom will the poor now carry their plea, since the good king is dead, who loved them so much?" In the Golden Legend of France he has no peer but Joan of Arc.[8]

CHAPTER IX

The Lost Centuries: 1270-1380

✍ THE BLURRED PATH

We are now coming to the most puzzling chapter in French history, a period of over two hundred years (1270–1483), unnamed, unnamable, neither repose, decay, nor joyous advance, the perfect example of a time out of joint. Transition, an empty term, will not answer the riddle: all history, even the most self-assured classical age, is transition. France was ruined by a century of warfare, bad government, banditry, pestilence; but the tragedy lies deeper than the dramatic events. The essential problems, the harsh contrasts of brutality and refinement, the perplexities ill concealed under an elaborate cloak were evident under Philip the Fair well before the second Hundred Years' War broke out; and the same atmosphere, a stormy, anguished twilight, still prevailed under Louis XI, when the physical wounds had been healed.

It was a time with a damaged soul, and we are impelled to turn for an answer to the keeper of the world's soul, the Church. Just as we have ascribed—an unprovable but attractive hypothesis—the great revival of the eleventh century to the Church reforms of the tenth, so we are tempted to explain the great bewilderment of the fourteenth and fifteenth centuries by the confusion and conflicts that existed within the Church. The eye of the world ceased to be "single," and the whole body was full of darkness. The Papacy had issued triumphant from the long contest with the empire; but it was morally weakened because of the ruthless means it had been compelled to use, and materially enfeebled, because there was no substitute for the secular sword it had broken. Three years after the great Jubilee of 1300, in which Boniface VIII had appeared as the supreme lord of Christendom, the pontiff was humbled by a Roman noble and a French envoy. The age was to see the "Captivity of Babylon," when at Avignon the popes were little more than the retainers of the French crown; then the scandal of a long schism; leadership falling to a series of councils, all infirm of purpose; open religious rebellion in England and Bohemia; in Italy, a daring, destructive critical spirit.

To these quarrels within the Church must be added, as a source of weakness and confusion, the ferocious repression of heresy throughout the thirteenth century. Not that the persecution of dissenters was a new departure, but the very greatness of the age made resorting to methods of barbarism more flagrant. Unity could not be enforced except by considering independent thought as the most heinous of sins. The repression was efficient: the Inquisition was no vain show, and the "hounds of the Lord," *Domini canes,* were perfect in their holy and terrible office; they created peace through spiritual devastation.

Perhaps the very success of St. Thomas Aquinas contributed to the sterility that came over Scholastic philosophy. The work was done once for all. There was but one alternative to his masterly reconciliation of faith and reason: to pronounce, as Duns Scotus and William of Occam did, that the two existed on absolutely separate planes. For the believer this divorce had the result of discouraging thought; and the rationalist, debarred from the highest realms, found his intellect devitalized. Thus theology, once so earnest and so profound, turned into that instrument of fearful intricacy which, under the name of Scholasticism, has remained a byword. "The second light of the world," the University of Paris, was wasted in pedantic futility.

Yet while medieval thought in France was losing itself in a maze, Italy was boldly seeking a new path. As France had reared the finest cathedrals of stone, Italy had produced the supreme "cathedrals of the spirit," the great syntheses of Bonaventura, Thomas Aquinas, Dante; and immediately after Dante, without any rebellion against Dante's art and faith, came the first conscious humanists, Petrarch, Boccaccio. Why did Italy escape the blight that struck France? She was not spared the ordeal of war. But the memories of the classical world had remained more vivid: Dante was guided by Vergil. Perhaps the very existence of the Papal State in the center of the peninsula freed the Italians from excessive awe: the pope was an Italian potentate with whom other Italians were constantly bickering.

The same process which turned Scholasticism from a philosophy into a technique affected all forms of life. Elaborate form was accepted as a substitute for substance. Knighthood became all trappings and pageantry while true chivalry disappeared. After the death of St. Louis, the crusade idea faded into mere wishful thinking. There could be no more impressive ceremony than the famous "Oath of the Pheasant," by which, in 1453, Philip the Good, Duke of Burgundy, solemnly bound himself to lead a crusade against the Turks; but the vow led only to lavish entertainments and increased taxation. The duke half-consciously enjoyed the romance of it all, as though he were a Froissart or a Walter Scott. It was an age of make-believe.[1]

If religious thought lost its way, political thought, too, stumbled in the dark. What we called the dissolving picture, feudalism melting into national monarchy, to most of the contemporaries offered nothing but a blur. It took three hundred years at least to clarify the principles which we, with easy retrospective wisdom, discern at work under Philip Augustus. The king's sovereign right to raise an army and levy taxes, not merely to summon a feudal host and call for feudal aids, became permanent *de facto* with the everlasting English wars; but even under Charles VII, that basic right was not yet fully established. Louis XI himself, often considered as the first truly modern king, intrigued with rebellious nobles against his own father and later had to sign humiliating treaties with his great vassals, just as in the worst days of feudal chaos.

⚖ PHILIP IV, THE FAIR, AND HIS LEGISTS

Nothing memorable marks the reign of Philip III (1270–1285). He was called the Bold: but Jean de Meung, who completed the *Romance of the Rose* in 1277, was bolder still, and better worth remembering. The actual head of the Capetian family was then Charles of Anjou, brother of St. Louis and king of Sicily; he was responsible for the disasters which marked both the beginning and the end of his nephew's reign. It was he who had steered St. Louis' second crusade toward Tunis; and in 1270 Philip, sick himself, brought back from Africa and buried at Saint-Denis the remains of five Capetians. In 1285 he was waging war on Aragon in the interest of his uncle [2] and at the behest of the pope. He suffered a severe defeat and, in the course of the retreat, died at Perpignan.

Of Philip IV himself (1285–1314) we know but one thing: that he was handsome. His reign was eventful, and he never was accused of weakness or indifference; yet to his contemporaries he was an enigma wrapped in a mystery. A bishop complained: "He is the best looking of men; but all he can do is to look and look and say nothing." They compared him with the Great Owl, whose splendid golden eyes, by daylight, are fixed and expressionless. Here we find sharply focused one aspect— and perhaps the most important—of that Protean concept, the French monarchy. St. Louis was the perfect Christian knight, Francis I, on his accession, stood for gay adventure, Louis XIV represented magnificence: Philip the Fair is the model of the figurehead.

With the increase of the royal domain had grown the number and importance of the king's agents, *les royaux*. Their influence was already felt under Philip Augustus and St. Louis. Under Philip the Fair we find them in actual control. He reigns, they govern. Not in their own name and not primarily in their own interests: they are intensely, jealously loyal, not to the royal person but to the institution. They are literally more Royalist than the king. No doubt that in magnifying the monarchy, they are increasing their own prestige. But they are devoted to an idea: they are creating that mighty and unlovely idol, the State, they are the State.

Their ideal is neither theocratic, nor feudal, nor democratic, although they can use, realistically, any principle that will serve their purpose, "for the greater glory of the kingdom." The king to them is the Lord's Anointed and the universal feudal suzerain and the father of his people; but above all, he is the incarnation of the law, of which they are the servants. They are themselves *légistes,* versed in the law; and they try to substitute everywhere a single law founded on reason (i.e., on the Roman tradition) for the welter of local customs. A process which will consume exactly five hundred years: it was only under Napoleon and with his codes that customs, the edicts of the kings, the heritage of Justinian, the rationalism that culminated in the Enlightenment were finally blended. The state councilors who served the First Consul so well were the heirs of the *légistes* under Philip the Fair.

For a later period Charles Seignobos uses the expression, "the *impersonal* absolute monarchy." [3] This would excellently define the trend already clear under Philip IV. In five centuries there was perhaps only one king who had a national, a popular, policy apart from that of the bureaucracy: Henry IV was truly a leader, because, in a desperate crisis, his name and his personality alone stood as the symbols of order. But on the whole, throughout the ancient regime the administration of the kingdom was in the hands of the king's men, the bureaucrats. When king and courtiers interfered, as they did all too frequently, they were disturbing elements, out of harmony with the majestic flow of national life. If France grew and prospered, in spite of the caprices, the prodigalities, at times the follies of her kings, it was thanks to the vast body of men who, in his name, were serving the monarchy and the nation.

We call these men bourgeois, because as a rule they did not belong to the feudal nobility. Yet the word could be misleading. They may come from the merchant class, but their outlook is entirely different. The bourgeois in the true sense of the term are attached to the interests and privileges of their own city: the king's men embrace the whole kingdom. The bourgeois are in business and think in economic terms; the king's men can be rapacious enough, yet profit is not their acknowledged motive. The time would come when, forming dynasties of their own, the

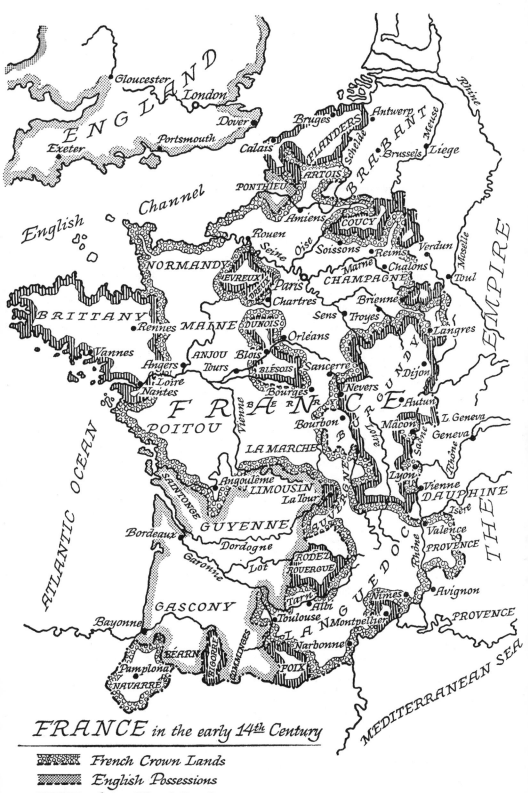

FRANCE *in the early 14th Century*

French Crown Lands
English Possessions
Other Vassal Lands

king's men were to separate themselves from the *bourgeoisie,* and secure recognition for a distinct order, the "nobility of the gown," opposed
to the "nobility of the sword."

If the king's men resembled any other class, it was not the feudal
caste and not the mercantile *bourgeoisie* but, rather, the clergy. Like the
clergy they were well educated, like the clergy they preferred legal
methods to open violence, like the clergy their horizon was not limited
to the local scene. For a long time trained clerics served as the king's
counselors. If they fought Rome, as they often did, it was not on matters
of faith—the king's men were good Christians, and even pious—it was as
a rival administration.

This conception of the ideal monarchy, superior to the whims of the
individual monarch, found its expression in the Parlement.[4] This body,
a tribunal, was, as we have seen, an offshoot of the vague *Curia Regis*
gathered by the king to give him advice. It never was fully separated
from the Court of Peers, which also had judicial functions. But, in usual
affairs, appointed members of the Parlement judged without the presence
of king or lords, ecclesiastical or temporal. Before edicts became the law
of the realm, they had to be registered by the Parlement; and that body
assumed the right of pointing out to the king that a new edict was in
contradiction with earlier ones, or at variance with the principles and
traditions of the monarchy (right of *remonstrance*). The king had the
last word: he could command the Parlement to register an edict. But
the judges thus possessed a sort of suspensive veto; and in ordinary
cases at least, their cumulative collective wisdom acted as a steadying
force. It was a brake on capricious rule; it became, in later ages, a brake
on progressive policy. The *légistes* were indeed radicals: they wanted
to substitute general principles for haphazard custom, but their juris-
prudence itself became an oppressive mass of precedents.

The foreign policy of Philip IV was active but neither systematic nor
particularly successful. He had litigations rather than quarrels with
Aragon and England. In Flanders he suffered a severe setback. The
active communes of that rich country resented his interference. When he
tried to crush them, his chivalry was massacred at Courtrai (1302);
golden spurs by the hundred were picked up on the battlefield. It was
an omen of Cressy, Poictiers, Agincourt. The disaster was partly relieved
at Mons-en-Pévèle (1304); but Flanders remained hostile, more favorable to England, from which it bought much of its wool, than to France,
which stood for oppression.

The great difficulty of all Capetian kings was financial. They wanted
to carry on a policy which reached beyond feudalism; their vast administrative machinery, their wars, their court were abysses of expense; yet

they had only feudal dues at their disposal. So, following the precedent of their great exemplar Philip Augustus, they sought resources everywhere, and with a rapacious hand. It is this constant stringency that accounts for the most dramatic events in the reign of Philip IV: the clash with the Papacy and the suppression of the Templars.

The pope protested against the taxing of the French clergy by the king; the king countered with a threat to put an embargo on French gold and silver sent to Rome (1296): it was a draw. But linked with the money question was a test of power: which things are Caesar's? A few years later, the king's officers arrested a bishop for *lèse-majesté;* the pope menaced the king with excommunication. The king then appealed to public opinion, by convening representatives of the three orders, the States-General, which met at Notre-Dame (1302).[5] Fortified with their support, he dispatched his ruthless chancellor, Guillaume de Nogaret, to Anagni, where the pope was residing, with orders to have him arrested and dragged before the council. Boniface VIII, insulted and perhaps maltreated by his Roman enemy Sciarra Colonna and by Nogaret, was rescued by the people of the town; but he was a broken man and soon died of humiliation and despair.

His successor Benedict XI was ready to prosecute Nogaret when he died with convenient and suspicious suddenness. The papal throne remained vacant for nearly a year. Then, bowing to necessity, the Sacred College elected Bertrand de Got, Archbishop of Bordeaux, who assumed the name of Clement V. The new pope yielded to Nogaret on every point. The "zeal" of Philip was declared "good and just"; the seat of the Papacy was transferred to Avignon (1309–1377);[6] and the king was allowed to prosecute, that is to say to despoil and destroy, the Knights of the Temple.

They were a tempting prey. Now that the crusades were over, those fighting monks had no fighting to do; and they had grown tremendously wealthy through bequests and through their banking activities. For, with branches everywhere, they had become the treasurers of kings, as the Rothschilds were to be in the first half of the nineteenth century. It is not inconceivable that their faith and morals had deteriorated, but their riches were their most patent crime. The Jews could be squeezed at any moment: were they not the enemies of Christendom? But to deal with a religious order, once the proud flower of the crusading spirit, more elaborate methods were needed: the knights had to be tortured and dishonored before they could be robbed. Nogaret proceeded implacably. Their landed estates were, in principle, to be turned over to the Hospitallers: in France their funds went to the hungry royal coffers. The people did not rebel; the Templars were too rich to be popular, and the pope sanctioned, or at least condoned, the deed (1307–1312). A sinister epilogue: in March, 1314, the grand master, Jacques de Molay, and three other knights were finally sentenced to death. Two were walled up alive; Molay and another were burned at the stake. They showed great fortitude; tradition has it that Molay summoned the evil king to appear, within a year, before their Maker. In November Philip was dead.

The brief reign of Philip's eldest son, Louis X (1314–1316), was a period of reaction, confusion, tumult: hence the quaint name *le Hutin,* loosely translated the Quarrelsome. Enguerrand de Marigny, who had been Philip's right hand, was brought to trial and hanged at Montfaucon with the common thieves. Yet it was under this king, so dim in our memory, that the French were proclaimed "free according to the law of nature," a bold principle which was not to be fully implemented for nearly four hundred years. He had a posthumous son, John I, who lived but a few days; the claims of his infant daughter were set aside, and he was succeeded by his brother Philip V the "Long," i.e., the Tall (1316–1322). The States-General in 1317 endorsed the ruling. Philip V died without male issue, and again the crown passed to a brother, Charles IV, the Fair (1322–1328), who likewise had no son.

Under these three kings the impersonal momentum of the monarchy went on; new provinces were added to the domain, the services were more clearly separated, the administration gained in power and definiteness. Philip V, in particular, issued a vast number of ordinances. The lesser vassals had been reduced to proper subordination; of the major ones, only four were still powerful enough to cause trouble: the duke of Brittany, the duke of Burgundy, the count of Flanders, and the duke of Guienne.[7] There were no devastating wars; and in spite of a harsh government, the country was prosperous. The direct line of the Capetians ended without brilliancy, but without disgrace.

⚔ VALOIS *vs.* PLANTAGENETS: PHILIP VI, JOHN II, EDWARD III

For the third time the king had no son. The rule adopted in 1316 was applied: women could not inherit the throne, nor transmit rights which never were theirs. So a cousin of the late three kings, Philip of Valois, received the crown instead of their nephew, soon to be Edward III of England. The decision was neither absurd nor inevitable. Authority was still linked with leadership in battle; but on the other hand, women, like Eleanor, had been suffered to inherit vast feudal domains. To give this practice the prestige of antiquity, it was later called "the Salic Law." But the French royal house had forgotten for many centuries that they ever were Salian Franks. Edward III was in no position to press his claim. His father had been forced to abdicate in 1327; he himself was but fifteen. Probably unconvinced, he did homage to his cousin for the duchy of Guienne.

On the accession of Philip VI the French monarchy had reached the height of its medieval power. The pope was at Avignon, not a prisoner but under French influence. There were Capetians on the thrones of Naples, Provence, Hungary; and kings—Navarre, Mallorca, often Scotland—flocked to the French court. John, King of Bohemia, felt at ease only in Paris, "the most *chivalric* sojourn in the world." By chivalric, we must understand a paradise for gentlemen, a perpetual round of festivals, jousts, and tournaments, in the spirit of the best romances.

The contest over the succession and the clash of interests in Flanders reopened the latent conflict between France and England which St. Louis had hoped to end forever. At first, the struggle was indirect: the contestants backed opposite parties in Flanders and in Brittany. And it was indecisive as well, although Philip's friends got the worse of it; a French fleet was destroyed at Sluys (l'Écluse) near the mouth of the Scheldt. But Edward, encouraged by dissenting French nobles, decided to renew his bid for the French throne. He harried central France, came close to Paris (Saint-Germain), and retired northward with the spoils. Philip, with a much larger force, caught up with him at last at Cressy (Crécy) (1346). The French king put his trust in his feudal cavalry, a brilliant anachronism, which was defeated as ignominiously as it had been at Courtrai. Calais was lost, after a long siege (1347), and England was to preserve that key to the continent for over two hundred years. The Black Death ravaged the kingdom, and financial chaos paralyzed the country: a swift and thorough downfall in a single decade (1340–1350). Yet the momentum of the monarchy was not completely spent: the bankrupt and defeated king managed to acquire Montpellier on the Mediterranean and Dauphiné in the Alps.

Philip VI, coarse under his knightly trappings, had been a disastrous ruler; John II was worse. He was known as the Good, i.e., the good fighter and the good fellow, not the kindly or the wise. He was brutal, unscrupulous—the currency was constantly altered under his reign— capricious, and extravagant. He had managed to turn against him many of his vassals, and even his son-in-law Charles of Navarre, when the son of Edward III, the Black Prince, took advantage of the disorder to march north from Guienne. John II barred his way at Maupertuis near Poictiers (1356). It was Cressy over again. The French had the advantage of numbers; the king, dismounted, fought with the bravery of a born soldier, but his generalship was so inept that his army was destroyed and he was captured.

ENGLAND

London
Dover
Southampton
Calais
Boulogne
English Channel

Utrecht
Antwerp
FLANDERS
Brussels
Liége
ARTOIS
PONTHIEU
Crecy
Amiens
COUCY
Rethel
Soissons
Reims
Verdun
BRABANT
Meuse
Moselle
Rhine
Toul
Rouen
Seine
Oise
Marne
Châlons
CHAMPAGNE
BAR
Bayeux
NORMANDY
EVREUX
DREUX
Paris
Chartres
Bretigny
Sens
Troyes
Brienne
BAR
BRITTANY
MAINE
Rennes
ANJOU
Angers
DUNOIS
Orléans
Langres
Dijon
BURGUNDY
Vannes
BLÉSOIS
Tours
Bourges
Autun
Nantes
Loire
Nevers
Châlon
L. Geneva
F R A N C E
BERRY
Loire
Saône
Rhône
Poitiers
POITOU
BOURBONNAIS
Mâcon
LA MARCHE
Lyon
Limoges
La Tour
FOREZ
DAUPHINÉ
Angoulême
LIMOUSIN
AUVERGNE
Valence
GUYENNE
Bordeaux
Dordogne
Lot
ROUERGUE
Mende
Isère
Garonne
QUERCY
Rodez
LANGUEDOC
Rhône
Avignon
Adour
GASCONY
Albi
Tarn
Nîmes
Arles
PROVENCE
Bayonne
NAVARRE
BIGORRE
COMMINGES
Toulouse
FOIX
Narbonne
ARAGON

ATLANTIC OCEAN

English Channel

HOLY EMPIRE

MEDITERRANEAN SEA

The
Peace of Bretigny, 1360
The First English Invasion

French Crown Lands
English Possessions
Other Vassal Lands

The king a prisoner, the nobility shattered, the dauphin,[8] heir-presumptive and regent, a puny, sickly boy—the country, thrown upon its own resources, had now the opportunity of reforming its institutions. For such a movement the instrument was at hand, the States-General. And able leaders were not lacking. One was Robert Le Coq, a typical "king's man," who, after a brilliant administrative career, had become archbishop-duke of Laon and peer of the realm. The other was Étienne Marcel, provost of the Paris merchants, one of the wealthiest men of his time.

The young dauphin was not foresighted or independent enough to cast his lot with the reformers; he was shrewd enough, in his apparent weakness, to be their deadly opponent. Marcel used methods of terror: he had two of the king's councilors killed before the dauphin's eyes and made him wear a red and blue bonnet, the colors of Paris: we might be in 1792 instead of 1357. A Great Ordinance was passed by the States-General; although it dealt with finances and administration rather than with the political structure of the state, it could be considered as the embryo of a modern constitution. It is a surprisingly sane and able document: the kings were to follow with profit some of its indications. But as a French Magna Charta, it remained the merest might-have-been.

The situation was exceedingly confused. The dauphin managed to escape from Paris. Many, even in the capital, resented the forceful methods of Étienne Marcel and remained obstinately loyal to the royal house. The States-General, in which the common people were not represented, was wavering. The nobles, the clergy, and the rich *bourgeoisie* were frightened by an uprising of the desperate peasant masses, the *Jacques.* Marcel, his power shaken, thought of joining forces with the *Jacques,* and also with Charles the Bad, king of Navarre: that sinister personage, flitting ominously from party to party, had a title to vast holdings including Normandy and even advanced claims to the throne of France. But Charles, instead of backing the *Jacques,* helped defeat them. Still, Marcel as a last resort against the dauphin, was perhaps planning to bring Charles into Paris when the Royalist faction killed the great provost (1358) as a rebel and a traitor. Paris has not forgotten him: his equestrian statue guards the City Hall.

At Brétigny (1360), peace was signed with England and Navarre. Guienne was rounded off with Poitou, Saintonge, Agenais, Périgord, Limousin: the whole Southwest was in English hands. A ransom of three million gold pounds was demanded; the king was unable to raise this enormous sum, and he returned to his captivity in London. Nothing loath: for the English treated him royally. The king took his defeat lightly enough: a fighter and nothing else, conscious of having fought valiantly, he was a good loser, we might even say a good sport. He was popular with his captors, and Edward gave him a splendid funeral at St. Paul's. It was the common people who felt the burden and the shame (1364).

✒ SLOW RECUPERATION: CHARLES V, THE WISE

So the dauphin became King Charles V (1364–1380). He was a new departure, and remains a unique exception, in the long royal line. Weak in body, of scholarly mien and tastes, a "seated king" after so many fighters on horseback, he shunned the battlefield and did not crave knightly glory. He was called the Wise, which, in the language of the time, meant the Learned, but also the Prudent. He refused to gamble the fate of the kingdom on a single throw like Cressy or Poictiers. He held fortified cities, harried the enemy without pitched battles, won minor engagements, engaged in diplomacy. He was well served by studious men like himself, but he also found two great commanders who added a touch of heroism and picturesqueness to the gray fabric of his shrewd and modest policy. One was Jean de Vienne, his admiral; the other, a Breton knight whom he made constable of France, Bertrand Du Guesclin.

Much of the Hundred Years' War is admirably described in Shakespeare's stage direction: "Alarums; excursions." The fighting was desultory and inconclusive, but it was ubiquitous. The worst enemies were not the organized troops of the English king but the irresponsible bands of armed men, the "Great Companies," hirelings when they found a customer, out-and-out brigands when royal business was slack. When one province was devastated, they moved to another which was repairing its ruins. Du Guesclin managed to take many of them with him to Spain, thus ridding the kingdom of a pest and incidentally bolstering up French policy in the peninsula. But they returned and grew: Du Guesclin fell at the siege of Chateauneuf-de-Randon, where he had cooped up a number of bandits. It was this nameless curse, rather than formal war, that all but destroyed the fair land of France.

The wide negotiations, the piecemeal continuous warfare of Charles V form a pattern intricate to the point of confusion. But the trend is clear. When the Black Prince died in 1376, and Edward III in 1377, they could see their work crumbling. The sedentary ruler, who collected in the Louvre such a fine library, had quietly conquered the men-at-arms. At his death in 1380—he was only forty-three years old—the English held just five cities, Calais, Cherbourg, Brest, Bordeaux, Bayonne. Above all Charles V had taught the French that if the monarchy was the cause of all their disasters, it alone could provide the remedy.

CHAPTER X

The Lost Centuries: 1380-1483

⚑ A MAD KING, A DISTRACTED KINGDOM

Charles VI (1380–1422) was a child of twelve showing but little promise. Power fell to his uncles, the dukes of Anjou, Berry, Burgundy, and
Bourbon. The royal system, as organized under Philip the Fair, was
still so precarious and so ill-understood, it had proved so oppressive
and at time so incompetent, that there was a demand for the suppression
of all taxes and a complete return to feudal custom. The new rulers
yielded: they were feudal in spirit themselves and wanted to court
popularity. The Paris mob, called the *Maillotins* because they were
armed with heavy mallets, the peasantry of the South (*Tuchins*), the
communes of Flanders were in open revolt. The rebellions were crushed
and the taxes restored. Not, however, in the interest of good government,
for the royal dukes proceeded to ransack the treasury for ambitious purposes of their own. Naturally, the bourgeois counselors of Charles the
Wise, contemptuously called the *Marmousets*,[1] were dismissed.

In 1389, on attaining his majority, the young king thanked his uncles
and recalled the *Marmousets*. But three years later, Charles VI, whose
frail wits had not been able to stand a mad pace of pleasure, went insane; and, although he had lucid moments, he was unfit to rule for the
remaining thirty years of his life.

The question now was: Which princely faction would control the
demented sovereign? His uncle Burgundy counted on the support of the
queen, Isabel (Ysabeau) of Bavaria, whom the poor king greatly loved;
for it was Burgundy who had brought her to the throne. The king's
brother, Orleans, did not have the maturity, the material power, the
international connections of Philip, Duke of Burgundy; but his great
charm made him a dangerous contender. When Philip died and was
succeeded by his son John the Fearless (1404), Queen Isabel veered toward Orleans, to the extent, it was rumored, of becoming his mistress.

John had a short way with rivals: in 1407 Orleans was brutally assassinated in a Paris street.

This murder changed a court rivalry between cousins into a savage feud which clove France asunder. The Orleanist party became known as the Armagnacs, for they were led by Bernard, Count of Armagnac, father-in-law of the young duke. It is idle to seek principles in the vendetta of headstrong and unthinking nobles. But it is roughly true that the Armagnacs, from the deep South, represented the purely aristocratic tradition; while Burgundy, who better realized the importance of public opinion in Paris, had to assume more democratic colors. A paradoxical alliance was struck between the reckless Burgundian, the powerful guild of Paris butchers led by the skinner Jean Caboche, and the University of Paris. Feudal pride, demagogic violence, and Scholastic learning in unison concocted a remarkable document, a new Great Ordinance called *Cabochienne,* even bolder than that of Étienne Marcel (1413). But the coalition was unstable; a Paris faction overwhelmed the *Cabochiens* and forced John the Fearless to flee from the city; the Armagnacs returned and exacted ferocious vengeance. All hope of intelligent reform vanished with their victory.

The English had given little trouble since 1380: the uneasy reign of Richard II—with fruitless expeditions into Scotland and Ireland, the Wycliffite agitation, the Lollard movement, the conspiracies of Henry Bolingbroke, Duke of Lancaster—had little energy to spare for Continental ventures. Bolingbroke became Henry IV in 1399. His son, Henry V (1413–1422), twenty-seven years old, ambitious and energetic, wanted to give the luster of victory to his usurping and still uncertain line. The quarrels of the French nobles under a mad king gave him a perfect opening. So, formally reviving the claims of Edward III to the French crown, he landed at Harfleur (1415). The season was far advanced, and he decided to head for Calais and safety. On October 25 he was intercepted by a force much larger than his own. At Agincourt (Azincourt) the pattern of Courtray, Cressy, Poictiers was scrupulously followed. The brilliant disorderly cavalry of the French—mostly Armagnac nobles—was routed. Henry V, in whom there was no magnanimity, spared the knights who could pay ransom and had all the other prisoners slaughtered in cold blood.

The conduct of John the Fearless had been equivocal. He may even have encouraged Henry V; at any rate, he sent no contingent to the French army. He took advantage of the Armagnacs' discomfiture to seize Paris and the king. But the dauphin had escaped, and the game was not finally won. We need not say that when they entered Paris, the Burgundians massacred every Armagnac they could seize.

ENGLAND

Gloucester

London

Dover

Portsmouth

Exeter

English Channel

Cherbourg

Harfleur

FLANDERS

Calais

Agincourt

Arras

Antwerp

Liége

Rhine

Meuse

Schelde

THE

EMPIRE

Moselle

Amiens

Rouen

PICARDY

Reims

Châlons

Verdun

Bayeux

St.Lô

Caen

NORMANDY

Falaise

Evreux

Laigle

Verneuil

Seine

Oise

Marne

Meaux

Paris

CHAMPAGNE

Domremy

Troyes

BRITTANY

MAINE

PERCHE

Chartres

Orléans

Dijon

BURGUNDY

ATLANTIC OCEAN

Angers

ANJOU

Loire

Nantes

Blois

BLESOIS

Bourges

Nevers

Saône

L. Geneva

Mâcon

FRANCE

Vienne

BERRY

POITOU

LA MARCHE

LIMOUSIN

AUVERGNE

Lyon

Vienne

DAUPHINE

Valence

Rhône

Loire

Bordeaux

GUYENNE

Castillon

Dordogne

Lot

Garonne

ROUERGUE

LANGUEDOC

Rhône

Avignon

Arles

PROVENCE

GASCONY

Tarn

Toulouse

Narbonne

BÉARN

ARAGON

MEDITERRANEAN SEA

FRANCE in 1422

Territory which recognized the English King
as King of France

Territory which remained loyal to the Dauphin

French Allies of the English

But, his vengeance slaked, John the Fearless hesitated. He negotiated both with the dauphin and with Henry V, and he kept Charles VI and Isabel as hostages. A meeting was arranged with the dauphin at Montereau (1419). It was hinted—and it is perfectly possible—that John meant to capture the young prince, but it was he who was murdered.

His son Philip the Good at once went over to the English side; he carried with him Queen Isabel and the old allies of his house, the *bourgeoisie* and the University of Paris. The dauphin was disowned as responsible for the crime. At Troyes, on the twentieth of May, 1420, a treaty was signed which, at the expense of the Armagnac faction, united the other three parties, mad Charles VI, the duke of Burgundy, and Henry V. The English king, proclaimed regent, would marry Catherine, daughter of Charles VI; and, on the latter's death, he would inherit the French throne.

We are irresistibly tempted to interpret history in the light of our present knowledge and feelings. France and England were to emerge as separate nations: the Treaty of Troyes appears therefore as the most shameful of capitulations, a craven surrender to a foreign conqueror. To the contemporaries it was nothing of the kind. Generation after generation, the royal houses of England and France had intermarried. The union which was contemplated was of the same kind as the one which ultimately closed the interminable feud between England and Scotland. Henry V stood as a lawful heir, not as a conqueror. The king and queen, the most powerful of the vassals, the capital itself gave their approval to the arrangement. It was simply the end of a long family litigation. Henry V had all the trumps in his hands, ability, power, possession, a legal title, and public opinion. It is a sheer accident that he died at thirty-five, leaving a son only nine months old. A few weeks later, Charles VI, almost forgotten, passed away in his turn (1422).

JOAN OF ARC

The boy Henry VI "ruled" in Paris, solemnly recognized by the burgesses, the Parlement, the University, the Burgundian party. The Dauphin Charles refused to acknowledge the Treaty of Troyes, which disinherited him. However, he was powerless. In the North his partisans attempted to assert his authority in Champagne and Maine, but they were defeated at Cravant (1423) and at Verneuil (1424). Much of the South remained loyal to the legitimate heir (if he was legitimate, for scandal did not spare Isabel), but his power there was hardly more than nominal. In truth, he was what his enemies called him in derision, "the king of Bourges." His chief weakness was within. He had no self-confidence and no ambition. He was as indifferent to feats of arms as Charles V, but out of apathy not wisdom. Life was not unpleasant in the castles of his little kingdom—Mehun-sur-Yèvre, Chinon—but state affairs were exceedingly annoying. No sooner had he become attached to a favorite—Pierre de Giac, Le Camus—but someone had him murdered "for the good of the state." His constable Richemont [2] forced upon him the adventurer La Trémoille, and then La Trémoille and Richemont started fighting. The "man of the family," the one who kept his cause alive, was his mother-in-law Yolanda, "Queen of the Four Kingdoms," Sicily, Naples, Jerusalem, and Aragon, Countess of Anjou and Provence; the titles were nearly empty, but the queen herself was no shadow.

If Charles was helpless, Bedford, regent for his nephew Henry VI, found the governance of France no easy task. He was undoubtedly an able man; but the country he had to rule was thoroughly ruined, large tracts were depopulated, even the rich plain of Beauce had turned into a wilderness. If there had been a recovery under Bedford's administration, Henry VI would have been safe; but to wring taxes from an exhausted people was the surest way of fostering discontent. Henry V had understood, realistically, that he was king of France by the grace of the duke of Burgundy; Bedford resented the power of one who, in theory, was only a vassal. Little help, financial or military, was to be expected from England, where his brother Gloucester had a very difficult time. So, for several years the struggle was half-hearted. It became sharply focused when the English besieged Orleans (1428), still held in the dauphin's name. If Orleans fell, the shaky kingdom of Bourges was doomed. The city became a symbol, a Verdun, a Stalingrad. The inhabitants resisted as those of Rouen had done in 1419. And still Charles did not move. Then Joan of Arc came.

A beautiful legend must be approached with reverence and sympathy. There is nothing iconoclastic about the term "legend," which the Middle Ages used for the lives of the saints. Legend does not mean falsehood or delusion: it means that the sentimental or spiritual value of a story is immensely greater than its material details. Joan is no figment like William Tell: she did live, lead, fight, achieve, suffer. She appears in history not as a vision shimmering in a golden haze but as a young woman of robust flesh and healthy blood, full of courage and tenderness, of common sense and racy humor. All this is uncontroverted, although both Shakespeare and Voltaire failed to understand. But beyond the plain facts, clearly stated in the full report of her trial, admirably told by Michelet,[3] there rises Joan as a symbol. For posterity she imparted mystic prestige to the cause of that sorry personage Charles VII. She made him one in the spirit of Christian France with Clovis, Charlemagne, St. Louis. She redeemed the "realism" of a Philip the Fair and later of a Louis XI. She crystallized for the French people the sentiment of their nationality. History must deal with facts; but we cannot forget that material events are not the only facts, nor the more significant.

Joan was born at Domrémy, a village on the uncertain border of Champagne and Lorraine,[4] about 1410. She was the daughter of a ploughman and early tended the sheep: a peasant girl with no book learning, gentle and pious. Even a remote countryside such as Domrémy was not free from the depredations of armed bands, and tales would reach her of the kingdom's piteous plight. But as a rule, the common man, absorbed in his own hardships, has little compassion for sufferings not under his own eyes—else how could there be any ease and mirth among us today? The first and greatest miracle is that the distress of the whole realm filled a little shepherdess with shame and sorrow.

The second miracle is that she felt it her personal mission to heal the wounds of the land. The inspiration came to her in the form of visions and voices, St. Michael's, St. Catherine's, St. Margaret's. In those days the veil between heaven and earth would often melt away: the other-worldly was not rejected as antinatural. The first visions were a sign of Joan's piety not of her patriotism: they told her simply to be good and go assiduously to church. The call to action came later.

Joan did not at once convert her family to her conviction. Her father swore that he would rather drown her with his own hands than let her go venturing among the soldiers. Five years elapsed between her first vision and her leaving her father's house. Finally, an uncle, believing her, took her to the Sire de Baudricourt, Captain of Vaucouleurs. A prophecy was abroad that the kingdom, "lost through a woman [Isabel], would be redeemed through a woman." Baudricourt, prudently, sent word to the dauphin. The answer was: Let her come. Joan set forth; the people of Vaucouleurs had bought her armor, the duke of Lorraine had provided her with a horse. Five men were her escort.

The third miracle is the extraordinary definiteness of Joan's mission in her own mind. She did not sally forth to save the kingdom in a vague mystic glow. She had two objectives: to raise the siege of Orleans, to have the dauphin crowned at Rheims. The importance of Orleans was not beyond the grasp of sound peasant sense. The coronation was the link between Joan's piety and her loyalty to her side. She identified France with the dauphin, not with Henry VI; and she felt that her liege should be the Lord's Anointed, if he were to bring peace to the distracted kingdom.

The listless, divided court at Chinon seemed an unfavorable ground for her message, but even the skeptics were not hardened freethinkers. Queen Yolanda supported her; there is no evidence that the queen "invented" her, primed her, used her as a piece of propaganda. Joan was tested and found no impostor and no lunatic, but clear-eyed and pure. There was no sudden flare of enthusiasm; but the king gave her a small troop, and she threw herself into besieged Orleans.

No story is more familiar than the brief career of Joan, and we need not rehearse it in detail. It must be noted that miracles, to be manifested on an earthly plane, must be translated into earthly terms. The "realistic" historian will find little to wonder at in the campaign of 1429. The events in themselves were not so "miraculous" as the victories of Cressy, Poictiers, and Agincourt. The English did not have an overwhelming force before Orleans; the material and moral aid brought by Joan was sufficient to turn the tide. In a few days (April 29–May 8) the English were driven away. At Patay (June 28) Sir John Talbot, a famous fighter, was defeated and captured. Joan did bravely on the battlefield, but she was not in actual command. She showed in her truer colors when she pitied and comforted the wounded soldiers.

Philip of Burgundy, whom Bedford had recently snubbed, was not displeased that the English should receive a sharp lesson. So he did little to hinder the march of the dauphin toward Rheims, although much of it was through territory he controlled. On July 17 Charles VII was crowned in the city where Clovis had been baptized. During the ceremony Joan proudly held her own banner: it was her only reward. Her mission was accomplished.

Yet she was induced to remain and play a part in strategy and politics which she little understood. She led an assault on Paris (September 8). It failed, and she was wounded. It is surmised that, unwilling to offend Burgundy, the all-powerful neutral who had many friends in Paris, the royal forces did not heartily support the Maid.

In May, 1430, she went to the relief of Compiègne, which was besieged by the Burgundians. She managed to enter the city on the twenty-third; the same evening, in a sally, she was captured. No effort was made to rescue her: the commander was an agent of La Trémoille, the king's favorite, who resented Joan's prestige and influence. She was turned over by her captor to Jean de Ligny, a vassal of Burgundy. He held her for months, expecting a bid from Bourges which never came. Then he sold her to the duke of Burgundy, who delivered her to the English.

They could have killed her outright or allowed her to waste away in prison; the trial was obviously a piece of counterpropaganda. The miraculous claims made on her behalf seemed to prove that Heaven itself ratified the Salic Law and endorsed Charles VII: it was Bedford's cue to prove that her power was not of God. So she was brought before an ecclesiastical court at Rouen on a charge of witchcraft. Out of a hundred clerics only two or three were of English origin; most of them were Normans; a few came from the University of Paris; all were committed to the Anglo-Burgundian cause. The president was the bishop of Beauvais, Pierre Cauchon.

No one wishes to defend Cauchon and his associates: their judgment has been reversed twice over, by the rehabilitation trial of 1456, by Joan's canonization in 1920. But apart from their flagrant political bias, their attitude is intelligible. They stood for the hierarchy: the Church alone has the right to pass on the validity of individual revelations. The Maid professed to be an obedient child of Rome, but *Dieu premier servi,* God to be served first of all. Ignoring official channels, divine inspiration could come straight to the chosen soul. This direct allegiance to the Supreme Power is the stand of the mystic; it is that also of the heretic and the freethinker.

Joan fought her inquisitors honestly, bravely, with delightful flashes of homely common sense. She uttered the words which first focused French nationalism: "I know not whether God loves the English or hates them, but I know they will be thrown out of the kingdom of France." Yet, weakened by the harsh prison regime, the interminable ordeal, the pressure of learned men in high office, she recanted and was sentenced to life imprisonment (May 24, 1431). Her enemies were not satisfied. They trapped her into a technical "relapse": she was forced to don once more man's clothing, one of her most heinous crimes. Roused by this supreme injustice, she abjured her abjuration. This justified her being sent to the stake as "Heretic, Renegade, Apostate, and Idolater." Broken in spirit, she retracted once more, without any hope of saving her life. She was burned in the Old Market Place, at Rouen, on May 30, 1431, with the name of Jesus on her lips. Charles VII had not stirred a finger to save her; the Holy Chrism had made a king of him, but not a man.

CHARLES VII, THE WELL-SERVED: RECOVERY

Here we have to face a striking discrepancy between the Golden Legend of Joan and the plain, sullen, stubborn facts. We take it for granted that her miraculous mission was the turning point in the war: the French felt a new assurance, the English lost heart. Chronology tells a different story.

For six years after Joan's great campaign, nothing of note happened. There was no recrudescence of activity on the part of the French, no crumbling away of English power. In 1435 the decisive event took place: alas! it was a deal of a drab, realistic nature. It was through the defection of Burgundy that Henry V had been able to conquer. For years the powerful duke played a cautious, and at times a capricious, game. At last he was reconciled with Charles VII by the Treaty of Arras. But not as a repentant vassal: it was the king who had to humble himself. Amends of every kind had to be made for the murder of John the Fearless at Montereau sixteen years before. Cities on the Somme were to be turned over to Burgundy, thus opening the way to Paris whenever he chose; above all, the duke was recognized as a sovereign prince for life, free from any allegiance to the king. It is bitter to think that this capitulation secured for Charles VII what the Maid had failed to win, his capital, Paris. The city was recovered in 1436; the king formally entered it in 1437 and was appalled at the havoc wrought by twenty years of war.

Even then, there was no spontaneous movement such as the liberation of vast parts of France in 1944. For the next thirteen years there was to be very little military activity: Henry VI, a weak and distressed ruler, favored conciliation. But the truce did not mean peace for the harassed land. The armed bands, no longer fighting one another, preyed on the population: they were called the "Flayers" or "Knackers" (*Ecorcheurs*). La Hire and Xaintrailles, prominent in the king's service, also amassed wealth as freebooters. With anarchy came its grim attendants, famine and pestilence. The incurable feudal nobility still rose against the king with the complicity of the dauphin, Louis (1440).[5]

But if Charles himself hardly improved, he began deserving his title in history, the Well-Served. The richest man in France, the great merchant, shipowner, and banker Jacques Coeur, was his *argentier* or finance minister; like Joan, he experienced the king's ingratitude. The Bureau Brothers provided France with an excellent artillery. Above all, the States-General recognized the need for a regular army supported by regular taxes. The king ceased at last to be a mere feudal lord and had the means to pursue a royal policy.

In July, 1449, the truce was broken. Richemont and Dunois[6] swiftly reconquered Normandy; Rouen effected its own liberation thirty years after the terrible siege of 1419. The battle of Formigny (1450) led to the surrender of Caen and Cherbourg. English rule was ended north of the Loire.

The recovery of Guienne proved a harder task. After three hundred years of profitable association with England, the people of Bordeaux were loyal to their traditional suzerain. Conquered by Dunois in 1451, they submitted but soon rebelled and called for English assistance: Joan's message, "Throw the English out of France!" had evidently not reached Gascony. Talbot, now earl of Shrewsbury, was sent to the rescue; but the grim veteran, hated and admired, was no great general. At Castillon (1453) he was defeated and slain. The reconquered provinces were treated with the utmost rigor. Since their return to French allegiance interfered with their London trade, they remained resentful for a long time.[7]

✒ CHARLES VII, THE WELL-SERVED:
THE GALLICAN TRADITION

We should constantly bear in mind that events of European scope were affecting France, although they do not specifically belong to French history. Religion was the center, if by no means the whole, of medieval life. The humiliation of the Papacy in the person of Boniface VIII, the Babylonian Captivity at Avignon, the Great Schism (1378–1423, and again 1440–1449), the bold challenges of Wyclif and John Huss, the Councils of Pisa, Constance, Basel, striving to restore harmony, reform abuses, and repress heresy: all these were of more vital importance to earnest souls than the endless squabbles of royal cousins.

The religious life of the time can be seen at its best in the person of Jean Charlier, known from his place of origin as Jean de Gerson (1363–1429). Scholastic philosopher, ecclesiastical statesman, seeker after spiritual consolation and peace, he ran the whole gamut of priestly activities. He was chancellor of the University of Paris and the last glory of that medieval source of light. He adopted the nominalism of Occam: general ideas, to him, were abstractions, mere names, not eternal patterns. This implied that reason could never bridge the chasm between material realities and the absolute. Scholasticism thereby acknowledged defeat; but the way was open for science and secular philosophy. Gerson was the dominant influence in the councils which attempted to heal the Church. In his desire for unity he was averse not to reform but to disruptive change, and so he was among the opponents of John Huss. His fame as *Doctor Consolatorius* was such that the *Imitation of Christ* was persistently ascribed to him. He reaped the reward of the wise: although we feel that his humane, well-balanced spirit should have guided his contemporaries, he is eclipsed in our minds by fanatical leaders who seem vigorous only because they are crude. Many French children who dutifully memorize the names of famous assassins— Tanneguy du Châtel, Poltrot de Méré, Jacques Clément, Ravaillac— have never heard of Jean de Gerson.

The troublous condition of the Christian commonwealth had a definite influence on the French monarchy: it strengthened what is known as the Gallican tradition: the autonomy, or liberties, of the French Church. The roots of Gallicanism are deep: from earliest times the king was, ambiguously, both the servant and the protector of the Church, and there was a sacred element in his earthly power. The virtues of St. Louis gave substance to such a claim. Even under rulers of questionable wisdom and integrity like the Valois, the spiritual aura that surrounded the monarchy did not disappear: witness Joan of Arc's faith in the coronation rite.

This contest for primacy had a darker shadow, the scramble for riches. The Church was opulent, thanks to the generosity of the faithful and to her own careful husbandry. Two great organizations sought to control this vast store of wealth, the papal and the royal. But in this realistic domain a compromise was not impossible, and no article of faith was involved. The Gallicans never were heretics or schismatics: they had no desire to rend the seamless garment. But they insisted on national autonomy in matters of administration and finance, and a national church would almost inevitably become a part of the national government. It is easy to understand why the king's men should be more ardent Gallicans than the king himself. The king was an individual Christian with a soul to save: his spiritual advisers wielded great influence. The ideal for which the king's men were working, the absolute supremacy of the state within its own frontiers, had no thought for the hereafter and was indifferent to the thunders of the pope.

In 1438 the Gallican tradition was crystallized in a royal document, the Pragmatic Sanction of Bourges.[8] This particular instrument was canceled by Louis XI, but the tendency it represented was too deep-seated to be reversed. We shall find it again in the Concordate of Francis I (1516), in the Declaration of the Clergy under Louis XIV (1682), and in the Organic Articles of Napoleon (1802). Throughout the ages Gallicanism found support among royal officials, particularly in the Parlements, among members of the secular clergy, and among the national-minded bourgeois. The Gallicans, we repeat, were sincerely religious: their doctrine took it for granted that the government was devoted to the Catholic faith. When the state became thoroughly secularized, when it granted full civil rights to Jews, heretics, and freethinkers, Gallicanism lost all meaning and slowly disappeared.

SPIDER AND JAILBIRD:
LOUIS XI AND FRANÇOIS VILLON

The reign of Louis XI (1461–1480) enjoys in French history a sinister eminence which it scarcely deserves. Like Charlemagne, Joan of Arc, Richelieu, Napoleon, Talleyrand, the crafty ruler is a figure of legend. He had the questionable fortune of tempting two great romancers, Walter Scott in *Quentin Durward,* Victor Hugo in *Notre-Dame de Paris,* with the dramatist Casimir Delavigne as a poor but honest third. His life was chronicled by a sagacious servant of his, Philippe de Commynes, a Flemish Machiavelli, who dilates complacently on his master's cunning as well as his own. Viewed without romantic or realistic spectacles (I know not which are the more delusive), the reign of Louis XI appears in every way as the continuation of his father's. Like Charles VII, Louis was plagued with rebellious nobles; like him, he built up the central power; like him again, he had to fight an unceasing duel with the house of Burgundy.

Louis found himself confronted with a conspiracy of his great vassals, Alençon, Burgundy, Bourbon, and, as their nominal head, the heir-presumptive, his own brother Berry: a familiar refrain in French annals, which must have awakened in the king's mind rueful memories of the *Praguerie*. The coalition adopted a most virtuous name, League of the Public Weal. Beaten at Montlhéry, Louis had to sign treaties with his rebellious subjects at Conflans and at Saint-Maur (1465). Each grabbed some benefit; the Public Weal alone was forgotten.

Louis XI pursued the organization of the kingdom with the assistance of bourgeois officials. This was no new departure: we have seen that the work, well begun under Philip Augustus, was continued by Philip the Fair and Charles V, and further advanced by Charles VII. In some respects, Louis XI perfected the framework which was to last until the Revolution. He had a rigorous, and indeed a grinding, system of taxation; it made him unpopular with all classes, but it enabled him to have a strong army, which he seldom used, and a well-stored treasury, a more effective weapon in his hands. Perhaps his chief contribution to the structure of the modern state was his organization of a royal postal network, relays at his instant service on all the high roads of France. This made him effectively and beneficently what the duke of Burgundy had called him, "the universal spider."

Above all the reign of Louis XI was, like that of Charles VII, overshadowed by the constant struggle with the dukes of Burgundy. From 1419, when John the Fearless was killed at Montereau, to 1477, when Charles the Bold perished under the walls of Nancy, this conflict, open or latent, affected the whole policy of the kingdom. It was more than the rebellion of a feudal vassal: a new state aspired to be born and to secure complete independence from France.

The duchy of Burgundy had reverted to the crown in 1361; but in 1363 John the Good gave it as an appanage to his son Philip the Bold, who, a mere stripling, had stood bravely by his side at Poictiers. Philip acquired the countships of Burgundy [9] and Flanders by marriage, Charolais by purchase. He thus possessed two separate groups of domains, both among the richest in Europe. It may be excessive to speak of a deliberate plan: if the dukes of Burgundy sought to increase their possessions, they wanted even more to dominate the whole of France by controlling the king. Still, the line that their ambition would take was obvious: they desired to link the Low Countries (they later secured Holland and Brabant) with the Burgundies; and for that purpose, they needed Lorraine and parts of Champagne. Then they would revive the *Francia Media* of Lothair, coequal in rank as it was in wealth, with Germany and France. They may also have remembered that once the "kingdom" of Burgundy extended far into the valley of the Rhône. By the Treaty of Arras (1435), Philip the Good had secured full sovereign status, for his own lifetime, a first step, and a long one, toward complete and permanent independence.

The dukes were powerful, although in constant difficulties with their fractious Flemish subjects. In their capital, Dijon, they lived in a state which outshone the petty court of Bourges and even that of Paris. There was a vigorous Burgundian Renaissance several decades ahead of the French one. The ducal order of the Golden Fleece (1429) enjoyed at once a prestige which it preserved through long centuries. It was expected of the Burgundian ruler that he should lead in a crusade; and, in a grand manner, Philip the Good toyed with the idea.

Philip the Good died in 1467 and was succeeded by his son, hitherto count of Charolais, known as Charles the Fearless.[10] Charles already had had a brush with Louis, in the War of the Public Weal. Louis, with overweening trust in his own craftiness, sought an interview with his powerful rival at Péronne (1468); at the same time he had secretly encouraged against him the burgesses of Liège. The move was fool-hardy as well as deceitful: Louis, who had placed himself in the duke's power, was found out. He could extricate himself only by confirming Burgundy in the possession of the key cities of the Somme. He had to accompany Charles in a punitive expedition against the Liégeois, who fell under his eyes crying, *"Vive France!"*

Charles, pursuing the great plan of his house, secured Upper Alsace in 1469 and the right of moving his troops across Lorraine. But the Alsatians rebelled; and the Swiss, their allies, egged on by Louis XI, declared war upon him. At Granson and Morat near Neuchâtel (1476) he was sharply defeated by those hardy mountaineers, for ages the best soldiers in Europe. Meanwhile, the elaborate coalition he had set afoot against the king—England, Brittany, and the inevitable discontented nobles—melted before the arms or the gold of France. Charles was besieging Nancy, to make himself full master of Lorraine, when the Swiss came to the rescue of the city. The garrison, at that sight, sallied forth. A confused combat ensued in the winter gloaming; when the routed Burgundians rallied, the duke was missing. His body was found later, stripped, among the anonymous slain. With him ended the dream of a new Lotharingia.

In this contest, Louis XI had shown neither conspicuous valor nor infallible skill. He did not so much win as wait for his adversary to lose, for the fiery Burgundian charged as blindly as a mad bull. The odds were heavy against Charles: Louis had merely to preserve an ancient and fairly compact kingdom; Charles was attempting to create a new one out of disconnected patches.[11] With his death the danger created by the appanaged houses disappeared. Of the great feudatories Brittany alone was still semi-independent, and its duke had no male heir.

Louis confiscated at once the duchy of Burgundy in punishment for Charles's felony. But the rest of the rich heritage escaped him: Marie, the duke's daughter, married Maximilian of Austria, taking with her Flanders, Artois, and Franche-Comté. These provinces were not recovered for two hundred years; and of Flanders, which had been within the French orbit throughout the Middle Ages, only a fraction was ever regained.[12] Luck, however, was with Louis: in 1481 the second house of Anjou died out, and Maine, Anjou, Provence were added to the royal domain.

The closing years of Louis XI lacked serenity and even dignity. The victor, the most powerful prince of the time, was hated and despised; so he lived in constant terror of assassination. His cruelty was almost pathological, although he did not keep *all* his prisoners in cramped iron cages. Moreover, he was ailing and in abject fear of death. He showed a puzzling blend of miserliness and luxurious display. He wore a greasy cap with a band of leaden medals in honor of his favorite saints, but he was also noted for the gorgeousness of his gowns. He had great statesmanslike projects of the centralizing, totalitarian kind associated in our minds with Richelieu, Napoleon, and Hitler; but he suddenly relapsed into arrant superstition. At the last his secret frustration was revealed: he desired to be represented on his tomb in his youth and strength, in hunting habit, with hound and horn.

The fascination of the period—and of the royal figure itself—lies in its twilit, chiaroscuro character. The medieval quality of the fifteenth century comes out more pungently because we feel that the Middle Ages were already dead. Overripeness appeals to the jaded taste; but it attracts the healthy-minded as well when new life is seen burgeoning by the side of corruption. The Lost Centuries were decadent, yet they were not weak.

All this is admirably expressed in the works of François de Montcorbier (or des Loges), B.A. and M.A. of the University of Paris (1431–*ca.* 1489), better known as François Villon. He too had lost his way; he fell among thieves, to rob, riot, and revel with them. He too felt the lure of the gruesome, of the macabre, and described with Baudelairian power the hanging corpses preyed upon by the worms and the carrion crows. He too had a sense of beauty and could evoke with a few marvelous notes "the fair ladies of old." He too had a soul gnawing and yearning under the grossness of his flesh. He still had faith, but that faith was to him a pageant rather than a direct experience. It is not the Virgin whose praises he sings in a luminous and tender ballad, the jeweled epitome of the Middle Ages, a Sainte-Chapelle among poems: it is his mother, whom he admires with a smile and envies for her holy simplicity. Even Boileau could not be deaf to the song, so strange and so pure, of that elfin jailbird. The last words on the Middle Ages—and perhaps on all human history—were spoken by him:

"Where are the snows of yesteryear?"

BOOK III
CLASSICAL FRANCE

CHAPTER XI

The Renaissance and the Italian Wars

✍ THE GREAT SURGE OF THE SIXTEENTH CENTURY

Three themes are dominant in the confused history of France during the first half of the sixteenth century. The first is the long series of wars that had their start in the lure of Italy and expanded later into a struggle for European supremacy. The second is the surge of confidence and energy in every field, which we call the Renaissance. The third is the recrudescence of religious passions, which led to magnificent and stormy heights, but also to disruption and disastrous, most un-Christian strife. The three themes are not independent: they form an intricate counterpoint. The keynote of the whole epoch is will power, daring, *virtú*. In absolute purity this quality is best exemplified in Machiavelli's hero, the princely ruffian Cesare Borgia. But the same intensity, the same boundless hope, the same lust for action are found among the discoverers and the apostles, the scholars and the artists. They are manifest in Vasco da Gama, Columbus, Luther, Calvin, St. Ignatius, as well as in Michaelangelo, Leonardo da Vinci, and Rabelais. It was in truth a world of giants.

It is safe to assume that there are powerful personalities in every age and every country. But the cultural climate may favor or hinder their development. Born sixty years earlier, Napoleon would never have risen to the throne. In periods of anarchy strong men waste their lives in hand-to-hand fighting; in ages of oppressive conformity they are stifled or crushed. For a Renaissance to occur, there must be a sense of release. But there must be also a sense of direction, of inner discipline; for chaos destroys the spirit even more surely than servitude. In the sixteenth century there was a triumphant escape from obsolete custom, from formal, unreasoning authority, in a word from decadent medievalism. And positive guidance was found in two forces so closely allied that they appeared identical: the wisdom of antiquity and the power of human reason. This was true of religious reformers as well as of scholars and artists. Both Luther and Calvin were vigorous logicians; and both sought their inspiration in truth yet uncorrupted, the undefiled fountain of apostolic faith. This dual reign, this bimetallism, as it has been called, of antiquity and reason, constitutes classical humanism; and it was to dominate European culture for three hundred years.

It will be remembered that we failed to account for the earlier—and perhaps the greater—Renaissance, that of the eleventh century. Like all spiritual movements, the mighty surge of the sixteenth century cannot be forced into a formal pattern and cannot be assigned indisputable causes. No single event created the Renaissance. Those events which are oftenest mentioned as determinants were only symptoms.

The fall of Constantinople in 1453, for instance, is undoubtedly of commanding significance; but it marks the end, not the beginning, of an era. That victory of the infidels, that disastrous epilogue of the crusades, proved that medieval Christendom was dead: it gave no inkling of greater glories to come. It was long seriously taught that a few Greek scholars, fleeing from the doomed city, brought Greek learning with them as though it were a germ; from them Italy "caught" the Renaissance, and the rest of Europe, from Italy. To this convenient hypothesis there are a number of objections. Byzantium had remained in full possession of ancient lore and nevertheless was decadent. Why wait for the exodus of a few grammarians? There never had been any complete severance between the Mediterranean East and the West: Venetians and Genoese constantly traded with the Greeks. The Latins had had possession of Constantinople in the thirteenth century: they could have had access to ancient manuscripts if they had cared, but they were more interested in jewels and relics. Finally, the Renaissance spirit was astir in Italy long before 1453. The rediscovery of antiquity, the "revival of learning," was not a material revelation, the unearthing of a long lost treasure: it was the result of an inner growth. It was because man was "renascent" that he at length understood and loved antiquity.

The printing press accelerated, but did not create, the movement. Lorenzo Valla, master of critical scholarship (1405–1457), was dead before Gutenberg's invention was perfected. The full consequence of printing, the democratization of culture, would not be felt for generations, indeed for centuries. The discovery of America was simply a manifestation of the new daring; it must be noted that in the evolution of Germany, France, Italy, the sudden expansion of the geographical horizon played at the time an extremely limited part.

Finally, it has been claimed that the promulgation of the Copernican system marked an era in the history of thought. But the work of Copernicus was not published in full until 1543, when he was on his deathbed, and by that time the Renaissance had already yielded its richest fruit. It is surprising, incidentally, to see how little the Copernican revolution affected the lives of men and even their philosophies. There had been sublimity of thought before Copernicus, embracing the whole universe, dwarfing the paltry concerns of our earthbound life; there was no lack of petty conceit after Copernicus, just as though our globe had not lost its throne in the center of the cosmos. The great economic expansion, first well marked in Italy and Germany, was well under way before the gold of Spanish America reached the shores of Eurcpe. In other words, vast trends like the Renaissance and the Reformation are not single events, and cannot be reduced to a single chain of events. We realize how vague, how illusive, how unscientific such a conception must seem. Yet it is only the awareness of such trends that distinguishes history from haphazard chronicling.

We have seen that Renaissance and Reformation were interwoven. At times they are in accord, at times they clash; but they cannot ignore each other without suffering a mutilation. In the political history of France, however, there is some justification for discussing them in separate chapters. Under Francis I the religious problem could not be dismissed; but it could be, and was, deliberately subordinated and deferred. The king was absorbed in his Italian and European ambitions; and he enjoyed, as a voluptuary, not as a philosopher, the luxury of the new culture. He strove hard, against all extremists, to remain tolerant. His frank subordination of the religious to the secular is apparent in his foreign policy. He, His Most Christian Majesty, allied himself with the Grand Turk and the German Protestants to thwart the temporal head of the Catholic Commonwealth, the emperor. For his successor, Henry II, on the contrary, the religious issue was paramount: his one desire was to extirpate heresy. But on momentum he was compelled to keep up the fight against the other great Catholic powers. Peace had been signed at last, and he was free to devote himself to his chosen task when a stupid accident ended his life. So it will be possible for us, as it would not be in the case of Germany, to postpone the religious theme until 1559. Thereafter, and for nearly forty years, its predominance will be indisputable.

THE ITALIAN WARS: CHARLES VIII AND LOUIS XII

When King Spider, Louis XI, died, his son Charles VIII was a lad of thirteen, small of stature, weak of body, will, and wit, his enormous head reeling with vague dreams. His sister Anne, twenty years of age, seized control. Her old cynic of a father had called her "the least foolish woman in France: there is none that is wise." Anne was married to Pierre de Beaujeu, a younger son of the Bourbon family; and, without a formal title, they governed, not unwisely, in the name of the odd and foolish child.

But not without opposition: Louis of Orleans, next of kin, sought the regency. The States-General was convened in 1484. This assembly, which the southern provinces ignored, was little more than a sorry farce. There were great festivities in Paris; the hated barber of Louis XI was sacrificed to those who had lived in dread of him when he was a favorite; Orleans was granted no power, but some money. Brave words, however, were spoken, notably by a Burgundian, Philip Pot: "All power comes from the people, all power goes back to the people, and by the people I mean all who dwell in the land. It is by the people that kings are made, it is for the people that they must rule." Jefferson, Mirabeau, Lincoln could not have been more definite. Reversing Hugo's dictum, we may say that there is nought so weak as an idea out of due time.

Unsatisfied, the feudal lords rebelled again (1485–1488), led by the duke of Brittany, and aided by unfriendly neighbors, Navarre, Lorraine. Finally, at Saint-Aubin-du-Cormier, they were defeated, and Louis of Orleans was captured. The aimless flare-up was dubbed "the Foolish War"; Pierre and Anne retained their hold.

But a sharper crisis was impending. The duke of Brittany died in 1488, and the young heiress was besieged with suitors. A vast coalition was formed against France: Henry VII of England, Ferdinand of Aragon, Maximilian of Austria. Maximilian, known to history both as "the Last of the Knights" and as "Scant-of-Pelf," followed what was to be the strategy of his house: "Let others fight: thou, happy Austria, marry." Now a widower, he hoped to settle the Breton succession as he had settled the Burgundian, by wedding the heiress. However, his remote courtship achieved nothing more than a marriage by proxy; and it was Charles VIII who, in 1491, became the husband of Duchess Anne. The duchess considered the union as purely personal and herself as sovereign in her own domain. So to make doubly and trebly sure, Louis XII had to marry her on the death of Charles VIII, and the next king, Francis I, married her daughter and heiress, Claudia. This threefold knot settled the question of Breton independence until 1940, when the Nazis attempted to revive it, with no result but a vast shrugging of shoulders.

Charles VIII was now of age. He dismissed Sister Anne and fell into far worse hands: those of his valet, De Vesc, and of a former merchant,

Briçonnet. It was they, now mighty personages—De Vesc was seneschal, Briçonnet a bishop—who encouraged his Italian dreams. The lure of Italy was potent already. Many Frenchmen had seen the peninsula, as pilgrims or traders, and felt the magic of its rich and refined life. But the kings so far had refused to be embroiled even in the fairest of lands. "The Genoese give themselves to me," Louis XI had said, "and I give them to the devil," with more political wisdom than Christian charity. Charles was too callow to resist the temptation. The weaker the mind, the more gigantic the schemes. He was not content with Naples, as heir of the Anjou dynasty founded by the brother of St. Louis: with Naples went elusive crowns, Jerusalem, Constantinople, mirages which he accepted as realities.

He had the means: the army, the treasury, well-husbanded on the whole by Charles the Well-Served, by Louis XI, by Anne and Pierre de Beaujeu. The tempting opportunity came: Charles was summoned by Lodovico Sforza, "the Moor," tyrant of Milan. So he gave up solid gains, Roussillon and Cerdagne to Ferdinand of Aragon, Artois and Franche-Comté to Maximilian, gold by the shovelful to Henry VII, in the hope of securing their good will. Then he sallied forth, a royal young Quixote, on his knightly quest.

The paradox is that at first everything seemed real. Charles was welcomed in divided Italy: by Lodovico in Milan, by the Florence of Savonarola, hailing him as the Sword of God. And his army was no shadow. The solid masses that followed him, Swiss and German mercenaries, alert Gascons, heavy French cavalry, an artillery without a peer, dazed the Italians, used to the delicate shadow fighting of the *condottieri*. It was a blitzkrieg. The pope, Alexander VI, had misgivings: Rome ever dreaded a strong power north and south of St. Peter's Patrimony. But Charles was too well armed to be denied a blessing. So through Rome he went and reached Naples in triumph. On May 12, 1495, he made a solemn entry into the city, on his head the crown of the defunct Eastern Empire.

But his cosmopolitan troops behaved like the barbarians they were. Italy, recovering from the first shock, noted that the French were not supermen, and that they were not so many after all. A Holy League arose against Charles. His neighbors, their appetite whetted, were closing in on all his frontiers. He was lost in a hostile land, a thousand miles from home. He rushed back faster than he had come. The bubble chasing would have ended in complete disaster if the impetus of despair —*la furia francese,* the Italians called it—had not swept aside at Fornovo the armies that barred his way (July, 1495). The lesson was not wholly lost: Charles, only twenty-five, saw and deplored some of his faults.

But before he could learn riper wisdom, he cracked his head against a low lintel in his castle at Amboise (1498).

Since the children of Charles had died in infancy, his heir was a distant cousin, Louis of Orleans. Louis was the son of that Charles, Duke of Orleans, who after Agincourt had spent a quarter century in English prisons, a "caged songster," the most delicate poet of his time —but how thin his princely chirp by the side of Villon's poignant note! The new king was thirty-six: but, of a frail constitution, he was prematurely old. His will was no stronger than his body; he followed with docility his second wife, Anne of Brittany, and his favorite counsellor, Georges, Cardinal of Amboise. He had a kindly heart, for his French subjects at any rate, for he showed little mercy in his Italian campaigns. Under him the country knew internal peace: no "Foolish War," no "League for the Public Weal." Prosperity was abounding: his reign and the first decade under Francis I are among the happy moments in France's checkered life. And the government did its best to foster the people's welfare. Banditry was repressed, and dishonesty among officials. Taxes were reduced. State finances were submitted to strict auditing. The Ordinance of Blois, in 1510, was a very creditable program of administrative reform. The royal household was not wasteful, to the chagrin of not a few courtiers. "I'd rather have them sneer at my parsimony," said the king, "than have the people groan at my extravagance." In 1506 the States-General of Tours conferred upon Louis the finest of titles, Father of the People. Official praises cannot be accepted at their face value; but the flattering name is remembered, and does not sound ironical, like John "the Good," or Louis XV, "the Well-Beloved." Not a strong man, Louis XII has left a good name.

Unfortunately, although better balanced and more mature than Charles VIII, he proved just as unable to resist the lure of Italy. He inherited his predecessor's claims to Naples; and he advanced rights of his own on Milan, as the grandson of Valentina Visconti. The expedition of Charles VIII had been brief: a dash, a pageant, a scurry. Those of Louis XII were protracted, but they followed the same pattern: early victories, complex Italian intrigues, threats of a European coalition, disaster barely averted, frustration.

In 1499 Louis XII wrested Milan from Lodovico Sforza, the Moor, and was greeted with enthusiasm by the fickle population. Sforza—the best mind among Italian rulers, the patron Leonardo da Vinci had chosen as the most enlightened—fled but returned at the head of Swiss mercenaries. Because he was unable to pay them, they betrayed him, and he spent the end of his life in a French prison. Then, in alliance with Ferdinand of Aragon, Louis conquered Naples. Soon, however, the confederates quarreled; the French were defeated by the famous Gonsalvo de Cordoba (1504), and all claims to Naples had to be relinquished. Unable to disentangle himself from Italian affairs, Louis first put down a popular revolution in Genoa (1507). Next he joined the League of Cambrai (1508), with the pope and the emperor, directed against Venice; and the Venetians were duly defeated at Agnadello (1509). No sooner was the Queen of the Adriatic humbled than the pope reversed his stand: Julius II was an energetic, ambitious ruler, statesman rather than pontiff; and he revived the Holy League to expel the French from the peninsula. The king's nephew, a brilliant young leader, Gaston de Foix, Duke of Nemours, won lightning victories at Brescia and Ravenna but died in the hour of triumph (1512). Milan had to be evacuated. The end of the adventure was inglorious. The defeat of Novara compelled Louis to withdraw from Italy altogether. Attacked in the north by Henry VIII and Maximilian, the French fled in such haste at Guinegatte that the brief combat remained known as the "battle of the spurs." A series of lame and costly peace treaties followed. One thing was clear: for the second time Italy was lost.

Out of the French commanders, only one, Gaston de Foix, was a military genius; but he was a meteor and died at twenty-three. Several, however, have remained alive in French tradition. La Trémoille, for one, a good and honest soldier—although not above trickery when required in the king's service—redeemed the name damaged by his grandfather, who had been Joan of Arc's persistent enemy and perhaps her betrayer. La Palisse, a valiant captain, at his best in defeat, whose name is ironically connected with outrageous platitudes, *vérités de la Palisse*.[1] And above all Bayard, the perfect knight, "without fear and without reproach." Bravest of the brave—on the Garigliano he held a bridge single-handed against an army—he was no mere mass of heroic brawn but a skilled commander, humane, scrupulously loyal, courteous and gentle, respectful of the ladies, modest to a fault: a Sir Galahad in an age of brutality, lust, and deceit. Miracles will happen, as M. de la Palisse would say.

A sadder man after so many frustrations, Louis XII showed no sign of becoming a wiser one. The ailing quinquagenarian married Henry VIII's sister, a rich-blooded girl of sixteen. He tried to please her, changed his habits, went to dances, kept late hours, and in a few months was sped to his eternal rest (January 1, 1515).

✣ THE CULT OF SPLENDOR: FRANCIS I

The hereditary principle is a lottery. The remote kinsman who succeeded Louis XII might have been a sickly child, a dullard, a morose old man:

fate brought to the throne, at that golden hour of the young Renaissance, an ideal Renaissance prince. The count of Angoulême, now Francis I, was twenty years old, vigorous, radiantly handsome, a lover of chivalric romance. Immediately upon his accession, at Marignano, he gave evidence of his prowess; and—a charming gesture—he wanted to be made a knight on the battlefield by the stainless hero, Bayard. Fond of luxury, even of display, he dazzled England and posterity with his Camp of the Cloth of Gold. But in his prodigality he was a connoisseur: he sought out Leonardo da Vinci and brought him over to France. He was a friend of scholars and poets, and, in the words of an old rhyme in his praise, "he honored learned men equally with warriors." He showered upon them fair words and at times substantial benefits. He sided with Budé against Béda, with humanism against the obscurantism of the Sorbonne.[2] He established Royal Lecturers for the free study of classical languages: the origin of the glorious *Collège de France,* where the utmost liberty of teaching and learning is preserved. He was the Prince par excellence, the hero, the lover, the protector of arts and letters.

It is difficult to be the spoiled child of fortune without becoming spoiled. Francis I was a disappointment; the young athlete of 1515 died at fifty-two, a tragically decayed charmer, gnawed by the Nemesis of his amorous pleasures. The knight of Marignano was to be eleven years later the inept and luckless commander of Pavia, the captive of Madrid. The friend of humanism did not prevent Louis de Berquin and Etienne Dolet from suffering death. Historians do not agree in gauging his enigmatic personality. The fact which cannot be denied is that for good or ill he gave a new luster and almost a new meaning to the kingly office. He was in many respects a prototype of Louis XIV, with less sustained and self-assured perfection, but with the color, the bravado, the dash of Italian *virtú* which made the Renaissance so much more fascinating than the age of Boileau.

Under him the court, an ancient institution, assumed an unprecedented significance. The enhanced prestige and power of the monarchy required an exalted standard of magnificence. The court nobility came into being. This transformation denoted not a rise of the aristocracy but its inner decay. The feudal caste had lost power: no castle could withstand artillery fire, and the king alone could afford to keep an irresistible ordnance. But their wealth also was declining. The whole period was marked—long before the influx of American gold—by a steady rise in prices, a veritable inflation. Now the dues collected by the feudal lords were fixed by custom: their real value sank, and the nobles, impoverished, debarred by their prejudices from any gainful occupation, had to turn to the king as to the sole fountain of wealth.

They became gilded retainers. Ultimately, the parasites stifled the monarchy upon which they were preying: Louis XVI became the prisoner and the victim of his court.

Although Paris was safely entrenched as the administrative capital, the court followed the king, and the king followed his whim. Like his predecessors Francis had a marked preference for the Loire region, the famed "garden of France": he added a wing to Blois and constructed Chambord. He began rebuilding and enlarging the Louvre. Fontainebleau was his favorite: the mighty hunter loved the great forest; the decoration, entrusted to Il Primatice and Il Rosso, well fulfilled his ideal of sensuous splendor. He also built Madrid, Villers-Cotterets, and Saint-Germain on the impressive bluff that commands the meandering course of the Seine. When he moved from one castle to another, not only did the whole court with its innumerable staff follow but even the furniture and the hangings. These rapid changes explain why the royal residences of the Renaissance impress us as magnificent rather than livable: they were not homes in any sense but mere stations in the eternal quest for pleasure. Chambord, a dream palace in its sylvan solitude, was but a gigantic hunting lodge.

If "the King's Pleasure" (*le bon plaisir*) meant first of all pleasure, the formula, which became official at that time, assumed a deeper meaning with the king's men. In their eyes, absolutism was not caprice, but law. Under the frivolous and prodigal ruler they patiently pursued the work initiated three centuries before: to make the central power truly and irresistibly sovereign. The Ordinance of Villers-Cotterets in 1539 was one of the great codes of the monarchy. It embraced many subjects, from the prohibition of workers' "Companionships" to the introduction of the king's French as the sole official language. It was a definite step in the deliberate creation of a France "One and Indivisible."

An abuse of ancient origin, and akin to feudalism, acquired under Francis I almost the dignity of an institution: many offices were openly bought and became the property of their owners, to be transmitted to their descendants.[3] Thus was strengthened a hereditary bureaucracy which, with its many faults, was none the less a check on despotism. The levity of kings and favorites might cause the monarchy to lurch; but thanks to the king's men and their traditional skill, the huge machine escaped disaster. Streamlined by Napoleon, it still carried, ponderously, the bewildered Fourth Republic. So the name of Francis I, the royal rake and spendthrift, is also connected with the strengthening of the state, like the names, respected or hated, of Philip Augustus, Philip the Fair, Louis XI, Richelieu, Louis XIV, Napoleon.

✒ "BALANCE OF POWER": KING FRANCIS I AND EMPEROR CHARLES V

A king with a taste for magnificence is a costly luxury. The prodigality that erected Fontainebleau and Chambord might be condoned: France could afford such jewels. But the lust for conquest, conquest as a splendid game without any regard for national interests or geographic realities, was ruinous indeed. Francis was not the first offender. But the expeditions of Charles VIII and Louis XII might have remained regrettable episodes; the policy of Francis I set a pattern. Down to Napoleon III French sovereigns would indulge in wars for the sake of prestige. Kings were afflicted with an "occupational disease" known as martial glory: the most acute case perhaps was that of Charles XII of Sweden. Undeterred by the Italian failures of his two predecessors, Francis, in the first year of his reign, rushed into the bewitching and fatal land.

He brilliantly defeated at Marignano (1515) the Swiss who were supporting Massamiliano Sforza, son of the hapless Lodovico. So Milan was in French hands again; and with the Swiss the king made a "Perpetual Peace," which, for a wonder, was to deserve its name. The new pope, Leo X (Medici) (1513–1521), a true Renaissance prince, a lover of arts and letters, was less combative and perhaps shrewder than Julius II; he and Francis I agreed on a Concordat which likewise endured as long as the French monarchy. A triumphant start: Francis, intoxicated with success, made his bid for the most prestigious title of all. As early as 1517, two years before the death of Maximilian I, he was preparing his candidacy to the empire. He already dreamed of leading Christian Europe against the Turks, redeeming the Holy Sepulcher, and reuniting East and West under a single crown.

The dream was grandiose but certainly not ignoble. The reality against which it broke was sordid. The Electors had little thought for Christendom, or even for Germany: their one desire was to line their own pockets. Accepting bribes impartially from every side, they had the decency to offer the crown to Frederick the Wise, Elector of Saxony, who, unwisely perhaps, declined. This limited the contest to Francis, King of France, and Charles, King of Spain. Francis was the richer, but Charles was backed by the great Augsburg bankers, the Fuggers. The conscience of the Electors steadily rose in value; every qualm was worth a fortune. Finally, the credit of the Fuggers beat the bullion of the French king, and Charles, the grandson of Maximilian, became Charles V. He was only nineteen.

Francis I was six years older, already brilliantly successful, more vigorous, more charming, the favorite of fortune. He considered his defeat as due to an unworthy trick. This keen frustration suffices to explain his constant desire to thwart his rival. Moreover, he felt encircled, and encirclement, *Einkreisung,* is the eternal nightmare of powerful states. He found Charles pressing on every frontier. In the great game of marriage and heritage, no one had ever drawn such an accumulation of prizes. From his father, the new emperor held the Netherlands and the county of Burgundy (Franche-Comté) since 1506. On the death of his grandfather, Ferdinand of Aragon, he had inherited the Spanish kingdoms.[4] Maximilian, his other grandfather, left him the Austrian domains. Soon Württemberg fell into his lap. Both from Maximilian and Ferdinand, he had claims to the choicest parts of Italy.

The contest seemed unequal. The lands that Charles V controlled far outweighed France; the treasures of the Americas were beginning to pour into his treasury. And although no genius, he was astute, self-possessed, hard-working; whereas the large, boldly modeled nose, the shapely beard, the regal smile of Francis I adorned an empty head. But Charles's incredible dominions were scattered and ill-assorted. He commanded no profound loyalty: to the Spaniards, he was a Fleming; to the Germans, a Spaniard; to the Italians, a German. Francis, had he not been prodded by jealous vainglory, could have left his rival to the incessant propping-up of his ramshackle empire.

But, in a sense, the provocation came from Charles. We think of him as a Spaniard or a German: at heart he was a Burgundian. He was born at Ghent, the son of Philip of Burgundy: his constant desire was to recuperate the duchy of Burgundy and accomplish the design of Charles the Bold. This was a threat not to the prestige of Francis I merely but to the very existence of France, for Burgundy was the keystone of the realm. And Charles would seek allies in England, and among the highest French nobility.

For bluff King Hal across the Channel was ever ready to revive his claims to the French crown—and drop them for a consideration—to sell his neutrality for a stiff price, and then to offer a "diversion" to a still higher bidder: there were realists in those days. Francis tried to avert the English peril. The two young and lusty kings met with great cordiality at a camp between Ardres and Guines, near Calais, in 1520. They and their retinue vied with each other in vulgar display. French nobles sold farms to adorn their backs: the meeting was called the Camp of the Cloth of Gold. Wolsey, Henry's adviser, was playing so complicated a game that he himself lost the thread. Besides, the nimbler

Francis most undiplomatically bested the beefier Henry in a wrestling bout. Henry repaired at once to Gravelines, where Charles V was waiting for him.

One of the chief pieces in Charles's game was the highest noble in France, Charles of Montpensier and Auvergne, Duke of Bourbon. Rich in his own name, he had inherited the vast estates and princely privileges that Anne and Pierre de Beaujeu had secured for themselves. He was considered the wealthiest noble in Europe, and he made his city of Moulins a veritable capital. Honors followed riches, not undeserved, for he was a brave and skillful commander: he was made constable of France and governor of Milan. It is said that he had spurned the king's mother, Louise of Savoy: in a fury of greed and revenge she had him deprived of some of his possessions. Goaded by this injustice, Bourbon "transferred his allegiance": for a quasi-royal personage, treason would be too crude a term. While still in command of French troops, he was striking an alliance with the emperor and the king of England. He was to have a kingdom of his own made up of his present domains with Dauphiné and Provence added. He was to recognize Henry VIII as king of France. But the plot was discovered, and he had to flee. His downfall was swift: from an associate he sank into a hireling, the leader of famished and irresponsible hirelings.[5]

The rivalry between Francis I and Charles V offers a fairly definite general pattern; the details are not simply intricate, they are bewildering. Charles V's attempts to carry on a policy remind us of Alice's croquet game: everything is alive and with a perverse will of its own; the hoops walk away, the hedgehog-balls unroll themselves and scurry, the flamingo-mallets gaze reproachfully at the player. If the possessions of Francis I were more firmly knit, it was his mind that created chaos. With imperious mien he followed contradictory advisers. The utter confusion of the times is most patent in the politico-religious attitude of the two sovereigns. Charles was His Catholic Majesty of Spain and Holy Roman Emperor to boot; yet it was his troops that stormed and plundered Rome as though he had been an Alaric. Francis was His Most Christian Majesty, and the Eldest Son of the Church; yet he struck an alliance with Suleiman the Magnificent, whose cavalry dashed as far as Vienna. The contest was a princely game, although not invariably chivalrous. There was no deep-seated hatred between peoples, or even between their rulers. In a lull (1539–1540) Charles went through France as a friendly guest, and was imperially entertained.[6]

Reduced to the barest facts, the struggle flared up no less than six times. In 1521 Charles took Milan from the French and in 1522 turned it over to Francesco Sforza. There were devastating but indecisive invasions of Italy by the French, of southern France by the imperial forces. Francis recaptured Milan; but, utterly defeated at Pavia and made a prisoner (1525),[7] he was forced to sign the Treaty of Madrid (1526), as disastrous as the Treaty of Troyes. He renounced Italy, he agreed to restore Bourbon in his lands and honors, and he gave up Burgundy. This *Diktat* he had no intention of respecting. To salve his conscience, he had the States (Assembly) of Burgundy refuse to accept it as valid. The Burgundians declared that the king had no right to barter them away and that their desire was to remain under the French crown.[8] Thus the democratic doctrine of self-determination was clearly proclaimed four centuries ago. On the part of the king it was only a trick; but with the trick started, unperceived, a revolution which is not fully accomplished even today.

In 1527–1529, second war: Francis was now allied with the pope, Venice, and Francesco Sforza. It was then that the imperial mercenaries sacked Rome. Lautrec invaded Naples, Genoa rebelled against the French, the plague paralyzed operations, and, in weariness, the Treaty of Cambrai established a *modus vivendi*.[9] For the fourth time France gave up Italy, but Burgundy was—provisionally—retained.

Third war in 1536–1538: Francis claimed Milan again. More fruitless inroads on either side; Suleiman attacked Charles by land and sea. The Truce of Nice—they could not call it a peace—was signed for ten years. But in 1542 the fourth war broke out. Again Milan was the pretext. This time northern France was invaded; and the emperor, allied with Henry VIII, advanced as far as Soissons, sixty miles from Paris. By the Treaty of Crespy-en-Valois (1544), Francis renounced Naples but secured Milan for his second son (who, however, died in 1545). Flanders and Artois were abandoned, Burgundy retained.

In 1547 the tarnished paladin died. Henry II (1547–1559), darkened perhaps by a long and harsh captivity in Madrid, did not possess his father's ambiguous charm. His piety had a somber fanatical Spanish cast: although far less able, he resembled Philip II. He too was the plaything of favorites. His mistress Diane de Poitiers is best remembered as a model for magnificent classical statuary; in politics the influence of "the Moon Goddess" was erratic. The irrepressible religious conflict which had set Germany aflame was ready to break into open war in France also. Yet the bigoted king, keeping up his father's feud, did not scruple to ally himself with the German Protestants. In 1552, for the fifth time, France was at war with Charles V. She had secured, in payment for protecting "German liberties," the three bishoprics, imperial cities but French-speaking, of Metz, Toul, and Verdun. The emperor attempted to recapture Metz; but he was foiled by Francis, Duke of Guise. Weary, Charles signed the Truce of Vaucelles and abdicated.

The sixth war was waged by the emperor's son, Philip II, King of Spain, with England as his ally. The French under Coligny were severely defeated at Saint-Quentin (1557), and from his retreat Charles exclaimed: "Is my son in Paris?" But, with excessive caution, the Spaniards failed to follow through. In January, 1558, Guise, in a rapid, well-concealed march, reached Calais and captured the key city in a week.

The Treaty of Cateau-Cambrésis (1559) ended the forty-year strife between Francis I and Charles V, inherited by their sons. Religion not empire was now to be the dominant theme. As usual, the peace was accompanied by a series of princely marriages. In the festivities Henry II, a stout horseman himself, wanted to tilt with Montgommery, captain of his Scottish Guard, noted for his skill and vigor. A rare accident happened: the spear went through the visor of the king's helmet, and a splinter reached his brain: Ambroise Paré could not save him. The crown went to a pathetic adolescent couple, the pale Francis II, already in the shadow of death, and his bride, Mary Stuart.

✍ RABELAIS AND PANTAGRUELIAN HUMANISM

A history of France limited to the capricious adventures of kings would be a sorry caricature. The substance of national life was provided, then as it is now, by a quick-minded people, hard at work. Above them were the kings, not invariably idolized; above the kings, the monarchy, a slowly growing body of traditions, doctrines, techniques; and above the monarchy, the potent shadow which we must call vaguely "the spirit of the time." The Renaissance was more real than the Valois dynasty; and of the Renaissance, Rabelais is a better symbol than Francis I:

> For that time was darksome, obscured with clouds of ignorance, and savoring a little of the infelicity and calamity of the Goths, who had, wherever they set footing, destroyed all good literature; which in my age hath by divine goodness been restored into its former light and dignity. . . . Now it is that the minds of men are qualified with all manner of discipline, and the old sciences revived, which for many ages were extinct. Now it is that the learned languages are to their pristine purity restored.[10]

These words, addressed by Gargantua to his son Pantagruel, express the very spirit of the Renaissance, a deliberate condemnation of "Gothic" barbarism, an eager return to the light of antiquity. They apply perfectly to the work of Guillaume Budé (1467–1540), an admirable Hellenist and historian, and to the activities of Robert Estienne, the scholarly printer, father of the famous Henri. But "the revival of learning" is not the whole, nor even the major part, of the Renaissance. Our impression of history is to a large extent derived from bookmen who are inclined to exaggerate the importance of bookish knowledge and literary fashions. Rabelais himself will help us correct the purely antiquarian and philological conception of humanism.

Let us note that the Renaissance in France and throughout northern Europe was the discovery of Italy rather than of ancient Greece or Rome. Italianate elements were at once adopted in northern architecture, but it was not until the end of the eighteenth century that Greco-Roman buildings were sedulously pastiched. Even the authority of Aristotle in literary matters was imposed, not directly but through Italian commentators such as Scaliger and Castelvetro. The poets who were to form a glorious "Pléiade," with Ronsard and Du Bellay as their leaders, produced only stillborn monstrosities when they directly copied antique models; the part of their work which is still fragrant is the one which combines the French tradition with Italian influences, in particular their sonnets. Rabelais, Du Bellay expressed their scorn for mere pedantry. It was the Middle Ages that idolized the remote past: the Renaissance loved it, but with the love of an equal.

Paradoxically, that period which is supposed to have "revived" the ancient tongues is the one that made them "classical" in the sense of "dead." Greek did not conquer even the whole learned world: to most Frenchmen it remained—Greek; and Latin actually receded in the sixteenth century. French was imposed as the language of justice and administration. Du Bellay in his *Defense and Illustration of the French Language* urged modern poets to trust themselves and their vernacular; if they have power and daring enough, they will be able, without forfeiting their originality, to enrich their works with the spoils of antiquity and also with whatever treasures their hands can reach. Luther, a fine Latinist, composed in German; Calvin translated his *Christian Institution* into French. The Renaissance was a joyous and grateful "Commencement": school was left behind, and life was ahead.

The Renaissance men were not unaware of the vigorous sap they were drawing from their own soil. Du Bellay advises borrowing from the racy speech of the provinces and the trade; and Rabelais's work, with its opulent vocabulary, is of the streets, the fields, the open road, the high sea far more than of the studious cell. He chose the framework of an ancient folk tale to pour out his vast learning as a priest, a medical man, a classical scholar. His pages are filled with *fabliaux,* mocking realistic stories, such as merchants had swapped at fairs for at least four hundred years.[11]

This is true of architecture as well as of literature. The best monuments of sixteenth-century France are not antique: even though they follow Italian fashions, they remain profoundly French. With their high roofs, their turrets, their bristling ornamental chimneys, they are still Gothic in outline, even the Paris City Hall, ascribed to an Italian artist. Chambord, which Rabelais was to adopt as a pattern for his ideal Abbey of Thélème, is a feudal castle that has dropped its armor and put on festive ornaments. The best churches of the time have nothing in common with antique temples or basilicas. Many are still completely Gothic; some of the most impressive, like Saint-Eustache in Paris, offer a delightful blend of Gothic structure and Italian decoration.

So the keyword of Rabelais, the essence of his "Pantagruelism," is not, "Back to Greece and Rome!" but *Vivez joyeux,* live in joy. He picked out for his subject a merry old tale of giants: a happy choice, for the human mind, released from its fetters, free from the anguish of the night, felt like a young giant gamboling on a young earth. Rabelais's heroes go through the world with Gargantuan and Pantagruelic appetite for all good things: for tripes and sausages, hams and cheeses, beefs and muttons roasted whole and washed down with torrents of wine; but also—for Rabelais is a bibber and glutton only in jest and symbol— they are craving for all experience and all knowledge, for the Trivium and the Quadrivium of old, and "all the lore of the Cabbalists," for "Greek, Hebrew, Arabic, Chaldean, and Latin," for "all sorts of herbs and flowers that grow upon the ground," and "all the various metals that are hid within the bowels of the earth"; as Rabelais is no bookworm or pedant, his characters are eager for all sports, games, pleasures, and exercises, for swimming, riding, fencing, and jousting; and at last, he makes them hunger and thirst for righteousness, knowing full well that "science without conscience is but the ruination of the soul."

This triumphant Pantagruelism inspires the chapters, full of quaint erudition, practical knowledge, and poetic enthusiasm, which at the end of the third book he devotes to the praise of the blessed herb Pantagruelion. Literally, Pantagruelion is mere hemp; symbolically, it is human industry. Rabelais caps the wildest achievements of his own times with wilder boasts and prophecies. The spirit of the great adventure, the onrush of man's endeavor, devouring space, annihilating time, yea, Bergson would add, perhaps conquering death itself, has never been more gloriously expressed than in these pages of gigantic, gorgeous, and lucid humor.

And there is much solid truth in his most daring flight. His Abbey of Thélème was not Utopia but anticipation. Thélème is not, as men unread in Pantagruelism might imagine, a refuge for the sensualist and the slothful: it is purely the perfection of a twentieth-century American university. Thélème is in truth a university not an abbey. Its ideal is not selfish reclusion: when the time comes, youths and maidens leave their Alma Mater; friendships formed in Thélème "increase to greater heights in the state of matrimony"; and the Thélèmites bring to their struggling brothers without the walls a reflection at least of their serene vision.

No philosophical label will fit this Pantagruelism: it is like the clear cool water of the Divine Bottle which the heroes of Rabelais had sought, all things to all men, according to their nurture and fancy. Of all possible tags materialism and sensualism would be the most misleading; rationalism is thin and cold; Pantheism sounds well but, unexplained, is mere sound. Naturism would do better. Rabelais loves Nature in all her shapes and moods, even the lowliest; and he hates only those who struggle in vain against good Mother Nature and who worship the sullen idol *Antiphysis*. But nature, for Rabelais, is life; and life is the life of man. His philosophy is humanism in the wider and deeper sense—the love, respect, and service of Man, in whom we are taught to see the image of God.

CHAPTER XII

The Reformation
and the Religious Wars

✎ RENAISSANCE AND REFORMATION

It is inaccurate to speak of *the* Renaissance, as though it were a unique experience in the annals of the Western world. It is even more misleading to speak of *the* Reformation. By 1500 the Church had already gone through several great crises of purification and renewed energy. The tenth and eleventh centuries saw a thorough reformation with the driving force of the Cluniacs behind it and spearheaded by vigorous popes. In the thirteenth century the Friars led another movement of rejuvenation. It reached the highest spheres of theology, but it was in truth an evangelical revival, a return to the poverty of the early Church, a missionary zeal that sent the new apostles to the crossroads and the market places. Disruption was averted, and the reformers were canonized; but at one time they had denounced the worldliness of the papal court as vehemently as Luther was to do, and the most spiritual among the Franciscans had adopted the daring doctrines of Joachim of Floris, which came to the very brink of heresy.

The critical conditions of the Church in the fourteenth and fifteenth centuries—the Babylonian Captivity and the Great Schism—inspired a demand for drastic change. Even the men who, because they wanted above all to preserve unity, opposed the movements of Wycliff and Huss favored none the less a rigorous cleansing of abuses, a purification and revival of faith. Such was, as we have seen, the attitude of Jean de Gerson; and we shall find his heirs in Lefèvre d'Étaples and his group. It may be safely assumed that if the Reformation had not taken the Lutheran path, or the Calvinistic, it would inevitably have come under some other form. Schism is not indispensable to a reformation any more than civil war to a revolution.

A second aspect of the sixteenth-century Reformation is frequently either neglected or distorted. Renaissance and Reformation are presented as antagonistic: it was against the gloriously pagan Rome of Leo X that Martin Luther rebelled. As a matter of fact, the two movements were at first so closely parallel as to be indistinguishable. They resulted equally from the revival of confidence and energy manifest in every field. Humanism in the fullest sense of the term would break away from the narrow cell of decadent medievalism and seek new worlds to explore and conquer, both in space and in time, both in the past and in the future, both in the realm of matter and in that of the spirit. The Renaissance is first of all a Reformation. It is significant that the perfect epitome of the Renaissance spirit, Erasmus, whom Rabelais revered as his master, should be not only a free mind but a pious soul.

The humanistic Reformation in which Erasmus believed, respectful of tradition yet untrammeled, suffered apparent defeat: it was not clearly endorsed by any church, and it created no sect of its own. But as a source of free religious inspiration it never lost its vitality. We must not be deluded by material statistics: a spirit may be so strong that it does not need the prop of institutions or the enrollment of formal members. We must insist on this neglected aspect of the Reformation, for, under many names, it has remained an essential factor in the religious life of France. Man, then, dared to seek emancipation from what seemed the senile childishness of the old order. A Reformation of that kind was obviously the fruit of the teeming activity, the enhanced courage of the time, like the revival of learning, the flowering of the arts, the great inventions, the epic discoveries. Luther, a monk like Rabelais, felt like Rabelais that the human mind had emerged at last out of "Gothic night." There was at the basis of the Reformation something of the joyous ardor that filled Pantagruel. It can be felt in Luther's table talks. It is admirably voiced by Ulrich von Hutten: "O century! It is a joy to be alive! The wind of freedom blows!"

Unfortunately, this spirit did not prevail in the later stages of French Protestantism. No wind of freedom blew where Calvin reigned, nor was it a joy to be alive. Rabelais was consistent when he denounced Calvin as "demoniacal," for here the two Reformations clash irremediably.[1] Rabelais had in abundance faith, hope, and charity; yet for the Calvinistic theologian his naturism was the most deadly of heresies. He believed in Man, as though fallen man were not totally depraved. He stressed the loving-kindness of God instead of His undying anger. He preached Joy here below, as though this world were not a vale of tears in preparation for a probable eternity of torment. Not in his obscenities, which never hurt a soul, but in his large indulgence for his fellow men did the Orthodox of the Dark detect his damning sin. The problem, of course, transcends any set of dogmas. Non-Christians or imperfect Christians—Buddha, Voltaire, Schopenhauer, Thomas Hardy, Jean-Paul Sartre—may be more pessimistic even than Calvin; and very orthodox believers—St. Francis, Leibniz, Fénelon, Robert Browning—were no less optimistic than Rabelais.

The Reformation was akin also to the other side of the Renaissance, the narrower humanism, the bodily return to antiquity. Pantagruelism was looking forward; it heralded Bacon's profession of scientific optimism, "The Golden Age is ahead of us, not behind." On the other hand, classical scholarship, Vergilianism, Ciceronianism, the Aristotelian tyranny in logic, rhetoric, and poetics were forms of antiquarian superstition, text-worship, literalism, in a word, bibliolatry. This element entered for a large part into the Reformation and warped its course. Hitherto, the supreme authority in religion had been the living Church: she was the appointed guardian of a tradition anterior to the New Testament, and of which the sacred writings were only a part; she was the interpreter of a continuous and expanding revelation. Now fifteen Christian centuries were pronounced dead and ruled out of spiritual history in the same way as they were contemptuously brushed aside from literary history.

Now we come to the conflict between these two mighty efforts of the sixteenth-century mind. The Reformation took a very definite theological turn, and its history is often written in terms of doctrines alone. But its very essence was not theological, it was moral. The corruption of Christendom was flagrant: the Church herself set about to reform it and succeeded in a very large degree as she had repeatedly done before. But this time, self-reformation came too late to avert a schism. At the point of departure we find the denunciation of palpable evils; the next step was an attack on the powers that condoned such evils; the third, a denial of the doctrines or traditions that these powers invoked in their defense; the fourth, only, was a consistently revised theology. The luxury of the Roman court, the sale of indulgences, the existence of Purgatory, the worship of the saints were thus challenged in order. Ultimately, this led to the denial of papal authority and to the substitution of the Bible for the Church as the sole rule of faith and life. Puritanism, therefore, is not a by-product of the Reformation but its starting point and its greatest glory.

We do not mean that all Protestants were virtuous and that they had a monopoly of virtue. Few Protestants could rival the devotion, the energetic asceticism, the thirst for martyrdom, found in the annals of many religious orders. The Huguenots had not a few leaders who fell far short of holiness, like Châtillon or Condé, or, in a less exalted station, Baron des Adrets. Henry of Navarre was no saint, even when he was the champion and idol of French Protestantism. Still, it was moral indignation and the love of virtuous living rather than theology that impelled men to the utmost sacrifice. In France particularly the necessity of a desperate struggle further deepened this original austerity. In their Puritanism the Huguenots were obviously at odds with the relaxed Catholics of the Valois court; but they opposed also the indulgent naturism of Pantagruel, which might so easily lead to self-indulgence; and they hated most of all the revived paganism, the unmoral *virtú* of the Italian humanists and artists. In this respect the Renaissance and the Reformation diverged irremediably.

It was their yearning for a righteous and sober life that was the compelling motive of the Huguenots, not their desire for freedom. Their faith, which is so often praised as the triumph of liberty, denies liberty at every turn. There is no freedom of thought in orthodox Calvinism: the infallibility of Scriptures allows of none; neither is there any freedom of action, and the freedom of the human will is emphatically denied. Yet out of this doctrine of enslavement some of the strongest characters in history did arise. The creed itself would lead to a somber and passive fatalism: what saved the Huguenots was the attitude of rebellion which was forced upon them. To break away from ancestral belief, to defy spiritual and secular authority, to face persecution, torture, and death undismayed demanded fearless and vigorous souls. A time would come when the new faith would turn into a safe and respectable harbor, when people called themselves Calvinists out of respect for tradition and conformity, when their Protestantism no longer voiced the spirit of protest. Then the salt of the earth lost much of its savor.

In the sixteenth century the greatness of Protestantism is not the cogency of its thought but the heroic power of its will. We shall see that it was matched by an equal intensity, an equal singleness of purpose, among the leaders of the Counter Reformation. Philip II too showed inflexible pertinacity; St. Ignatius was as completely the slave of his faith and the master of his own frailties as John Calvin or John Knox. Worldly wisdom, admirably represented by Michel de l'Hôpital, Henry of Navarre, and Michel de Montaigne, turned against the fanatics, Catholics as well as Protestants; and worldly wisdom was wise. But the devouring zeal on either side is impressive. It makes caution, reasonableness, and even humanity seem timid, tepid, almost futile. Like the Supermen of Nietzsche, the leaders of the Reformation and Counter Reformation attempted to surpass, to transcend, their ordinary selves.

The result was war, and therefore disaster. But it also offered a tragedy of Miltonic grandeur.

✍ THE CONCORDAT

Human destiny is a drama played on many levels. Above, we find the mighty conflicts of ideas, like the battles of the gods in the ancient epics. Among men of flesh and blood we meet the sharpest contrasts: saintliness and crime under the same banner, at times within the same breast. There is an intermediate plane which is neither ideal nor purely personal. There, the protagonists are powers, institutions, collectivities: the monarchy, the churches, the nobility, the officials. Each claims to stand for some great cause; each is swayed also by immediate material interests often at variance with its principles. History is chiefly concerned with events on that plane: ideas in their abstract purity belong to philosophy and the fate of individuals, to biography. But we must recognize that the political scene is affected by ideas and also by the energy, intelligence, or frailty of particular men. The ambiguous personality of Francis I kept the course of the Reformation uncertain in France for nearly two decades. The rigorous personality of Calvin forced the issue. The complex and attractive personality of Henry IV could not evolve a final solution but did restore peace. At every turn, *it might have been otherwise*.

The rapid successes of the Reformation in northern Europe were not entirely due to religious earnestness. A large part of the population followed the princes with docility: even before the doctrine was formally acknowledged, it was true that to a great extent "he who rules the land commands the religion," *cujus regio ejus religio*. It was very tempting for the head of a state to make himself supreme over the religious establishment. It increased his prestige, his power, and his wealth: Church property was an irresistible bait. Many princely conversions to Lutheranism were strongly influenced by such worldly motives, and they had their share in the secession of Henry VIII. Such a Reformation did not take place in France, because it was not needed. France already had a deeprooted policy of her own, that Gallicanism which we have previously attempted to define.

The charter of the Gallican tradition, as we have seen, was the Pragmatic Sanction of Bourges issued by Charles VII in 1438. Louis XI played fast and loose with Gallicanism but with no thought of forfeiting its benefits. He abrogated the Pragmatic in 1461, but he held it in reserve as a threat in case the Papacy should prove obdurate. The king's men, and particularly the Parlement, were, and remained throughout the ancient regime, out-and-out Gallicans. They formed a lay clergy, as it were, devoted almost to the point of fanaticism to a doctrine, the supremacy of the state. This doctrine the Parlement would defend even against the king. When Louis XI abolished the Pragmatic of Bourges, the Parlement refused to register his order. The conflict lasted as long as the reign; the Parlement outlived the king, and the Pragmatic was restored.

The regime sanctioned by the Pragmatic, and dear to the clergy and the people of France, contained elements of democracy as well as of national autonomy. The general councils were proclaimed superior to the popes; and the right of the chapters of cathedral churches, collegiates, and abbeys to elect clerics to vacant positions was recognized. Francis I needed, for his Italian policy, the support of the pope; the pope desired above all things the suppression of the hated Pragmatic. The result was the agreement known as the Concordat, signed at Bologna in 1516. That instrument was to regulate the relations between the Church and the French State until the Revolution, and the Concordat of Bonaparte (1801–1905) may be considered as its prolonged shadow.

The chief point of the Concordat is that it conferred upon the king the right of nominating a candidate to a vacant see, abbey, or priory. The pope alone could give the canonical "institution" or investiture: but, since he was not at liberty to withhold his confirmation, the royal nomination amounted to an appointment. If in theory the Concordat recognized in the pope a greater power than had been admitted under the Pragmatic Sanction, in practice the king not the pope was supreme in the French Church.

The Concordat was far less simple than this summary indicates. Diplomatic compromises seldom are clear-cut and logical, and the Ancient Regime, so respectful of vested rights, seldom attempted sweeping changes and never succeeded in carrying them out. Many benefices were conferred not by the king but by ecclesiastical, or even by lay, patrons; the pope preserved direct powers in a number of cases; finally, the right of capitular election was retained by certain abbeys, particularly by the wealthiest and most powerful of all, Cluny and Saint-Denis.

But the tendency of the Concordat was unmistakable. Gallicanism was actually strengthened by this treaty, which was supposed to endanger it, and which the Parlement fought tooth and nail: only it was royal Gallicanism. The church lost much of her independence not from the pope but from the king. France remained self-governing within Catholic Christendom; the French Church no longer was fully self-governing within the monarchy. She ceased in fact to be a sovereign body and became merely an Order: a transformation similar to the one which was turning the independent feudal caste into a court nobility. Without disloyalty to either spiritual or temporal power the Church of France would have liked to manage her own affairs, and especially to dispose freely of her own immense resources: in 1516 the two rulers came to an agreement at the expense of the national clergy.

The material prize won by Francis I was magnificent. Marino Giustiniani, Venetian ambassador to France, noted with awe: "The king disposes of ten archbishoprics, eighty-two bishoprics, five hundred and twenty-seven abbeys, an infinitude of priories and canonries. This prerogative assures him of the utmost servitude and obedience on the part of prelates and laymen, because of their desire for benefices. . . ." This great strengthening of the king's hand had far-reaching consequences.

First of all, let us repeat that there were for the French king none of the inducements that tempted some German princes away from the Catholic fold. The French Church was already his own; he freely used ecclesiastical preferment to reward his friends and servants, including his Italian political allies, and even writers whose religious qualifications were of the scantiest: under the successors of Francis I, Brantôme and Ronsard became abbots.[2] Many a courtier, it was said, "inditing a sonnet, was dreaming of a bishopric." A reformation on Lutheran or Anglican lines formally making the king the ecclesiastical head of the nation would neither greatly enhance his prestige nor serve his material interests. Had the Pragmatic endured only a very few years longer, until the open rebellion of Luther and his excommunication, the history of France might have taken a different turn. As it was, when the crisis broke out, the monarchy was committed to the defense of Catholicism through self-interest as well as through conviction. The vaguely liberal sympathies of Francis I, the influence of his gifted and loving sister Marguerite of Navarre, the necessities of his European policy which made him the ally of Protestants and Turks, could not prevail against that fundamental fact.

Conversely, at a critical hour the royal character of French Catholicism caused the masses of the French people to rally to its support, for royalism in those days foreshadowed the patriotism of a later age. So the balance never was even between conservatives and reformers: the Protestants were from the first and in spite of themselves considered as rebels against the State as well as against the Church. The Catholicism of Ronsard in his *Discourses on the Evils of the Times,* the hazy Catholicism of Montaigne, were political, not theological creeds.[3] These men—and most men in France, as we shall see—were more interested in law and order, as embodied in the monarchy, than they were in transsubstantiation. Royal Gallicanism on the practical plane, the humanism of Rabelais on the spiritual, left but a rough and narrow field for the Huguenots.

✍ A MILD ELUSIVE DAWN: LEFÈVRE D'ÉTAPLES

The humanism of Erasmus and Rabelais, the Gallicanism of the Pragmatic Sanction and of the Concordat had elements in common with what we now call Protestantism; twisting a well-known phrase, we might say that all three were for a time "fellow travelers." But their ways soon parted. Although humanists and Gallicans were not devoid of religious feeling, they did not wrestle with some of the essential problems of Christianity. They either left theological disputes behind, or they accepted without question the traditional tenets. This reserve was dictated at times by worldly prudence. In other cases it was the result of simple faith, indifferent to subtleties.

With Lefèvre d'Étaples (1455–1537), we reach the realm of definite Protestant thought, although he and his friends remained a group or a school and did not attempt to create a church. Lefèvre believed in faith above works, in grace and not in human merits: in this he was at least as radically opposed to the "Naturists" such as Rabelais as to the upholders of a superstitious ecclesiasticism. Against spurious authorities and corrupt traditions he appealed to Christ alone and to the pure doctrine of the apostles. A true Renaissance scholar, he wanted a "return to antiquity" and the restoration of the original sacred texts, in the same spirit as Budé or Estienne attempted to give correct editions of the classics. He desired to cleanse the very sources of religious life from the agelong deposit of medieval legends; and he wanted also to make these living waters accessible to all men through French translations of the Old and the New Testaments. His thought was fully formed by 1508, long before Luther could have any influence upon him; and he gathered around him a number of earnest men, Budé, Farel, Cop, Roussel.

He was in particular the spiritual center of the "group of Meaux," thus named because Briçonnet,[4] a friend of Lefèvre's became bishop of that See in 1526. In 1523 Lefèvre was made Briçonnet's vicar general. This purely French and peaceful Reformation enjoyed the sympathetic and active support of Marguerite d'Angoulême, sister of Francis I and queen of Navarre. She herself was an excellent example of the group. Her religious attitude would win the approval of many Protestants today: it was a gentle mysticism seeking direct support in the promises of Scripture. But she had no desire for a violent rupture with ecclesiastical authority: whatever changes were necessary should be effected quietly and from within. So her theology was never clearly formulated, and she did not openly challenge the essential Catholic dogmas or the main points of Catholic discipline.[5]

This moderate Reformation was destined to be swept aside. In theology Lefèvre was soon left behind by Luther, and more strikingly still by Calvin. Briçonnet, in his diocese, forbade the reading of Luther's works (1523), and, while not persecuting on his own authority, he did nothing to avert persecution by others. Perhaps the worst obstacle to the success of the school was that it insisted on piety and righteous living rather than upon dogma. Francis I might conceivably have accommodated himself to any doctrine: we can imagine him as a landgrave of Hessen or as a Henry VIII. But the quiet and austere mysticism of the Meaux group was out of harmony with the pleasure-loving spirit of his court. Thanks to Marguerite and to his own moderation, Briçonnet escaped censure and died in peace in 1534. Lefèvre found refuge in Marguerite's little court at Nérac until his death in 1536 or 1537. The school thus faded away without any tragic crisis; it shared the melancholy fate of most half-revolutions.

✒ JOHN CALVIN

On October 31, 1517, Martin Luther nailed his ninety-five theses upon the door of the Court Church at Wittenberg; in 1518 Zwingli initiated his reform movement in Zürich. Their names and their activities were almost immediately known in France. Lefèvre and his friends were at first favorable. But when Luther was excommunicated in 1520, the French reformers were hopelessly divided. Some, such as Clichtove, who had been among the most active lieutenants of Lefèvre, rallied to the strictest orthodoxy taught by the Sorbonne. The principal leaders, Lefèvre himself, Briçonnet, Marguerite, persisted in their gentle dream of a change of heart without any dogmatic upheaval. Many went over to the bolder doctrines from Germany and complained that they were abandoned, and even persecuted, by their former friends and masters. About 1530, a Protestant party was already in existence, and between 1530 and 1536 we see the definite beginnings of a Protestant Church.

During these critical years French Protestantism was without a leader: Lefèvre and Briçonnet wanted to stop on the hither side of heresy and schism. It was therefore a ubiquitous and spontaneous growth. Not of learned origin by any means: artisans rushed in where humanists feared to tread. It was not until 1533 that Calvin sprang into prominence; and it was only two years later that, with his *Christian Institute,* he assumed the spiritual guidance of the movement.

John Calvin (or Cauvin) was born at Noyon in 1509. In November,

1533, the rector of the University of Paris, Cop, opened the session with a speech which had been prepared for him by young Calvin. This speech was neither radical in its theology nor defiant in its tone. The Blessed Virgin was solemnly invoked, divisions were deprecated, and the spirit of peace extolled. Yet it was so virulently denounced by the conservatives that Cop and Calvin found it necessary to flee.

The king, however, was still reluctant to be forced into the camp of the Sorbonne extremists. Thanks to this hesitating policy, Calvin was able to return to Paris, while Béda, the most violent of the reactionaries, was exiled for the second time. But the neophyte zeal of the new faith left little room for compromise. Already in 1528 a statue of the Virgin had been desecrated in Paris, and that sacrilege had caused an explosion of Catholic passion. Of this angry mood Louis de Berquin was the victim in 1529: accused of being in sympathy with Erasmus and Luther, he was not the first martyr but the first martyr of note. In October, 1534, placards posted in Paris and in the provinces violently attacked the Mass as idolatrous. This lashed to fury the fanaticism not of the Sorbonne only but of the whole population. Terrible reprisals followed: hundreds of men were arrested, scores were taken to the gallows or the stake; Clement Marot, a personal favorite of the king, had to run away. On January 21, 1535, in solemn expiation for the blasphemies of the placards, a great procession was ordered in Paris; it was devoutly followed by the king, his head bared, a wax taper in his hand. Now Francis I had been forced to take his stand; but even then, he still strove for peace. In 1535 he offered an amnesty and was hoping against hope for reconciliation. More decisively, Calvin had made his choice. He went again into exile, never to return.

Calvin sought refuge first in Basel, then in Geneva (1536). Banished from the latter in 1538, he was recalled in 1541. Henceforth and until his death in 1564, he ruled the little republic with a rod of iron. His life and work at Geneva belong not to our special theme but to world history. Suffice it to say that Geneva became the Protestant Rome, the school of doctors, and the training ground of martyrs. Théodore de Bèze (Beza) was chief among the field agents of the new church. The French Protestants or Huguenots [6] now had a head, an organization, a doctrine.

But as Calvinism became a mounting threat, it was met with ever-increasing rigor. The Edict of Fontainebleau in 1540 directed the systematic extirpation of heresy. The Waldensians, whose quiet evangelical faith had survived since the twelfth century, were among the innocent victims of the new terror: three thousand of them were massacred in Provence. In 1546 the humanist Etienne Dolet, who had printed the works of Lefèvre d'Étaples, was burnt in Paris on Place Maubert, where an expiatory statue stood for many years. Those responsible for the cruel policy of the enfeebled king were the friends and counselors of his successor, Henry II. There was not even a gleam of Renaissance liberalism in that bigoted sovereign. Persecution under him was no longer spasmodic but constant in its ruthlessness. A special Court of Parlement was created to deal summarily with the heretics; it was popularly called *la Chambre Ardente,* for most of the accused were promptly sent to the fire.

In the fierce struggle the faith of the Huguenots grew more resolute. In 1559 they dared to convene a synod in Paris and to draw up a *Confession of Faith of the Reformed Churches of France,* and many nobles subscribed to their creed. But as yet there was no armed resistance. It was not until the reign of the weak child Francis II that the conflict between the two churches blazed into civil war.

THE POLITICO-RELIGIOUS WARS

In 1560 a daring Protestant gentleman, La Renaudie, plotted to remove the evil counselors of the king. The conspiracy was ill-concerted; the leaders found their enemies alerted, and the sporadic uprisings were easily crushed. But the feeble attempt justified a ferocious repression. The castle of Amboise, where Francis II was in residence, was surrounded with a forest of gallows; and everywhere the boy king, nervous and ailing, could see severed heads stuck on pales or pikes. From that moment (1560) to the abjuration of Henry IV in 1593 France was not to know peace.

For this horrible welter in which the country nearly perished the conflicting creeds were only partly to blame. No doubt, throughout the land Catholics and Protestants fought fanatically for or against the doctrines of transubstantiation and election; both sides committed atrocities whereever they had the upper hand; Blaise de Montluc, who left us such gusty, racy memoirs, was no whit gentler than Baron des Adrets. But these wars soon became political, or rather factional, like the Wars of the Roses. Their true name should be War of the Guises and Bourbons, not Wars of Religion.

The Guises were a junior branch of the great house of Lorraine. They served France brilliantly and became French, but with a difference. Allied with sovereigns—a Guise married the king of Scotland, and her daughter, Mary Stuart, became queen of France—they considered themselves as on a higher level than even the Bourbons-Condés. They broadly hinted that, as descendants of Charlemagne, they had a better claim to the French crown than the "usurping" Capetians. They held vast domains in France; and for three or four generations there always was a younger brother who made it a point to collect, and almost to corner, the richest bishoprics and abbacies: Charles, Cardinal of Guise, was, among innumerable titles, Archbishop of Rheims, Abbot of Cluny, Abbot of Saint-Denis, with all the rights, privileges, and revenues thereunto appertaining. The head of the family under Henry II, Duke Francis, a great military leader (it was he who recaptured Calais) of princely mien and, with his friends, of most generous spirit, was the idol of his troops and a favorite with the populace. For a decaying dynasty the Guises were disquieting subjects indeed.

At first their chief rival was a Catholic whose faith was as unswerving as theirs, Anne de Montmorency, Constable of France. A rough soldier, not invariably successful, cruel with the defeated, a grasping politician, Anne lost favor under Francis I but was restored to honors and influence by Henry II. He remained a foe of the Huguenots to his dying day. But his nephews, Admiral de Coligny, Dandelot, and Cardinal de Châtillon, veered toward Protestantism. They united forces with the Bourbon-Condé-Navarre connection: Jeanne d'Albret, Queen of Navarre, was an ardent supporter of the Reformed Religion. The struggle between the two groups recalled the reckless fury of the feud between Armagnacs and Burgundians during the Hundred Years' War. Both sides sought support from abroad. The Huguenots were aided, fitfully, by the Netherlands, the German Protestants, Elizabeth. The Guises allied themselves with Spain.

Between the two raging parties the monarchy was helpless. Under the three degenerate sons of Henry II—Francis II, Charles IX, and Henry III—their mother, Catherine de Médicis, was if not the actual ruler at least a constant and trusted counselor. She was unequal to the responsibility. She had been married frankly for her money—it was a shocking misalliance for the House of France to be linked with the Medici, a minor parvenu dynasty, whose wealth was rooted in banking—and the desperately needed dowry had proved disappointing. Her Italian cunning likewise was inadequate in the political and religious storm. She worked from day to day for her brood, not with pertinacity and caution but with sudden bewildering shifts in policy. Some modern historians, following the unsafe lead of Balzac, have praised her methods as masterly: since she was disingenuous and cruel, she must have been realistic. To the candid student her tricks denote not Machiavellian profundity but merely confusion and panic. There was a man in high office who wished to steer a wise, generous, and moderate course, the chancellor, Michel de l'Hôpital. "Let us forget," he said, "those hate-filled terms, Papists, Huguenots, and only remember that we are Christians." The Conference at Poissy (1561), inspired by him, offered a last hope of religious peace. But the chancellor's purpose was defeated by the Guises, and there is no sign that Catherine ever understood him.

The chances for reconciliation, or even for compromise, were blasted by the massacre of two hundred Protestants at Vassy in 1562. The duke of Guise denied premeditation and claimed that he himself had been threatened, but the outrage took place in his domains and was perpetrated by his troops. He was present and did nothing to stop the murderers.

Historians count no less than eight religious wars; as a matter of fact, it was a thirty-year struggle punctuated now and then by an insincere truce. The first war ended when Francis of Guise was killed before Orleans (February, 1563): a month later the peace of Amboise recognized freedom of worship not to all Protestants but to the nobles only. In 1567 the Huguenots attempted to kidnap the king and to capture Paris; then it was, at Saint-Denis, that the old constable, Anne de Montmorency, met his death. The peace of Longjumeau (1568) restored the conditions of Amboise. Hostilities broke out again in 1569. The contest was disastrous for the Protestants. At Jarnac, Condé fell; at Moncontour, Coligny was wounded. But the victor was the duke of Anjou, Catherine's third and favorite son; the king, Charles IX, out of jealousy made his success fruitless. Stubborn Coligny, well supported by the queen of Navarre, advanced toward Paris and defeated the royal troops in Burgundy. Enmeshed in complicated intrigues even within her own family circle, Catherine, distracted, agreed to the peace of Saint-Germain (1570). Liberty of conscience and worship was recognized to all Protestants. In addition Coligny secured four fortified places; the most vital of them was La Rochelle, an Atlantic port through which he could maintain contact with his sympathizers, the English and the Dutch.

This was indeed a sudden twist of the kaleidoscope: not only was Coligny forgiven for his rebellion, but he was taken into the confidence and favor of the king. Charles IX, unstable, half-demented, could yet respond to high merit: Coligny's military talents, his integrity, his patriotism had won the respect even of his enemies. He had great plans, to help the Dutch rebels against Philip II, thus pursuing the policy of Francis I, and to embark on a vast scheme of colonization. Uniting all parties in a common enterprise, he hoped to assuage the fierceness of their religious differences. For a while the young king saw exclusively through the eyes of the great Huguenot leader, whom he called "Father." To seal this reconciliation, Henry of Bourbon, King of Navarre, now the head of the Huguenots, was to marry the king's sister, Margaret of Valois.

But Catherine swiftly reversed herself: she now dreaded the prestige of Coligny. An attempt was made on the admiral's life, and the king professed—perhaps felt—the most vehement indignation. Italian advisers urged Catherine to strike boldly: on St. Bartholomew's Eve (August 24, 1572) the Huguenots, who had flocked to Paris for the wedding of their chief, were slaughtered by the thousand. Coligny's dead body was brutally flung out of the window. Navarre and Condé escaped death only by renouncing Protestantism. The plot was not improvised: massacres took place in many parts of the country. So poisoned with hatred were the times that the crime was hailed in Europe as a victory for the faith and a medal struck in its honor.

The Huguenot cause seemed desperate. Death and forced conversion had robbed the party of its leaders; pastors and common people were beginning to suspect the motives of the Protestant nobles. But the Catholics were not united either. Some sincerely deplored the massacres, others were jealous of the Guises, not a few dreaded Spain. So a moderate element forced a new compromise, and the Edict of Boulogne ended the fourth war.

The entente between the Protestants and the moderate Catholics, however, was a precarious one; for among the *Politiques,* as the latter were called, there were many whom no Huguenot could trust, least of all Catherine's fourth son, Alençon. So the pretense of a peace was soon discarded. Navarre and Condé, escaping from Paris, recanted their forced abjuration. German troops were coming to their aid, but a detachment of that army was defeated at Dormans (1575) by the young Duke Henry of Guise. A fortunate slash in the face won for him the affectionate nickname *le Balafré* (Scarface). Now the Catholics had again a popular leader.

This alarmed Catherine, who urged another truce. By the peace of Beaulieu (1576) the monarchy was stripped to appease the factions. The disastrous policy of appanages was resumed: Alençon was to have four rich provinces in central France, Navarre was given Guienne, Condé, Picardy. The Guises, in compensation, secured no less than five of the thirteen "governments" in the realm; the king retained only three under his direct control. The Huguenot rank and file obtained most generous terms: except in Paris their freedom of worship was almost complete.

The uncompromising Catholics felt themselves betrayed. They formed a Holy League which, while professing loyalty to the king, had for its first aim the destruction of heresy. It worked in full harmony with the pope and with the avowed champion of the Catholic cause throughout Europe, Philip II of Spain. It offered a unique blend of princely intrigues, demagogy, and fanaticism: monks with a rough, popular eloquence, aristocratic ladies, and the turbulent Paris rabble vied with each other in their anti-Protestant ardor.

Henry III (1574–1589), who, in spite of his notorious corruption and effeminacy, did not lack political intelligence, made himself the nominal head of the League, in the hope of wresting from Guise that powerful instrument. In 1577 and in 1580 he demonstrated his orthodoxy and attempted to justify his leadership by waging two more "wars," the sixth and seventh, against the Huguenots. As a result, the privileges granted them at Beaulieu were curtailed. He hoped that victory would enable him to suppress both the Protestant Union and the Catholic League: then he would be king indeed.

THE CROWNED MONTAIGNE: HENRY OF NAVARRE

The death of Alençon (now duke of Anjou), the fourth Valois brother, made Henry of Bourbon, King of Navarre, heir apparent to the French crown. This caused a curious readjustment of doctrines. The Huguenots, hitherto inclined to republican ideas, rallied to the principle of heredity, now that it favored their leader. The ultra-Catholic Leaguers, formerly devoted to the cause of legitimacy, now asserted their right to disown an unworthy king, a "relapsed heretic." Henry of Guise, their chief, "descendant of Charlemagne," became almost openly a contender for the throne.

Then began the eighth war, the War of the Three Henries.[7] The king was still officially the head of the League: he suppressed Protestantism by a stroke of his worthless pen. But in the field his favorite Joyeuse was defeated at Coutras by Henry of Navarre, while Henry of Guise was victorious over the German auxiliaries of the Huguenots. Against the king's orders Guise boldly came to Paris; the populace rose and besieged Henry III in his Louvre (Day of the Barricades, May 12, 1588). It seemed as though Guise had but to stretch his hand: he hesitated and quieted his supporters. Henry III fled from his unsafe capital, convened the States-General at Blois, and ordered Guise to attend. Confident in the king's confirmed cowardice, Guise and his brother the cardinal obeyed the summons: "He would never dare!" was their reply to all warnings. On December 23, 1588, both were assassinated by the king's bodyguards. Catherine de Médicis praised the deed with her dying breath, "Well cut, my son; now you have to sew up the pieces."

The result was not peace but an open rebellion of the Leaguers under Guise's brother, fat Mayenne. Henry III, forced into an alliance with Henry of Navarre, was attempting to recapture Paris when he was murdered in his turn by a monk, Jacques Clement.

The League proclaimed the old cardinal of Bourbon king as Charles X; but according to the law of the land, Navarre was now Henry IV of France. A "legitimate" king, but without a capital, and with an army so small that he was little more than a guerrilla leader in his own realm. He was counting on Elizabeth of England, but the aid sent to the Leaguers by Philip II of Spain was more effective. Twice Henry IV defeated Mayenne, at Arques in 1589, at Ivry in 1590, where his waving white plume was to serve as a rallying point and as an assurance of victory.[8] But Philip's general, Alexander Farnese, Duke of Parma, compelled him to raise the sieges of Paris and Rouen.

Henry IV was a good fighter, but he was no mere fighter. He had been schooled by twenty years of tortuous intrigue. He recognized that the situation was a stalemate. Obviously, France showed no sign of turning Calvinist. The Huguenots were but a devoted minority; the great lords among them cared little about theological and ecclesiastical niceties; in France the reform spirit had taken other channels. On the other hand, Catholicism had not merely held its own, it had regained ground. Of this aggressive revival, the Jesuits were both the instrument and the symbol. They were active everywhere. The old Gallicans distrusted them, for the sons of Ignatius, "the militia of the Holy See," stood for Romanism in all its rigor. But their power was undeniable. Constantly under suspicions, the Jesuits were to remain a great factor in French culture and French politics for two hundred years and more. The whole education of the ancient regime bore the Jesuit stamp. Even art was fashioned by their hands: what in other countries is called the Baroque is properly known in France as the Jesuit style. This reinvigorated Catholicism was not ready to acknowledge defeat.

Among these warring elements—Huguenots, Jesuits, Gallicans, humanists—the traditional monarchy, weak as it had become, was the only possible center of authority. To the legitimate king rallied all the moderate and patriotic elements, all those who were not Huguenots first of all, and not Holy Leaguers, but Frenchmen; in a word the *Politiques,* those who placed *polity,* i.e., law, order, and peace, above sectarian strife. This spirit found expression in the clever *Satire Ménippée,* the work of a few witty and sensible bourgeois.

Henry IV declared that "Paris was well worth a mass," and proclaimed himself ready to "turn somersault." These cavalier expressions show clearly enough that theology and mysticism had very little to do with the king's change of heart. At Saint-Denis, he abjured Protestantism for the second time. He even took the oath of exterminating heretics: had the white plume turned into a white feather? He was crowned at Chartres; and he could at last enter his capital, which as a Huguenot he had besieged in vain. With his unique combination of military talent, diplomacy, genuine kindness, and Gascon bluff, he defeated, wheedled, or bribed his last enemies, and pieced together his tattered kingdom. He signed peace with Spain at Vervins (1598), confirming the forty-year-old Treaty of Cateau-Cambrésis. To his former companions, the Huguenots, he granted complete liberty of conscience and full equality before the law with mixed courts as a guarantee of justice. Realizing that they were a small minority and that the new regime was still precarious, he gave them also, temporarily, places of refuge with Protestant garrisons paid by the state. This was the Edict of Nantes (1598). In spirit it was generous; under the circumstances it was statesmanlike. Yet it created a situation which a modern state, averse to a plurality of authorities and laws, would find it hard to tolerate.

Monarchical unity appeared to the French mind as the sole method of salvation: this was the political lesson taught by thirty-three years of war. From the religious point of view the natural conclusion was the tolerant and somewhat skeptical common sense which had finally guided Henry IV and the *Politiques*. The evils of fanaticism were patent: fanaticism therefore was the enemy—as Voltaire would say many generations later, "l'Infâme," the monster to be crushed. This second lesson was drawn, for all time, by the philosopher of the age, Michel de Montaigne. Are we not prizing our own opinion too highly when we "roast people alive" because they do not agree with us? Is not the record of human beliefs a chaos of contradictions and absurdities? (*Apology for Raymond de Sebonde*) "What do I know?" "Man is so fluctuating and diverse!" All this, after so many trenchant affirmations supported by fire and sword, was wisdom indeed, and wisdom that remains useful and true. But it was a modest, a negative, almost a despairing, wisdom, the weary soberness that comes after an orgy. In Montaigne's *Essays* we find not a book but a man, human, humane, sensible, congenial, delightful. But that man is also a trifle selfish, unpoetical, and not heroic in the least. The splendor of hope had faded that we found in the hymn to the sacred herb Pantagruelion.

CHAPTER XIII

The Foundation of Classical Order: Henry IV, Richelieu, Mazarin

✍ ABSOLUTISM BY WEARY CONSENT RESTORES ORDER

After four decades of anarchy France was yearning for order almost at any price, and the monarchy seemed the only institution capable of enforcing peace. The five Bourbon kings from 1589 to 1792 (more accurately from 1594 to 1789) stand as the representatives of absolutism. Yet, paradoxical as this may sound, their absolutism, in practice and in theory, was far from absolute. It was neither sheer tyranny nor blind obedience to an abstract principle. It was actually government by consent, the consent tinged with resignation rather than enthusiasm.[1] The king's authority was the least of many well-known evils. We must not be deluded by the high-sounding phrase, "Divine Right." It merely imparted prestige to a conscious and rather weary compromise. The sacredness of the kingly office had been far more evident in the Middle Ages when royal authority was checked and challenged at every turn. To consider Louis XV—or for that matter Henry IV—as "the Lord's Anointed" demanded not naive faith but a transcendent sense of irony.

The situation in 1594 was not unexampled. Repeatedly, and in particular under Charles V and Charles VII, we have seen the monarchy serve as a rallying point. All its possible rivals had been found wanting. The feudal "system" was a Utopia: baronial power, born of anarchy, invincibly reverted to anarchy. A Christian commonwealth, a genuine theocracy, never came down to earth: the Church needed the secular arm and was forced to condone its abuses. In France, at least, an economic democracy founded upon the trades was not even a brief and blurred vision: before the cities and the guilds had reached maturity, the selfishness of the vested interests had destroyed their vitality. The king alone was above all petty wrangling. He alone belonged to all classes: to the nobles he was the first of their order; to the Church, her Eldest Son; to the masses, a father.

There was no sudden revelation, no revolution in thought or feeling, when Henry IV, the royal adventurer, was at last recognized as the legitimate king. French history counts a few miraculous dawns: the accession to power of Francis I, Louis XIV, Bonaparte. The rise of Henry IV was not one of them; it was clouded and slow. It took him a full decade of fighting and negotiations to master his kingdom; even in 1598 the conquest was still incomplete; it remained precarious to the very end. Neither his hereditary title nor his victories had sufficed to win the crown: his recognition was the result not of a clear-cut triumph but of a "deal." Although there was no express bargain, every-one understood, with a wink, that "Paris was well worth a mass." It was not the white-plumed knight of Arques and Ivry that reached the throne but a shrewd realist, expert at computing the price of a conscience, including his own. This explains why he could not purely and simply reduce the rebellious nobles to submission: it was he, the nominal con-queror, who had to be absolved by the pope and who joined their ranks as a penitent.

The leaders of the Holy Catholic League, in open alliance with Spain, had entrenched themselves in the government of provinces and were creating a new feudalism. In a ruined kingdom Henry IV had to find enormous sums to bribe them. One after the other, they sold out: Brissac surrendered Paris for 480,000 livres; Vitry gave up Meaux for 169,000; Villars yielded the fortresses of Normandy for 4,000,000; Mayenne re-ceived 3,500,000 for Burgundy, Guise nearly 4,000,000 for Champagne. Another Guise, Mercoeur, attempted to make himself hereditary duke of Brittany and quasi-independent; he was the last to give in, and the greediest; in 1598 he exacted more than 4,000,000 livres. A rude de-feat for poetic justice: the great nobles, far from being punished, retired from the contest their coffers bulging with gold, new honors heaped upon their heads, their daughters marrying into the royal family. To his com-panion and adviser Sully, who hated squandering good money on rebels, Henry replied, "If we have to fight, it will cost us ten times more." For a miracle this dangerous method proved almost successful: with a few exceptions the men Henry paid for remained bought.

They gave up their claim to feudal independence and fully acknowl-edged the king, but they were nonetheless hard to manage. The discipline maintained by Francis I—Bourbon the one glaring exception—had been ruined by a whole generation of strenuous chaos. No majesty did hedge round a king whom all had known as an enemy, a hated heretic, the leader of a tough, starveling band. In making their peace with a successful rival, such men as Mercoeur, Epernon, Soissons had no thought of submitting to the common law. The contagion of this unruly spirit affected even the king's personal friends. Biron, whom he had made a duke and peer, marshal of France, governor of Burgundy, plotted against him with Savoy and Spain and planned for his assassination. Forgiven once by Henry, Biron betrayed him again and was beheaded in 1602. Not only did Joinville and Bouillon conspire with Spain but also a woman he dearly loved, Henriette d'Entragues, and her family.

The cities followed the example of the nobles: they too refused to surrender unconditionally. They stipulated that the king should maintain within their walls a limited garrison, or none at all. The Huguenots, who felt themselves abandoned by their leader, insisted on preserving an organized republic within the state. The Edict of Nantes gave them more than their religious liberty: they needed the right to protect themselves, for they knew that the king could not adequately protect them. In 1598 the peace established by Henry IV looked like another truce which might well prove as deceptive as the six or seven that went before.

The same confusion prevailed in court society. Henry, his companions, and his former adversaries could not turn suddenly from a life of violence, treachery, and adventure to one of decorous restraint. It was a mischievous prank of fate that had made the gay, lusty, bawdy, profane [2] Gascon the hero of the Calvinists. Before his marriage with Margaret of Valois was annulled, he lived openly with Gabrielle d'Estrées, and their children were brought up at court. After he married another bag of Medici gold, he preserved the rough freedom of a soldier. Amorous to the end, the graybeard was ready to drag France into war, partly for the purpose of chasing pretty Charlotte of Montmorency, Princess of Condé, whom an exclusive husband had removed from his court.

Decency, order, refinement had to seek another center. Then it was that Catherine de Vivonne, Marquise de Rambouillet, developed, away from the court, that admirable institution of the classical age, the *salon*. Under her scepter tongues and manners were disciplined and refined to the utmost. This reaction against brutality led to sophistication: for fear of vulgarity, plain speech was banned; over the simplest thoughts was spread a veil of metaphors and allusions, diaphanous to the initiated, cryptic to the common herd. Instead of sudden cavalier amours, the Rambouillet circle cultivated a meticulous strategy of love: Julie d'Angennes, the marquise's daughter, kept up that subtle game with her suitor Montausier for two decades. Because the ladies of that society were known as *les Précieuses,* the Precious Ones, their affectation took the name *préciosité;* and its bane was felt for two centuries at least in polite literature. But the educative work of the marquise de Rambouillet is not to be despised. The best writers of the day, as well as the highest society, flocked to her famous Blue Room. They had to abjure looseness, uncouthness, pedantry. When, through the robust bourgeois spirit of Molière and Boileau, the morbid refinements of *préciosité* were cured, what remained was urbanity, the greatest and most lasting achievement of the Classical Age. We cannot forget that among the *Précieuses* were counted Madame de La Fayette and Madame de Sévigné, in whom extreme delicacy never stifled natural sentiments and a vigorous intellect.

✁ THE GREAT ASSET: HENRY IV'S COMPLEX PERSONALITY

Reconstruction is an appalling task, as the world found out after World War II. Henry IV had been part of the chaos which had overwhelmed France; he had to heal himself as well as his country. When the difficulties of the undertaking are considered, and the imperfection of the instrument, the results seem astounding. Much of the recovery, of course, was due to the spontaneous efforts of the common people. Our intricate civilization might be wounded irrecoverably by forty years of destruction; but in the local and primitive economy of those days, the healing power of nature and the elementary activities of man could be trusted. Simply stop devastation, allow the peasant to sow and reap in peace, and in a few years the traces of war will be effaced.

Henry IV, however, was not satisfied with *laissez faire*. He had the fundamental instinct of the good ruler: he felt that authority is to be sought not for prestige but for service. And he did bend his efforts to the restoration of his ruined land. He found in Maximilien de Béthune, whom he made duke of Sully, an ideal collaborator; but the initiative was his, and on certain points he was more far-sighted than his great minister.

Sully, an able general, was also a treasurer of unexampled efficiency. At court, he was the needed frown and tight fist, while Henry was the smile and the open hand. He managed to fill his arsenal with ordnance, and his vaults with a war chest, enormous at the time, of 20,000,000 livres; yet, for a wonder, he contrived also to lighten the *taille,* the chief tax on commoners. He vigorously promoted agriculture and public works. He gave a decisive impetus to highway building, and his plan, continued for two centuries, was one of the glories of old France. The roads were lined with elms which the peasants long called by one of his names, *Rosny*. The first French canal with locks, the canal of Briare, was begun between the Seine and the Loire; the great canal between the Mediterranean and the Garonne was projected.

Henry believed with Sully that "ploughed field and pasture land are the two fountains of life"; he read assiduously the famous treatise of Olivier de Serre, *Théâtre d'agriculture*. But while Sully had a Jeffersonian prejudice against manufactures, Henry favored industry, foreign trade, luxury. He planted mulberry trees so that France could produce and weave her own silk; he gave privileges to the makers of artistic glassware, challenging the supremacy of the Venetians; he started the tapestry works of the Gobelins. He extended the Louvre in a stately gallery along the Seine so as to link it with the neighboring palace of the Tuileries. Even a despot can order a dream palace: it takes a wise ruler to think of civic improvements for the common good. Under him— and we may say in his spirit—was built the Place Dauphine, the first of the symmetrical and ornamental plazas in Paris, delightfully intimate in its moderate size and its modest brick, stone, and slate architecture, an urban development which might serve as a model today. And Paris owes to him its hoary "New Bridge," *le Pont-Neuf,* robust and elegant with a chain of spirited grimacing masks under its parapet: a charming touch of baroque fantasy like the gleam in the wary eyes and the smile on the seamed features of the king. There, in that incomparable center of historic beauty, stands his equestrian statue.

There is no key to the reign of Henry IV except the personality of Henry IV; and there is no better definition of his character than Montaigne's formula for man in general: "fluctuating and diverse." Compared with him, the most complex, the most subtle of modern rulers—a Franklin Roosevelt for instance—will seem rigid and cold. This elusiveness was imposed upon him: throughout his career he could never be the single-minded servant of an obvious cause; he had to feel, to fight, to insinuate, to smile his way in a world of fanatics and assassins. He mastered the difficult art of yielding without creating the impression of weakness. Even when he had reached power, he still preferred to use diplomacy: he was, with excellent reason, prouder of his charm than of his sword. He used the velvet glove with such deftness that he made his opponents believe in the iron hand within—which perhaps was not there.

The opening words of a speech to the Assembly of Notables, convened at Rouen in 1596, offer an excellent example of his method: "I did not call you, as my predecessors did, merely to have you endorse my decisions; I brought you together to hear your counsels, to believe them, to follow them, in a word to place myself entirely in your hands. . . ." Is this a complete surrender? Henry does not mean it so and does not want his words to be so misinterpreted. So he adds, "Such a desire is not customary with kings, graybeards, and conquerors. . . ." Naturally, the Notables advised and granted everything he wanted. The Parlements were harder to manage. "My predecessors," he said to them, "were afraid of you and did not love you. I love you, and I fear you not." When he rammed the Edict of Nantes down their throats, he used the same masterly mixture of familiarity, persuasion, and authority: "I am the King now: as King do I speak, and mean to be obeyed. . . ." Was this tone too peremptory? He hastened to correct the impression: "Grant to my entreaties that which you would deny to my threats. You will not do it for my sake but for your own, and in the interests of peace." Purring and growling, the Parlements yielded, and the wise edict became the law of the land. Thus was authority rebuilt, without bluster, like a delicate work of art. It was autocracy—Henry never convened the States-General—but autocracy by persuasion, with barely a hint of the Big Stick in reserve: *Bâton porte paix.*

Henry IV was popular and knew that his popularity was an asset: he cultivated it for the good of the kingdom. Like Napoleon he contributed actively, consciously, to the growth of his own legend—a legend more amiable than that of the Corsican, and with a firmer foundation in fact. He was not insincere: he played a part, and played it for all it was worth, but that part was himself. He was expected to be gay, impulsive, familiar; he did not have to wear a mask, he had only to show the public that side of his nature which the public wanted to see. Benjamin Franklin in Paris exploited his own personage with exactly the same kind of shrewdness, calculating, not deceitful; on the stage, yet not histrionic.

Of no other rulers are there so many friendly anecdotes reported, so many wise and kindly sayings, at times homely and folklike, at other times more flamboyant, with a waving of the white plume. His very weaknesses served him: he was no plaster saint but "the triple-threat man, who could drink, fight, and make love." He is still remembered as *le Vert Galant,*[3] the ardent but not too exclusive lover. His affair with *la Belle Gabrielle* (*d'Estrées*) with its mysterious and tragic ending endeared him to the Gallic heart. At his most fallible he was human and amiable. There was shrewdness in his smile, but the good humor and the profound kindness were genuine. He hated to hurt, and he loved to forgive. With St. Louis, far above the indefinite Louis XII and the heavy-witted Louis XVI, he ranks among the rare rulers who did not ignore the common man. His wish that every peasant should have "a chicken in the pot of a Sunday" is more than an admirable election slogan. Others might have spoken, as La Bruyère did later, of "not lacking bread." Henry's phrase evokes a vision not of food merely but of a modest, homely festivity. In its gay realism it is delicate and touching; it is not the word of a dutiful philanthropist: it is the greeting of a friend.

Through the affection he inspired, Henry IV built up the Bourbon monarchy. When the Revolution broke out in 1789 as an explosion not of anger but of hope and loyalty, the Parisians wrote on the pedestal of Henry's statue, "He is restored to us," a "directive" which Louis XVI failed to understand. But his opportunistic, pragmatic policy built up also something very different from royal leadership: it strengthened the caste of hereditary officials. Henry was not responsible for this development: for ages offices had been openly bought and transmitted like other forms of property. But, on the advice of a financier, Paulet, the king granted more definite recognition to this practice in exchange for a substantial contribution from the officeholders.[4] Established purely as an expedient, and for nine years only beginning December, 1604, "la Paulette," as this tax came to be known, survived until the Revolution. We must never forget that under the "absolute" monarchy the king's men were to a large extent independent of the king.

In home affairs Henry felt his way with great caution but not without steadiness. In the foreign field his policy was far more puzzling. He liquidated, as we have seen, the interminable war with Spain. He rèsisted the lure of Italy and was glad, after a brush with the duke of Savoy, to exchange the marquisate of Saluzzo for lands that were manifestly French, Gex, Bresse, Bugey. But he could follow no clear principle. His inclinations were anti-Hapsburg and anti-Spanish. But the queen and the Jesuits were urging him to ally himself with those very powers, champions of Catholicism. Just because he was a convert, he did not feel free to follow the course of Francis I, later resumed by Richelieu, and openly to support the Protestants. The precarious peace of the kingdom, and his own life, were at stake. He may have been thirsting for glory: success breeds ambition. But, wiser than Louis XIV, he negotiated from day to day and avoided commitments.

What plans were maturing in his mind we do not know. He once expressed the conviction that all "Frenchmen"—probably meaning all who spoke French—should come under his rule: an anticipation of the "principle of nationalities," later propounded by Napoleon III, that ill-fated forerunner of ill-fated Woodrow Wilson. But his words may have been a chance remark not a doctrine. As for the "Grand Design" that goes by his name for a sweeping reorganization of Europe, we find no trace of it except in the memoirs of Sully. The minister, in retirement and semi-disgrace, was indulging in a grandiose retrospective project—

the sheerest might-have-been. Like the plan of Pierre Dubois three hundred years before, Sully's posited the supremacy of France. "This way wisdom does not lie."

Strangely enough, it was Sully the thrifty who was urging Henry IV to war—naturally against the Hapsburgs. The pretext was the succession of Cleves and Juliers (Jülich), duchies on the lower Rhine, a minor problem fraught with tremendous consequences, as all problems must be among jealous great powers. The dubious enterprise was cut short by the dagger of a fanatic, Ravaillac, (May 14, 1610): Henry IV, the kindly and wise, had the same fate as Henry of Guise and Henry III.

✍ FROM CHAOS TO IRON DISCIPLINE: THE ADVENT OF RICHELIEU

The boast of monarchy is to promote stability. Causes and leaders pass away, but the dynasty endures: "The king is dead, long live the king!" When a child of nine succeeds a Henry IV, this fine formula does not tell the whole story. The Parlement of Paris, delighted to assume political authority, entrusted the regency to the queen mother—bloated flesh and shrunken mind—Marie de Médicis. Under her a camarilla seized power, the companion of her childhood, Leonora Galigai, and Leonora's husband, Concini. The pair had no thought but for their fortune; Concini became marquis and marshal of France. Back of the Italians strong influences, particularly Father Coton and the papal nuncio, were at work for an aggressive Catholic policy: the Counter Reformation was vigorously proceeding throughout Europe. Sully, still a Huguenot, had to retire.

Sully's hoard was soon drained. The nobles grumbled because of the favors heaped upon the Concini; so they had to be appeased with lavish bribes. Then they rebelled anew, virtuously denouncing the very prodigalities by which they had profited. The Parlements were openly voicing dissatisfaction. The Huguenots, under the threat of Catholic reaction, were girding themselves for resistance. So feeble was the regent that she had to sign a formal treaty with the malcontents at Sainte-Menehould. As a last resort, perhaps as a face-saving device, the States-General were convened in 1614. No light and no strength came from that distracted assembly. The three orders, unequally privileged but equally indifferent to the welfare of the people, could only bandy recriminations; they could not frame a policy. The institution survived in vague memory and dusty reserve; but the States were not to be called together again until 1789.

In 1617, with the complicity of the young king, the Concini were overthrown. The marshal of Ancre, as he was now called, was shot down when entering the Louvre; his wife was sentenced to death as a witch. The queen mother herself had to leave the court. With her went a young prelate, her protégé, Armand du Plessis de Richelieu, Bishop of Luçon.

The sole result was a change of worthless favorites: Charles d'Albert de Luynes, a gentleman from Provence, had amused the boy king with his skill in falconry. He made himself constable of France and marched against the southern Protestants, goaded into rebellion by the forcible restoration of Catholicism in Béarn. De Luynes failed to reduce the fortified city of Montauban; death saved him from impending downfall (December, 1621).

It took three more years for "the man of destiny" to make himself supreme. In April, 1624, Richelieu, a cardinal since 1622, entered the royal council. By August he had the chief minister, La Vieuville, arrested, and himself appointed in his place.

Then began a tense silent drama which was to last eighteen years. Louis XIII had no liking for Richelieu; yet he supported him against the whole court and his own family. When the queen mother turned against her former protégé, it was she who was forced into lifelong exile. The young queen, Anne of Austria, the king's brother, Gaston d'Orléans, had to abase themselves before the Red Robe. As for the great nobles who dared to challenge Richelieu's power, their meed was banishment, imprisonment, or death. Montmorency, "first baron of the realm," went to the scaffold. Once it looked as if the spell were broken, and the whole court rejoiced; but again the king rallied to the support of the cardinal, and the episode remained known as "the Day of Dupes" (November 10, 1630).

Was Louis XIII as weak as his mother, imposed upon by the Concini? Weak minds are unsteady and easily resort to violence, as Charles IX did when he allowed the massacre of the Huguenots. Louis XIII's consistency is not weakness. Had he given a nod, great lords would have been eager to arrest the cardinal and lead him to Vincennes or the Bastille. Louis was urged to give that nod: by his mother, by his brother, by his wife, by the two women whom he loved in his reticent fashion, Mademoiselle de Hautefort and Mademoiselle de La Fayette. Not to give that nod required on the part of the king constant vigilance and energy. His voluntary servitude was a triumph of the will. He must have understood Richelieu. He must have placed the interest of the monarchy above his personal pride; and his handsome, melancholy figure, half-effaced in the background of his own reign, acquires thereby a strange and somber nobility.

Richelieu at the beginning of his ministry expounded his plans to

Louis XIII; at the end, he summed them up in his *Political Testament:* there is no clearer example of lucid, inflexible determination. Yet we must not forget that he was a man of ailing flesh and ardent blood, not a formidable robot of steel. If he was not a Henry IV, neither was he a Calvin or a Robespierre, the incarnation of a radical doctrine. The most authentic forerunner of the Jacobins, he was no Jacobin himself. He had to feel his way, very deviously at times, in the accomplishment of his purpose. But the purpose was unmistakable: to make the king's power absolute in France and supreme in Europe. It was not an ideology but a tendency, a tendency, however, with the intensity of a passion, served by an energy which grew more ruthless with the years.

Richelieu was not cruel: he was too great to find pleasure in the suffering of the fallen. But the sentiments, the rights, the liberty, the life of his opponents were as naught in his eyes when *la Raison d'Etat,* the paramount interest of the State, had spoken. Henry IV wanted to be loved; Richelieu accepted hatred if it was reduced to impotence by fear: *Oderint dum metuant.* The contrast was due, first of all, to a difference in temperament. In spite of premature infirmities Henry was a *bon vivant:* he knew the joy of animal well-being. In spite of his commanding presence Richelieu was constantly fighting for health: when he killed his last enemies, he was himself a living corpse. But the difference is better explained by the origin and station of the two rulers. For Henry IV, and for lesser men like Francis I and Louis XIV, the State was no Leviathan but something natural, accessible, personal, human: their own domain, their own family, themselves. For Richelieu, of comparatively modest origin, a son of the provincial nobility allied with the *bourgeoisie,* the State, far above the great lords, was an awe-inspiring idol to be served by methods of terror. Few hereditary monarchs can be as ruthless as the great parvenus, usurpers, ministers, dictators.

THE TRIPLE GOAL: TO CURB PROTESTANTS, NOBLES, AUSTRIA

Every child in France learns by heart, like a magic formula, the three points of Richelieu's policy: to suppress the political privileges of the Protestants, to reduce the nobles to strict obedience, to humble the House of Austria.[5]

First the Protestants: Richelieu's absolutism could not tolerate that a minority should have its own fortresses, its own army, its own diplomacy. The temporary expedient had worked well enough under Henry IV, thanks to his skill and prestige. The fitful violence and weakness of his successors exasperated and at the same time emboldened the Huguenots. They had a vigorous leader in Rohan and allies in the northern countries. The key to the situation was La Rochelle, their maritime capital. Richelieu cut it off from the sea with a mighty dike; English support, under Buckingham, failed miserably; the obduracy of the defenders, led by their mayor, Guiton, found its relentless match in the besiegers (1627–1628). Finally the heroic little city was starved into submission; resistance was crushed in the Cévennes Mountains; Montauban was reduced, Rohan fled; and the rebellion was ended at Alais in 1629 not with a negotiated peace but with an "Edict of Grace."

Richelieu, a rigorous Catholic, hated heresy. But he respected the word pledged by Henry the Great. The ruin of Protestant power was followed by no persecution. Religious freedom was not abridged. Huguenots were employed by the state: three years after Alais, Rohan was in command of a royal army.

The subjugation of the great could not be so swift and thorough. Conspiracies, as we have seen, were repressed without pity, whether the culprit be a Montmorency or a mere upstart, a boyish favorite of the king such as Cinq-Mars. As a Christian and as a statesman, Richelieu attempted to put down dueling, which often was deliberate murder and which was the last trace of that ancient feudal curse, the right of private warfare. He did not fully succeed: attenuated traces of dueling survive to this day. But he would not be openly flouted: Bouteville, another Montmorency, who had ostentatiously fought a duel in defiance of the edict, was executed. Richelieu ordered all fortified castles not on the frontier to be dismantled: a symbolic gesture, for these picturesque survivals could not have stood modern ordnance. He was the first of the terrorists and the first of the levelers.

Offices traditionally held by the greatest nobles, such as that of Grand Constable, permanent head of the army, were suppressed: he could brook no power beside his own. The authority of the aristocratic governors in the provinces was curtailed. Richelieu did not originate, neither did he develop to the full, the institution of the intendants; but it made decisive progress under him. The intendants were middle-class officials, appointed by the minister, responsible to him only, sent out to observe and to check the governors. Ultimately all real power fell into their hands, and France was transformed from a semifeudal kingdom into a centralized bureaucracy. The prefects of Napoleon were the heirs of the intendants.

The "humbling of Austria" was far from a simple process. Indeed the diplomacy of Richelieu, admirably seconded by his alter ego, "the Gray Eminence," the Capuchin Father Joseph, was incredibly tortuous and his military achievements by no means an unbroken series of triumphs. A prince of the Church and the servant of His Most Christian Majesty, Richelieu sought to achieve the ruin of Spain and Austria without weakening the Catholic cause they were upholding. Hence the hesitancy, the shiftiness, of his policy, so unexpected in a man dreaded and admired for his inflexible will.

Like Henry IV he wisely abandoned not all action in Italy but all desire of permanent conquest in that field. Henceforth, in the great game of European politics the North will be all important. Italy, even in the most brilliant campaigns like those of Bonaparte in 1796 and Napoleon III in 1859, will be considered as a secondary issue. Like Henry again Richelieu refrained as long as he could from direct, all-out intervention. Germany was torn by a war, civil and foreign, political as well as religious, which was to last thirty years and leave the country ruined for generations. By a secret treaty Richelieu subsidized Gustavus-Adolphus, King of Sweden, to fight against the emperor.

But Gustavus was no mere tool; he made himself supreme in North Germany as far as the Rhine, and Richelieu was relieved when the Lutheran hero died in victory at Lützen (1632). Casting for an instrument, Richelieu thought of Wallenstein, who had raised a large army of his own with profit as his avowed motive: the cardinal urged him to carve a kingdom for himself in Bohemia, thus holding the Hapsburgs in check. But Wallenstein, last and greatest of the *condottieri,* was murdered in 1634. Then Richelieu hired the army of Bernhard of Saxe-Weimar, who had worked with Gustavus-Adolphus, and avenged his death at Lützen. Bernhard, after conquering most of Alsace, was planning to make it a principality of his own. Again Richelieu must have sighed with regret and relief when the ambitious adventurer died in 1639. His troops and his conquests remained with the French.

In the meantime Richelieu had been forced to unmask his batteries, and the first impact was not favorable to his arms. The imperial forces advanced as far as Saint-Jean-de-Losne; the Spaniards as far as Corbie on the Somme, seventy miles away from Paris: there was panic in the capital (1636). France rallied, and for the next six years she and her allies—a motley array, Bernhard, the Swedes, the Dutch, some German princes, some Italians, the Portuguese—more than held their own. The final helplessness of Spain and the empire was due to internal causes rather than to any blow dealt by the French armies. It was after Richelieu's death that young Condé defeated at Rocroy the renowned veterans of Castile. Still the policy of the cardinal, continued by Mazarin, is invariably credited with the triumph sealed in 1648, after seven years of haggling, by the Treaties of Westphalia. It was he who made the supremacy of Louis XIV in Europe a possibility; and even today, the diplomacy of Richelieu remains a prestigious and perilous model.

He made France, as he made himself, great: in both cases a word of dubious praise. The price was heavy. His magnificent game on the chessboard of Europe was expensive, and he was no financier. He was prodigal in his own household and in the king's service. He was too conservative in social matters and too much engrossed in loftier problems boldly to tackle the essential evils of the ancient regime, absurd privileges in taxation, faulty methods of collection, absence of any definite budget. He was superbly ignorant in economic affairs: because he signed grandiose charters for trading companies conceding the exploitation of a continent to a few men without experience and without capital, he thought he had done enough for the prosperity of France. As a matter of fact, this glorious minister was in constant financial distress; and, although the middle class suffered deeply, the burden fell most heavily upon the common people. The cardinal, ruthless with the great, was not tender with the poor. There were repeated insurrections due not to disloyalty but to sheer despair; and they were repressed, as the rebellions of the nobles had been, with the crushing iron hand.

THE HEROIC WILL:
ST. VINCENT DE PAUL, CORNEILLE, DESCARTES

The picture of France would not be complete if we failed to present, by the side of Richelieu, the beloved figure of St. Vincent de Paul (1576–1660). Vincent, a Gascon of humble origin, devoted himself to those who suffered, beginning with the deepest circle in the social inferno, the galley slaves. He was not content with almsgiving and personal service: realizing the hideous extent of the evil, he attacked it with the decision, the far-sighted strategy, of a great conqueror. He organized the Sisters of Charity, the Lazarist missionaries, homes for foundlings. He awakened vocations among the lowly and among the great: some of the noblest ladies in France were proud to serve under him. A self-made minister of social welfare, he managed his immense enterprises with smiling gentleness and with the passionate energy of an empire builder. The Treaties of Westphalia have long been torn to shreds: the foundations of St. Vincent de Paul endure.

Intensity of will power was eminent in Richelieu but not unique: it was a characteristic, and almost a fashion, of the time. St. Vincent was charity and mildness—plus will power. Pierre Corneille the dramatist, with the education and at times the tortuous mind of a pettifogging Norman lawyer, was of will power all compact. He rose stiffly but naturally to the heights of ancient heroism. He is not an idealist, as he has been called, offering a purified vision of mankind; he is by no means the poet of duty; he compels us to admire his characters—Medea, Cleopatra in *Rodogune*—even when they are criminals. For him as for the supermen of the Italian Renaissance, virtue means not goodness but force. With a difference: force in his tragedies is not blind instinct, it is a passion tamed and harnessed by sovereign reason. The true Cornelian is the reverse of the Romanticist, tossed by dark impulses he neither controls nor understands. With his naive ingenuity and his antiquated bombast Corneille still stirs us to the depths. He anticipated Pascal: man is greater than that which crushes him, when he refuses to bow his head and close his eyes.

We find the same spirit in René Descartes, soldier of fortune, mathematician, physicist, physiologist, and philosopher. The key word of his *Method* is not detached rationalism but rationalism at the service of the heroic will. Quietly, Descartes brushes aside all external authorities. He ventures into the depths alone. There he meets doubt, as his master Montaigne did; but for him doubt is no comfortable haven. Doubt is thought; thought proves the existence of the thinker: *Cogito ergo sum*. But thought counts only when it is free, fearless, sustained, orderly. Thus, in radically different domains do we find, with Richelieu, St. Vincent de Paul, Corneille, Descartes, the same quality of conscious disciplined energy. We have spoken of "lost centuries": it is possible that we are living in such an epoch. Here we have a generation of men who had sought and found themselves.[6]

COMEDY ON AN EPIC SCALE: MAZARIN

The life of Giulio Mazarini (1602–1661) is a picaresque novel on the heroic scale. Of Sicilian origin, educated by the Jesuits at Rome, he spent some time at the Spanish university of Alcalá. There, we are told by Morse Stephens, he was distinguished for gambling and gallant adventures rather than for studiousness; but "he mastered that romantic fashion of Spanish love-making which was to help him greatly in after life." After taking at Rome his doctor's degree in both civil and canon law, he turned up a captain of infantry. Then he rose rapidly as a diplomat in the papal service and was sent as nuncio to the court of France (1634–1636), although never ordained as a priest. Richelieu appreciated his skill, made him a Frenchman, secured for him a cardinal's hat; and when the great minister died, Louis XIII simply ordered all his officials to report to Mazarin.

Within six months Louis XIII followed his masterful servant to the grave (December 4, 1642–May 14, 1643). A child of five, Louis XIV, came to the throne; a Spanish queen was made regent. A new reign meant as a rule a reversal of policy and a purge of the old personnel. Already a clique of self-important persons believed that they had captured the queen, who hated Richelieu, his works, and his minions. But Mazarin had up his sleeve the art learned at Alcalá. It was miraculously successful: the queen "detested work and loved Mazarin," and for eighteen years the incredible adventurer and secret prince consort ruled her and France.

At home he was a grafter on a monumental scale, a grander Concini, able not only to grab but to hold; in foreign affairs he was a marvelous chess player, unhampered by pride or scruple. The French did not submit easily to this equivocal personage who, with his farcical singsong accent, seemed to them half buffoon and half rogue. The war and the Mazarin family were expensive—for the cardinal was an excellent uncle—the people jeered and grumbled, and the Paris air was thick with jests, songs, and lampoons about the minister.

The Parlement had been asked to alter the will of Louis XIII: it felt itself confirmed in its political claims. So it gave official form to the universal discontent. In June, 1648, the four "sovereign courts" united (Parlement, Great Council, Chamber of Accounts, Court of Aids) drafted a joint resolution in twenty-seven articles, which might have been a Magna Charta. It demanded the suppression of the intendants, instruments of absolutism; the right of the Sovereign Courts to confirm all edicts relating to taxes and to supervise their application; and the interdiction of all arbitrary arrests. A purely administrative reform: yet it would have substituted the rule of law for "the king's pleasure." The queen-regent shuffled for a while; then, nerved by a brilliant victory at Lens, she had the leaders of Parlement arrested. Among them was Broussel, renowned for his private and professional virtues. At once (August, 1648) barricades went up throughout Paris. The haughty Spaniard had to yield; but, at the first opportunity, she fled from the capital to Saint-Germain. She took with her the Palladium of France, the young king (January, 1649).

The Great Rebellion was raging in England at the time: perhaps the French Parlement was influenced by the example of its British namesake. But the British Parliament was a cross section of the country; the French was a court of justice. And judges, although they may resist tyranny, are ill-prepared to turn into aggressive revolutionists. Soon, the fight against Mazarin passed into the hands of noble military leaders; and what might have been a decisive contest for principles became the most erratic, the most frivolous, of civil wars. It was called *la Fronde,* the sling, in derision, as though it were a game for children with toy catapults as weapons. To the common people it was no laughing matter. Its worst effect was to make Mazarin shine, in comparison, as an efficient and patriotic statesman.

The rebellious princes had no guiding principle but their old unruly spirit, no substitute for Mazarin's corrupt rule but their fantastic anarchy. We find them changing sides according to the caprices of fortune and the swing of their ambitions. Now Condé, the victor of Rocroy and Lens, was with the crown, and now allied with Spain; and it so happened that his great rival Turenne, shifting likewise, was generally on the other side. An element of romance made the conflict even more unaccountable: noble ladies, Mademoiselle de Montpensier, Madame de Longueville, Madame de Chevreuse, cast themselves into heroic parts and were blindly followed hither and thither by their adorers. To make confusion more abysmal, a born agitator, Paul de Gondi, Bishop Coadjutor of Paris, was constantly brewing mischief. With incomparable verve—his *Memoirs* are among the most vivid productions of the Classical Age—and a genius for intrigue, he plotted indefatigably for a variety of purposes, to oust Mazarin and succeed him, to be confirmed as bishop of Paris, to secure the cardinal's hat, as he finally did under the name of Cardinal de Retz.

The whole affair lasted five years (1648–1653), and France lay in ruins. Mazarin, as supple, as humble as Richelieu had been haughty, yielded to the storm. He went into semivoluntary exile at Brühl in the Electorate of Cologne, returned too soon, and withdrew again, this time at Sedan in the duchy of Bouillon. Out of sight and out of danger he did not relax his hold on the regent. He did not conquer his enemies; he allowed them to wear themselves out. He represented, however unworthily, the monarchical principle, which once again seemed the only guarantee of national interest, order, internal peace. So this man, who had been so bitterly hated and so justly despised, finally returned in triumph. To the end he displayed his power and his semiregal state as insolently as Richelieu had done. He had amassed, in the distress of the country, a fabulous, a scandalous, fortune. Louis XIV, although he had been declared of age in 1652, never dared to assert himself so long as the omnipotent cardinal lived. In 1661 Mazarin left France to Louis XIV with the nobility thoroughly tamed and even servile; the Parlements, which had so badly fumbled their legitimate resistance, hopelessly discredited; the people putting their whole trust in a strong royal government; and the French monarchy, thanks to the Treaties of Westphalia (1648) and the Peace of the Pyrenees (1659), without a peer in Europe. That such a consummation should have come through a Mazarin is one of history's most exquisite ironies.

CHAPTER XIV

The Grand Monarch:
Personal Reign of Louis XIV,
1661-1715

✍ THE MAJESTY OF CLASSICAL HARMONY

On the death of Cardinal Mazarin crown officials asked the young king, "To whom should we henceforth report?" and the answer came, "To me." For over half a century Louis was his own prime minister. He was not merely the State, he was France: the identity of dynasty and country was then a truism. In the most literal sense his word was law. There was no suggestion of convening the States-General, or even that safer substitute, an Assembly of Notables. The Parlements administered justice but no longer dared to remonstrate. The nobles ceased to rebel. They had even forgotten how to plot: their intrigues were the merest cabals to secure some lucrative or honorific favor. Not a whisper of criticism was heard for twenty-five years. A few sporadic peasant revolts quelled with swift rigor barely ruffled, in obscure corners of the land, the majesty of that Augustan peace.

Never was absolutism more calmly proclaimed, and more wholeheartedly accepted. The best symbols of the age are the magnificent portraits of Louis XIV and Bossuet by Hyacinthe Rigaud: we are struck first of all by their invincible self-assurance and repose. Monarch and bishop do not gesticulate and do not frown. There is no trace of bluster in their authority: it pervades their whole being. Here we reach serene and sunlit heights: Catholicism, Classicism, Monarchy in perfect harmony.

No wonder this miracle impressed the contemporaries, in France first of all, but also throughout Europe. No wonder its afterglow survived defeat and death: Voltaire, the embodiment of the critical spirit, remained awed by the grandeur of the epoch and of the sovereign. Throughout three centuries, in spite of many revolutions, the figure of Louis XIV has aged gracefully. The king and his times were lusty and often brutal: now they are veiled in noble melancholy. There may have been a parvenu gaudiness about the fresh glories of Versailles: today gildings and brash allegories are muted, and the stately walks are at their best when strewn with autumn leaves. In our Atomic Age the ideal of 1661 is still professed, not as a vanished Utopia but as a practical goal, by one of the most thoughtful, the most cultured, the most dignified, of our spiritual guides, T. S. Eliot.

This impression is not shattered by such disparaging studies as *The Seamy Side of the Great Century*.[1] The adverse critics have a case. It is a fact that the splendid beasts of prey, the last feudal barbarians, were not yet fully tamed. Under the ceremonial, the intelligent luxury, the elaborate courtesy of Versailles, we find traces of primitive coarseness: in the great Condé himself there was a hero, a courtier, and a brute. The fine Italian hand of the Borgia had disciples: the black melodrama of the famous poisoner, Marquise de Brinvilliers, reached further than the judges dared publicly to probe. The palaces of the time lacked elementary sanitation; the aristocrats bathed less frequently than they did in the Middle Ages; stench was fought with perfume. In the same way lewdness and violent temper were fought with decorum. But no ideal is to be judged by the failures of individuals: there were knaves and self-seekers among the early Christians. Society under Louis XIV was no Arcadia. Still, the manners of the aristocrats were greatly improved, if not their morals; and in the *bourgeoisie* could be found a quiet certainty of taste, an unostentatious piety, a robust dignity of life hard to match in any other age.

The unity, or if the reader prefers the totalitarianism, of classical France at its point of perfection was not the result of tyrannical rule. The generation tutored by Descartes, Corneille, Pascal did not suddenly abandon self-reliance and self-respect to turn into a rabble of flunkeys. On the contrary, we are struck by the freedom of mind, the vigor of character, of the great classicists, Boileau, Molière, Racine. These men chose the rule they lived by deliberately. If they praised the king in terms which would sound fulsome today, it was as the symbol and instrument of the rational order they craved. They were loyal to him as we are to the flag and to the law.

It might even be said that classical France imposed her stamp upon Louis XIV, not the reverse. He had unruly appetites: in a chaotic age he might have been a capricious despot, like the last Valois. He was no genius: in a duller period he would have been a lackluster figurehead. If both his solid qualities and his secret dream were given full scope, it was because a France replete with conscious energy demanded "a great king." He responded to the call; he plied with unrivaled application what he proudly called "his kingly trade." A great king he was, as he had vowed to be. Grandeur is a perilous ideal: in later life, drunk with twenty years of power and pride, he turned "great" according to his own lights, which were crude. But there is even in grandeur a saving grace: rejecting all that is mean, it strives for, and may attain, greatness. Louis preserved dignity even in sin, error, defeat. In the tragic twilight, in the melancholy sunset, of his reign there was still incomparable majesty.

The traditional conception of the Grand Monarch seems to us a "legend" in the more favorable sense of the term, truth simplified, amplified, adorned, but, for all that, essentially true. Neither Saint-Simon nor Michelet, and a long way behind, neither Thackeray nor Félix Gaiffe were able to debunk his glory. Even Napoleon had to borrow his method, and the great dome which covers the emperor's tomb was built by Louis XIV.

Yet, although it has an indestructible core of truth, this legend carries with it two delusions. The first is that the splendor which shone for a few years under Louis XIV was due to a profound, all-pervasive harmony. This notion springs from that craving for unity at all cost which is properly the totalitarian fallacy. The second is the belief that, in the classical ideal, the world had reached an "eternal verity," a formula which in essentials could still be applied today: this we may call the static fallacy. At one moment and from a particular angle, the picture offered by classical France was admirably in focus. But that moment was fleeting, twenty years at most, probably not more than ten. And its striking unity was more superficial than its present admirers are ready to admit. No doubt it was, to use an expression now in vogue, a "way of life." But a way of life may be a style rather than a philosophy. Against these deep-rooted delusions we must appeal to the historical spirit. There are no simple and no permanent solutions in human affairs. Under the obvious unity and the impressive stability of the classical style we must seek the living realities, which were then as they are now, complexity, conflict, and change.

✍ LOUIS XIV AND HIS CONCEPTION OF DIVINE RIGHT

To Louis XIV divine right was no empty phrase. His crown was that of Clovis, Charlemagne, and St. Louis, the one which God Himself had miraculously confirmed through St. Joan.[2] His function was sacerdotal: he was the Lord's Anointed. If, in the chapel of Versailles, the courtiers turned their backs on the altar when the king appeared, they had at least this excuse, that the Royal Presence bore an element of divinity. A very ancient tradition, as we have seen: in Louis XIV himself it acquired a singular fervor. Henry IV had perhaps been a crowned Montaigne. But both Louis XIII and Anne of Austria were ardently religious: Anne's Spanish piety must indeed have been indestructible to survive close association with Cardinal Mazarin. The birth of Louis XIV had been a special answer to prayer, the result of a solemn vow, after twenty-two years of barren wedded life. He was therefore the Child of the Miracle, God's gift, *Dieudonné*.[3] He had cause to believe he had been singled out by Providence.

In other ages this conviction would have made him an oddity: even the Legitimists in 1873 thought that their pretender, another "Child of the Miracle," the count of Chambord, was unduly stressing his divine appointment. In 1661 the king was not out of harmony with public opinion. The old Roman tradition which deified the State and its living emblem, a genuine revival of piety, the yearning for authority as the sole refuge against anarchy: all converged and united to make divine right a national tenet. It is significant that it was best formulated not by a visionary or a fanatic but by a robust and sensible representative of the middle class, Bishop Bossuet. But the unanimity of France on this essential point, while perfectly sincere, was also to a large extent verbal. For some divine right was hardly more than a convenient legal fiction, a synonym for the majesty of the law. For others it was a pious wish: "May the king be the instrument of God's will!" For Louis it was literally an article of faith.

This would go far to explain, if not to justify, the central event in the whole reign, the ruthless suppression of heresy, the revocation of the Edict of Nantes (1685). Louis was merely applying, with belated logic and after persuasion had failed, the formula already found under Louis XII: *Une foy, une loy, un roy,* one faith, one law, one king. But this was after the royal sun had passed its zenith. In the ascending years the rule of Louis XIV had been singularly free from theocratic intolerance. Conversions were welcomed and rewarded but not forced. Here we come to a paradoxical but essential element in French classicism: the lack of doctrinaire rigidity. France and Louis XIV believed in divine right, but within reason; and in absolutism, but in moderation. The classical ideal is not a devastating unity but a sensible compromise. Between traditional authority and the free exercise of the human intellect, the French of the seventeenth century refused to make a choice. They took it for granted that the two must be in secret harmony. This coexistence of two standards has been aptly called a cultural bimetallism.

The solution was transitory, but for a few decades it provided a resting place. Many minds today would welcome even such an illusion of spiritual peace.

The great classic virtue, therefore, was neither blind worship of the past nor blinder faith in formal logic but *measure*.[4] Such wisdom had often been expressed in antiquity and was fully alive in the Middle Ages: *démesure* was then considered as the flaw which proves the undoing of heroes. The "reason" which Boileau bids us not merely to honor and obey but to love is not "reasoning" but common sense. The Grand Monarch possessed to a surprising degree that humdrum, that bourgeois, quality. It has been said that, in his intense piety, in his addiction to pomp and punctilio, in his impressive gravity, he was Spanish rather than French: if it be so, the Spanish strain in him included Sancho Panza no less than Don Quixote.

He earnestly believed that the source of his authority was divine, and he must have nodded approval when Bossuet asserted, in biblical language, "O kings! Ye are like gods!" But when a provincial monk dedicated to him a thesis in which he was compared with God Himself, "in such a manner as to show that God was only the copy," Louis XIV, on the advice of Bossuet, had it suppressed. Madame de Sévigné, who reports the incident, comments sagely, *Trop est trop,* too much is too much. It was this innate feeling that *trop est trop* which, for two decades at least, preserved Louis XIV from irreparable mischief.

Saint-Simon taxes him with mediocrity; but he had a quality rarer and more precious than brilliance, a sense of his own limitations. He dabbled in poetry, and he loved praise; but he played a delightful and cruel joke, as good as a scene in Molière, on a foolish old courtier, Marshal de Gramont, who was ready to damn or extol a madrigal on the slightest hint of the sovereign: the wretched poem was by Louis himself. He listened to reason: he, who for half a century decided alone, never decided on the spur of the moment and never without consultation. Deliberations in council were no farce as they had become under Mazarin. He, the source of all authority, recognized superiorities. He appeared to grace with his august presence certain operations of war— the crossing of the Rhine, the surrender of a citadel—but he never wrenched actual command from the more capable hands of his generals. When he asked Boileau, "Who is the greatest writer of the time?" Boileau answered, "Sire, Molière." The king remarked, "I did not think so, but you know better about these things than I do," an admission which Napoleon I, Adolphe Thiers, or Mussolini could never have been brought to make.

Louis XIV was no radical. He might have attempted a royal revolution clarifying, simplifying, rationalizing the chaos of ancient France; he worked in that direction, unconsciously perhaps, but he did so with very cautious steps. He curbed the powers that limited his own: he did not attempt to suppress them altogether. Closely, jealously, he watched the nobility: he could not forget the *Fronde* and the hurried flight of the royal family from Paris. But he treated nobles with scrupulous courtesy, heaped favors upon them, and respected their privileges. He tamed his Parlements, but the Parlements survived. He reduced to a show most of the ancient liberties of provinces and cities; but the show, which was no vain thing in his eyes, went on undisturbed. His respect for local customs and autonomy explains the ease with which Alsace was reconciled to what, at the time, was undoubtedly alien rule. His reign was long unblemished by any act of arbitrary violence. Until the Revocation there was nothing that could be called a *coup d'état* or a purge. His treatment of Fouquet at the very start of his personal reign (1661) was not inspired by personal spite. Fouquet, Superintendent of Finances, a survivor of the corrupt Mazarin era, was condemned to banishment for graft on a monumental scale: Louis, on his own authority, aggravated the sentence to life imprisonment. With good reason: Fouquet was ambitious as well as grasping [5] and a danger to the state. He had friends and accomplices in high places, and the light penalty meted out by the judges was a scandal. Few modern governments have as clear a record. Granted that it was the king's mental sluggishness rather than philosophical balance that acted as a check: the result was at any rate closely akin to instinctive wisdom.

✒ THE SUN KING AS A MAN

Louis was able to keep up the elaborate ritual of the court and the exacting duties of government without being fatigued and without being bored. He was served by a vigorous physique. He was not handsome: of medium height and stocky, he lacked the aristocratic mien of Charles I. The famous Bourbon nose, both aquiline and fleshy, was impressive rather than beautiful. A droop in the full lower lip revealed his descent from the Emperor Charles V. He was a voracious eater in spite of bad teeth and early stomach troubles. Robust rather than agile, he was fond of all physical exercises; he was keen on the hunt and, almost up to the last, a fine horseman. He loved to dance: long past adolescence, he appeared in ballets, clad in mythological garb. But dancing was sedate in those days: we cannot imagine Louis XIV cutting capers.

There was nothing gloomy about his constant stateliness. He was the reverse of an Oriental despot, an Ahasuerus before whom even his favorite trembles. His court never was an Escorial. It is true that he did not indulge in the gay Gascon sallies, the relapses into soldierly coarse-ness, the easy familiarities practiced—not unconsciously—by Henry IV. Every inch a king, every moment a king, Louis XIV never attempted to be popular. But he achieved the miracle of remaining erect for half a century without stiffness. He came to power a very young man, long overshadowed by his "stepfather" Mazarin, eager to rule, eager to work, and no less eager to play. In 1664 he gave at Versailles, then still a minor royal residence, a series of entertainments called *The Pleasures of the Enchanted Isle,* in the planning of which Molière played a leading part. The title was a program. He wanted his life, and that of his com-panions, to be "the Life Enchanted."

Hunting, dancing, card-playing filled the many hours not devoted to ceremonies and affairs of state. He preserved among the pleasure seekers who thronged his halls a reasonable amount of decency: boors and sharpers were soon warned off. Above all he established a standard of elegance which has not lost its appeal. It is not every sovereign, de-sirous of having a good time, who can be served by a Molière, or even by a Lulli. No doubt the pleasures he provided would sit heavily on modern shoulders: the dinners were interminable and overabundant, the furniture massive, the men's wigs formidable. The monuments of whale-bone and brocade which adorned the opulent charms of Madame de Montespan would appall the slim and lightly clad woman of today. But the contemporaries bore the burden with a smile. Versailles has been compared to a gilded cage in which the king kept a tamer's eye on his nobility: the memoirs of the time give a totally different impression. Few were the lords who, of their own accord, chose to live on their own domains and among their local friends. To be exiled from court meant a loss of opportunity and prestige; it made a man ridiculous; but above all it kept him away from the fountain of delight. Madame de Sévigné was not in constant attendance—she was the friend of men upon whom the king had frowned, Retz, La Rouchefoucauld, Fouquet. She was of a free and sprightly disposition; yet, whenever she mentions the king, she conveys the impression of perfect naturalness. Louis was a gentleman entertaining his friends. His tremendous pride created no obstacle; he knew so intuitively his own position, and everybody else's, that, himself at ease, he made almost everyone feel at ease.

His appetite for pleasure expressed itself in innumerable love affairs, from passing fancies, "the small change of adultery," to prolonged liai-sons flaunted with Jovelike cynicism. He found a Molière to condone this pagan freedom: *Un partage avec Jupiter—n'a rien du tout qui dés-honore,* There is nothing shameful about sharing with Jupiter. Bourda-loue alone, a Jesuit, dared to preach at court against his flagrant sins.

The royal lover acknowledged his bastards and gave them princely rank: he had none of the virtuous scruples which impelled Henry VIII to wed and kill. Anecdotic history dwells with delight on his paramours: the elegiac La Vallière who loved him truly and became a religious; Fontanges, best remembered for her headgear; above all, the superb Montespan, his true mate in magnificence and imperiousness, of whom Madame de Sévigné gives us a glowing vision, "all clad in gold upon gold, embroidered with gold." We said anecdotic history, for the king's amours did not interfere with his policy. Madame de Maintenon, the pious companion of his old age, belongs to a different period. The bourgeois decency of his secret marriage with her bears no resemblance to the scarlet splendor of his maturity. She was not one of his sins but part of his repentance. Contrition, unfortunately, proved more disastrous than transgression. Madame de Maintenon cannot be made responsible for the Revocation, but the favor she enjoyed and the destruction of religious freedom sprang from the same roots in the king's heart.

⚔ THE BOURGEOIS IN CONTROL: COLBERT

When we think of Louis XIV, we have two pictures in mind. The first might be an actual scene: the king at Versailles surrounded by his gorgeous courtiers; a nobleman himself, the head of their caste, their master no doubt, but a courteous and liberal master, living their life and thinking their thoughts. The other is a composite, an ideal vision, such as official artists love to paint on the walls of state palaces: the "Century of Louis XIV" and its makers. In the center the king again, inevitably; but by his side Bossuet, his ecclesiastical right arm; Colbert, his regent in economic and administrative affairs; Louvois, de Lionne, who prepared his armies and his diplomatic campaigns; Vauban, who cuirassed his kingdom with fortresses; Boileau, the dictator of Parnassus, with his friends Molière and Racine; Lulli, his musician; Le Brun, his court painter and autocrat of the fine arts; Mansard, Le Nôtre, architects in stone and living foliage; all the representatives of that classical spirit which was focused in his person; all bourgeois to a man, and some of them very modest bourgeois.[6]

Of the great servants of the regime, only the military officers belonged to the nobility: Turenne and Condé were both princes of the highest degree. In social life Louis was the leader of the nobles; in practical work he was the executive head of the *bourgeoisie*. The court was the ornament of his reign; the middle class, the instrument of his rule. Saint-Simon was conscious of this contradiction, and he denounced the age as one of "vile *bourgeoisie*." His paradox is now accepted as sober truth.

Saint-Simon was mistaken only in considering this bourgeois character as a new departure: it was almost as old as the Capetian monarchy. It is not certain that Louis XIV was conscious of the fact: no crowned Charles Maurras, he was not given to rationalizing.

This double policy—a striking example of the Classical Compromise —was ultimately to ruin the nobility and the monarchy with it. Privileges accompanied with responsibilities have some justification; the privileges of social parasites inevitably become intolerable, while the class which does the actual work will grow weary of being denied corresponding prestige. And—this is an essential theme in the history of the Ancient Regime—the king, living among his nobles, was in constant danger of becoming their prisoner in his turn. They formed a glittering screen between him and his people. Louis XIV achieved the paradox of creating the most brilliant court in history, and the most useless. The result still dazzles the world, but it was an absurdity.

Louis XIV was not Louis-Philippe, the Citizen King: he did not place his confidence in the *bourgeoisie* as a class but in individual bourgeois who were his instruments and whom he could dismiss at will. Ancient France was a tangled mass of privileges: without destroying them, Louis established everywhere, as a growing substitute, the authority of his agents. It must be noted that these privileges were not all nobiliary or ecclesiastical. Many were possessed by bourgeois: the franchises of the cities, the monopolies of the guilds, the hereditary transmission of many administrative and judicial functions. The royal officers who were working for the king—and incidentally for themselves —were thus frequently in conflict with the middle class from which they sprang.

The chief instruments of government were the intendants and the secretaries of state, or ministers. We have seen that the institution of the intendants had been greatly developed by Richelieu, but it was only under Louis XIV that the system became definite. By the side of the governors—mere titled figureheads—and of the provincial states or assemblies—historical shadows wherever they still existed—the intendants held the substance of power. They were the prototypes of Napoleon's prefects, who survive to this day.

At the controls of the huge machine were the secretaries of state, and the greatest of these was Colbert. He never was prime minister— Louis XIV would not share his absolute power—but he was the universal manager in home affairs and the economic dictator of the reign. Colbert (1619–1683) came directly out of the commercial class: his father had been a clothier at Rheims (although, like Molière's *Bourgeois Gentilhomme,* he would rather veil that awkward fact). He managed

Mazarin's scandalous fortune, and the cardinal "bequeathed" him to the king as a faithful and efficient servant. Colbert compassed the downfall of Fouquet (1661), stepped into his position, and followed his example: like his master Mazarin, he amassed a vast fortune. We must remember that under the Ancient Regime the profit motive was not accounted shameful.

It may be said that until his death the whole economic system of the realm was in his hands: he was the king's factotum. He rejoiced in hard work; he was called "the North Pole" by courtiers begging for favors; he had vast visions of maritime and colonial expansion; in his public works he showed the taste for disciplined magnificence which is the hallmark of the Louis XIV style. In the spirit of Henry IV he fostered royal manufactures, which gave France, down to our days, a place second to none in decorative arts. Thanks to his energy and to his strict accounting, France could afford for twenty years the crushing luxury of a Grand Monarch. He was the model of those great servants of the state whose breed, fortunately, is not extinct in France.

Yet it was a losing fight: for all the incomparable ability of Colbert his economic dictatorship ended in failure. The essential flaw was at the very core of the system, to which his name remains attached, Colbertism. Colbert had in economics the same conception as the old-fashioned diplomats in politics: wealth, like power and prestige, exists in limited quantity and can be acquired only at the expense of less successful rivals. The kingdom should sell more and more, buy less and less, and hoard the gold which is the ultimate reality. Although veiled in splendor, it was in fact a miser's dream. Colbertism is at present held to be an economic heresy: the prosperity of others is a condition of our own. But there are still many heretics in the councils of modern nations.

As a result of this preconception Colbert, who admired the Dutch, considered them as the natural enemies of France simply because they were a prosperous trading community. He did not overtly promote the disastrous policy which first ruined the good understanding between France and Holland and then led to a long duel in which the Sun King was finally humbled. He was not an advocate of war: he and Louvois were antagonists. But his conception of commerce was bellicose.

The second cause of Colbert's failure was the prodigality of the king: in this respect Louis forgot that *trop est trop*. Colbert could say "No" when approached by aristocratic plunderers, he could check the accounts of his subordinates, but against his sovereign he was disarmed. Louis, generous to a fault, would, like his model Jupiter, pour a shower of gold on a favorite and let Colbert do the worrying. France may be justly grateful to Louis XIV not merely for roads, canals, and manufactures

but for works of sheer beauty, for palaces, gardens, city embellish-
ments, which added much to her patrimony without imposing upon her
an intolerable burden. The Place des Victoires, the Place Vendôme, the
Colonnade of the Louvre, the Invalides, the triumphal arches of the
Saint-Martin and Saint-Denis gates bear his royal imprint, even though
they were not all due to his initiative. But the aqueduct of Maintenon
was a costly blunder; and Versailles engulfed untold millions. It may
be cheap democratic sentimentality, as Louis Bertrand would have it,
to think of the blood, sweat, and tears with which its stones are cemented. But enormous size is not beauty. It rather detracts from the
charm of the palace that its garden front should be five hundred and
eighty meters long and could boast of nearly four hundred windows.

Perhaps the deepest cause of Colbert's failure was the refusal of the
bourgeoisie to follow his lead. Until the seventeenth century, at least,
there prevailed in France a curious antieconomic prejudice. No class
was afraid or ashamed of riches, not even the clergy: Bossuet's sermon
on "The Eminent Dignity of the Poor" fell on indifferent ears. But
everyone spurned "a gainful occupation." The nobles fought (and
danced), the clerics prayed, for the good of the kingdom; but even the
bourgeois professed to despise trade and industry. Their dream was to
retire on a competence and live like gentlemen. Traces of that prejudice,
even after the revolutionary eighteenth century, were found under Napoleon: to express his bitterest contempt for the English, he called
them "a nation of shopkeepers." Only yesterday, any employment under
the state enjoyed greater prestige than a more profitable position in
commerce. Under Louis XIV France's business was not Business. The
Dutch and the English won in the end.

FUTILE MAGNIFICENCE: THE WARS

The most obvious causes of ruin were the protracted wars: four covering no less than twenty-eight years out of the fifty-four of his personal
rule. Louis himself, on his deathbed, repented his prodigality and his
thirst for glory: let us not be more Royalist than the king. All were
caused by his gluttonous craving for prestige. The French did not demand them or rejoice in them. It is highly to the credit of Boileau, a
staunch Royalist but a stauncher believer in common sense, that in his
first *Epistle* (1668) he warned the king in no equivocal terms. Playing
Cineas to Louis XIV's Pyrrhus, he was "the very sensible adviser of a
very imprudent king." Louis admired the lines, greedily swallowed the
praises, gave Boileau a pension, and disregarded his advice. When his
grandeur was at stake, he could not listen to reason.

The curse of the reign, however, was not of his own making. He found it when he began to rule in the form of that "hegemony" which had been won for France by the treaties of Westphalia and the Pyrenees. It is still the boast of conservative historians that these diplomatic triumphs had made France supreme in Europe. Louis XIV would have felt himself recreant if he had not taken full advantage of this privileged situation. As Richelieu had striven to "humble the House of Austria," so did Louis seek to keep all princes in their proper places, satellites to his sun. His ambassadors claimed precedence over all others; his flag must be saluted first on every sea. The doge of Venice was dragged to the French court to apologize for an alleged slight. Even the pope had to erect in Rome a monument commemorating some misdeed of his Corsican Guard and the full reparation the French king had exacted. It is true that after Louis XIV had provoked all Europe, even his traditional allies the Swedes, even the England of Charles II, who was in his pay, his enemies sought to pare his talons; and Royalists like Jacques Bainville claim that his wars were in defense of the national interest: a familiar fallacy, not fully exploded even in the middle of the twentieth century.

The first war started with a lawyers' quibble. When Louis married a Spanish princess, she formally renounced all claims to Spanish possessions. But since the queen's enormous dowry was not paid, it was ruled that this default voided the contract. The queen was then entitled to the reversion (*dévolution*) of certain lands, and war was made to support her "rights." In 1667 Turenne easily conquered Flanders and Condé, Franche-Comté. But England, Holland, Sweden, in alarm, formed a triple alliance. Louis had not yet lost touch with classic reasonableness; to the dismay of the war party he signed at Aix-la-Chapelle (Aachen) in 1668 a moderate peace. He kept only twelve towns in the Spanish Netherlands (the Belgium of today), the most important of which was Lille.

But Louis was incensed that the stodgy Dutch merchants should have dared to oppose him. He detached from them their allies, Sweden and England; and in 1672 he crossed the Rhine with Condé and Turenne. The doom of the little republic seemed inevitable. But the Dutch overthrew the aristocratic party, accused of timidity; the brothers John and Cornelius de Witt were massacred, and William of Orange assumed leadership. The sluices were opened; the flood protected the province of Holland and the city of Amsterdam. The spirit of the Dutch won them new allies—the elector of Brandenburg, the emperor, and even their old enemy Spain. The intended punitive expedition turned into a full-scale European war, with operations ranging from the Mediterranean to the Baltic. Condé and Turenne were still at the height of their power:

Condé, a spirited butcher, Turenne, more cautious and more humane. But it was Turenne who applied to the Palatinate a scorched-earth policy which Germany was never to forget.[7] Finally, in 1678–1679 a series of treaties were signed at Nimwegen, Fontainebleau, Lund, Saint-Germain. Louis had been checked, but he had more than held his own. He kept Franche-Comté and several places in the northeastern frontier. He could boast: *Nec pluribus impar,* not unequal to many.

Louis assumed that his fiat was law on the Continent as well as in his own realm. In 1680–1683 French courts of claims decided what lands should be "reunited" with France as a result of the recent treaties. Their decisions were immediately executed by the king's troops. Among the cities thus acquired was Strasbourg (1681), which made a show of resistance and whose loss was deeply felt even by the divided and impotent Germany of those days.

Louis was still eager for new increments to his grandeur. The Elector Palatine had died in 1685 without issue. His sister (whose uncouth manners greatly amused the French court) had married the king's brother, the duke of Orleans. But this claim was merely a starting point: the real issue was not just another province, it was European hegemony. William of Orange was the soul of resistance. The Revocation had caused indignation in Protestant Europe; the "reunions," nibbling into the Germanic body, had created dismay. So, in 1686 the League of Augsburg united the Emperor, Sweden, Spain, Bavaria, Saxony, and the Palatinate. In 1687 Savoy joined the allies. The decisive factor was the English Revolution of 1688. The Stuarts, if not the English people, had hitherto been benevolent neutrals; now William of Orange could turn the naval and economic power of the island kingdom against the pretensions of Louis XIV. It was indeed "the Grand Alliance."

After three years of cold war hostilities began in 1688. The Palatinate was invaded and, by order of Louvois, ravaged a second time with even greater thoroughness. Louis still had excellent generals, Luxembourg, Catinat, but also inept court favorites like Villeroy. He had a great admiral in Tourville, a dashing corsair in Jean Bart, the popular hero who dared to smoke his pipe at Versailles. On land he was on the whole successful, but by a slim margin. At sea the defeat of La Hougue marked the beginning of England's unquestioned naval supremacy. By the Treaty of Ryswick (1697) France lost little except some of the cities "reunited" since 1680; Strasbourg she preserved. Yet it was not a drawn peace. The Dutch were allowed to garrison fortresses in the Spanish Netherlands; and Louis XIV, abandoning his protégé and coreligionist James II, had to recognize William III as king of England.

The prestige of the king was sadly impaired; his once prosperous realm was already ruined. In his *Characters,* which appeared in 1688, La Bruyère gives a harrowing picture of rural distress even before the third war had begun. Many years of peace and economy would have been needed to restore the kingdom: four years after Ryswick Louis XIV engaged France in a desperate, gigantic, and purely dynastic adventure.

Spain was then—nation and royalty alike—the sick man of Europe, but a sick man with world-wide dominions and at least the memory of formidable power. Austria, France, and Bavaria all had claims, through the female line, on the heritage of the childless Carlos II. It would have been wise to divide the ill-assorted possessions of the Spanish crown; and two different treaties were made to that effect. But Carlos wanted his loose and crumbling empire to remain united; and he bequeathed it entire to Philip, Duke of Anjou, grandson of Louis XIV. The French king pondered, took counsel, and finally decided to accept the opportunity and the challenge. Although his grandson had formally renounced his claims to the French crown, Louis XIV uttered the fateful words, "The Pyrenees are no more."

Europe united at once into another Grand Alliance. The leading spirits (William III died in 1702) were Eugene of Savoy, Imperial general, Marlborough, consummate politician as well as strategist, and Heinsius, Grand Pensioner of Holland. France had no ally except Bavaria and Spain herself. There was no lack of able military leaders, Catinat, Villars, Vendôme, Berwick; but the Villeroy breed had multiplied. The French suffered a crushing series of defeats: best remembered is the one inflicted on Tallard by Eugene and Marlborough at Blenheim (1704).

By 1708 all seemed to be lost. France, exhausted, was fighting that last war with spendthrift's expedients. The king sold offices wholesale for cash. He sent his gold plate to the mint to be melted into bullion. He was compelled to beg for a loan from the banker Samuel Bernard; worse, he had to entertain him at Marly, his private sanctuary, where, with a few particular friends, he fled the gilded mob of Versailles. Saint-Simon witnessed what he fiercely called "this prostitution of the King."

France, however, was saved from unconditional surrender. The allies had proposed impossible terms: Louis was asked to wage war against his own grandson. He appealed to his people—for an autocrat it was an abdication—and the struggle went on. Malplaquet (1709) was another victory for Eugene and Marlborough but a costly one: the French had retired unbroken, inflicting losses greater than their own. The Whigs fell in England, and Marlborough's opponents assumed control. At

Denain (1712) Villars, to whom Louis had solemnly entrusted the last army of the kingdom, brilliantly defeated Lord Albemarle.

So the treaties of Utrecht, Rastadt, and Baden (1713–1714), which closed the long conflict, did not compass the complete downfall of France. The duke of Anjou was acknowledged as king of Spain and retained the vast Spanish colonies. France lost some of her North American possessions but preserved her European conquests. Still, the French could not forget the initial folly, the gross mismanagement, the intolerable hardships of this dynastic war. We, detached observers, may admire the somber dignity of the great king in defeat; but the sufferers hated and despised him. They turned his funeral into a festivity. As the royal procession skirted Paris on its way from Versailles to Saint-Denis, it passed by a long line of men singing, jeering, and carousing. The union of France with her dynasty was not wholly shattered. But faith in traditional authority could no longer be entire. Reason, long held in check, freely asserted itself. The days of the classical compromise were numbered.

⚜ THE STIFLING OF RELIGIOUS DISSENT

It was, however, in the domain of religion that Louis XIV dealt the severest blow to the ideal of classic reasonableness after practicing it for nearly two decades.

The Catholicism of the seventeenth century, although not so rich in violent contrasts as that of the Middle Ages, was far from offering absolute unity. Within the fold could be found scholars such as Bérulle, founder of the Oratorians, and Olier, who created the great Saint-Sulpice Seminary; ascetics such as Rancé, who fled the world and started the rigorous Trappists; aggressive laymen such as Henri de Lévis, Duke of Ventadour, who was the moving spirit in the Company of the Holy Sacrament; practical men like St. Vincent de Paul and Bossuet; pessimistic fatalists like the Jansenists ("Grace given to but a few"); optimistic fatalists like the Quietists [8] ("Rest in Him Whose purpose is our good"); not to mention Laodiceans and pious worldlings innumerable. The king in the first twenty years of his personal reign admirably preserved his equilibrium: to listen to Bourdaloue and keep Madame de Montespan was in itself a marvelous balancing feat. "Libertines" were discouraged (at that time the term denoted freethinkers), but so were religious bigots. The Company of the Holy Sacrament, a secret society to promote Catholic interests, was dissolved in 1666. The king accorded his protection to Molière; and the public performance of *Tartuffe* (1669), a daring satire on hypocrisy, proved that the French would brook no inquisition, whether of the Dominicans or of a "devout cabal." Peace was imposed for a decade (1669–1679) upon the theologians fiercely battling over free will and predestination.

In that quest for the middle road, the king's hardest task was to reconcile Gallicanism, asserting the ancient liberties of the French Church, and ultramontanism, devoted first of all to the Holy See. Louis freely quarreled with the pope as a secular sovereign; he even threatened to confiscate Avignon. He allowed the assembly of his clergy, under the leadership of his confidential adviser Bossuet, to vote a Declaration in four articles (1682) which reasserted Gallican autonomy. Many of the secular clerics, and most of the king's officers, particularly the judges in Parlement, were Gallicans at heart. To some foreign observers France seemed on the brink of a schism. On the other hand the confessors of Louis XIV were Jesuits. It was even claimed that the king was secretly affiliated with their order known as the Militia of the Holy See. In 1693 a compromise ended the deadlock but not the ambiguity. Gallicanism remained officially condemned in Rome, officially enforced in Paris. No one knew for certain, at any moment, whether the king would stand by the Holy Father or by his own courts of justice; and the two parties, contending with mellifluous acrimony, were officially on the best of terms. The vaunted Anglican compromise was child's play in comparison.

The same tremulous balance was preserved with regard to Protestantism. The Huguenots had remained quiet during the *Fronde*. They were no longer a political party but useful citizens whom Colbert appreciated. Turenne was a great personage at court as well as a trusted commander in the field, although he was not formally converted until 1668. Schomberg, a Protestant, became a marshal of France and Duquesne, an admiral. Conrart, Permanent Secretary of the Academy, to which prelates eagerly sought admission, was a Huguenot.

There was no sudden change of heart on the part of Louis XIV. Twenty years of autocracy slowly corrupted him. The new generation had been brought up in an atmosphere of enthusiastic submission; almost unconsciously, the king had weeded out or snubbed all would-be critics. With age he grew more austere but also more fanatical. He felt increasingly that the survival of heresy in his kingdom was a scandal, that even dissent was an insult. Perhaps he saw the need, in his conflict with the pope, to reassure his clergy and himself about his orthodoxy.

Of this more rigorous attitude the Jansenists were the first victims. The "Peace of the Church" ended in 1679. Arnauld, their head, had to flee. The king's wrath vented itself on the pitiful remnants of the group. Finally, in 1709–1710, the survivors, aged and indomitable nuns, were dispersed into different convents, the buildings of Port-Royal destroyed, and the very tombs of the leaders desecrated.

Against the Huguenots, Louis proceeded at first with slow, barely conscious steps. The Edict of Nantes remained the law of the land, but it was construed in the strictest possible manner, whittling down the privileges granted by Henry IV. Conversions were encouraged; Bossuet, skilled in controversy and master of spiritual diplomacy, showed himself efficient in that work, as in all others. Converts like Pellisson were used to entice or bribe their former coreligionists. Madame de Maintenon herself was the niece of the great Huguenot poet Agrippa d'Aubigné, and she founded at Saint-Cyr a school for the daughters of converts. Louis was possibly half sincere when he professed to believe that the R.P.R. (religion pretending to be reformed) was moribund. In 1682 methods of violence were frankly restored to by the intendants. Quartering dragoons in the homes of recalcitrant Huguenots began in 1684. By 1685 the outward manifestation of the "disease" had practically disappeared. Officially, there were no more Protestants except a handful of perverse agitators. So, amid the acclaim of classical France and Catholic Europe, the Edict of Nantes, no longer needed, was revoked (1685).

The miscalculation was soon apparent. A vast exodus took place, causing the severest hardships. A whole population of grave, well-educated bourgeois, prosperous merchants, skilled artisans left France: the silk industry of Tours, for example, was entirely ruined. England, Holland, Brandenburg received with joy these valuable recruits. French Huguenot names still survive among the Boers of South Africa, and among the most anti-French families of the Prussian aristocracy. The peasants of the Cévennes Mountains rose up in arms, and held the royal troops at bay: they could be quelled only through the skill, diplomatic as well as military, of Marshal Villars.

For a whole century the Protestants had no legal standing, and the clergy constantly grumbled at the grudging tolerance which permitted them to exist at all.[9] Persecution does at times achieve its object. The Huguenots were crushed and even under a regime of liberty never could regain their former importance. Jansenism flared up several times in the eighteenth century, and the suppression of the Jesuits in 1762 was to some extent the belated revenge of Port-Royal. But royal orthodoxy prevailed. Only it was a Pyrrhic victory. The result was that free thought, instead of austere Christian churches, became the sole force of opposition to oppressive bigotry. The dragoons of Louis XIV had cleared the path for Voltaire.

⚔ THE LONELY SUMMIT: PASCAL

In closing this study of the Classical Compromise, so successful for twenty years that it seemed eternal, we cannot forget that it never represented the whole of French culture. Men conformed to a style, and a most impressive style it was; but their thoughts remained free, and therefore diverse. The books of the skeptics Montaigne and Charron were still the breviaries of educated men. Descartes was a power; and cautious as he was in his practical life, he had uttered the irrevocable words, "We should never accept a thing as true unless we know it clearly and evidently to be such." In Molière there is no trace of supernatural Christianity: his ideal—moderation, sanity, honesty, courage—is that of the pagan philosophers, of the average sensual man, the sensible man of the world, *l'honnête homme.*

A compromise means not wholeness but duality. This essential duality of the French classical soul—humanistic rationalism on the one hand, the Christian and monarchical tradition on the other—never worried Louis XIV, who was no philosopher. But it was most tragically felt by Pascal: Pascal was a genius and a saint, whilst Louis was neither.[10] The most pitiless of logicians, the most ardent of believers, he was hoping, in his *Apology for the Christian Religion,* to bring together the two extremes of his being. He died at thirty-nine and left only a heap of sublime fragments. The mystery, the contradictions, the abysses of human destiny he expressed with a quivering dread unique in literature. The absolute victory of faith, the personal union of the soul with God, he also voiced in words of fire. But what of the bridge across the chasm, what of the attempted reconciliation between reason and historical Christanity? At one time—a counsel of despair—Pascal urges us to stifle reason, to seek refuge in "practices" that will stupefy our intellect. At another time he advises us to "bet on Christianity": again an abdication not a demonstration. Pascal was too great to find comfort in the classical compromise. In the perspective of centuries his tragic figure dwarfs all those who followed the middle road. An age, a country, which produced a Pascal cannot be summed up in a Louis XIV.

CHAPTER XV

Louis XV: The Absentee King and the Enlightenment

⚔ THE REGENCY

Louis XIV had his son, the grand dauphin, trained by Bossuet; his eldest grandson, the duke of Burgundy, by Fénelon. Both died before him, and the crown went to his great-grandson, a child of five. The one principle of the new government was to reverse in all things the policies of its predecessors. The duke of Orleans, who became regent, was almost driven in self-defense to adopt such an attitude. Louis distrusted him: not daring to deprive the first prince of the blood of the Regency, he had attempted to rob him, in advance, of any real power. One of his bastards by Madame de Montespan, the duke of Maine, made a legitimate prince, was to be in actual control. The regent thus had to exorcize the ghost of the Grand Monarch, tyrannical beyond the tomb. The will of Louis XIV was set aside by the Parlement, which thus recovered its quasi-political prerogatives. Whilst Louis had waged a ruinous war to establish his grandson on the Spanish throne, France, now in alliance with England, aided her in destroying the navy, the fortresses, the arsenals of Bourbon Spain.

As for thirty dreary years morose piety had been the rule, incredulity and licentiousness were now given free scope. When morality becomes discredited because of excessive gloom, hypocrisy, or intolerance, an antipuritanical reaction is inevitable: so it was in England under the restored Stuarts; so it was to be in France when the Thermidorians overthrew Robespierre, apostle of terror and virtue. The regent himself and other great lords like Vendôme set the fashion. The aura of elegant wickedness which appeared under the Regency lasted to the very end of the Ancient Regime, in spite of a notable upsurge of "virtue" under Louis XVI. Great minds, Montesquieu, Voltaire, Diderot, Mirabeau, were not free from the taint; the last years of the monarchy saw the works of Choderlos de Laclos, Louvet, and the Marquis de Sade.

The regent himself was an equivocal, a disquieting personage. Accused of monstrous vices, he was confessedly a rake, a roué, too honest to pay virtue even a hypocritical homage. Self-indulgent, he was indulgent with others. This facility, this freedom from prejudices, gave him the renown of being liberal and humane. But he was too indolent to be genuinely kind: he could be high-handed if he thought brutality would save him trouble. Too slothful to govern by himself, he never thought of consulting the people. So, under the posthumous influence of Fénelon (who died in 1715) and that of Saint-Simon and of Boulainvilliers, the reaction against Louis XIV's tyranny took at first an aristocratic turn. For the seven or eight ministers, accused of being servile instruments of royal despotism, seven or eight councils were substituted in which the nobles had a predominant voice. But the nobles were unprepared for this responsibility, and the cumbrous "Polysynody" collapsed after three years (1715–1718).

So, Philip of Orleans fell back upon the usual expedient of lazy princes: he turned the government over to a factotum. He had already entrusted the conduct of foreign affairs to his old tutor, Abbé Dubois; he now made him in fact a prime minister. Dubois may not have been "the battle ground of all the vices," as Saint-Simon described him; at any rate, he was fit company for the regent. His greatest achievement in his adventurous career was to secure for himself a cardinal's hat, less as an honor than as a safeguard; for in France it is not etiquette to hang a prince of the Church. The precaution was unnecessary: Dubois died in office, and Philip followed him within four months. The great financial experiment under the Regency, John Law's bold banking scheme and its collapse, will be discussed in its place.

✍ THE BORED IRONIST: LOUIS XV AND HIS FAVORITES

The King reached his technical majority in 1723. He was, of course, unfit to govern. For three years the duke of Bourbon, chiefly advised by the financier Paris-Duverney, was a very indifferent prime minister. At last the boy king, who hated new faces and responsibilities, asserted himself enough to call in his old tutor Abbé (soon Cardinal) Fleury: his irresponsible childhood could thus be indefinitely prolonged. The septuagenarian cleric administered the kingdom honestly, economically—of course the courtiers called him parsimonious—and above all, cautiously. His guiding thought, at home, was to let sleeping dogs lie; abroad, to preserve the peace. In this he was in agreement with his contemporary Sir Robert Walpole, and to these tranquil years France owed much of the prosperity which characterized the middle of the century. A lenitive regime: but France had never been more keenly awake. Fleury was unable, however, to avert the foolish War of the Austrian Succession. He died in office, at ninety, in 1743.

France expected that, at long last, the king would now assert himself. Monarchical sentiment had not waned: the prolonged effacement of the monarch had served the royal cause. The errors of Louis XIV were ascribed to his insane pride not to the principle of his rule. The handsome, timid little boy, so frail, surviving alone amid the ruins of his race, had appealed to the heart of his people. When he assumed personal power in 1743, there was a tremor of hope. When in 1744, on his way to the front, he fell dangerously ill at Metz, masses by the thousand were said for his recovery. He deserved then the title which was to become so bitterly ironical, the Well-Beloved.

But he refused his place at the head of the state and in the hearts of his subjects: he remained a figurehead. As such he was not devoid of majesty and grace. He preserved in public ceremonies an Olympian aloofness which was but a kingly mask for his utter indifference. He was no coward: once at least, at Fontenoy, he displayed physical courage. He was not stupid: taciturn, even sullen, in his boyhood, he had been turned by the sisters De Nesle—three of them in succession—into a courtly gentleman. With his friends he was pleasant, even witty. Madame de Pompadour retained her empire over him through her cleverness, her delicate taste, her social charm, rather than through mere physical attractiveness. A deplorable husband, even as royal husbands went in those days, he was an excellent father; with his daughters in particular he could be unaffected and cheerful. There was nothing morbid or monstrous about him as there was about Nero or the last three Valois. He was simply spoiled, but spoiled unto rottenness.

Alone on his artifical Olympus, untrained except to laziness, prejudiced and unprincipled, timid at heart while absurdly proud, superstitious and skeptical, he yawned his life away. State business, which had engrossed his predecessor, bored him unutterably. In council he hardly opened his mouth, and then only to reveal the vacuity of his mind. He found more pleasure in petty intrigue: he had his secret police, his secret diplomacy; he was accused of speculating secretly on the wheat market. But these pastimes failed to amuse him for long: he could not take them seriously enough to play the game. All his life was a pretense; he was himself a pretense. He had flashes of Voltarian irony in which the utter futility of it all was revealed to him. "Do not invest in royal securities," he advised one of his business agents, "they say it is not safe." And posterity remembers his cries of cynical despair, "Bah! the old machine will last out my time, at any rate!" and "After us, the deluge!"

What wonder if in this wasteland he should clutch at pleasure, "the one thing as certain as death?" Louis XIV had shown the way; the regent had flaunted his vices. The court was even less squeamish than the king: temptation was forced upon him. Courtiers affected to admire the "constancy in inconstancy" that impelled him to take three sisters one after the other; and the one objection raised at first against Jeanne-Antoinette Poisson, Dame d'Étioles and later marquise de Pompadour, was that she, a mere bourgeoise, was poaching on the preserves of the nobility.

Madame de Pompadour's career was a triumph of the will. She had consciously—we might say conscientiously—prepared herself for her dazzling destiny. Louis, as soon as he saw the young queen of financial society, was subjugated. But mere beauty would not have preserved his favor many months: she kept it for twenty years until her death in 1764. Her daily existence was a combat: against the Church, against the nobility, against possible rivals, against the eternal *taedium vitae* that was devouring the king. In the chaos that reigned in France's diplomatic and military affairs it is hard to tell whether the foreign policy she advocated was worse than any possible alternative; since it failed disastrously, she had to bear the blame before the contemporaries and before posterity. At home, at any rate, her influence was fairly steadily on the liberal side. She protected Voltaire, like herself a parvenu of wit; and, according to Condorcet, she even wanted to make him a cardinal. She helped the *Encyclopedia*.

Above all she deserved to give her name to a period in French culture akin to the Regency but less crudely immoral and decidedly more enlightened. An artist of some talent herself, a consummate actress, of course, a musician, a painter, etcher, engraver, she was a generous and intelligent patroness. Her group—her fatherly protector Tournehem, her brother Marigny—officially directed French art for two generations; and the result of their guidance is not to be despised. Strangely perhaps, her predilections in art were chaste; she reacted against the rococo, a prettified baroque which may truly be called "dissolute." It was in 1752, when she was at the height of her influence, that Gabriel drew the plans for the Place de la Concorde, unique in its gracious stateliness.

Even the marvelous resourcefulness of the marquise, however, failed to monopolize the interest of the king. She had, willy nilly, to share the fate of legitimate queens and acknowledge the existence of rivals; she had even to treat them with friendliness, as Louis XV's consort, placid and kindly Marie Leczinska, treated her. Legend has no doubt magnified the debauchery of Louis XV, and his private establishment of the *Parc aux Cerfs* was in all likelihood not so horrific as it has remained in popular imagination. But advancing years neither moderated nor refined the lust of the monarch.

The court, so hostile at first to Madame de Pompadour, a bourgeoise, welcomed without a qualm Marie-Jeanne Bécu, Countess du Barry, a mere courtesan (1769–1774). The king had become merely an old man seeking amusement and illusion. The Du Barry was pretty, vivacious, refreshingly vulgar, madly prodigal, yet not sordidly grasping. They played housekeeping together in their cozy little apartment, an oasis in the dreary splendor of Versailles; and when their coffeepot boiled over, she cried: *Eh! La France! Ton café fout le camp!* [1] At councils of state she would sit on the arm of the royal chair making faces at the ministers and interfering in national affairs with the irresponsibility of a pet monkey. Her influence was not wholly pernicious: since she was a mere instrument, she served at times defensible causes without an inkling of the real issue.

We should not have mentioned this prolonged and shameful affair if it did not throw such a glaring light upon hereditary absolutism. France offered for sixty years the strange spectacle of an acephalous autocracy, a crown without a head. The absentee king, bored by etiquette as well as by business, could find no escape except in pleasure; and he finally accepted a priestess of pleasure from the gutter. Once he was teasing Choiseul about some love scandal, "Be careful, Choiseul, your soul is in peril!" The minister dared to reply, "What about your own, Sire?" "Oh!" the king answered, "my case is different: *I am the Lord's Anointed.*" The magnificent fallacy of Bossuet about the divine right of kings needed such a *reductio ad absurdum*.

✍ VELLEITIES OF ENLIGHTENED DESPOTISM

Yet, at the end of his reign the crushing part of an "enlightened despot" was forced upon Louis XV. It was one of the most confusing episodes in an age of universal confusion.[2]

Three ministers, D'Argenson, Machault, Choiseul, had made spasmodic efforts to remedy the abysmal disorder of the kingdom. All three found themselves opposed by the profiteers of anarchy, courtiers and hereditary bureaucrats. The stronghold of their resistance was the Parlement of Paris, posing as the defender of "ancient liberties." We have seen that the Parlements had been curbed by Louis XIV and reduced to their primary function, the administration of justice. But they had never given up their claims to be "sovereign courts," co-ordinate with the monarchy. They were confirmed in this exalted view of their office by the regent, who needed them in order to annul the testament of Louis

XIV: the right of "remonstrating" was restored to them. Such an abridgment of absolutism might seem a conquest for liberty, and it would have been if the Parlements had represented anything but themselves. As it was, they formed a small, selfish, reactionary caste; the restoration of their privileges was a victory for the spirit of privilege.

Finally, Choiseul's successor, Maupeou, boldly attacked this central fortress of abuses. In 1771 the magistrates of the Paris Parlement were exiled from the capital. Their offices were confiscated, and other judges appointed. Their investment in their function was declared redeemable, but the further sale of judiciary positions was abolished. The unwieldy territorial jurisdiction of the Paris Parlement was divided into five Supreme Councils of Justice. Some provincial courts were reorganized on the same pattern. The sweeping reform was heartily approved by liberal opinion, particularly by Voltaire and Turgot. Even some conservatives applauded: the Parlement, with its Gallican and Jansenist tendencies and its hostility to the Jesuits, had incurred the enmity of many Catholics.

Unfortunately, France had little confidence in the ministers [3] and even less in the king. The new courts, called in derision the Maupeou Parlements, were not free from the worst abuses of the old. By immemorial tradition the judges were entitled to presents (called *épices,* or spices) from the parties. The Maupeou judges did not frown upon that profitable custom; at least, they allowed their wives to collect perquisites. Unfortunately, one of them, Goezman, ran afoul of the redoubtable adventurer Beaumarchais, one of the cleverest men in that century of cleverness. Openly defrauded by the judge's wife, repeatedly condemned and censored as well as robbed, Beaumarchais carried the case before the tribunal of public opinion in a series of *Memoranda* (1773–1774) which anticipated the brilliancy and the comic power of his Figaro plays. Beaumarchais himself was on the liberal side. He was to aid, very efficiently, the struggling American colonies; and he is considered one of the fathers of the French Revolution. Unwittingly, as a result of private wrong, he had struck a blow for privilege. When Louis XV died, his successor restored the old Parlements.

WAR IS THE SPORT OF PRINCES

The foreign policy of such a regime may easily be imagined: it was sheer caprice on an epic scale. When thought is paralyzed, tradition fills the interim: for many years, dazzled by the success of Richelieu and Mazarin, French diplomats, on sheer momentum, were still bent on "humbling the House of Austria." The policy of the reign was purely dynastic: it was Bourbonian not French. It succeeded ultimately in link-ing through a rather uncertain family pact the Bourbons of France, those of Spain, and those of Naples (1761). Like those of Louis XIV the conflicts in which Louis XV was engaged were wars of succession: the confused aftermath of the Spanish Succession (1718–1720), the half-hearted and rather disgraceful War of the Polish Succession (1733–1738), in which a French diplomat, Count de Plelo, quixotically showed the world "how to die for Danzig"; the full-size, many-angled, protracted War of the Austrian Succession (1740–1748). Even the last and most disastrous of all, the Seven Years' War, was at first but a renewal of the feud between Austria and Prussia, the second war caused by the Austrian Succession. Back of the two great wars there was in fact a duel for colonial empire between England and France; they were episodes in what Seeley called the Third Hundred Years' War (1688–1815). But of this neither the French leaders nor the masses of the French people were fully aware.

War was then the sport of princes for the benefit of princes. In the gamble they might win or lose a province: Belgium, Sicily, Tuscany, Sardinia, Lorraine changed rulers without any thought of the sentiments or interests of the population. Louis, royally bored, was not even interested in the stakes: when peace was discussed at Aix-la-Chapelle, he superbly declared that he was waging war like a king not like a merchant. This lofty indifference to gain, this Art-for-Art's-Sake attitude, gave rise to a brace of proverbial expressions, "As stupid as the peace. . . ." and "To work for the king of Prussia."

To this dynastic sport the common people and many elements in good society were utterly indifferent. Hirelings led by foreign hirelings, such as Löwendahl, and above all Marshal de Saxe (Maurice of Saxony, bastard of the Polish king), were fighting—beyond the confines of France, fortunately—for lawyers' squabbles which even the lawyers did not understand. The victory of Fontenoy (1745) created some official elation, because the king had deigned to grace the slaughter with his presence. It is said that the French, with true Louis-Quinze courtesy, bade the English fire away first: eight hundred men fell, and the line was broken; but it was a *beau geste*. Saxe and Löwendahl retrieved the day. It was a glorious victory, duly celebrated in an elegant and frigid poem by Voltaire, at that time in favor with the court.

But as a rule, indifference prevailed. The French had to pay the pipers, and the fees were heavy. They could not call the tune, but they reserved the right of hissing the performers. When the marshal-duke of Richelieu, grand-nephew of the cardinal and a noted profligate, conquered and ransacked Hanover, he won for himself the nickname, "Little Father Plunder." When Soubise was defeated by Frederick of Prussia at Rossbach (1757), a mocking Parisian song had him say, "Where the deuce is my army? I am sure it was there yesterday morning!" How could patriots (the word was just starting on its great career) be loyal to an incompetent, self-seeking, cosmopolitan crew? At any rate, this indifference saved them from hatred. Never have England and France stood so close in culture as during this century of constantly recurring warfare. Not only between campaigns but in the thick of hostilities English visitors flocked to Paris and were received with cordiality. Society in the eighteenth century was singularly civilized and considered war as a "gothic" anachronism. Yet Frederick II of Prussia, the Philosopher-King, who liked to speak French and to surround himself with Frenchmen, was a great favorite with his official "enemies" in Paris. He could hardly be considered as an angel of peace, but *philosophie* does not imply consistency.

In Europe these four futile wars cost France blood, treasure, and prestige but no territorial loss. On the contrary, the situation of Lorraine, long ambiguous, was favorably settled at last. It was given for life to Stanislas Leczinski, dethroned king of Poland and father of the French queen. At his death (1766) the duchies of Bar and Lorraine, long French in culture, reverted to the royal domains.[4]

The naval and colonial contest with England, on the other hand, was wholly disastrous. Until 1756 France had held her own: the peace of 1748 had arranged for the mutual restoration of conquests. A vigorous governor, Dupleix, had started in India a policy of active intervention in the quarrels and ambitions of the local princes. The English did not fail to imitate this method, which ultimately changed a trading company into an empire. The vast holdings of France in North America, Canada and Louisiana, linked by the Ohio and Mississippi valleys, formed a barrier to the westward expansion of the British colonies. But this immense line was tenuously held; the French were few in their boundless possessions, and even with their redskin allies they could hardly hope to stem the progress of the more numerous and richer British settlers. Aid from France would have been needed; and France was compelled, then as under Napoleon, to consider continental Europe as her prime concern. When Montcalm asked for reinforcements in Canada, the minister replied, "When the house is on fire, no one has time to bother about the stables." By the Treaty of Paris in 1763 France had to acknowledge England's predominance in India; Canada was lost ("A few acres of snow!" said Voltaire); Louisiana was turned over to Spain in compensation for Florida, which she had ceded to England. France made repeated efforts to reconstitute her colonial empire, and, under the Third

Republic, she succeeded at last. But at no time could England's supremacy be seriously challenged again.

🖎 A BANKRUPT STATE, A PROSPEROUS FRANCE

At the death of Louis XIV France was ruined. Peace and hard work could restore the prosperity of the country, but not the solvency of the state. For the financial practices of the ancient monarchy seemed perversely devised to create and perpetuate chaos.

The most obvious cause of this abysmal confusion was the irresponsible prodigality of the court. As the king's word was law, so his signature was gold, and he gave it with lordly munificence. Splendor was his attribute and almost his duty: any bourgeois limitation on his spending would have been *lèse-majesté*. In spite of Louis XIV's deathbed repentance his successors could never learn wisdom. Not even Louis XVI, whose intentions were upright and whose personal tastes were simple.

A second cause of financial distress was the extreme reluctance of the privileged orders to submit to taxation. There was in this more than common selfishness: it was a point of honor, a last survival of the feudal spirit. The lords still considered themselves as petty sovereigns: to their suzerain they owed loyalty and service, but a monetary tribute would have been humiliating. As for the Church, her property belonged to God and to the poor: it stood among those things which were not Caesar's. All that the clergy consented to do was to vote, in solemn assembly, a "free gift" (*don gratuit*) to the crown. When pride, prejudice, and interest unite, their combination is formidable indeed. The monarchy was increasingly striving to carry on a national policy, but with a fiscal system which was still to a large extent feudal. The same difficulties are encountered today by those countries which are attempting a policy of social welfare, while their mode of raising revenue remains that of the capitalistic era.

Had the feudal nobility and the clergy alone claimed exemption, there would have been definite limits to the evil. But, for reasons both of pride and of profit, the richest bourgeois bought themselves either offices or estates which made them nobles and saved them from the disgraceful necessity of paying taxes like commoners. The sale of such immunities was therefore a desperate expedient: the king received immediate cash payment but forfeited future returns.[5]

Finally, the method of collection was faulty in the extreme. It was based on the principle that private enterprise is invariably more efficient than bureaucratic management. So the taxes were leased, or farmed out, to contractors, individuals or companies, like the publicans of ancient Rome. These *fermiers généraux, partisans,* or *traitants,* as they were called, wrung from the people the uttermost farthing, and returned to the king as little as they dared. Thus men like Crozat or Samuel Bernard acquired enormous fortunes and could impose their terms upon the sovereign himself.

The situation seems intolerable to us, and so it appeared to enlightened contemporaries. Boisguillebert in his *Détail de la France,* a searching inquiry (1695), dared to propose a radical simplification of the fiscal system; and Marshal Vauban, the great builder of fortresses, advocated a royal tithe.[6] Both were sternly rebuked. This resistance to reform is easy to understand. Chaos was immemorial, and therefore hallowed, in an age which still revered tradition; reform was radical, that is to say crackbrained. In the defense of the past all the elites were united: nobility, clergy, magistrates, bourgeois eager to turn gentlemen, financiers and their retainers. Only the common people suffered, and, apart from the lone daring cry of La Bruyère, they had no voice.

The regent was open-minded, well-meaning, and, in reaction against the repressive methods of Louis XIV, not averse to radical measures. So he favored the dazzling scheme of the financial wizard John Law: he picked out as his adviser the one Scot who was the reverse of thrifty. John Law (1671–1729), however, was no swindler and no quack. The son of a banker, he had, after a stormy youth, studied commercial methods where they had reached their utmost development, in Holland. He offered his system to Louis XIV in 1708, but he was expelled as a Protestant and a suspicious character. The Regency gave him his chance. His full plan was nothing less than an economic revolution: a Royal Bank was to manage the trade and currency of the kingdom, collect taxes, and, incidentally, free the country from debt.

In 1716 the Banque Générale was created as a private institution. It absorbed much of the depreciated government paper and eased the treasury. As a bank it was an instant success. This auspicious beginning enabled Law to extend the field of his operations. He felt that an expansive economy was the only permanent way out of the financial morass. So he bought from Crozat the monopoly of the Mississippi trade and created the Louisiana Company. This undertaking was also sound in principle, and it started well: ports, cities, vessels were actually built. In December, 1718, Law's bank became a state institution. Next, he consolidated with his own the old Companies of the East Indies and of China: he had now a practical monopoly of France's overseas trade. Finally, he took over the management of the national debt. All was developing according to plan; it was breathtaking, but not frenzied.

The frenzy was provided by the subscribers. Totally unprepared for this revolution in finance, they thought that an era of miracles had opened. Speculation was not checked by experience or common sense. The Rue Quincampoix, where the bank had its offices, became a riotous open-air exchange. In the crazy mob ladies of fashion jostled their own valets. Fortunes were made in a few hours: slower and safer was the rise to affluence of a hunchback who rented his hump as a writing desk.

Law had clearly felt the need of solid activities as a basis for this dizzy paper wealth. But neither the Louisiana swamps nor the hazardous trade with the Far East was capable of sudden returns. Meanwhile, the nominal value of the shares went skyrocketing. The "bubble" was bound to burst, as did the South Sea bubble in London a few months later. Law himself might have saved something of the enterprise, for he was resourceful as well as honest. But he was swept aside and died in exile, impoverished and forgotten. Titled investors, the duke of Bourbon at their head, sent trucks to the company's headquarters and carted away gold in exchange for their paper: by the same stroke, they started the panic and made it irremediable. Four financiers, the brothers Pâris, opponents of the system, liquidated the situation with ruthlessness. The baseless fabric of Law's vision left not a rack behind.

The moral—more accurately the demoralizing—effect was great and lasting. The brief fever had further confounded the social anarchy which marked the Regency. For a few months both aristocratic blood and honest toil were at a discount: luck, daring, and freedom from scruples opened the way to riches. This fever abated, but the crash created in France an invincible distrust of credit finance. The bourgeois, chastened, went back to their exclusive faith in saving one by one their hard-earned pennies until a field, a house, or a government bond could be bought. This pardonable timidity of the middle class was never fully conquered, even during the Second Empire, financially the most modern, the most "American," of all French regimes. Thrift and caution are still solid virtues, but fortune favors the bold.

If the people as a whole remained averse to credit, in which they saw nothing but gambling and profiteering, the professional financiers had learned a few tricks which increased their power. They were a rising class even before the advent of Law, and they assumed a conspicuous place in society. They bought titles, and they bought noble connections. Great families were only too willing to "regild their scutcheons," as the saying was, or in cruder terms, "to manure their lands" with the wealth of a successful commoner. They had their handsome *hôtels* or private residences in the Faubourg Saint-Honoré, their *"folies"* in the suburbs, their *châteaux* in the country. They patronized magnificently art and literature. They were on friendly terms with philosophers: Madame d'Épinay was the friend of Grimm and Diderot and gave Rousseau a home. Indeed, they might be philosophers themselves, like Helvetius, or scientists of the highest order, like Lavoisier. More vital, freer from prejudices than the old aristocracy, they might have been a power for liberal reform, and at the same time for stability. But their position, however brilliant, remained ambiguous. Distrusted by the people, they were not frankly accepted by the nobles; "the sword" and "the gown" both spurned the parvenu moneybags and treated them with insolence while accepting their riches. There is more wounded vanity than democratic feeling in the deadly epigrams of *Figaro;* and Beaumarchais, who heralded the Revolution, was an adventurer of finance.

Corruption and extravagance, shameful failures in war and diplomacy, blind opposition to reform, cynical profiteering: our view of the Louis XV era, so far, has been almost uniformly dark. But if we were to accept this view as a complete picture of France, it would be totally misleading. Repeatedly—and down to the time of the Fourth Republic—the French have been better than their government. France was then creating wealth and artistic masterpieces; and, in politics, science, philosophy, religion, thinking more intensely and more lucidly than ever before. Never had her social and cultural prestige stood so high. In spite of the royal figurehead this was truly, as Michelet called it, "the great century."

Our theme has been the growth of France through the Capetian dynasty; but the boundless egotism of aging Louis XIV, the incurable indifference of Louis XV, had inexorably destroyed this identity of king and country. France was outgrowing her crown. It would take perhaps two hundred years for the divorce to be complete. But the rift was apparent in 1715 and became irreparable in 1789.

So, in the eighteenth century, the traditional institutions, monarchy, nobility, aristocratic higher clergy, the hereditary magistracy, the universities, were all in decadence; but the country itself was sturdier than ever. France knew internal peace. In this the reign of Louis XV was eminently successful. The intrigues of factions might lead to the overthrow of a favorite but did not create the slightest threat of civil war. The incompetence of diplomats and commanders was not punished by invasion. The breaking down of prejudice, so manifest under the Regency, released energies which were felt even in the economic field. On the whole the eighteenth century, from 1715 to 1789, was a period of expanding prosperity. This has left traces visible today. The refined luxury of innumerable private residences would not perhaps be conclusive evidence: it gave employment, at any rate, to a host of unrivaled craftsmen. More striking is the extent, solidity, and finish of the public works. The highways of Sully and Colbert were perfected by Trudaine and remained a model until the automobile revolution. In spite of the long naval wars the ports were thriving, particularly Nantes and Bordeaux. Their wealth expressed itself in splendid urban developments. Under King Stanislas, Nancy was turned into a gem: a city which is at the same time a park, a palace, and a drawing room. Even the wall erected round Paris by the hated tax contractors, to the loud grumbling of the populace,[7] was adorned at every gate with the charming pavilions of Ledoux, all different, all picturesque, impressive, and daring, yet with a smiling classic grace.

This prosperity reached deep: even the eternal victim, the peasant, had his modest share. He had to be constantly on his guard against the official plunderers, but he managed to outwit them. The most curious document on this point is provided by Jean-Jacques Rousseau. Lost in one of his aimless wanderings, tired and hungry, he asked a villager for supper. He was offered the most miserable fare, skimmed milk and coarse barley bread. When the farmer found out that he was a bona fide traveler and not an agent of the dreaded tax gatherers, he brought out from a secret recess an excellent wheat loaf, a delicious ham, a bottle of wine, and prepared a thick omelet for good measure. The man was well off: he had to simulate poverty, so unjust and so crushing were the taxes. Rousseau then swore "unextinguishable hatred" against the oppressors.[8] A man who is wholly destitute may sink into listless despair; one who is prospering but prevented from enjoying his well-earned comfort will inevitably rebel. It is this sharp contrast between official France, wasteful, incompetent, oppressive, and real France, wide awake and energetic, that was to cause the Revolution.

⚜ THE ENLIGHTENMENT: *The Salons*

While the French state was threatened with bankruptcy, while the French arms were disastrously defeated on land and sea, French culture reached its zenith. Its language, its arts, its manners, its thought had peacefully conquered Europe. It was a moment comparable with the thirteenth century, when *Opus Francigenum,* the French style of architecture, was followed from Scandinavia to Portugal and Cyprus, when the University of Paris was the spiritual center of the world, when the French tongue was declared "the most delectable and the most familiar to all people."

This period is known as *le Siècle des Lumières,* the Enlightenment, an apter term than "the Age of Reason." It did not burst upon the world on the death of Louis XIV. As historical units centuries, of course, are the merest conventions. Reigns, whether of autocrats like Louis XIV or of figureheads like Victoria, have greater validity, but even they are arbitrary divisions in the life of a people. Between the France of 1648, the France of 1668, the France of 1688, the France of 1708 there were profound differences in prosperity, power, and temper which the majestic presence of the same sovereign could not fully conceal. Even cultural patterns, so dear to anthropologists, are apt to be delusive. Pascal soars above his age: to understand him we should think of Job, St. Paul, St. Augustine, Kierkegaard, not of Cardinal Mazarin, and least of all Jean Chapelain, nominal head of literature.

A genius defies classification, but lesser men likewise were out of harmony with the solemn music of the Grand Reign. Some were in exile. Saint-Évremond, the gifted amateur, lived in England from 1659 to his death in 1703: he escaped the discipline of Versailles altogether. Pierre Bayle, the Huguenot scholar, completed in Holland his curious *Historical Dictionary,* which was to provide an arsenal for the Voltairians. Others dwelt undisturbed in France in outward conformity but dissenters at heart. La Fontaine, author of charming fables for young and old, a day-dreamer, a spoiled child, satirized the predatory great as wolves and bears, not sparing even His Majesty the Lion. One of his apologues, *The Danubian Peasant,* extols primitive virtue and condemns the corrupting influence of civilization in terms which anticipate the Rousseau of 1750. La Bruyère, a dependent of Condé, dared to write, "The people have no wit, the great have no soul. If it comes to a choice, I want to be with the people." Yet he was elected a member of the decorous French Academy.

Long before the end of Louis XIV's interminable rule, decisive words had been uttered which ruined the foundations of the classical compromise and heralded the Enlightenment. By Descartes: "Trust your own common sense." By Corneille: "I believe in the precepts of Aristotle not because they are Aristotle's but because they are in agreement with human reason." By Molière: "The ancients are the ancients, and we are the people of today." By Charles Perrault: "Our century stands on its own merits and need not ape the century of Augustus." By Bayle: "Errors are none the better for being old." By Fontenelle, the centenarian who linked the age of Corneille with that of Voltaire: "Authority has ceased to have more weight than reason."

Cultural history therefore is not altogether a matter of chronology: the Enlightenment existed before Voltaire was born. Even in the arts, which are swayed by the prevailing style, history revels in anachronisms. *Turcaret* is a satire on ruthless finance; it might be called *Business is Business* (or perhaps *The Gold Digger,* for the profiteer is preyed upon by the adventuress). In tone and technique it resembles the plays of Henry Becque in the late nineteenth century. It was written by Lesage and performed in 1709. Watteau, the delightful painter whose silken puppets dance or play the lute in dreamy gardens or embark for the vaporous isle of Cytherea, appears as the perfect interpreter of the Pompadour era: he died in 1721, and much of his work was done in the tragic years of the Spanish Succession. The conformities imposed by a prevailing style are not the deeper realities of a people's life. Wigs alter human nature, but not to the very core.

Monarchy had abdicated leadership; the court, more numerous and more lavish than ever, had become a mob torn into cliques; the scepter fell to a new sovereign, Public Opinion. That phantom power, amorphous, ubiquitous, irresponsble, *Monsieur Tout-le-Monde*, the collective mind, proved mightier than the king and wittier than Voltaire.

A unique phenomenon without exact equivalent in our days. Under the Second Empire opinion, although officially curbed, had a definiteness, a quiet authority, which it has lost in our vociferous, bewildered age; yet Alexis de Tocqueville, comparing ancient France and the France of Napoleon III with its daily press, its legislative body, its plebiscites, could say, "France today is muffled, echoeless: then it was vibrant. It was sufficient to raise one's voice to be heard afar."

The key to this paradox is "society." Information was transmitted, opinions vented, measures suggested or opposed, ministers made or unmade by word of mouth—an epigram, a song, perhaps even a glance, a smile, a shrug. By society we should not understand in this case a formal, exclusive set, the "Four Hundred": society had no single center and no recognized hierarchy. It simply meant conversation. Wherever people gathered informally and talked—in a public garden like the Palais-Royal, in the pit of a theater, in a coffee house like Procope or La Régence, in a club like l'Entresol or Clichy—there a cell of society came into being and went into action. Between a chance conjunction of idlers at the fair and the exclusive *salon* of Madame du Deffand there was apparently an abyss, but between the most remote circles there existed innumerable channels of communication. The rumor that originated among the newsmongers of *La Petite Provence,* a sheltered spot in the Tuileries gardens, would be discussed the same evening in an aristocratic company; the song that amused the Pont-Neuf would at once proceed to the Faubourg Saint-Germain, bastion of ancient pride; and conversely, a witticism whispered under a crystal chandelier in the Faubourg Saint-Honoré would find its way, with mysterious swiftness, to the workshops of the Faubourg Saint-Antoine. Paris, high or low, was curiously cohesive in those days. In spite of social barriers, there existed a freemasonry of wit, which the Revolution, industry, science, democracy have actually weakened and all but destroyed. It was that unorganized and invisible empire that was called society.

Public opinion, struggling for consciousness, found in the drama a powerful instrument. A theater was an open club. Not only did the common people have their own spectacles in the farces at the fair, particularly that of Saint-Laurent, but they thronged the Théâtre-Français. The pit was open to all those—and they were innumerable in Paris— to whom the language of the classics was not a sealed book. They were not seated: this made that part of the audience, thus jammed together, more responsive and more irresponsible. A joke, a jibe, a biting allusion, and the offender, in the confusion of laughter, applause, or protest, would duck under the sea of heads and elude the police. Allusions were found even in Racine's biblical *Athalie*. Playwrights knew the possibilities of this incomparable instrument. Even Marivaux, the sophisticated analyst of love, was not averse to a "philosophical" touch in the midst of his badinage. The "lachrymose comedy" of Nivelle de La Chaussée, the "middle-class tragedy" of Diderot and Sedaine were social manifestoes, the glorification of bourgeois virtues. Voltaire, who wrote plays for sixty years, never failed to preach against abuses, prejudices, superstitions, intolerance. The performance of Beaumarchais's *Marriage of Figaro* (1784) was a victory against the tottering world of privilege.

The *salon* was not therefore the only temple of society, but it shows society in its perfection; and the eighteenth century saw the unquestioned reign of the *salon*. It was not a literary or political institution: the pleasure of meeting congenial acquaintances was its essential aim, *philosophie* only a by-product. If a secondary purpose existed, it was flirtation, the highly expert fencing of wit and sentiment so well reported by Marivaux. Society did not allow itself to be infected with the pedantry of *philosophie:* it was *philosophie* that was tinged with what may be called the pedantry or convention of society, a tone of artificial levity, a gesture of apology for every lapse into boorish seriousness. It was this tone, first consistently practiced by Fontenelle, that Montesquieu carried to perfection in his *Persian Letters*. He could never discard it altogether: even in his masterpiece, *De l'esprit des lois* (*On the Spirit of Laws*), we find at times *de l'esprit sur les lois* (witticisms about the laws). The deep earnestness of Voltaire is often veiled in graceful flippancy.

The great hostesses of the time would repay detailed study: we can merely mention the most prominent, from Madame de Tencin, the resolute adventuress who conquered the regent and Dubois, gambled heavily in the days of Law's "system," and managed to make her brother a cardinal, to Madame Necker, the virtuous wife of the Genevan banker called *in extremis* to save the finances of the monarchy. The two most impressive, and the most sharply contrasted, were Madame du Deffand and Madame Geoffrin.

Madame du Deffand was a great lady, cool and sharp; Voltaire respected her as an equal. She derided the romantic eloquence and sentiment of Rousseau: yet, at seventy, and blind, she fell in love with Horace Walpole, to the infinite embarrassment of that middle-aged worldling. Madame Geoffrin, at fourteen, married Money, forty-eight years of age. After a long apprenticeship and with marvelous pertinacity the modest bourgeoise turned her *salon* into "the Kingdom of Rue Saint-Honoré," the most brilliant social empire of the time. She could not be presented at court, but she counted Catherine of Russia and Gustavus III of Sweden among her friends. Stanislas Poniatowski, King of Poland, with many other celebrities in Europe, loved to call her "Maman."

The leaders of the Enlightenment, the *philosophes* of the *Encyclopedia,* had their favorite *salons:* those of Julie de Lespinasse (who had seceded from her protectress, Madame du Deffand), Madame d'Épinay, Holbach, Helvetius, Necker. It was in that exhilarating atmosphere that Germaine Necker was brought up, who was to be the redoubtable Madame de Staël; all through the Revolution and the Empire she yearned incurably for that lost Paradise.

Society not *philosophie* [9] was the queen of the age, but *philosophie* was one of its favorite games. The social, the conversational, nature of eighteenth-century thought must ever be kept in mind. It was lively, daring, amusing; it shunned jargon like a plague; it spurned the lone wrestling of the metaphysician with the Absolute: for the Absolute is not fit for polite society. It was tolerant, except of intolerance, the arch-monster, "the Infamous One to be crushed," to quote Voltaire's famous battle cry; for fanaticism is the deadly enemy of urbanity.

This drawing-room or coffee-house character explains both the popularity of *philosophie* at the time and the discredit in which it fell in later ages. For conversation is evanescent. Even if we had a full record of the words, if we could follow the dazzling bout of paradox, irony, and repartee, the setting would be lost, the animated scene, the soft lights, the exquisite decorations, the tones, undertones, and overtones, and especially the smile—that unique eighteenth-century smile, shrewd, mocking, and tender, preserved in the marvelous pastel portraits of La Tour.

The impression still prevails that the *philosophes* of the Enlightenment were shallow, because they spoke and wrote for a Pompadour audience. They were lucid, which is the first requisite of courtesy; and turbidity is easily mistaken for depth. As a matter of fact, the great men of the time were hard and conscientious workers. Montesquieu labored for eighteen years over his *Spirit of Laws,* which our Founding Fathers quoted with reverence. Voltaire sought original documents for his *Charles XII* and his *Century of Louis XIV;* and if his *Essay on Manners* is necessarily based on secondary sources, it remains the most keenly critical and the most thought-provoking of all universal histories. Buffon, the naturalist, wrote too well—"never without his lace cuffs," it was said—but he was a careful observer and a masterly architect of thought: his book, *Epochs of Nature* remains impressive to this day. Diderot, who started as a hack writer and a bohemian, had nonetheless an incredible capacity for hard and serious work. Not only did he organize and edit the mighty *Encyclopedia*, fighting every inch of the way for twenty years; but his own articles, those on the arts and crafts, for instance, are models of conscientious research.

Neither should we believe that the *philosophes* were satisfied with mere talk or mere theory, that they reared "heavenly cities" in the clouds, that they deluded themselves and mankind with vague prophecies of a new heaven and a new earth. They were singularly realistic: they—and most of all Voltaire—fought definite abuses and urged definite reforms. They did not advocate violent upheaval, for they loved the world in which they lived: "What a happy time is this Iron Age!" They had no blind faith in human nature, or in any metaphysical panacea. They knew how slow and checkered the progress of mankind had been, how precarious its achievements. Those who accuse the Enlightenment of vapid optimism seem never to have heard of Voltaire's *Candide.*

What is the Enlightenment? Simply the working out of Fontenelle's dictum, "Authority has ceased to have more weight than reason." There were to be no privileged castes or doctrines. Any vested interest that would not submit to the test of free criticism, and fled to Tradition for sanctuary, was declared an abuse, a prejudice, or a superstition. Many cobwebs had to be swept away. But the *philosophes* were not mere scoffers, rejoicing in destruction. Their aims were positive.

It has been said that Voltaire was "England's best gift to France.' This might be extended to the whole Enlightenment. Montesquieu studied and expounded the English constitution. Voltaire's sojourn in London revealed him to himself; his first decisive contribution to liberal thought was his *Lettres philosophiques,* or *Lettres anglaises.* Diderot knew English well; the starting point of his *Encyclopedia* was Chambers' *Dictionary.* Buffon's favorite authors were Milton and Richardson. The masters of French thought then were Bacon, Locke, Newton, and, secondarily, the "Deists," Toland, Collins, Woolston, Tindal, Shaftesbury. It must be said that the England they admired had never been so Frenchified: it was the age of Addison and Pope, of whom Boileau himself would have approved. Culturally, the eighteenth century was an Anglo-French condominium, and under that sign America was born. Jefferson was such a typical American because he was so true to the spirits of both England and France. Englishmen were later to revel in "the wisdom of prejudice." But when they take pride in their freedom from clear thinking, we cannot forget that they were the initiators and masters of the Enlightenment.

ROUSSEAU'S REBELLION AGAINST *Philosophie*

Now we come to a strange crosscurrent of doctrines which, after two centuries, is still bewildering us: the sudden rise of Rousseauism, out of the Enlightenment, and against the Enlightenment.

In 1750 an obscure musician approaching middle age, a minor member of the Encyclopedia set, Jean-Jacques Rousseau, won a prize for a discourse on this subject: Whether the restoration of sciences and arts had contributed to corrupt or purify morals? [10] He took the paradoxical side, attacked progress and civilization, and woke to find himself famous.

In this first essay, and in his greater works, *On the Origins of Inequality, The New Heloise, Emile, or Education, The Social Contract,* he attacked prejudices, like the *philosophes,* and more radically than any of them. The positive side of his doctrine also was derived from them: long before he wrote, they had voiced their faith in "natural" rights, "natural" laws and "natural" religion. And it had long been the fashion to extol the virtues of the "natural" man, the Noble Savage. If Rousseau squabbled with the Encyclopedists, it seemed but a family quarrel. They were persecuted by the same enemies. The Revolution ranked Rousseau as well as Voltaire among its forerunners; and their remains were placed in the national Pantheon.

Yet Rousesseauism was exactly the reverse of the Enlightenment. Voltaire believed in civilization, in refined society, even in luxury: Rousseau denounced them and fled from the sophisticated life of the Paris *salons.* Voltaire's method was a cautious, many-sided critical inquiry leading to the gradual suppression of manifest abuses, the gradual creation of rational order. Rousseau grandly said, "First of all, let us sweep aside the facts!" and proclaimed one essential principle which had come to him in a sudden revelation. Voltaire was conscious of the stupidities and criminal propensities of man: civilization was in his eyes a slow, laborious conquest, ever threatened by an offensive return of barbarism. Rousseau put his whole faith in the natural goodness of human nature. From 1750 to our own days the spirit of France has been the scene of a three-cornered battle: tradition, the Enlightenment, and Rousseauistic primitivism in sharp conflict, unexpected alliances, and incurable confusion.

BOOK IV

THE BOURGEOIS-LIBERAL
REVOLUTION: 1750–1848

CHAPTER XVI

A Golden Twilight:
The End of the Ancient Regime,
1750-1789

ENGLISH INFLUENCE AND POLITICAL LIBERTY

Louis XV died of smallpox in 1774. But long before his unlamented demise, France and the king himself had been conscious of impending change. A deplorable ruler, the Well-Beloved had proved a true prophet: he had safely won his race with "the Deluge," and "the old machine" was to creak and balk for fifteen years after his death.

In the tangled history of culture, it is difficult to discern starting points, and especially turning points. Sensational events, as a rule, are symptoms rather than causes: revolutions do not break out in the streets until they have progressed very far in the minds. The explosions of violence which shook France between 1789 and 1794 were but episodes in a vast cycle that extended over a full century. This long process was the formation of the bourgeois-liberal regime. In France the new synthesis was clearly formulated by Abbé Sieyès in 1788–1789: "What is the Third Estate? Nothing. What should it be? Everything." It won its decisive victory in 1830 with the advent of the bourgeois monarchy. It felt itself for the first time radically challenged by democracy, with a tinge of socialism, in 1848. These dates stand out clearly enough. But the moment when the bourgeois ideology was first definitely focused is much harder to determine. The date 1750 is a mere indication.

The *bourgeoisie* had been a power in France for ages, perhaps from the remote days of Louis VI. That class had reached a high degree of wealth and influence under Louis XIV. Molière, who may be called the average Frenchman at his best, was fully conscious of his dignity as a bourgeois: when he derided "would-be gentlemen," he was not espousing nobiliary prejudices. The aristocrats in his plays, when they are not the merest fops, are adventurers and sharpers. If Monsieur Jourdain and Georges Dandin are branded as fools, it is because they are ashamed of the sturdy, self-reliant, useful class in which they were born. Still, for three-quarters of a century after Molière the social hierarchy was not openly challenged: only particular abuses were denounced. It was a great temptation for an ambitious man to seek his share of privileges rather than fight for their abolition. There was a *bourgeois gentilhomme* even in Voltaire.

England and France were so delicately attuned in those days that we find it hard to ascertain in which direction an idea first crossed the Channel. Richardson's *Pamela* (1740), which unmistakably voiced the bourgeois spirit, was immensely successful in France; but the same elements were found in Marivaux's *Marianne,* started ten years before. One could distinctly hear the rumblings of social change in the middle-class dramas of Diderot and Sedaine: the bourgeois refused to be exclusively a figure of fun; he wanted to be taken seriously, and even tragically. These dramas owed not a little to the plays of Lillo; but at the same time as Lillo, and independently from him, Nivelle de La Chaussée had fought for the bourgeois virtues (including conjugal faithfulness) in his "tearful comedies." On the whole, however, there is little doubt that the English showed the way. The London merchants had supported the Revolution of 1688, and they had reaped their reward: Voltaire was delighted with their high standing in the community when he spent in England two or three years of most profitable exile, and he insisted on that point in his *English Letters.* The military and economic prestige of England, the Enlightenment, the early stages of the Industrial Revolution: all contributed to the steady rise of political consciousness in the *bourgeoisie.* By the middle of the eighteenth century that progress had been so substantial that the French aristocracy and its close associate, the higher clergy, were beginning to turn into transparent ghosts.

In 1748 Montesquieu brought out his *Spirit of Laws:* "Mankind had lost her title-deeds," said Voltaire, "M. de Montesquieu has restored them to her." In 1749 came Diderot's *Letter on the Blind,* so daring that he was jailed, to the great benefit of his fame and influence; he was already preparing his monumental *Encyclopedia,* which appeared, in the din and smoke of constant battle, between 1751 and 1766. The year 1750 saw Rousseau's first triumph, significant not so much for the intrinsic merits of the work as for the instant and enthusiastic response of the public. Most striking of all as a symptom of radical change was Voltaire's new attitude. In his sixties, at the summit of his fame, he grew not mellower but more belligerent. Until 1752, for all his freedom of thought, he had sought a definite place in the existing society, as the protégé of great lord, favorite, or king. Now he was fully emancipated at last. In 1754 he established himself on the border of France and Geneva and turned his principal seat, Ferney, into a sort of international capital of the spirit, a Supreme Court of Public Opinion. He had become King Voltaire, by the divine right of human reason. He had privately accomplished his revolution: the Voltairian *bourgeoisie,* a generation later, had only to follow his example.

The modern reader is struck not by the daring of eighteenth-century thought but by its obviousness. He is apt to shrug away the doctrines of Montesquieu as too safe and too sane, the criticism of Voltaire as shallow, the declamations of Rousseau as sophomoric. This, of course, is a delusion created by the very thoroughness of their victory. In 1750 it was by no means so easy and so safe to be a *philosophe.* Diderot was repeatedly imprisoned. Voltaire, who was Paris incarnate, found it advisable to live three hundred miles from the City of Light. (He distrusted the Calvinistic Republic of Geneva almost as much as the Catholic monarchy of France and was ready, with four different homes in that region, to play hide-and-seek with both.) The Parlement, just because it suppressed the Jesuits to the applause of the *philosophes,* turned sharply against the *philosophes* in order to vindicate its own orthodoxy. Rousseau's arrest was ordered, and he had to flee for a long period of wandering and exile. A mere child, the Chevalier de la Barre, for foolish acts of impiety, was beheaded and burned (1766). The regime of the Well-Beloved, so delightful in its social aspects, could be ruthless. Fortunately, sheer incompetence, inveterate urbanity, and divided counsels conspired to make its persecution fitful and ineffectual.

Many people realized that the *Encyclopedia* was not merely an admirable epitome of useful knowledge but also, and very deliberately, a war machine against the abuses of the existing order. It was condemned, confiscated, destroyed, with an outward show of rigor; it survived all ordeals, thanks to complicities in high places, even in the very highest. Malesherbes, son of the chancellor, Lamoignon, member of one of the finest families among the "nobility of the gown," had charge of supervising all printed publications; he warned the Encyclopedists of their perils and even stored the subversive volumes in his own residence. It was not a betrayal of his trust: he believed the monarchy would be strengthened, not destroyed, by the new spirit. He was to prove his loyalty in a tragic hour: he defended Louis XVI before the Convention, and the guillotine was his reward (1794). Voltaire shows us Louis XV, Madame de Pompadour, and a small group of friends delightedly scanning the forbidden work. When a *philosophe* heard an impressive carriage stop at his door, he never knew whether it meant an invitation to some aristocratic château or a season in some grim fortress.

The four decades that preceded the outbreak of the Revolution have often been called "the twilight of the Ancient Regime." They were no less obviously the dawn of the new world. There was no foreboding of darkness engulfing mankind, as in the last two centuries of the Roman Empire. There was none of that nameless anguish that tortured the "Lost Centuries," the fourteenth and the fifteenth, and made the Dance of Death their favorite theme. There was none of that mounting dread of inevitable catastrophe that marked the eve of the Russian Revolution. Under Louis XV and Louis XVI, in spite of defeat, maladministration, and financial confusion, France was prosperous, self-confident, and cheerful. The rising class, the Third Estate, was filled with hope, and irritated, not depressed, by hope deferred. Among the aristocrats many had adopted liberal views: Lafayette is only the best remembered in an "enlightened" generation. The obstinate defenders of prejudice were either too stupid or too frivolous to fight effectively. They were not even as intelligent as Louis XV, who at any rate foresaw the Deluge.

It is this freedom from dread, this unconquerable hope, that made "the twilight of the Ancient Regime" so delightful and so pathetic. Society at that time enjoyed the best of two worlds: the mellowed luxury, the elegance, the urbanity of the old, the generosity, the eagerness of the new. It is this unique blend that justifies Talleyrand's oft-quoted dictum: "Whoever has not lived before 1789 does not know the sweetness of life."

We, fully aware of the catastrophes ahead, are inclined to call this optimism foolish. We are grievously unjust to a very intelligent generation. Their hope of rapid change without disruption was not unreasonable. After all, England had shown the way for nearly a hundred years: what was an obvious truth beyond the Channel need not be an error a few miles south. And beside the constitutional solution offered by England, there was an alternative, truer perhaps to the French tradition, "enlightened despotism." Europe was filled at that time with sovereigns who were also *philosophes:* Frederick II, Catherine II, Joseph II, his brother Leopold of Tuscany; the kings of Sweden and Poland breathed with delight the air of the Paris *salons;* in other states, even in the most backward, Spain, Portugal, Naples, "enlightened" ministers were vigorously attacking abuses. Choiseul, not unblemished by any means but free from prejudices and energetic, had shown that the old monarchy could be revitalized (1758–1770).[1] The bold stroke by which Maupeou had swept aside the old Parlements was hailed by the *philosophes* as the first and essential step in a progressive policy. Under Louis XVI, as we shall see, "enlightened despotism" very nearly won the day; ultimately, the ideas of the *philosophes* were to prevail throughout Europe. It was not therefore the desire for change that was an accident, a deviation of France's normal course: it was blind resistance to change.

CONFLICTING TRENDS

The unique fascination of the period is due to this very pluralism: old and new lived side by side, in contrast, in conflict, yet in outward peace, and often in gracious friendliness. As in the heyday of Louis XIV, unity was provided not by an ideology but by a style: and what a style it was, robust under its extreme refinement! Perhaps the best symbol of the age is offered by the charming sphinxes, worthy of Clodion, with the coquettish smile of society ladies: the effect is absurd but delightful.

To describe this age, we should have to accumulate antinomies. It was a time of general prosperity, yet there might be distress, and even famine, among the people. It was an era of liberalism and indulgence but capable of sudden fits of intolerance and cruelty. The Parlements, it will be remembered, were facing both ways: champions of "liberties" which in truth were privileges. Rousseauism, the rise of the *bourgeoisie,* and, after 1776, sympathy for those "noble savages," the American insurgents, had spread the cult of nature and simplicity, but a nature, a simplicity, deeply tinged with sophistication. The English gardens, which superseded the majesty of Le Nôtre's classical style, were "landscapes" indeed, but most artfully contrived. Fashionable ladies nursed their babies at the Opera; Marie-Antoinette played dairymaid in the toy village of Trianon. It was also the triumph of sentiment and of virtue: Rousseau, Diderot, and Sedaine in their dramas, Greuze in his paintings were preaching purity, innocence, the uplifted eye, and the ready tear; the French Academy was (and remains) entrusted with the awarding of the Montyon Prizes, for virtue in humble guise. Louis XVI was unquestionably a blameless husband. But the prestigious old rakes, Richelieu, Choiseul, survived impenitent. Diderot wrote *The Indiscreet Jewels;* Greuze's *Broken Pitcher* is wilfully equivocal; and the most extreme examples of salacious literature, Louvet's *Faublas,* Choderlos de Laclos' *Liaisons dangereuses,* the crazy works of the Marquis de Sade [2] belonged to the very end of the period.

It was the Age of Reason, but also the age of riotous make-believe. Never had fakers and charlatans found such an eager public. Saint-Martin, "the Unknown Philosopher," Saint-Germain, the Man of Mystery, Cagliostro (Joseph Balsamo): all hinted that they had lived for centuries; they were theurgists, faith healers, cabalists, alchemists;

they were heirs to the secret lore of the ages, and the future was unveiled before their eyes. Mesmer blended convincingly science—the idol of the Encyclopedists—mysticism, and the most arrant mystification. He created a furor with his "animal magnetism": to mesmerize has remained a common word. His *baquet* or vat was a bold modern version of the witches' caldron. The government offered him a fortune for his "secret": since the state was in a desperate plight, it was tempting to consult a quack. He founded a Society of Harmony, and among its members were the fighting Parlement leader d'Espréménil, the noted chemist Berthollet, and the overenthusiastic Lafayette. Paris in 1778 saw the triumph of dying Voltaire, whose critical wit was an acid test; of Franklin, the embodiment of science and plain common sense; and of Mesmer, astrologer, magnetizer, and magician extraordinary. The Rosicrucians flourished, and the Masonic lodges clothed the unceremonious, blunt philosophy of the Enlightenment with a rich mantle of mystery.

It was likewise characteristic of the period that art should move in two directions at once without any violent disruption. Architecture and painting were growing more severely classical. Compared with David's early pictures, Corneille's tragedies would seem almost frivolously modern. The Abbey of Saint-Genevieve (now the Pantheon), by Soufflot, offered tremendous blank walls of aggressive, self-righteous austerity. The rediscovery of Herculaneum and Pompeii had contributed to this vogue. The temples of Paestum, with their massive Doric columns, were accepted as models. A description of classical Greece by Abbé Barthélemy enjoyed immense popularity. The only true poet of the time, André Chénier, composed elegies, eclogues, idyls, and epic fragments in the purest Hellenic vein.[3] The movement was fully started which was to lead to that rigid pastiching of the antique, the Empire style. But at the very same moment Romanticism, still unnamed, was invading French literature through the Oriental tale, the exotic, the "Gothick" or romance of mystery and terror,[4] the primitive. The pseudo-Gaelic poems of Ossian-Macpherson threatened to displace Homer from his ancient throne; the great realist Napoleon traveled with an Italian version of Ossian.[5] The etcher Piranesi, whose *Albums of Classical Ornaments* had such an influence on domestic decoration, also depicted *Roman Antiquities* with a bold quest of the dramatic and the picturesque; and his *Dungeons* (*Carceri*) are a gorgeous collection of architectural nightmares. All these external contradictions were fused and absorbed in the essential contradictions we have already pointed out: divine right represented by a Louis XV, an absolutism too skeptical to enforce its own claims, a *philosophie* which embraced, but could not reconcile, the progressivism of the Voltairians [6] and the primitivism of the Rousseauists.

✒ THE PATHETIC PAIR:
LOUIS XVI AND MARIE-ANTOINETTE

Louis XVI, when he came to the throne on the death of his grandfather, was barely twenty. "We are so young!" he cried in dismay. Youth was his best asset. France had grown weary of the old rake, and the new royal pair was hailed with delight.

In an age of settled government, Louis XVI, virtuous, well-meaning, not stupid by any means, would have been a very honorable sovereign: shall we say the equivalent of a Victoria? Even in times of stress, his reign could have been successful if, like so many of his predecessors, he had entrusted power to a vigorous prime minister. Of his own accord he was absolutely incapable of leadership. The wild gamble of hereditary rule gave France, at a critical hour, the man least fitted to meet the emergency.

Louis XIV had natural majesty; Louis XV had a vacant but handsome presence; Louis XVI, of larger build than either, was heavy, clumsy, and waddling. He was so perfectly commonplace that, in a crowded scene, he would seem to disappear. He was the despair of his valets: his most impressive trappings invariably went awry. Like the Grand Monarch he was incredibly voracious: the menu of his informal breakfast would have astounded Paul Bunyan himself. (It is true that waste was a sacred rule at Versailles; there were numberless functionaries on the lookout for perquisites.) As a result he would doze at state functions. He read with extreme slowness, could not dance, had little taste for music or the drama. His favorite entertainment was the hunt. There again his pleasures were massive rather than refined: he shot heads of game by the thousand, and kept elaborate statistics of these massacres. A day without hunting was accounted wasted: on the fourteenth of July, 1789, he entered in his diary, "Nothing." He had a hobby; since Rousseau's ideas were in the air, he had, like Émile, taken up a trade and become a proficient locksmith. He was deeply pious; he sincerely practiced the most Christian, the most unkingly, of all virtues, humility. He was incurably shy: he had kind words in his heart and could not bring them to his lips. The least haughty of men, he could not be affable and lost the benefit of his genuine good will.

Had his responsibilities been limited to the family table, the hunting field, the workshop, and the church, he might have led a happy and blameless life. It seemed as though Providence had planned to illustrate three different ways in which hereditary kingship could go wrong: the pride of Louis XIV, the cynical indifference of Louis XV, the invincible sluggishness of Louis XVI. But his dullness did not suffice to stifle loyalty: for fifteen years the people obstinately fixed their hopes on him. In theory he was all-powerful; he was known to have a good heart. It took two full years of Revolution to reveal the sinister but inescapable aspect of his flabbiness, duplicity. It requires energy to speak and act the truth.

His faults were brought into sharper relief by the merits of his consort, Marie-Antoinette, an Austrian archduchess and the daughter of the Empress Maria Theresa. She had dazzling beauty and a charm of manners which at first conquered the whole of France. In her presence the king's awkwardness appeared in a more comical light. And with the cruel irresponsibility which was one of her constant traits she could not refrain from calling attention, publicly, to the painful contrast.

He adored her, and she despised him. A purely physical curse blighted their private life (but kings have no private life): a congenital impediment on his part made their union incomplete. After a number of years it was remedied by a surgical operation. The psychological effect of this protracted ordeal must have been profound: his humiliation, her frustration and scorn. When they had children at last, she had taken the habit of reckless pleasure-seeking, and her reputation for frivolity and extravagance was indestructibly established.

She was madly fond of luxury and could never be brought to consider the price. She was, of course, an easy prey; when simplicity became the fashion, her plainest frock still cost a fortune. Her love of jewelry was so notorious that the Cardinal de Rohan, Archbishop of Strasbourg, easily imagined that her influence, if not her favors, could be bought with a diamond necklace; and public opinion agreed with him.[7] She gambled wildly at cards to the consternation of her more sensible husband. Above all she squandered millions on her favorites, the princess of Lamballe, the duchess of Polignac, and their rapacious connections. Her one excuse is that she never realized the financial distress of the crown: how could she, when the king and the superintendent of finances were ever ready to provide money for her whims? But her blindness was also deliberate. Abbé de Vermond, who had been her tutor and remained her confessor, spoke words of wisdom; her mother Maria Theresa, her brother Joseph II did not spare their warnings. But there was in her frivolousness a vein of iron—that obduracy which was to wreck the monarchy. Granted that her extravagance was but a minor cause of the threatened bankruptcy: it was more plainly visible, and more deeply resented, than the rest. She became a symbol: she won for herself the ominous name, *Madame Déficit*.

Modern historians agree that she was virtuous. Her very faults protected her: she was too proud, too self-centered, and too shallow to be a prey to passion. Such was not, however, the opinion of her contemporaries. Long before the Revolution, and in the most aristocratic circles, her reputation was fiercely assailed. Gouverneur Morris, anti-democrat and prince of snobs, took it calmly for granted that she had lovers and that her devoted knight, Fersen, had enjoyed his reward. She had courted such obloquy by the flightiness of her manners at a time when decency had been restored to favor. She, daughter of staid and punctilious Austria, could be unconventional to an extraordinary degree. Some of her friends were notorious for their looseness. She loved the irresponsible promiscuity of the fancy-dress ball: under the mask and cloak she could forget that she was queen of France. It was natural that people should wonder how far she forgot it. Perhaps the aptest judgment on her morals was passed by her brother Joseph II. She asked him: "How do you like my coiffure?" and he replied: "Rather flimsy to bear a crown."

Frivolity would have been no mortal sin, if the queen had been satisfied with the scepter of fashion. But she must interfere in state affairs. Popular as she was for a season, she suffered from a great handicap, her Austrian birth. For three centuries Austria had been considered as the hereditary foe of France; the shift of policy which turned Versailles and Vienna into allies seemed to many a grievous error. The result of that alliance had been the disasters of the Seven Years' War: unless the new queen had become unquestionably French at heart, that ingrained hostility could not be allayed. It was felt from the beginning, at court, in official circles, among the common people, that on the French throne Marie-Antoinette had remained a loyal Austrian. She never truly liked, never thoroughly understood the French, although once she called them prettily *mes charmants mauvais sujets,* my charming naughty subjects. Her influence was constantly thrown on the side of her own family: Vergennes, the able minister of foreign affairs, had to use eternal vigilance against her. We know for certain today what contemporary opinion could only surmise: we have the correspondence of Maria Theresa with her daughter and with her ambassador in Paris, Mercy d'Argenteau. They take no trouble to disguise the fact that the queen of France was to be consistently the tool of Austrian policy. So to her name *Madame Déficit* was added a deadlier one, The Austrian Woman, *L'Autrichienne.*

✒ *Philosophie* AT THE HELM: TURGOT

At the very beginning of the new reign the discord was struck which never found its resolution. Intelligence and good will are not enough, if plain *will* be deficient.

Choiseul, whose fall late in 1770 had roused indignation, was holding himself in readiness; but he was not called back to power. The direction of affairs was entrusted to Maurepas, who remained at the helm until his death in 1781: the seven crucial years when it was still possible to avert "the Deluge." It would be unfair to dismiss Maurepas as merely an old courtier, frivolous and ineffectual. The son of a respected cabinet minister, Pontchartrain, he had been in government from the absurd age of fourteen. He took his duties, when they became effective, with some seriousness, and in naval affairs sought and followed intelligently the best expert advice. Like many members of high society he was genuinely interested in scientific matters; he skirted the coasts of the *Encyclopedia* in a friendly spirit. His enlightenment was of the mildest: at any rate it was not darkness. And he picked out a ministerial team which filled the *philosophes* with hope.

On the other hand, after twenty-five years of retirement he had a great desire to retain office. In 1749 he had been dismissed for an epigram against Madame de Pompadour: more cautious in his seventies, he would take good care not to offend the legitimate favorite, the queen. He was secretly jealous of his fellow ministers when their popularity or their influence with the king threatened to outstrip his own. He did not exactly betray Turgot at the beginning of his administration, or Necker at the end; but he failed to give them wholehearted support. And he committed at once a fatal mistake: instead of reforming the Maupeou courts of justice, he gave up the experiment altogether and restored the old Parlements.

The minister of foreign affairs was Vergennes, a diplomat of ripe experience. Vergennes, resisting the queen, refused to let France be embroiled in continental affairs as the cat's paw of Austria. His moderation and his disinterestedness repaired to some extent the damaged prestige of France. He was a cautious friend of the American cause, but there was little of the Lafayette spirit in him. During the war he had the skill to secure the friendly neutrality of most European states; and, although a determined adversary of England, he negotiated a reasonable peace which left no rancor. His fame survives in honored twilight.

What gave the new ministry its significance was the appointment of Turgot. With him the Enlightenment was reaching power. The defenders of ancient abuses like to accuse their opponents of being theorists and irresponsible dreamers: this could not be said of Turgot, the son of a great public servant and himself a tried practical administrator. As intendant in Limoges from 1761 to 1774 he fostered agriculture and industry (it was he who started there the manufacture of fine china, destined to become world-famous), abolished compulsory labor for public works, improved the roads, and lessened the glaring injustices of taxation. In a year of famine (1770–1771) he used vigorous and modern methods of relief instead of haphazard charity. But if he was no mere theorist, he had seriously reflected upon economic problems. With Quesnay the physiocrat, Dupont de Nemours, Gournay,[8] he belonged to the earliest group of economists in Europe. Adam Smith was his friend, and his works still rank among the classics in the history of the science.

We have already insisted upon the contrast between the vigorous activity of eighteenth-century France and the obsolete character of customs and regulations: the dead hand of the past was stifling the present. The remedy was to restore liberty: free trade, free industry, or, in the phrase which became the motto of the liberal school, *laissez faire, laissez passer*. Perhaps, in their radical liberalism, Turgot and Adam Smith had not fully realized the collective nature and the monopolistic tendencies of mechanized industry, which was just arising. Perhaps the fine, energetic optimism of their thought made them believe too easily in a "Guiding Hand" harmonizing the selfishness of individuals for the common good. In its anarchistic or Rousseauistic aspects their doctrine was obsolete as soon as it was formulated; but in so far as it attacked manifest abuses, it was valid, and was accepted as a legitimate form of the Enlightenment.

Turgot, soon promoted to be comptroller general, promised to relieve the financial situation without catastrophe: "No bankruptcy, no increased taxation, no further borrowing." A paradox of simplicity: but when the state is impoverished in a rich country, the obvious remedies are order, honesty, efficiency, rather than any nostrum. He advocated strict accounting—a budget at last!—rigorous economy, better management of taxgathering and the royal monopolies. Beyond these immediate measures he wanted to remove all obstacles to the energy of the people, and first of all to allow the free circulation of grain. Unfortunately, a bad harvest brought about a rise in the price of bread, and this was ascribed to the minister's new-fangled schemes. Bread riots broke out in several places, so widespread, so carefully timed, so well engineered that they were manifestly not spontaneous. Turgot repressed this "War of the Flour Mills" with a firm hand. The king supported him; and

Malesherbes, entering the ministry at this anxious moment, strengthened the position of the *philosophes*.

Early in 1776 Turgot submitted to the king's council six notable edicts, two of which were far-reaching, and indeed revolutionary. One abolished the *corvée,* or forced labor in lieu of taxation, as he had done in Limoges. The other suppressed the privileges of the medieval guilds or corporations. These edicts had to be rammed down the throat of a recalcitrant Parlement. Then all the threatened profiteers made a common front against the reforms: feudalists and financiers, masters of the old guilds, and pensioners of the court. The queen could not forgive Turgot for opposing her lavish grants to her favorites. Turgot believed that, in a civilized age, it was sufficient to be right: he could use lucidity as a method of persuasion but not diplomacy. He made his policy so clear that "any village judge could explain it to the peasants." But to his opponents it was only too clear. The resolute support of his chief and of the king was needed for him to win the contest: Maurepas failed him and went over to the queen's side. The attitude of Louis XVI was typical: a good heart, a sound mind, no backbone. He had told Turgot, "You and I alone truly love the people," and regretfully dismissed him. It was the first, and perhaps the most decisive, of his capitulations.

Turgot's successor was at hand, and most willing: Jacques Necker, a rich banker from Geneva and the representative of his country in Paris. He had fingers in many financial pies; he was a director of the French East India Company and had loaned money to an embarrassed and embarrassing customer, the Royal Treasury. His chief asset was his charming and ambitious wife. She ran a brilliant *salon,* the peer of Madame Geoffrin's; there *philosophie,* finance, and government put their heads together and proclaimed Necker a genius. It helped his cause that, as an expert (Had he not made a fortune speculating in grain?), he wrote a weighty essay against Turgot's free-trade policy.

Necker was no wizard and not even a statesman. But he was an excellent man and a good banker. He applied the well-tried methods of the counting house to the welter of state finances; in particular, he attempted to fund, that is to say to reduce to intelligibility, that vast and loose monster, the national debt. It is hard to tell whether his plain and cautious methods would have restored the treasury to health, for the American war broke out and upset every prevision. In 1781 he published his *Compte-rendu,* or balance sheet of the country. The book, although technical, was immensely successful. It was far too optimistic and not wholly ingenuous: it announced a surplus when Necker knew there was a deficit. But it brought some light, however imperfect, into the chaos of the regime; and for that very reason it was resented by those who were thriving in the dark. Necker had committed the crime of thwarting a protégé of the queen, the duke of Guines. So he was dismissed and had to be satisfied with his luxurious and sociable private life. But he was not satisfied, and we shall meet him again on the eve of the Revolution.

THE WAR OF AMERICAN INDEPENDENCE: BEAUMARCHAIS

Everything, in that brilliantly dubious period, appears in a double light. This is particularly true of the American war—our War of Independence. It was fought by French conservatives and French liberals side by side, for totally different reasons: a situation which was to be repeated in the two world wars of the twentieth century. It is difficult to appraise, in the country as a whole or even in the case of individual men, which of the two motives was paramount: to avenge the disasters of the Seven Years' War or to promote the cause of liberty everywhere in the world. One thing appears probable: without a combination of these two incentives the war would not have taken place. And a second thing amounts almost to a certainty: without such a combination victory was inconceivable.

If the advocates of intervention were not one at heart, neither were the believers in neutrality. Turgot wanted peace, because he foresaw that a costly adventure would kill every chance of orderly reform. Louis XVI was averse to war through a mixture of Christian meekness, common sense, and lethargy. It was not very natural even for the mildest of autocrats to espouse the cause of insurgency. The cry, "No taxation without representation" might be expected to reverberate across the Atlantic.

The main facts of the American war are familiar to school children and need not be repeated here. But no single interpretation of these facts is accepted as final, either in America or in England, and least of all in France. If we want to keep free from doctrinaire cocksureness, we must constantly bear in mind that, even though the major trends in history be "inevitable," actual events are affected by chance. It might have happened otherwise. In the short run individualities do count, although principles and permanent interests invincibly assert themselves in the end. The mad obstinacy of George III changed—apparently at least—the face of the world. The course of French intervention was determined by three sharply contrasted personalities, Beaumarchais, Lafayette, Franklin.

In the spring of 1775 when the news of Concord and Lexington reached Europe, Beaumarchais was on a secret diplomatic mission in

London. It was he who first informed Vergennes of the state of public opinion in England; it was he also who first urged the minister to support the cause of the insurgents. Who was this Beaumarchais, now best remembered as the author of two sparkling comedies, *The Barber of Seville* and *The Marriage of Figaro?*

His career had been a breathless picaresque romance, a wilder *Gil Blas,* unique even in that age of prodigies. Pierre-Augustin Caron (1732–1799), who was to style himself de Beaumarchais, was the son of a Paris watchmaker. He first showed genius in his father's trade: he invented a remarkably simple and effective escapement. Through a lady friend, whom he later married, he secured a minor post at court. He thus had some contact with society: he was appointed the music teacher of four pathetic old maids, the daughters of Louis XV. His talent, his wit, his charm conquered them. Through them he was able to be of service to the great financier Pâris-Duverney, who rewarded him by taking him into partnership (1760). On the death of his protector (1770), a law suit brought him into the limelight. As we have seen he felt himself mulcted by the wife of a judge in the newly created Maupeou Court, and he carried the case before "the Parliament of Public Opinion." Officially censored, deprived of his civic rights, he became a popular hero. Now the watchmaker, courtier, musician, financier, and pamphleteer was ready for a new avatar: he offered himself, and was accepted, for secret diplomatic missions. The first was promptly successful. The second took him to London again to make terms with an adventurer as fantastic as himself, and more ambiguous, the Chevalier, or Mademoiselle, d'Éon, whose sex was an enigma. This androgynous agent was blackmailing the ministry; thanks to Beaumarchais, his (her) retirement from the scene was quietly purchased. "Mademoiselle" d'Éon henceforth wore feminine clothes; but on *his* death in 1810, all doubts were removed.

Meanwhile Beaumarchais had been introduced to John Wilkes, the fiery politician who had sworn a feud against George III and was at that time lord mayor of London. At his house he met the most advanced of the Whigs, in hearty sympathy with the grievances of the Americans. Beaumarchais so far had been too busy making several careers and several fortunes to devote much attention to political philosophy. But he was of modest origin, with a keen mind and a generous heart. He was then, through Britain and America, sincerely converted to liberal ideas. His mission to London had the same effect upon him as Voltaire's exile a generation before.

Reporting to Vergennes on the D'Éon affair, Beaumarchais also put in a plea for the Americans. Vergennes was favorably inclined, not as a liberal, but because he had an old score to settle with England. The king could not be moved. But one thing he could do, most naturally: he could close his eyes. It was then that Beaumarchais started, with the complicity of Vergennes, a lend-lease system on his own initiative. He formed a concern, Roderigue Hortalez and Company, for the intensive smuggling of arms and ammunition to the insurgents. He did so with the greatest energy and efficiency: we must remember that for ten years he had been the close business associate of a prince of finance. He got the ships and even, to convoy his argosies, a man-of-war of his own, "Le Fier Roderigue." He got the supplies by ways which had to be devious; and he managed to effect the payments through marvelous devices of international banking. The business, even at its peak, was exceedingly precarious: some of the king's officers refused to understand the winks from above and treated him as a mere smuggler. But, on the whole, the job was admirably done. The supplies were of the utmost importance to America; what is perhaps even more important is that his private initiative gradually committed France and her government. The country had to pass through Beaumarchais's war and then Lafayette's before it was ready for Rochambeau's.

The accounts of such a vast, complex, and mysterious enterprise were bound to be involved. Beaumarchais knew many tricks; but, strange to say perhaps, he was honest. His motives had been genuine liberalism and a devouring thirst for activity rather than downright greed. The beneficiaries of his efforts affected to believe that he was too clever by half. He never was fully repaid for his advances, and his heirs, in 1835, had to accept a very inadequate settlement. The moral debt of America to Beaumarchais has never been repaid at all. He was too equivocal a character to figure in the noble company of the Founding Fathers.[9]

⚜ THE WAR OF AMERICAN INDEPENDENCE: LAFAYETTE, FRANKLIN

If Beaumarchais bewilders us with his infinite variety, Lafayette puzzles his biographers with his transparent singleness of mind and heart. Realists, in his own time and in ours, found it impossible to admit that a man could be so purely devoted to his principles. So, because they could not accuse him of being a play actor or a profiteer, they must conclude that he was a simpleton. Such was the verdict of Mirabeau and Talleyrand, and they were certainly free from the reproach of "innocence." This accusation has created a counter-legend following like an ironic shadow "the Hero of Two Worlds."

Lafayette (1757–1834) was of a wealthy and noble Auvergnat family. At sixteen he married into a still wealthier and far more influential connection, that of the Noailles. He was captain in the Dragoons of the Guard when the American colonies declared their independence: he threw himself at once into their cause. His family, his military chiefs, advised against any quixotic rashness. The king himself forbade him to go, and, upon the request of the British government, ordered the ship that Lafayette was fitting out at Bordeaux to be seized. Undeterred, Lafayette managed to slip through French and English obstacles. His ship, "La Victoire," sailed from a Spanish port and eluded the British cruisers. After two weary months he landed at last near Georgetown, South Carolina. He was nineteen, and had left behind him a young wife and a baby daughter. De Kalb, a cosmopolitan professional soldier, was his companion and thought himself his mentor.

Silas Deane, the American agent in Paris, had promised De Kalb and Lafayette the rank of major general. When the lad turned up in Philadelphia, Congress was dismayed. But the young man refused to insist on his bond. He was serving as a volunteer, without pay, and was ready to accept any assignment. Impressed by his generous attitude, Congress turned the matter over to Washington, who took at once to the generous boy. His rank was confirmed. It was expected that he would serve on the staff of the commander-in-chief in a purely honorary capacity. But Washington soon entrusted him with actual command. No one claims for him a Napoleonic genius. But he did remarkably well, and in circumstances which demanded skill and fortitude rather than juvenile dash. He was at the head of an expedition against Canada; left without support, he extricated his troops in a masterly retreat. He took a very creditable part, again on the defensive, in the Rhode Island expedition.

Meanwhile France had officially entered the war. Lafayette returned to place himself at the service of his sovereign. He was received with the utmost enthusiasm: the king graciously forgot having ordered his arrest. The visit was in fact a mission in which he submitted to Maurepas and Vergennes the needs and the desires of their American allies. He went back to the States after six months, received the warm commendation of Congress, and was entrusted with the defense of Virginia. The victory of Yorktown, in which he had an important share, brought his active military career to a close.

Lafayette's part in the War of Independence was no mere *beau geste*. His personal initiative influenced opinion and the government. But there might have been a ludicrous discrepancy between his crusading zeal and his performance. On the contrary, he showed himself modest and efficient, a good comrade and a good soldier. Prejudices against "the Boy" soon disappeared.

It would not have been unnatural if such glory had turned a head of twenty-five. Considering the temptation, Lafayette on his return to France behaved with great moderation. He kept away from public affairs for several years, until abstention would have become cowardice. If Jefferson noted his "canine appetite for popularity," it was with an affectionate smile.

The star witness in the defense of Lafayette—for, strangely enough, he has to be defended—is George Washington. Washington was no sentimentalist, but he loved Lafayette as a son [10] and respected him as an equal. It was to Lafayette, and in a spirit which he knew to be that of Lafayette, that he wrote his admirable letter of August 15, 1786, in which he prophesied peace through freedom of intercourse, and called himself "a citizen of the great Republic of Humanity at large." [11]

Just before Christmas, 1776, Benjamin Franklin reached Paris, as American commissioner, and established himself at Passy, then a quiet suburban village on a height overlooking the Seine. Quite apart from the cause he came to serve, Franklin was received with universal enthusiasm. He stood at the same time for the Enlightenment—science, freedom from prejudices, rejection of the supernatural—and for Rousseauistic simplicity. The double halo of the "noble child of Nature" and of the "virtuous Quaker" surrounded this shrewd and rather loose-living businessman, who had little claim to either. He played, with matchless skill, the role which was expected of him and which, after all, was in accord with his own nature. He might have been awkward in court dress: it was a stroke of genius for him to reject the powdered wig and all that frippery. He was revered for his scientific fame—had he not "robbed the heavens of their thunder"?—and beloved for his kindly wit. Even more than Jefferson, he found in France a most congenial spiritual home. He enjoyed the sophisticated, yet idealistic, society of those golden days; he loved to have elegant young ladies call him *Bon Papa,* and he carried on an *amitié amoureuse,* a flirtation with a touch of genuine sentiment, with the brilliant widow of the *philosophe* and financier Helvetius.

All this, of course, immensely aided his mission; and, although without a wig or lace cuff, he proved more than a match for the professional diplomats of his day. This cordial fusion of the French and the American spirit is best symbolized by the meeting in Paris of Voltaire and Franklin. Both were then at the summit of their glory; both were sincerely devoted to the service of mankind; both were willing to be carried aloft by the enthusiasm of their admirers; both had deep reserves of irony. Franklin pushed his grandson toward Voltaire; and the Patriarch of Philosophy, laying his hand on the lad's head, blessed young America in the names of "God and Liberty."

On the sixth of February, 1778, France signed a treaty of commerce and a formal alliance with the United States. Eleven days later Lord North proposed the plan of conciliation which, three years before, might have averted rebellion and secession. European opinion, on the whole, was against England. The neutrals of the North leagued and armed themselves to protect their rights. Spain joined France in 1779.

The war was extensive and indecisive. Admiral d'Estaing's attack was beaten off, a plan to invade the British Isles came to nothing, and all efforts against Gibraltar proved fruitless. On the other hand, Suffren won brilliant victories in the Indian Ocean, and De Grasse was able to convoy Rochambeau's expedition. It was high time: the British, still holding New York, were advancing in the South. The French troops, seasoned and ably led, helped stem their progress. Cornwallis entrenched himself in Yorktown. When he was compelled to surrender (October 19, 1781), it was felt that the war was over.

The desultory negotiations for peace, however, lasted for nearly two years. Finally, overruling Franklin's scruples, the American commissioners made a separate agreement with England. The definitive treaty was signed in Paris on September 3, 1783. Spain recovered Florida, but did not return Louisiana to France. A few scattered colonies were regained including those five towns in Hindustan which the French were to keep until India became independent. England's naval supremacy had not been shattered, but it had been successfully challenged. It was a very honorable page in French history. But the bill was appalling.

⚓ FINANCIAL GASPS OF ABSOLUTISM

For three years (1778–1781) Necker, through skillful management, had been able to finance the war not out of current resources but with moderate loans. When he fell, his successors, Joly de Fleury and D'Ormesson, had to borrow recklessly and at exorbitant rates. While liberal sentiment was at its height, they carried on a policy of blind reaction: a half-forgotten eddy in the turmoil of that period, yet of singular significance. Feudal rights, so obviously obsolete, were more strictly enforced. The army and the navy were made more rigidly aristocratic than ever before. Under Louis XIV a bourgeois, Vauban, could become a marshal of France; under Louis XVI he could barely have been a captain.

In 1783 Calonne was entrusted with the finances of the kingdom. He solved the problem with smiling ease through prodigality camouflaged by falsification. He was neither a madman nor a swindler: he had held high and responsible offices. There was method in his recklessness: his theory was that prosperity depends upon confidence, and that confidence could only be stimulated by free spending. To spend one's way out of a depression is a hazardous but defensible paradox: economy can only contract and slow down production. But the trouble from which France was suffering was not depression, it was faulty financing; and to spend one's way out of debt is a manifest absurdity.

For a few years Calonne delighted the queen and the courtiers: he anticipated their every wish. The day of reckoning was approaching. Then the spendthrift was suddenly converted to sanity: he fell back upon the social reforms of Turgot and the orthodox financing of Necker, and he wanted his plans to be endorsed by an assembly of notables. The reactionaries, whom he had led into a fool's paradise, brought about his downfall (1787).

A brilliant ecclesiastic, Loménie de Brienne, Archbishop of Toulouse, assumed the desperate task. He too was compelled to propose sweeping changes. But the notables, chosen for their pliancy, refused to accept such a responsibility and evoked the ghost of the States-General, never convened since 1614. The idea appealed both to the "enlightened" constitutionalism of Montesquieu's disciples and to the democratic sentiments of the Rousseauists: to consult the nation meant a solemn renewal of "the Social Contract." Brienne was not ready for this solution, a curious blend of antiquarianism and radicalism. He tried "beneficent despotism" *in extremis:* reform by royal edicts. But the edicts had to be registered by the Parlement, and that body was in a combative mood. It refused to endorse the new measures; threatened with punishment, and even with destruction, it boldly stood its ground and appeared, in a false melodramatic light, as the champion of popular liberties. In the heat of battle the Parlement also appealed to that ancient institution, the States-General. The autocracy of the four Louises was thus challenged not by the new France alone but by the old.

The king was checked at every move. His moral authority as the arbiter of the nation's destiny had vanished. He had, sensibly enough, refused to allow Beaumarchais's *Marriage of Figaro* to be performed: "It is detestable! That man is deriding everything that ought to be respected! If it were played, the Bastille would have to come down!" Beaumarchais repeated in everybody's hearing, "The King does not want my comedy to be played; *therefore it shall be.*" And it was performed early in 1784, to the delirious applause of the courtiers themselves. Then the scandal of the Diamond Necklace revealed—although in this case it was on unjust grounds—the distrust and hatred of the people against the queen.

Helpless, bewildered, the king was still free to capitulate: it was the last of his prerogatives. In 1788 Loménie de Brienne was forced to retire, Necker was recalled to office, and the States-General were convened for May, 1789. The Ancient Regime was at an end, and the Revolution was accomplished. But the old world, unable to survive, could still lash convulsively. Hence the tragedy of the next five years.

CHAPTER XVII

The Revolution: 1788-1792

⚔ CAUSES OF THE REVOLUTION

Many theories are current about the causes of the Revolution. They cannot be ignored, for they determine the selection and interpretation of the events. The shallowest of all is that the French made a revolution because they are of a revolutionary temper: Alfred, Lord Tennyson, honestly contrasted the "red fool-fury" of the Celt with the majestic and equable course of England's history, "a land of settled government." Nothing is so delusive as national psychology. For eight centuries the French had been obstinately loyal to the same dynasty, under the most tragic circumstances, when the king was a child and when he was a prisoner, when he was a wastrel and when he was a madman. It was England, on the contrary, that had given glaring examples of religious instability in the sixteenth century and of political fickleness in the seventeenth. It was men of English stock, on both sides of the Atlantic, who had first revealed a radical turn of mind and rudely shattered the majesty that doth hedge round a king.

The most familiar interpretation is the one long official in the schools of the French Republic: the Ancient Regime was a mass of corruption and oppression, and the long-suffering French were at last goaded into rebellion. This view survives in the Anglo-Saxon world, quaintly blending with a strong antirevolutionary prejudice, through that incomparable handbook of misinformation, Dickens' *Tale of Two Cities*.

We are not ready to accept too rosy a view of the old monarchy, either in its heyday or in its decline. There were famines in the fair and fruitful land; men were actually killed because they attempted to evade the preposterous salt tax; torture was used to wring out the confession of imaginary crimes; serfhood still lingered; feudal rights, onerous or humiliating, could still be enforced; men could be arrested with no warrant but a royal letter, kept in jail without judgment, and there allowed to waste away if the powers did not choose to remember. These facts cannot be brushed away by Talleyrand's wistful sigh for "the sweetness of life," or by the nostalgic optimism of Franz Funk-Brentano.[1] But most of these abuses were vestigial. Only a few abbeys still owned serfs; on Malesherbes' initiative the torture was on its way out; the Bastille held but a handful of prisoners; the victims of arbitrary arrest were mostly unruly members of the nobility, imprisoned, like Mirabeau, at the request of their families. We must never forget that the Revolution was not started by the downtrodden but by the *bourgeoisie,* a solid, wealthy, rising class; Brittany and Vendée, which took up arms for the defense of the old abuses, were among the poorest parts of France.

Then there is the theory propounded by Hippolyte Taine, in his monumental *Origins of Contemporary France.*[2] According to him the Revolution was a disease of the mind, and its starting point was in the intellect. Jacobinism (or radicalism, as we would call it) is the fruit of *philosophie;* and *philosophie* is the embodiment of "the classical spirit," by which Taine means faith in general ideas, and abstract logic forcing its way in scorn of paltry realities. An ancient conception: it was originated and defended in England by no less an authority than Edmund Burke. It was to find ironical expression in the song that Victor Hugo, in *Les Misérables,* places on the lips of dying Gavroche:

> *Je suis tombé par terre:*
> *C'est la faute à Voltaire;*
> *Le nez dans le ruisseau:*
> *C'est la faute à Rousseau.*[3]

This school is alive today, not only with the reactionary historians who prepared the Vichy regime, Maurras, Bainville, Madelin, Gaxotte, but with those conservatives everywhere who affect to consider any demand for reform as the result of some unpractical abstract doctrine, some "crackpot ideology" or "-ism."

We have seen that the true classical spirit bore no resemblance to Taine's caricature: it was characterized by reasonableness, moderation, realism, not logic run mad. The Revolution of 1789 was not inspired predominantly by Rousseau but, on the critical side—the attack on abuses—by Voltaire; on the constructive side—constitutionalism—by Montesquieu. Neither Voltaire nor Montesquieu was a logician; both were keen, realistic observers and historians of the highest merit. Both derived their "Enlightenment" from cautious and practical England.

Principles with a Rousseauistic ring were voiced, as we shall see, even in the early stages of the Revolution. They were no doubt in the air, although they found it difficult to assume concrete form. But these

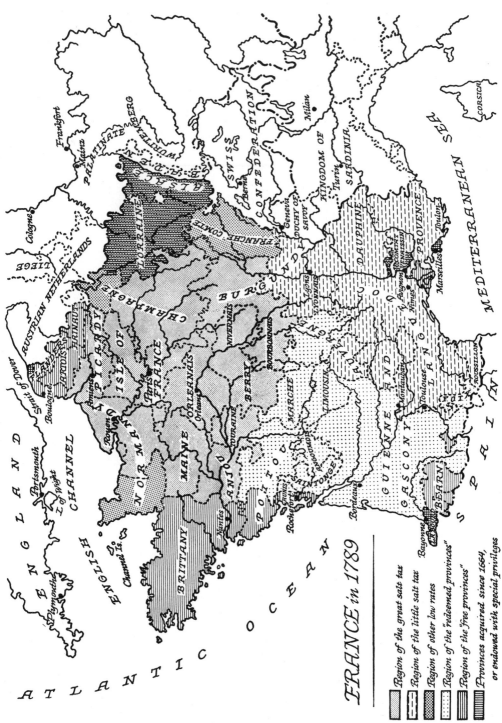

FRANCE in 1789

Region of the great salt tax
Region of the little salt tax
Region of other low rates
Region of the "redeemed provinces"
Region of the "free provinces"
Provinces acquired since 1664,
or endowed with special privileges

principles were scrupulously those which had been formulated by our Founding Fathers, and which, embodied in the Preamble of our Constitution, are considered by the most conservative among us as eternal verities. The rights of man, natural liberty, natural equality were not newfangled sophistries but commonplaces of ancient standing, professed, oddly enough, even by the old Capetians. In a charter of 1147 we read: "A decree of divine Providence has ordained that all men, being of the same origin, be endowed at their birth with a sort of natural liberty. . . . It belongs to Our Royal Majesty to raise them again to liberty." In 1315 Louis X, the Quarrelsome, issued an ordinance which breathed the purest Jacobinism: "In accordance with the law of Nature, every man should be born free. . . . We, considering that our kingdom is called the kingdom of the Franks, that is to say of the Free, and that reality should be in agreement with the name, have ordered, etc. . . ." [4]

As for a purely economic interpretation of the events, it will take us some of the way, but not very far. The immediate cause of the crisis was undoubtedly fiscal: the Revolution occurred when both ends could not be made to meet. In addition the temper of the people was made less patient, in 1788–1789, by a poor crop and a harsh winter. But the needed fiscal reform would not have been beyond the capacity of a Necker if it had not involved a change in the structure of society. The nobles resisted that change not exclusively out of greed but even more out of pride. The bourgeois, on the other hand, did desire to be relieved from excessive and unjust burdens; but they desired even more not to be snubbed by aristocrats who, in Figaro's words, "had merely taken the trouble of being born." The real issue was social equality rather than a balanced budget.

THE STATES-GENERAL

We have seen that the demand for the States-General had come both from the reactionaries and from the liberals. The Parlement proposed that the assembly be formed according to the procedure that prevailed in 1614. But public opinion protested angrily. The rules finally adopted for the elections were complicated but, on the whole, surprisingly generous. The lower clergy, for one thing, would actually be represented; and in the crisis of 1789 the parish priests proved a decisive factor. The Third Estate would not be entirely dominated by official and rich bourgeois. And that Third Estate was accorded as many delegates as the other two orders combined. But all these concessions would have been nullified if, as on previous occasions, the orders were to vote as units and not the representatives as individuals. Then the privileged classes would constantly outvote the commoners two to one. This vital question was left in suspense. Both Louis XVI and Necker were well-meaning and timid souls and preferred to put off the awful hour of decision.

The campaign afforded excellent political training: we should never forget that the Revolution began not with an insurrection but with a thorough and ubiquitous inquiry. Everywhere grievances were aired and duly consigned in *cahiers* or memoranda. These show a remarkable likeness throughout the land, although there were no nationally organized parties. There was at least one *philosophe* in every village, and a few obvious patterns were pretty generally followed. What we would call the proletariat, the poorest peasants, the journeymen in the cities, did not voice their special desires. Perhaps they were conscious of none so far and accepted the bourgeois reforms as a first installment. It is the great fermentation of that period that created the France we know. Until 1788 the royal dominions had no unity but the person of the king; they were provinces and cities acknowledging him as their liege, but each with its own customs and traditions. It was then, and then only, that the people of Brittany, Navarre, Flanders, Alsace, Dauphiné began to feel themselves actually French.

It was a new departure, in very truth the birth of a nation. Yet this growing sense of unity was the perfection, not the destruction, of the work obscurely and unconsciously accomplished by the Capetians over eight hundred years. The new "patriotism"—the word then came into fashion—was accompanied by a recrudescence of royalist feeling. Louis XVI had never been so popular as he was in May, 1789. Dynasty and nation could have remained fused, but the curse of Versailles destroyed that hope. Louis XIV had drawn the nobility to his enormous court: now the king appeared as the head of the court, not of the people. He could not, with his flabby good will, tear himself apart from his natural associates. The queen, at any rate, knew her own mind. She threw her whole influence in support of the crumbling old order. So far, she had understood nothing but pleasure and pride; now the days of frivolous pleasure were over, and pride became her sole passion.

When the States assembled on the fifth of May, 1789, the bias of the king was manifest. They were convened at Versailles, not in Paris, so as not to interfere with the king's prime concern, his hunting. All the resources of etiquette were strained to keep the commoners humble. The privileged orders appeared in splendor: the Third Estate had to wear a plain black uniform. The king's opening speech and Necker's long exposé were both noncommittal. The essential question was not answered: would the States be a mere antiquarian show, each order voting separately, or would they be recognized as a genuine representative assembly?

For six weeks there was an irritating deadlock. On June 17 Abbé Sieyès, the theorist of the bourgeois revolution, moved that the States declare themselves a National Assembly. This motion was carried by a meeting of the Third Estate. The other orders were invited to join. A number of the lower clergy and a few nobles were ready to do so.

The court's countermove was fumbling: when the deputies were to meet in the accustomed place, they found the hall closed in preparation for a royal sitting to be held three days later. They refused to disperse and sought shelter from the rain in a covered tennis court (*Jeu de Paume*). There they took an oath not to separate until they had given France a constitution (June 20).

On the twenty-third there was a plenary royal session. The king did his best to be haughty, resolute, threatening. He ordered the Assembly to meet in three separate houses. The privileged orders followed him out of the hall. The Third, disregarding his command, remained. The Grand Master of Ceremonies, Dreux-Brézé, came to remind them of the king's decision. Mirabeau answered him with the dramatic voice, the flashing imperious glance which made him unique in that curiously tame and drab assembly, "Tell your master that we are here by the will of the people, and shall not leave except under the force of bayonets." Fateful words! They contained the whole of the bourgeois revolution—and more. "The will of the people," like our own, "We the people," implied the fullness of democracy for which Sieyès and Mirabeau themselves were not ready.

The man who had hurled that challenge was a powerful and disturbing figure. Forty years old, pock-marked, of an expressive ugliness, he had become famous for his wild adventures, which included abductions, duels, imprisonments, daring escapes, exiles. His life had been an even more exciting picaresque romance than Beaumarchais's, only far more disreputable. In particular all France knew of his quarrels with his volcanic father, the marquis of Mirabeau, who had repeatedly put him under lock and key. Oddly enough, the fiery marquis was also an economist of some note, and was known by the bleating title, "The Friend of Mankind." Gabriel, his son, had the raffishness, but also the histrionic power, which was so completely absent from the personality of Lafayette. He had shown himself a good publicist: his work on the Prussian monarchy, on an ambitious scale, showed penetration and rare political sense. Rejected by the nobility as a black sheep, he had himself elected by the Third Estate of Provence. He was to be, for the next two years, a portent rather than a power: the pride, the dread, and the scandal of the Assembly.

The reference to "the force of bayonets" might have been taken as an indication by a headstrong king: the bourgeois knew they could not fight, and they had no appetite for martyrdom. Mirabeau almost hinted that to a show of force there would be no physical resistance, only a moral protest. But the king shrank from the decision. He followed his invariable line, sullen acquiescence. He sent word to the privileged orders to unite with the Third Estate: the National Constituent Assembly was thus tacitly recognized.

Louis yielded, and yielding was wisdom; but he could never yield with a good grace, a clear mind, or a clean heart. He was easily persuaded to take back, by stealth and violence, what he had granted out of apathy. So, early in July foreign regiments were moved into the vicinity of Paris: the French Guards were suspected of sympathizing with the Assembly and the people. These mercenaries were palpably intended to be the instruments of a *coup d'état*. Public opinion was intensely aware of the projected move. When suddenly Necker was dismissed (July 11), the act was understood to be a declaration of war on the Revolution.

✄ FALL OF THE BASTILLE. FEUDALISM ABOLISHED. RIGHTS OF MAN PROCLAIMED

Necker, a banker, was the very symbol of the *bourgeoisie*. His downfall meant the frustration of their hope; it might also portend what they most dreaded, bankruptcy, "hideous bankruptcy," to use Mirabeau's dramatic words. It was among the bourgeois that resistance was first conscious and vocal: the people were used as a willing instrument. The revolt originated not in workingmen's suburbs like Faubourg Saint-Antoine but in the Palais-Royal gardens.

The gardens were the delightful and equivocal creation of an equivocal character, the duke of Orleans, grandson of the regent. Dissolute and intelligent, prodigal and enterprising, ambitious and infirm of purpose, he had wasted his vast substance, and sought to recoup himself through a bold real-estate proposition: the gardens of his palace [5] in the heart of Paris were lined with handsome apartment houses with shops on the ground floor. The gardens themselves, and the arcades surrounding them, became, and remained for three-quarters of a century, the center of fashion and vice, a rendezvous for gallant adventure, gambling, gossip, newsmongering, and politics. It was an open-air drawing room and a free-for-all arena of opinions, like Hyde Park in our time on a Sunday afternoon; but active on every day and at every hour, with a cohesiveness, a quickness of response seldom found in Hyde Park.

The duke of Orleans had his agents in that whirling mass of the best and the worst: there was at least the velleity of an Orleanist movement. The Palais-Royal crowds, inflamed by the inspired voice of a publicist, Camille Desmoulins, were seething with anger; they stuck in their hats, as a rallying badge, leaves from the sheltering trees—and green happened to be the color of the Orleans household. But the Orleans faction, all yea-and-nay, went no further: its chance was to come only forty years later.[6]

No formal decision but a sure instinct carried the people to the Bastille on July 14. The pretext was to obtain weapons against the expected *coup d'état* and to disarm the old fortress, whose obsolete batteries could still have raked the populous eastern districts in deadly fashion. The bundle of frowning medieval towers was defended by a handful of retired veterans with a few Swiss guards. The governor, De Launay, hesitated, parleyed, fired feebly upon the crowd. The besiegers, enraged by his apparent treachery, carried the fort by storm and killed the garrison. A few insignificant prisoners were liberated. Before the smoke of battle had blown away, Paris had started pulling down the ancient stones, dark with the grime and hatred of four centuries.

There is no clearer case of a legend, in the sense now familiar to our readers: an event of limited intrinsic importance magnified into a symbol. The Bastille meant everything that was arbitrary and oppressive in the past; it was a gloomy ghost in the Paris, in the France, of the Enlightenment. The significance of the deed was realized at once. When Louis XVI was informed, he said, "But then, it is a revolt?" and the messenger wisely answered, "No, Sire: it is a revolution." It was *the* Revolution. In Koenigsberg Immanuel Kant, living aloof in the serene temple of pure reason, took notice of the world of men and was fired with enthusiasm. In St. Petersburg, according to Ségur, people hugged each other in the streets and wept for joy. When France, a year later, celebrated her new birth, the "Federation" of all Frenchmen, she picked out, for that solemn day, the anniversary of the fall of the Bastille.

The usual pattern was wearily repeated. The king submitted, sent away the foreign regiments, recalled Necker to the ministry. As a token of reconciliation he came to Paris and was received in state at the City Hall. He even adopted the new national cockade, the red and blue of Paris with the royal white in between. "Take these colors, Sire," said Lafayette, the commander-in-chief of the newly formed National Guard, "they will go round the world."

Necker, palladium of the bourgeois, had been the center of the storm; but the decisive blow had been struck by the people of Paris. *The people of Paris!*: that is to say democracy, demagogy, and enlightenment in unstable proportions. The fourteenth of July marked the beginning of that fitful dictatorship of the capital, to some a messianic hope, to others an apocalyptic menace, which was to be an erratic factor in French history at least until 1871.

The long, obscure tussle, the bitterness of hope deferred, the irritation and contempt caused by the shiftiness of the court party had fevered not Paris alone but the whole nation. There was first a curious collective neurosis, the "Great Fear": rumors of brigandage and destruction spread throughout the land. But beside this nameless and passive dread, there were definite disorders. The people were taking the law into their own hands, storming the châteaux, burning the feudal title deeds. Any attempt at repression would have meant universal anarchy. The menace was met more intelligently and more courageously by giving up the hated vestiges of the feudal regime. On the night of August 4, 1789, members of the nobility, friends of Lafayette and liberals like himself, proposed the abolition of privileges, and gave the example by formally renouncing their own. They were followed by other nobles and, a little more cautiously, by members of the higher clergy.[7] This willing sacrifice, which was not extorted by fear, which, on the contrary, robbed fear of the initiative, roused the enthusiasm of the whole Assembly. Realists may call the scene theatrical and sentimental, but it was an unprecedented triumph of generosity and reason. The Ancient Regime did not disappear in a fit of idealistic hysteria: the act was eminently sensible. It did not blast the foundations of society: it merely swept away useless rubble. The majority in control were shrewd bourgeois. They saw to it that, if every trace of feudal domination was erased, all contracts involving property were respected. All feudal dues which were a form of rent and did not imply class privileges were not suppressed outright; they were only made redeemable.

We find the same spirit, the purest bourgeois orthodoxy, in the Declaration of the Rights of Man, voted on August 27. It is a Jeffersonian document.[8] Only it is more conservative than its American prototype. It names "property" among the inalienable rights of man: the Founding Fathers had declined to proclaim such a dogma and substituted for "property" the innocuous "pursuit of happines." Burke, his great mind clouded by "the wisdom of prejudice," failed altogether to understand the nature of the French Revolution. Its moderate, realistic, bourgeois character, under the fine philosophical phrasing, is apparent to every unbiased observer.

THE KING'S FUMBLING RESISTANCE

The submission of the king after the fourteenth of July was insincere. At any rate it was not sincere enough to preclude reactionary plotting at court and amid the royal circle. From Versailles it was easy for the king to move farther away from the capital, gather loyal troops, and march on Paris to end the Revolution "by the force of bayonets." Breteuil, who had been active in the abortive *coup d'état* of July 11, still urged such a course. At a banquet of loyalist officers the presence of the queen evoked delirious enthusiasm. They sang with tears an air by Grétry, "O Richard! O my King! The whole world forsakes thee!" The national tricolor cockade was torn off and trampled underfoot; the royal white, or the Austrian black of the queen, took its place.

Again a provocation, again a fumbling, irresolute one; the king had not made up his mind to fight. Again, the bourgeois, threatened in *their* revolution, took up the challenge, but by proxy. Cautious, used to legal procedure, they were reluctant to meet force with force. So, as on the fourteenth of July, it was the people that served as cat's paw. Against the ladies of the court, emblems of frivolous extravagance, marched the women of the central market, *Les Halles*. Famed for their fearlessness of speech, like their congeners of Billingsgate, they were easily roused to action. On the fifth of October they trudged in grotesque array to the royal residence, some twelve miles away from the Halles. The pretext was a scarcity of food; they affected to believe that if the king were in their midst, they would no longer lack bread. So, they went in quest of "the Baker, the Baker's Wife, and the little Baker Boy." Lafayette and his National Guards followed, unwilling to disperse the pitiful rabble, still more averse to support its vague wild demands.

At any moment the farce might have turned into bloody drama; the queen had to flee, half-dressed, from her apartments; and a few guards gave their lives in her defense. Lafayette's protection was more effective. He risked his reputation, his popularity, for the sake of a queen who distrusted and hated him. He brought her out on a balcony and, respectfully bending, kissed her hand. The crowd cheered; the royal lives were saved.

But the cause of absolutism was lost. It was too late now for Louis XVI to hack his way to freedom: Lafayette had calmed the crowd, but he was also holding the reactionary troops in check. So, on October 6 the riotous adventure ended riotously. The king, yielding to the entreaties of his subjects, went back to "the bosom of his family," the good people of Paris. And from Versailles to the Tuileries there roared a fantastic, indescribable parade: royal carriages, royal retainers, a few loyal officers, Lafayette's troops, and pell-mell, cheering and jeering, workingmen, dubious characters, and the nominal victors, the vociferous ladies of the Halles.

Once more the king had stolidly bowed to the facts. Once more he had a chance: Lafayette could have made a respectable constitutional sovereign out of him. But he did not play fair with Lafayette, because he was congenitally unable to play fair. No sooner had he reached the Tuileries than he sent a secret message to the court of Spain: henceforth, he said, he considered himself a prisoner, and no public word or act of his was to be accepted as expressing his own volition. The Assembly followed the king to Paris; but over two hundred members resigned, and already a number of aristocrats were leaving the country. The Revolution by general consent, the Revolution that was meant to be not civil war but reconciliation, had appeared for a few hours in the night of August 4. That holy flame was waning.

Had any other solution assumed definiteness—Orleans, Lafayette, a republic—the end of Louis XVI's reign might have come on October 6, 1789, instead of August 10, 1792. The momentum of eight centuries carried the monarchy for those three years of mental and moral confusion: deceit and self-deceit, distrust and self-distrust. Naturally, it would have been folly to give such a king an absolute veto on legislation: the weapon would have been in the hands of the queen, and she would have wielded it to destroy the new regime. She was called *Madame Veto* as she had been called *Madame Déficit*.

The king acted his part well enough: it was difficult to tell whether his sullen co-operation was the result of good sense, resignation, dullness, or duplicity. On the fourteenth of July, 1790, when France celebrated her rebirth in a grand "Festival of Celebration," the king appeared on the altar of the Fatherland, in the Champ-de-Mars, and duly swore allegiance to the still incomplete constitution. But the solemn mass in that ceremony was celebrated by Talleyrand, and this gave to the whole affair a Mephistophelean tinge.[9]

The court party made a last move to break down the power of the Assembly: they bought the most eloquent, the most clear-thinking, of the deputies, the formidable Mirabeau. The word "bought" is literally true: his services were heavily paid for in cash. Morally, the case is not so clear: Mirabeau would have served the same cause without compensation. He felt, rightly enough, that some power was needed not to stem the Revolution but to steer it in such a crisis. He was ready to provide that power behind the throne. If his activities had to be secret, it was not wholly Mirabeau's fault: the jealousy of his colleagues and the nemesis of his notorious past were blocking his way. Had he lived, it is likely that the king would have failed to support him in any energetic course, and the queen in any intelligent one: for he wanted the restoration of order, not of the old order. He died on April 2, 1791, his secret dealings not yet exposed; and he was admitted to the nation's Pantheon. Strangely enough, his tumultuous disreputable youth and his final intrigues have not destroyed his popularity even yet. If his remains were removed from their usurped place of honor, his name is perpetuated in streets, bridges, and monuments. All that is remembered is that, at the crucial hour, he had roared out "the will of the people."

Mirabeau had advised the king to move to Rouen and there to rally his partisans against the Assembly: thus any sign of collusion with foreign powers would have been avoided. After the great statesman's death the court party realized that, in a civil war, their chances would be slim without support from abroad. So, when on June 20, 1791, the royal family escaped at night from the Tuileries, their aim was to join Bouillé and his loyal forces, with headquarters at Metz on the eastern border. That dramatic episode has been admirably told by Carlyle, Michelet, Dumas, Lenôtre: the details, rich with incident, suspense, and even comic relief, belong to anecdotic history. The king was recognized at Sainte-Menehould by the postmaster, Drouet, and detained at the next relay, Varennes. He was brought back to Paris between living hedges of somber silence. Suspended from his functions, he was granted another respite. The official version was that he had been "abducted" by enemies of the Fatherland and providentially "rescued" by his faithful subjects. Louis swore again (September 14, 1791) to support the constitution, now completed. By that time his oath was heavily discounted. The monarchical principle did not die suddenly on August 10, 1792: its life had been oozing away for three years.

✒ THE CONSTITUENT ASSEMBLY:
FINANCIAL, ADMINISTRATIVE, ECCLESIASTICAL MEASURES

It is time to revert to realities, the work of the National Assembly. On June 20, 1789, absolutism had ended; on August 4 the remains of feudalism were destroyed; on August 27 the "rights of man" were proclaimed: three great affirmations of principle rather than constructive measures. The Assembly now addressed itself to its positive tasks, the financial problem, the administrative reorganization of the kingdom, the constitution.

The new France, once upon her feet, might be able to keep her financial balance. But before any reconstruction the impending bankruptcy of the state had to be averted. An enormous hoard was at hand, the property of the clergy. The thought had crossed many minds, from Law's to Calonne's. It was formally proposed by Talleyrand, still a bishop in good standing; as Abbé de Périgord he had been one of the agents of the Assembly of the Clergy; he knew more about ecclesiastical resources, and ecclesiastical abuses, than any man living. This utilization of Church property was conceived in a spirit not of vengeance or greed but of justice. It was hardly safe for the clergy to be absurdly rich in the midst of a bankrupt kingdom; it was even less safe for it to starve its hardest workers, the parish priests, in order to pamper a few aristocrats like Rohan. The necessity of a redistribution was felt by all, and not least by the most loyal Catholics. The clergy having ceased to be a separate order in the state, its property was placed at the disposal of the nation. The first use to be made of this property was to assure the adequate support of all priests who were actually ministering to the religious needs of the people. This done, a vast surplus was left which could be applied to the reduction, or even to the extinction, of the national deficit. Since the need was pressing, and since the whole bulk could not be sold outright, mortage notes bearing interest were issued on the security of the nationalized domains and were called the assignats.

So far, the plan was statesmanlike; and much as certain conservative elements may have disliked it, they found downright opposition a very unpopular attitude. If the assignats later depreciated, it was because of civil and foreign war: wild inflation is a phenomenon all too familiar in our age. We may add that this measure, radical as it was, never was reversed. When the Church, after nearly ten years of estrangement (1792–1801), resumed friendly relations with the French State, the principle adopted in 1789 was not seriously questioned.

The reshaping of French administration was also done with commendable efficiency. We must remember that, in spite of all efforts on the part of the kings, France in 1789 was still a tangled mass of local customs: England was then by comparison a model of logical simplicity. For the capricious overlapping divisions of the past the Assembly substituted new units, the largest of which was the *département*. The eighty-three departments were of such a size that one could travel to the local capital (*chef-lieu*) in one day. With the increased rapidity of communication it is now felt that the units might well be larger, twenty "regions" for instance, but the solution adopted by the Assembly was the more practical at the time. It is important to note that if the Assembly introduced standardization in local government as a rough-and-ready method of bringing order swiftly out of chaos, it did not impose centralization. The departments were endowed with a large measure of autonomy. The dictatorship of the central government came as a tragic necessity under the Convention; and that wartime concentration of power was made permanent by the supreme war lord, Napoleon. Centralization, of course, had been the constant goal of the old monarchy: "one faith, one law, one king." The Convention and Napoleon were perhaps truer to the Capetian-Valois-Bourbon tendency than the Constituent Assembly had been; but they undoubtedly overshot the mark.

The reconstruction of France involved one mistake which proved fatal to the Revolution, the attempt to reorganize the Church on the same lines as the other branches of national activity. The Church had always been so intimately connected with the monarchy that the reform of the one seemed to carry with it the reform of the other. When the State took over the property and assumed the liabilities of the clergy, the union became even more complete. There was no thought of persecution, heresy, or schism: the spiritual primacy of Rome was not disputed. The most sweeping of the changes proposed, the election of the priests by the community, was in agreement with the practices of the early Church. The policy of the Assembly was not anti-Christian and not anti-Catholic: it was, however, Gallicanism carried to its logical extreme, the doctrine of the Pragmatic Sanction of Bourges and of the Declaration of 1682, inspired by Bossuet.

Rome had found it possible to compromise, albeit reluctantly, with some degree of Gallican independence. But the king was His Most Christian Majesty, the Lord's Anointed; his Gallicanism had therefore a religious character. The Gallicanism of an Assembly was a totally different affair: for one thing the Assembly was not subjected, as the king was, to the guidance of a confessor. It would have been hard enough for the Church to retrace her steps after so many centuries and to accept the principle of popular election even if the faithful alone had been entitled to a vote; but according to the Constitution, all the political electors, including Jews, Protestants, and infidels, could take part in the choice of priests.

In spite of these very great difficulties the Holy See preserved for a while an expectant attitude, and cautious diplomacy might have averted an open rupture. But the king's ambassador at Rome, Cardinal de Bernis, represented the irreconcilable aristocratic element within the Church: the vast body of French Catholics had no way of manifesting their desire for conciliation. Furthermore, at the request of the inhabitants France annexed Avignon, which had been a papal domain for five hundred years. So the pope finally condemned the whole ecclesiastical legislation of France and forbade the priests' taking the "civic" or loyalty oath to the Constitution. This proved to be the formal declaration of war between the factions. Conservative clerics and nobles henceforth felt that they were fighting not for pride and privilege but for their faith. In many provinces the devout peasantry stood with them; even in Paris the liberal nobles and the middle class began to waver. So far, Louis XVI had yielded to the pressure of events, fitfully, reluctantly, but his ultimate acceptance of the new order was not inconceivable. He was too torpid and too kindly to offer much of a fight. But when Rome had spoken, his wavering ceased. He obeyed not merely with the passivity of a good Catholic but with inner alacrity, because the words of the pope crystallized his latent misgivings.

When we consider all these obstacles, we wonder, not that the Constitutional Church failed in the end, but that it came so near succeeding. Its start was not absolutely discouraging, its personnel far from despicable; and through many trials it managed to survive for ten years until it was suppressed by Bonaparte's Concordat.

The political regime evolved by the Assembly was a constitutional monarchy of the orthodox type. It was doomed from the first but not through its own faults; it suffered from circumstances beyond the scope of any constitution. The king, in normal times, would still have had power enough to act as a check on the single Assembly; only this particular king was at heart a traitor to his own government, and the Assembly felt it.

The constitution was purely bourgeois in character: that is to say, it was frankly plutocratic. In the matter of elections it was less generous than Necker had been in 1788. All Frenchmen were citizens; but the poor were merely passive citizens. To be an active citizen and take part in the elections of the first degree, you had to pay a due amount of direct taxation ("No representation without taxation"). To be an elector and vote in the second degree, the minimum required was higher; and to be eligible for office, it was higher still. So, there were actually four classes with a hierarchy of rights according to their wealth. France's business was Business; the ruling power was an assembly of shareholders, men who had a "stake in the country." This was exactly the political philosophy which Guizot so magisterially taught until 1848, and which remained official in Prussia until 1918.

THE LEGISLATIVE ASSEMBLY.
FAILURE OF THE CONSTITUTIONAL MONARCHY

In a quixotic fit of disinterestedness the Constituents decided that they would not be eligible for the new Legislative Assembly. But a vast political personnel had been prepared ever since 1788. France, with a deluge of newspapers and pamphlets, with a constant hubbub of eager conversation, had become a huge debating society. The clubs, in particular, were exceedingly active. They came to be known not by their formal title but by their meeting place, usually some former monastery. Thus Lafayette was a "Feuillant," Marat and Camille Desmoulins were

"Cordeliers," Danton, both a "Cordelier" and a "Jacobin," Robespierre, a "Jacobin." The ghosts of the ancient monastic orders survived strangely into the new era.

The Legislative Assembly met on October 1, 1791. Of the 745 members—lawyers, many of them, and, with a few exceptions, men of little note—the monarchical Right was a dwindling minority: the most ardent Royalists were emigrating; the liberals had lost faith in the king. On the Left were found eloquent and inexperienced constitutionalists verging on republicanism: Vergniaud, Guadet, Isnard, Gensonné, Barbaroux, a chance grouping called loosely Girondists, because several of their leaders came from Bordeaux, in the department of Gironde. The Girondists were not at that time sharply divided from the Cordeliers and the Jacobins, whose strength was in their clubs rather than in the Assembly. Outside, the Commune of Paris was already casting a threatening shadow: it was no mere municipal body but, with its forty-eight "sections," a well-knit insurrectionary force.

The ministry was colorless but might be described as Feuillant: that is to say, it stood for the waning constitutional compromise. Leadership was lacking. Mirabeau was dead; Lafayette had lost his popularity by his chivalrous defense of the throne. Necker had been sent packing as early as October, 1790, this time not through the caprice of a despot, but because everyone had grown weary of his ineffectual financial juggling. With him went Montmorin who had, not ineptly, directed foreign affairs; but although he had sought advice form Mirabeau, he had never been taken into the king's confidence. The survivors were nonentities; for a few months a brilliant man, Narbonne, was minister of war. Soon all party squabbles were reduced to insignificance by the mounting threat of foreign conflict.

Threat is perhaps a misleading term; although the age was eminently civilized—much more so than our own—all parties, more or less consciously, were desiring war. It seemed the only way out of inextricable ambiguities. Robespierre and Marat, the half-crazy doctor turned demagogue, were among the few publicists who resolutely advocated peace.

The irreconcilable French nobles, following the king's brothers in voluntary emigration, had formed a little anti-Revolutionary army at Coblentz on the Rhine; that this army should be tolerated and even encouraged by the elector-archbishop of Trier was in itself a *casus belli*. The German princes who held feudal property in Alsace protested against the suppression of their rights on August 4, 1789. The pope was denouncing not only the reorganization of the Church in France but the whole policy of the Revolution. The problem was of European scope. The example of France, the oldest monarchy and the center of the most brilliant culture, was likely to prove contagious. Even liberal princes were beginning to feel uneasy. Moreover, hungry neighbors might want to take advantage of France's troubles: France had profited often enough by their division.

When on April 20, 1792, France declared war on Austria and her ally Prussia, the purely domestic phase of the Revolution came to an end. That war, with brief delusive lulls, was to last twenty-three years: it completely warped the course of France's destiny. It called for centralization, dictatorship, terror at home; for victory and annexations abroad: *Salus populi suprema lex esto.* Eventually, the efforts of the European reaction were to fail: the political conquests of 1789 remained firmly established, the Ancient Regime was not restored. But on the other hand, that quarter century of titanic achievement was for France utterly wasted. Her European frontiers remained practically unchanged; no democratic progress made after 1792 survived; the word Revolution caused a shudder even in liberal minds; in Paris and in all the European capitals the upper classes were less enlightened, less generous in spirit, after the storm than they had been before. The lightning conquests of the Republic and the Empire are credited with the downfall of the ancient regimes throughout the Continent; but a peaceful constitutional France, through the example of her success, would have more surely achieved the same goal. All that resulted out of the formidable catastrophe was an array of glorious, lurid, and conflicting legends.

CHAPTER XVIII

Martial Interlude: 1792-1815: The Revolution: Legislative Assembly, Convention, Directory

WAR DEFLECTS THE REVOLUTION

It is a truism that the course of human events is fitful. There are periods of apparent stagnation, like the half millennium of the Dark Ages, and eras of swift, determined progress, like the early sixteenth century or the middle decades of the eighteenth. The four years we have just considered (1788–1792) tumbled like rapids: the stream of French tradition was not broken, but it rushed perilously. The twenty-three years ahead of us, which ended at Waterloo, were to be a series of whirlpools, an impressive display of wasted energy: it is possible for a generation to be lost, although engaged in titanic efforts. Here we clearly see the difference between romance, even when it is based on true facts, and history as a scientific pursuit. Romance seeks awe and wonder; history traces deep and lasting trends. But we are telling the biography of France: perhaps the epic of a nation's life is its essential reality. No one could expunge from the annals of France the names of Robespierre, Danton, Marat, Carnot, Bonaparte any more than those of Joan of Arc, Francis I, Henry IV, Richelieu, or Louis XIV. Without these vivid protagonists how drab would be the tale! The general reader is an incurable romanticist; in simpler terms he is human.

The story does not belong exclusively to our field. It is European rather than specifically French. No war can be fully understood from the standpoint of a single participant. The French saw but dimly, beyond the battle line, the forces that opposed them. They evolved, for instance, a horrific dual entity, *Pittetcobourg*, Pitt and Coburg, which to them explained everything, and to us seems ludicrously wide of the

mark. On the other hand, the heroism of the Republican armies, undeniable as it is, does not properly account for the dazzling victories of
1793–1795: we have to keep in mind, as the French did not, the secret
jealousies of the allies and the martyrdom of Poland.

On August 27, 1791, Frederick William II, King of Prussia, and
Emperor Leopold II had met at Pillnitz. They had issued a proclamation
which, although carefully worded, carried a threat of interference. After
all, crowned heads form a brotherhood, and the queen of France was
the emperor's sister. On February 7, 1792, a formal alliance was formed
between Austria and Prussia. On March 2 Leopold II died: his moderation, his sincere enlightenment had been the last prop of peace: it would
be more difficult to talk reason with his successor, Francis II. It was this
increasing menace that caused the downfall of the moderate Feuillant
ministry, suspected of excessive subserviency to the king and to "the
Austrian committee."

It was a curiously assorted team that assumed power in March, 1792.
Clavière was, like Necker, a banker and a Genevan. Roland, an elderly
man, able, austere, a trifle pompous, had a young, handsome, ambitious,
idealistic, insufferable wife. The key man was Dumouriez, an old soldier
of fortune turned secret diplomatic agent; youthful at fifty-six, he was
as clever and an unreliable as his checkered past would indicate.

On April 20 France declared war: her three main armies were to be
led by Rochambeau, Luckner,[1] and Lafayette. The forces were disorgan-
ized by the emigration—it might well be called the desertion—of so
many aristocratic officers. The new levies were unseasoned; they broke
into a panic at the first encounter and shot their officers. Soldiers and
people felt themselves betrayed. The reaction in Paris was an invasion of
the royal residence, the Tuileries, on June 20. The pretext was to frighten
the king into signing the Assembly's decrees against recusant priests and
fugitive nobles. For once the passivity of Louis XVI reached the level
of courage. He faced the rabble with dignity, uttered no menace, and
made no promise. The Assembly proclaimed that the country was in
danger, and everywhere volunteers flocked to the standards. The Phrygian bonnet, the red cap of liberty, became the emblem of patriotism.

The duke of Brunswick, Prussian commander-in-chief, issued a
blustering manifesto threatening to destroy Paris if any harm should
happen to the monarch or his family: thus the solidarity between the
royal cause and that of the nation's enemies was made evident. The
blunder was so egregious that it might seem intentional: there were
Royalists who felt that Louis XVI would be worth more to the cause as
a martyr than as a leader. The reaction was immediate. The more radical
elements seized control of the Paris Commune, and on the tenth of

August the people marched again on the Tuileries. This time blood was shed. The king gave in; he ordered the Swiss guards to cease firing and sought refuge in the Assembly. Suspended from his functions, he was imprisoned in the tower of the Temple.[2] Danton, Lebrun, Monge, Servan, Roland, Clavière formed a provisional government. A National Convention elected by universal (i.e., manhood) suffrage was to determine the nature of the new regime.

The mass hysteria that followed is not hard to understand. No nation engaged in a life-and-death struggle has ever shown much mercy to traitors. The fact that disloyalty was ubiquitous did not dilute its venom: it only made the plight of the country more appalling, and more implacable the resulting mood. Lafayette, after a last effort to contain the flood, was arraigned in his turn and had to flee: an Austrian prison awaited him. Verdun, bastion of the eastern frontier, was captured. So the "Fifth Columnists"—they were simply called suspects in those days —were rounded up until the prisons were choked. From the second to the seventh of September the mob stormed the jails, improvised People's Courts, and massacred almost at random. Danton, Minister of Justice, humane and energetic as he is held to be, did nothing to stop the slaughter.

The Prussians were advancing into Champagne. At Valmy their well-trained army officered by veterans of Frederick the Great met the unsteady troops of Dumouriez and Kellermann (September 20). An indecisive artillery duel was fought in the mist. The French stood their ground and even started a counterattack. Astounded at this unexpected resistance, the enemy paused, turned back, and slowly retreated. Goethe, who was present, claims to have said, "On this day, at this place, a new era opens in the history of the world." The Convention, which met on the morrow, agreed with Goethe: the monarchy was declared abolished, and September 22 was proclaimed as the first day of the Year One of the Republic.

The French pursued their counteroffensive. Custine took Speyer, Mainz, Frankfort on the Main. By the victory of Jemappes (November 6) Dumouriez conquered the whole of Belgium. Since the king of Sardinia had joined the war on the side of the allies, Savoy and Nice were occupied. A dramatic reversal, which the French ascribed altogether to the holy wrath of an awakened people. Already the battle song of democracy, the "Marseillaise," composed by Rouget de Lisle at Strasbourg, was hovering like a spirit over the marching battalions.

The king was brought to the bar of the Convention. He was manifestly guilty of treason: 683 deputies out of 721 returned that verdict. But only 321 against 320 voted for immediate capital punishment. On January

21, 1793, Louis XVI was decapitated. The queen, whose moral responsibility was far greater, had to wait until the sixteenth of October.

France had only followed an English precedent: but within ten days she found herself at war with the Empire, Holland, Spain, Great Britain. In March a Royalist revolt broke out in the Vendée on the Atlantic coast. Dumouriez, beaten at Neerwinden (March 18), went over to the enemy, and Belgium was lost. The situation of France was unexampled. Her noble officers had deserted almost in a body; no priest could remain faithful to the pope without being in flagrant rebellion against the Constitution. More than one-fourth of France, in the West (Vendée, Brittany, Normandy), in the Center (Lyons), in the South (Toulon), had risen against Paris. Republican France was a besieged fortress torn by strife within. The result was a state of exasperation verging upon madness. Of this "preternatural suspicion," as Carlyle calls it, of this "obsidional fever," Jean-Paul Marat is the sinister symptom. The Friend of the People, as he liked to call himself, had at first found few sympathizers. But as his worst predictions came to pass, he seemed to incarnate the somber resolve of a people at bay. The ferocity of many had slowly risen to the pitch of his own. When he was stabbed in his bath by Charlotte Corday (July 13), he was worshipped as a martyr.

THE REIGN OF TERROR. ROBESPIERRE

Terror feeds upon itself. A cowed adversary cannot be trusted: the very wrongs inflicted upon his friends make it more likely that he is harboring plans of vengeance. So the circle of victims widened endlessly. The initiative and the driving power were from the first in the hands of the extremists, the Mountain.[3] But they were only the official spearheads of the Jacobins, with their network of societies covering the whole of France. The Commune of Paris was their tremendously effective weapon: it was close at hand, controlled an armed force, and could unleash the multitude. Many Convention members who were known as Terrorists themselves lived in terror.

The Mountain did not stand for an ideology but for a desperate will to victory. Clemenceau, in so many respects a *petit bourgeois* conservative, was the true heir of the *Montagnards,* with his defiant watchwords, *Jusqu'au bout,* to the bitter end, and *Je fais la guerre,* I am waging war; and the Tory Winston Churchill was, in that sense, a perfect *Montagnard.* No doubt the Convention did vote, perfunctorily, an ultrademocratic constitution. But it was piously enclosed in a cedar Ark of the Covenant for the duration of the war. Before the Ark was opened, the constitution was dead. No doubt an appeal was made to "the peoples" everywhere against "the oppressors," and so the war assumed (on both sides) the dignity of a crusade. But (on both sides also) principles were compounded of conviction, camouflage, and propaganda. The one problem was to survive, to save the country.

That is why the Committee of Public Salvation (*Salut Public*) was created: the usual rendering, Public Safety, is far too tame, and fitter to translate *Comité de Sûreté Générale*. Measures of safety are purely defensive; of salvation, dynamic.[4] The committee was a dictatorship of twelve; the persons might shift from month to month; the policy, for one crucial year, remained steady.

The instruments of that dictatorship were the Representatives on Missions and the Revolutionary Tribunal. The Representatives were sent to the armies and to the provinces, to put the fear of the Convention into the servants as well as the enemies of the Republic. They were the all-powerful agents of the concentrated national will. The decentralization provided by the Constitution of 1791 disappeared: the word from Paris was law. When many provinces were in a state of open or latent insurrection, local autonomy appeared suicidal. From the Jacobin point of view it was a crime of *lèse-patrie* in the Girondists that they appealed to regional sentiment against the central authority: they were splintering the national will. So they, at one time the vanguard of the Revolution, were arrested, on June 2 and executed on October 31, 1793.

After these moderate republicans—overpraised by posterity, especially through the romantic eloquence of Lamartine—came Terrorists nauseated at last by the reek of blood. Camille Desmoulins, who had provided the spark for the Fourteenth of July, 1789, Danton, who had engineered the tenth of August, 1792, had to expiate on the guillotine the crime of "indulgence" (April 6, 1794). Desmoulins was but a pamphleteer, witty and sentimental; Danton was a giant, a rough and powerful orator, more vital even than Mirabeau. Under his bluster and his flaunted vulgarity he was at heart moderate, and even easygoing. He was willing to negotiate at a point short of unquestionable victory. To the tough-minded, the soft easily appear rotten. Danton was no Spartan; there was in him a craving for ease and enjoyment; he may have flirted with appeasement; he may, like Mirabeau, have set a price on his services. Somehow, like Mirabeau again, he has not forfeited his place in the hearts of his countrymen: posterity has a weakness for phrase-makers, and Danton's phrases are quoted to this day.

The home policy of the Assembly and the committee passed into the hands of a triumvirate, Robespierre, Couthon, Saint-Just. Couthon was an attractive cripple. Saint-Just, handsome, energetic, scornful, inexorable, "the Archangel of Death," remains an enigma. Robespierre was Rousseau's *Social Contract* incarnate: beware of the man of a single book! Immaculate in his sea-green coat, precise, pedantic, he was un-flinching and incorruptible. He wanted to turn the whole of France into a Geneva under the iron rod of Virtue. He sent even his friends to the scaffold without a qualm, just as Calvin had sent Servetus to the flames. He was the Grand Inquisitor, the Torquemada, of Democracy. To Voltaire he would have been *l'Infâme* in absolute purity, Fanaticism made flesh.

He could strike to the left as well as to the right of him: no deviation from the line revealed to him alone! The Hébertists perished for being extremists (*exagérés*) (March 24, 1794), just as the Dantonists were to be struck down for being indulgent. Like Rousseau he was profoundly religious. There had been at Notre-Dame a silly ceremony in honor of the goddess Reason, flatteringly personified by an opera girl: in the eyes of Robespierre, this shallow desecration was one of the crimes of Hébert and his friends, Chaumette, Anacharsis Cloots. He himself professed the natural religion which was that of our Founding Fathers. The climax of his career was the Festival of the Supreme Being (June 8, 1794), in which, as president of the Convention, he assumed the part of high priest.

A provincial lawyer, he preserved a curious respect for legal forms. He disapproved of random massacres: he codified and centralized the Terror. At any rate, there was some show of a regular trial. Compared with the holocausts of our days, the Parisian Terror of 1793–1794 was benign. But sentiment is not a matter of statistics; the age was still civilized, and shuddered. Many victims deserved their fate: they gambled and lost. But some were young and fair, some bore illustrious names. Posterity rightly remembers three crimes. Condorcet, one of the noblest minds of the age, was hounded to death. Lavoisier, the great chemist, paid the price for having been associated with the hated tax contractors. André Chénier, a true poet and a true republican, perished because he had dared to denounce the tyranny.[5]

Robespierrism died of victory. So long as the country had to be saved, people stoically accepted the Terror. By the middle of the year 1794, Revolutionary France was victorious everywhere. In October, 1793, Lyons had been reconquered, and the *Vendéens* or *Chouans* in the west decisively defeated. The allies had been driven back across the Rhine, the British forced to abandon Toulon. In the North a brilliant series of victories, Wattignies, Charleroi, Fleurus (June 26, 1794) forced Coburg out of Belgium. The country was no longer in danger. It was no longer necessary to impose the rule of Virtue by cutting down every one less pure than Robespierre.

The tragic irony of it all is that Terrorism was not overthrown through a rebellion of the sane and the humane: Robespierre was tumbled from his bloody throne by a coalition of the vilest, men who had terrorized out of cowardice and who felt the cold of his accusing glance. Ill fares the nation that is "saved" by a Tallien and a Barras.

Accused in the Convention on Thermidor 9 [6] (July 27), Robespierre was rescued by the Commune. But, a stickler for legality to the very end, he refused to start an insurrection against the official power of the State. While he hesitated, the City Hall was stormed, a pistol shot shattered his jaw, and he died on the guillotine without another word. The democratic revolution, hopelessly entangled with tyranny, war, and Terror, was at an end. The power of the Commune was broken. Soon the Jacobin clubs were closed, and the last radicals sentenced to transportation. The field was free for the realists and profiteers of the Plain.

ACHIEVEMENTS OF THE CONVENTION

According to orthodox republican history the Convention, torn by factional strife, engrossed in civil and foreign war, harassed by an acute economic and financial crisis, found time and energy to continue the reorganization of France. An impressive list of creations is adduced: the Polytechnic School, the Institute of France, the introduction of the decimal system. Had the Convention achieved much of permanent value in those years of tragic confusion, it would indeed have been a miracle; much more probably, it is a myth. No doubt the Mountain and the Plain had leisure enough to legislate, and to legislate wisely, in the lulls of the storm. Not all the Assembly's time was wasted in entertaining grotesque delegations. After a century of teeming *philosophie* it was to be expected that innumerable proposals for reform should be ready, and that some of them should be elaborate and sensible enough. Most to the credit of the Revolution is the fact that it did recognize the primordial importance of popular education. Talleyrand and Condorcet had been aware of it; Danton proclaimed it in long-echoing words; the great plan drawn by Lakanal would do credit even to a modern democracy. An actual start was made, to wither under Napoleon. Much remained merely on paper. A new name tagged on to an ancient institution—the "King's Garden," for instance, a great scientific establishment under Buffon, became the "Museum of Natural History"—is but a shadowy victory for progress. The record of the Convention is creditable enough; it is not superhuman.

If the Convention did not create on the epic scale claimed by its admirers, neither did it destroy as wantonly as its foes would have us believe: it was too busy purging itself and winning the war. Richelieu and the classical architects have played greater havoc with the heirlooms of ancient France than the Terrorists. Revolutionary vandalism is a myth, like revolutionary Prometheism. The wholesale destruction of historical buildings (e.g., the Temple in Paris, the Abbey of Cluny) was perpetrated by profiteers not by radicals. It reached its climax under Napoleon I and continued even under the Restoration: young Victor Hugo denounced the depredations of "the Black Gangs."

The social legislation of the Revolution was, in principle, purely conservative. Private property remained an "inalienable and sacred right." Individualism was still the official philosophy: the revolutionists did not foresee the industrial transformation, already well on its way in England, which was to make economic individualism obsolete. Employers and employees were to discuss their contract man to man, without considering that in a large enterprise such a theoretical equality is delusive. Any association, temporary or permanent, among the workmen was banned by law under the names of coalition and conspiracy. Unions and strikes were not to be legally authorized until three-quarters of a century had passed, under the Saint-Simonian emperor, Napoleon III. The thought of economic equality filled the various assemblies with virtuous horror: death was to be the punishment of anyone who should propose a share-the-wealth measure or, as it was called in memory of the Gracchi, an "agrarian law." At the height of the crisis price-fixing by the state (known as the *Maximum*) was adopted as a desperate remedy, but it was abandoned at the fall of Robespierre and profiteering knew no bounds. The Thermidorian reaction and the Directory were the paradise of classical liberalism, and the *nouveaux riches*.

There was, no doubt, a vast transfer of real property. Not only were the peasants relieved of all feudal dues, but they had a chance of appeasing their land hunger by purchasing the confiscated estates of the *émigrés* nobles and of the clergy. In payment for these estates the fast-depreciating assignats were accepted at their face value, while the farmers sold their produce at ever-mounting prices. In this way they got the land for a song. Not all of it went to the tillers of the soil. Many nobles were shrewd or popular enough to keep their estates; others managed to repurchase them secretly through agents; the landed aristocracy was to remain a power in France for generations, especially in the West. The urban middle class was not likely to let such a splendid opportunity go by, and the bourgeois, too, secured their share of nationalized property. But on the whole the class of peasant proprietors which existed before the Revolution was enormously increased. It became the impregnable rock that prevented a complete return to the Ancient Regime, but it stood likewise across the path of social progress. Henceforth, such words as "the people" and "the masses" had a dual connotation: the industrial workers were radical, the agriculturists conservative. In June, 1848, that cleavage between the two lower classes became tragically apparent.

Above all the essential problems which were tormenting France in 1789 were still unsolved. It was the fear of bankruptcy that had caused the downfall of the Ancient Regime, but the treasury was in more desperate condition in 1795 than it had been under Calonne and Loménie de Brienne. The monarchy had perished: the finances were not saved. And the ecclesiastical problem remained hopeless. The Convention repented from its strange religious vagaries—the Cult of Reason, the worship of the Supreme Being—and in 1794 it voted the complete separation of Church and State. But it was unable to create the atmosphere that would have made genuine liberty possible, and thus it left an opening for Napoleonic reaction.

CARNOT, THE ORGANIZER OF VICTORY. THE BASEL TREATIES

The one all-devouring reality, we repeat, was war. Humanity, liberty, progress, like the constitution, were suspended for the duration. The Terrorists could claim in their defense that they had saved the armies from being stabbed in the back: the guillotine made fewer victims than a single battle.

Within three years the ragged hosts of the Republic, led by boyish impromptu generals, had defeated Europe. A man was found who evolved a strategy adequate to the resources, the needs, the spirit of the time. To the small, carefully drilled armies brought to perfection by Frederick the Great, Lazare Carnot opposed fighting hordes of unprecedented magnitude: the *levée en masse,* universal conscription, gave him twelve hundred thousand men. For the learned chess game of maneuvers and countermaneuvers, he substituted a war of swift motion with no lull in midwinter: it was indeed a blitzkrieg. But Carnot's genius, so unjustly eclipsed by the fame of Bonaparte, was not the single decisive element. He was only the organizer of victory. It was the whole momentum of France's tradition that carried her through the desperate struggle. The revolutionary recruits were not steadied into genuine soldiers until they were amalgamated with veterans. The ordnance used by Carnot and by Napoleon was that of Gribeauval created by the Ancient Regime. In the more scientific and less aristocratic branches of the service, the artillery and the engineers' corps, many officers, like Carnot himself, had loyally accepted the Revolution. The new liberty fired the enthusiasm of the fighters; but no less ardent was their pride in the ancient fame of France. The nation and the Republic were one, but the victory was national even more than it was republican. France, formed by the dynasty, discarded the dynast, but clung to the monarchical tradition of prestige, glory, predominance. The war of defense was forgotten; the crusade for

Liberty, Equality, Fraternity became a phrase; in sober fact the Convention turned into a collective and far more formidable Louis XIV.

The crucial decision came in 1795 when, at Basel, victorious France signed treaties of peace with Prussia (March 5) and Spain (June 22). Carnot, a professional soldier but a true republican, wanted to keep the old frontiers with minor rectifications. The mirage of extending France to the Rhine proved an irresistible temptation. The French persuaded themselves that for the thousand years and more of their history they had consistently striven for that one goal; and as "Nature" was in fashion ("natural" rights, "natural" religion), they called the Rhine the "natural" limit of France.[7] It would have taken a miraculous blend of moderation and strength to make such an extension of French power acceptable to Europe. Strength was achieved under Napoleon; moderation never was. The course of the next twenty years was determined when France decided to keep the left bank of the Rhine. It was not Napoleon who won the decisive victories or forged the instrument of conquest, and it was not Napoleon alone who made war inevitable and permanent. He was the product, the symbol and the victim, of a situation created when he was still an obscure brigadier general.

THE THERMIDORIAN REACTION AND THE DIRECTORY

The Convention survived Robespierre by fifteen months. The period is known as the Thermidorian Reaction. In Paris the "gilded youth," flaunting its royalism, hounded the survivors of Jacobinism; a White Terror raged in many provinces; in the South the "Companions of Jesus" massacred the "patriots." The Thermidorians, who had been revolutionists themselves, had to guard their precarious power against both the Left and the Right. The last spasms of demagogic violence, the riots of April 1 and May 20, 1795, only led to more rigorous repression: the last six *Montagnards* were driven to spectacular suicide, each handing to the next the knife with which he had stabbed himself. But on Vendémiaire 13 (October 5, 1795) it was a Royalist uprising that had to be quelled with "a whiff of grapeshot." This heavy lurching between factions also characterized the regime that succeeded the Convention, the Directory.

The new constitution provided an executive commission of five, the Directors, under whom served six ministers. The legislature was divided into two councils, the Elders (quaintly named the Ancients) and the Five Hundred. The bourgeois features of the 1791 Constitution were revived: the distinction between passive and active citizens, and suffrage in two degrees, with a scale of property qualifications. But, reversing the quixotic disinterestedness of the Constituents, the Convention stipulated that two-thirds of the new legislators were to be chosen among its own members. The converted regicides henceforth formed a mutual protection society. If they dreaded a resurgence of Jacobinism, they knew that a restored Louis XVIII [8] would give them short shrift. They had to maintain themselves in power in order to save their skins.

So they were condemned to a weary game of seesaw, now against the Left, now against the Right. They suppressed the Communist uprising of Caius Gracchus Babeuf in April, 1796. When defeated by the Royalists in the elections of 1797, they called for assistance from the army: under the protection of General Augereau, a lieutenant of Bonaparte, they quashed the elections in forty-nine departments. Carnot himself, the organizer of victory, was eliminated from the Directory as too moderate (Fructidor *coup d'état,* September 4, 1797). In 1798 thanks to this stern rebuff to the Rightists, the Jacobins were regaining ground: once more, the results were arbitrarily altered in thirty-seven departments, and ninety-eight deputies were excluded (Floréal *coup d'état,* May 11, 1798). In April, 1799, the elections strengthened both extremes at the expense of the center. This time it was the Directory that was forcibly modified by the councils: three directors were driven out (Prairial *coup d'état,* June 18). It was a government by *coups d'état,* which called for its own death by a *coup d'état.*

The victors of Thermidor did not have the moral authority to form the needed center party. They were unable to solve the two pressing problems which had harassed the Convention: the restoration of peace and of sound finances. The fault lay neither with the people as a whole nor with the constitution but with the small class in power, the scum of the *bourgeoisie.* The Thermidorian Reaction and the Directory, which form a single period (1794–1799), are a grease spot in French history. The age resembled the Restoration in England, the Regency in France, the moral slump in America after World War I: in all three cases desperate tension and enforced puritanism were followed by utter demoralization. But the Stuart Restoration and the Orleans Regency were partly redeemed by a certain aristocratic elegance. The American crisis was far more superficial, for the country was enjoying at least the illusion of peace and prosperity: pleasure-seeking, however hectic, is more pardonable when the frontiers are secured and the people at work. France in 1794–1799 had no such mitigating circumstances.

The central character in those five years, the chief instrument of Robespierre's downfall, the one perennial director, was Barras, an aristocrat who smiled complacently when he was called "the King of the Rotten." Talleyrand, returned from exile, found the atmosphere of the Directory most congenial. Paris was a carnival: *Muscadins* and *Merveilleuses* sported the most extravagant fashions, wilfully grotesque or classically indecent; gambling and dancing seemed the chief end of man.

It must be noted, however, that this familiar picture is not true of France as a whole. Directorial corruption was only a local skin disease, disfiguring but not fatal. Even in the political world most of the directors were able and honest men, and the two councils were no worse than the common run of assemblies. Profiteering and graft in business and politics, glaring immorality in private life were confined to a small circle in Paris and a few great cities. Internal peace had been restored: Hoche, with a blend of masterly strategy and generous diplomacy, had at last pacified the Vendée. Prosperity was timidly returning in spite of the fact that public finances were still in chaos. When Lafayette came back from imprisonment and exile, he was surprised to find France so definitely on the upgrade. It is a grievous injustice to say that a country always gets the government it deserves: the France of 1794–1799 was not Barras any more than the France of 1799–1815 was Bonaparte.

The one imperious necessity was peace; and the Directory was unable, and even unwilling, to make peace. Its palpable weakness created a temptation for the powers still at war with France: surely such a rotten government could not hold its conquests much longer. On the other hand, war was for the Directory the one source of prestige and profit: the crusade of 1792 had turned into a predatory expedition. Perhaps the government was secretly afraid of the soldiers' return, for the army represented patriotism, efficiency, glory. So that regime of bourgeois profiteers proved to be the most bellicose in the long history of France. It started a policy of wild expansion by creating, beyond the so-called "natural frontiers," satellite states, the Batavian, Helvetian, Cisalpine, Ligurian, Roman, Parthenopean republics. It was not Napoleon who initiated that megalomania. For fifteen years he tried to prop up the crazy fabric built up by the Directory. His one original touch was to turn puppet republics into feudatory kingdoms.

CHAPTER XIX

Martial Interlude: 1792-1815: Napoleon Bonaparte, General, Consul, Emperor

⚹ THE DAZZLING ITALIAN CAMPAIGN

In 1795 Prussia, Spain, and a few German states had made peace with the Republic. England, the empire (Austria), and Sardinia (Piedmont) remained at war. England was both impotent on the Continent and inexpugnable at home. Against Austria Carnot conceived a gigantic plan. Three armies were to march on Vienna, two north of the Alps under Jourdan and Moreau, one through Italy under Bonaparte.

Napoleon Bonaparte, then twenty-six years of age, was a Corsican, that is to say, the son of a detached, recently acquired, totally unassimilated province. His father had rallied to the French cause; as a reward Napoleon received a military education in France and was commissioned as second lieutenant in the artillery of the royal army. But he was not a Frenchman at heart, and at one time he espoused the cause of Corsican independence under Paoli. He distinguished himself at the siege of Toulon and was promoted to brigadier general. In October, 1795, he was in Paris without a command: his friendship with the Robespierre brothers had placed him under suspicion. A Royalist insurrection broke out. Barras, chief of the Thermidorians, called upon Bonaparte to save the Convention. In a trice the young artillerist quelled the uprising; those who resisted to the end were mowed down on the steps of the church Saint-Roch (Vendémiaire 13, October 5, 1795).

Barras rewarded the Corsican with the hand of a discarded mistress, Joséphine de Beauharnais, one of the merry widows of the Thermidorian carnival. The penniless, uncouth, provincial officer fell madly in love with the aristocratic demimondaine, his senior by six years. The command of the Italian expedition was a handsome wedding gift.

When the veterans of that neglected force caught sight of their new leader, small, dark, and sallow, they were amused and called him Puss-in-Boots. His first address to them was worthy of a robber chief: "Soldiers! You are destitute: I am going to lead you into the richest plains in the world." Soon, raillery yielded to wonder. The youngster knocked the king of Sardinia out of the war, imposed terms upon the pope, and marched resolutely against the Austrians.

In Carnot's mind, which the Austrians had accurately read, the chief effort was to be north of the Alps. But Jourdan was badly defeated, and Moreau, left unsupported, had to operate a retreat, which, however masterly, was an acknowledgment of failure. The Austrians were slow in realizing the shift in the operations. They still considered the Italian theater as secondary. They sent one army after another into the valley of the Po, and each one was successively defeated by the well-knit and alert forces of Bonaparte. On May 15, 1796, he entered Milan. The pope, the king of Naples, the dukes of Parma and Modena were placating him with tribute in cash and art treasures. He fought, organized, negotiated as though he were the sovereign of Italy. The Directory could not rebuke the upstart of their own creation, for he was shedding glory on their pitiful regime and replenishing their yawning coffers.

Mantua, the last obstacle, was at last taken. Bonaparte was crossing the Alps toward Vienna when, in April, 1797, he decided to make peace. The best Austrian general, Archduke Charles, was at last to be his antagonist. The mountaineers of Tyrol were being called to arms. In addition Hoche and Moreau had started a lightning campaign north of the Alps, which might have compelled him to share his glory with them. The preliminaries, dictated by Bonaparte, were signed at Leoben on April 18; the final peace, which closely followed the same pattern, at Campo Formio on October 17. That peace was brilliant and realistic, that is to say, unscrupulous. Bonaparte, without a qualm, gave away the Republic of Venice to the Austrians: it took seventy years to repair that injustice. The complicated secret articles were at least as important as the published terms. It was not peace, but a deal: the kind of settlement for which neither side could feel any respect.

⚔ THE EGYPTIAN ADVENTURE AND THE EIGHTEENTH OF BRUMAIRE

England remained. Bonaparte declined to take command of an expedition in Ireland. He agreed—the thought may have originated with Talleyrand—to lead a campaign into Egypt: the idea was as old as Leibniz, and even as St. Louis. Since there was no Suez Canal at the time, the possession of Egypt would be vital only as a steppingstone through the barren Near East to the fabulous empire of India. The enterprise was therefore gigantic and vague; the means, without command of the sea, wholly inadequate. Bonaparte himself had a romantic hankering for the "gorgeous East"; excellent historians believe that it was the key to his whole career.

Miraculously, the French fleet eluded the far superior British squadrons. On the way Bonaparte captured Malta from its Knights. He took Alexandria, marched on Cairo, and defeated at the Pyramids the colorful and antiquated cavalry of the Mamelukes. "Soldiers," said the general, "from these Pyramids forty centuries are looking upon you."

As he had done in Italy, Napoleon in Egypt showed himself a born ruler no less than a soldier. He had with him a scientific mission which did excellent work. He reorganized the country with due regard for the customs of the inhabitants. A thorough Voltairian, not quite sure that Jesus had ever existed, he found it easy to flirt solemnly with Islam. But Egypt was of little value except as a starting point, and the French were hemmed in. Their fleet was destroyed by Nelson in the bay of Abukir (Battle of the Nile). A campaign into Syria proved a failure: Bonaparte could not capture Acre, and his plague-stricken troops hastily returned to Egypt. Warned of the desperate plight of the Directory, Bonaparte escaped, abandoning his own army. His successor, Kléber, was assassinated; and Menou had to capitulate. It was, on a much smaller scale, as complete a disaster as the Russian expedition in 1812; yet it enhanced Napoleon's prestige, and to the present day it has preserved its romantic glamor.

In the meantime Russia, hitherto neutral, had struck an alliance with England. Austria, Naples, Portugal, the Ottoman Empire had joined them; the second coalition was more formidable than the first. The French were driven out of Italy by the Russian Suvorov and the Austrian Melas, and the British effected a landing in Holland. The situation, not so desperate as in 1793, was ominous; and people yearned for the wonder worker of Italy, Bonaparte.

In politics and history impressions count for more than plain truth. The contemporaries and posterity closed their eyes to the palpable fact that the country was saved before the savior returned. On September 19, 1799, Brune defeated the English at Bergen, and they hastened to reembark; on September 26 Masséna crushed Korsakov at Zürich. The great Suvorov himself had to retreat; Russia, disgusted with Austria's incompetence, withdrew from the coalition. On October 6, Bonaparte landed at Fréjus.

It was not, therefore, the fear of invasion that caused the downfall of the Directory: the conspiracy was "an inside job." Sieyès, the con-

stitutional oracle and a director, was plotting against his own government. He needed a sword, and Bonaparte appeared exactly at the right
moment. But in Sieyès' scheme the general was to be merely a tool.
At the decisive hour Bonaparte, unused to parliamentary intrigues,
stammered and fumbled. The day seemed lost: his brother Lucien,
President of the Five Hundred, saved it. As the Assembly, threatened
with a *coup d'état,* was growing tumultuous, Lucien called upon the
Grenadier Guards to restore order. The deputies, in the prophetic words
of Mirabeau, yielded to the force of bayonets. The councils were dispersed; a few stragglers created then and there a Provisional Consulate.
Although Sieyès was made a member of the triumvirate, he understood
that his Machiavellian plan had miscarried. He wanted a cat's paw, and
he had summoned a lion (Brumaire 18, November 9, 1799). Soon a
permanent consular regime was set up with Bonaparte as First Consul.
His colleagues, Cambacérès and Lebrun, appointed by him, were purely
ornamental. When the constitution was formally submitted to the people, an illiterate woman asked, "What is there on that big placard?" and
the answer came, "Just one word: Bonaparte."

Brumaire is Napoleon's Rubicon. It must be remembered, however,
that the initiative did not come from him: he probably would have
preferred his path not to be so messy. He reached power because
Thermidorian rottenness had collapsed at last. Somehow, the able and
moderate men, Lafayette, Carnot, Cambon—and Talleyrand might have
counted among them—never had a chance to work together. It must
be said also that if the Grenadier Guards struck the final blow, Brumaire
was only by accident a military *pronunciamiento* of the Spanish type.
Napoleon had a commendable bourgeois respect for civil government.
As First Consul he discarded his military uniform, attended the meetings of the Academy of Sciences, and pronounced a sincere eulogy of
Washington. He was a Bonapartist not a militarist: one of the reasons
was that politically he did not trust his generals. In 1800 the army was
still profoundly republican. Men like Moreau, Brune, Bernadotte,
Masséna, Macdonald were personally hostile to him. As emperor he
never entrusted his marshals with civil authority.

It is not impossible to retire from the conquering business: Frederick
the Great was a man of peace from 1763 to his death in 1786. The First
Consul fulfilled France's first desire, peace. The Austrians, defeated by
Desaix and Bonaparte himself at Marengo (June 14, 1800), by Moreau
at Hohenlinden (December 3), signed peace at Lunéville (February 9,
1801). England, victorious on the seven seas but helpless in Europe,
followed suit at Amiens (March 27, 1802) amid the delirious enthusiasm
of the London populace. After ten years the guns were stilled at last;

but all treaties were signed with the treacherous secret ink of realistic diplomacy, and it was not peace.

RECONSTRUCTION UNDER THE CONSULATE

While working for a victorious peace, the First Consul was also clearing up the debris left by the revolutionary storm. In a few years he gave France a framework which survived for a hundred years and more. His institutions were in many cases crippling; but they were immediately effective, and they remain impressive. The Consulate was long cherished as a golden epoch in the memory of the people.

The most spectacular of his achievements, the one which most endeared him to the *bourgeoisie,* was the swift restoration of financial order. Confidence in the new leader worked the miracle: immediately after the *coup d'état,* the French *rentes* began to rise. The Consulate and the Empire had their difficulties, but bankruptcy never threatened again. Until 1812 the burden of war fell on the conquered. Even after three disastrous campaigns and two invasions France, in 1815, was financially sound. Napoleon was an admirable efficiency manager; and Gaudin, the one minister that remained with him from first to last, was his most able assistant.

The political institutions, on the other hand, were an elaborate camouflage. In fact, the First Consul, elected for ten years (later, for life), was omnipotent. The Council of State, a body of technicians entrusted with the preparation of the laws, was appointed by him. The nucleus of the Senate was picked out by a committee of four: it remained subservient, and even servile, until the end. The Tribunate, supposed to discuss the laws, was chosen by the Senate; but, because it dared to express opinions, it was first purged of half its members and then suppressed altogether. The Legislative Body was in no sense a popular assembly. The voters could only choose one-tenth of their number to form a communal list; the same process was repeated: one-tenth of the communal lists forming the departmental list, and one-tenth of that, the national list. But these lists were merely panels out of which the government chose its functionaries, and the Senate chose the Legislative Body. There were so many assemblies that people could easily forget that democracy had been completely volatilized. This ingenious system originated with Sieyès: "Confidence comes from below, authority from above." The plebiscites confirming the consular and imperial constitutions were solemn and empty shows. People voted by signing on open registers; in many cases, long lists of names were written by the same hand.

The administrative system destroyed all local autonomy. The intendants were restored under the name of prefects as the agents of the central power. Justice and finances were reformed on the same hierarchical lines. The system was rigid and undemocratic: at any rate, it was simple, and it worked. The French could speak of "that administration which is the envy of Europe"; with the years that famous phrase elicited a bitter smile.

Higher education, except in technical fields, was stifled: Napoleon wanted competent servants not independent minds. Secondary education (the *lycées*) lost the modern progressive character of the Republican Central Schools. Popular education was totally ignored. In 1808 the emperor created a vast monopolistic teaching order, the University of France, under a Grand Master; its discipline was half-monastic, half-military. In this domain the Second Empire repaired to some extent the errors of the First. French scholarship and science were saved only by institutions of the Ancient Regime, such as the Collège de France and the Museum of Natural History.

Two great measures are attached to the name of Napoleon, the Concordat and the Civil Code.[1]

The Concordat (1801) ended the quarrel between the Holy See and the French State; for French Catholics it softened and veiled the conflict between their political and their spiritual loyalties. It suppressed the moribund Constitutional Schism. It secured from the Church a quitclaim for her confiscated property. It gave the clergy security and prestige as officials of the state. The government resumed the right of appointing bishops who had to be confirmed by the pope. Catholicism was acknowledged as "the religion of the majority, and that of the Consuls." But Protestantism and Judaism secured a corresponding status.

Like the Lateran Agreement of Mussolini the Concordat seemed a masterstroke. Liberal opposition was not allowed to become vocal. A hundred years were needed to restore true religious freedom with complete separation of Church and State. During that long century, the Church was devitalized by close association with a purely secular authority. Napoleon cared very little for religion: he cared for order and, above all, for power. He considered the episcopate as a mitred police: he spoke of "my bishops, my prefects, my gendarmes." He had no thought of sharing a particle of his absolute rule with the pope: in his own dominions he alone was sovereign. The so-called Organic Articles, which he tagged on to the Concordat without consulting Rome and which Rome never recognized, were in the purest Gallican tradition. Napoleon went further. When he became emperor, he modeled his attitude on that of his "predecessors," Charlemagne and Constantine. He considered himself as sovereign over the Church universal, the pope being no more than his ecclesiastical lieutenant. As a result within ten years of the signing of the Concordat, the pope was a prisoner, and the emperor was excommunicated. Napoleon was clear-sighted enough to call the Concordat his worst mistake.

Of the Civil Code, on the contrary, he said, "I am prouder of it than of any of my victories." A fine group of jurists, as a committee of the Council of State, harmonized the teeming traditions of old France and the confused legislation of the Revolutionary Assemblies into a consistent whole, within the framework of Roman law. Both in organization and in style, the Code is a model of definiteness and simplicity: Stendhal sedulously read it to purge his own language of pomposity or mistiness. The Code was used as a pattern in many countries, and it remains the foundation of the French legal system.

If the work was done by the experts, it must be said that Napoleon prodded and stimulated them. He attended many of their meetings and took a very active part in their discussions. He had a large share in the labor and must not be denied his full share of the glory. We are apt to forget, however, that his personal intervention was almost invariably on the reactionary side; he whittled down the principles of 1789 as much as he dared. Napoleonic legislation placed woman, politically, economically, morally, under an eternal tutelage. It established class inequality: in case of a conflict between employer and employee, the court must take the word of the employer. Slavery was revived in the colonies. Under the Empire Napoleon was to create a new nobility and to restore in its favor the right of primogeniture. Arbitrary imprisonment was practiced once more: there were not one but eight Bastilles for the enemies of the regime. In the eyes of Europe Napoleon might appear as the Revolution with crown and sword; to the French he was the man who arrested and sought to destroy the Revolution.

The nefarious consequences of the Consulate appeared gradually and were increasingly felt during the nineteenth century; even today, the Consular virus has not been completely eliminated. We can understand, however, the enthusiasm of the contemporaries. Napoleon appeared as the Enlightened Despot, that dream of the *philosophes,* a Frederick the Great on a vaster scale. To the peasants he confirmed their possession of Church land; to the bourgeois he was the defender of property and the hierarchy of classes; to the clergy he brought appeasement after a decade of anguish; to all he meant security. To be sure, that security was purchased at the expense of liberty, initiative, dignity. It turned French culture into a wasteland. All the great writers, Chateaubriand, Madame de Staël, Joseph de Maistre, were in opposition or in exile. The official poets and dramatists of the time reached the very limit of correct vacuity. But all this was not apparent at first: Lunéville and Amiens, the Concordat and the Code, had the glow of a marvelous dawn. That was the first Napoleonic legend: Bonaparte the wonder-worker. It had paled before 1814; but in our own days, beyond the frontiers of France, there are many who denounce Mussolini, Hitler, or Stalin, and who remain orthodox Napoleon-worshippers.

✍ THE EMPIRE

Bonaparte was served both by his own achievements and by the attacks of his enemies. On December 24, 1800, a bomb or "infernal machine" failed to touch him but killed or wounded some eighty people. This permitted him to proscribe or imprison a number of his republican opponents, although his police knew full well that the attempt had been made by Royalists. The peace of Amiens won him the consulship for life with the right of appointing his successor. In February, 1804, a new conspiracy was discovered. Pichegru, who had led republican armies, died mysteriously in prison; the Royalist George Cadoudal was executed; Moreau, whose military fame balanced that of Napoleon, fled to America. The Regicides, those members of the Convention who had voted for the death of Louis XVI, were still a power—among them Fouché, the Minister of Police, who held so many mysterious threads. As a pledge to them Napoleon had a Bourbon prince, the duke of Enghien, arrested in Baden, a neutral country, on the flimsiest of accusations; a special court condemned him to death, and he was shot the same night at Vincennes (March 20–21, 1804). This single deed created an effect of concentrated terror. It was "worse than a crime: a blunder." It precluded any genuine reconciliation between old France and old Europe, on the one hand, and the Corsican dictator. The ghost of Enghien was his Banquo.

The imperial title followed in logical sequence. It was part of the classical revival: it may be said that in France the imperial style preceded imperial institutions. If the Vendôme Column and the arches of triumph in Paris were pure Roman pastiches, so was Soufflot's Sainte-Geneviève (the Pantheon), designed in 1764. Rome, after the kings and the republic, assumed imperial form. The philosophy of Rousseau confirmed the lessons of history: the master had taught that only small communities could be republics. The Empire, however, was not altogether pseudoantique. Romanticism, as we have seen, was growing by the side of the curious Greco-Roman revival. Napoleon felt himself the new Charlemagne even more than the new Augustus. As a matter of fact, he was a Louis XIV streamlined into formidable efficiency.

No upstart regime could have a more auspicious beginning. Lenin,

Mussolini, Hitler had their origins in national humiliation, Napoleon in reconciliation and triumph. The pope came to Notre-Dame to enhance the splendor of his coronation: characteristically, Napoleon set the crown on his head with his own hands. He created marshals to be his paladins. He set up a court, magnificent, frigid, meticulous, with sudden lapses into Revolutionary vulgarity: the new Lord's Anointed had streaks both of bourgeois economy and of soldierly roughness. He conjured up out of the motley mass of his followers a new nobility: marshals and prominent ministers became dukes, some of them even princes, and there was a rich crop of counts and barons. He used as much as he could those survivors of the Ancient Regime who could be bribed to rally: "Those people alone," he said, "make good servants." He created kingdoms not only for his own Corsican clan, Joseph, Louis, Jérôme, his brother-in-law Murat,[2] but for his German supporters: the ancient electors of Saxony and Bavaria, the duke of Württemberg were proud to receive royal crowns from the usurper.

He was the Parvenu *in excelsis:* he could have borrowed Fouquet's motto, *Quo non ascendam?* What heights shall I not scale? His most dazzling achievement was to marry into the oldest and proudest of ruling families, Austria. His wedding Marie-Louise appeared to him the climax of his incredible career: imagine Hitler winning Princess Elizabeth of England. It enabled him to say, with studied casualness, "My uncle Louis XVI." No wonder the *bourgeois gentilshommes* throughout the world consider the Napoleonic saga as the greatest success story ever told. Talleyrand smiled and was not impressed; neither was Metternich, although it was he who found the name for the imperial heir, the king of Rome. Napoleon's mother, Madame Letitia, shook her shrewd old head and said, "If only it would last!"

It might have lasted if England had not been an island. So long as England remained unreconciled and unsubdued, nothing was achieved. The peace of Amiens had been earnestly desired by the two peoples; it was signed by the two governments with a damning array of mental reservations. Trust was lacking on both sides: it is difficult to adjudge which party was more responsible for the breaking of the truce. Napoleon had no thought of receding within the "natural frontiers": to free his satellites would be a humiliation. England would not give up Malta, key to the Mediterranean.

England by herself was as powerless against Napoleon as Napoleon against England: she could not even make a threatening gesture matching the Camp of Boulogne, where the best troops of France were constantly drilling for invasion. But England could find and finance Continental allies. Austria was not resigned to her loss of influence in Italy and Germany. Prussia could not forget the glories of Frederick the Great. Before Napoleon ascended the throne, there was already rising through the huge and ill-compacted Germanic body a new consciousness of pride, and romantic visions of the medieval emperors in their might.

Napoleon's task was easier than Hitler's. French culture was still supreme among the ruling classes. The French were bringing with them genuine reforms, ideological and practical. They roughly and efficiently swept away the cobwebs of medievalism. But Napoleon, like Hitler, was incapable of treating his satellites with consideration. His "New Order" was geared to the interests of France not of Europe as a whole. The Continental Blockade (Berlin Decree, 1806), closing the Continent to all English goods, might have been a decisive weapon. Only Napoleon disregarded altogether the interests of the local populations, Holland, the Hanseatic Cities. Association with France, meant ruin; so every bight in the immense coast line became a nest of smugglers. The conquered learned that the first "natural right of man" for a German or an Italian was the right not to be a Frenchman. The economic hardships sharpened national consciousness. The French not only plundered, with Napoleonic efficiency, the lands nominally associated with the Empire, but they also destroyed their sources of wealth. It was not Fichte in his *Addresses to the German Nation* who created German patriotism: Herder had laid deep foundations before. But there was fraternity in Herder's soul; Fichte, inspired by Napoleon's oppression, fostered the nationalism that is filled with hate, and which still poisons Europe today.

✍ VICTORIES WITHOUT PEACE

In spite of several delusive truces it was the same war that raged from 1803 to 1814, with a brief epilogue in 1815. Large-scale hostilities did not break out until 1805. Napoleon had a gigantic scheme to reduce England. Nelson was to be lured to the West Indies; the French fleet would rush back, pick up the allied Spanish squadrons, and, for a few hours at any rate, have command of the Channel. This required perfect timing in the capricious days of sail, a commander with a genius on the Napoleonic or Nelsonian scale—and such cannot be produced by an emperor's fiat—and above all, an instrument, an efficient fleet. The Republic had forged admirable land armies but allowed the navy to deteriorate. At Trafalgar (October 21, 1805) Nelson defeated, crippled, and all but destroyed the navies of France and Spain. England remained sole mistress of the sea.

Already Napoleon had broken up the Camp of Boulogne to face the third coalition, Austria, Russia, and Sweden. On October 17 he compelled Mack to surrender at Ulm; on November 14 he was at the palace of Schoenbrunn in Vienna; on December 2, the anniversary of his coronation, he won over the combined armies of Austria and Russia the most brilliant of all his victories, Austerlitz. On December 26 he dictated to Austria the Treaty of Pressburg. Then he felt that he could shape Europe as he pleased. A haughty command, and the Bourbons of Naples had ceased to reign. He watched the German princes scrambling for German spoils. He fostered a Confederation of the Rhine under his protectorate. The ghost of the ancient Holy Roman Empire disappeared.

Prussia, under a weakling, had shilly-shallied; she had accepted Hanover as a bribe from Napoleon; now she felt that her very existence was at stake and joined Russia. Again a lightning campaign. At Auerstedt Davout routed the main Prussian army; at the same time Napoleon destroyed the rest at Jena (October 14, 1806). Berlin was occupied.

Russia remained in the field. The Battle of Eylau (February 7-8, 1807), one of the fiercest under the Empire, was a draw. But the French were victorious at Friedland (June 14), the last border strongholds were captured, and Napoleon had reached the Niemen. Moreover, Russia had another enemy on her hands: Turkey, spurred by French diplomacy, had started war. So the two autocrats, tsar and emperor, met on a raft on the Niemen at Tilsit. Alexander professed to be the friend and admirer of Napoleon, the troops fraternized, and Peace reigned again, with her tongue in her cheek. Prussia was drastically cut down and enrolled willy-nilly among France's allies. A truncated Poland was restored under the name of Grand Duchy of Warsaw.

Emperor of the French, King of Italy, Protector of the Rhine Confederation, with Austria, Prussia, Warsaw, Spain, Holland among his vassals or allies, and Russia as a friend, Napoleon had reached a power greater than Charlemagne's or Charles V's, and nearly equal to that of Hitler in 1941. His first check occurred in Spain. It was a gratuitous move: the Bourbon king had been a most docile instrument of French policy. Believing that the Spanish people would accept anything from him, he swept aside the worthless royal family, father and son in bitter quarrel, and the queen's lover, Godoy, "Prince of the Peace." He promoted his elder brother, Joseph, from Naples to Madrid. Spain had accepted a French dynasty in 1700; in 1808 she resented being treated as a puppet state. The people rebelled. And for the first time since the rise of Napoleon French troops suffered a sharp defeat: improvised Spanish forces obliged Dupont to capitulate at Baylen.

Ironically, Napoleon, in his high-handed career, encountered the fiercest opposition where his case was best. The Spanish royal house was beneath contempt; the French ended the Inquisition and brought

Central Europe
in 1812

~~~~~ Boundary of the Confederation
of the Rhine

liberal ideas and modern legislation into the peninsula. Among the *Afrancesados* (the Frenchified, or collaborationists) were many Spaniards who believed that their country was in need of thorough reform. The resistance was inspired by patriotism and superstition, a formidable alliance.

Napoleon's trouble was England's opportunity. For six years Wellesley, the future duke of Wellington, played a seesaw game in Spain and Portugal, advancing whenever the French forces were depleted, beating a retreat whenever they assumed the offensive. Madrid repeatedly changed hands. The warfare was conducted on both sides with unexampled ferocity. Finally, when the French had been defeated in Russia and Germany, Wellington drove them out of Spain and advanced into southern France as far as Toulouse and Bordeaux.

This minor but fiercest struggle roused Europe. In April, 1809, Archduke Charles started a war of liberation and invaded Napoleon's ally, Bavaria. The hope was premature. Napoleon moved as swiftly and inexorably as ever. In May he was in Vienna again. This time, however, Austria put up a better fight. For weeks Napoleon's army was pinned down in the island of Lobau, and the battle of Essling and Aspern was a draw. Finally, the victory of Wagram (July 5–6) left Austria no choice but to sign at Schönbrunn another treaty of peace, the fourth in twelve years. Officially, she was now part of the French system. The marriage of Napoleon with Archduchess Marie-Louise (April, 1810) confirmed the alliance. When on March 20, 1811, the booming guns of the Invalides told Paris that an imperial heir was born, the emperor could well have said, in Victor Hugo's words, "The future is mine!"

Tilsit proved, if proof were needed, the hollowness of an entente among big powers. They carve the world into spheres of influence by the divine right of force; but, because of their very realism, they are unable to trust one another. Russia and France passed from effusive to cool friendship, from correct frigidity to barely veiled hostility. Revived Poland remained a source of irritation. Napoleon could not make up his mind to restore the martyred kingdom: he could have done so only in the name of self-determination, and that principle would have worked against him in Germany, Italy, and Spain. But he kept tantalizing the Poles with blurred visions of independence. His half promises were considered by Alexander as threats: Russia did not like a French satellite on her border. On the other hand, Napoleon had no faith in the liberal and seductive Alexander: under the enlightened despot he could see the Byzantine and the Tartar. Caulaincourt sought in vain to avert a break and was called a Russophile for his pains. Talleyrand pursued a more devious course: he secretly advised the tsar that Napoleon, drunk with power, no longer was quite sane and that the days of his rule were numbered.

Napoleon still believed in the virtue of force; he thought that even a mere show of force, provided it be overwhelming, would enable him to impose his will on the shifty Russian autocrat. He gathered six hundred thousand men on the Niemen. Barely one-half of them came from old France: Poles, Italians, Rhinelanders, and even Spaniards had been pressed into his service. Prussia was among his auxiliaries and was to do some sharp fighting on his side. The tsar refused to be impressed. Reluctantly, Napoleon crossed the Niemen, that other Rubicon. He occupied Wilna and destroyed Smolensk: no peace messenger came. He was plunging blindly, in late summer, into the vast mystery of Russia. Only Cossack patrols were visible on the rim of the boundless plain. All supplies had been removed or burnt.

The gigantic expedition was ill-conceived, ill-prepared, ill-conducted. The task of managing such an unwieldy army in hostile territory was beyond the technical resources of the time, and Napoleon, the great technician, should have known it. He had his service of information: it was no secret that there were no good roads in Russia. His own bitter experience at Eylau should have taught him that winter, in those regions, came early, and with a rigor unknown in the West. He went on, somberly fatalistic, trusting to his star: one smashing victory, a change of heart of the unstable Alexander, perhaps a palace revolution. One weapon he declined to use: he did not call upon the oppressed peasants to revolt. He stood for order, not for revolution. He chose to come as a conqueror, not as a liberator.

There was one fierce battle at Borodino on the Moskva River (September 7, 1812). Kutuzov had to retire and was unable to block the way to Moscow. But the losses on both sides had been appalling. On September 14 Napoleon was at the Kremlin waiting for offers of peace.

Alexander ignored the rules of the game and remained silent. Moscow had been deserted; on September 15–19 most of it went up in flames. Now it was the victor's turn to propose a truce: his advances were ignored. The emperor waited for five weeks. His line of communication was precarious; winter was approaching. On October 19 the retreat began. By November winter had set in. The soldiers had to drop first their loot then their equipment; the horses were devoured. Kutuzov's regulars, Cossacks, armed peasants harried the straggling horde. The crossing of the Berezina (November 26–28) remains an epic nightmare. Ney, the hero of the disaster, was still able to perform feats of valor. But only a few units, under Davout and Eugene, preserved a semblance of discipline: the rest was a mob fleeing in distress and panic.

Of barely one hundred thousand men that reached Smolensk, not one-third were in formation.

"His Majesty," said the twenty-ninth bulletin of the Grand Army, which gave an inkling of the reverse, "has never been in better health." This was not simply monumental egotism: at the time Napoleon felt that he was France's supreme asset; he alone could retrieve the appalling disaster. News had reached him which revealed how purely personal his power was. On the false report of his death a general under police supervision, Malet, had boldly attempted to seize power in Paris. The coup had failed, but several high functionaries had shown themselves ominously torpid. So, on December 5 at Smorgoni Napoleon left his shattered army and headed for Paris by swift sleigh and coach with Caulaincourt as his sole companion. He rushed through Warsaw and Dresden and reached his capital on December 18.

He found the yes-men of his Legislative Body critical for the first time and France apathetic. The coalition against him was gathering momentum. The generals and the people forced the craven king of Prussia openly to rebel against him. Even Sweden, where Bernadotte, one of his marshals, was now crown prince, declared war. Austria was still playing a waiting game.

It is a miracle that for nearly a year Napoleon was able to hold back this array of enemies. He still held strategic points; Saxony and Bavaria were still on his side; Austria had not yet declared herself; and his military genius, slumbering in the Russian campaign, again showed itself at its best. He could still win victories, Lützen and Bautzen on May 2 and 21. Perhaps they proved his undoing: he remained unchastened and overweening. Had he shown moderation, he might have withdrawn within the "natural frontiers," where he would have been impregnable. The diplomacy of that fateful year, more important than the strategy, remains an enigma. The problem is an equation with too many unknown quantities: neither side was ever sincere. The allies, who had the upper hand, were averse to a compromise peace; Napoleon still had faith in his genius and in his star. He lost the diplomatic campaign: the armistice he accepted worked against him; by refusing to answer categorically and in time, he forfeited the last shred of Austrian support.

The end came at Leipzig, "the Battle of the Nations" (October 16–19, 1813). In midcombat, as he was weakening, Bavaria and Württemberg turned against him. Again he abandoned his troops to reorganize resistance from Paris. Luckier than their comrades in Egypt and Russia, his soldiers made good their escape. As late as November 8 the allies were still offering Napoleon their willingness to respect the "natural frontiers." They knew his unyielding temper, and they wanted to expose him as the sole obstacle to peace. Perhaps, remembering 1793, they had misgivings about attacking those frontiers which had become dear to the French, and which might be defended with savage energy. Napoleon gave an evasive answer. No further compromise was possible.

By the end of 1813 the allies had crossed the Rhine and entered old France. Schwartzenberg and his Austrians, Blücher and his Prussians were converging on Paris. For three months Napoleon played a magnificent game worthy of his greatest achievements in Italy. With raw recruits, some of them eighteen years old, he rushed from one invading army to the other and sent them reeling back at Champaubert, Montmirail, Château-Thierry, Vauchamp, Nangis, Montereau. Once more victory went to his head: he dreamed of reconquering all that he had lost and refused a last offer, with the boundaries of 1792. The French were of clearer sight than their leader: they shrugged their shoulders wearily when a fresh victory was announced. Every passing advantage won by Napoleon brought about a drop in the Paris stock exchange: the same realistic barometer that had indicated his rise served to register his fall. All the prodigies of tactics and endurance proved unavailing; the imperial troops were beaten at Laon, Arcis-sur-Aube, La Fère-Champenoise. The allies captured the heights of Montmartre, and Paris capitulated. The British were at Bordeaux.

Napoleon at bay still refused to understand: he heaped abuses on Marmont for surrendering Paris and urged his marshals to make a supreme effort. They shook their heads. He may have attempted suicide: reports on this point are at the same time definite and irreconcilable. Then, at Fontainebleau, he abdicated, at first in favor of his son, then, under allied pressure, unconditionally (April 11). He took a well-staged, heart-rending farewell of his Old Guard. Already his Senate had turned against him and declared that he and his race had forfeited the throne.

The allies, many of whom had professed to be his friends, one of whom was his father-in-law, treated him with singular consideration. He kept his imperial title; he was given, instead of a jail, a toy kingdom, the island of Elba, with an army of four hundred men. France deeply felt her defeat but not the fall of the autocrat. As he himself had prophesied, his exit was hailed with a sigh of relief. If he had few friends left, he still had bitter enemies: he was insulted on his way to exile and had to disguise himself to escape lynching. On May 4 he arrived at Elba. The strangest chapters of his career were still to be written.

CHAPTER XX

The Constitutional Monarchy: 1814-1848

✍ THE FIRST RESTORATION AND THE HUNDRED DAYS

By 1810 the Bourbon cause in France seemed as hopeless as the Jacobite one in England. The return of the old dynasty was chiefly the work of Talleyrand. He had become thoroughly convinced that the sole foundation of the Empire was the prestige of the emperor, and that the character of the autocrat was disintegrating. Ostensibly, Talleyrand served the master well. He was an ideal diplomat, although he would line his pockets in true Directory style. Napoleon distrusted him, despised him, admired him, dreaded him. He called him "filth in a silk stocking." (I soften the emperor's soldierly bluntness). But he also recognized in Talleyrand those qualities which were eminently lacking in himself: easy wit, subtlety, and good breeding. As early as the interview at Erfurt between Napoleon and Alexander (1808), Talleyrand had secretly dissociated his fate from that of his sovereign.

A true prophet, he had given the Corsican ten years; and as the term approached, he was casting out for a possible successor. A republic seemed out of the question: the Convention reeked, and the Directory stank. The imperial personnel was, apparently, subservient to the ruler. In 1809 a Bernadotte-Fouché combination seemed to emerge: at least the jealous eyes of the emperor detected such a possibility. But Fouché, the ex-monk, ex-Terrorist turned into the superpoliceman, had no appeal by himself; and Bernadotte, through a bold comedy of misunderstandings and intrigues, was called to become the crown prince of Sweden. The duke of Orleans, unknown in France, shunned by his fellow exiles, had no party. No foreign prince would do. Talleyrand was almost inevitably led back to the Bourbons: they at least had a historical claim. When he was approached by a Royalist agent, Montrond, he responded with his wonted caution. Although in semi-disgrace, he remained one of the great dignitaries of the Empire, vice-grand elector (the shadow of a shadow) and prince of Benevento in the Napoleonic nobility.

As late as 1814 the allies were not clearly committed to the return of Louis XVIII. Austria favored Marie-Louise as regent: she would have been Metternich's puppet. Alexander promoted, but with no excessive eagerness, the candidacy of Bernadotte. It took the subtle machinations of Talleyrand and Fouché and a vigorous pamphlet by Chateaubriand, the recognized head of French literature, to make a Bourbon restoration appear as the inevitable solution.

Talleyrand, in so far as he had principles, was a man of 1789, a disciple of the Enlightenment. He did not want to see the Ancient Regime come back with all its abuses and absurdities. In this he was in accord with England and Russia, for Alexander was a liberal abroad. Louis XVIII understood that he would have to accept a constitution: the clock was to be set back to 1792 not to 1788. By the Declaration of Saint-Ouen (May 2, 1814) the pledge was given—with mental reservations. As a reward the allies signed with France a surprisingly generous treaty (Paris, May 30). All the conquests of Napoleon, of course, went by the board, and the "natural frontiers" were disregarded. But France kept some minor acquisitions and recovered some of her colonies. No indemnity was imposed upon her; she even preserved the art treasures looted during the war.

A congress met at Vienna to reorganize Europe after the collapse of the Napoleonic order. It remains the supreme achievement of old-world diplomacy, a nostalgic dream for traditionalists even today. There was no democratic nonsense about it: the Liberation War had been a crusade of the peoples, but the peoples and their desires were rigorously kept out of the discussions. The emperor of Austria, in his famed capital, was a generous host. Royalties of all degrees were duly entertained. The various delegations vied in lavishness. "The Congress dances," as old Prince de Ligne remarked. He was to provide one of the most impressive shows of the season, his own funeral.

France attended and was represented by Talleyrand. At first the allies were tempted to snub her as a reprobate. Talleyrand's point was that Louis XVIII had his place among the victors: it was Napoleon who had been defeated, and legitimacy was triumphant. For immediate success the move was masterly: France became almost at once one of the Big Five and was spared the long penitence imposed upon Germany after 1918 and after 1945. In a larger perspective Talleyrand's cleverness was disastrous. It had the effect of committing France and Europe to the obsolete principle of legitimacy, which, in spite of all quibblings and compromises, meant dynastic rule by divine right. It was not the only possible course: we must repeat that the peoples were already fully awake and that the two great powers which had never been subdued by Napoleon, England and Russia, did at least lip service to liberalism. But Talleyrand, a passionate whist player, thought only of winning the game at hand. This made him a consummate artist at the green baize table and, in the course of generations, an influence for evil.

The Restoration began in a fog of ambiguities. The constitution was liberal enough: all the essential achievements of the Revolution were preserved; there were to be a hereditary Chamber of Peers and a House of Representatives on the orthodox plutocratic basis. But the wording was ominous. The constitution was not a covenant between ruler and people: it was a charter granted by the sovereign. It could therefore be amended, suspended, or withdrawn by him at his pleasure. The white flag of absolutism was restored. The charter was dated "the nineteenth year of our reign": the Republic and the Empire were obliterated by a stroke of the royal pen.

Had the king possessed personal prestige, had he fought bravely for his own rights, his chances would have been more substantial. But Louis XVIII, fat and gouty, was no majestic figure. His wit (he had preserved some of the graces of the eighteenth century) appealed only to a small circle of friends and never reached the people. With him returned the *émigrés* and at their head the king's brother, the count of Artois, haughty, thirsting for privilege and for revenge, ghosts in a France which had lived ardently during the twenty years and more of their exile.

In March, 1815, an incredible rumor reached Vienna and Paris: Napoleon had escaped from Elba and landed near Cannes. The vanity of the Talleyrand solution was cruelly revealed. France had accepted the Bourbons out of weariness, but she had no faith in them and no love for them. Traditions may be kept alive indefinitely, but once they are dead, they stay dead. Before this single man the dynasty collapsed ingloriously. Ney, who had rallied to the king, was sent to halt the usurper and fell into his arms. Louis XVIII fled to Ghent; no finger lifted in his defense. It was an unequivocal negative plebiscite: the Bourbons were through.

But it was not a positive plebiscite in favor of Napoleon. His eagle "flew from steeple to steeple to the towers of Notre-Dame," and on March 20 he entered the Tuileries, his supporters frantic with joy. The great realist, however, was not deceived: France had remained listless. "They let me return," he remarked, "just as they let the others [the Bourbons] go." Glory no longer appealed to the French: they had known the surfeit of victory and the bitterness of defeat. And although he brought back the tricolor flag, Napoleon was careful not to rouse again revolutionary passions. At Lyons he had been hailed as a savior by the populace, and he had recoiled: he would not be the emperor of the Jacobins. As in 1799 he appealed to the *bourgeoisie* not to the masses. He simply offered to be a more vigorous and more intelligent Louis XVIII.

He had a charter drawn up by a former opponent, a friend of Madame de Staël, Benjamin Constant: limited monarchy, two Chambers, the civil conquests of the Revolution guaranteed. As a face-saving device this un-Napoleonic instrument was called "Act Additional to the Constitutions of the Empire." He sought the support of the safe and sane to embark upon the most desperate of adventures, a fight to the finish with the whole of Europe. No wonder they remained cool. The constitution was duly ratified by an apathetic plebiscite, duly inaugurated by a pompous and frigid ceremony at the Champ-de-Mars. Everyone knew that if Napoleon were victorious, he would tear up the constitution; if he were defeated, the allies would toss it aside.

Europe did not hesitate. A ban was at once declared against Napoleon. Austria, England, Prussia, Russia each pledged 180,000 men; with the minor allies, the total contingents reached over a million. On the other hand, there was no *levée en masse* in France as there had been in 1792–1793. Marshal Davout, the very able Minister of War, could only raise a force of 300,000 men.

Napoleon, still capable of swift motion, struck the first blow. His troops were victorious at Charleroi, Ligny, Quatre-Bras. But Wellington, in Brussels, was concentrating an army of Englishmen, Dutchmen, and Hanoverians. The Battle of Waterloo (June 18, 1815) was uninspired on either side. Napoleon attempted no subtle maneuver: he made a series of frontal attacks which Wellington stubbornly withstood. Evening was falling. Cannon was heard approaching. It was not Grouchy, Napoleon's lieutenant, but Blücher and his Prussians. This was the end. The emperor fled, as after Moscow and Leipzig. Panic seized the shrunken remnants of the Grand Army; even the Old Guard surrendered.[1]

The question has often been asked, "What if Napoleon had won at Waterloo?"[2] The answer is as certain as any mere hypothesis can be: Waterloo would have occurred a few weeks later under a different name. Physically, the disparity of forces was too great. Morally, France had lost heart.

The Assemblies of the brief Empire were not Napoleonic, but they were even less Bourbonian. They accepted the second abdication of Napoleon and proclaimed his four-year-old son emperor. The shadowy reign of Napoleon II actually lasted for a few days. But Fouché, who was the arbiter of the situation, was aware that the renewed Empire was stillborn and secretly made terms with the Royalists. Napoleon had planned to flee to America; but, hoping against hope for a popular movement in his favor, he waited too long. Trapped at Rochefort, afraid of falling into implacable Royalist hands, he surrendered to the British, "entrusting his destiny to a generous foe." The British ignored the fine gesture and remembered Elba. The warship "Bellerophon" carried him to St. Helena, where he died on May 5, 1821. Even then, it was not the end: it was at St. Helena that he achieved the most indestructible of his creations, the Napoleonic legend.

The strange interlude of a Hundred Days proved costly, besides the lives and the millions wasted in a futile war. France was the first victim. The second Peace of Paris (November 20, 1815) was much harsher than the first. A heavy indemnity was imposed; foreign troops were to occupy French territory until full payment had been made; the frontiers were pushed back at several points (Saar, Savoy). Above all, the allies distrusted more than ever the incorrigible disturber of the peace: for a full quarter of a century Europe was constantly prepared to unite against her. The Bourbon dynasty suffered: its weakness had been revealed; it returned, unwanted, in the baggage of the invaders. The whole of Europe had to pay a heavy price: for the Hundred Days were interpreted (wrongly) as a recrudescence of the revolutionary spirit, and stern reaction prevailed. The Holy Alliance was formed, dedicated to the glory of God and the oppression of the people. In Central Europe, the leaden Metternich system was to be supreme until 1848.

THE SECOND RESTORATION

After their inglorious fiasco the Royalists returned not chastened but enraged. A White Terror reigned in the South; the Napoleonic veterans were treated like bandits.[3] The rich landowners had elected a Chamber so monarchical in sentiment that it was called *Introuvable* ("beyond the wildest dreams"). Fortunately, Louis XVIII was not such a fanatical reactionary as his ultra-Royalist supporters. Well-advised by the duke of Richelieu, he dissolved the overzealous assembly, and the moderates secured a majority. With Richelieu, Dessolle, Decazes, there was genuine appeasement and a degree of liberty unknown under Napoleon. The war indemnity was paid in full (1818) and the occupation troops withdrawn.

In 1820 a madman, Louvel, murdered the duke of Berry, nephew of Louis XVIII, in the hope of extinguishing the Bourbon line.[4] The result was a return to violent reaction. A new electoral law was devised to give still greater influence to the landed nobility, the bulwark of extreme royalism. The liberty of the press was curtailed. Bourbon France was proud to act as the sword of the Holy Alliance and to restore to absolute rule the worthless Ferdinand VII of Spain (1823).

Villèle, from 1821 to the end of 1827, with courteous pertinacity attempted to restore the social hierarchy of the Ancient Regime. In 1825 compensation amounting to $200,000,000 was given to those *émigrés* whose property had not yet been returned. The conservative element within the Church took the upper hand; through a religious brotherhood directed by the Jesuits and vaguely known as "the Congregation" it influenced the course of government. Sacrilegious acts were made punishable by death. Absolutism and theocracy were frankly advocated. Joseph de Maistre, French in culture if not in nationality, was the spiritual guide of the age.

Louis XVIII died in 1824. He was neither very strong, nor very clever, nor very good; at any rate, he had common sense and a deep-rooted desire not to suffer exile again. So he was, under very difficult circumstances, an acceptable constitutional sovereign. His brother, "Monsieur," count of Artois, succeeded as Charles X. A rake in his youth, once a spiteful enemy of Marie-Antoinette, he had in his old age turned into a religious bigot. Under him the uneasy truce between the dynasty and the nation came to an end.

For nearly ten years the Bourbons had been aided—unaware—by a mighty current in French and European culture, Romanticism. For our immediate purpose let us define that trend as a great surge of imagination and sentiment in rebellion against the cool and gray rationalism of the Enlightenment. Romanticism, as we shall see, could blend with many causes; in the first quarter of the nineteenth century it took, in France particularly, a historical turn. It exalted, in the spirit of Edmund Burke, the wisdom of prejudice and the holiness of tradition; with Chateaubriand, the esthetic, almost the sensuous, appeal of ritual, sacred stories, mysteries, and symbols; with Walter Scott, the colorfulness, the chivalric glamour of the past. It was no accident that the greatest writer of the age, Chateaubriand, Romanticism incarnate, should have contributed so much to the revival of religion (*The Genius of Christianity,* 1802) and to the return of the ancient monarchy (*On Bonaparte and the Bourbons,* 1814). For his brilliant services he was made ambassador to London and minister of foreign affairs.

This Burke-Chateaubriand-Walter Scott mood reached a climax with the coronation of Charles X at Rheims in 1825. The great church was magnificently decorated; the old rites were scrupulously followed. The king duly touched the sick to heal "the king's evil" as his ancestors had

PROVINCES and DEPARTMENTS

done for eight hundred years. The miraculous vial which since the days of Clovis had held the Holy Chrism was found miraculously filled again. The greatest poets of the time, Lamartine at the height of his glory, the young prodigy Victor Hugo, were enrolled as official bards. It was an orgy of make-believe; after a century of Voltairian irony it was too much. Before the smoke of incense had cleared and the pealing organ was hushed, a snicker was heard throughout the *bourgeoisie* and the people. All too obviously, Louis XVIII bore no resemblance to St. Louis, nor Charles X to Charlemagne. Elderly relics of the eighteenth century, they were wholly devoid of glamour. From that moment the romanticists began losing interest in the royal pageant. The fact that Villèle, unwisely, had snubbed Chateaubriand and dropped him from the Cabinet greatly aided in their conversion.

Two other events, of a politico-cultural nature, accelerated this evolution. The first was the struggle for Greek independence. The Holy Alliance was in a quandary. Founded on Christian principles, it should have supported a Christian population fighting to shake off the yoke of the infidels. But as defender of vested interests (perhaps the deeper meaning of "legitimacy") the alliance favored the established authority, the Turks, against revolutionists. The naval battle of Navarino (October 20, 1827), in which the Egyptian fleet was destroyed, was deplored by Wellington as "an untoward incident, threatening to disturb the balance of power." The Liberals had espoused the Greek cause as a combat for the rights of the people; the romanticists, because it was Oriental, picturesque, a brilliant epilogue of the crusades. The immense fame of Lord Byron cast its aura over the contest: on his death at Missolonghi, the great egotist and rebel was hailed as a martyr of liberty.

The other event was the growth of the Napoleonic legend. So long as he had even a distant hope of regaining power, for himself or for his son, Napoleon at St. Helena had posed as the restorer of order, the protector of property, the foe of revolution. He claimed, not without reason, his place among the crowned superpolicemen. When the dynasts ignored his plea, Napoleon effected the most amazing, the most successful, of his maneuvers. He turned himself into a martyr, the Prometheus of democracy, chained to his South Atlantic Caucasus with dull and precise Sir Hudson Lowe cast in the role of the vulture. His death in 1821 had caused no stir. But soon the gospel from St. Helena, Las Cases's *Memorial,* spread among the *bourgeoisie.* Compared with the feeble and antiquated protagonists of the Restoration, the Corsican was vivid, virile, dynamic. His deathbed conversion to liberalism opened a vast horizon, whereas the Bourbons stood for peace, conservation, unimaginative orthodoxy. Soon the emperor, clear-cut and realistic, efficiency manager and supreme martinet, was to become one of the vague gigantic myths of Romanticism, with Prometheus, Don Juan, Faust, and the Wandering Jew. Hugo, son of a Napoleonic general, had started as a loyal Legitimist: already in his *Orientals* (1829), Napoleon's shadow, "dazzling and somber," appears on the fiery horizon.

Villèle was conscious of growing discontent. The country was honeycombed with secret societies, in particular the *Carbonari* of Italian origin. As a precaution Villèle disbanded the National Guard, the stronghold of the urban *bourgeoisie*, suspected of liberalism. Charles X dissolved his obedient Chamber in the hope that the taxpayers would confirm his conservative policy. But on November 17-24, 1827, a Liberal majority was returned. The king yielded grudgingly, and early in 1828 he called in a middle-road minister, Martignac, who satisfied neither side. Judging that conciliation had failed, Charles reverted to stronghand methods. Polignac was appointed in Martignac's place (August 8, 1829).

Now Polignac was an "ultra of the ultras," a determined and purblind reactionary. The Chamber protested against this disregard of parliamentary practices: it was dissolved. But the new elections (May 16, 1830) were again unfavorable to the king. True to his policy of "thorough"—had not everyone blamed his brother Louis XVI for his weak vacillations?—Charles accepted the challenge, sent the new Chamber packing, muzzled the press, and altered the electoral law so as to bring the French to their senses. This he did in the form of five Royal Ordinances, stretching to the breaking point the emergency powers conferred upon him by the Charter. He hoped that the capture of Algiers, and perhaps inchoate plans for expansion toward the Rhine, would reconcile the French to the loss of their liberty. The suppressed deputies, the gagged journalists, the University students, the workingmen of Paris, all rose against him. In his overweening confidence, he had taken no precaution against an uprising. Marshal Marmont could not cope with the barricades. In three days (July 26-29, 1830) Charles X was taught, to use Bossuet's resounding phrase, a great and terrible lesson. Unhurriedly, not without dignity, he went again into exile.[5]

✒ THE BOURGEOIS MONARCHY

All revolutions offer the same ambiguity: it is easy enough to tell who was defeated, but much harder to determine who was victorious. The conservative *bourgeoisie* wanted no radical change in the monarchy: it was Charles X who had committed a revolutionary act, a *coup d'état* against the Charter. But if the *bourgeoisie* had been the first to protest, the working people and the students of Paris had borne the brunt of the fighting; it was they who refused to be put down by the force of Marmont's bayonets.

The old king eliminated, four solutions were possible. On his way to Cherbourg Charles X had stopped to abdicate in favor of his grandson, the duke of Bordeaux, "Henry V," with the duke of Orleans as lieutenant general of the kingdom. Thus change would have been reduced to a minimum; but in the anger of battle this last gesture was ignored. The Napoleonic legend had already caught hold of the people's imagination. But there was no organized Bonapartism. The pretender, Napoleon II, was merely the duke of Reichstadt, a sickly adolescent in the clutches of Metternich. A moderate republic was not unthinkable: the man to head it would inevitably be Lafayette. He had been very active in the Liberal opposition, and his triumphal tour of the United States had greatly enhanced his prestige. Finally, there was the Orleanist solution, which, as we have seen, had already flickered in 1789–1791.

There was no popular demand for the duke of Orleans. France was definitely averse to extreme solutions: ultra-Royalism or a Jacobin dictatorship. But Henry V under a regency or Lafayette as president of a bourgeois republic would have been good working compromises. The Orleans candidacy, in modern parlance, was "put over." It was the result of a "deal," closely resembling those which, in a smoke-filled hotel room, traditionally mark the climax of American national conventions. The most active agent in that intrigue was the brilliant young journalist and historian Adolphe Thiers (1797–1877). To his dying day he was the champion of the *bourgeoisie,* all the more so perhaps because he was himself of humbler origin. He wanted the reign of the middle class to be acknowledged without equivocation. Even a chastened Bourbon would still be closely linked with the Ancient Regime; even an anti-Jacobin republic might not hold the gate firmly enough against radical democracy. Terms could be imposed upon the duke of Orleans who had no valid claims of his own.

The authors of the Orleans compromise were deeply impressed by English precedents. The Charter followed the English pattern; during the Restoration the *Doctrinaires* had constantly held up English parliamentary practice as a model. The parallelism between the two histories was too striking to be ignored. A stubborn king who refused to heed the nation's representatives and in consequence was beheaded: Charles I, Louis XVI. A Commonwealth or Republic, turning into the dictatorship of a soldier: Cromwell, Napoleon. A Restoration, with a first king cautious and skeptical enough to end his days peacefully on the throne:

Charles II, Louis XVIII. A brother who was a religious bigot and brought discontent to a head: James II, Charles X. The year 1830 in France was 1688 in England. It was time to adopt the carefully balanced solution which had worked so well north of the Channel: a prince of royal blood, but not in direct line of descent, a constitution not merely granted by an absolute monarch, but binding upon the king as a solemn compact. There are few cases in history of such deliberate imitation.

Paris, vibrant with the "Three Glorious Days" of the barricades, might be an obstacle; and Lafayette might come to terms with the radical elements in the capital. But Lafayette was seventy-three and not in a combative mood. Although he loved popularity and was not afraid of responsibility, he had no craving for the empty pomp of office. Moreover, like his friend and model Washington, he was at heart a moderate, attached to liberty but unwilling to "open the flood gates of democracy." So Lafayette was easily prevailed upon to lend his influence to the Orleanist cause. He went to the Hôtel de Ville (City Hall), center of Leftist power, and presenting Louis-Philippe, said, "Take him: he will prove the best of republics." He lived to doubt the wisdom of his choice. At any rate, like every other action in his long career this move was scrupulously disinterested. Talleyrand, discarded by the Restoration, inevitably endorsed the new regime and served it well as the supreme virtuoso of diplomacy. He was to die not exactly in odor of sanctity but formally reconciled with the Church and honored as a senior statesman (1838).

Politically, France was going back to 1791. Like Louis XVI Louis-Philippe [6] was not king of France, but king of the French, with the tricolor flag of the bourgeois revolution. The vote was still the privilege of heavy taxpayers, although the franchise ceased to be the quasi-monopoly of the great landowners. The Upper House was retained, but the new peers were appointed for life. Liberty and property; no more autocracy, whether of the king's pleasure, of the mob, or of the sword. The solid enlightened *bourgeoisie,* slowly rising through the centuries, was officially enthroned at last.

Louis-Philippe (1773–1850) was by birth a prince but in his faults and his virtues a bourgeois. He was hard-working and well-informed, blameless in his private life, shrewd, parsimonious, and not averse to strictly legal trickiness. In his youth he had, like his father, supported the Revolution, joined the Jacobins when they were still moderate, served very creditably under Dumouriez at Valmy and Jemappes. With Dumouriez he had escaped into the Austrian lines in 1793 and taken no part in the Terror. He refused to fight against Republican France and was kept at arm's length by his fellow exiles. Louis XVIII, however, bore him no grudge and restored to him his titles, his rank in the army, and his immense fortune. An excellent businessman, he soon was one of the richest men in France. In the Chamber of Peers he belonged to the Liberal opposition. He had his sons educated in public high schools (*lycées*) with the children of the *bourgeoisie*. He was therefore admirably prepared to become "the Citizen-King."

At first he played his bourgeois part with great gusto and success. Before the revolutionary fever of July, 1830, went down, he was always ready to appear on the balcony of the Palais-Royal and sing the "Marseillaise"—off key, the enemies of the regime remarked. Even after he had moved to the stately Tuileries, he entertained there the haberdashers of Rue Saint-Denis, who came to the ancient palace in their unpretentious hacks. Villemain, professor and statesman, one of the great personages of the reign, went to royal parties at Compiègne with a clean shirt in a brown paper parcel. The king strolled the streets unattended, a good bourgeois among bourgeois; and with bourgeois forehandedness he carried with him an umbrella, far more to the point than either scepter or sword. He knew the meaning of money. The old kings "espoused France" at their coronation; their private wealth became part of the national domain. Louis-Philippe kept his own fortune separate. He haggled with his bourgeois parliament over his civil list and the allocations to his numerous progeny; they fought back but admired him for his ability to drive a bargain.

No regime was ever more frankly plutocratic. Even Victorian England preserved at least the trappings and some of the traditions of an aristocracy; America in her most business-worshipping moments still did lip service to democracy. Under Louis-Philippe, the divine right of property was officially beyond question. Property was not a privilege but the just reward of thrift and the guarantee of independence. Why should those who could not manage their own affairs meddle with the conduct of the state? Guizot, an austere Huguenot, a philosophical historian of the highest merit, an upright and competent statesman, said with flawless logic, "If you want a vote, get rich!" *Enrichissez-vous!*

From the economic point of view, however, the reign was not merely bourgeois, but *petit bourgeois:* short-sighted and timorous. The Industrial Revolution, the first effects of which were clearly felt under Louis XVI, had been interrupted by the political revolution and by the military adventure of the Empire; it progressed but slowly under Louis-Philippe. Adolphe Thiers, the king-maker, the sharpest intellect among the Orleanists, derided the railroads as new-fangled toys, just as, twenty years later, he was to brand the reconstruction of Paris by Haussmann as sheer extravagance. There was notable progress in spite of Thiers; but it was halfhearted and sluggish. Constructive capitalism of the modern type had to wait until Napoleon III.

THE PROTEST: ROMANTICS AND UTOPIANS

It is this combination of rapacity and timidity that makes the economic life of the Constitutional Monarchy so unlovely. It was marvelously described by Balzac who knew it from within: he calls the business world of his day a basket of live crabs seeking to devour one another. The *Human Comedy* of the great realist is a Dantesque inferno, and the deadliest of its sins is meanness. Balzac, himself a frustrated businessman, could stand above that blind struggle for profit: the great sculptor Rodin rightly represented him recoiling before the vision he had evoked. He claimed to write "by the light of those two eternal luminaries, Monarchy and Religion," but this was to a large extent a pose; as a matter of fact, he was at heart a captain of industry of the Saint-Simonian, Second Empire, or American type, redeemed from sordid greed by the exhilaration of adventure, the joy of creation, and perhaps the hope of service.

Thanks to Balzac, we know the era of the Constitutional Monarchy better than any other period in French history: his only rival, the duke of Saint-Simon, limited himself to court circles. But Balzac was a romanticist as well as a realist, and both tendencies distorted his vision. We must not yield to the temptation of viewing the reign of Louis-Philippe altogether in this lurid light. In spite of its one deadly sin the rule of the *bourgeoisie* was mild and not stupid. France labored on quietly and not unhappily. All the Philistine virtues flowered; but the middle class was still Voltairian, keen-minded, critical, and, on many essential points, liberal. The atmosphere was not stifling as under the rule of Metternich. It was easier to think freely in the Paris of Louis-Philippe than in the London of Victoria's first decade.

With tame rabbits in the seats of the mighty the age was, intellectually, a glorious jungle. With the drab present it embraced, far more than we do today, all the past and all the future. Legitimism was still a power, and Berryer, its defender, was one of the greatest orators of the time. There was a splendid revival of religion, democratic with Lamennais, aristocratic-liberal with Montalembert and Lacordaire, plebeian-ultramontane with Veuillot. The Revolution was at last studied with sympathy, and Michelet was to write the glowing epic of that great fight for freedom and justice. Napoleon was reinterpreted, in fantastic but generous fashion, as the Messiah of Democracy. And before the Industrial Revolution had materially transformed the land, prophets had arisen, struggling with the moral and practical problems that it was to create:

the pre-Marxian socialists so unjustly dismissed as Utopians, Saint-Simon,[7] Fourier, Louis Blanc, Cabet, Proudhon.[8] Romanticism, the great revolt against the conventional, the drab, and the mean, was now exploring the future as well as the past. The greatest writers, Chateaubriand their ageing master, Lamennais, Lamartine, Hugo, Michelet, Quinet, George Sand, even Alfred de Vigny in his austere ivory tower, felt their responsibility as spiritual leaders.

The redeeming point about the July Monarchy was its being limited: limited no doubt in its outlook and sympathies but also limited in its repressive action. It did not seek to impose a single way of life. Official platitudes only gave greater pungency to audacious paradox. If the ruling class was more dully utilitarian than Bentham, Théophile Gautier could profess the proud doctrine of Art for Art's Sake. If Louis-Philippe, his peers, and his deputies turned property into a fetish, Proudhon dared to assert: Property is theft. If Guizot preached the inevitable and ever-lasting triumph of the middle class, Lamennais the priest, Hugo the poet, Sand the novelist, Michelet the historian, Eugène Sue the popular romancer proclaimed their faith in the people. Hence the puzzling and vital fact that the quietest period in French life, the dreariest in French politics, should also be the most ardent in French culture.

PEACE WITH (BORROWED) GLORY

Louis-Philippe, king by the grace of the barricades, believed that a revolution is a major surgical operation, which demands a long and cautious convalescence. His first care was to reassure Europe. The allies were afraid of a new crusade for the rights of the peoples—ending with the reconquest of the "natural frontiers." Europe is one in spite of dynasties and nationalisms: July, 1830, had shaken the whole of the Continent; everywhere the oppressed were turning their eyes toward Paris. But Louis-Philippe and the class that had put him on the throne were not qualified to start a holy war. Very sensibly, the king believed in peace, even in peace at any price; in his eyes as in Franklin's there never had been a good war or a bad peace. The test was the Belgian question. The Belgians broke away from the Dutch with whom they had been forcibly united in 1814. Many wanted to become French; the more moderate desired independence, but with a French king and a customs union with France. Louis-Philippe realized that either solution would be interpreted, by England and Prussia at any rate, as a direct challenge; Austria and Russia would inevitably follow their lead. The compromise then adopted —an independent and neutral kingdom linked by dynastic ties with Germany, England, and France—was a masterpiece of diplomacy.

The anchor of Louis-Philippe's policy was friendship with England.

The two liberal parliamentary monarchies should be natural allies, and in 1832 a great electoral reform made England almost as purely bourgeois as France. That is why Louis-Philippe sent to the key position, the court of St. James, the most skillful and the most prestigious of diplomats, Talleyrand. This very reasonable understanding worked, but it did not work very smoothly. Palmerston, a power in English politics, was headstrong, blustering, even brutal; his bad manners, even more than his patriotism and his ability, endeared him to the British public. So France and England, who ought to have co-operated in closest harmony, were repeatedly on the brink of war.

At times the cause was futile, like the commercial activities and political plottings of a missionary, Pritchard, in Tahiti. Once at least it was a major issue: in 1840 France found herself alone in supporting Egypt, while her former enemies of 1814 were once more united against her in favor of Turkey. Thiers drew up a feverish program of armaments, including the last fortifications of Paris. The king swallowed his humiliation, got rid of bellicose Monsieur Thiers, and saved the peace. In 1843, after pleasant meetings between the two royal families, an *entente cordiale* was openly proclaimed. It had ceased to be a verity by the time it had become official: Guizot had already veered toward an understanding with his fellow conservative, Metternich.

Peace could be preserved only if the great powers would refrain from intervention in the affairs of the lesser countries. Louis-Philippe was a resolute noninterventionist. His rule of conduct was excellently formulated by Dupin the Elder, a typical bourgeois: *Chacun chez soi, chacun pour soi,* let everyone stay at home and mind his own business. Calvin Coolidge could not have been more explicit. If France moved against the Dutch at Antwerp, it was with an international mandate and without any thought of conquest. If she occupied for six years (1832–1838) the papal town of Ancona, it was only as a check to Austria, who had seized Bologna. In the second part of his reign, the foreign policy of Louis-Philippe was negative: *quieta non movere,* let sleeping dogs lie. On the positive side it became almost entirely dynastic: he had to find suitable matches for his numerous children. The affair of the Spanish marriages was an Anglo-French tragicomedy.

Louis-Philippe was exceedingly clever—he was often compared with the much-traveled and cunning Ulysses—and he rejoiced in his cleverness. He believed in peace; but he knew that the nation, as much attached to peace as he was, also thirsted for glory. Ximénès Doudan, a very orthodox Orleanist, was right: the French bourgeois wanted at the same time to "bestrew with his corpse" (*joncher de son cadavre*) all the battlefields in Europe and to toast his toes by his cozy fireside, Don

Quixote and Sancho Panza rolled into one National Guard. So Louis-Philippe provided two safe outlets for the martial spirit.

The first was the conquest of Algeria. He might have withdrawn his troops in 1830 as soon as the dey of Algiers had been properly chastised for his insolence to a French consul; he decided, on the contrary, to defeat one after the other the barbaric principalities nestling in that mountainous region. It was the romance of the homespun July Monarchy. Romantic in its setting, it lent itself to brilliant episodes; as England growled, it enabled Louis-Philippe to beard the British lion without excessive risk. The Orleans princes won their spurs in the fight against Arabs and Berbers. It took eighteen years to subdue the beautiful country with its rocky fastnesses and its fanatical population. Deeds of heroism were performed, and atrocities also: a whole tribe was smoked up in a cave. The warfare was ideal for dashing cavalry lieutenants: it caused French generals to unlearn modern strategy. It brought out one strong man, Marshal Bugeaud, Duke of Isly, colonizer as well as conqueror; and it added to the folklore of the French one romantic figure, their brilliant and chivalrous enemy, Abd el-Kader.

The second outlet was Napoleon-worship. Louis-Philippe gorged the people with retrospective glory by reviving the memories of the Empire. The legend had no more sedulous propagandist than the peace-loving Citizen-King. He surrounded himself with survivors of the heroic period even though they were third-rate administrators like Maret, Duke of Bassano, or the policeman Savary, Duke of Rovigo. No ceremony was complete without "an illustrious sword," or, at any rate, "an illustrious scabbard." The show piece was Marshal Soult, Duke of Dalmatia. President of the Council in 1832 and 1840, he was for years the nominal head of the Guizot cabinet; he was a military "vicar of Bray" who had served all regimes without ever neglecting his perquisites. The statue of Napoleon was restored on top of the Vendôme column; the great Arch of Triumph was completed. Finally, the Orleanists organized the grandest celebration of all, the "Return of the Ashes," as it was called in classical style. The sailor-prince, Joinville, brought back the sacred remnants from St. Helena on a frigate incongruously called "The Beautiful Chicken" (La Belle Poule). Survivors of the epic, "bronzed with the sun of the Pyramids, stiff with the ice of the Berezina," [9] surrounded the magnificent catafalque; and under that spiked helmet, the gilded dome of the Invalides, Napoleon was laid to his final rest, according to his wishes, "on the banks of the Seine, amid those French people I have loved so well."

The dangerous game worked perfectly. The popularity of the Orleans dynasty was undoubtedly enhanced by this reflected glory. The Bonapartists did not profit by the growth of the legend. In 1836, when Prince Louis-Napoleon, son of Napoleon's brother Louis, king of Holland, attempted a military coup at Strasbourg, he was soon arrested and packed off to America: France did not stir.[10] In 1840, when the legend was reaching its climax, the prince tried again, at Boulogne; and the fiasco was even more pitiful. On the eve of the Revolution of 1848 the police could report that Bonapartism was a negligible element.

"FRANCE IS BORED"

The home politics of the July Monarchy offered a dreary spectacle except for the few who took active part in the game. A middle road for the middle class is a narrow path, and by no means a straight one.

Louis-Philippe, who, we repeat, was a very intelligent prince, genuinely attempted to reconcile the battling traditions of the country. Versailles, for instance, was reopened not as a royal residence but as a historical museum dedicated "to all the glories of France." It was duly decorated with acres of battle scenes by the very best of Philistine painters, chief among whom was Horace Vernet. To exorcize the memories both of Louis XVI and of the guillotine, a perfectly neutral Egyptian obelisk was erected on the Place de la Concorde. The regime had no sufficient vigor to create a new synthesis; it could at least practice eclecticism. So eclecticism was the order of the day; and Victor Cousin, the official philosopher of the age, took cool, clear French rationalism, added a few drops from the Gospels, a dash of Neo-Platonism, a jigger from Kant and another from Hegel, and felt that he had said the last word on the True, the Beautiful, and the Good.

We must never forget the ambiguous origins of the regime. Was the Revolution of 1830 merely a lesson to the absolutists, or was it a first step toward "the best of republics"? It was the time when De Tocqueville went to America to find out whether democracy was a promise, a menace, or a blank. From the beginning the victors of July, 1830, split into Conservatives and Liberals: they were soon to be known as partisans of Resistance and partisans of Movement. At first Louis-Philippe gave the Movement a chance with the banker Laffitte, a friend of Lafayette's. He knew that the first months were the hardest and that Laffitte would soon wear out his thin popularity. Then came Casimir Périer, a Constitutionalist with an authoritarian temper. He believed that the executive should be limited but not weak: in this respect he was the heir of Mirabeau. He repressed with a vigorous hand an insurrection in Lyons (November, 1831), one of the very first symptoms of a proletarian movement. He was carried off by the great epidemic of cholera of 1831–

1832. Louis-Philippe did not mourn: he craved for personal power and had no use for too strong a prime minister.

Between 1832 and 1840 Soult, Broglie, Thiers, Molé (the king's personal favorite), Soult again for a moment, Thiers for the second time occupied the center of the small parliamentary stage. The period had to its credit the Elementary Education Act sponsored by Guizot: this marked a definite progress in a field that Napoleon and the Restoration had shamefully neglected. Guizot, a Protestant but first of all a conservative, placed the State schools under the influence of the Catholic Church. In 1834 there was a renewal of radical agitation and rioting in Paris and Lyons: the "best of republics" had turned sour.

Adolphe Thiers was the rising man; but if he represented the Movement (so long as property was not challenged), he stood also for a spirited foreign policy which might embroil France in a European war. As a result of the Oriental (Near Eastern) crisis in 1840, Thiers fell from power, and Louis-Philippe had his wish at last.

Guizot was in perfect harmony with the king: both wanted peace abroad, strict conservatism at home. Guizot had great talents as an orator, as a practical politician, as an administrator, as a philosopher and historian; but he was too aloof to command wide popularity and eclipse his sovereign.

Guizot believed in the mission of the propertied classes. To him the electors, i.e., the richest taxpayers, alone constituted the country "legally speaking." Proletarians and bohemians had no place in his scheme: they were subversive elements. He manipulated his bourgeois parliament with great skill. Scrupulously honest in his private life, he felt justified in bribing a constituency or a deputy. Many members of his well-disciplined majority were at the same time state officials whom he could control through fear or hope. The Movement with Thiers, the Dynastic Opposition with Odilon Barrot were allowed to criticize him as much as they pleased, thus proving that the July Monarchy was in truth a liberal regime; but when it came to a test division, Guizot had the votes in his pocket. In seven years of an upright and competent administration he achieved the miracle of accomplishing absolutely nothing. For every change is a leap in the dark, and he was a practical man.

This marvelous stability was the sign not of a firm purpose but of a creeping paralysis. The king, as he grew older, was more and more confident in his own wisdom, that is to say, more and more averse to novelties. His liberal-minded heir, Ferdinand, Duke of Orleans, had died in a carriage accident in 1842. Guizot was increasingly the prisoner of his own doctrinaire infallibility. The government did nothing wrong:

a few scandals in official and aristocratic circles, an economic depression would not in themselves have seriously weakened it. But it closed the door to every hope. In the words of Lamartine, "France was bored."

While secret societies were flourishing again, while Barbès and Blanqui were attempting futile insurrections, while Utopians were propounding fantastic schemes, the Liberals had a simple remedy to offer: a reform of the electoral system. Nothing so radical as manhood suffrage, merely an extension of the franchise to the men who, through their positions, had proved their capacity, even though they did not pay the stipulated amount of taxes. Louis-Philippe and Guizot, impregnable in their parliamentary majority, declined to move a single inch. The reform campaigns spread to all parts of the country and to all classes. It was supported by the Legitimist die-hards (who did not believe in suffrage at all), by a handful of Bonapartists, and by the increasing host of Republicans, who wanted to go much faster and much further than Thiers and Odilon Barrot.

Lamartine, in his fanciful and eloquent *History of the Girondists,* set forth his conception of a generous and moderate republic. An orator as well as a poet, he became the leader of the whole movement. He soared above parliamentary factions; he claimed to represent "the constituency of the ideal." Political meetings were not allowed; but banquets were, with speeches to follow a Spartan feast of cold veal and salad. In 1847 there was a nationwide campaign of banquets. It was to find its climax in a great banquet in Paris on February 22, 1848.

Excitement was running high; the government fumbled lamentably. The meeting was prohibited, authorized, prohibited again. Each false move made Paris more restless. A mere accident, a random shot followed by a panicky fusillade, turned the agitation into a riot. Again the twisting lanes of old Paris bristled with barricades. Louis-Philippe jettisoned Guizot, called in Thiers, Odilon Barrot, the popular strong man from Africa, Bugeaud. Each step came a few moments too late. It was no longer the ministry that was under attack but the regime. Louis-Philippe was no coward: he had faced assassins with royal calm. But he hated bloodshed. Perhaps his conscience was uneasy: he knew his title was precarious. His bourgeois National Guard had turned against him and shouted, "We want the Reform!" The barricades of Paris had given him his crown: they had the right to take it away. So, like Charles X, he abdicated in favor of his grandson. But Charles had retired slowly, a king to the last: Louis-Philippe fled and reached England under the bourgeois name of Mr. Smith.

BOOK V
MODERN FRANCE

CHAPTER XXI

The Second Republic
and the Second Empire: 1848-1870

⚔ THE "MAD AND HOLY YEAR"

February, 1848, is the belated second phase of July, 1830. There is a striking similarity between the two revolutions. In both cases the initiative came from the liberal *bourgeoisie* against the senile obstinacy of the king. In both cases agitation flared up into violence. In both the material victory was won by the working masses of Paris led by a handful of radicals. This time, the victors were determined not to be cheated again as they had been eighteen years before. The Hôtel de Ville, the historical headquarters of Parisian insurrections, had a firm purpose, whereas the bourgeois Palais-Bourbon (Chamber of Deputies) was confused. The Hôtel de Ville easily prevailed. The Republic, One and Indivisible, was proclaimed. Alphonse de Lamartine headed the provisional government. Among its members were Garnier-Pagès and Ledru-Rollin, leaders of the radicals, and, as an afterthought, one workingman, Albert.

The new Republic had a distinctly reddish tinge: it was officially called democratic and social. The "right to a job" was affirmed. Louis Blanc, the socialist, was placed at the head of a commission to inquire into economic and social problems. And National Workshops (the name was borrowed from Louis Blanc) were created as an emergency measure against unemployment.

Provincial France accepted passively the decisions of Paris: it was not organized to resist the prestigious capital. And no one desired to fight for the Orleanist compromise: the wonder was that such a rootless regime should have endured so long. The country had grown weary of the interminable Guizot government with its myopic cleverness, its futile technical skill, its doctrinaire infallibility, its invincible standpattism. The Golden Mean, rule of the July Monarchy, had perished of its own meanness.

The revolution was a vindication of idealism, and it seemed natural that Lamartine the poet should guide the young Republic. There was a moment of superficial but genuine good feeling. Even the clergy, no friend to radical change, blessed the trees of liberty which were solemnly planted everywhere. Ominously, they refused to grow.

The problems that faced the new government were exactly the same as in 1830, only a great deal worse. The most urgent need was to adopt a foreign policy. Europe, we repeat, was already one, although the governments were wilfully blind to the fact. Within a few months insurrections had broken out in most European capitals: even London, proud of its immunity to Continental fevers, was soon to see tremendous Chartist demonstrations. Once again, Paris was expected to take the lead. The issue was lead or perish, for if the popular uprisings were crushed throughout Europe, it would be difficult for a democratic and social republic to survive in France. The people of Paris were clamoring for a crusade. In particular, they wanted to liberate Poland from her triple yoke.

Lamartine was forward-looking, courageous, and generous to a fault. But for an elegiac poet he had a very keen sense of reality. He knew that France was divided and that Russia's enormous weight would buttress the dynasties, that the German democrats distrusted the French, and that liberal England, for fear of French hegemony, would side with reaction. The enterprise would not merely be costly, it was doomed in advance. So Lamartine had to adopt the homely dictum of Dupin, "Let everyone stay at home and mind his own business." With great skill he managed to reassure Europe without forswearing his principles. This meant the abdication of his idealistic Republic, but a European crusade would have been even more suicidal.

For over three months Lamartine wielded the dictatorship of eloquence at the service of common sense. He tamed the mob not with bayonets but with sensible and impassioned words. The elections to the Constituent Assembly—manhood suffrage was adopted as a matter of course—were a victory for the tendency he represented, moderate republicanism and peace (April 23). It won five hundred seats. The Orleanists, who might easily rally to Lamartine, had two hundred; the extremists—Legitimists on the right, radicals and socialists on the left—a hundred apiece. Lamartine was confirmed as president of the Council. The Executive Commission—Arago, Garnier-Pagès, Marie, Lamartine, Ledru-Rollin—was decidedly left of center. But it contained no socialist. Ledru-Rollin, too much of a Jacobin, was ardently opposed; and even Lamartine lost votes because he had endorsed him.

The economic problem was now to the fore. The preceding years had been unfavorable. Parisian trade depends largely on luxury and is extremely sensitive to political crises. So unemployment was mounting perilously. The National Workshops, had they been true to Louis Blanc's conception, could have served as a transition from *petit bourgeois* economy, with its jealous and timid individualism, to large-scale enterprise, still unfamiliar in France. But such was not the intention of Marie, the minister in charge, and Thomas, the director. Both chose to consider them purely as temporary charities. No long-range plans were prepared, no useful work undertaken. The vast horde of the unemployed was sent to scoop out the Champ-de-Mars, and then level it up again: a Gargantuan sandpile to amuse Demos. After a while the workers, many of them skilled artisans, dropped their shovels, lit their pipes, and talked politics. An army of discontent was thus mobilized on the outskirts of Paris.

On May 15 the Parisian workmen, feeling that the democratic and social republic was slipping away, invaded the Assembly, declared it dissolved, and proclaimed a new Provisional Government. They were easily put down, and the challenge was accepted by the bourgeois majority. The Red Specter, communism, was already haunting those men who thought that social order and property were inseparable. Proudhon, with his audacious blasphemies ("Property is Theft; God is Evil"), became a one-man Terror. Because of their distant socialistic implications, the National Workshops were suppressed with as much clumsiness as they had been managed. This was intended to be a showdown. On June 23 the Paris masses rose in formidable insurrection. Lamartine and his fellow commissioners felt unable to cope with the uprising and resigned. Cavaignac, a general trained in Africa to ruthless warfare, defeated the insurgents in the bloodiest street fighting Paris had ever known. The archbishop of Paris, Monseigneur Affre, nobly attempted to bring words of peace and died a martyr.

Cavaignac, although he was to be bitterly remembered as the Butcher of June, was an upright republican. He did his duty and restored order. But it was the old order. The generous, idealistic Republic of February 1848, "democratic and social," yearning for the fraternity of classes and nations, was dead. The regime which nominally survived until December, 1852, was guided, far more than Louis-Philippe ever was, by its hatred and dread of the proletariat.

Cavaignac, the successful dictator, was made provisional chief executive. The constitution was taking shape. It was drawn up by a very competent commission including, among noted jurists, Alexis de Tocqueville, the author of *Democracy in America*. Its faults, which were undeniable, were not the cause of its ultimate failure: after June, 1848, the Second Republic lived on sufferance, constantly menaced by a monarchical restoration or another democratic revolution. No paper instrument could have made it secure.

One point was discussed with great heat: how should the president be elected? Jules Grévy proposed that there should be no president at all, thus ensuring his own election thirty years later. Lamartine in a magnificent speech supported a direct election by the people and won the day. Perhaps he knew that the choice of the Assembly would undoubtedly be Cavaignac, and he remembered his own popularity before the Days of June. More probably, he was sincere and disinterested in his advocacy of the democratic principle, "Let God and the people decide! *Alea jacta est!*"

The elections were held on December 10, 1848. Cavaignac, who had "saved society" in June, received but 1,400,000 votes; Ledru-Rollin, the democrat, 370,000; Raspail, candidate of the Socialists, 36,000; and Lamartine (*Alea jacta est!*) 17,000. Prince Louis-Napoleon headed the polls with 5,400,000.

That one vote determined the course of the next twenty years, and requires careful interpretation. It was not purely and simply the triumph of the legend: in 1840 the legend was more virulent than in 1848, yet the Boulogne attempt failed miserably. It was certainly not due to the personal magnetism of the candidate. To most people he was known only for his two abortive and somewhat ludicrous gestures. When he appeared in the Assembly, his short stature, his shuffling gait, his lackluster eyes, his halting speech with traces of German accent fully reassured those who had thought him dangerous. There was some Bonapartist propaganda, vigorously led by the fanatical Persigny; but its resources were limited and its personnel not outstanding. No doubt the reactionaries—including Thiers, whom the Days of June had pushed very far to the right—thought it clever to support Louis-Napoleon against Cavaignac since they could not yet present a candidate of their own. But the enormous majority he obtained—without any suspicion of fraud, for his rival Cavaignac was in control of the election machinery—was not entirely composed of reactionary votes.

The truth is more complex than any of these partial hypotheses. The confusion which reigned in Louis-Napoleon's mind was at that precise moment in perfect harmony with the national confusion. France wanted contradictory things, and Louis-Napoleon in all sincerity offered them all. By certain aspects of his puzzling character he was "the Common Man," or the common denominator. His name stood for order, discipline, a strong executive: Cavaignac had done the work, but Louis-Napoleon represented the principle. But he was not committed to reaction, open or hypocritical, as the Royalists were suspected to be. He was a believer in manhood suffrage, a Caesarian democrat: his very able program-pamphlet, *On Napoleonic Ideas,* had made the point clear. While the bourgeois and the peasants thought of him as the super-policeman sworn to defend their property, the Socialists knew that he stood for a more generous policy than that of the Orleanists and of many Republicans. His short book *On the Extinction of Pauperism* was not forgotten; it was known that he considered Louis Blanc as his master. He was fortunate enough to have been out of France during the Days of June: he was compromised neither in the uprising nor in the repression. For the ultra-patriots, his accession to power would finally tear up the hated *Diktat* of Vienna: for the victors had then decided that France should never again be ruled by Napoleon or his heirs. Above all a Napoleonic regime, by whatever title, promised surcease from the two evils France most hated—and hates today—disorder in the street and party squabbles.

THE PRINCE-PRESIDENT

Louis-Napoleon, who was to hold for twenty-two years the center of the stage, was born in 1808, the son of Louis Bonaparte, King of Holland, and of Queen Hortense, daughter of the Empress Josephine. He was educated in German Switzerland and in Bavaria; one of his tutors was Philippe Lebas, son of the noted Robespierrist. In 1831 he and his elder brother (who died in the brief adventure) took part in a liberal insurrection in Romagna, a province of the Papal States. After the death of the duke of Reichstadt (1832), he considered himself as the legitimate Napoleonic pretender: he was the only Bonaparte who had faith in the mission of his house. He asserted his claims, as we have seen, both in political writings and in two audacious bids for power, at Strasbourg in 1836, at Boulogne in 1840, sorry caricatures of the return from Elba. His six years of imprisonment at Ham were his university: he read extensively and with a very serious purpose. In the intervals of conspiracy he spent a few seasons in England; he was well received in the most aristocratic circles, for he was an excellent horseman. Disraeli, himself something of a paradox, a sphinx, and an adventurer, gave a very flattering picture of him in his romance *Endymion.* He was interested in a Nicaragua Canal scheme, and was offered the crown of Poland by liberal conspirators. All in all, his was a curiously equivocal figure—prince, dreamer, and bohemian. He went pretty rapidly through the fortunes of Hortense and Louis. When his chance came, between 1848 and 1851, he had to be financed by friends, particularly by a lady of great and profitable charms, Miss Howard.

With the Revolution of February 1848 the ban against him had been lifted. He entered French politics cautiously, even modestly; for his unswerving purpose and his daring always wore a veil of reticence. As a child, he was timid, silent, and gently stubborn; and twenty years as a conspirator had deepened his secretiveness. In appearance he was, we must repeat, unprepossessing: the admirable portrait by Hippolyte Flandrin is an interpretation, not a candid likeness. In manners he was quiet, extremely courteous, with a background of kindness and of mystery. The voluble Adolphe Thiers, his very antithesis, thought him a dolt.

His mind was richly stored, bold, generous, and confused: images of the future are bound to be blurred. He had grown with the legend: his hero was the mythical Napoleon of the thirties, not the sharp, competent, reactionary autocrat of 1810. He believed in the modern Caesar as appointed by Providence to serve international and social democracy. He was a fatalist but by no means a quietist: he knew that Destiny needed the co-operation of human energy. By training, experience, sympathy he was European rather than purely French: born a Dutch prince, he had lived in Switzerland, Germany, Italy, England, and was to marry a Spaniard. He belonged to what the French call the generation of forty-eight: he was a romanticist, a mystic democrat, a free believer, a Utopian socialist. The irony of fate brought him to power just at the moment when the spirit of forty-eight had suffered a crushing defeat. His rule for twenty-two years offered the disquieting combination of secret persistent idealism with the trappings of a coarsely materialistic regime. This, and not any moral obliquity, caused the distrust that doctrinaires of the right and of the left felt for him. Even his closest friends were nonplussed. All those who approached him were impressed by his extreme gentleness, but they did not understand. To the present day no scrupulous historian can draw a clear-cut portrait of him and say with assurance, "This is the authentic Napoleon III."

In 1849–1850 Louis-Napoleon was a correct constitutional president. He chose a moderate cabinet headed by Odilon Barrot, an Orleanist but leader of the "dynastic opposition" under Louis-Philippe. The Roman Expedition, which was to be the incubus of his reign to the very end, had been decided upon by Cavaignac. In 1848 the Papal State had not been spared the ordeal of revolution. A moderate minister, Rossi, was murdered by a radical; the next day, November 16, an insurrection forced the pope to appoint a democratic cabinet. Pius IX, in alarm, fled to Gaeta under the protection of the king of Naples (November 25). The French government then thought it advisable not to intervene but to watch. It might be necessary to forestall any action by Austria: it was over again the story of Ancona in 1832. On February 9, 1849, a Roman Republic was proclaimed. On April 14 the French Constituent Assembly voted funds for an expedition which ten days later landed at Civita-vecchia.

What followed was a tragicomedy of errors. Mazzini and Garibaldi, knowing the present temper of French official circles, did not welcome Oudinot's troops as friends. The French met with resistance. According to a lamentable tradition which still survives, such a repulse "engaged the honor of the flag." The diplomat De Lesseps, later of Suez and Panama fame, negotiated a sensible agreement; but he was overruled by the military, and Rome was besieged. On June 30, 1849, it capitulated. This defeat was the end of the Roman Republic. The pope was restored. Louis-Napoleon desired even then to secure from him some promise of a liberal policy. But Pius IX, who, on his accession, had been the hope of the democrats, had been driven by the revolution into extreme conservatism. To challenge his rule was a sacrilege: absolutism seemed to him inseparable from his sacred character. Rome became a key position in the great conflict which was raging throughout Europe: everywhere the reactionaries considered the pope's temporal power as the symbol and bulwark of order against subversive tendencies. Louis-Napoleon found himself trapped into standing as the protector of a pontiff who had already declared war on liberalism, modern civilization, and progress.

The purpose and the issue of the Roman Expedition were still uncertain when the elections to the Legislative Assembly were held (May 13, 1849). The moderate majority of a year before melted away. The conservatives were now in control. But the radicals also came out of the test greatly strengthened. This nerved them to attempt, on June 13, 1849, another Parisian insurrection. It was easily suppressed; the President showed himself a good policeman, and Ledru-Rollin, a dubious leader at best, had to flee. The reactionary temper of the Assembly was sharpened by this victory. Louis-Napoleon did not start an open conflict with the legislative; but, to some extent, he disengaged himself by dismissing Odilon Barrot and appointing a purely presidential cabinet: men unknown to fame, capable administrators, who later—especially Rouher—were to be good servants of the Empire.

On March 10, 1850, complementary elections resulted in a moral victory for the "Reds." The majority resolved to conduct "a Roman Expedition at home," a campaign to suppress all subversive activities. The Falloux law was intended to increase the influence of the Church in education. A new electoral law, while respecting the principle of manhood suffrage, managed, through stricter residence requirements, to disfranchise 3,000,000 out of 10,000,000 voters: the axe fell chiefly on urban workers who were suspected of favoring the Reds. Thiers, the liberal of 1830, denounced "the vile multitude."

The President knew that this rightist turn did not truly represent the sentiment of the nation. Without openly breaking with the majority he, as the elect of the whole people, began a political campaign of his own. He toured the country, promising everywhere order without reaction. He was received with universal acclaim. In great military reviews the soldiers, primed by their officers, shouted, "Long live the Emperor!" But the strength of the movement was in the rural masses rather than in the army.

⚔ THE *Coup d'État*

Everyone was looking forward to 1852 with dread. Then the term of office of Louis-Napoleon would expire, and, according to the constitution, he could not be re-elected. Standing above parties, he was the only element of stability in a distracted land. An amendment that would have enabled him to succeed himself failed to obtain the required three-fourths vote. The President then asked for the repeal of the antidemocratic electoral law: this was rejected by a bare majority. He stood therefore as the sole representative of the people's will against a dominant party committed to reaction and a minority openly preparing for revolution.

The way to lawful reform being barred, he had to consider other methods. He carefully matured his plans. He first secured the right instruments: Saint-Arnaud as minister of war, Magnan as commander of the Paris garrison, Maupas as head of the Paris Police, and, as minister of the interior, his illegitimate half brother, who had only recently rallied to him, Morny. On December 2, anniversary of Napoleon's coronation and of his victory at Austerlitz, the Rubicon was crossed. In the night the key members of the Assembly were placed under arrest, and the walls were placarded with proclamations. In the bleak light of a winter morning the Parisians could read: "The Assembly is dissolved. Universal suffrage is restored. The final decision will be left to the people in the form of a solemn referendum."

Paris received the news without enthusiasm and without indignation. The most common reaction was, "Well played!" The bourgeois thought, "At last we may go back to business!" The people did not rise. There were a few barricades here and there: in the narrow streets of that time a handful of men with an overturned omnibus and a few paving stones could improvise a fortress. But there was nothing to match the millennial ardor of February, 1848, or the despairing wrath of June. Mere patrols sufficed to clear the obstructions. The most famous episode of the *Coup d'État* proves the listlessness of the population. A Republican deputy, Baudin, was urging workingmen to defend a barricade. They shrugged their shoulders: "To get killed so as to save your twenty-five francs a day? No fear!" "Citizens," Baudin replied, "I am going to show you how one dies for twenty-five francs." He went up to the barricade and was instantly shot. Victor Hugo, who was very active in the resistance, had to admit that it was sporadic and half-hearted.

On the fourth of December affairs took a different turn. Eager for a showdown, the leaders of the *Coup d'État* withdrew their patrols, thus encouraging the resistance and enabling it to gather momentum. Then, with a great display of force, the barricades were easily reduced. The responsibility for this Machiavellian strategy is not fully established: Saint-Arnaud, Magnan, to magnify their share in the operation? Morny, to create a breach between the President and the people and save his half brother from his dangerous socialistic propensities? More simply, Maupas, Prefect of Police, may have lost his nerve and blundered into useless violence.

Then, as a regiment was marching down the Grands Boulevards thronged with idle passers-by, a shot was heard. Some trigger-happy soldiers, believing themselves attacked, fired a volley at the windows and into the crowd. In a moment the madness spread from file to file, and the whole boulevard was ablaze. Before sanity could be restored, several hundred people had been wounded or killed.

The tragic blunders of the fourth completely altered the complexion of the *Coup d'État*. We must not forget that it was made in the name of democracy against a reactionary Assembly: two days later, the conservatives were exulting. Intended as a bold appeal to the people, it had turned into a deed of treachery and violence. Victor Hugo and Gambetta were justified in calling it a crime. Before it was born, the future Empire was thus a damaged regime, just as Louis-Napoleon himself, for all his generosity and kindness, was a damaged soul.

To cover up the gesture of witless rage, the Red Danger had to be magnified. Society had to be saved: for weeks the police hounded the Communists, as all dissenters were then called; improvised courts sent them to convict camps in Algeria, Guiana, or New Caledonia. A few, like Victor Hugo, went into exile. It looked as though Paris had been cowed into submission; the working classes never forgave Louis-Napoleon.

On December 20–21 a plebiscite ratified the President's action by 7,440,000 to 646,000. Even a radical historian such as Charles Seignobos admits that it genuinely mirrored the opinion of the country. In the elections of February 29, 1852, Louis-Napoleon was further endorsed:

out of 261 deputies there were only eight opponents, three Legitimists, two Independents, three Republicans. The rest were "official candidates," a term which remained familiar for the next two decades. It was not the use of force that made the *Coup d'État* a success: it was the popularity of the President and of his program that made the French condone the fusillade on the Boulevards.

Even before the *Coup d'État* Thiers, narrow-minded but keen-sighted, had said, "The Empire is made." No one expected the Bonapartist Republic to be permanent. The Prince-President took another tour through central and southern France: he was everywhere greeted with shouts of *Vive l'Empereur!,* to a large extent spontaneous. There was but one obstacle in his path: the French were attached to peace, and the Empire seemed the exaltation of martial glory. At Bordeaux on October 9 Louis-Napoleon gave the pledge which France and the rest of Europe were anxiously awaiting, *L'Empire, c'est la paix,* "the Empire stands for peace." The Senate, a hand-picked body, declared that the restoration of the Empire should be submitted to the people. The plebiscite taken on November 21 approved the proposal by 7,-824,000 to 253,000. The President was officially notified of the result on December 1, and on December 2 the new regime was formally inaugurated.

⚜ THE EMPIRE: MATERIAL ORDER, MATERIAL PROSPERITY

From 1852 to 1867 political life was almost suspended in France. Until 1859 the regime was frankly authoritarian. There was no opposition: the Republicans would not take their seats because of the loyalty oath. Only the liberal Catholic Montalembert, who had approved of the *Coup d'État,* dared openly to criticize the government. After 1860 the Empire took a more liberal turn: the consequences of the Italian war had disturbed the harmony between the Conservatives and the government. Still, the Republican opposition counted only five members, the most eloquent of whom were Jules Favre and Emile Ollivier. After 1866 the physical decay of the emperor, the reverses of his foreign policy, the sheer lassitude that comes after nearly two decades under the same leader gave both the Royalists and the Republicans a chance. There was also a third party, an opposition loyal to the regime yet determined to assert its independence. Finally, at the end of 1869, the Empire became strictly constitutional with a ministry responsible to Parliament. And the head of that ministry (January 2, 1870) was a liberal, a former Republican, Emile Ollivier.

Perhaps it would have been more accurate to say that the parliamentary life of France was a blank, rather than the political. For, in spite of the dull unanimity that made elections almost senseless, in spite of laws restricting the freedom of the press, France was intellectually and even politically extremely active under the Second Empire. The regime, radical in its democratic principle, bold and even adventurous in its economic policy, was supported, with misgivings, by the Conservatives: its hybrid character acted as a stimulant to thought. There was no single French way of life to impose its commonplace stamp upon every individual. The emperor is reported to have said: "How could you expect the Empire to run smoothly? My wife is a Legitimist; my cousin Napoleon, a Republican; Morny is an Orleanist; I am a Socialist; there is but one Bonapartist in the lot, Persigny, and he is mad." *Se non è vero.* . . . The repressive laws were for the journalists a blessing in thin disguise. If, until the closing years, writers could not indulge in violent personal attacks, the loss to genuine freedom was small. If they had to use wit, allusiveness, and irony in the exhilarating game with the censor, the result, in thought and art, was clear gain. Napoleon III was spared, but Tiberius of Rome and Soulouque (Faustin I) of Haiti were mercilessly criticized. And if an old republican craved for stronger fare, he could always import a plaster bust of Napoleon III from Belgium, smash it, and find inside a copy of Victor Hugo's great lyric and epic satire, *Les châtiments.*

The real history of the Second Empire is not to be found in the debates at the Palais-Bourbon or the Luxembourg but, at home, in economic expansion; abroad, in a series of questionable but not ignoble adventures.

Under Napoleon III France moved consciously into the Industrial Age. The material progress in those eighteen years (1852–1870) was spectacular, and its chief manifestation was the sudden development of the railroads: 2,200 miles in 1852, 10,000 in 1870. The same change had taken place in England two decades earlier, and it involved not France alone but the whole of western Europe and North America: evidently, the Second Empire was not the originator, but merely the beneficiary of this new Renaissance. A regime, however, may either foster or hinder the evolution of a country. The spirit of French business, under Louis-Philippe and again under the Third Republic, was *petit bourgeois:* an economy of small shopkeepers, artisans, and peasant proprietors. The Second Empire was practical but bold.

As Hippolyte Taine—no Bonapartist—put it in his *Travel Notes,*[1] the emperor understood his time better than any man: we feel that he would understand the atomic revolution today. Railroads, sea ports, mining were undertaken not grudgingly but with with alacrity and on a generous scale. Nothing was too bold for the engineers of the time. They went beyond their English masters in daring and in technical skill. They planned a Paris metropolitan railway, which was not realized until thirty years later; a Paris ship canal and a Channel tunnel, which are still mere projects: the Empire fell too soon. They bored the first Alpine tunnel under Mont-Cenis. Their most sensational achievement was the Suez Canal, completed just before the fall of the Empire. England, who was to profit so greatly by the enterprise and to seize a controlling interest in its management, had fought it tooth and nail against the gentle pertinacity of Napoleon III.

No less striking was the transformation of the great cities, in particular Paris. This was conceived personally by the emperor, who chose Haussmann as his instrument. Wide, tree-lined avenues were traced through the old districts of the city, new quarters developed beyond its ancient limits, parks created, churches and hospitals, markets and railroad stations built on a scale and with a rapidity hitherto undreamed of. Belgrand carried out a modern system of water supply and sewerage. The Seine was lined with stately quays, and spanned by bridges of Roman robustness. The Louvre was at last linked with the Tuileries after three hundred years of desultory efforts. Few of the buildings of the Empire are of commanding merit, not even the gaudy Grand Opera of Charles Garnier, pastiched throughout the world; many intimate, old-world corners, many quiet and charming edifices of the past were needlessly sacrificed by the Boeotian prefect. Still, on the whole, the work was nobly planned and efficiently done. The Third Republic, instead of striking new paths, did not manage even to finish the work started by Haussmann; although not kept up to date, it became obsolete only after seventy-five years.

That Napoleon's motives were mixed does not detract from the merits of his achievement. All dictators like to show off: this policy, which after all was that of Louis XIV, was followed by Porfirio Díaz, Mussolini, and Huey Long. There was also an attempt, which proved unsuccessful, to bribe the great cities, citadels of opposition. There was likewise, no doubt, a strategic consideration: wide and straight avenues lend themselves to cavalry charges and even to artillery fire, against which insurgents would be powerless. The emperor did not anticipate that he would fall without even a pistol shot fired in Paris. But above all this there was a desire to create a new city and a new nation, proud of their past yet looking boldly and confidently into the future.

There were two aspects to this immense prosperity. On the one hand, the age was frankly materialistic. The fault, however, lay neither with science nor with industry nor with Napoleon III. The fraternal spirit of

1848 had been crushed in June: what triumphed with the troops of Cavaignac was order and common sense, no doubt, but also "realism" as an inveterate distrust of generosity. Romanticism survived only in the older writers whose thought was darkened by defeat: Hugo, Michelet. The younger ones were wounded souls who, rejecting the naive hopes of their elders, abandoned hope in any form: Baudelaire, Flaubert, Leconte de Lisle expressed their horror of the world in which they were condemned to live. The vanished dream left the world in cynical mood: the harsh conception of life affected socialism with Marx ("iron law"), science with Darwin ("struggle for life"), liberal economics with the Manchesterians ("Devil take the hindmost"), politics with Bismarck ("Blood and iron"). Progress was sneered at, but the undiluted reaction of the ultramontanes and Pius IX offered no consoling refuge. Physically, man had grown tremendously richer and more powerful; spiritually, he was pauperized. This was the price that had to be paid for "saving society" in June, 1848.

Hence the triumph of materialism in all its forms: morose realism in the arts, material wealth, material power, material pleasure. So the fifties and sixties were a "Gilded Age," of a type all too familiar on both sides of the Atlantic. It was a parvenu period: get rich quick, show off, enjoy. Gamblers, profiteers, and demimondaines held the center of the stage: Zola has described them with "naturalistic" accuracy, if with a touch of epic amplification, in *La curée* ("The Kill") and in *Nana*. When tourists flocked from all parts of the world to see the great Exposition of 1867—the apotheosis of the regime—they expected to enjoy, and virtuously to condemn, the wickedness of the modern Babylon. It is then that *La vie parisienne,* as a play, as a magazine, and as a mode of life, became a byword for meretricious gaiety. The best symbol of that Bacchanalian frenzy, more striking than the operettas of Meilhac and Halévy, even with Offenbach's sprightly music, is Carpeaux's group on the facade of the Opera, "The Dance."

Even the highest members of the imperial circle had a bohemian tinge: the clerical aristocracy and the solid *bourgeoisie* were silently disapproving the loose manners of a regime which they openly supported as the lesser of two evils. Napoleon III was frankly an adventurer; so was, on a less exalted level, his devoted henchman, Persigny; so was (with no slur on her virtue) the beautiful empress, née Doña Eugenia de Montijo y Teba; so was (with no restrictions) her all-too-vivid mother. The best epitome of that cynical, pleasure-loving society was the duke de Morny,[2] financier, profiteer, gambler, and statesman. He was no coarse caricature: in his speculations and in his amusements he preserved a high degree of Louis XV elegance. He was an ideal president of the Legislative Body; with his practical sense, his personal prestige, his exquisite manners, his elaborate entertainments he made the deputies forget what a small part they played in the government of France. His death in 1865 was an irreparable loss for the Second Empire.

But there was, we have said, another aspect to the period. Although the Empire was a paradise for the get-rich-quick promoter, the emperor himself had deeper views. Without being formally associated with the Saint-Simonian school, he was animated by its spirit. Now Saint-Simon's neo-Christianity was in truth a religion, the service of God through the service of man. Its fundamental principle was that the first duty of a government is to promote the welfare, material and moral, of the most numerous and poorest class. In his new order the thinkers, scientists, artists, and poets were to form the clergy; and the "captains of industry" were to be the nobility, making the riches created by modern technique available to the people at large. It is significant that a number of Saint-Simonians, Father Enfantin, the Pereires, without abjuring the messianic hopes of their youth, became prominent business leaders under the Second Empire, and that Sainte-Beuve hailed Napoleon III as "Saint-Simon on horseback."

Nor was the emperor's sense of social responsibility merely a pious wish. In favoring the creation of wealth, he was incessantly concerned with its distribution. He thought, as Napoleon and Louis-Philippe never did, in terms of hygiene, slum clearance, the common luxury of public buildings, theaters, promenades. He was not an anticapitalist, but he made the essential instrument of enterprise, credit, more democratic. Under him were founded those great companies, Société Générale, Crédit Lyonnais, which drained the small savings of artisans and peasants and directed them into large projects: thus property preserved its individual character yet lost its sterile isolation, and was enabled to work for great collective ends. The Crédit Foncier, a national building and loan corporation, also financed the public works of the cities. The Crédit Mobilier, although it went through a severe crisis in 1867, greatly helped in the prosperity of the era. Napoleon III was thus moving cautiously toward a mixed formula, the co-operation of state capitalism with collective private enterprise; he had reached about the same point as America when the Reconstruction Finance Corporation was established. He was in favor of free trade, and, in spite of determined opposition, he took a practical step in that direction through a commercial treaty with England.

The vastly increased number of industrial workers intensified social problems: Zola's *Germinal* was among the first, and in some respects remains the most powerful, of all proletarian novels. But the emperor was not indifferent to the claims of the working class. Strikes and unions, which the Revolution and all subsequent regimes had outlawed, were at last authorized. The infamous Article 1781, according to which the word of an employer was to be accepted by a court against the word of an employee, was finally abrogated. If the working classes had not been haunted by the word "republic" and the memories of December 4, 1851, they would have recognized that the Second Empire was not absolutely committed to mesocracy, or middle-class rule.

"Frivolous materialism," therefore, is not an adequate summing up of the Second Empire. Few ages have taken such a profound interest in religion. There was the usual crop of commonplace and sedative apologies with the usual accompaniment of cheap scoffing. But it was also the time when Renan's *Life of Jesus* became a best seller, and his first lecture at the Collège de France a national event; when Guizot was penning his *Meditations on the Christian Religion,* and Proudhon his great treatise on *Justice in the Revolution and in the Church.* Sainte-Beuve, a liberal Bonapartist and in some ways the most complete embodiment of the age, had written a long and austere study on Jansenism, *Port-Royal.* Auguste Comte was blending humanitarian religion and social reaction in his positive philosophy. Taine may be stiffly systematic: he can hardly be accused of levity, even though he did contribute to *La vie parisienne.* In science it was the age of Claude Bernard and Louis Pasteur, the full maturity of Marcelin Berthelot. All this is "France of the Second Empire," no less than the antics of Princess Pauline Metternich and the lively tunes of Offenbach, than the shallow Voltairianism of Edmond About, or the scurrilous ultramontanism of Louis Veuillot. Between the reign of Napoleon III and the various totalitarian regimes in our own century there is an abyss.

"THE EMPIRE STANDS FOR PEACE": CRIMEA, ITALY

Louis-Napoleon had pledged his word, "The Empire stands for peace." The assurance was not superfluous: there had been some saber rattling in the uncle's career; the nephew in 1840 had promised to avenge Waterloo, tear up the Treaties of Vienna, and recover for France her natural frontiers. Europe took the fair words at Bordeaux in a strictly Pickwickian sense. In eighteen years the Empire waged four major wars, with two or three minor expeditions (Rome, China, and Syria).

The first, with Russia (1854–1856) was an old-fashioned war of European equilibrium. The actual pretext—a quarrel between Orthodox and Latin monks in Jerusalem—was forgotten before the opponents drifted from intrigue into bluster, and from bluster into open hostilities.

France, and especially England, wanted to keep Russia away from the Mediterranean. Both, and especially France, wished to curb an enormous irresponsible power which, in 1848, had been the mainstay of reaction. The allies landed in the Crimea and besieged Sevastopol. The expedition was marked by glaring inefficiency on all sides. Repeatedly, "someone blundered," and the most brilliant episode was rated as "magnificent, but not war." Strangely enough, although the Western allies operated two thousand miles from their home countries, it was Russia that suffered from imperfect communications; it was easier to ship men and ammunition from England and France than to have them wade through the trackless mire of southern Russia; the factors which had once defeated Napoleon now paralyzed the tsar. The irreconcilable autocrat, Nicholas I, died. His successor, Alexander II, agreed to negotiate when Sevastopol was finally stormed and when the Russian troops— never surrounded—had retreated. The peace congress took place in Paris (February–March, 1856). It was presided over by the French minister of foreign affairs, Count Walewski, the Polish son of Napoleon. Napoleon III, the parvenu sovereign, appeared as the arbiter of Europe. He tried to turn the congress into a United Nations meeting: an international regime for the Danube was prepared. To enhance the festivities, the prince imperial was auspiciously born. Honor and vainglory were satisfied. France had nothing else to show for the waste of lives and money.

The Italian war was briefer, more brilliant, more perilous also, and infinitely more complex. Not national prestige merely but three or four different principles were involved.

Napoleon III, as a Caesarian democrat, believed in the will of the people manifested through plebiscites. This implied self-determination, which in those days was known as "the doctrine of nationalities." Populations should not be held down by force or bartered away without their express consent: they had the right to unite and separate as they chose. The principle applied particularly to Italy, Germany, Poland, Romania. The emperor was instrumental in creating the Romanian nation with a Hohenzollern as its prince. He wanted, with the support of all parties in France, to see Poland reconstituted; but he was paralyzed by the indifference of his indispensable ally, England. The case of Italy was dearest to his heart. Italy had been almost united under Napoleon I and then parceled out again at Vienna. In his youth Louis-Napoleon had fought in the ranks of the Italian liberals. Intervention in Italy would enable him to recover Savoy, which was French in culture, and Nice, which was on the French side of the Alps and had been French for twenty years. In addition this would give him a chance to "humble the House of Austria," a tenacious tradition inherited from Richelieu.

A dramatic episode may have determined him. An Italian patriot, Felice Orsini, hurled a bomb at him (January 14, 1858) and missed him. The first result of this outrage was a series of repressive measures; the second, an outburst of vituperations against England, where the plot had been hatched. But Orsini, from his cell, wrote a noble letter to Napoleon urging him to espouse the cause of Italian independence. The emperor may or may not have been a *carbonaro* in his youth; at any rate, it seems established that the pathetic appeal impressed him, stirring dormant aspirations and forgotten promises. On July 20, 1858, at Plombières the emperor met secretly with Camillo Cavour, Prime Minister of Piedmont.

On April 20, 1859, a threatening ultimatum of Austria to Piedmont brought the alliance into operation. The French emperor promised to liberate Italy as far as the Adriatic. On June 4 Mac-Mahon won the battle of Magenta; and four days later, Napoleon entered Milan in triumph. On June 24, in actual command, he was victorious—or at any rate Francis Joseph believed himself defeated—at Solferino. Then, suddenly, Napoleon III offered his adversary a personal interview and an armistice. The terms agreed to by the two sovereigns at Villafranca (June 11) were confirmed by the formal Treaty of Zürich (November 11): Austria gave up Lombardy but not Venice. This lame peace was a timely move. Napoleon had realized that the hardest task was ahead: Austria still held a "quadrilateral" of formidable fortresses; Prussia was arming on the Rhine; England's neutrality was less than benevolent.

The emperor's moderation infuriated the Italians: his portrait disappeared from the shop windows of Turin and Milan and was replaced by that of Orsini; Cavour resigned. In spite of these excessive gestures the Italians realized that Napoleon's intervention had been decisive. In France, at any rate, his triumph was complete. On his return to Paris (August 14, 1859) when, on the Place Vendôme at the foot of his uncle's victory column, he passed his troops in review, he was wildly cheered, even by the workingmen of the Republican suburbs. His reign had reached its zenith.

But he was already conscious that the Italian problem was a hornet's nest. The solution he favored was not a centralized Italy but a federation of Italian states with the pope as member and as president. The extreme conservatism of Pius IX, however, and his outspoken hatred of liberal Piedmont made such a consummation unthinkable. Parma, Modena, Tuscany drove out their princes, who were Austrian satellites, and voted for union with the new Kingdom of Italy. But so did Romagna, a papal province. Garibaldi, with his thousand Red Shirts, conquered Sicily and Naples. Napoleon, a believer in Italian unity, had given to all this an approving wink: "Go ahead, but do it quickly."

It was evident that Italy, now a nation, would demand her historical capital, Rome. But the temporal power of the pope, it must be re-membered, had become a symbol for all conservatives: if Napoleon III ceased to protect the pope, it would signify that he had gone over to the Reds. Had he been tempted to do so, the fourth of December, 1851, had created a gulf between the Empire and the Republican Left. Thus Napoleon was caught, and for ten years he could not extricate himself. He was at heart with the Italians, but he could not afford to break his alliance with the Church. In 1864 a compromise was reached: the French would evacuate Rome in 1866, a papal army was organized, and the Italian government, now established in Florence, pledged itself not to attack the Holy City. But Garibaldi, not bound by this compact, led his volunteers against Rome; the French landed once more at Civita-vecchia; at Mentana (November 3, 1867) they defeated the great *condottiere,* whom liberal Europe considered a hero. So Rome was still occupied by French troops when the Franco-Prussian War broke out. Victor Emmanuel II expressed himself willing to join Napoleon III if Rome were evacuated. The empress vetoed such a move: was not the pope the godfather of the prince imperial? The French did not leave Rome until the fall of the Empire. Less than three weeks after Sedan, on September 20, 1870, the Italians could at last enter their own capital.

THE MEXICAN IMBROGLIO

The Mexican affair was an imbroglio in which the best intentions jostled with the worst motives. Mexico was in the throes of a civil war caused by the liberal reforms of Benito Juarez. A conservative, Miramón, had seized the presidency; but at the end of 1860 he was driven out by the Juaristas. In 1861 the Mexican government suspended payment on foreign debts. On December 17 England, France, and Spain jointly occupied Veracruz to safeguard their interests. The story had a troublous background: a Swiss banker, Jecker, held outrageous bonds issued by Miramón and wanted Juarez to be responsible for them. It was known that Morny protected Jecker, even if he was not an outright partner to the swindle. But so far, the sordid story was of an all-too-familiar type. A deeper plot was in the making.

A number of Mexican exiles persuaded the empress that only a strong monarchical government could restore peace and save Catholicism in Mexico. They represented the docile and pious population of that country as misled and terrorized by a few radicals. The emperor was tempted: the Mexicans should at least have a chance freely to express their preference. Pardonably, he thought an empire would suit them best: had not a democratic Empire been brilliantly successful in France? Had not all republics failed in America, even the United States, then torn by a fratricidal war? The only country in the hemisphere to enjoy peace was Brazil, under the enlightened rule of Dom Pedro II. By strengthening Mexico he would block the advance of the "Anglo-Saxons," who had recently taken nearly one-half of the country: he vaguely considered himself as the protector of the whole "Latin" world. Of course, a friendly Mexico, although not a colony, would offer a fruitful field for French enterprise. As a candidate for the hypothetical throne he accepted Maximilian of Hapsburg, who had been a good viceroy in Lombardy and who was wasting his days at Miramar.

When Spain and England understood that France might wish to intervene in Mexican affairs, they wisely withdrew. A deplorable misunderstanding occurred. By agreement with the Juaristas, the French were allowed to move from fever-stricken Veracruz to higher and healthier grounds. But when they advanced on Puebla, dangerously close to the capital, they were sharply checked (May 5, 1862). To have repulsed the finest army in the world greatly heartened the Juaristas, and made them less amenable to a compromise. On the French side, as in the case of Rome in 1849, the honor of the flag was declared engaged. A full-sized expedition was organized; and on May 19, 1863, after a three-month siege Forey captured Puebla.

By this time Napoleon had misgivings about his Mexican scheme; honor was satisfied, and he would gladly have stopped the adventure. Now it was Maximilian and particularly his wife, Charlotte (Carlotta) who were reluctant to give up their dream crown. An honest plebiscite would have settled the question: either Maximilian would have received an unequivocal call, and even the United States would have been bound to respect the will of the Mexican people; or, clearly rejected, he would have stayed at home. But Forey, as soon as his lieutenant Bazaine had entered Mexico City, rigged up a pseudo government which elected Maximilian. Forey retired with a marshal's baton leaving Bazaine in charge of military affairs; and, in political power, a junta of extreme reactionaries.

Napoleon still hoped that Maximilian would refuse this unconvincing call. Maximilian was weak, stubborn, conceited; he was also conscientious and filled with noble ambition. He accepted what he thought to be a mission, and on June 12, 1864, he entered Mexico City. Bazaine, a rough soldier but very competent for that kind of warfare, conquered the whole of Mexico for him. Juarez was driven to El Paso, and his isolated supporters were treated as bandits. Wherever they went, the emperor and the empress were blessed by the clergy and cheered by the multitudes. For a season the Mexican Empire looked almost real.

Maximilian, like Napoleon, wanted a modern, enlightened regime; but the reactionaries who had engineered his candidacy and his election hated the very thought of liberalism. On the other hand, the Juaristas remained irreconcilable. At times the imperial pair thought that the French army alone stood between them and the love of "their people": yet without French troops Maximilian could not have maintained himself.

The French troops were withdrawn: Napoleon had realized at last that "the greatest thought of his reign" was a fiasco. The situation in France and in Europe was uneasy. The War Between the States was over, and Secretary Seward urged that the occupation should end, with a firmness which was almost menacing. Bazaine left Mexico City on February 5, and Veracruz on March 12, 1867; and Maximilian was given the fullest chance to retire with him. He declined, still believing that there was an immense imperialist party in Mexico. He soon discovered his helplessness. Carlotta went to Europe to beg Napoleon for aid: in vain. The poor empress, her dream shattered, took refuge in lifelong madness.[3]

Almost to the last Maximilian could, safely and honorably, have left the country that rejected him; a few dangerous friends told him that a Hapsburg could not desert his partisans. So he fought to the bitter end, was betrayed and captured at Querétaro, and shot according to the very ordinance he had passed against the Juaristas (May 19, 1867). On May 30, when the Paris Exposition was at its height, and awards were being distributed in an impressive ceremony, the tragic news reached the French sovereigns: the imperial group silently withdrew from the hall. Mexico was left to a half century of civil wars and military dictatorships: there are some Mexicans, like the philosopher and historian José Vasconcelos, who have come to think that Maximilian might have been a very acceptable ruler. In France and in Europe the failure of the Mexican adventure irreparably damaged the prestige of Napoleon III; in the United States it created an invincible prejudice against him.

"LIBERTY CROWNING THE EDIFICE": THE CONSTITUTIONAL EMPIRE

In 1866 Prussia and Austria went to war. The other large German states, Hanover, Saxony, Bavaria, sided with the Confederation, that is to say, with Austria. On July 3 the Seven-Week Campaign was abruptly ended by the complete triumph of Prussia at Königgrätz (Sadowa). When the news reached Paris, the capital started illuminating, and the government seemed to share the popular elation. There was no reason why France should mourn the discomfiture of her recent enemy, reactionary Austria. Then the word was passed that the rejoicings were mistaken: it was France that had suffered defeat at Sadowa.

It was plain that Prussia had smashed the bicephalous and impotent Germanic Confederation only to establish a closer, more dynamic union under her own exclusive leadership. Prussianized Germany could be seen to emerge as a formidable power. Now it was a tradition of the French that, their own country proudly "one and indivisible," Germany should be kept divided. That tradition is alive today. The War of 1870 is supposed to have proved its wisdom. But the cause of that war was not German unity: it was the declared intention of the French to fight it tooth and nail. *Gleichberechtigung,* which may be freely translated as, "What is sauce for the French goose is sauce for the German gander," is not an unreasonable plea.

According to his own principles Napoleon III should have welcomed German unity; and in his secret heart, he probably did. He was maneuvered into the position of considering Sadowa as a personal rebuff. As a matter of fact, his previsions had proved false: he had fully expected a long and exhaustive struggle; at the proper moment he was ready to offer his mediation and appear again as the arbiter of Europe. He did tender his good offices: they were accepted with ironical courtesy after the terms of peace had been settled. The only shred of prestige he secured from the transaction was that Venice was handed to him, not directly to Italy: Austria hated the thought of yielding a province to an upstart country she had just beaten on land and sea. It was the merest face-saving device.

From the day of Sadowa Napoleon was urged to secure at least some compensation so as to retrieve the prestige of France. He arranged for the purchase of Luxembourg from the king of the Netherlands: the inhabitants were not unwilling. Unfortunately, Luxembourg was a federal German fortress. Bismarck vetoed the deal and disdainfully remarked that Napoleon was not entitled to any "tip" for services not rendered. In 1867 Luxembourg became a war cloud. An acceptable solution was devised: the grand duchy would become independent and neutral, its fortress would be dismantled, and it would join the North German customs union.

The situation at home from 1866 to 1869 was uneasy. The opposition, both Royalist and radical, harped on the humiliation that the emperor had brought upon France: any stick to beat the party in power.

They were urging a spirited, a defiant, attitude, while the weary emperor stood for moderation and peace. But at the same time, they denied the government the means of implementing the policy they advocated. The military law prepared by Marshal Niel would have given France a modern army: it was sabotaged by the Chamber. The *bourgeoisie* hated the thought of universal military service: hitherto, they had always managed to buy themselves off. The Republicans claimed that the Empire was essentially a militaristic regime and that its strength was constantly used to keep the people in subjection. After the brilliant but sultry festival of the Exposition, 1868 and 1869 were agitated and anxious years.

A more liberal press law had let loose a flood of scurrilous abuse: every week, Rochefort insulted the emperor in his paper, *La lanterne*. A subscription was opened to erect a monument to Baudin, a victim of the *Coup d'État;* the promoters were prosecuted, but Gambetta took advantage of the trial to denounce the "crime" which was the origin of the regime. Napoleon III, only sixty years old, was suffering from a painful bladder complaint; and sedatives left him in a sort of stupor. The government still had a majority at the polls, but the great cities, especially Paris, cast an adverse vote. The end seemed to be near at hand.

Yet at the eleventh hour there was an unexpected favorable turn. Napoleon had got rid of his trusted instruments, the devoted Persigny, the resourceful and hard-working Rouher, for years a veritable vice-emperor. Soon the great prefect, Baron Haussmann, was to go. The sovereign frankly accepted the necessity of a thorough reform. The Empire ceased to be Caesarian: it became "constitutional," i.e., parliamentary, with a cabinet responsible to a freely elected Chamber. The first prime minister fully under the new dispensation (January 2, 1870) was Émile Ollivier, son of a stalwart Republican, himself for years a leader of the Republican opposition. Orleanists, moderate Republicans, liberal Bonapartists united in a tacit and workable coalition.

On May 8, 1870, a plebiscite was taken to pass on these sweeping reforms. It was freely debated, and it proved a great victory for the regime, 7,358,000 approving, against 1,571,000. As usual with plebiscites the figures did not tell the finely shaded truth. How many "yes" votes endorsed the record of the Empire since 1852, how many were cast in favor of the new liberal trend? Above all France wanted to avert another revolution: the established government, with all its faults, stood for continuity and material order. Still, the figures were impressive. With a whole new generation going to the polls, Napoleon counted more supporters than on December 10, 1848. He said, "We can face the future without fear." And Gambetta, with bitterness in his heart, was compelled to agree, "The Empire is stronger than ever."

In May and June there was a curious lull, a feeling of euphoria, as though a new spring had come for the regime which, a year before, had seemed so hopelessly decayed. Even the health of Napoleon III improved. There was a resurgence of good will: "We shall give the emperor a happy old age," promised Émile Ollivier. And, surveying the European scene, a statesman could calmly affirm, "Not a cloud in the sky." On July 3 came the thunderbolt: a Hohenzollern prince was a candidate to the Spanish throne.

CHAPTER XXII

The "Terrible Year"
and Its Aftermath: 1870-1880

THE TRAP

In September, 1868, the long scandal of Queen Isabella's reign was ended by an uprising of the Spanish army and navy. In 1869 a constitutional assembly under the leadership of Serrano and Prim decided to preserve the monarchical principle. The problem was to find a prince willing to accept the uneasy crown. In 1870 it was offered to Prince Leopold of Hohenzollern-Sigmaringen.

Immediately, France—that is to say, a few diplomats and politicians —shuddered at the thought of encirclement. The dreaded empire of Charles V was being reconstituted. A partial and biased knowledge of history may be more dangerous than ignorance. As John Lemoinne pointed out in the liberal *Journal des débats,* dynasties count for very little nowadays. Prince Leopold was only a remote cousin of the Prussian king, and he belonged to the Catholic branch of the family. No objection had been raised when, in 1866, Napoleon III had helped another Hohenzollern-Sigmaringen to become prince of Romania.

But the fact that Prim had acted without previously consulting France seemed to mark the end of French hegemony. We have seen that the opposition was at the same time hostile to militarism and in favor of a spirited foreign policy. Gambetta, Jules Favre, Jules Simon, all considered that the move was a secret coup of Bismarck, and a *casus belli.* It was imperative that the Hohenzollern candidacy be vetoed.

It was, and the prince, after some hesitation, withdrew. France had scored a diplomatic point. But the fiery patriots wanted to press their advantage. Now was the time to humble Prussia and avenge "the shame of Sadowa." The king of Prussia was asked to pledge his word that no prince of his house would be a candidate to the Spanish throne. The ultra-Imperialists had joined the Republican opposition in their truculent attitude: a successful war would revive the tarnished prestige of the regime and enable it to do away with all liberal nonsense. The empress may not have said, "It will be *my* war." But her most devoted apologists, Maurice Paléologue, Augustin Filon, make it quite plain that she stood for defiance not for conciliation.

The king of Prussia, then at the health resort of Ems, acted with diplomatic and constitutional correctness; he refused to take any formal engagement while away from his ministers. His last conversation with the French ambassador, Benedetti, was brief but not curt.

Bismarck had perhaps not baited this particular trap. But for years he had been preparing for a possible conflict. One of his most unscrupulous and cleverest moves had been to talk vaguely with Benedetti about the possibility that France might annex Belgium: this would be the "compensation" French diplomats so desired. An informal memorandum, totally unauthorized by the French government, was drawn. Bismarck kept it in his pocket ready to use it at the right moment. Although he liked to appear in the uniform of a white cuirassier, Bismarck was first of all a diplomat, not a soldier. He believed in *List,* or cunning, even more than in *Blut und Eisen,* blood and iron. But if force were needed, he had it at his disposal: Moltke and Roon had assured him of that. He also knew that the French army, in the early stages of reorganization, was no match for his own.

So he trumped the French move to humiliate Prussia: he touched up the report of the interview between the king and Benedetti at Ems and made it appear that the king—a thorough gentleman—had deliberately snubbed the ambassador. This was the tenor of the famous Ems dispatch which was sent to the press of all the great capitals. If the French accepted the rebuff, Prussia would have won the third round in the contest for prestige. If they did not, so much the better: Bismarck needed a victorious war to weld Germany together, or rather to make Prussia supreme in Germany.

"France" fell into the trap. By "France" we do not mean the deep masses of bourgeois, workers, and peasants, but the very vocal groups which claimed to represent public opinion: the Chamber of Deputies, the metropolitan press, a noisy crowd on the Boulevards shouting, "To Berlin!" Thiers, almost alone, opposed the general hysteria. He was a patriot; he had even been bellicose; but he saw no reason to charge like a mad bull because of a mere press dispatch. He was hooted down as a coward and a traitor.

Caesarian democracy might have saved the day: the emperor and the masses wanted peace. But Napoleon III was too weary, his prestige had been too severely damaged, for him to defy the clamors that filled Paris. He had abdicated as a dictator: he was now a constitutional sovereign. So with his eyes tragically open, he yielded to martial madness. The man in actual power was the prime minister, Émile Ollivier; and he accepted the responsibility for war "with a light heart."

War had caught Napoleon III unprepared. His armies were years—perhaps only months, but vital months—behind the formidable instrument of precision created by Prussia. And his diplomacy also had been lax. He had vaguely counted upon the support of Italy, and even of Austria: had he been successful at the outset, they might indeed have rushed to the aid of the victor. As it was, they thanked their stars that they had not rashly committed themselves. He was expecting that the southern German states, so recently defeated by Prussia, would at least remain neutral; but he found himself alone against a united Germany. Bismarck published his secret trump: Benedetti's memorandum about Belgium. This made France appear, especially in British eyes, as the unscrupulous intriguer and bully. Materially and morally, the war was lost before a shot had been fired.

THE DOWNFALL

The very first encounters were disastrous. One of the main French armies, under Bazaine, had to seek refuge under the walls of Metz and was at once pinned down. The other, under Mac-Mahon, retreated to Châlons. It might yet have been reorganized using Paris as the pivot of defense. But the empress, now regent, claimed that there must be no further retreat: only an aggressive strategy could save the regime. So Mac-Mahon was ordered forward to relieve Metz and free Bazaine. But he was maneuvered into the deadly pocket of Sedan. Wounded, he appointed Ducrot as his successor; and Ducrot might still have extricated at least part of his army, but a senior general, De Wimpfen, appeared, claimed authority, stopped the retreat, and engaged the battle under the worst possible conditions. From all the surrounding heights artillery fire plunged into the helpless horde that had been the proud French army. Napoleon III, tortured by illness, had followed his troops, an encumbrance rather than a figurehead. When all hope was lost, he attempted to get himself killed, failed, and resumed command in order to stop the slaughter. He surrendered with a hundred thousand men (September 1–2, 1870). When the news reached Paris, the Empire, four months after the triumphal plebiscite, melted away without a show of resistance, and the Republic was proclaimed (September 4, 1870).[1]

It was, and it was not, the Republic. The Republican deputies of Paris, chief among them Jules Favre and Léon Gambetta, formed a Government of National Defense; but the nominal head was the military governor of Paris, General Trochu, a Conservative. Soon, however, Paris was invested; Trochu remained in the capital. A branch, or "delegation," of the central power was established at Tours to direct resistance in the provinces. Gambetta, escaping from Paris in a balloon, became the dictator of the war effort.

The situation offered not a glimmer of hope. Mac-Mahon's army was captive; Trochu's was surrounded; on October 27 Bazaine surrendered Metz with 173,000 men: no traitor, but a mediocre man who had lost heart. Europe was indifferent or hostile. Under these circumstances it was most unrealistic to continue the hostilities. But there was in France a legend of 1792, as there was a Napoleonic legend: neither is completely extinct even today. The young Republic had stamped the soil with her foot, and legions had sprung up, filled with holy enthusiasm, invincible. The most ardent Republicans of 1870 had a mystic faith in their cause and hoped to repeat the miracle. We know that the legend was to a large extent a fairy tale; raw recruits are no match for well-organized, well-armed, and seasoned soldiers. Above all the spirit of 1792 did not exist in 1870. The French were not fighting for immortal principles; they were engaged in a foolish contest for prestige, an illusion which did not appeal to a realistic generation. There were admirable patriotic episodes, recorded almost *ad nauseam* in French literature and art in the next three decades; but there was no sacred flame sweeping the whole country.

Under these circumstances it is highly to the credit of Gambetta and his chief lieutenant, De Freycinet, that they did manage to raise large armies and to keep them supplied with food and ammunition. These improvised troops gave a better account of themselves than the veterans of the Empire. D'Aurelle de Paladines and Chanzy on the Loire, Faidherbe in the North, Bourbaki in the East escaped annihilation and inflicted minor defeats upon the Germans. If Paris had played its part in the general scheme, the outcome might not have been so one-sided. But Trochu was a military pedant without imagination; he distrusted and even feared the rabble that formed his army. Although he had more men than Moltke and occupied a central position, he never dared to strike. When, urged by public opinion, he attempted to break through the iron ring, he did so halfheartedly, as if to demonstrate the folly of such a move. Paris was in a heroic mood; it submitted with grim gaiety to cold, famine, and bombardment. But the man in control, like Bazaine at Metz, had lost faith. On January 28, 1871, Paris capitulated. An armistice was arranged. A National Assembly was to be elected at once to decide on the issue of peace or war.[2]

The verdict of the country was overwhelmingly for peace (February

8, 1871). The Empire had started the war; the Republicans wanted to keep fighting to the last ditch; both were defeated at the polls. In the sudden political vacuum the voters turned to local worthies, country squires or substantial bourgeois who had not been compromised in the disastrous adventure. As a result the Assembly which met at Bordeaux comprised a large majority of Monarchists. On February 16 it elected as chief of the executive power Adolphe Thiers, clear-headed, patriotic, and above all champion of immediate peace. The terms dictated by Bismarck were harsh: Alsace, part of Lorraine, and a war indemnity which seemed astronomic and was intended to be crushing, one billion dollars. But they were accepted by 546 votes to 107. Gambetta, of course, was among the opponents. So was Georges Clemenceau who, forty-eight years later, was to tear up the hateful *Diktat*. The formal treaty was signed at Frankfort on May 10.

Most countries, and France herself, had suffered defeat before. Under the old dispensation, the Treaty of Frankfort was not more unjust than many others. But Bismarck himself, for all his mastery of up-to-date technique, was an anachronism. He did not realize that the principle of self-determination was an essential part of the modern conscience. The deputies of Alsace-Lorraine, elected in the presence of German troops, protested at Bordeaux against "an odious abuse of force, which tore them away, against their will, from their mother country." The first delegation of Alsace-Lorraine to the Reichstag of the new German Empire voiced the same opposition. Many of the plebiscites held in our own days in the name of self-determination are under legitimate suspicion: no doubt is permissible about Alsace-Lorraine. That is why the case was to remain for generations a crucial instance: antiquarian or pseudoscientific claims *vs.* the plain will of the people or, in cruder terms, *Faustrecht,* sheer force, *vs.* democracy.

⚔ THIERS AND THE COMMUNE

Paris was smoldering with rage. It had resented as a slur Trochu's refusal to fight. It was fevered with protracted excitement, inadequate food, loss of sleep. Paris was a convalescent that should have been treated with the greatest consideration. The reverse was the case. No thanks were offered for its heroic resistance, no sympathy expressed for its sufferings. It was not spared the triumphal entry of German troops. The moratorium on debts and rents was abruptly ended before normal conditions had been restored. The scanty pay of the National Guard, which alone kept many from starvation, was stopped. As in June, 1848, it looked as though the conservative Assembly was deliberately affronting the people. As the worst insult of all the rank of capital was taken away from the great city.

The Assembly decided to move from Bordeaux not to Bourges or Tours, which might have been justified for strategic reasons, but to Versailles, the symbol of the Ancient Regime. When Thiers made an effort to disarm the Paris National Guard, his troops fraternized with the people, and two generals were killed (March 18, 1871). On March 26 municipal elections were held. Thus began the brief and tragic episode known as the Commune.

The term has nothing to do with socialism, and still less with Marxian communism. All the municipal bodies in France, with the exception of a few cities, are known by the medieval term communes. In this case there was a deliberate attempt to link the new governing body with the Jacobin Commune so powerful under the Revolution. Among the supporters of the Commune in March, 1871, were men like Clemenceau, who all his life was a patriot, an individualist, and an anti-Socialist as well as a radical Republican, and Jules Méline, destined to become the leader of the Conservative Agrarians.

The German troops still quartered near Paris could watch the conflict with *Schadenfreude,* that rejoicing in the ills of others for which German alone has a name, although it is not a German monopoly. This, it is alleged, is the Commune's unforgivable sin: rebellion in presence of the enemy. But the insurrection of March 18, 1871, made in defense of the Republic, was not more "criminal" than that of September 4, 1870. It is worse to rise against the established government in the throes of a foreign war than after the end of hostilities; and the Second Empire, confirmed by three plebiscites, was at least as legitimate as the month-old and still unnamed regime of Adolphe Thiers. Even after the eighteenth of March a generous policy might have averted a civil war. But since the Days of June Thiers abominated the "vile multitude." He welcomed the chance of teaching the people of Paris a lesson. The regular troops were withdrawn, and the second siege of Paris began.

During the two months of its rule the Commune evolved very rapidly in principles and personnel. When they saw that provincial France had not followed the lead of Paris, the moderate elements gradually retired; and a strange crew of radicals, many of them foreign adventurers, came to the fore. Even then, there were no massacres, no looting, no confiscation. The Bank of France was respected; the Commune showed itself curiously *petit bourgeois* in its moderation. When the Versailles troops shot captured leaders of the Commune without judgment, the Communards, after due warning, executed a few hostages in reprisals, among them Monseigneur Darboy, Archbishop of Paris. Finally, Mac-Mahon's army, released from captivity for the purpose, reached the western gates of Paris. They fought their way slowly, through a whole bloody week, to the eastern districts, where the *Fédérés,* as they were called, made their last stand in the cemetery of Père-Lachaise (May 21–28). A few public buildings went up in flames, among them the ancient royal and imperial residence, the Tuileries.

The chief cause of the insurrection had been the despair of defeat: it was first of all a gesture of impotent rage. The repression partook of the same character, only tragically aggravated. Seventeen thousand men were killed in cold blood after the fighting had ceased. Twenty thousand more were arrested, often on the flimsiest denunciation, and shot, imprisoned, or transported after a drumhead court martial. It was an orgy of vindictiveness. The legend of the Commune, more lurid than its plain history, was to a large extent a by-product of the repression. As in June, 1848, the victors, when their lust was sated, sought to assuage their conscience by believing that they had saved society from nameless horrors. When sanity returned, the Conservatives found that "Commune, Communards, Communeux" were magic words to scare the timid and make them vote blindfolded for the right—and Rightist—candidates. Correspondingly, the Revolutionists everywhere, led by Karl Marx, interpreted the Commune as the first conscious and large-scale proletarian uprising.[3] Thus the same misreading was officially adopted by the two contending parties. In this welter of partisan hatred, plain history would feel isolated and puny if it were not for the testimony of Victor Hugo. The great poet, who had become a national hero with the fall of the Empire, and who had lived through the agonizing months of the first siege, denounced the delusions and the errors of the Commune; but he also understood the provocations and sympathized with the sufferings. He dared to plead for understanding and mercy. He was driven into exile again by an explosion of conservative fury; he was not safe even in Brussels. Yet he was of clearer sight than either Adolphe Thiers or Karl Marx.

⚔ THE BOURGEOIS REPUBLIC EMERGES

Thiers, seventy-four years old, was an indefatigable executive. He managed to restore some self-confidence in the shattered army. A very competent financier, he paid off the war indemnity ahead of time, thus shortening the term of German occupation: he was justly called "The Liberator of the Soil." His official title was, since August 31, 1871, President of the Republic; and he developed a pardonable fondness for the pitiful young Republic entrusted to his care. Reversing the words of Lafayette in 1830, he might have told his Orleanist supporters, "Am I not the best of bourgeois monarchies?" The majority noted that dangerous tendency and, in spite of his services, formally censured him as "not sufficiently conservative." On May 24, 1873, he most reluctantly resigned, and made way for Marshal Patrice de Mac-Mahon. The Rightists were sure that the old soldier, the hero of Malakoff, Magenta, Sedan, and Paris who did not conceal his monarchical convictions, would never be guilty of flirting with even the Left Center.

With a safe man as chief executive there was but one obstacle to a restoration, the presence of two pretenders: the Legitimist, the count of Chambord, grandson of Charles X, and the Orleanist, the count of Paris, grandson of Louis-Philippe. The difficulty seemed settled when the Orleanists acknowledged the prior claims of the count of Chambord: he was childless, and his Orleans cousin would be his heir. But the Legitimist leader happened to be a Legitimist; he believed in the divine right of his race and in its symbol, the white flag. He would not consent to come to terms with the Revolution, to be an Orleanist in disguise, and to keep the throne warm for the hated usurping line. He was anxious to reign, but only according to his own principles. When he made it plain that he would never abandon the white standard, his *raison d'être,* and his religion, the Orleanists knew that the game was up. For the Legitimists, with the aid of the Republicans and the Bonapartists, could easily block an Orleanist restoration; and if the count of Chambord attempted to return with the symbol of the Ancient Regime, "the Chassepot rifles," according to Mac-Mahon himself, "would go off of their own accord." All that the Royalists could do was to prolong the powers of the marshal for seven years.

Meanwhile France, with her wonted resiliency, was recuperating from the traumatic shocks of the war and the Commune. It became evident that the Assembly, elected on a single issue, did not represent the normal tendencies of the country. Bonapartism, which still had strong roots, found itself leaderless: Napoleon III had died early in 1873, and no one desired a return of the empress as regent. The Republican cause was greatly helped by the reconciliation between Thiers and Gambetta. They had been united in fighting the Empire; but Thiers, antiradical and opposed to the last war, had called Gambetta a "raving lunatic." The young firebrand, matured by his responsibilities in power, ignored the insult and paid generous tribute to the elder statesman. This greatly reassured the middle class: it looked as though the Republic were indeed the regime that would least divide the French, provided, of course, that it be a Republic without the Republicans. The more liberal among the Orleanists and Bonapartists rallied to this middle way; and when at last a Law on the Organization of the Public Powers was introduced early in 1875, the Right Center and the Left Center were ready to co-operate.

On January 21, 1875, Henri Wallon proposed an amendment: it contained the crucial words, "The President of the Republic," and it was adopted by 353 votes to 352. Two other laws completed the Constitution of 1875. It provided for a president elected for seven years by the Congress, i.e., a joint meeting of the two houses; an upper house or Senate of three hundred elected by indirect suffrage with the vote heavily weighted in favor of the rural districts; a Chamber elected by direct universal (manhood) suffrage; a cabinet responsible to the Chambers. It was a streamlined British constitution with the essential feature of the English system left out: in England the cabinet can order a dissolution; in France if Parliament and cabinet disagreed, it was the ministry that went out—every few months. It was an Orleanist compromise voted with little faith and less hope by a disheartened monarchical majority. It was inspired by a deep-seated distrust of the masses, which, unless properly curbed, might turn Red; and by an equal distrust of the chief executive, who might have a will of his own and become another Charles X or a new Napoleon III. It was intended to be a *grand bourgeois* regime: at one time it was indeed a Republic of Dukes.[4] With the years it became *petit bourgeois,* even *tout petit bourgeois,* but never democratic. With its King Log president, its cabinets constantly at the mercy of the assemblies, its assemblies divided into splinter parties and overlapping groups it was impotence deliberately organized. Yet, constantly tottering but saved by being pulled in antagonistic directions, it managed to survive, through many crises, scandals, threats of revolution, rumors of *coups d'état,* war clouds, and finally the great ordeal of World War I, until the summer of 1940.

The foreign policy of the period was passive: France was licking her wounds. The most ardent Catholics or ultramontanes dreamed—audibly —of a crusade to liberate the pope, whom they considered a prisoner in the Vatican. Since Italy would inevitably have been supported by Germany, it would have meant 1870 over again under worse circumstances. As a result of their warlike prayers "to save Rome and France in the name of the Sacred Heart," the ultramontanes, many of them Legitimists, lost much of their influence with a peace-minded electorate.

A second danger was more definite. France was reorganizing and strengthening her army. The privilege of the bourgeois not to serve unless they chose was not completely abolished but whittled down: the common people were drafted for five years, the rich for one year only. A new earnestness prevailed among the officers: under the Empire too many of them had been scatterbrained swashbucklers. France after Sedan was not unlike Prussia after Jena. The measures taken by the French government were of course purely defensive; still, Bismarck had misgivings. He knew that France would never accept the Treaty of Frankfort as a just and permanent settlement. He thought he had eliminated France as a factor in European politics if not forever at any rate for a long generation, and he was alarmed by the swift revival of her economic and military strength. There were distinct threats of preventive action: an inspired article appeared in the Berlin *Post* asking, "Is War in Sight?" Duke Decazes, the French Minister of Foreign Affairs, appealed to England and Russia and was more successful than Thiers had been in 1870. Bismarck had to realize that the supremacy of Germany was not absolute. Gorchakov, after some sharp discussion with Bismarck, was able to wire, "Peace is now assured." It was an anxious armed peace, hard to distinguish from a cold war; but it lasted miraculously until 1914. The abortive crisis of February–May, 1875, so easy to overlook, set the pattern of European relations for nearly forty years. In 1914 the same coalition faced William II that once had checked Bismarck.

LAST EFFORT OF THE "UPPER CLASSES"

As soon as the constitution went into effect (it was not submitted to popular approval), the National Assembly dissolved. It left conflicting memories with mediocrity as the dominant note. Its patriotism, its honesty, its good will were beyond question; but even original personalities lost much of their character in that glutinous mass of country squires. Elected for the single purpose of signing a treaty of peace, it maintained itself in power and, long after the emergency was over, it attempted to shape the future of the nation.

The new Senate had a Conservative majority, not fanatically committed to the monarchy. The Chamber was frankly Republican: the conjunction of Thiers and Gambetta had prepared this victory. MacMahon, very correctly, appointed a moderate liberal to form his first cabinet. He had some merit in choosing Jules Simon, who had once attacked him with unwonted acerbity and who was among those responsible for the change of regime on the fourth of September—a crime in the eyes of the old soldier. Simon was a popular philosopher, a disciple of Victor Cousin; he had written mildly eloquent books on natural religion, freedom of conscience, duty, the family. In manners, he was so smooth, ingratiating, and diplomatic that his opponent, Monseigneur Dupanloup, a fiery bishop, jestingly remarked, "He will beat me to a Cardinal's hat."

Jules Simon was an eminently reassuring personage. But the Royalist and Catholic camarilla surrounding the marshal could descry behind his bland platitudes the dread specter of radicalism. The Left was undoubtedly anticlerical: that is to say, it was opposed to the intervention of the clergy in politics. Especially in foreign affairs. We have seen that a recrudescence of militant ultramontanism was a threat to peace. A monster petition was drawn up urging the government to secure, by every available means, "the independence of the Holy Father." Some bishops took an active part in this campaign. Now, under the Concordat, they were also functionaries of the State, and Jules Simon felt justified in rebuking them. Gambetta uttered his ringing challenge, "Clericalism is the enemy!" The Chamber passed a resolution deprecating "ultramontane activities": Simon did not dare to oppose it. Evidently he was not sufficiently alive to the peril from the Left; he believed in a Republic from which the Republicans need not be ostracized. Mac-Mahon bided his time; on the sixteenth of May not on the clerical issue but on a couple of minor pretexts he forced Jules Simon to resign.

This opened a crisis which affected the whole life of the Third Republic, and even that of its pale shadow, the Fourth Republic of 1945. The lines were then sharply drawn between the presidential system of government, with a strong executive largely independent of the Chambers, and the parliamentary, in which the cabinet is merely a joint committee of the two houses to be recalled at will. Mac-Mahon appointed as premier the duke of Broglie, an able man, son of a prominent statesman, and member of an illustrious family. But on June 19 the Chamber, by 363 votes to 158, refused him a vote of confidence. Thereupon Mac-Mahon, with the consent of the Senate, used his presidential prerogative and dissolved the Chamber for the first and only time in the history of the Third Republic.

The Conservatives waged a determined battle to reconquer power. Church and State, bishops, prefects and generals, large landowners and employers of labor united in exerting the utmost pressure upon the electorate: they had vowed to "make France walk the right way." Napoleon III had assumed—modestly—the responsibility for material order. Broglie and his friends went further: they wanted to restore and enforce moral order—the phrase became their slogan—that is to say, proper respect for the social hierarchy.

The campaign was ardently fought on both sides. The government pressed into service the old prefects of the Empire: those men knew how to "cook" an election. The Conservatives had a stroke of luck: the octogenarian Thiers died on September 3. Now it had been understood that if the Left were victorious, Thiers would replace Mac-Mahon as President. The presence at the Élysée (the French White House) of the man who had crushed the Commune would reassure the most timorous bourgeois. Gambetta parried the blow. The workingmen of Paris, although they had not forgotten the Bloody Week, turned the funeral of Thiers into a great national and republican demonstration. The most conservative of *petits bourgeois,* Jules Grévy, was nominated to stand for Thiers's constituency in Paris.

The Conservatives used the modest fame of Mac-Mahon for all it was worth, and more. The brave, competent, and uninspired officer was paraded through the provinces and hailed as "the Bayard of our days," the symbol of "glory purest in defeat." He embarrassed his supporters by his soldierly artlessness. He blurted out abysmal platitudes which greatly amused a nation of Voltairians. If he was the modern Bayard, he was even more plainly a reincarnation of Monsieur de la Palisse.[5]

Gambetta had prophesied that the Republicans would return four hundred strong. But the strenuous campaign for moral order had not been without effect. In the elections of October 14–28, 1877, the Left lost thirty-six seats. Still, they commanded a clear majority. On November 19 Broglie faced an adverse Chamber and was forced out by 312 votes to 202. There were rumors of another dissolution and a military *coup d'état:* the marshal had promised to carry through his policy "to the bitter end." Saner counsels prevailed. Mac-Mahon made a last gesture of resistance: he appointed General de Rochebouet as premier without any regard for the wishes of the majority. Rochebouet was summarily rejected. In the course of the campaign Gambetta had said, "When the sovereign voice of France has been heard, it will be necessary to submit or to resign." Mac-Mahon, who had never craved power, who "regretted the fall of every regime except his own," was only too willing to quit. He was requested to remain in office, as a pledge of national unity and stability, on account of the difficult international situation— the Russo-Turkish War was in progress—and for the sake of the Exposition to be held in 1878. He consented and appointed as premier Jules Dufaure, a colorless man acceptable to the victors. On January 5, 1879, the Republicans conquered a majority in the Senate. On January 30 Mac-Mahon felt free at last to leave his uncomfortable post. He died in 1893, his dictatorial velleities fully forgiven, surrounded with respectful affection.

But the crisis, known as "the Sixteenth of May," ruined for two generations at least the chances of a strong executive in France. No President dared again to dissolve the Chamber: that useful provision became a dead letter. Mac-Mahon's successor, Jules Grévy, was picked out for his ideal absence of glamour. In 1848 he had proposed that there should be no President: in 1879 he was thought to be eligible as the next best thing to zero. No fool by any means, he had the cautious and somewhat rapacious mind of a small-town attorney. Practically all his successors were chosen for the same reason. The strong men who, through some accident, reached the presidency, had an uneasy time of it. Casimir-Périer and Alexandre Millerand were forced out of office. Poincaré was so closely watched that he became perfectly innocuous.

Clemenceau, at the very height of his glory, was rejected because, at eighty, he still had a will and a temper of his own. The drab political record of the Republic (in nonpolitical fields, the life of the country was healthy enough) is due to the unfortunate experience of 1877. Because presidential power was once misapplied, it remained paralyzed forever.

✍ CULTURE: A DRAB, EARNEST DECADE

The year 1878 marked the first normal year of the new regime. The victory of the Republic at the polls had not been overwhelming, but it was decisive. Soon both the presidency and the Senate were to pass under Republican control. France appeared at the Congress of Berlin (June–July, 1878) not as one of the protagonists, with Russia, England, and Germany, but as a land of settled government with a ripe diplomatic tradition and armed forces inspiring no terror yet commanding respect. The French plenipotentiary, William Henry Waddington (a Rugby and Cambridge man, who had rowed to victory against Oxford), kept silence in two languages with the most consummate dignity.

Of greater weight perhaps than France's sword was France's purse. The spectacular prosperity of the Second Empire was not all glitter. France paid off her war indemnity, repaired her ruins, and found herself, until the middle eighties, still better off than victorious Germany. Of this healthy economic condition the Exposition of 1878 was the sign. It did not eclipse the breath-taking display of material progress, the somewhat gaudy show of imperial magnificence, the meretricious appeal of luxury and pleasure, which made the Exposition of 1867 unique to this day among World Vanity Fairs. It was serious, honest, efficient, and, in its sober bourgeois way, eminently successful. It had its unexpected flight of fancy: on the bluff of Chaillot was erected an enormous edifice in Hispano-Moorish style, a sort of mosque with two minarets and two colonnaded wings. This was the Trocadero at which old Parisians smiled with fond irony, and which they secretly regret.[6] It evoked Marshal de Mac-Mahon in gala uniform and the Honorable Monsieur Jules Dufaure, five times prime minister of the Third Republic. France was well beyond convalescence, since she could indulge in such an elaborate architectural pleasantry.

From the cultural point of view the decade 1870–1880 is a trough between the waves. Many noted figures disappeared just before or soon after the downfall of the Empire: Baudelaire in 1867, Sainte-Beuve and Lamartine in 1869, Jules de Goncourt, Alexandre Dumas Père and Mérimée in 1870, Gautier in 1872; although Michelet survived until 1874 and George Sand until 1876, the days of their glory were over.

Flaubert's trio of supreme novels had come out before 1870. The poet Leconte de Lisle, the dramatists Augier and Dumas Fils also had done their best work before that date. Verlaine was enjoyed by but a few; Rimbaud was totally unknown.

Even for Ernest Renan, still engaged in his studies of religious history, the period was one of comparative twilight between the great battles of the sixties and the serene sunset of his indulgent irony in the eighties. Taine, once considered as a vanguard philosopher and critic, had been thrown off his balance by the apocalyptic events of 1870–1871: he was now preparing his passionate arraignment of the Enlightenment, the Revolution, and democracy in general, *The Origins of Contemporary France* (1876–1893). Zola was slowly conquering the respect of the public with his massive and powerful series of documentary novels, *The Rougon-Macquart, Natural and Social History of a Family under the Second Empire* (1871–1893). But his fame, already noisy, was something of a scandal. It was only in 1880, with *Nana* and *Evenings at Médan,* that he was safely established as the head of a vigorous and bitterly attacked school.

The hush that had come on the heights of French literature (the lower reaches were vociferous enough) gave greater relief to the glory of Victor Hugo. The "prodigious boy," the handsome fighting leader of the long-haired poets, had become a white-bearded demigod. He was revered as an ancestor, as a living classic, as a prophet. He was the sole survivor of the Romantic era, the laureate of patriotism and democracy, the outstanding enemy of the Empire. He was a senator, and the world high priest of free thought and peace. The fiftieth anniversary of his drama *Hernani* (1880) was celebrated as a national event. All this Hugolatry, which he endured with courtesy and perhaps relished for a while, was to find its climax in his grandiose funeral in 1885. Not even Goethe had so obviously stood at the summit of his nation's culture. To match Hugo's fame, we must go back to the last years of Voltaire.

Trop est trop, again to quote Madame de Sévigné. The next generation was to wreak a cruel and unjust vengeance on the memory of the dead poet. Because he had been prodigal with sonorous commonplaces, because he had won the applause of the multitude, the fastidious were to brand him as a ranting Philistine. They chose to ignore the weird, the shuddering, aspects of his genius, the depths of his sympathies, the tremendous range of his imagination, the unique, unearthly notes of his music. Baudelaire and Rimbaud knew the greatness of Hugo: André Gide for many years failed to understand.

The decade opens tragically with Sedan and ends tamely with wise old Grévy ensconced in the presidential armchair. At any rate the Hugolian spirit of social pity, the spirit of *Les Misérables,* won a belated victory: on July 11, 1880, an amnesty was voted freeing the Communards who were still in convict settlements or in exile. The government had moved back to Paris: the Republic, established by the monarchists but conquered at last by the Republicans, could start with a clean slate.

CHAPTER XXIII

The Third Republic: Opportunism, 1880-1900

⚑ GAMBETTA FRUSTRATED

In the elections of 1869 the Republicans were united only in their opposition to the imperial regime. The followers of Barbès and Blanqui, those two monomaniacs of insurrection, stood apart from the more law-abiding elements. Jules Favre, an old parliamentary hand, was victorious in his district over the marquis of Rochefort-Luçay (Rochefort), the aristocratic journalist whose witty and scurrilous *Lanterne* had won immense applause. On the other hand, Gambetta defeated Hippolyte Carnot, a veteran of 1848, the son of Lazare Carnot, the Organizer of Victory. At Belleville, a workingmen's quarter in Paris, Gambetta offered the following program which was generally accepted as representing the aspirations of the whole party: liberty of the individual, liberty of the press, freedom for meetings and associations; the separation of Church and State; elementary education to be secular, free (i.e., without fees), and compulsory; the election of all public officials; abolition of standing armies; economic reform, social justice, and social equality.

This last clause was intentionally vague. Gambetta was far less of a socialist than that "Saint-Simon on horseback," Napoleon III. He believed there was no such thing as a single, fundamental social question: there were many definite social problems to be solved in accordance with the principles of 1789 and within the framework of political democracy.

The Belleville program remained in abeyance for ten years. First came the war, then the Commune, then, after a long confused interlude of halfhearted reaction, the final establishment of the Republic in 1875 and the necessity for the Republicans to conquer the regime thus grudgingly created. When finally they reached unquestioned power, in 1879, the Belleville program stood evidently in need of sweeping revision. The standing army could, of course, not be abolished in presence of the German menace. The election of all officials, including prefects and judges, no longer appealed to the victors: they meant to take full advantage of the centralized system perfected by Napoleon: local autonomy would not do, when in many parts of France either the Royalists or the Bonapartists still controlled a majority. The other reforms were to be effected, but *seriatim,* not as a single cohesive "new deal." "Opportunism," said Gambetta in 1880, "is an ugly word, but a sound policy."

"Opportunism" was to guide the Republic for two decades. According to its opponents it consisted in declaring steadily that the opportune moment for any given reform had not yet arrived; the Belleville program of 1869 had the force of the sign on the barber's shop, *"Tomorrow, shaving free of charge."* The agitators of yesterday, turned statesmen in their maturer years, thought that the essential goal of all Republican efforts was attained since they were the government. As practical men they were persuaded that the daily responsibilities of their office were enough to absorb their full attention. Gambetta, an obvious candidate for the premiership, had turned Opportunist and gloried in the name.

Georges Clemenceau, forty-year-old doctor, journalist, and politician, remained faithful to the original Republican commitments and was the guerrilla leader of the Radicals: he was too much of a fierce individualist, a bohemian, and an *enfant terrible* to be the actual chief of an organized party. Here we find again the natural opposition between "Resistance" to change, and "Movement," as under Louis-Philippe; between Conservatives and Liberals, as in Victorian England. The doctrinaires of the parliamentary system hoped that the two tendencies would become sharply focused; and they rejoiced when, in 1895–1896, there was a brief homogeneous radical ministry under Léon Bourgeois to be followed in 1896–1898 by a much longer-lived, solid Conservative ministry under Jules Méline. It looked as though the ideal seesaw, dream of all orthodox constitutionalists, had at last been established.

This, however, never was the essential feature in French politics. Although the Republicans were sharply divided, they had to remain united against a possible aggressive return of the Royalists and Bonapartists. So, every cabinet until 1895 was a coalition. And after 1898, when monarchism had ceased to be of vital importance, two new factors interfered with the simple division, Opportunists *vs.* Radicals. The first was sudden, violent, and accidental, the Dreyfus Affair; the second gradual and permanent, the growth of organized socialism. So, coalition again became the rule and prevails to the present day. All that can safely be said is that until 1899 it was the Opportunist element that dominated in the various coalitions; from 1899 to World War I, it was the Radical (which had turned opportunistic). Between the two there never was any doctrinal opposition, only differences in temper and method. All Republicans from Méline to Clemenceau were patriots not internationalists. All wanted to maintain administrative centralization, the better to defend the Republic, "one and indivisible": regional home rule became a Royalist tenet. All wanted the state to be free from militarist and clerical influences. All were attached to individual property. Whenever any one of these pillars of their society was threatened, from the right or from the left, they would rally to its defense.

For ten years Gambetta had been foremost on the battle line for the Republic. In 1879 he became president of the Chamber of Deputies. In that capacity he revived the Morny tradition of gracious hospitality, perhaps not without a trace of his unconventional bohemian days. Many had agreed with Thiers in considering him a raving maniac; but now that the danger was long past, his energy during the war was remembered with admiration and pride: he had saved the honor of France. With his heavy frame and his beard already half-silvered, he now looked the part of a responsible statesman; even Bismarck appreciated and respected him. He was the obvious choice for the premiership. But President Grévy, who had the best reasons for not liking strong and vivid personalities, exhausted every possibility—Waddington, Freycinet, Jules Ferry —before calling on Gambetta.

At last Gambetta's hour could not be deferred any more. Everyone expected a great ministry, a cabinet of all the talents (1881). But the other prominent men in the party refused to serve under a chief whose popularity was all-absorbing. He had to form his cabinet not with nonentities but with younger and lesser-known men. This personal regime encountered the barely veiled hostility of the Chamber: Gambetta was considered a potential dictator. His administration lasted only ten weeks (November, 1881–January, 1882). Gambetta, who was only forty-three, fully counted on another chance. But he died on December 31, 1882, under circumstances—an accidental pistol shot—which at the time seemed melodramatic and mysterious. His funeral on January 6, 1883, enabled the French to bring their tribute to their fallen leader. His fame has suffered no eclipse. There is hardly a town in France without a street or a monument perpetuating his name. His memorial, vehement like his eloquence and not in the purest taste, was given the finest site in Paris, the historic gardens between the two wings of the Louvre. An informal plebiscite, conducted a generation later by a popular newspaper to name the greatest Frenchmen in the nineteenth century, placed him after Louis Pasteur and Victor Hugo but ahead of Napoleon.

In the dusty Jules Grévy era there was no dearth of able men in French

politics. Charles de Freycinet, Gambetta's right-hand man in 1870–
1871, was not merely a shrewd parliamentary manipulator but an excellent engineer. He gave his name to a comprehensive plan of public
works which bears the hallmark of his personality and of the whole
regime: he encouraged innumerable minor improvements so that every
section of the country might be satisfied but had a positive dread of the
bolder projects; in other words, his regime was one of extravagance
under the mask of moderation. The "little white mouse" outlived his
generation with the sole exception of Clemenceau. In 1914, at eighty-
six, he was a symbolical member of the Sacred Union ministry. He died
in 1923, dimly and coolly remembered. Léon Say was a very competent
financier of the most orthodox type; Paul Bert, a natural scientist of note,
a devoted educator, a hidebound freethinker, who wandered into the
colonial field as governor-general of Indochina. But the strong man of the
period was Jules Ferry.

⚓ JULES FERRY: SECULAR EDUCATION, CONFLICT WITH THE CHURCH

Ferry (1832–1893), from the Vosges Mountains in eastern France, did
not possess the southern eloquence and the personal magnetism of
Gambetta. His side whiskers gave him the austere appearance of a
French judge;[1] his heavy, broken nose seemed to discourage levity and
familiarity. Yet he first owed his rise to fame to a marvelous pun. His
attack on the costly transformation of Paris was entitled *Les comptes
fantastiques d'Haussmann:* in French *comptes* (accounts) and *contes*
(tales) are pronounced alike, and Hoffmann's weird stories were a minor
classic. The memory of Jules Ferry is inseparable from three major developments in the eighties, the expansion of popular education, a sharp
conflict with the clergy, and the creation of a vast colonial empire. Few
statesmen were so virulently attacked as this earnest and capable servant
of the Republic. Even among his supporters he commanded respect
rather than enthusiastic loyalty. He is not forgotten, but there is no glow
about his fame.

Danton had said, "Next to bread, education is the first need of the
people." The first Republic with Lakanal, the second with Hippolyte
Carnot had led bold attacks against ignorance; in both cases reaction
intervened and frustrated their endeavors. Modest efforts were made
under Louis-Philippe by Guizot and under the Second Empire by Duruy.
Still, in 1880 the masses were illiterate to an incredible degree. Already
before 1870 the Republican party had made universal education "secular, free, and compulsory," an essential item in its program. The war
gave a new impetus to this idea; it was currently said that the true victor

at Sadowa and Sedan was not the needle-rifle but the Prussian school-master. (Two generations before, it is said, Wellington had asserted that the Battle of Waterloo had been won on the playing fields of Eton.) The unquestioning faith in science, which characterized the age, con-firmed the demands of patriotism and democracy. As soon as they had gained power, the Republicans tackled their enormous task.

It should be noted that the Republic of Jules Ferry was still, emphati-cally, a bourgeois republic. The masses were to be taught the three R's; but secondary education, the gateway to all the professions, was made neither compulsory nor free. It remained the preserve of the middle class, protected both by custom and by a financial barrier. A worker's son could hope to become a better mechanic, artisan, or foreman, a clerk, a small shopkeeper, an elementary teacher; but only in excep-tional cases could he aspire to be a civil engineer, a manager, a pro-fessor, a doctor, a judge, a diplomat, or an army officer. The few who conquered all obstacles were expected to forget their proletarian origin and to aggregate themselves with the *bourgeoisie*. Full equality of op-portunity was not even attempted until after World War I; then it was bitterly combated as demagogic and extravagant. The mesocracy has not fully capitulated even yet.

The vast extension of the school system envenomed the latent con-flict between the Church and the Republic. It was of long standing. After a few fraternal weeks in 1848 the Catholic Church in France had frankly espoused the cause of reaction. Adolphe Thiers, a Voltairian himself, frightened by the Days of June, exclaimed, "Let us rush to the feet of the bishops!" The uncompromising attitude of Pope Pius IX, fulminating his anathema on liberalism, progress, and modern civiliza-tion, had been scrupulously followed in France by the ultramontanes, particularly by the powerful journalist Louis Veuillot. In the crisis of the Sixteenth of May (1877), the Church had wholeheartedly supported the authoritarian, antidemocratic move of Marshal de Mac-Mahon. So Gambetta voiced the opinion of all militant Republicans when he de-fiantly said, "Clericalism is the enemy!"

Now the Church had had, for centuries, a quasi-monopoly of educa-tion and resented any encroachment on her domain. The government scheme was antagonistic to Catholic interests on three points. First of all, it proposed to substitute lay teachers, women as well as men, for the thousands of Brothers of the Christian Doctrine and Sisters of Charity then employed in state-supported schools. It debarred unauthorized re-ligious orders from teaching even in private establishments. It declared that education under the state was to be "lay," or nonsectarian, that is to say, not specifically Catholic. The Church chose to interpret neutrality as hostility and branded the new schools as "godless." The accusation was undeserved. Even the most Voltairian bourgeois believed, with Voltaire himself, that a religion was good for the people. The essential dogmas of "natural religion" were preserved under the Third Republic. Jules Simon, one of the founders of the regime, could rub his hands and boast that he had had "the existence of God passed in the Senate by a handsome majority."

But the crucial battle was fought on the question of the unauthorized teaching orders, for this involved the spiritual control of the essential class, the *bourgeoisie*. The Jesuits were the center of the storm. The history of their company in France had been extremely checkered. The old Gallican elements, the Parlements and the University, had always distrusted that militia of the Holy See. Pascal had attacked them on moral grounds, with masterly eloquence and irony, in his *Provincial Letters*. They had been officially banished from France in 1762 and suppressed by the pope throughout Christendom in 1773. Their alleged influence over Charles X had been one of the causes of his downfall. The Liberals, under the Constitutional Monarchy, had a morbid dread of the Jesuits. Quinet and Michelet wrote a violent denunciation of them (1843). In 1844–1845 Eugène Sue's vast popular romance, *The Wandering Jew,* spread the legend of a Jesuit conspiracy for world mastery. Such phantoms of popular imagination, the Napoleonic legend, the Red International, the Black International, play a loose, elusive, yet potent part in human affairs. They are among the facts that realistic history cannot ignore.

The Jesuits, officially banished, quite openly maintained their schools in France; they were staffing with their alumni the army, the navy, the diplomatic corps, the judiciary. Article VII of the Ferry bill, stating that orders which had no legal status would not be allowed to teach, was passed in the Chamber by a safe majority but was rejected in the Senate. Thereupon Ferry decided to enforce the existing laws by ministerial decrees: the orders were requested to apply for authorization or leave the country. The Jesuits did not avail themselves of the first alternative, knowing full well that it would only lead to a refusal: they chose to wait for a show of force. Ferry's strong-handed but perfectly legal methods led to a miniature rebellion on the part of the ultramontanes. Army officers and judges resigned rather than take part in measures which they considered as a persecution. When the Jesuits left their establishments, they were escorted by affectionate crowds of their former students, men of substance and standing who enjoyed the respect of their fellow citizens. The sight was impressive and moving; yet it was followed by no movement of indignation among the masses. Even in

Catholic circles the Jesuits had few ardent supporters. So they were ejected from their houses *manu militari* and went theoretically into exile. Soon new schools sprang up which were known to be managed by the Jesuits.

This crisis, symptom of a profound and permanent conflict, had long echoes. For years the lay teacher replacing a religious in a village state school was treated as an enemy by the Conservatives; the women teachers in particular had to face implacable hostility, for the Sisters had been particularly beloved. No wonder the state teachers considered themselves as the embattled defenders of the Republic; no wonder many went over to belligerent free thought and sought the support of Freemasonry, an association condemned by the Church. The lay school and the parish church became two political poles.

The situation after the open hostilities of 1882 remained uneasy for many years. No doubt Boulanger had a number of clericals among his supporters: any tool was welcome that would sap the godless Republic. Leo XIII was neither a democrat nor, in the partisan sense of the term, a liberal. But he was both a realist and a lover of concord. He sought to heal the breach between the Church and the Republic. Cardinal Lavigerie, Archbishop of Algiers, Primate of Africa, a vivid and energetic figure, implementing the pope's indications, advised all believers to rally to a government supported by the people. This was a bitter pill for the intransigent Legitimists and ultramontanes (1890). Nor did the rabid anticlericals such as Clemenceau welcome the move; they thought the clergy less dangerous as an open antagonist than as an insidious friend; and they held that the bishops should abstain from any political pronouncement, even in favor of the Republic. The Opportunists, on the other hand, accepted the advances of Monseigneur Lavigerie. In 1894 a minister of education, Monsieur Spuller, could speak of the "new spirit," seeking conciliation through common sense, justice, and charity. Anticlericalism lost caste. Unfortunately, a few years later, the Dreyfus Case brought about a recrudescence of bitterness and strife.

THE BOULANGER CRISIS

The record of the Republic, so far, had been unsensational but creditable. Yet there was in the country a feeling of uneasiness and disenchantment. The hope of *revanche* (not revenge but restitution) and Gambetta's faith in "immanent justice" had faded; France was thoroughly sensible but had ceased to be heroic. A war against nuns and priests, even though necessary, never enhances the prestige of a government. Opportunism is a policy devoid of glamour. Forain was to draw later a marvelous cartoon: the Republic with her liberty cap, as a shapeless, middle-aged hag with tired eyes and sagging jowls; an elderly gentleman comments wistfully; "Ah! How beautiful she was under the Empire!" This cruel satire was already true in 1885.

As a result the Conservatives in that year won 176 seats on the first ballot, the Republicans only 127. On the second ballot the Republicans closed their ranks and retrieved their losses: they had 372 seats against 202. Still, the Right had made sensational gains, and the warning could not be ignored.

The situation grew worse with a scandal at the Elysée. Old Grévy had played his negative role so well that in 1886 he was re-elected. The French liked to jest at his parsimony as they did later with Armand Fallières's, but they had to acknowledge that it was only the exaggeration of a bourgeois virtue. At any rate his personal integrity could not be questioned. Now it transpired that his son-in-law, Daniel Wilson, who made the Elysée his business headquarters, was using his influence —not gratuitously—to get the Legion of Honor for certain clients of his. It was found that the affair had many ramifications, involving in particular a noted general and former minister of war. It was at once evident that the President should go. But with senile tenacity, Jules Grévy clung to his position. There was no legal means of forcing him out. The Chamber had to organize a ministerial boycott against him: no reputable politician would serve under him, and he had to resign.

Ferry was the strongest man in France; but this of course counted against him as a candidate for the presidency. He was hated by the Radicals for his colonial policy, by the Catholics for his "godless schools." After some hesitation Sadi Carnot was elected (December, 1887). He was a quiet, upright man, faultless in manners and in attire, black-bearded, handsome in a lifeless and almost funereal way. He was a good second-string politician, well trained as an engineer, and with a fine military record during the war. Above all he was the grandson of Lazare Carnot, the great strategist of the Revolution, and the son of Hippolyte Carnot, still alive, now one of the revered survivors of 1848; a boulevard wit remarked, "Now we have the Carnotvingian dynasty." Clemenceau is reported to have advised his friends, "Vote for the dullest." The word was unfair, but undoubtedly the French parliamentarians remembered that the best figureheads are made of wood.[2]

It was under the blameless rule of this ideal King Log that King Stork made his boldest bid: in 1888–1889 General Boulanger was a serious menace to parliamentary institutions. In command for a short time of the French troops in Tunisia, he had entered politics through the influence of Georges Clemenceau. It is easy to understand how the Radical leader was trapped into such an egregious mistake. The French army was then, and remained until after the Dreyfus Case, the stronghold of Royalists and Bonapartists: Boulanger himself owed his first stars to the duke of Aumale, son of Louis-Philippe. Clemenceau could see the peril of such a situation; he was on the lookout for a general who could make the spirit of the army less antagonistic to democracy. It seemed as though Boulanger might serve that purpose: he had a good reputation as a soldier and was not of aristocratic origin. In January, 1886, under Freycinet, he became minister of war. He had at once started a series of minor reforms which showed that he understood the needs and the feelings of the common soldier. His popularity was increased by his professions of ardent patriotism. When in April, 1887, a frontier incident, the Schnaebelé Affair, created serious diplomatic tension between Germany and France, Boulanger appeared as the "General *Revanche*" of destiny. With his blond beard and his blue eyes, on his black charger Tunis, he made a fine soldierly figure. The great parade and review on Bastille Day seemed to be held in his honor. The crowd shouted gaily the inane ditties that Paulus, a music-hall idol, had created to his praise. Broadsheets made his features popular. It was a loud vulgarized version of the Napoleonic legend—minus the victories and the Code. Naturally, Clemenceau, who hated military dictatorship even more than he craved *revanche,* turned against the political upstart of his own making.

We find in Boulangism a well-known pattern, that of the two Napoleons, of Mussolini, of Hitler. Only in his case the pattern was blurred, for he was served by no outstanding talent and not even by a fanatical belief in himself. The first element in modern Caesarism is national pride: he was fated to avenge the humiliation of 1871. But even stronger was the purely negative factor: France in 1799, in 1848, in 1888, Italy in 1922, Germany in 1933 were utterly disgusted with the mediocrity, fumbling, and corruption of the parliamentary world. They wanted a stronger, simpler government not committed to the defense of special interests, appealing directly to the people. Boulanger was not a force in himself: he was the symbol of a protest.

The Republicans, aware of the danger, dropped him from the ministry: the crowd hailed him all the louder. He was assigned to the command of an army corps at Clermont-Ferrand in Auvergne: a delirious mob attempted to prevent his departure, yelling, "We want Boulanger!" For insubordination (he had come twice to Paris without leave) he was deprived of his command, then removed from the army list: this gave him the prestige of a martyr and released him for open political activity. He offered himself as a candidate everywhere and won every contest. Finally he was triumphantly elected in Paris (January 27,

1889). His partisans shouted, "To the Élysée!" Had he heeded the cry, he might have staged a successful *Putsch*. When midnight came and the general had not moved, Georges Thiébaud remarked, "From this moment, Boulangism is ebbing."

His followers were, like those of all would-be Caesars, an amazingly motley crew. The diffuse chauvinist and revanchard spirit helped him; but he was supported also by the docile masses, peasants and bourgeois, who wanted authority in high places. At the opposite pole were found the unquiet spirits who love turmoil for its own sake, failures and adventurers, the disciples of Blanqui the eternal insurgent: Henri Rochefort, the pamphleteer, once vaguely a Communard, still more vaguely a socialist, rallied to him. The Bonapartists were split: the demo-Caesarians under Prince Napoleon (*Plonplon*), the Conservatives under his son Prince Victor. Naturally, Prince Napoleon aided Boulanger: both believed in an appeal to the people. More strangely, many Royalists, rather shamefacedly, rallied to him: the duchess of Uzès gave him financial backing, the count of Paris allowed his partisans to support him. Their one common point was: "Down with the Parliamentary Republic!" The general's program was perfectly simple and perfectly vague: dissolution of the Chamber, revision of the constitution, a Constituent Assembly.

The Republicans—Opportunists and Radicals now working in close harmony—did not abandon themselves. They called in as minister of the interior Ernest Constans, famed for not being overburdened with scruples either in business or in politics. He was to be "a Morny in reverse," the man whose energy was to avert a *coup d'état*. Constans simply brought out a warrant for Boulanger's arrest (April, 1889), and, no less simply, Boulanger fled. Popular support was fast abandoning him for a reason peculiar to French politics: an international exposition. Political disorder would be bad for business: let the general stay in exile. So Paris celebrated in peace, with Carnot as President, the centennial of the great Revolution.[3] In October, 1889, Boulanger was tried *in absentia* for conspiracy and condemned. On September 30, 1891, he shot himself at Brussels on the tomb of his mistress. To the end he was the hero of popular romance, a facile charmer with a touch of vulgarity, without principles, and without backbone.

✍ THE PANAMA SCANDAL

Had the Panama scandal broken out a few months earlier, Boulanger might have had his chance. The Panama project, under the direction of Ferdinand de Lesseps, who had promoted the Suez Canal, was not a swindle. Lesseps, who was well over eighty and had never been an engineer, could not supervise the actual construction. The builders encountered difficulties for which Suez provided no precedent, sliding earth under a tropical sky and, worst of all, health conditions which could not be controlled by the methods then available. Soon the funds judged adequate for a sea-level canal were exhausted. The plan was changed to a canal with locks: even then it became evident that the scheme, if it could be completed at all, would not be the gold mine that Suez had turned out to be. Bonds were sold with increasing difficulties. The most massive issue of them was of a type familiar in France, combining moderate interests with a lottery feature. It could not be floated without the authorization of Parliament. Realizing the desperate plight of the company, a number of senators and deputies, and even a few cabinet ministers, insisted upon their cuts. The thing was so widespread that it was difficult to keep it an absolute secret. Still, the revered name of Lesseps, the complicity of the press—at a price—the desire not to ruin a national enterprise had kept the general public from realizing the whole truth, even after the collapse of the company in 1889. Ironically, by the time of the financial disaster in Paris the construction difficulties in the Isthmus were being conquered. Bunau-Varilla, energetic and resourceful, had evolved a proper technique, and Gustave Eiffel had become one of the chief contractors.

It took three more years for the scandal to burst forth. Not until November, 1892, were Ferdinand de Lesseps and his associates prosecuted. Their chief agent, Baron Jacques de Reinach, threatened with blackmail, committed suicide. It could no longer be denied that innumerable small investors had lost their savings: in those days $300,-000,000 seemed a fantastic sum. Indignation ran high: the legal outcome was something of an anticlimax. Only three parliamentarians out of 104 under suspicions were found guilty; only one minister, Baïhaut, served a prison term. The promoters, including Lesseps, then eighty-eight years of age, received heavy sentences; but the judgment was quashed by the Supreme Court (*Cour de Cassation*) under the statute of limitations. Meanwhile, Bunau-Varilla had reorganized the company and valiantly kept up the work, though at a crawling pace. He managed at last to sell the concern to the United States after staging a revolution in Panama.

A financial crash combined with corruption in high places is a commonplace occurrence in the modern world. Frenzied finance and graft are not French monopolies. The unique importance of Panama was not due entirely to the magnitude of the losses, but to the fact that it provided weapons for the enemies of the regime. The whole Republican personnel, except that Sir Galahad automaton President Carnot, was under suspicion. It was a retrospective justification for the Boulangist movement: "Ah! If only the great sweep of the broom had been given in time!" It turned indeed to be the revenge, although not the vindication, of the Boulangists: the men who had barred the way to the general were the grafters in the pay of the canal company. Maurice Barrès, an admirable novelist who was also a politician, had been a lieutenant of Boulanger: now he was active in a fierce campaign against the Panamists. The highest were not spared: Clemenceau himself was bespattered. He was not directly accused of pocketing bribes, but he was unfortunate enough to have among his protégés an international adventurer, Cornelius Hertz, who knew most of the secrets of the Panama affair and managed to keep them undisclosed. The presence among the protagonists of Reinach and Hertz gave a strong impetus to a feeling alien as a rule to the French mind, anti-Semitism.

The rise of anti-Semitism antedated Panama. The Catholics had once attempted to break what they called the Jewish ring in finance. But their banking venture, L'Union Générale, after an auspicious start, had badly failed. This had created a bitterness of which the somber and passionate books of Edouard Drumont, *Jewish France* (1886) and *The End of a World* (1888), were the symptoms. Now Edouard Drumont, whose sincerity and talent were no less patent than his irrational spite, could distill his venom in his widely read daily, *La Libre Parole*. Fate would have it that this forerunner of Adolf Hitler should look like an extreme caricature of a Semite. Drumont's influence was not central in the Dreyfus crisis; neither was it negligible.

The judicial epilogue of the Panama Affair took place in June, 1894: October 15 of the same year marked the opening of the Dreyfus Case. The reader will gather the impression that the life of the Third Republic was an uninterrupted series of scandals: *Le scandale est mort: vive le scandale!* This, to some extent, is the ransom to be paid for a free press, and for peace: under absolutist regimes, scandals are hushed, and in war times they are drowned. We must also remember that in France the Parliamentary Republic was not established beyond challenge. In England and America a scandal will affect only a small group of men, seldom a whole party, never the fundamental institutions. In France an affair of this kind is inevitably used by the monarcho-Catholic opposition against the freethinking democratic state, by the anarchists and socialists against bourgeois plutocracy. The malfeasance of a few men is thus given a symbolical, a quasi-apocalyptic, significance.

Neither should we forget the radical discrepancy between political history and social history in the widest sense. The politics of the Third Republic were dismal enough: apart from a few leaders like Ferry and

Clemenceau the best men were dingy, the worst were dirty. But the life of France was wholesome and not unhappy. In spite of Panama the economic condition of the country was sound. Prosperity was not so spectacular as under the Second Empire, and Germany was progressing with far swifter strides; but employment was steady, prices were stable, the savings banks were bursting with deposits, the state funds were well above par. National education was developing admirably; the provincial universities, so long neglected, had a most promising revival. The colonial empire was expanding at a breathless pace. And cultural life, although it did not accurately mirror the temper of the whole people, was extremely active. This story of health, confidence, and progress is hard to relate, because it is made up of innumerable facts in many domains. Perhaps in future ages history will become more realistic simply by eliminating the political side altogether.

✍ THE DREYFUS AFFAIR

On October 15, 1894, Captain Alfred Dreyfus, a probationer in the intelligence section of the General Staff, was arrested on a charge of treason. On December 22 he was sentenced by a court-martial to life imprisonment. On January 5, 1895, he was publicly degraded; on April 13 he arrived at Devil's Island, which, oddly enough, is part of the Salvation group (*Îles du Salut*) off the coast of French Guiana. The first reaction in France was one of indignation at the leniency of the sentence: for offenses far less heinous common soldiers had been put to death. Dreyfus had never wavered in affirming his innocence. His counsel, Maître Leblois, was convinced that the evidence against him was of the flimsiest and was astounded at the verdict.

There was no deep-laid anti-Semitic plot in the accusation against Dreyfus. Only we must remember that the high posts in the army were almost a monopoly of a Catholic-monarchical caste. For them the service of France was identical with their own traditions. This implied a belief which Charles Maurras was soon to turn into a doctrine: the monarchical idea is "integral nationalism," and we have seen throughout this book that there is sound historical foundation for such a faith. The conservative officers could not understand why a Jew should attempt to force his way into the General Staff; there must be some sinister purpose. When leaks were discovered, he was immediately under suspicion.

In 1896 Lieutenant Colonel Georges Picquart, recently appointed head of the Intelligence Section, came across documents which incriminated a certain Major Walsin-Esterhazy. Picquart was at once sent on a mission in Tunisia. In 1897 Leblois, Dreyfus' counsel, informed Senator Scheurer-Kestner of Picquart's discoveries. Scheurer-Kestner, an old Alsatian, was vice-president of the Upper House, and one of its most respected members. His open letter on the subject created a sensation. Esterhazy faced the storm boldly and requested to be tried by a court-martial.

He was the very antithesis of Dreyfus. Dreyfus had been a model officer; he was well to do and led an orderly life. Esterhazy was a cosmopolitan adventurer of Hungarian origin who had entered the French army through the Foreign Legion; eternally in financial straits, he was known to be engaged in many shady transactions. But the military, furious that civilians should interfere with their affairs, were determined to maintain their position. Esterhazy was triumphantly acquitted. Prince Henry, of the Royal House of Orleans, embraced him with effusion (January 11, 1898).

Two days later, Emile Zola published his great manifesto *J'accuse!* in the newspaper *L'Aurore*. In an open letter to the President of the Republic [4] he charged the judges with having obeyed orders in whitewashing Esterhazy. He was courting prosecution with the purpose of bringing light into the tenebrous affair, but at his first and second trials (February, and May–July, 1898) the judge refused to have the essential questions asked of the witnesses. Zola was condemned and fled to England. But the obstructive attitude of the judge made it evident that there were mysterious depths to the case. The French are very fond of a mystery, provided they are allowed to work out its solution. The claim of the military to be a law unto themselves and unto everyone else roused the anger of a people not brought up in Prussian reverence for the officers' caste.

There was a swift succession of war ministers torn between their loyalty to Republican institutions and their devotion to the army. One of them, Godefroy Cavaignac, a man of high integrity, a trained historian, the son of the Chief Executive in June, 1848, was conscientious enough to seek for additional proofs; the General Staff provided them, they seemed decisive to him, and he read them publicly in the Chamber. But the Socialist leader, Jean Jaurès, submitted them in his newspaper *La Petite République* to a masterly critical analysis and demonstrated, from internal evidence, that they were spurious. On August 13 it was discovered that they had been forged by Lieutenant Colonel Henry of the Intelligence Section. Henry, arrested, conveniently committed suicide. Madame Dreyfus applied at once for a new trial of her husband, and the government agreed to submit the case to the Supreme Court (*Cour de Cassation*).

By this time the Dreyfus Affair had gone far beyond the fate of an individual victim. It had become an epic duel between the defenders of tradition and those who cherished freedom first of all, even though it might disrupt hoary prejudices and time-honored institutions. On the one hand were arrayed the monarchists, a notable and most vocal element in the clergy, the patriots of the Paul Déroulède type for whom a bugle call was the supreme argument, the authoritarians of all schools like the classical critic Brunetière, a large portion of the rich *bourgeoisie:* a formidable coalition of the most respectable citizens. Their motto might have been, "My country, right or wrong!" and for them country, flag, and army were one and the same. Their militant organization was the League of the French Fatherland, and they rightly assumed the name Nationalists.

On the other side were the "Intellectuals"—a term intended to be scornful—writers such as Zola, Anatole France, Mirbeau, the young Marcel Proust; scholars and scientists such as Havet, Buisson, Picavet, Hadamard, Duclaux; the Jews—not unanimously—the Protestants; radical politicians like Clemenceau, and finally a rising force, the Socialists.[5] Jules Guesde, leader of the orthodox Marxians, wanted the party to remain neutral in this quarrel among bourgeois. Jean Jaurès, heir to the more generous, pre-Marxian tradition, saw in socialism first of all the defense of liberty and justice; an injustice against a single individual, whatever his class might be, was the common concern of all citizens. These men placed truth above the "sacred egoism" of the tribe: for that reason they were accused of being the agents of foreign interests. Their rallying ground was the League of the Rights of Man. Thus, after a hundred and ten years of revolution, the problem was sharply stated: the historic past, the "wisdom of prejudice," or universal principles? It was stated, it was not solved then; it is still debated now.

The Nationalists were so sure of their essential rightness that they were not long disconcerted by Lieutenant Colonel Henry's tampering with evidence. They claimed that he was in possession of proofs which were irrefutable but of so dangerous a nature that they must be kept secret. Patriotically, he "drew a check on the bank of truth." A subscription was started to erect a monument to Henry the Martyr. The fact that Dreyfus had manifestly been condemned on the strength of documents communicated neither to him nor to his counsel seemed to the military mind incompetent, immaterial, and irrelevant. The Supreme Court, with a more fastidious sense of legal procedure, quashed the 1894 judgment and sent Dreyfus to another court-martial, which was held at Rennes from August 7 to September 9, 1899.

In the meantime the anti-Dreyfusists had lost two political battles.

President Félix Faure was their man: he died suddenly, and in February, 1899, Émile Loubet was elected to succeed him, against Jules Méline. Loubet, in accordance with his placid and cautious temperament, had been scrupulously neutral in the crisis. But, by opposing him violently, the Nationalists turned his election into a sharp defeat for themselves. As a consequence Premier Charles Dupuy, a burly and awkward trimmer, fell and was replaced by Waldeck-Rousseau. This former lieutenant of Gambetta, a great lawyer, cold, dignified, faultlessly conservative, was a determined Dreyfusist. His cabinet opened a new era in the history of the Republic and will be considered in our next chapter.

The trial at Rennes left no doubt whatever in the minds of unbiased observers. Outside of France public opinion, which took an extraordinary interest in the affair, was unanimous. But the military were still unwilling to admit their own fallibility. In maintaining an error they thought they were defending the honor of the army, discipline, the flag, the Fatherland; and, by the same token, sound economic and political doctrine, the established social hierarchy, against the onslaught of international subversive forces. The evidence, however, was too strong even for their willful blindness. They arrived at a lame verdict: Dreyfus was condemned by five votes to two, but with "extenuating circumstances."

Evidently this could not be the end. But once more there appeared the *deus ex machina* of French politics, an international exposition. Principles could wait: peace must be patched up so as not to discourage the tourist trade. Dreyfus was "pardoned" (September 19). And the minister of war, old General de Galliffet, issued the order, "The incident is closed."

In spite of this heavy moral sacrifice the Exposition of 1900 was only a qualified success. Artistically, it did not fulfill the modest but distinct promises of 1889; it abandoned steel construction and reverted to lath and plaster. It was *art nouveau* at its meretricious worst, technically known as "noodle style." Visitors came in unprecedented numbers, but miracles had been expected, and many "concessions" were richly deserved failures. The enormous effort left an impression of frustration and fatigue. Paris swore, "Never again."

The Affair was only slumbering: poetic justice triumphed at last. In 1906 the Supreme Court, stretching its power to the uttermost, quashed the Rennes judgment *absolutely,* i.e., without ordering a new military trial. Dreyfus, completely vindicated, was reinstated, promoted, decorated on the very spot where he had suffered degradation. In World War I he served as lieutenant colonel. He died in 1935. Lieutenant Colonel Picquart, who had suffered for justice's sake, became a general and minister of war. The remains of Zola [6] were transferred to the

Pantheon. Jaurès and Clemenceau were the chief powers in the Republic. In 1923 a destitute outcast died at Harpenden, England: he had once been known as Major Esterhazy.

⚜ COLONIAL EXPANSION. ANGLO-FRENCH RIVALRY

Whilst the stodgy opportunist Republic was saving pennies, knocking down ministers, and indulging in unsavory crises, she was, unawares, engaged in a tremendous adventure: the conquest of a colonial empire second to England's alone. Overseas expansion was not a new departure for the French. It might be said that in the eleventh and twelfth centuries England and the Holy Land were in fact French colonies. The French had shown their mettle in India and in North America: if they had lost out, it was only because they were constantly absorbed in Continental politics from which England could withdraw at will. By 1815 only vestiges of their once far-flung dominions remained. The Restoration started, the July Monarchy continued, the Second Empire completed the conquest of Algeria. Under Louis-Philippe a few South Sea islands were acquired. Under Napoleon III a foothold was secured in Cochin China, and Faidherbe extended French rule inland from the modest coast establishments in Senegal. The expeditions in China (1860), Syria (1860–1861), Mexico (1861–1867) had something of a colonial character. France never lacked great navigators: La Pérouse, Bougainville, Dumont d'Urville. Furthermore, she always played a great part in Catholic missions, and her various governments considered themselves as the traditional protectors of Catholic interests in the Levant and the Far East. Even Gambetta had said, "Anticlericalism is not an export article."

At the Congress of Berlin (1878) Bismarck hinted to Waddington, "Why do you not take Tunis?" This suggestion was probably as Machiavellian as his "offer" of Belgium to Benedetti. When France did take Tunis three years later, it embroiled her in a quarrel with Italy, who thought she had prior and more substantial claims. Italy thereupon joined the Triple Alliance, intended to guard Central Europe both against Russia and against France. When Ferry decided upon intervention, the military task proved easy; and the formula adopted—a protectorate respecting native institutions and customs—worked on the whole very satisfactorily (1881).

France suffered a setback in Egypt. Throughout the nineteenth century that country had been politically, economically, and culturally in close relations with France. The extravagance of a Khedive led to a Franco-British condominium which was resented by the Egyptian nationalists. When an antiforeign insurrection broke out in 1882, France and England were expected to act jointly. But Gambetta was out of power, and his successor Freycinet, intimidated by Clemenceau, refused to move. So the British alone bombarded Alexandria, defeated Arabi Pasha, and occupied the country "provisionally." As late as 1956 that "provisional" regime had not yet been fully liquidated.

Ferry, returning to power in 1883, extended French rule in Indochina. Tonkin, the northern province of Annam (now Vietnam), was under a shadowy Chinese protectorate. This brought the French into conflict, first with Chinese irregulars, then with the enormous decrepit empire. A minor rebuff at Langson (March 28, 1885), amplified by rumor into a disaster, roused the indignation of the French people: they had no desire for expansion in southeastern Asia and refused to waste lives and millions in that remote and unhealthy region. Ferry, fiercely attacked by Clemenceau, was driven out of office. He was branded as "the Tonkinese" and became the most unpopular of French politicians. This was the chief obstacle to his being elected President in 1887; he died in 1893 without having returned to power. Yet France kept Indochina. An energetic governor, Paul Doumer, dispelled the dark legend which had so long cursed the colony. And as late as 1950 France could still hope to retain this distant and alien empire as a free and independent member state within the framework of the French Union.

Meanwhile, from the various settlements in West Africa soldiers, administrators, engineers were pushing inland. Joffre, the future marshal, linked Senegal and Niger by a railroad. The ferocious despotism of Behanzin in Dahomey was put down by a mulatto general, Alfred Dodds (1892–1893). Thus another huge federation was built, encircling British, Portuguese, and German possessions, the A.O.F. (*Afrique Occidentale Française,* French West Africa).

A naval officer of Italian origin, Savorgnan de Brazza, explored the Gabun and reached the banks of the Congo, where his claims clashed with those of Stanley. No two men engaged in similar work could have been more different. Stanley was ruthlessness incarnate and gave the Congo Free State an ominous start. Brazza, although not an evangelist like Livingstone, was humane, sought the friendship of the native chieftains, and came to be known as "the Father of the Slaves" (1880–1898). After his retirement the material success of the Congo Free State induced the French to copy its realistic methods of exploitation. The results were disastrous, even financially, and no one deplored them more deeply than the gentle and enlightened founder, Savorgnan de Brazza. This region has not fully outgrown its sinister reputation: André Gide found it still in 1927 "the heart of darkness." An odd twist of fate made for a while Brazzaville, in French Equatorial Africa, the capital of France, that is to say, of the Free French under General de Gaulle.

Finally, Madagascar was added to the bulging French dominions. The claims of France in that region were ancient, although misty: they went back to Cardinal Richelieu. There were constant bickerings with the native authorities over the extent and validity of these claims. The master tribe, the Hovas, were encouraged in their resistance by English Protestant missionaries, who had converted a notable portion of the population. There was a brief war in 1883–1885: the second downfall of Ferry left it inconclusive. In 1895 the French landed at Tamatave and pushed on to the Hova capital, Tananarive (Antananarivo) in the central highlands. Their little column was nearly wiped out not by enemy fire but by the murderous climate. General Galliéni was sent to pacify the island. He deposed the queen (February 28, 1897), restored order, promoted sanitation, education, and public works, and especially protected the masses against the feudal tyranny of the Hova aristocracy: he was the master and the model of Lyautey. Both were enlightened administrators anxious not to crush the spirit of the conquered. Thanks to them colonialism is not altogether a term of reproach.

This sudden expansion, undesired, only dimly realized by the people, was bitterly opposed by the Radicals and the Socialists at home, and by England in Africa and Asia. Every move of France was considered by England as a "pinprick" intended for her annoyance. The whole period was a snarling cold war. Once the two countries came to the very brink of open hostilities. The French government had the fantastic idea of reopening the Egyptian question through the back door. Under Captain Marchand a mission was sent across Equatorial Africa to the upper reaches of the Nile. There it was to be met by forces of Menelik, Negus of Abyssinia. When General (Sirdar) Kitchener had led his Anglo-Egyptian army up the Nile and defeated the Madhi at Omdurman (September 2, 1898), he found to his intense surprise the French flag waving over Fashoda (September 19). Marchand refused to lower it, or to retire without explicit orders from his government. The French had a case: the Upper Sudan, abandoned for fourteen years, could be considered as *res nullius*. But the British had, according to the old jingo song, the guns, the ships, and the money, too. There were anxious hours; finally the French withdrew; the Bahr el-Ghazal was not worth the bones of a single French private. No wonder, however, that this humiliation made the French ardent supporters of the Boer cause.

These colonial difficulties had a very unfortunate effect upon European politics. Normally, France, England, Italy should have stood together, the pillars of the liberal West, against the *Dreikaiserbund,* the natural alliance of the three military empires, Germany, Austria, and Russia. But Italy broke with France over the Tunis conflict, and England, although not formally committed, was at that time wholeheartedly pro-German: many shared the dream of Cecil Rhodes, the world ruled by the Anglo-Saxon powers with scant consideration for the lesser breeds. This breach with her neighbors virtually forced France into an alliance with Tsarist Russia (1891–1893).[7] There was no love lost between the two governments, although the two peoples indulged in strangely sentimental manifestations. But Russia had in abundance what France lacked, i.e., manpower; and France had what Russia needed, viz., capital. So ideologies were realistically ignored. At any rate it was impossible for two such ill-assorted partners to plot an aggressive war: the Dual Alliance was a defensive measure and served its purpose well. When, after the Russian Revolution, its secret terms were published, they were found to be exactly what the French public had always known and understood.

FIN-DE-SIÈCLE ANARCHISM

From the cultural point of view the ascendancy of opportunism does not form a single period. Materialism, which had triumphed with the "realistic" reaction after 1848, prevailed almost unchallenged until about 1890. At its best it appeared in the positivism of Littré (more pedestrian than that of Comte), or the scientific determinism of Taine. Romantic sentiment and imagination were derided, and the ancient creeds were studied as curious fossils. Even though Renan's mind was subtly shaded to the point of ironic elusiveness, his philosophy remained scientific at the core. He reaffirmed it by publishing, toward the end of his career, his youthful profession of faith, *The Future of Science* (1890).

For the common people the scientific gospel was blended with a touching faith in reason, progress, and social service. The teachers in Ferry's elementary schools were apostles of a naive but not ignoble creed, which revealed its full power in the Dreyfus crisis. But among the leaders scientific dogmatism was still colored with the cynical realism of the post-forty-eight era. Darwin and his struggle for life seemed to justify the harshness of Manchesterian economics, the power politics of Bismarck, the dialectic materialism of Marx.

About 1890 this somber synthesis crumbled. *The Disciple,* a novel by Paul Bourget, attempted to prove that scientific determinism, per se, could not be a moral guide: a degenerate imbued with modern materialistic ideas experiments criminally with a human soul. Soon Ferdinand Brunetière could proclaim the bankruptcy of science: to the orthodox secularist this was as outrageous a blasphemy as Proudhon's paradoxes, "God is Evil; Property is Theft."

The reaction against naturalism (which claimed to be the scientific, experimental spirit applied to literature) assumed many forms. There was a determined return to traditional values, with Brunetière in particular, the Irving Babbitt and T. S. Eliot of his day; it was at the end of the century that Charles Maurras began his long fight for "Classicism, Catholicism, and Monarchy." If the anti-Dreyfusists battled so ardently, it was because they were defending not individual interests but a resurgent ideology. This was to lead, in our century, to a great revival of Catholic literature with Paul Claudel as its outstanding representative.

But the same reaction was also transforming naturalism from within. Zola himself, who kept in close touch with the masses, reverted from materialistic determinism to the spirit of 1848, democracy, humanitarianism, and science fused into a religion. His last books were sermons, not experiments in filth: *The Three Cities* (*Lourdes, Rome, Paris*), *The Four Gospels* (*Fruitfulness, Labor, Truth, Justice*). This apostolic zeal was best exemplified by Jean Jaurès, who, although he had to do lip service to Karl Marx, had transcended the antiquated materialism of the master. And it was this counter-faith that led the Dreyfusists in their crusade, while Jules Guesde, the orthodox Marxian, stood aside. So the dim and stodgy Opportunist Republic served as a background for a spiritual contest of magnificent intensity.

The clash of ideals, however, had an inevitable result: in many minds the old and the new faiths canceled each other and left a void. So the nineties were also an age of nihilism. But anarchism is a protean conception. The fanatics like Ravachol, Vaillant, Émile Henry, Santo Caserio, who could stab a harmless personage like President Carnot or hurl a bomb into the Chamber of Deputies, called themselves anarchists because the term was in fashion; and philosophical anarchists like Jean Grave and Élisée Reclus did not wholly repudiate them. Anarchistic also was the endorsement of their outrages by a poetaster, Laurent Tailhade: "What does it matter that vague human beings should die? The gesture was beautiful!" Anarchistic were many of the manifestations of Art for Art's Sake, symbolism, decadence: a rebellion against both tradition and reason. Anarchistic the influence of Renan in his later years, and the popularization of the same mood by Anatole France. Anarchistic, on a loftier plane, the potent influence of four foreign writers: the radical individualism of Herbert Spencer and Henrik Ibsen—twins in thought, if poles asunder in art—the neo-Christianity of Tolstoy, the transcendental egotism of Nietzsche.

This anarchism had its lunatic fringe and its commanding heights;

it had also its frivolous aspects. The French like to rationalize even un-reason: so the carnival misrule of bohemians, worldlings, and profiteers justified itself with the plea of anarchism. For this willful indulgence in moral chaos, the expression *fin-de-siècle* was coined. The phenomenon was by no means purely French: not only the Latin world, Italy and Spain, but England and Germany had their decadent strains. Anarchism, however, was only an eddy: the deeper reality was the conflict of mighty forces, each seeking justice and truth by its own lights. It was in that hectic *fin-de-siècle* era that the combat reached its climax; and the whole world waited breathlessly for the outcome.

CHAPTER XXIV

The Third Republic:
Radicalism and World War I,
1900-1918

✍ WALDECK-ROUSSEAU AND "REPUBLICAN DEFENSE"

The Third Republic was founded in 1875 by the Royalists; the long rule of the Radicals was inaugurated in 1899 by the most conservative among the Opportunists, René Waldeck-Rousseau. In both cases the change was a dissolving picture rather than a revolution. Thanks to the existence of many overlapping groups, French political life, in spite of a stormy surface, proceeds with remarkable continuity: rare are those swings of the pendulum, those sudden landslides, which are considered normal in England and in America.

Waldeck-Rousseau had served with distinction under Gambetta and Ferry. Then, although he retained a seat in the Senate, he had practically retired from politics and made a fortune at the bar. In particular, he had vindicated Gustave Eiffel at the time of the Panama trouble. He was steeped in the legal tradition of the *bourgeoisie*. In his masterly speeches he seemed to be the contemporary of Royer-Collard, Guizot, and the Doctrinaires of the Restoration, rather than the colleague of Jaurès and Clemenceau. His deliberate formality, his limpid and icy eloquence, the hard lucidity of his legal mind composed a unique and consistent personality. The Chambers were frozen into admiration; connoisseurs appreciated him as a finished work of art.

Waldeck-Rousseau evolved a political formula which was not altogether new, but which had never been applied with such bold and conscious definiteness: his ministry was an emergency coalition founded not on compromise but on harmony upon a single dominant point. He and all the members of his cabinet were Dreyfusists and meant to draw the inevitable consequences from the affair. Most of his colleagues were Radicals; he was a Conservative himself. To show that Dreyfusism was not in principle hostile to the army, he chose as his minister of war a picturesque and almost legendary survivor of the Second Empire, General de Galliffet (1830–1909), a splendid cavalryman in his day, a *beau sabreur* and a gay aristocrat withal, no less dashing in the ballroom than at the head of his troops. Moreover, Galliffet had taken part, with a heavy hand, in the repression of the Commune: no one could accuse him of subversive opinions. To balance this brilliant figure from the past, Waldeck-Rousseau picked out Alexandre Millerand (1859–1943) for the Department of Commerce and Industry, which at the time dealt also with labor questions. Now Millerand, who had been nominated for the position by Jaurès, was at that time a Socialist in good standing; he had even formulated the program of the party in a notable speech at Saint-Mandé. For a bourgeois regime to place a Socialist at the head of economic affairs was a startling new departure. Waldeck-Rousseau knew that Millerand was a hard worker, a level-headed administrator, almost as great a business lawyer as himself, and perhaps at heart even more of a conservative.[1]

The Waldeck-Rousseau administration was called Ministry of Republican Defense. The Dreyfus Case had been a *cause célèbre*—the most sensational since the affair of the diamond necklace—a spiritual storm, and also a political crisis. The Nationalist movement was in fact a new Boulangism: the parliamentary republic was threatened once more by a coalition of clericals, militarists, and demagogues. Nationalism, as the movement was called, had no single leader, which made it harder to crush. Marchand, the hero of Fashoda, was groomed for a while as a new Bonaparte returning from Egypt. On the day of President Félix Faure's funeral, the revanchard poet Paul Déroulède had urged General Roget, a militant anti-Dreyfusist, to lead his troops against the Elysée. Fortunately, it was said at the time, the general's horse was Republican and refused to heed the call.

General de Galliffet, with his personal prestige, had quelled the incipient rebellion of the officers. He retired as soon as quiet, if not peace, had been restored. To his successor, General André, a convinced Republican, was left the ungrateful task of weeding out the most disloyal elements. The chief danger, however, had come not from the army but from the Church. It was the Church schools, particularly the Jesuits', that had trained the anti-Republican generals. Another order, the Assumptionists, edited widely read popular papers, exceedingly virulent in tone; they had openly called for a clerico-military *coup d'état*.

This menace revived the latent anticlericalism of the Republicans, and not exclusively of the Radicals. They could not forget that the Church had fought the first Revolution, inspired the absolutism of Charles X, applauded the *Coup d'État* of December 2, 1851, and supported Mac-Mahon's reactionary attempt. In 1899 it was not the secular clergy, the parish priests and their bishops, who were directly incriminated: officials of the state, their attitude had been correct enough. The men who had fought and lost were the members of the militant religious orders, who were often compared with the fanatical monks at the time of the League (*ca.* 1580). This hostility to the Regulars was, we have repeatedly noted, an old tradition in the French *bourgeoisie* and even among members of the secular clergy. It might be considered as a last trace of Gallicanism: many French Catholics distrusted the activities of men who were the agents of an international authority. It is a paradoxical fact that the orders, backbone of the Nationalist movement, were combated on nationalistic grounds.

The measures against the orders were not direct, like Ferry's closing of unauthorized establishments. They took the form of a liberal law. Ever since the Revolution, French legislation had frowned upon associations of all kinds; a law was now passed making it considerably easier for Frenchmen to combine for legitimate cultural and political purposes. But all such associations, in order to be authorized, had to submit their statutes, bylaws, and membership lists to the government. A few orders, of a charitable or missionary character, had in the past been formally recognized by the state; these were not disturbed. The others had to comply with the general rule. Many did not even take the trouble to apply: they knew full well that permission would not be granted as their vow of obedience to a power outside France was an insuperable objection.

The Waldeck-Rousseau ministry, born of an emergency, lasted longer than any other under the Republic. Its policy was endorsed by the general elections of April–May, 1902. In spite of scattered victories, notably in Paris and in Algeria, the Nationalist movement was crushed. The opposition was now composed mostly of "Progressists," i.e., of moderate Republicans, the old Opportunists with a more euphonious name. This emphasized the fact that the cabinet, although headed by a Conservative, was definitely Radical in its general tendencies. To everyone's surprise the victor, Waldeck-Rousseau, resigned a few days later. The simple cause, which he had stoically concealed from the general public, was the dangerous condition of his health. He went into almost complete retirement and died two years later, a proud, reserved, lonely figure to the end.

⚰ ÉMILE COMBES AND ANTICLERICALISM

Waldeck-Rousseau's victory at the polls had given him the right to designate his successor. Ritually, the premiership was offered to the nominal leaders of the Radical party, Léon Bourgeois and Henri Brisson. Both declined. So President Loubet, not without the knowledge and consent of Waldeck-Rousseau, summoned Senator Émile Combes, a third-string politician educated for the priesthood and noted only for his rabid anticlericalism. It meant that the Association Law was to be enforced without favor.

The orders which had not applied for authorization were at once declared dissolved; those which did apply saw their requests rejected in the large majority of cases. In 1899 there had been more religious in France than at the end of the Ancient Regime: now many had to go into hiding or into exile. The Carthusian monks of the Grande-Chartreuse went to Tarragona in Spain: for a time their famous liqueur was contraband in France, since a secular company had acquired the right to manufacture it in their old location. Because the orders ceased to exist—or rather because they had never existed in the eyes of the law—their property reverted to the state. It was earmarked for social benefits, thus keeping faith to some extent with the intentions of the original donors. Unfortunately, not a few of the receivers (*liquidateurs*) appointed by the government were incompetent, dishonest, or in collusion with the former owners. Of the $200,000,000 thus nationalized, only part went to its worthy purpose. The affair left an unpleasant aftertaste.

At the same time General André was devoting his energy to the task of republicanizing the army. For generations conservative opinions had been the key to promotion: now the tables were turned. It became a demerit to be known as a practicing Catholic. The minister accepted the services of Freemasons [2] among the officers, who, embittered by long years of disfavor, did not scruple to denounce their clerical and Royalist comrades. It was a "loyalty purge," with all the unpleasantnesses and injustices that such a process inevitably entails. When the system of personal spying in the army was revealed, the first results were a wave of duels among officers and a feeling of nausea in the general public.

Although the secular clergy was not officially under attack, Premier Émile Combes and the Radical party made no secret of their anticlericalism. The separation of Church and State was one of their goals; and if Combes had expressed himself in favor of preserving the Concordat, it was only in order to keep under control an institution he thoroughly distrusted. So the last two years of the Concordat regime were filled with unpleasant incidents, and even with open quarrels. In 1903 the apostle of appeasement, Leo XIII, had been succeeded by Pius X, whose very name sounded like a challenge: it seemed to declare his intention of resuming Pius IX's warfare against the modern spirit. The pope attempted to dispel an ambiguity which for a whole century—and perhaps for ten centuries—had confused the relations of the Holy See with the temporal powers. It had never been made explicit whether the head of the French state—king, emperor, or president—appointed or merely nominated bishops: the verbs *nominare, nommer,* were capable of both interpretations. The pope, of his own authority, added *nobis,* "to us," which made the meaning perfectly clear: "The government presents the candidates to us, but their actual appointment, not a mere confirmation, rests in our hands." The development was logical enough: it was a scandal that bishops should be made by an anticlerical politician. But a solemn treaty cannot validly be modified on the sole initiative of one party. The pope's move simply exposed the absurdity of the Concordat.

The long "marriage of inconvenience" between Church and State lasted until March, 1904. Then President Loubet paid a courtesy call on the king of Italy. This visit to the "usurper," the "jailer of the Papacy," offended the Holy Father who protested in vigorous terms, perhaps all the more vigorous because the document was intended to remain confidential. The secret, however, was not well kept; it found its way into the Radical press. The pope's censure, once made public, had to be construed as an insult to the French government; and as a consequence the French ambassador to the Vatican was recalled (May 21). This was equivalent to a declaration of war, and the Concordat was *ipso facto* suspended.

Some substitute had to be devised. The cabinet prepared a bill for the separation of Church and State. Combes, however, fell from power on January 19, 1905; and the bill that became law was mostly the work of Aristide Briand, who directed its drafting and steered it through the Chamber.

Briand was an independent Socialist, and the Socialists had never been such fierce anticlericals as the Radicals. Moreover, he was throughout his career a man of peace with a genius for conciliation. The law he sponsored was a model of statesmanlike moderation. Liberty of conscience was fully guaranteed. The Church property, hitherto part of the national domain, was to be turned over to the Catholics themselves, who, for the purpose of receiving and administering these holdings, would form in each commune a special organization called Association for Public Worship. The state could not give the property outright to the pope with whom relations had been broken. Moreover, this would have been contrary to the immemorial traditions of the French Catholics. But it was stipulated, so as not to encourage heresy and schism, that the associations so formed must be in spiritual communion with Rome.

This legislation was rejected by the pope on three grounds. As an immediate issue nothing done by a godless government in open conflict with the Papacy could be recognized as legitimate by true believers. In a more general way the very principle of separation is wrong: the Church should be associated with the State as its appointed spiritual guide. (This theoretical condemnation applies to the United States as well as to France or Mexico.) Finally, it is not the individual Catholics who constitute the Church in France: this would imply a sort of congregationalism. The Church is first of all the hierarchy. The property should be owned and managed by the shepherds not by the flock.

The French bishops, meeting for the first time in generations as a national council, voted an address to the pope in which they first assured him of their obedience and loyalty. They also confirmed his doctrinal rejection of the separation; but they urged that, in practice, the moderate Briand Law be accepted. The pope chose to acknowledge the two propositions which endorsed his policy and to ignore the third. So, the associations provided for by the statute could not be formed. The Church lost at once the minor benefits of the settlement: the episcopal palaces, manses, and seminaries, which were to have been left to their users rent free for a number of years, reverted at once to the state. The churches themselves were never closed to the faithful; but full title to them remained in doubt. The state did not desire to keep them, but found no legal party ready to accept them. This made the problem of their upkeep a tangled one, and a few fell into disrepair. All those which were of historic or artistic interest were protected as national monuments.

Before Church property and State property, long associated, could be disentangled, it was necessary to take a full inventory. A few fanatics, mostly Royalist rowdies incited by Charles Maurras and Léon Daudet, affected to consider this simple legal precaution as an outrage. They barricaded themselves in the churches against the agents of the government and declared themselves ready to stand a siege. Every sacred edifice in France could thus be turned into a citadel of disorder. This was done against the desires and instructions of the clergy. Monsignor Gardey, the venerable vicar of Sainte-Clotilde in the most aristocratic district in Paris, told his self-appointed defenders, "This is pious hooliganism!" (*Vous êtes des apaches pieux!*)

If the Royalists had hoped to use the religious crisis as a weapon against the Republic, they were disappointed. Their militant paper, *L'Action Française,* was ably written with an impressive show of dogmatic infallibility on the part of Charles Maurras and a great display of picturesque scurrility by Léon Daudet. It was good literature of its kind, but it was mere literature and of no more significance than the antics of the Royalist youths who chose to call themselves "the King's Peddlers," *les Camelots du Roy.* Literary Paris was amused, but France voted steadily for the Republic. Armand Fallières, who succeeded Emile Loubet as President in January, 1906, was almost as colorless as his predecessor, but noticeably more to the left. In May the general elections confirmed the progress of the Radicals and Socialists: they won sixty seats from the Conservatives. The people thus solemnly ratified the Briand Law.

Its effects on the religious life of the country were excellent. The Concordat had made the Church somnolent; with freedom from official trammels there came a magnificent revival of thought and fervor. Catholic philosophers such as Leroy, Sertillanges, Jacques Maritain renewed a tradition long in abeyance. Catholic novelists such as François Mauriac, Catholic poets such as Paul Claudel were in the forefront of literature. There were a number of significant conversions. At no time since the Middle Ages was church building so active as between the two world wars. As soon as the threat of clericalism disappeared, anticlericalism sickened. After the death of the uncompromising pope, Pius X, a *modus vivendi* was reached. The Church did accept the Separation Law: the only concession by the State was that the Associations for Public Worship were formed on a diocesan basis instead of using the township or commune as a unit. Diplomatic relations were resumed between Paris and the Vatican. Napoleon himself had come to consider the Concordat as his worst mistake: after over a hundred years the error was corrected at last.

WANING OF THE DREYFUSIST HOPE

To the victors went the spoils: the Dreyfusists, mostly Radicals supported by Socialists, consolidated their political position. Meanwhile, however, the great hope of the Dreyfus crisis had grown dim. No movement had ever been so purely idealistic. But victory has to be achieved by realistic means and inevitably assumes a realistic cast. Materially, the triumph was complete: full justice to the victim, his defenders in office, the religious orders punished, the Royalists in the army curbed. But the bourgeois republic remained as shy of generous reforms as in the days of Opportunism, and party squabbles were just as unedifying.

The resulting disenchantment was heightened by dissensions within the Socialist party. Under the inspiration of Jaurès, socialism had attracted a large number of young men; it had even converted an inveterate ironist such as Anatole France. But the party was faced with two alternatives, each entailing a frustration. Collaboration with bourgeois Radicals, advocated by Jaurès, had robbed the movement of its revolutionary and quasi-messianic prestige; the Socialists became merely a progressive group, enmeshed in all the intrigues, smeared with all the compromises, of parliamentary politics. Able men like Alexandre Millerand, René Viviani, Victor Augagneur, Aristide Briand, who still called themselves Socialists, could hardly be distinguished from *petits bourgeois* Radicals. They might even be termed Opportunists: the revolution to which they were still doing lip service was forever to be postponed until tomorrow.

On the opposite side stood the Marxists of the strictest obedience, with Jules Guesde. They triumphed at the Amsterdam Congress in 1904: no truck with bourgeois politics. But the French Socialists, workingmen and intellectuals alike, did not relish the iron orthodoxy imposed by the Marxians, nor a discipline dictated by the dominant German social democracy without any regard for French conditions. Jaurès submitted for the sake of unity, thus disbarring himself from a ministerial position for which he was so eminently qualified. But his submission was bitter to many of his followers.

Worst disappointment of all: the Dreyfusists had combated the martial spirit, sought an understanding with all their neighbors, Germany, England, Italy; and now peace was more insecure than ever. The clearest result of the Entente Cordiale, as we shall see, was to impair Franco-German relations. In 1900 a possible solution of the age-long strife was in sight: had Germany neutralized Alsace-Lorraine, or simply given it a liberal autonomous status, the French were ready to abjure any thought of *revanche*. By 1905, however, it was evident that a new era of distrust and hatred had begun. Both at home and abroad the fraternal dream of 1900 was paling.

Of this disenchantment two writers, Anatole France and Charles Péguy, offer the clearest examples. Anatole France had had his period of elegant, all-dissolving anarchism: *The Rôtisserie of Queen Pédauque* is the breviary of thorough-going skeptics. The Dreyfus Affair had turned this *Montaigne Fin-de-Siècle* into an earnest defender of truth and justice, and even into a militant Socialist; the sordid and uneasy atmosphere that followed victory revived his old nihilism, but with a new touch of despair, with a Swiftian ferocity. *Penguin Island* (1908), under a grinning mask, is pitiless; it ends in weariness and gloom. The French Revolution had been the Holy of Holies for all orthodox democrats, Michelet, Victor Hugo, Clemenceau: in *The Gods Are Athirst* (1912) Anatole France lashes the fanatics, profiteers, dupes, and craven followers of the Left even more bitterly than the effete supporters of the Right. In his long and sinuous career he was to go through two more periods: he became a patriot in 1914, a Communist after 1920. Just because he was delicate rather than robust, his mind was a sensitive thermometer of intelligent public opinion.

Charles Péguy, too, was an ardent Dreyfusist and a believer in "the Universal Socialist Republic." His was a curious mind, candid and tortuous, rich, searching and strangely limited, generous and perverse. He expressed himself in a unique style made up of infinite repetitions with minute variations, monotonous and irresistible like a rising tide, its wearisome wordiness touched up suddenly with a gleam of rarest beauty. By 1906 he had lost faith in the Radical, anticlerical, and Socialist leaders, all absorbed in their dismal parliamentary game. And he felt quiveringly, like Clemenceau, the lash with which at that time William II sought to secure the co-operation of the French. He was thus converted to traditional values. He had never lost them altogether: from the first his heroine had been Joan of Arc; she stood for "the soil and the dead," as Maurice Barrès, the theorist of nationalism, had put it, the common people, the common earth, the common faith of France, against the levity of aristocrats and the scoffing of sophisticates. He became increasingly a patriot and a Catholic but, like Joan herself, not wholly reassuring to vested interests and comfortable orthodoxies. He died in World War I, having sung in advance his own Requiem in the noblest poem inspired by patriotic faith:

Heureux ceux qui sont morts dans les grandes batailles . . .

⟡ THE *Entente Cordiale.*
MOROCCO. FRANCO-GERMAN CONFLICT

After 1905 international questions took precedence over home affairs. France had never been able, and, even under Louis-Philippe, had never desired, to live in isolation: foreign problems never were alien to her, and the enslavement of Poland, for instance, weighed upon her conscience like a mortal sin. Still, her prime concern in peacetime had been with reform and progress within her own boundaries. In 1905 she was made to realize that it was impossible for her to think exclusively or even primarily in terms of French interests. This consciousness has been increasingly forced upon her in the following decades. What happens in London, Berlin, Moscow, Washington is far more important than conditions in Landerneau or Montmorillon. What had always been true in periods of international crises has now become a permanent condition. Frenchmen of this century know that Europe is one, that the world is one, and that every local question has to be viewed in that perspective.

Paradoxically, the most advanced elements, in England as well as in France, were the last to realize intensely this solidarity, for good and evil, of all the nations. Their first thought was still, according to the formula of the British Liberals, "peace, retrenchment, and reform." The universal principles they professed were not translated into a constructive policy: the vague optimism of the Hague Conferences satisfied them. It was the Nationalists who were most conscious of the international danger. Their methods of meeting it may have been wrong: increased armaments and a tough policy have never been avenues to peace. At any rate preparedness was not quite so unrealistic as willfully ignoring the palpable facts and relying passively on a good will that was not there. The Socialists, and Jaurès first of all, knew the peril and offered a remedy. But they were a minority: in France in 1910 one-eighth of the electorate; even in Germany in 1912 little more than one-fourth; and it is doubtful that, on either side of the Vosges, they were as truly international in their thought as in their party slogans.

The men who came to power in 1899, the Dreyfusist coalition, were with few exceptions antimilitarists and anti-imperialists. They were patriots without bluster and without hatred, very different from Paul Déroulède with his exasperating "Bugle Calls." For France's *revanche* they counted on "immanent justice" not on the force of arms. We have noted a lull, about 1900, in the Franco-German feud. The pressing problem was now to check the insensate rivalry between France and England. It would have been the height of folly if two great civilized powers had come to blows over the marshes of the Bahr el-Ghazal, or in order to determine whether in 1713 lobsters were classified as fishes.[3]

Reconciliation required a determined effort. In addition to the many colonial squabbles culminating in Fashoda, the Boer War had aroused burning indignation in France; some French papers, in the worst possible taste, had insulted the venerable symbol of England's traditions and power, Queen Victoria. Fortunately, the efforts were not one-sided. If Joseph Chamberlain could be considered as a rank enemy of France, Balfour was too much of a gentleman and a philosopher for vulgar animosity. And France at her Frenchiest had a great friend in Albert, Prince of Wales, who in 1901 became King Edward VII. Thanks to his personal popularity, this inveterate Parisian could pay an official visit to

Paris (May 1–4, 1903) and be politely received. President Loubet returned the courtesy, and London gave him an even warmer welcome (June 6–9, 1904). It took a year to turn these official amenities into a veritable understanding called (at times not without irony) the *Entente Cordiale* (April 8, 1904). All the minor causes of contentions were removed; the larger questions were settled by trading spheres of influence. France would no longer question England's predominance in Egypt, and England recognized France's paramount interests in Morocco. On both sides of the Channel the peoples greeted this arrangement with delight, as a hundred years before they, wiser than their rulers, had hailed the Peace of Amiens.

But the Entente, intended for peace, inserted itself in a chain of events that made for war. For one thing in order to win Italy over to the Franco-British agreement, a free hand was promised her in Tripoli (now Libya). This led to the Italo-Turkish War of 1911, which in turn, by revealing the weakness of Turkey, encouraged the Balkan allies; and World War I began as an extension of the Balkan conflict. Then, and especially, it embittered the relations between France and Germany. The maritime ambitions of the kaiser—"Our future lies on the water"—seemed a challenge to Britannia, appointed by Heaven to rule the waves. Incidentally, the two sovereigns, Edward VII and William II, nursed this particular grudge against each other: that they were uncle and nephew. England and France had wooed Italy, Germany's ally; and France was anxious that her two friends, England and Russia, should be reconciled, after the longest cold war in history. All these were peace moves, but Germany construed them as *Einkreisung,* encirclement. Since England was still impregnable behind the inviolate sea, since Russia, perhaps easy to defeat, was too vast ever to remain conquered, the kaiser turned against that member of the Triple Entente which was least protected against attack, France. His aim was to convince France that she could hope for no effective aid from either England or Russia, and that the safest policy for her was to be Germany's docile friend.

Circumstances at first favored Germany: Russia was engaged in a war with Japan (February, 1904–September, 1905); in the Manchurian mud, she no longer appeared invincible. So, on March 31, 1905, against the advice of his best diplomats, William II made a defiant gesture. In a speech at Tangier, he made it plain that he refused to recognize the validity of the Franco-British agreement. The French Radicals and Socialists were still committed to peace. They blamed their minister of foreign affairs, Delcassé, who had held his post for seven years, liquidated the Fashoda incident, and signed the Franco-British Entente. They accused him of having "ignored Germany," and they forced his resignation. Rouvier, then prime minister, assumed the direction of foreign affairs and accepted the German demand for an international conference to settle the status of Morocco. Germany had scored a point.

The conference took place at Algeciras, near Gibraltar (January–April, 1906). Germany found herself almost isolated, supported only by her brilliant second, Austria-Hungary. France, England, Italy, and Spain were bound together by previous agreements. Russia had issued from the Far Eastern war with her prestige damaged, but with her power still formidable in the West. Theodore Roosevelt, under the forms of strict neutrality, gave his moral support to the Anglo-French side. The result was a convention which reaffirmed in theory the unity and independence of Morocco, assured all countries of equal economic rights in that area, but placed the police of the ports under the control of France and Spain in their respective zones, with a special regime for Tangier.

If Morocco alone had been at stake, this would have been a very acceptable solution: Germany's material interests were safeguarded, and her pride had suffered no deep wound. But in the game of prestige, it was a setback. She had forced the dismissal of France's strongest foreign secretary in a generation, but her further bluff had been called. German public opinion, and in particular the critics of the imperial regime, chose to consider Algeciras as a deep humiliation.

So, in 1907 there was a new alarm. At Casablanca three Germans, deserting from the French Foreign Legion, had been recaptured, although they had placed themselves under the protection of the German consul. The matter, in which both sides were at fault, was submitted to arbitration; an agreement was arrived at recognizing France's political interests and pointing to an economic collaboration in Morocco between the two countries. In 1909, as the pacification of Morocco was proceeding apace, Germany once more reopened the question. The French by this time were persuaded that Germany intended to keep this sword perpetually dangling over their heads. This time, Germany sent a gunboat, the "Panther," to the undeveloped port of Agadir under the plea of protecting interests which were nonexistent. Lloyd George from the time of the Boer War had been considered a pacifist, but in a belligerent speech he assured France of England's full support. The French premier, Joseph Caillaux, however, made a last effort for appeasement. In payment for recognizing (it was the third time) France's position in Morocco, Germany was given two large strips of territory in the French Congo, odd tentacles which actually cut the French possessions into three. Peace was preserved; but hardly anyone in France, except Caillaux and perhaps a rising young Socialist by the name of Pierre Laval, believed in the possibility of a free and equal collaboration between the two neighbors. The French had an old expression, *Querelle d'Allemand,* a German's quarrel, for one picked up under a flimsy and mendacious pretext: they were confirmed in their age-long prejudice. They felt now certain that, if a war broke out either between Germany and England or between Germany and Russia, France would be dragged into it. Too strong to be tolerated as a neutral, she would have to fight Germany or become her satellite: exactly the choice that Hitler offered Poland in 1939.

REVIVAL OF FRENCH NATIONALISM

The German menace brought about a sharp revival of French nationalism. Maurice Barrès, whose position had been eccentric, was now acknowledged as an authoritative voice: his novels on Alsace and Lorraine under German rule were read with avid interest. The *Action française* writers were taken more seriously. Officers were no longer apologetic about their calling; the workers, without showing any greater fondness for military service, ceased to consider it as sheer penal servitude. The French discovered at that time the colonial empire they had absent-mindedly acquired: since it had brought them to the brink of war with England and with Germany, it must be worth preserving. The work of a few great proconsuls, Paul Doumer in Indochina, Galliéni in Madagascar, Lyautey in Morocco, was duly appreciated. It was realized that France had acquired not only territories but a doctrine: neither domination nor assimilation but association, the cross-fertilization, the gradual converging of cultures. For that great and delicate task, their total freedom from race prejudices gave the French a decisive advantage. The colonies, once a receptacle for disreputable officials, became a field for the energetic with a touch of the missionary. It is not claimed that these fine ideals worked miracles overnight: still, materially and morally, the French Union was becoming a reality.

The change in the national temper was particularly marked in three radically different personalities, Alexandre Millerand, Raymond Poincaré, Georges Clemenceau.

Millerand, as we have seen, was a Socialist who, refusing to accept the ruling of the Amsterdam Congress, had become an Independent. He moved rapidly toward the center and further right. In 1912 he became minister of war, and he did his best to restore not only the efficiency but the morale and the prestige of the army, even by such rudimentary means as torchlight parades. The people again cheered the soldiers in the streets, and the old Boulangists wept with joy: Paulus alone was lacking. As Abbé Ernest Dimnet noted, "France was herself again": the martial spirit was aflame once more.

Poincaré, like Millerand a noted lawyer, was coolly respected as an expert in finances. Hard-working but without any glamour or magnetism, he would have remained merely one of the supporting cast if his Lorrainer patriotism had not so admirably fitted the mood of the time. He was a reserve captain in the Alpine Chasseurs, the famed Blue Devils, and this, in the popular mind, offset the stolidity of his countenance and the frigidity of his oratory. It was as a patriot, as the man who would stand up to Germany or to any foreign power, that he was carried to the forefront of French politics, to the premiership in 1912, to the presidency in 1913.

But the coming man, the best symbol of the resurgent spirit, was the veteran Radical leader, Georges Clemenceau. For many years only the destructive aspects of his character had stood out. It was claimed that he had overthrown nineteen cabinets: "Nineteen?" he would snarl, "only one: they were all the same." His private life, without being disreputable, was not a model of bourgeois decorum. He was dreaded rather than respected for his cruel wit, his brutal manners, and his physical courage; for he was as fearless in a duel as in a verbal encounter. His innumerable enemies rejoiced when, after the Panama scandal, he was under a cloud. He lost his senatorial seat because he was accused, absurdly, of being in the pay of Great Britain. He threw himself heart and soul into the Dreyfus affair: with Zola and Jaurès he was the intellectual leader of the movement. Yet, even after the victory of his cause, he was not called to office: the old prejudice caused by his uncertain temper and his rejection of every discipline was too strong.

Now France began to appreciate the consistency that lay under his apparent willfullness. His opinions had not changed, but France was at last in step with him. In 1906 as forty years before, he was an individualist, a philosophical anarchist of the Herbert Spencer type. He neither loved nor trusted the people overmuch: if he was a democrat, it was because he resented every false assumption of superiority, every privilege not justified by actual service. He combated both militarism and clericalism, because to him they meant passive obedience, the silencing of free thought. He was an anticolonialist for the same reason that he was a patriot: he did not want to impose upon others an alien rule, however well meaning and enlightened.

It was only in 1906, at the age of sixty-five, that he became a minister for the first time. Even then, he had to go through a period of probation: he was subordinated to a neutral and reassuring personage, Jean Sarrien (March–October). In spite of widespread misgivings, he proved to be a competent executive, clear-headed, swift to decide, courageous in action. Finally, he assumed the premiership and held it for nearly three years. He lost power in one of his old fits of temper through an unjust attack on Delcassé; so it was said that he was again at his game of smashing cabinets, not sparing even his own.

Clemenceau and Poincaré, great Frenchmen both, were merciless antagonists. To Clemenceau, Poincaré was insufferably *petit bourgeois,* plodding and stuffy; to Poincaré, Clemenceau was irremediably bohemian. The conflict with Jaurès was on a higher plane. The international and social ideal of Jaurès did not frighten Clemenceau: he had preserved his father's faith, the faith of 1848, and he placed truth and justice above tribal or class interests. But he was, at close range, extremely keen-sighted; and he thought that the boundless dreams of Jaurès were still in the clouds. There were splendid debates between them, unblemished by personal animosity or partisan narrowness. Parliamentary eloquence in France has never reached greater heights.

In those years France waded wearily through the usual minor scandals, the Rochette affair, the Caillaux-Calmette affray; they would not be worth recording except that they created a false impression abroad. On the history-making plane the lines were sharply drawn. Both sides recognized the mounting danger of war. The Socialists and many Radical-Socialists (a pink hybrid), following the lead of Jaurès, wanted to meet the peril with a great campaign of international education. The peace sentiment so evidently present among the masses was to be mobilized. At Basel and, at the eleventh hour, in Berlin Jaurès met the other European Socialists and urged them all to curb their respective warmongers. On the other hand, Poincaré, Barthou, Millerand, with the reluctant support of Clemenceau, were openly preparing for a war which they deemed—and made—inevitable.

The test was the proposal to increase the period of military service from two to three years in order to meet on more equal terms the mounting German menace. The argument of the Socialists was that the Three-Year Law created only a delusive impression of numerical equality with Germany. It did not add a single soldier to the total forces of France; in case of war every able-bodied citizen would be called to the colors, and two years were admittedly sufficient for the training of a private. Only the peacetime standing army would be larger. This would be an advantage exclusively in the case of a sudden attack, without mobilization, unheralded even by a period of diplomatic tension: a hypothesis which, we may note, was not realized either in 1914 or in 1939. The objection to the Three-Year Law, beside the enormous expenditure it entailed, was that it could be interpreted by Germany only as a gesture of defiance and even of provocation. It was exactly the attitude that would hasten a conflict: *Si vis bellum, para bellum.* The decisive argument on the other side was: "Yours not to reason why. The General Staff declared the Three-Year Law indispensable. In a crisis the man who votes against an additional burden is a traitor." By some this was called playing safe, by others, playing with fire.

The elections of 1914 were therefore of commanding importance. They had a complex and somewhat murky background: the current assorted scandals and the Income Tax bill. But the essential issue was the Three-Year Law. The Poincarists made it their battle cry, and they were soundly defeated. The French had voted down the policy of clenched fists. President Poincaré at first refused to heed the verdict. He called in as premier a noble-looking septuagenarian, Alexandre Ribot: the new Chamber shrugged him out on his first appearance. Poincaré, who had wanted to be a strong President, had to acknowledge his impotence. Clemenceau, who might have united the warring factions, was ruled out, as a personal enemy. So, Poincaré summoned the independent Socialist René Viviani.

WORLD WAR I: JOFFRE. THE MARNE. STALEMATE

The most tragic thing about history is not its inevitability but, on the contrary, the fact that it might so easily have been otherwise. In July, 1870, there was "not a cloud in the sky." On June 16, 1914, when Viviani took office, it seemed as though the war spirit had receded. In Germany as well as in France the people were alerted and had manifested their horror of war. Jaurès had actually won the day. Then war, kept out of the front entrance, sneaked in through the back door. On June 28 the crown prince of Austria, Archduke Francis Ferdinand, was assassinated at Sarajevo.

France had given but little thought to Balkan problems. Murders were not uncommon in that picturesque region; it was thought that this new outrage involved only one fanatic, at most a handful of terrorists. Neither France nor Germany was directly interested. We are here leaving the field of purely French history as determined by the will of the French people for that of general European politics. Austria, and particularly the more bellicose head of the bicephalous monarchy, Hungary, determined to have it out with Serbia once and for all. England, France, Russia urged Francis Joseph's government to observe due caution; but the shaky empire had reached the point when bluster alone could give the illusion of unity. So, in Rose Macaulay's words, Austria demanded that Europe let her have her little war in peace. If Russia, the natural champion of the Slavs, spoke firmly, this was interpreted as a threat. Germany suffered at this point from the curse of all entangling alliances: she had to say, "My ally, right or wrong!" And she was morally handicapped by the very perfection of her military preparedness. In a contest she would be weeks ahead of the lumbering Russian giant; she could not allow Russia to mobilize at leisure. This made her headstrong and hasty at the very moment when self-possession was the most urgent need.

Even when war had become imminent between Russia and Germany, France was not fully committed. She would have to decide whether Germany was the aggressor before the Franco-Russian alliance could come into operation. She was spared that problem, which still puzzles certain historians. Germany gave her no choice, or rather she offered as alternatives war or complete submission, with the key fortresses of Toul and Verdun as a pledge of good behavior. France refused to commit herself to vassalage. To make sure that no frontier incident could be invoked as a *casus belli,* Viviani ordered French troops on the eastern frontier to be withdrawn ten kilometers. But when the shadow of a pretext cannot be discovered, the phantom of a shadow can be invented: Germany asserted that French warplanes had violated German territory and flown over Nürnberg. On August 3 war was declared.

On July 31 a "patriot," crazed by the denunciations of the Royalist press, shot to death the one great force for peace, Jean Jaurès. At other times this event—a major disaster for France and for Europe—might have been the start of a civil war. But France was already swept by the martial spirit, and no one attempted to make party capital out of the crime. On the next day, August 1, general mobilization was ordered; it was carried out without the slightest protest. Never in her long history had France felt such perfect unanimity. The heirs of the Ancient Regime, the men who had killed Jaurès, rushed to the front out of traditional loyalty to the flag. The Socialists, with no less ardor, went to battle for the defense of Jaurès' ideal. All the other classes responded with the same determination, burning and somber, too deep for bluster.

This feeling of unity found expression in the formation of a National Defense Ministry. Viviani remained premier, and the strongest men in France accepted office under him, irrespective of party allegiance: Millerand took the War Department; Delcassé resumed his post at the head of foreign affairs; Ribot, the Conservative, directed the finances; Auganeur, an independent Socialist, the navy; Sembat, a regular Socialist, took over public works. As a symbol of this "Sacred Union," four elder statesmen became ministers of state, without portfolio: Charles de Freycinet, active in the war of 1870, who represented the tradition of Gambetta; Émile Combes, the militant anticlerical; Denys Cochin, sanest and most respected of Catholics and Royalists; and, greatest wonder of all, Jules Guesde, the inflexible Marxian who had so rigorously condemned any collaboration with the bourgeois parties. Only one personality was wanting, Clemenceau. His exclusion was not due exclusively to Poincaré's spite: even the strongest men in France were afraid of the formidable old man. He remained out of the government, the most uncompromising patriot of them all but also the most fearless critic of inefficiency in high places. When his paper, *The Free Man,* was suppressed, it reappeared at once, fiercer than ever, as *The Man in Chains.*

The military and diplomatic events of World War I belong to world history and cannot be told in terms of France alone. England joined the fight not because of the *Entente Cordiale* but because Germany had violated the neutrality of Belgium. At first it looked as though Germany's cynical disregard of her pledged word would swiftly bring victory. The fine resistance of Liège hardly delayed the invaders at all. Joffre's offensive in Alsace and Lorraine came almost immediately to a stop. The French, defeated at Charleroi, retreated at full speed, sacrificing a few units here and there to fight a delaying action. It seemed as though the end would come even faster than in 1870: the government hastily abandoned Paris for Bordeaux.

Suddenly, the face of events changed. Joffre—it was one of the greatest military feats in history—had kept his fleeing troops in constant control. Thanks to his magnificent fortitude and his organizing ability, the armies which the Germans considered as *unkampffähig,* incapable of further fight, had lost neither spirit nor discipline. So, at the first opportunity—a false move on the part of von Kluck—Joffre could give the word, and the Allies stood their ground, soon to assume the offensive. Sarrail firmly held Nancy. Foch, his two wings shattered, attacked with the center. Galliéni, governor of Paris, speeded reinforcements in taxicabs to the crucial point (September 5–12). Russia, not waiting for complete mobilization, had hurled troops into East Prussia, and the Germans, frightened, had withdrawn two army corps from the West. The Schlieffen Plan called for a lightning decision in the West: by September 12 it had failed.

The miracle of the Marne had saved the Allies, but they were too exhausted to turn the German retreat into a rout. They raced northward to save the Channel coast from the invaders and managed to rescue even a small strip of Belgium. But the Germans dug themselves in after a costly, indecisive battle on the river Aisne. And for interminable months trench warfare was to prevail on a continuous front of over four hundred miles.

Joffre had moral and technical qualities of the highest order, but he lacked imagination. As early as the end of 1914, noting the stalemate in the West, Franchet d'Esperey urged a Balkan campaign starting from Salonica. By enabling the Western Allies to join hands with the Russians, it might have averted the ultimate collapse of the Muscovite armies and a revolution which is still shaking the world. Neither Joffre nor Kitchener would hear of what they called a diversion. Joffre stolidly accepted trench warfare and was satisfied with "nibbling" the Germans; he forgot that the French were being nibbled too, and could not so well afford it.

The operations on the western front in 1915 were extraordinarily costly and indecisive. In 1916 the Germans attempted to end the stalemate. With the *Kronprinz* in command they started an all-out assault on Verdun preceded by a formidable bombardment (February 21). The epic duel continued throughout the year. Verdun was almost surrounded, linked with the rest of France only by one road and one local railway line, both exposed to constant artillery fire. Under Pétain, then under Nivelle, the French clung tenaciously to the symbolic city. They made good their boast, "They shall not pass!" Meanwhile the British, supported by the French, were attacking on the Somme. By the end of the year the small advances of the Germans near Verdun had been recaptured. But the British and the French had gained only a few miles in the mud of the Somme, churned up mercilessly by artillery fire. There the British lost 400,000 men, the French 200,000; at Verdun the French casualties mounted to 350,000. And still it was a stalemate.

Nineteen hundred and seventeen was a year of unrelieved gloom. The Germans withdrew of their own accord to a stronger position, the Hindenburg Line. Joffre had at last been removed, with an honorary position and the marshal's baton. His successor, Nivelle, the hero of Verdun, hoped to win a decision in Champagne. His advance proved terrifically costly and was checked by the enemy almost at once. The government stopped the senseless slaughter: few students of military affairs blamed this decision. The frustration, after the glowing promises of speedy victory, broke the spirit of the French army: there were mutinies in as many as sixteen corps. Nivelle was superseded by Pétain, whose first task was to restore, by humane means, discipline and confidence.

Once again, we find that French history cannot be isolated. The French had been resigned to the slow torture of trench warfare so long as they hoped that either they or their allies would ultimately break through. But the German lines proved impregnable, and one ally after another fell under Teutonic blows. Romania had cast in her lot with the Western powers only to be annihilated in a few weeks. Serbia, which had offered splendid resistance to Austria, was finally overwhelmed;

king and army, after a winter flight through trackless mountains, had to seek refuge in the island of Corfu. Italy, who thought that her belated intervention would prove decisive, was beaten back on the Isonzo and routed at Caporetto. For months, for years, the West had hoped that the enormous Russian "steam roller" would at last get into action; now Russia was irremediably defeated and in the throes of a revolution.

No wonder the splendor of August, 1914, grew faint, and the Sacred Union gave way to sharp recriminations. Talks of a compromise peace, a "white peace," if not peace at any price, could not be hushed. The Socialists and pacifists met at Kienthal and Stockholm, and their "cease firing!" propaganda appealed to the weary. Had the Germans offered generous terms early in 1917, the defeatists in the West—such men as Lord Landsdowne in England and Joseph Caillaux in France—would not have lacked supporters. But Germany, flushed with triumphs on every front, could only think of a victor's *Diktat*.

WORLD WAR I: WILSON. CLEMENCEAU. FOCH

The French, pardonably, might have lost heart had it not been for the intervention of the United States. Long before troops and supplies could arrive in appreciable quantities, the decision of the American people had restored the spirit of the Allies. It was first of all a moral tonic. President Wilson had been scrupulously neutral in word and deed: his final judgment, ratified by Congress and public opinion, confirmed the belief of the West in the righteousness of their cause. With this renewed faith and this illimitable hope they could hold a while longer, until the inexhaustible resources of the New World made their weight fully felt. So the West could face, without despair, the crushing disasters in Russia and Italy.

Without this blood transfusion it may be doubted whether Clemenceau himself could have nerved the French to "see it through" (*Jusqu'au bout!*). But so long as there was a gleam of hope, Clemenceau's indomitable will to fight on could not be called heroic madness, as was Gambetta's in 1871. After Viviani France had tried in quick succession Briand, a conciliator with a violoncello voice; Ribot, an eminent but weary parliamentarian; Painlevé, an illustrious mathematician: all excellent men, but not fighters. Finally, Poincaré's obstinate reluctance was conquered; he had to send for his adversary Clemenceau, who was then seventy-seven years old.

No sooner had the Tiger assumed power than hope sprang up again. His sole program was, *Je fais la guerre,* I am waging war. No doubt he was a dictator. He restored unanimity by suppressing dissent. Not only foreign spies and plotters, Almareyda, Bolo Pacha, Mata Hari, hitherto treated with strange longanimity, were swiftly judged and shot; but statesmen among the highest in the parliamentary world, Joseph Caillaux, Malvy, protected by a host of hangers-on and friends, were arrested and condemned for no other crime but that they did not believe ardently enough in total victory. The rough old man became the idol of civilians and poilus alike. And the inveterate cynic developed a deep tenderness, with no trace of sentimentality, for the men who were bleeding, freezing, rotting away in the trenches that the country might not die. All the time he could spare from office or Chamber he spent at the very front, never thinking of his own comfort or safety. His shapeless felt hat, his loose, shaggy overcoat, his Tartar face with high cheekbones, drooping moustaches, and burning eyes, his bluntness, his humor, the raciness of his speech, and above all his energy made him a familiar, a legendary, figure. The poilus were icily polite to Poincaré when, dutifully, courageously, he visited them at their posts. But it was Old Father Victory they loved.[4]

Only one thing was now lacking for victory, unity of command. Joffre had once exercised it, at least in theory; but his failure had weakened the very idea. Now the heroic king of the Belgians could hardly be treated as a subordinate; Pershing, in spite of one fine gesture and of repeated urgings from Washington, could not admit that American troops be placed under a foreign general; Pétain and Haig distrusted each other. On the contrary, Hindenburg and Ludendorff worked in close harmony and had full control on the German side.

This gave them a tremendous advantage, and they meant to use it to the full. They were able to move many units from the eastern front to the western; but they had to clinch their victory before America's growing power had changed the balance. So, they launched a sudden and violent offensive in March, 1918, actually breaking the British lines and advancing forty miles in a few days, as far as Noyon and Montdidier. French reserves managed to plug the hole. It was in that crisis, at Doullens on March 26, that Foch was called to co-ordinate operations on the western front. On April 9 the Germans started a new attack, south of Ypres. Again, they tore a gap in the British defenses; then Foch was made commander-in-chief (April 14). A fantastic gun, "Big Bertha," fired upon Paris, sixty miles away, and on Good Friday many worshippers were killed when a projectile hit Saint-Gervais, a church in the very heart of the capital.

Foch's appointment did not suddenly alter the situation. At the end of May the Germans delivered another tremendous blow in Champagne along that Chemin-des-Dames which had been the scene of Nivelle's ill-fated offensive. The French were driven back thirteen miles on the first day. On June 4 at Château-Thierry the Second American Division checked the German advance. It was the first great battle in which American troops had played an essential role, and they acquitted themselves well.

In spite of these German successes Clemenceau and Foch did not despair. On July 15 began the second battle of the Marne, and the last offensive on the part of the Germans. Ludendorff managed to cross the river, but his progress was soon arrested. On July 18 the Allies counterattacked. In an unceasing hundred-day battle the initiative was not wrenched from them until the armistice was signed.

Ludendorff saw clearly enough that all was lost; he urged his government to sue at once for peace. This disposes of the Nazi legend that the German army, undefeated in the field, was stabbed in the back by democrats and defeatists. Germany's allies were toppling down: Turkey under the blows of Allenby, Bulgaria under those of Franchet d'Esperey. The Serbs were forging ahead, reconquering their whole country and reaching Austrian territory. The Italians forced the Austrians back on the Piave (June 15–24), while the oppressed nationalities of the empire were in open rebellion. Even if Ludendorff had extricated his troops earlier and established a shorter and stronger line on the Meuse, the end would not have been long delayed: by December the Allied armies would have been in Vienna, Prague, and southern Germany.

It was the Imperial German Government, with Prince Max von Baden as chancellor, that appealed to President Wilson for an armistice as early as October 4. The mutinies and the revolution of November 3–9 were the result, not the cause, of the military collapse. The Germans, who until September had been told that absolute victory was only a matter of days, realized that they had been duped and rose in anger against their leaders. Even Hindenburg had to warn William II that he could not guarantee the loyalty of the army. The kaiser abdicated and fled to Holland. So it was the German republic that had to accept the terms of the armistice. On November 11, 1918, at 11 A.M. the order to cease firing became effective.

The armistice was at the same time severe and generous. It was not a truce between equals: it was an acknowledgment of defeat, and the Germans were deprived of every means of resuming the fight. It was not, like Leoben or Villafranca, a sketch of the peace to come. The agreement was strictly military. No political conditions were imposed upon the conquered, and no pledge was given that the Allies would be bound by President Wilson's Fourteen Points. But as a soldier Marshal Foch treated his fallen adversaries honorably. He recognized their skill and their courage. The troops did not capitulate: they were allowed to march home in formation, with arms, bands, and banners. Hitler was to make the French doubt the wisdom of Foch's chivalrous attitude.

The end of the nightmare was one of the supreme moments in French history. It was, of course, a personal triumph for Clemenceau, the only survivor among those deputies who, in 1871, had refused to ratify the peace dictated by Germany. His brief address to the Chambers on that great occasion bears no trace of rancor. It ends with the ringing phrase, "France, of old the soldier of God, today the soldier of humanity, ever the soldier of the ideal!" It was not a rhetorical flourish but a true profession of faith. It linked the crusades, the Revolution, the Great War together as three cantos of a magnificent epic. It was the fitting climax of a dramatic career, perhaps also the climax of a great national destiny. Henceforth the French, Clemenceau at their head, knew that patriotism is not enough, that "above France there is civilization."

On November 25 the French entered Strasbourg: the population was wild with joy. Poincaré and Clemenceau, reconciled for a moment by this fulfillment of a lifelong dream, fell into each other's arms.

CHAPTER XXV

The Anxious Truce: 1918-1939: Recovery, 1918-1929

✒ THE HALFHEARTED *Diktat:* VERSAILLES

The Inter-Allied Peace Conference met in Paris on January 18, 1919, forty-eight years to a day after the proclamation of the Bismarckian Empire: thus was confirmed Gambetta's faith in "immanent justice." France, among the major Allies, had suffered most and fought most tenaciously; the Marne and Verdun were the outstanding episodes in the long struggle, and the prestige of Clemenceau and Foch among war leaders was unrivaled. So the choice of the French capital seemed inevitable. Yet it must be pronounced a mistake. Paris never was a placid city; after the nervous tension of the last four years, it was feverish. The delegations caught that excitement and increased it. Diplomacy, home politics, business, and pleasure jostled uncomfortably. It would have been preferable if the Congress had assembled in a neutral city like Geneva, or in a quiet provincial French town like Angers. The weariness, the irritability, the frustration, the cynicism recorded by the best witnesses, Stephen Bonsall, James T. Shotwell, Maynard Keynes, Harold Nicolson, were due in a large measure to the hectic atmosphere of the great city. Peace-making is the most delicate of experiments; it should be conducted in a laboratory. Paris in 1919 was a world's fair.

The second great handicap of the Peace Conference was the presence of Woodrow Wilson. When he arrived in Paris on December 14, 1918, he was hailed as no Allied sovereign, no national leader, no victorious general had been. To the people of Paris he stood not for victory alone but for justice, the sole possible foundation of peace. But that immense moral force was not without flaws. Wilson did not know Europe and European problems at firsthand: an admirable staff of experts could not make up for that fundamental lack. He did not fully know his own country; and, most disastrous of all, he did not fully know his own mind. He jibbed at the principle of racial equality which the Japanese wanted to have explicitly stated in the Covenant. He stumbled even worse on the question of definite sanctions which the French experts, Léon Bourgeois, Larnaude, insisted upon as the solid core of international law. Just as Lloyd George had his reservation about the freedom of the seas, so Wilson had his reservation about the Monroe Doctrine. He was a sincere but incomplete idealist coupled with an astute but incomplete politician. The French understood well enough—better at any rate than many Americans—the nobility of his aims, the loftiness of his thought, the immense moral and material aid that he had brought to their cause. But they were made uneasy by his inconsistencies, ill veiled at times by bursts of prophetic eloquence, at times by strange fits of petulance.

Had Wilson chosen to fight for uncompromising Wilsonism, he would have found himself supported by the industrial workers educated by Jaurès, Zola, Anatole France, and back of them Victor Hugo; but he would have been opposed by the organized powers, the vested interests, the self-styled elites. On the fourteenth of December the heart of Paris went out to him, but *Le Figaro,* the organ of "Society," sneered at his ideals. He did try, halfheartedly, to appeal to the peoples of Europe over the heads of their governments. But can we imagine him, in temper and upbringing a fastidious conservative, leading a social revolution against Poincaré and Clemenceau, or against Lloyd George? So his crusade was the merest velleity. It increased the diffidence of the rulers without providing the common people with the definite and steady leadership they needed.

Moreover, Wilson was in 1919 a man defeated in his own country. He had some justification for believing that his world policy was endorsed by the American people, irrespective of parties; and he had communicated that conviction to his colleagues at the conference: they took it for granted that he stood for a solid United States. But he had ruined in advance the possibility of a truly national policy by remaining too faithful to party orthodoxy. Had he taken with him to Paris if not Henry Cabot Lodge at any rate former President Taft and President Lawrence Lowell, of Harvard University, the outcome would have been different.

Finally, the conference suffered a catastrophe which was not realized at the time. There was to be a preliminary conference of the Allies to agree on the terms which were to be presented to the Germans; then the conference proper would open, and the victors would discuss those terms with the defeated. But the preliminaries dragged on indefinitely. By imperceptible steps people came to believe that this elaborate and infinitely wearisome affair was the main conference. When the terms were at last drawn up, everybody's patience was exhausted. The delegates shuddered at the thought of starting all over again. The Germans were simply told to sign on the dotted line.

No peace was ever more fully, more openly, discussed: Wilson fought harder for his Fourteen Points than the Germans themselves could have done. Still, a judgment passed in the absence of the accused was bound to seem highhanded. A *Diktat* per se would have been in line with diplomatic traditions: the Treaties of Paris in 1814 and 1815, the Treaty of Frankfort in 1871, the Treaty of Paris in 1898 after the Spanish-American War were purely and simply imposed upon the conquered. But the Treaty of Versailles contained the Guilt Clause, Article 231, blaming the Imperial German Government for starting the war.

Now, after a free and fair trial democratic Germany might have been induced to accept the Guilt Clause. The German Revolution of November 9, 1918, was in fact an admission of that responsibility; had the kaiser fought a purely defensive war, it would have been treason to overthrow him. On the other hand, Germany, in a realistic spirit, might have resigned herself to the harshest terms of a dictated peace: Versailles was mild compared with Bucharest and Brest-Litovsk. But what she could not accept was the combination of the mailed fist and self-righteousness. No moral judgment can be imposed by force. This, in Germany's eyes, invalidated the Versailles Treaty altogether; and liberal opinion throughout the world had to admit she had a case.

The interminable debates in Paris are often presented as a duel between the forward-looking idealism of Wilson and the cynical realism of Clemenceau. Two expressions had a deplorable influence in that connection: "the Tiger" and *la revanche*. It was not realized that "the Tiger" was an affectionate nickname referring to Clemenceau's appearance and his manners, not to his political philosophy, and that *la revanche,* it cannot be repeated too often, stood for justice not vindictiveness. The real duel was not between Wilson and Clemenceau but between Clemenceau and Poincaré. Foch was asked, purely as a military expert, what would be the essential condition of French security, and he answered, the Rhine under French control. Poincaré, whose patriotism was more jealous and single-minded than Clemenceau's, fully adopted the marshal's view. Any peace that would not permanently establish the Rhine as the military frontier of France would, in his opinion, be a delusive truce. Not even Poincaré, however, advocated the annexation pure and simple of the whole left bank: the nefarious doctrine of the "natural boundaries" had been exorcized at last.

Clemenceau stood much closer to Wilson than to Poincaré. He had told Pershing, "Above France there is civilization." In fact, he agreed with Wilson better than Wilson agreed with himself. Lincoln Steffens tells us that Clemenceau asked Lloyd George and Wilson whether they knew what a genuine community of nations entailed: the end of privileges, of empires, of customs barriers, of racial inequalities; were they ready for all that?—Well, no; not quite; not yet. "Then, gentlemen, it is not peace you are preparing; it is war."

Clemenceau was seeking to harmonize his own ideal of a civilian, a civilized, a free world, with the harsh realities so clear to the eyes of Poincaré. He could not entrust the fate of France wholly to a League still in the making and bound to remain weak for a generation, but he was willing to give the League a full chance—with interim precautions. France would keep watch on the Rhine for fifteen years only; and, as a substitute for the strategic frontier demanded by Foch and Poincaré, the liberal democracies, England, France, America, would remain bound together in a defensive alliance. In Clemenceau's mind, this Pact of Mutual Assistance, signed on the same day as the Treaty of Versailles, was the keystone of the peace. His enemies were to say that he abandoned realities for a scrap of paper.

The treaty of peace was signed on June 28 in that famous Hall of Mirrors which had seen the birth of the German Empire.[1] The French Parliament ratified it, with great misgivings, on October 13, 1919. The general elections on November 16 sent to the Chamber a "horizon blue" majority, just as in England the House of Commons went khaki. This patriotic combination was known as the *Bloc National*. It professed to support all the war leaders, Clemenceau, Briand, but particularly Millerand and Poincaré. A number of Radicals, with the sympathy of the Socialists, formed under Edouard Herriot the Leftist coalition, or *Cartel des Gauches*.

Clemenceau was still "Old Father Victory." He was prevailed upon to be a candidate for the presidency of the Republic: the Elysée would thus be the temple of a living symbol. He did not crave the empty and wearisome honor any more than he desired membership in the French Academy: he was ready to accept both as unwelcome but inevitable consequences of victory. But a caucus of the Republican parties, swayed by the right wing, and particularly influenced by the Catholics, nominated Paul Deschanel, better known as Ripolin, a smooth, highly varnished nonentity. Clemenceau shrugged his shoulders, resigned the premiership, and retired into a long, studious, and snarling twilight (d. 1929). This was the first step in the liquidation of the world war (January 17–18, 1920).

The worst fears of the Poincarists were soon realized. The Treaty of Versailles failed of ratification in the American Senate for lack of a two-thirds majority.[2] Wilson, long an invalid, was stricken by sickness in his desperate attempt to rally public opinion. There is no provision in the American Constitution for the "solemn referendum" he had demanded. Traditional isolationism, frayed nerves, weary "normalcy," party politics, personal spite combined to defeat for a quarter of a century what had been first of all the American solution. The special alliance with England and France went down without even the courtesy of a debate. The fate of Clemenceau was even harsher than that of Wilson. The idealist attained at any rate the dignity of a martyr; the keener-sighted realist remained branded as a dupe.

TOUGH REALISM: MILLERAND, POINCARÉ, AND THE RUHR

Through some strange whim of fate Paul Deschanel, that perfect pattern of the safe and sane, lost his mind as soon as he had attained the goal of forty years. On September 15, 1920, he had to be removed. He was succeeded by Alexandre Millerand, now a thoroughgoing Nationalist and conservative.

Raymond Poincaré, released from the presidency that had cramped him for seven years, worked in close harmony with Millerand. Both considered Versailles as a feeble peace, and they were persuaded that Germany would never willingly fulfill its terms. So it was France's duty to enforce them with the utmost rigor. Millerand, massive and ruthless, was thinking in terms of plain coercion; Poincaré, no less unbending, was more of a stickler for legal procedure. Both were unimpeachable patriots; and within its narrow range their vision was singularly clear.

A vigorous hand was needed all the more because France felt strangely isolated. America had withdrawn from European, from world, affairs. In 1892 France had sought security in an ill-assorted alliance with Tsarist Russia: by 1917 that great counterweight to German power had disappeared. Not only was Russia defeated and in utter chaos, but, as the French saw it, she had deserted her allies. The Bolsheviki were hated as traitors to the common cause and as secret agents of Germany even more than they were dreaded as revolutionists: Clemenceau blocked Wilson's efforts to be fair to the new regime. The Soviet world was now both a void and a peril. The *Bloc National* supported all the White military adventurers, and particularly General Wrangel;

but they all failed. Italy was a broken reed: that country chose to consider herself, even in the middle of the peace conference, as an injured party rather than as a victor. The worst disappointment came from England. Both Britain and France had been loyal to the *Entente Cordiale,* and through the darkest hours they had fought bravely side by side. But the British obscurely resented the greater military prestige of France, the primacy of Marshal Foch, the selection of Paris for the pageant of triumph. Several hundred years of rivalry cannot be effaced in a single generation. England was constantly tempted to relapse into "splendid isolation." Influenced by the Dominions and the United States, she would not make herself responsible for peace and order on the distracted Continent; but neither would she allow France to assume the sole responsibility. So she reverted to the old balance of power, and the ancient Roman rule, *Parcere subjectis et debellare superbos,* to spare the conquered and humble the proud.

Thus, in Churchillian phrase, France was left alone "to lick her wounds and mourn for her dead." She felt both defrauded and maligned. The "Soldier of the Ideal," as Clemenceau had called her on Armistice Day, was degraded by open foes and alleged friends into a vindictive and rapacious bully. England and America, no less than Germany, needed to believe that France was wrong: it was their best alibi for having turned their backs upon the Wilsonian ideal. A ubiquitous and spontaneous campaign was started to prove that the great "Crusade for Democracy" had been altogether a fraud, that Versailles was not a judgment but a crime. Reputable historians propounded that paradoxical thesis. Oswald Garrison Villard, a true liberal, was to brand France as "the enemy of mankind." This was called "revisionism." Its influence was profound. It made Franco-German reconciliation more difficult. It implied the doom of German democracy: if the Imperial Government was blameless, then the revolution was indeed a "stab in the back," and Hitler was the heaven-sent avenger. Ultimately, it broke down the morale of the French themselves: they sought to appease Hitler because their conscience had grown uneasy.

Such was the situation that Millerand and Poincaré had to face. It was manifest from the first that Germany would pursue a policy of evasion. The trial of the men accused of breaking international law and committing atrocities was the merest farce. For a while an Allied Commission saw to it that the disarmament clauses were technically carried out; but the desire to rearm never disappeared, and the Weimar Republic, with its "pocket battleships," for instance, prepared the way for the bolder defiance of the Nazis. Reparations created an immediate conflict. The question was finally buried but never settled. In the meantime it had embittered Germany against her victors, and the victors among themselves.

Financial problems are tangled enough; when they are complicated by politics, sentiments, and morality, they become inextricable. It must be noted that these "reparations," true to their name, were never intended as punitive fines, like the war indemnity of 1871. Their sole purpose was to compensate for damage done; the main argument in their support was not victory but justice. That France instead of Germany had become a battlefield was due to the sudden and treacherous attack through neutral Belgium. Moreover, destruction had deliberately gone beyond military necessity: the avowed aim of the Germans was to cripple France for a generation. A "White Peace" without indemnities would therefore have implied a tremendous punishment for the victim and a great premium paid to aggression. The Germans themselves, before the armistice, had recognized the justice of compensation to France and Belgium on a scale which dwarfed the billion-dollar indemnity of 1871.

This plain issue was obscured by three factors. In the first place reparations appeared a consequence of the "Guilt Clause"; and this clause, dictated under the threat of starvation, was rejected by the Germans as not morally binding. In the second place the Allies went beyond strict reparations. It would have been to the interest of France that indemnities be limited to actual damages, for she had suffered most. When the cost of war pensions was added, on the suggestion of Lloyd George and to the apparent advantage of England, an element of unreality entered into the computation. The total was not so much astronomical as fantastic. No one could figure out the obligation, nor how long it would take to pay it off. In the third place even if Germany had been willing and able to pay, the transfer of wealth on such a scale created insuperable difficulties. This had been foreseen by Norman Angell just before the war, and by Maynard Keynes immediately after the peace. No payment in cash was possible unless Germany built up a favorable balance of trade, and this would have implied for German industry an unprecedented supremacy which the victors dreaded even more than default. The destruction might have been repaired exclusively with German materials and German labor. But the tender-hearted would have denounced this as a combination of looting and penal servitude. Anyway, this method did not appeal to the French. Reconstruction offered opportunities for juicy contracts, which shrewd businessmen desired to keep for themselves. Above all the population of the devastated regions was anxious to clear the very last German out of the country. So reparations in kind, in spite of the realistic

Loucheur-Rathenau Agreement, were kept down to a minimum. The man in the street did not realize these difficulties. Just as President Coolidge is reported to have said, "They hired the money, didn't they?" the average French voter could only repeat, "They did the damage, didn't they? The cost will have to come out of somebody's pocket; why should it be out of the pocket of the victim?"

The Allies thrashed that elusive problem in a series of conferences which, in retrospect, seem equally futile: Spa in 1920, Paris and London in 1921, London again in 1922. Lord Balfour suggested that war debts and reparations should both be canceled. This proposal, generous and wise from the British point of view, found little favor either in France or in America. France had been decimated and devastated as England had not: simply wiping the slate clean seemed to her a little less than fair. America was a creditor not a debtor; there would be no compensation whatever for the sacrifice demanded of her, except the general welfare of the world. But in those years the general welfare did not appeal to American minds: the country had washed her hands of Wilsonian idealism and declared that her only business was Business.

Diplomacy had failed. Those elements in France who considered Versailles as too lenient urged that at least the full letter of the law be enforced. Already in March, 1921, on a technical default of German deliveries, the French had occupied Düsseldorf, Ruhrort, and Duisburg. It helped them very little. In January, 1922, Poincaré returned to power. He struggled with the problem for a whole year. In December, 1922, Germany was again declared in default by the Reparations Commission. In January, 1923, French and Belgian troops occupied the industrial heart of the Reich, the Ruhr basin. It must be remembered that at that time France, already in control of the Saar, was attempting to secure the whole of Upper Silesia for her ally Poland: industrial Germany would thus have been reduced to impotence.

This "invasion" of the Ruhr could not be opposed by the force of arms; neither was it accepted as a legitimate argument. Passive resistance was organized with fanatical fervor and scientific efficiency. Yet it proved futile: the French, after some fumbling, did actually take hold of the huge industrial machine. By September 26 the German government had to acknowledge defeat: passive resistance ceased. The ordeal completely wrecked the frail edifice of German finance: the mark disappeared altogether in a vertiginous inflation.

Poincaré had won his suit; but at what cost! Between 1914 and 1918 German hatred had been directed against England not against France; in 1923 many Germans, not yet conscious Nazis, swore the destruction of the *Erbfeind*, the hereditary foe. The rift in the *Entente*

Cordiale grew deeper: England had formally protested against Poincaré's action. American opinion became definitely hostile. It does not invariably pay to get tough.

Sobered by his Pyrrhic triumph, Poincaré was willing to accept the advice of neutral experts. On April 9, 1924, the plan of the commission headed by General Charles Dawes was presented and was almost immediately accepted by Germany; in August it was ratified by an international conference held in London. It introduced a semblance of reality into the confused shadows of the reparations problem. The scheme started working and went on working as long as America kept priming the leaky pump with fresh loans.

THE LEFTIST COALITION. POINCARÉ TO THE RESCUE OF THE FRANC

The French masses were not so stubborn as their leaders: Poincaré's technical victory caused no elation. In the general elections of 1924 the voters turned definitely away from the *Bloc National.* The Leftist coalition, or *Cartel des Gauches,* came into power; it was led by Edouard Herriot, Paul Painlevé, Aristide Briand. President Millerand, instead of observing the neutrality of a constitutional sovereign, had thrown his whole influence on the side of Poincaré: he had to pay the penalty of defeat. No minister who could command a majority in the Chamber consented to serve under him; and the premier he picked out was brushed aside at the first encounter. Before this parliamentary strike, Millerand was compelled to resign; and his shaggy frown was replaced at the Elysée by the innocuous southern smile of Gaston Doumergue.

As a result of this change in French policy, the international situation rapidly improved. On October 28, 1924, full *de jure* recognition was accorded to Soviet Russia. The Ruhr was evacuated. This gesture of conciliation facilitated the conferences held at Locarno between Aristide Briand and Gustav Stresemann (October, 1925). These in their turn led to a series of treaties signed on December 1. A new spirit, the "Spirit of Locarno," had prevailed. France had shown herself capable of rising above victory, and Germany above defeat. Germany had won her point: she had achieved *Gleichberechtigung,* equality of status. Locarno was no *Diktat.* France also was satisfied: in fact if not in theory Locarno superseded Versailles, but it also confirmed its essential terms.

For three hopeful years every sign pointed to reconciliation, cooperation, and peace. Germany in 1926 was admitted into the League of Nations with a permanent seat in the Council, and Briand was her sponsor. The Inter-Allied Commission of Military Control in Germany was wound up. Service in the French army was reduced to one year (1928). Steps were taken toward a full Disarmament Conference (1926–1930). War was outlawed as an instrument of national policy (Pact of Paris, or Kellogg-Briand Pact, August 27, 1928). A substitute for the Dawes Plan, the (Owen D.) Young Plan for reparations, seemed to provide a workable settlement (July, 1929). Briand proposed a European Federal Union (September, 1929), and the left bank of the Rhine was evacuated five years ahead of schedule. In spite of an inveterate legend no major treaty was revised so soon and so generously as Versailles. It looked as though, within a brief decade, the sting had been removed from the bitterest conflict in history: the feud between the North and the South in America took much longer to die away. But for the economic depression which started in Wall Street in October, 1929, Europe would have succeeded in putting her house in order. It must be remembered that in 1923 the Nazis were a laughing stock in Germany and, as late as 1928, barely a nuisance.

The uncertainties of the international situation had their effect on French finances. Even before the treaties of peace were signed, the country was hard at work, more fully employed than ever before; but the state found it impossible to make ends meet. With her richest industrial regions in the hands of the enemy France had not been able to follow England's example and to pay during the war an appreciable portion of the staggering cost. The gap had to be filled with advances from England and America. The spirit was then that of "lend-lease" for the common cause, but the letter was a strict commercial obligation. The spirit died, and the letter remained. Men like Klotz, Clemenceau's minister of finances, could dismiss the nightmare with a flourish: "The Boches will pay!" At the time of the Ruhr occupation the flimsiness of that hope was revealed. There no longer was an inter-Allied financial front; while humbling the enemy, Poincaré had made it all the more difficult for him to settle his huge indebtedness to France. So, at the very moment when Poincaré seemed to triumph, the franc began to tumble.

On the diplomatic plane the situation was relieved by the *Cartel des Gauches,* but on the financial front it grew worse. Not that the new leader, Edouard Herriot, was an impractical dreamer: as mayor of Lyons he had proved himself a capable administrator. But, a *petit bourgeois* Radical, strongly attached to classical economic doctrine, he was averse to any revolutionary measure, such as a drastic levy on capital. Even if he had toyed with such a thought, his own party, especially in the Senate, would have refused to follow him. The Radicals, since 1900, had become a middle-road or moderate party: they failed not through radicalism but through timidity. Herriot's feeble efforts were stopped dead by *le mur d'argent,* the breastwork of moneybags. As soon as it was feared that the cabinet might try to get money from those who had it, there was a most unpatriotic "flight from the franc." Capital deserted without qualms and sought safety in London and in New York. In this age of alleged nationalism the Socialists are not the only ones to be internationally minded.

As a last resort Joseph Caillaux was twice called to the rescue. He was a trained financier, had repeatedly held the portfolio of finances in the last quarter of a century, and, among his unbusinesslike colleagues, had a reputation for wizardry. He had been under a cloud for his "defeatism," but had been exonerated, like Malvy, after Clemenceau's retirement. But his magic was of no avail. The franc was sinking fast.

The defense of the franc called for a Cabinet of National Union, like Waldeck-Rousseau's Ministry of Republican Defense, or Viviani's Ministry of National Defense. All party leaders—no less than six former premiers—united in preventing the franc from vanishing altogether, like the mark and the ruble. Poincaré was summoned to restore the franc that his "treat 'em rough" policy had imperiled. His patriotism, his integrity, his technical ability and experience were unchallenged. The Left had full confidence in his republicanism, the Right in his conservatism. Poincaré did not use his return to power to resume his bluster in the foreign field: Aristide Briand, the consummate conciliator, remained at the Quai d'Orsay. Without drastic medicine the decline of the franc stopped, and the patient even recovered some strength. The elections of April 22–29, 1928, approved of Poincaré's economic methods. So, on June 24, 1928, the franc was finally stabilized at just under four cents, roughly one-fifth of its prewar value.

This registered a quiet but profound revolution, perhaps the most thoroughgoing since 1789. The conservative lower middle class, the modest and cautious bondholders, long praised as the "backbone of the country," found themselves impoverished. With their power in French society waned certain unamiable but solid virtues: rigid honesty, a strong respect for the Code, and above all, unimaginative thrift. There was now a class of *nouveaux pauvres,* bewildered and resentful, who had lost faith in the regime. This affected the vast body of state officials. For generations many bourgeois had accepted positions under the state because of the prestige and security attached to them; the inadequate pay was supplemented by a private income. Now the bourgeois no longer cared, nor could they afford, to serve the government under such terms. Many observers have noted, since that time, a marked decline in the traditional qualities of the French bureaucracy.

The Poincaré administration, reorganized in November, 1928, remained in power until July, 1929—an unusual case of longevity among French cabinets. Poincaré had to retire because of his health and never returned to active politics. Respected not beloved, he was a curious example of intelligence without vision and character without generosity: an Adolphe Thiers with greater integrity but less vivacity.

The *petit bourgeois* regime, shaken but not completely shattered, could find some comfort in the thought that the cruel but inevitable sacrifice had been performed by a perfect exemplar of the bourgeois virtues. This completed, in the financial sector, the liquidation of the Great War. France could start again, sobered yet not dismayed. Like the Locarno Treaties, like the Dawes and Young Plans, the Poincaré franc was a realistic solution, disenchanted, plodding, close to earth; but it was not an admission of defeat. France and Europe in 1929 were convalescent. Had circumstances remained normal, this gradual improvement might have led to complete recovery. But the health of the stricken Continent, especially that of Germany, was still precarious and could not stand another shock. The shock came from America in October, 1929; and its immediate result was the rise of Hitler.

A CREDITABLE ACHIEVEMENT: RECONSTRUCTION

Clio, a romantic muse, gloats over disaster and spurns quiet progress. The healthiest part of a nation's life is usually ignored by historians. The decade of reconstruction after the Great War was by no means wasted. If there was frustration on the political plane and embarrassment on the financial, the economic life of the country was none the less booming, and so was the cultural. Compared with the periods that preceded and followed, it was an era of good feeling. There was at least an afterglow of the Sacred Union. The army, held in distrust since the Dreyfus Case, was genuinely popular again. Conservatives like Marshal Foch and Marshal Lyautey had become truly national figures. General Gouraud, the one-armed hero of Morocco and the Dardanelles, the colorful and beloved military governor of Paris, shook hands in public with Malvy and Caillaux. Even Charles Maurras, the vigorous hater, could write in the past tense, "When the French did not love one another," *Quand les Francais ne s'aimaient pas,* and spoke with respect of Anatole France. Romain Rolland alone was excluded from this communion for having attempted to remain "above the strife." He was accused of "speaking Swiss with a strong Esperanto accent."

One of the excellent effects of this reconciliation between the various spiritual families in France was the resumption of diplomatic relations with the Vatican (1921). This, as we shall see, had been made inevitable by the recovery of Alsace-Lorraine. A *modus vivendi* was then evolved between Church and State; the Associations for Public Worship which, on a parochial basis, had been rejected by Pius X, were accepted on a diocesan basis by Pius XI (1924).

France had appeared magnificently victorious on November 11, 1918. But her wounds were deep. She had lost 1,600,000 of her sons: in proportion to the population this would have meant five million American dead, one-fourth more than the total number of our mobilized forces. Her most prosperous regions had been occupied and looted for over four years; her best mines, in the North, had been destroyed with fiendish efficiency. The task for a wounded nation was appalling, and France received very little assistance from Germany either in cash or in materials. Yet the reconstruction of the devastated regions was completed in less than seven years, and on a generous scale.

To offset the loss of her coal mines, France had at her disposal, for fifteen years, the Saar basin, natural complement of Lorraine. The lack of manpower was made up by an influx of foreign workers, Belgians, Italians, Kabyles from North Africa (known as *Sidis,* and not great favorites with the population), even a few Chinamen, and Poles by hundreds of thousands. Between the two world wars France received more immigrants than America. Until 1930 they were attracted by the prosperity of the country; from 1919, but especially after 1933, France was flooded with political refugees, White, Red, or colorless, fleeing persecution in Russia, Italy, or Germany.

It would be an outrageous paradox to say that the destruction wrought by the Germans was a blessing in disguise. But it is a fact that France was much better off industrially in 1929 than in 1914. Under the Third Republic the French had been slow about modernizing their obsolete equipment: the Germans accomplished for them the overdue scrapping. For the first time since the Second Empire France was again abreast of modern developments. Wartime industries had been created, particularly in the Parisian region. They survived and were converted to peace activities: Citroën turned from armaments to automobile production. The newly recovered ore of Lorraine enabled France to produce at one time more pig iron than England and nearly as much steel. There were ample deposits of bauxite for the making of aluminum. Hydroelectric power, poetically called "white coal," compensated to some extent for the dearth of "black coal." The mountain streams of the Pyrenees and Auvergne were harnessed; great projects were started on the Rhône and the Rhine. Grenoble, a center for tourists, foreign students, and glove manufacturers, became industrial without losing its historical charm. Many ports, among them Le Verdon (an annex of Bordeaux), La Pallice, Saint-Nazaire, Cherbourg, Le Hâvre, Marseilles, were extended and thoroughly modernized.

The change was particularly noticeable, and not altogether fortunate, in Paris. A huge, sprawling, and at times ominous belt of factories and mushroom suburbs surrounded the capital. The Parisian region, on a smaller area than the city of Chicago, numbered well over five million inhabitants. Not merely the delicate masterpieces of the luxury crafts but automobiles and locomotives became *articles de Paris.* So did communism, encircling the City of Light with a menacing ring and conquering the sympathy, if not the full allegiance, of men like Anatole France, André Gide, Romain Rolland, Henri Barbusse, André Malraux.

But the new heavy industry did not obscure the ancient fame of the city. Paris fully regained its primacy as a world capital of pleasure and elegance, of art and learning. It was for a decade the universal Mecca of tourists and the literary capital of the Americas. The Exposition of Decorative Arts in 1925 was not so oppressive as the World Fair of 1900 and revealed a much healthier artistic temper. The University recovered its medieval glory as "the second light of the world": many learned institutes clustered round the old Sorbonne, and many nations erected residential halls in the new University City near Parc Montsouris.

A literary generation was passing away: France, Bourget, Barrès, Loti. Rolland was in spiritual exile, no longer a Frenchman, not fully attaining the stature of a world citizen. Rostand died without repeating the miraculous success of his *Cyrano de Bergerac* two decades before. But it was only after the war that Marcel Proust was to be revealed, a unique blend of traditional and ultramodern psychology. André Gide, long an esoteric writer, was imposing himself as the most definite apostle of uncertainty and the most assured of guides nowhither. All his works might be entitled *Le voyage d'Urien,* The Voyage of Nobody into Nothing. Paul Valéry broke the silence of twenty years and at one stride reached the summit, as the most tantalizingly lucid of cryptic poets. Paul Claudel conquered an audience at last for his symbolical dramas and his great religious odes. François Mauriac, André Maurois, Jules Romains, Georges Duhamel, Jean Giraudoux, Roger Martin Du Gard, Valéry Larbaud attained their full stature. Even Paul Morand, diplomat and globe-trotter, in spite of his incurable levity opened new horizons. If music halls and night clubs effaced for the first time the gaudiest memories of the Second Empire, never had the Parisian public, native and cosmopolitan alike, shown such an appetite for lectures, even of the most austere type. The venerable Collège de France itself became the rendezvous of fashion: society ladies sent their valets ahead to secure seats in the courses of Professor Henri Bergson.

THE REINTEGRATION OF ALSACE-LORRAINE

What did France secure by the Treaty of Versailles? Reparations which proved delusive and were offset by crushing war debts at home and abroad. African mandates—a slice of Togoland, the bulk of Cameroon, which France administered honestly and successfully but which brought her very scant political or economic advantages. Mandates in the Levant, Syria, and Lebanon which were to be a constant source of expense and worry. The one clear gain to show for the enormous sacrifice was the return of Alsace-Lorraine. The mourning draperies were at last removed from the statue of Strasbourg on the Place de la Concorde, and every Frenchman breathed a freer air.

From the moral point of view, the Alsace-Lorraine question was settled beyond dispute: no province ever affirmed more decisively its determination to remain French. The protest of her deputies in 1871, both at Bordeaux and in Berlin, had never been forgotten; and forty-seven years later, the French troops were received at Strasbourg and Metz with an enthusiasm which astounded American observers. Germany had acquiesced in advance in this inevitable *revanche* of international justice; and even Hitler, in a number of speeches, was to forswear every claim to the former Reichsland. But there were many problems of readjustment, of an economic, linguistic, and religious nature.

It was feared that Alsace-Lorraine would suffer a material loss by the change. The trade currents of forty-seven years would have to find new channels. Besides, Imperial Germany had been more daring in the economic field than Republican France. These misgivings proved unfounded. The transition from the German to the French economy was managed with great efficiency. Marks were exchanged for francs at a generous rate. The potash mines were exploited with greater energy than under German management; a great hydroelectric power plant was constructed at Kembs on the Rhine; the canals were modernized; the port of Strasbourg was extended; the foundations of the marvelous cathedral spire were consolidated with impressive skill. The university with a faculty drawn from the very best scholars and scientists in France, many of them of Alsatian origin, assumed a place second to none among provincial centers of learning.

The language problem was complex. In Lorraine the division was geographical: the greater part of the province, including Metz, spoke

French; a small northeastern fringe spoke German. In Alsace the division was mainly social: the upper classes spoke French, the masses clung to the local dialect, very different from standard High German. When the French returned, they did not prohibit the use either of Alsatian or of German. Sermons and plays in the language of Luther and Goethe could be freely heard in French Strasbourg. All officials who had direct contact with the population had to be bilingual. The Alsatians did not question the necessity of their learning the national language if they wanted to call themselves French; the debate was entirely on a question of method and tempo. Those Alsatians who were adults in 1919 were to some extent a sacrificed generation. To learn French was not easy for them, although most of them did not shirk the effort. Not to know French placed them in a position of inferiority; they were made to feel strangers or second-class citizens in their own land. The well-educated, however, already knew French, and the younger generation took to it with alacrity. Even the strong Alsatian accent, derided by Molière and Balzac, practically disappeared. Before the outbreak of World War II the worst of this problem was over.

The religious problem was harder to solve. Alsace-Lorraine still lived under the laws of the Second Empire: Church and State were still united through the Concordat of 1801, and the public schools were still under denominational control, Catholic, Protestant, or Jewish. The French government was only too glad to preserve in Alsace-Lorraine the Concordat which France had denounced in 1905: it made it possible to eliminate, or at least to hold in check, any cleric suspected of pro-German activities. The regime of the schools remained unchanged. But the Alsatians realized that it was an anomaly, and under a constant threat. It was an article of faith with the French Republicans that all state education should be secular. The Alsatian Conservatives—and there were many in all three religions—were chiefly afraid of the Radicals in their own midst: already the city of Strasbourg had voted to secularize its school system. On entering Alsace in 1914 General Joffre had promised that the customs and institutions of the province would be respected. That promise was interpreted by the Home Rulers or Autonomists as freezing the conditions that prevailed in 1914 and preventing any possibility of change, even though it should originate in Alsace itself.

When the *Cartel des Gauches* came into power, the problem grew more acute. The Autonomist movement assumed at times an unpleasant aspect. The loyalty of the Alsatian masses was unquestioned, but there were dubious elements among the leaders of the *Heimatbund* (Home Rule Union). Never did they dare to express a desire for a return to

Germany; but the Germans, naturally enough, "muscled in." So did the Communists and the ultramontanes, oddly associated. While the common people were thinking first of all in terms of Strasbourg, there were influences at work that came from Berlin, Rome, and Moscow. Four Autonomist leaders were condemned at Colmar in 1928; at the close of the trial, they cried, *Vive la France!* and were promptly pardoned, but this emotional reconciliation was not fully convincing. However, the problem was gradually losing its sting. An ever-increasing number of Alsatians were found in the army, in the colonies, in the national administrations throughout France. It is to be hoped that greater autonomy will be granted not to Alsace alone but to all the other regions. Strasbourg, the focal point of a Europe united at last, is now resuming its glorious destiny as a bridge between two great cultures.[3]

⚑ LYAUTEY IN MOROCCO

This decade of reconstruction was also marked by rapid progress in greater France beyond the seas. During the war the empire [4] had provided soldiers, laborers, raw materials. Ten years later, it was to cushion for a while the great depression. Without Mussolinian bluster the French had fine achievements to their credit. The Trans-Indochinese Railway was completed, also the sixteen-hundred-mile, standard-gauge line from Tunis to Marrakech. The celebration of Algeria's centennial in 1930 found that colorful "New France" booming; the colonial exposition at Marseilles and especially the one at Vincennes (1931) were a revelation.

All was not for the best in the best of empires. There were two Cinderellas: Guiana, handicapped by its torrid, malarial climate, burdened also with the incubus of a penal settlement, and Equatorial Africa, which, as we have seen, had copied the methods of Leopold II in the Congo Free State at the very moment when they were condemned by world opinion. The railroad from Brazzaville to Pointe-Noire proved costly in money and lives, and André Gide brought from the Congo a tragic and scathing indictment. The other colonies, on the whole, did well. An estimate of the French Union will be attempted in our last chapter. Only Morocco and Syria made history during the decade we are now considering.

Until the twentieth century Morocco, at the gate of western Europe, had remained a fragment of the Near East and a relic of the Middle Ages. It was at the same time lovely, barbaric, and decadent. The sultan's rule was sporadic as well as capricious. It extended only as far as he could send a foray to gather tribute, and this was known as *Bled el Maghzen;* when his raiders had retired, the country they had pillaged reverted to its status as *Bled el Siba,* the land of dissent or rebellion. This picturesque anarchy was perpetuated by the jealousy of the European powers. We have seen that a series of agreements, with England (April, 1904), with Spain (October, 1904), and, most laborious of all, with Germany (1906–1911), had finally assured France a free hand in Morocco. In 1912 the sultan had to accept the protection of France, and General Lyautey was appointed resident general.

When World War I broke out, the tribes were in open revolt against the sultan, and the sultan was a none-too-willing associate of France. It was taken for granted that the French would at best be able to hold a few coast towns, and Lyautey received instructions to that effect. On the contrary, he managed to increase the sphere of French influence while sending fine divisions to fight on the European front. It was a miracle of military and diplomatic skill which included a daring element of bluff. When world peace was restored, the pacification and development of Morocco could start in good earnest.

Lyautey brought to perfection the methods he had learned from Galliéni in Indochina and Madagascar. His first principle was gradualness. Bazaine had "conquered" the whole of Mexico for Maximilian in a couple of years: the work of bringing order to the whole of Morocco was not completed until 1932, seven years after Lyautey's retirement. Only the vital parts of the country were organized at once: the hill tribes could wait in their medieval fastnesses. Many of them were won by treaties with their feudal chiefs.

Lyautey's second principle was a sincere and effective use of the protectorate. The French did not reduce the sultan to a shadow: they actually strengthened his hands. Lyautey, an aristocrat, a soldier, and a believer, had profound affinities with the Moroccan ruling class: perhaps he preferred them to the agnostics and civilians who prated in Paris. He dealt with the feudal lords, the caids in their mountain kasbahs, or the omnipotent pasha of Marrakech, El Glaoui, as though he were one of themselves, the lieutenant of their legitimate overlord. He protected the mosques from the sacrilegious curiosity of the tourists; and though he let into Morocco a swarm of promoters who were frankly profiteers, he saw to it that they did not grab the property of the natives. He gave the old Moorish towns improved police and sanitation but otherwise left them untouched in their teeming picturesqueness. The new French cities were built at some distance so that the native quarters did not turn into slums like the deceptive white Kasbah of Algiers. He revived Moorish pride, Moorish industry, Moorish art. He wanted to be known not as the conqueror but as the restorer of Morocco. His tomb at Rabat is in Moorish style and watched over by the sultan's native bodyguard.

On the other hand, he favored European enterprise wherever it could achieve what the Moors had left undone. Fine cities were built under the direction of Prost and his brilliant team: Casablanca, Oudjda, Kenitra (Port-Lyautey), Meknes, Fez, Fedhala, Marrakech. In particular, the capital, Rabat, rich in ancient monuments, became a charming blend of modernism and local tradition. A French-Moroccan style was evolved, daring and delicate, which had its origins in both lands but was not a pastiche of either.

Lyautey's mind covered the span from Rome and the Middle Ages to the twentieth century. The new economic equipment of Morocco was generously planned and strictly up to the minute. Standard-gauge electric railways, perfect roads even in the Atlas Mountains, well-equipped ports, particularly Casablanca, the rich phosphate mines exploited by a state-controlled but autonomous office, a strong national bank: these turned medieval Morocco, in little more than a decade, into a prosperous and progressive country. For once, modern civilization did not generate ugliness and squalor. Economic equality for all nations was strictly respected: the Moroccan market was flooded with incredibly cheap Japanese goods. If France secured a lion's share of Morocco's commerce, it was in open competition, through initiative, hard work, and efficiency. This peaceful victory proved that the French were not necessarily timid and old-fashioned. Lyautey, of course, was a unique figure; but the magic transformation of the country was a collective achievement. The marshal—no *baton* was ever more amply deserved—knew how to pick his men, and the Republic had the sense to give this Royalist soldier a free hand.

Yet that magnificent career ended under a cloud. Lyautey had not fully foreseen the victory of Abd el-Krim in Spanish Morocco. The Riffian chieftain had inflicted a disaster on the Spanish troops at Anuel (1921) and, within the next three years, compelled them to abandon the interior. In April, 1925, he attacked the French: it was feared that even Fez might be threatened. On September 24 Lyautey resigned: he landed in France without any official welcome. An army of 150,000 men had to be gathered; it was guided, although not officially commanded, by Marshal Pétain. The combined French and Spanish forces defeated the Riffians, and on May 26, 1926, Abd el-Krim surrendered. Lyautey had his *revanche* when, at seventy-seven, he superbly organized the colonial exposition at Vincennes. This great demonstration of the empire's vitality was the only fair on record to be ready on time and to wind up with a profit.

Lyautey, the medieval knight, was a convinced and thorough advertiser. He invited foreign delegations and entertained them royally. He encouraged the steamship companies to create luxury hotels. It was excellent business and even better politics. The French have learned to love Morocco, a land even more picturesque and more richly contrasted than Mexico itself. After leaving Rabat, Meknes, or Fez, the traveler is apt to find Bordeaux, a city of great dignity and charm, just a trifle dingy and antiquated.

THE UNEASY SYRIAN MANDATE

The mandates created by the Treaty of Sèvres were the Arab lands liberated from the Turks. With an old and refined civilization of their own, they were not intended to remain under tutelage: they were to be trained as rapidly as possible for complete independence. The mandate period was to be merely the liquidation of Turkish misrule. But the Arabs had not understood, when they rebelled against the Ottoman Empire, that they would be subjected to this probationary stage. They resented being treated worse than the Turks, who, within their shrunken frontiers, were free from foreign control. They felt betrayed; and their best friend, Colonel Lawrence, shared that feeling.

The question was complicated by the rivalry of England and France. France claimed Syria as her share—and Syria at that time was supposed to include Palestine—on the strength of a tradition which went back to the crusades and had been kept up by Francis I and Napoleon III. French was the second language of the country, and many enterprises, like the Joppa-Jerusalem Railroad, were in French hands. It does not appear that French diplomacy, which thinks in terms of history rather than economics, had given much attention to the Mosul oil fields.

England strongly desired to keep France away from the Suez Canal, then a vital link in the defense of the empire. Moreover, if in Syria the Catholic Church was associated with the French tradition, the Protestant missions, English and American, were the rallying points of the anti-French elements.

Emir Faisal, with the tacit support of England, established himself as king of Syria and was driven out by the French (1920). A division was effected which took into account the natural differences in the country: Lebanon, Aleppo, Damascus, Alawites, Djebel Druse. Rational as it was, it savored too much of *Divide et impera* and was intensely resented by the Syrian Nationalists, eager to impose unity in the name of independence and even at the cost of freedom. The whole Near East was then in ferment: Greeks against Turks in Anatolia, Arabs against Jews in Palestine, and Egyptians against British rule.

General Gouraud and after him General Weygand as high commissioners restored a semblance of order. It was jeopardized again in 1925 under the unlucky Sarrail, whose command at Salonica had been such a disappointment. Known as a republican and a freethinker, he was sent to Syria by the *Cartel des Gauches,* anxious that France should not be committed to a "clerical" policy. Yet it was under Sarrail that the Druses rebelled, charging that the protecting power was unduly favoring the Christians. Damascus rose in its turn and had to be recaptured by ruthless methods.

Civilian commissioners did their best to patch up the quarrel. Their efforts led to a treaty, signed in 1933, which followed the pattern of the Anglo-Iraqi agreement. We shall take up later the tragic events which brought the mandates to an end. But it was evident by 1939 that the Syrian enterprise was a political failure. It was partly redeemed by a creditable road-building and educational program, which, however, could not compare with the spectacular achievements in Morocco. For all this fumbling, individuals cannot be absolved; neither should they be made scapegoats. The initial disappointment of the Arabs, the cross-purposes of the great powers, the secret yet evident influence of oil interests, the rivalry of the Christian churches, the determination of the Syrian Nationalists to crush minorities were such handicaps that success would have been a miracle. The use of force nearly ruined an ancient and mutually profitable friendship. Syria had never been quite a foreign land to the French, and many among the Syrian elite had found in France their second spiritual home.

CHAPTER XXVI

The Anxious Truce: 1918-1939: The Darkening Sky, 1929-1939

✎ FUMBLING IN THE DARK

We interpret the decade 1919–1929 as a period of recuperation, both material and moral. This was true of the whole Continent, but far truer of France than of Germany or England. When we bear in mind the extent of the devastation, the appalling loss of life, the resurgence of primitive violence and hatred which were the results of the war, the prompt recovery must be considered marvelous. Yet it was evident that, by 1929, this return to sanity was still precarious and exposed to a fatal relapse. Europe was not yet integrated enough to face the Russian problem courageously or to be independent of American support. When America fell into a severe depression and when Russia showed signs of returning vigor, Europe was struck with panic.

For the division which made Europe helpless, England must bear a heavy share of responsibility. The habit of "splendid isolation" is hard to cure: it takes unusual eyesight and very favorable circumstances to see the coast of France from the cliffs of Dover. As early as 1925 the British Tories, claiming the support of the Dominions, had rejected the Geneva Protocol, which, by defining aggression, would have enabled the nations to avert it. At Locarno Great Britain guaranteed the common frontiers of Germany, Belgium, and France, but declined any further commitments. She believed in semicollective, detachable security: "truth on the hither side of the Rhine, error beyond." Germany, although she had signed arbitration treaties with Poland and Czechoslovakia, would not agree to an eastern Locarno. The League was still a house of cards: France alone, a wounded nation, was left to guard the wounded peace. Fully realizing that *sacro egoismo* is suicidal, she assumed her responsibility and made treaties of mutual assistance with

Poland and Czechoslovakia. But any measure of defense is a sign of distrust: it was impossible to aid the lesser powers without seeming to challenge the potential—and potent—aggressor, Germany. As a result the Reich was haunted once more with the nightmare of encirclement; so long as this state of mind prevailed, it was difficult for peace to take root.

So, even in the Locarno era France was justifiably uneasy. Bled white in 1914–1918, she made up for the weakening of her active army by strengthening her eastern frontier: she started building the elaborate and costly Maginot Line, a poor substitute at best for the security England and America enjoyed. The attitude of the Weimar Republic was equivocal and indeed ominous. It was not reassuring that a military idol, Marshal Paul von Hindenburg, should have been elected President, although it was by a minority vote. The worst disappointment of all: after Stresemann's death, it was revealed that he had boasted to the former *Kronprinz* that, in his dealings with Briand, his system had been *finessieren.* The word might be interpreted as "subtle technique," which would be legitimate, for crude methods can never solve delicate problems. But it might also mean "deceit." The French had not forgotten the boasted Machiavellism of Frederick the Great nor the enormous trickiness in which Bismarck took such pride. This disappointment cost Briand the presidency of the Republic (1931); and the great Pilgrim of Peace, as he loved to call himself, died like Wilson a broken man (March 7, 1932).

The liquidation of World War I had been a wearisome series of compromises rather than a logical and triumphant process. Still, those compromises, although reluctantly accepted, appeared workable and indeed promising. France and Europe might reasonably hope that they were "muddling through somehow." The decade we have now reached was a rake's progress: a tale of squabbles, scandals, threats of upheaval, financial chaos, broken alliances, crushing and yet inadequate armaments. All these were the result of a divided purpose. France "muddled through" indeed, but into the abyss.

It would be easy but unprofitable to give in strict chronological sequence the details of this disheartening decline. They would remain bewildering to the reader, as they were to the actors themselves. They explain nothing: they are but the symptoms of a deep-seated disease.

The reasons generally adduced fail to account for this befogging of the sharp French mind and this collective paralysis of an energetic people. Both the constitution and the parliamentary personnel have been blamed. No doubt the hybrid instrument of 1875 was faulty. Meant for a limited monarchy rather than for a democratic republic, it provided no check against the omnipotence of the Chambers—the worst of tyrannies because it is the most irresponsible. Still, as we have seen, that constitution had weathered many storms: Boulanger and Panama, the Dreyfus Case and World War I. Whenever a definite crisis had to be faced, a coalition *ad hoc* could be formed to deal vigorously with the situation.

The whirligig of cabinets was evidently an evil. But the elements of stability in French political life should not be overlooked. The "new" ministers, as a rule, were old hands. Technically, Aristide Briand was eleven times at the head of affairs, Poincaré and Laval five times each, Chautemps four times. They did not have to learn the ropes. A "new" cabinet in most cases meant only a reshuffling of the familiar cards. When they were not in office, the political leaders kept in close touch with the affairs of the country, not merely as members of Parliament, but as heads of important commissions: it was because Clemenceau had led the Army Commission in the Senate that he was so well able to take hold of the War Office. It would not be paradoxical to compare the French parliamentary game with that marvel of efficiency, American football: two combinations on the same side, one offensive, the other defensive, succeeding each other in the field with many individual substitutions. The trouble was that the coach, French public opinion, was utterly befuddled.

Conditions were not so different as they seemed from those prevailing in English-speaking countries. Whenever there was a slight change of direction, inevitable in such troublous times, it was registered in France by a corresponding shift in personnel, in England and in America by a fresh inconsistency on the part of the men in power. In the twelve years of Franklin Roosevelt's incumbency there certainly were more than twelve such veerings and tackings. It is by no means certain that the policies of France between 1929 and 1939 were more ambiguous or less steady than our own. France consistently proclaimed her faith in collective security and was aware of the German peril while America sneered and pooh-poohed. When France fumbled, it was in order to conform with our own line. In addition it should never be forgotten that in France a strongly organized civil service, slow perhaps but permanent, well trained, and with a great respect for tradition, was carrying on efficiently enough, little concerned with the nominal heads of the departments.

The leaders were not appreciably worse than in the earlier stages of the Republic. No man reached the stature of a Gambetta, a Ferry, a Jaurès, or a Clemenceau; but it must be remembered that Gambetta held power for a few months only, that Jaurès never was actually in office, and that until he was sixty-five Clemenceau was known chiefly as a disruptive force. The Republic seemed to have done very well with men of smaller caliber. Louis Barthou, Edouard Herriot, Léon Blum, men of delicate culture, not unversed in practical affairs, and skilled in parliamentary strategy, would have been considered well above the average at any time and in any country. André Tardieu had intelligence and vigor unhampered by squeamishness; and Paul Reynaud, while he showed deplorable taste in the selection of his lady friends, did not lack foresight, intellectual daring, and administrative capacity. The sorriest representatives of the period were not—alas!—unprecedented. Camille Chautemps was probably no better and no worse than his father, whose career had been most honorable. If Pierre Laval rose during those years to equivocal eminence, he was hardly more disquieting than some of the great "realists" before him, such as Constans and Rouvier. No apology is offered for the manifest blemishes of the Third Republic. We simply want to observe that these flaws existed before 1929 and even before 1914. The causes of the downfall are not to be found in France alone, but in that bewilderment which France shared with Germany, England, and America. Germany fell first and worst because she was most sorely tried. England and especially America escaped the most tragic effects of the crisis, because they were materially secure.

The French common people and the *petite bourgeoisie* were genuinely attached to the Republic; the upper classes, *grand bourgeois* and aristocrats, were at least resigned to its existence. The Royalist *Action française,* as we have seen, attracted attention first of all because it was noisy. It was followed with some interest, in an extremely literary nation, because of the talent of its leaders, Charles Maurras, Léon Daudet, Jacques Bainville. It won a measure of approval because of its virulent denunciation of undeniable evils. But it had no constructive power. This was to be proved when, after July, 1940, under the Vichy regime, the *Action française* had an unimpeded field: the so-called National Revolution was unable to take any open step toward a royal restoration. The Republic seemed secure.

✼ SCHIZOPHRENIA OF THE MIDDLE CLASS

But for the bourgeois, great and small, the Republic was inseparable from private property. The "natural and inalienable rights of man" proclaimed in 1789 were "liberty, property, security, and resistance to oppression." The French Revolution was far more definite on that point than the American. If democracy were to challenge property, then the bourgeois would at least hesitate. To quote André Siegfried's pregnant phrase, "The heart of the French bourgeois is on the Left, but his pocket-book is on the Right."

To the traditional bourgeois order the Bolshevist Revolution was a deadly menace. At first the Bolsheviki [1] were righteously hated as traitors to the common cause: that was Clemenceau's excuse for sabotaging the Prinkipo conference proposed by Woodrow Wilson. But after the restoration of peace that excuse was no longer valid, and the hatred grew worse. It was not the violence of the Bolsheviki that roused indignation in the West: everyone knew that the Whites, wherever they had the upper hand, did not treat their foes in the purest spirit of Christian meekness. There had been revolutions before not free from terrorism and bloodshed. But the Soviets, by proclaiming socialism, were attacking the holy of holies. The issue was all the clearer because the French, encouraged by their government, had invested their savings in Tsarist bonds, which were at once repudiated by the new regime. This implacable opposition guided the policy of Clemenceau, Millerand, Poincaré. They applauded Noske when he put down the Spartakists, and Count Arco Valli when he shot Kurt Eisner, although these were the only Germans who fully admitted the guilt of Prussian militarism.

The violent period of bolshevism was not the worst from the conservative point of view; it could be met by aggressive countermeasures. If the White military leaders supported by Millerand failed in Russia itself, at any rate the Red tide had been stemmed in Bavaria, Hungary, Prussia; in Poland with the aid of Weygand, Foch's trusted lieutenant; in the Baltic countries and in Finland with the help of the Germans; it was soon to be halted in China also. But when Russia emerged staggering from foreign war and famine and started putting her enormous house in order, the "pluto-democracies" had cause for misgivings. The series of five-year plans, beginning October 1, 1928, was a more insidious threat than Trotsky's call to world revolution. Especially since the well-advertised beginnings of the plan coincided with the first symptoms of the American depression.

If we define the *bourgeoisie* as the class attached to private property, it includes in France a vast army of small shopkeepers and the deep masses of peasant proprietors. This means that it is overwhelmingly strong and should feel secure in a democracy. France might therefore have been expected to offer a solid front against the Communist peril. But many elements intervened to complicate the question. French industry, relatively quiescent during the first thirty years of the Republic, was expanding again, even before World War I. The industrial workers, although still a minority, were more aggressive and better organized

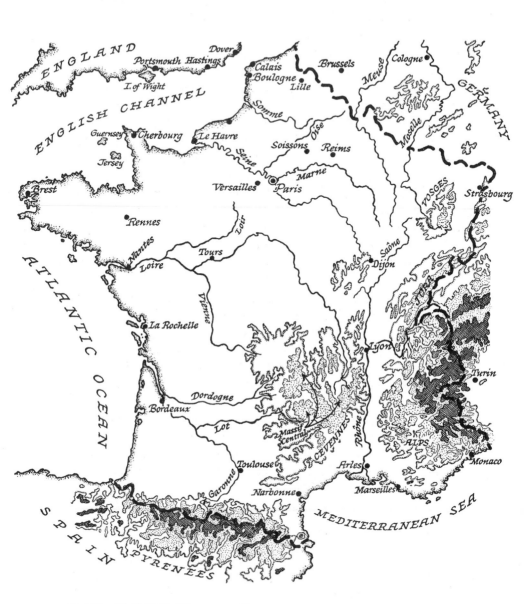

FRANCE — its Principal Rivers and Mountains

than the retailers and the peasants. Their strength was concentrated at strategic points. Then, if the rank and file of the believers in private property were attached to democratic institutions, their natural leaders were not: large landowners, financiers, industrialists were in the main extremely conservative, and even reactionary. The success of Mussolini seemed ominous to the French Republicans: they were not quite willing to save private property by sacrificing their political liberty. Finally, the growing menace of German nationalism confused both political and social issues: *primo vivere*. England was a most uncertain friend, America had chosen isolation, and the many smaller allies formed only a loose bundle of weaknesses. This compelled the French to look eastward again for possible support: the French kings had not scrupled to ally themselves with the Turks, with the German Protestants, with the regicide Cromwell. Thus a revival of the Franco-Russian alliance always remained a possibility: under Laval (May 2, 1935) it became a reality (as it did again under De Gaulle in December, 1944). Anticommunism could not be the supreme law.

There were still deeper sources of confusion. The bourgeois world was divided against itself. The *petite bourgeoisie* had always distrusted big business. As against the cartels, the trusts, the utility companies, the great department stores, the nationwide banking establishments, small shopkeepers and peasants had always been in favor of strict government regulation, and even of government control. Theoretically, their position was defensible: they were individualists first of all, and free enterprise on a large scale is inevitably collective.

On a higher plane, many intellectuals and many technicians were not averse to a new departure, for the bourgeois regime had grown stodgy. Not a few people of conservative tendencies were ready to accept a large measure of socialism. The profit motive, although it was as sedulously followed in France as anywhere else, had never become a national dogma. There was a long tradition that the service of the state (in the old days, the service of the prince) was somehow more honorable than private gain. In addition it seemed more secure; and by many Frenchmen property was considered not as an ideal in and for itself but only as a means of achieving security, the prime condition of liberty and dignity. Thus there were, within the bourgeois mind, several lines of cleavage. It was the law with certain "radicals" that they should have no enemies on the Left. But other "radicals" would add, "provided the extreme Left does not challenge the existing economic and social order." With French socialism, the tendency of Millerand, Viviani, Briand, Laval, a compromise was always possible. Its principles were acknowledged as ideally right, but the proper time for their realization had not yet arrived. The existence of a Communist state in Russia and of a Communist party in France raised the issue, *socialism now*. The "Radical-Socialists," who had hoped like Louis XV that the old machine would last their lifetime, felt exceedingly uncomfortable.

Hence, two phenomena which foreign observers often found puzzling. The Senate, the citadel of traditional radicalism, the great bulwark of the Republic, was also the irreconcilable enemy of socialism: it was the Senate which twice forced the retirement of Léon Blum. In the Chamber, cabinets, if they would survive at all, had to practice a policy of seesaw: in political issues they relied upon the support of the Left; in social and economic conflicts they called the Right to the rescue.

This duality in thought greatly hampered the evolution of French finances and their adaptation to a world radically different from the eighteenth century of Turgot and Adam Smith. It was impossible to restore unchecked *laissez-faire* capitalism, but any fiscal measure with the faintest collectivistic tinge was vetoed or at any rate sabotaged. The same men voted for the principle of an expensive social legislation and resented the taxes which such a policy entailed. The old monarchy was in constant straits, because it wanted to carry on a modern national government while its fiscal system was still partly feudal. The Republic likewise tried riding at the same time two horses, collectivism and economic individualism, which were proceeding at different speeds in different directions. The same hesitation affected foreign policies. Politically, France was compelled to renew the historic alliance with Russia against Germany. Socially, bourgeois France considered Germany as her shield against communism.

✍ THE DEPRESSION BEWILDERS THE FREE WORLD

In a healthy world it is possible for politics to be a constant series of illogical compromises: the home affairs of contemporary America would not fully satisfy René Descartes. When shooting the rapids, however, one must not drift but steer. In all countries during the decade that preceded World War I, the steering was hesitant. America, free from any foreign menace, could have led the way on a cautious and steady course. But America had abdicated leadership. Isolationism, a high tariff, curtailed immigration, laissez-faire economics were various ways of shutting tight our doors, our minds, and our hearts. Had the exasperating war-debt question been settled in a sensible spirit, had measures been taken for a fair exchange of goods and services, ailing Europe could have slowly recovered. Instead, America gave the world the financial crash of October, 1929.

The result was immediate: just under a year later, the German general elections returned to the Reichstag 107 Nazis, when in 1928 there were only twelve. It certainly was not the Versailles *Diktat* or the Ruhr invasion that caused the difference. The financial crisis hit Germany much harder than France. The economic machinery of the Reich was more powerful than that of the French Republic, but it was also more delicate. Soon there were as many as six million unemployed: it became an evil beyond traditional remedies. There settled over the country the aimless despair so well described by Hans Fallada in *Little Man, What Now?* In this crisis the politicians of the feeble Weimar regime fumbled helplessly. They tried to recoup their prestige by proposing an *Anschluss,* or customs union, with Austria (March 21, 1931). Economically, the scheme had nothing to recommend it: for Germany and Austria, suffering from exactly the same ills, were in no condition to help each other. Diplomatically, it created a conflict which Europe could not afford. It was considered by the French as another attempt to circumvent what little remained of the treaty system, sole basis of a legal and peaceful order on the Continent. The Versailles and Saint-Germain treaties had not precluded the union of the two countries: they had only stipulated that it should be submitted to all the signatories, since it interested the whole of Europe, and this the German and Austrian governments chose to ignore. The question was referred to the World Court, which sustained the French objection. But the episode affected Franco-German relations very unfavorably, and Franco-British relations also, for England had not concealed her sympathy with the German point of view. Ironically, the "liberation" of Austria from Nazi rule was to become one of the aims of the Allies in World War II.

The first public catastrophe occurred in the weakest of the European states, Austria: the *Credit Anstalt* collapsed in May, 1931, and a panic rocked the whole of Central Europe. England attempted to stop it by advancing a large sum to the Austrian National Bank. But by September the strongest financial power in Europe, and, for two centuries, in the world, was shaken in its turn: the Bank of England had to be supported by America and France and was forced off the gold standard. The Hoover moratorium was paralyzed by its timidity: President Hoover was unable to conquer the isolationist and anti-European prejudices of his own supporters. So his wise and generous measure was offered purely as a temporary expedient for one year only. Unrealistically, it refused to admit the connection between war debts and reparations; and it was not linked with any bold positive program such as a European *Zollverein,* or Common Market. It did nothing to cure the diseases which were undermining Europe, hopelessness and fear.

For two years France, with her well-balanced economy and her thriving empire, could stand the shock better than most of her neighbors. But she felt it at last. By their very caution the conservative methods which had cushioned the crisis were totally inadequate to bring recuperation. The orthodox economists could not see beyond "penitential measures": when in financial straits, reduce your expenditures. Anything bolder would have been a "New Deal," which the French bourgeois dreaded and hated even more than did his American counterpart. For a determined state initiative marks an undeniable socialistic trend; and in France, as well as everywhere in Europe, socialism was considered not as a mere theoretical menace but, thanks to the rising power of Russia, as an immediate peril.

France and Germany were thus fellow sufferers from the same conditions and should have sought a remedy in concert. But Germany was hit so hard, just as she had begun to hope, that, like Hamlet, she sought refuge in madness. When a convalescent organism is stricken with a new disease, its old troubles are apt to reappear. Germany had, like the rest of the bourgeois world, to face both the depression and the threat of bolshevism: Hitler chose to add to these very real difficulties his insane anti-Semitism and the angry ghost of Versailles. The Germans were saved from utter despair by being offered definite objects of hatred. Bewildered leader of the bewildered, Hitler was not clear in his own mind whether he wanted the humiliation of 1918 to be avenged or the promises of Wilson's Fourteen Points to be fulfilled. He professed to have no goal but independence and self-sufficiency, but he could not repress vague gigantic dreams of world empire. At one time he said that France must be utterly destroyed; at another, that Germany had no quarrel whatever with France and had given up any thought of recovering Alsace-Lorraine: all she wanted was to be treated as an equal by her sister nations. So he sang discordant tunes, but the one invariable refrain was the defense of Western culture against Russian barbarism.

It is only fair to say that there was at least as much confusion as duplicity in Hitler's thought. His was the inspiration of the demagogue: he would shout with the same passionate earnestness whatever brought a storm of applause from the multitude. He was no Bismarck, and even Bismarck was not so consistent a Machiavellian as he made himself out to be. But confusion and duplicity had the same effect: the French were thoroughly disconcerted. The prospect of reconciliation with Germany pleased the masses, profoundly attached to peace: it was sufficient to abjure Poincarism, and all would be well. The crusade call against communism found willing ears among the self-styled elite. So, the rise of Hitler did not create in France a spirit of united resistance. Not even in 1939; not even in 1940.

One statesman, at any rate, had a clear vision both of the danger and of the available means of defense: it was Jean-Louis Barthou. He was a conservative Republican, the lifelong companion and political heir of Poincaré; but he had Bearnese suppleness—the Bearn of Henry IV—instead of Lorrainer asperity, and he was a delicate man of letters, like Herriot and Blum, rather than a lawyer versed in the intricacies of the Code. He planned definitely for an understanding with Russia; at the same time he was drawing more firmly together France's allies, Poland and the Little Entente (Czechoslovakia, Yugoslavia, Romania). This policy was denounced in England and in America as imperialistic: France, it was said, wanted to assure her predominance and keep her former enemy in subjection through a network of alliances encircling the Reich. Moreover, she was ignoring the League. But the League, wounded to death by the abstention of America, had already proved its helplessness; and France, not contiguous with any of her alleged satellites, could not impose her will upon them. Theirs was a free association for mutual defense in which France gave far more than she received. But Barthou was murdered at Marseilles on October 9, 1934, with King Alexander of Serbia; his death was the greater tragedy, although the king's caused a deeper sensation. No one else was found with the singleness of aim, the authority, the skill to continue his work. The diplomacy of the main allies, France and England, became sheer chaos.

It was hoped that Mussolini would help check the growth of German power. Under English auspices a Franco-Italian agreement was arrived at. Although it was il Duce who was wooed, the terms that were made public were surprisingly favorable to France. Italy professed herself satisfied with minor rectifications of frontiers in the Sahara Desert. She admitted that the Italian settlers in Tunis would ultimately become French citizens and simply stipulated for a prolongation of their privileged status. Obviously, the essential truth was to be read between the lines: England and France had tacitly given Italy a free hand in Ethiopia. This Anglo-Franco-Italian Entente was the short-lived Stresa Front (April 11, 1935).

England and France may have hoped that Mussolini would be content with a sphere of influence and methods of peaceful penetration. But the Italian dictator desired to avenge the disaster of Adua (1896) and to win imperial laurels; he wanted victory and dominion. On October 3, 1935, Ethiopia was invaded; the League of Nations declared Italy at fault.

The people of England and France had had no share in the Machiavellian deal with Italy. They supported the League's demand for sanctions against the aggressor. But the French and British governments. secretly committed and anxious not to turn Italy into an irreconcilable enemy, saw to it that the sanctions should remain ineffective. America, of course, washed her hands of the whole affair. The Italian troops were to a large extent motorized, and the success of the campaign depended entirely on a steady supply of oil. Italy had no oil of her own; yet she had no difficulty on that score.

No wonder that, in presence of this eternal yea-and-nay, everyone should scurry from the wobbling Western Alliance. Pilsudski, the strong man of Poland, a ruler after Hitler's own heart, had shown the way: on January 26, 1934, he had signed a nonaggression pact with his fellow dictator. France was thus placed in a hopeless position. Her last efforts to maintain peace and order in Europe were denounced even by moderate Germans as "encirclement again," even by English and American "liberals" as imperialism. Now Italy was frankly, vociferously, hostile. The Poland of Pilsudski and of his political heir, Colonel Beck, the Yugoslavia of Prince Regent Paul were openly flirting with Hitler. Belgium under Leopold III had become an ambiguous ally: on October 14, 1936, the king denounced the military pact with France and resumed his liberty of action. The French Conservatives could not bring themselves to the point of accepting a wholehearted alliance with Russia. The only remaining hope of checking Nazi aggressiveness was the *Entente Cordiale* with England.

And now England under Stanley Baldwin and Neville Chamberlain deliberately deserted the common cause. Hitler's defiance of communism appealed to many a Tory. When Germany started rearming openly, England, instead of opposing her, granted her by a secret agreement the right to build a navy superior to that of France (35 per cent of the British fleet): the deed was signed on June 18, 1935, the anniversary of the Anglo-Prussian victory at Waterloo. When a military clique started a rebellion in Spain, the French premier, Léon Blum, wanted to assert France's right under international law and sell arms to the legitimate government. He was warned that if this were to lead to a conflict with Germany or Italy, he could not count on British support. Thus the sorry farce of nonintervention was started, and thus it was kept up for three years. To everyone's knowledge it meant very active but one-sided intervention, the strangling of a democracy by the united forces of the dictators.

In the Czechoslovakian crisis, England's attitude amounted to a betrayal. It is a mere technicality that France was bound to Czechoslovakia by a formal alliance, and England was not: England ought to have been, and her moral responsibility is not lessened. Without her France was evidently powerless against the Nazi-Fascist coalition. Lord Runciman, sent as an informal mediator, at once endorsed the German thesis. The semiofficial London *Times,* in a blazing indiscretion, suggested ahead of Hitler that the proper solution was not a more autonomous status for the Sudeten, but outright annexation by Germany. Chamberlain's interviews with the Führer at Berchtesgaden and Godesberg were barely concealed capitulations. They led to the agreement of the Big Four (ominous phrase!), Hitler, Mussolini, Chamberlain, Daladier, at Munich on September 29, 1938. Czechoslovakia, a liberal democracy, the bastion of anti-Nazi resistance in Central Europe, was ruthlessly sacrificed. The Poland of Beck acted at once as Germany's jackal and received her share of the spoils.

Ignoring Russia in such a crisis was more than a snub, it was an insult. It was plain that both Republican Spain and Czechoslovakia had been abandoned because they refused to consider Russia as an enemy. Under the sanctimonious mask of "peace in our times" Neville Chamberlain's policy was equivalent to a quasi alliance with Hitler. Even after Hitler, in March, 1939, had annihilated what remained of the Czechoslovak state, England was extremely reluctant to come to terms with Russia, and so was Poland. Chamberlain was still hoping to appease the Nazis with the offer of a substantial loan, while the negotiations with Russia were slowed down to a standstill. It was this inveterate hostility which finally drove the Soviet Union to follow America's example and proclaim her neutrality (nonaggression pact with Germany, August 24, 1939). A week later, the Polish crisis engineered by Hitler came to a head, and World War II began.

It would be grossly unfair to cast the English people as the villain in this squalid drama. The true spirit of England denounced appeasement at that time, as it had previously rejected the ignoble deals, secret or open, with Mussolini. Winston Churchill, then in the wilderness, showed with great force the folly of the official attitude. We cannot praise his foresight and his indomitable sense of honor without condemning the craven confusion against which he was protesting. England herself was later formally to repudiate Munich and the pro-Nazi, anti-Russian bias which had made Munich inevitable.

Obviously, the catastrophe which was to engulf not France merely but Europe and the world was not primarily due to the weaknesses of the Third Republic. There is no single scapegoat: all have erred. But England's share of responsibility (not to mention our own) cannot be overlooked. The degree in which the various nations suffered is no indication of their guilt: Norway and the Netherlands, wholly innocent, were completely overrun. It would be a sacrilege to consider war as God's final judgment.

✍ THE PROTO-FASCIST MENACE AND THE POPULAR FRONT

We have carried the story of France's international problems to the outbreak of World War II without a word about her home affairs. The foreign field and the domestic in such a country as France cannot be separated. But at this particular time the foreign factor was decisive. It made little difference whether France had as her nominal head Radicals like Sarraut, Chautemps, Paul-Boncour, or Daladier, Conservatives like Tardieu, Flandin, or Reynaud, an unprincipled "fixer" like Pierre Laval, or a Socialist like Léon Blum. The situation, we must repeat, was determined by forces which did not originate in Paris; they were also felt in Moscow, Washington, Berlin, and London. It was Laval who negotiated the Franco-Soviet agreement, and it was Blum who abandoned the Spanish Republic to its fate.

Individuals cannot be exonerated. They did their pitiful best, and it was not good enough. Yet most of the confused leaders who occupied cabinet positions during those years were intelligent and honest men, as politicians go. We doubt whether even a magnetic personality like Clemenceau could have altered the result. France was in too desperate a plight to be rescued by a smiling Roosevelt; she was too obstinately sane to accept a raving Hitler.

Many drastic remedies were proposed to mend—or end—the ailing Republic. There was, as we know, *L'Action Française,* with Maurras and Daudet: reactionary apostles of violence, Fascists without a Duce, Royalists and Catholics in rebellion against Church and king. There were the *Croix de Feu* [2] of Colonel de la Rocque: an association of veterans decorated at the front, with a nationalistic, vaguely Nazi program. There was the franker Naziism of Jacques Doriot, a converted Communist, placarding every wall with the prophecy, *Doriot vaincra!* Doriot shall win. There were the Communists themselves, the heirs of Jules Guesde's Marxian orthodoxy, who in 1920–1921 had completely broken with the Jaurès tradition: they were vitriolic in their denunciation both of bourgeois democrats and of opportunistic Socialists. As early as 1934 there were men like Gustave Hervé, once a fiery antimilitarist, who hailed old Marshal Pétain as the only possible savior.

In such a scene of economic uncertainty, political confusion, and international dread minor events assumed a tragic significance. They focused and sharpened the universal anguish. Thus the fate of a mere cosmopolitan crook, a "frenzied financier" of the Ponzi type, was able to rock the Republic. Serge Alexander Stavisky, a debonair swindler, repeatedly convicted, managed to elude justice through the protection of persons in responsible places. His last coup was the issuing of bonds, to an amazing amount, on the slender security of the Bayonne Municipal Pawnshop. When the police finally caught up with him, he was found dead—a most convenient suicide (1934). A magistrate connected with the case also died under mysterious circumstances. The most sinister feature of the case was that the prosecuting attorney who had repeatedly failed to secure Stavisky's arrest was the brother-in-law of Camille Chautemps, at that time prime minister.

France was seeking an outlet for her perplexity and exasperation: the Stavisky scandal admirably served that purpose. On the sixth of February, 1934, a great demonstration was staged on the *Place* ironically called *de la Concorde,* opposite the Chamber of Deputies. The masses which filled the great historic square were not animated by any common purpose: they only knew they were anxious and irritated beyond endurance. There was no concerted action, no definite leadership. Colonel de la Rocque, who stole the show, did not know what to do with it. Had the crowd forced the bridge and stormed the Chamber, the result might have been a veritable insurrection, the first in sixty-three years. The police themselves were puzzled: their chief, Chiappe, was no friend of the regime he had to defend, and was cashiered the next day. The government stood not firm but passively immovable. The scene looked more tragic than it actually was: confused turmoil, an inarticulate roar, and, in the winter night, the aimless angry billows fantastically lit by the flare of a burning autobus. There were only a few casualties in spite of the deadly power of modern weapons. But for the first time since Boulanger it was felt that the Republic had been shaken to its very foundations.

Daladier, who had just succeeded Chautemps as prime minister, was technically victorious but hastened to resign. Once more a Union Cabinet was formed to cope with the crisis. The veteran Gaston Doumergue, former President of the Republic [3] was called from his rural retreat to be "the dictator of appeasement." There was something pathetic and ludicrous about the selection of Doumergue to be the strong man of France. As a parliamentarian his career had been notable for its sustained mediocrity; as a President he had been picked out to be the perfect King Log and had fulfilled every expectation. But the sixth of February had scared the French people into unwonted docility. For a time they rallied to Monsieur Doumergue as the only available port in the storm. After a few months equanimity was partly restored. In the meantime Doumergue had taken his role as providential man with un-expected seriousness. He tried to combine a Mussolinian frown with his ineradicable Gascon smile. So, in November, 1934, he had to be gently removed and sent back to his belated marital bliss. In 1937 a grateful Republic gave him an impressive state funeral.

The sixth of February had more lasting effects than the brief and unconvincing autocracy of Gaston Doumergue. The parties of the Left realized the seriousness of the situation. Vague discontent, breeder of dictatorship, had not yet found its Hitler; but a French Hitler might appear at any moment. The rise of Naziism had sobered the Communists both in Russia and in France. They discovered at last that in self-defense it might be wise for them to co-operate with bourgeois democrats. Thus was created the coalition of Radicals, Socialists, and Communists which was to be known as *le Front Populaire* (November 3, 1935). It was Edouard Herriot's old *Cartel des Gauches,* but extended and more firmly cemented. The spasmodic and futile efforts of the French Fascists had determined a vigorous swerving toward the Left. In May, 1936, a *Front Populaire* majority was sent to the Chamber. In this coalition the Socialist party was at the same time the central and the most numerous element. So its leader, Léon Blum, assumed the premiership.

Léon Blum (b. 1872) was exactly the reverse of a demagogue. He came from a well-to-do, not wealthy, Jewish family; a scholar by train-ing, he had started his career as an art critic and literary philosopher. But he had practical experience as well: for years he was a member of the Council of State, a body which gathers the best authorities in public finances and administration. Not a born orator, he was an effective speaker, lucid, cogent, and of sterling intellectual honesty. It is greatly to the credit of the French proletariat that it could select such leaders as Jaurès and Blum. Men as different as Winston Churchill and William Bullitt endorsed the tribute paid to Blum by a political opponent, the Nationalist journalist and deputy Henri de Kérillis, "You are a great Frenchman."

Blum came to power with a handsome majority but under the most difficult circumstances. The extremists of the Right waged against him and his cabinet a campaign of unprecedented ferocity. They had already attacked him bodily, at the suggestion of the *Action française,* and with murderous intent. Their scurrilous sheet *Gringoire* harried his minister of the interior, Roger Salengro, into suicide, with accusations which a military Court of Honor had declared baseless. Their watchword was, "Rather Hitler than Blum!" They were advocates of direct and violent action: if Blum had helped the Spanish Republicans, as he felt it to be his right and his duty, he would have had to face an insurrection of the

French Fascists. Secret organizations, the CSAR (*Comité Secret d'Action Révolutionnaire*), the *Cagoulards* or Hooded Men, were preparing an uprising with the complicity of high-ranking officers; some of them were very close to Marshal Pétain.

The democratic swing, even before the elections, had been accompanied by a wave of sit-down strikes. Premier Albert Sarraut, a veteran Radical, had been unable to cope with them. The situation was so tense that the employers themselves urged the government to refrain from drastic action. It was felt even by the obstinate and the timid that the only way out was forward. The very Senate, so conservative in social and economic matters, speedily accepted a flood of reforms: not one of them of a revolutionary nature, most of them long overdue, the forty-hour week, vacations with pay, compulsory arbitration of labor disputes, nationalization of war industries, and a more democratic control of the Bank of France, that citadel of the "two hundred families."

For a few weeks the masses were swept by a wave of enthusiasm: the Republic was young and dynamic again. And the more generous among the Conservatives sighed with relief: it seemed as though France had effected a revolution without an upheaval. But it was a false dawn, like the Émile Ollivier ministry at the end of the Second Empire. Again, the hope was shattered from without. Hitler and Mussolini considered the presence of a liberal and a Jew at the head of French affairs as a personal insult. The British Tories were decidedly cool toward the declared enemy of privileges. The Spanish insurrection was making headway. The Communists, who were not represented in the government, were not very comfortable "fellow travelers." The conservative *bourgeoisie,* as soon as the worst of the peril was over, visited upon Léon Blum their fright and their capitulation of June, 1936. He had averted a revolution: they claimed that the menace was of his own engineering.

The *Front Populaire* showed no doctrinaire obstinacy. Against its somewhat rash promise it accepted an inevitable further devaluation of the franc. Blum, fully aware of the international peril, started a great rearmament program. He offered to call a halt to social reform: he understood that French economy, none too robust, needed a breathing spell.[4] He never forgot that Socialists and Communists, even if they were united, were but a minority; so he governed with socialist leanings but without infringing orthodox bourgeois principles. He offered to form a "Sacred Union," such as the one that had prevailed in 1914, embracing all parties, from Thorez the Communist to Marin the Rightist.

He failed. *Le mur d'argent,* the breastwork of moneybags, barred his way as it had previously stood in the path of Edouard Herriot. Joseph Caillaux, who, a generation before, had been so violently hated by the Right, was now the leader of the capitalistic opposition. The Conservatives, who had long claimed a monopoly of patriotism, were thinking of their social and economic privileges, not of the national interest. The France they wanted to save was their France. They saw everywhere in Europe a contest between communism and fascism, and they unhesitatingly preferred fascism: most literally, "Rather Hitler than Blum!"

Although supported by the Chamber, Blum was defeated in the Senate (June 19, 1937). The government, still nominally *Front Populaire,* was reshuffled, with Camille Chautemps as premier and Léon Blum as vice-premier. Chautemps broke with the Socialists and was overthrown. Blum tried his hand again (March 13–April 10, 1938). Once more the Senate forced him out.

His successor, Edouard Daladier (b. 1884), was a *petit bourgeois* Radical, well educated, honest and intensely patriotic. Minister of war under Blum and Chautemps, he was fully trusted by the General Staff. Whatever appropriation they demanded, Daladier secured it for them. There was in the French Parliament none of that haggling which characterized other legislative bodies on the eve of the conflict. The accusation that the *Front Populaire* starved national defense to pamper the working class is wholly unfounded. Yet Daladier was not a good minister, for he was a weak man. Not that he lacked moral courage, but there was some looseness in his intellectual fiber. He concealed his eternal perplexity under blunt manners. He liked to be thought brutal and to be called "the Bull." Those who knew him well shrugged their shoulders.

Even more than Léon Blum, Daladier sacrificed party shibboleths to the necessity of rearmament. He was still under the delusion that the Right was more patriotic than the Left; and he swerved to the right, reserving his display of energy for repressive measures against Socialists and Communists. Like Blum also, he understood that the *Entente Cordiale* was France's sheet anchor. The state visit of George V to Paris (July 19–21, 1938) was a striking demonstration of Anglo-French solidarity. To the necessity of following England's lead, Daladier sacrificed Czechoslovakia and Spain. Franco was formally recognized, and Marshal Pétain was sent to Burgos as the man who would best placate the triumphant *Caudillo.*

For a while it looked as though Daladier's efforts were to be rewarded. On January 26, 1939, England and France pledged themselves to place all their forces at the disposal of each other. Daladier was given by the Chamber the right to govern by executive decrees, the "plenary powers" which the Senate had denied Léon Blum. He was a quasi-dictator, and in a well-staged tour of Corsica, Tunis, Algeria, he tried to outfrown

Mussolini. Yet anxiety deepened: it could not be allayed by bluster any more than it had been by concessions.

On December 6, 1938, France and Germany signed a pact of amity and peace: a pathetic piece of make-believe which deceived no one. Madness was stalking abroad, served by fanatical courage and scientific efficiency. The men of Munich, Chamberlain and Daladier, drifted toward the catastrophe, their eyes fully open, their will strangely paralyzed. On September 3, 1939, after Hitler had started invading Poland, England and France declared war on Germany.[5]

FRANCE'S CULTURE STAYS ALIVE

Again, this somber tale of errors, perplexity, anguish, which is the surface of French history, does not give a true picture of French life. The confusion of the time was reflected in culture but did not affect the whole of culture. We can easily discern in the 1930's that cult of the abnormal, the insane, the exotic, and the primitive as a refuge from the torture of lucid thought, that flight into madness which is a constant element in romanticism, and perhaps its essence. In all epochs there have been men who refused to accept the discipline of the world without, and yet were not able to evolve an inner discipline of their own. Such were the devil-worshippers in the Middle Ages, the Marquis de Sade at the end of the eighteenth century, the ultra-Romanticists in the 1830's, then Baudelaire, Lautréamont, Rimbaud, many of the Symbolists and Decadents, and, between the two world wars, the Dadaists and Surrealists. It will be evident from the foregoing list that such writers are not to be considered as negligible. Their nihilism is at least a challenge to the tedium of bourgeois conformity; their venture beyond reason may be exploration and experiment. In the twenty years between the wars men like Louis Aragon, André Breton, Jean Cocteau, Louis Céline had undeniable talent not wholly obscured by the self-advertising pranks or hoaxes of their imitators. Aragon on the eve of the war turned into a vigorous, realistic novelist and, during the war, into a curiously traditional poet. But in self-assured periods the rebels are merely a fringe; to borrow Sainte-Beuve's phrase, they dwell in a remote *Kamchatka* of their own. In times out of joint they become central and find docile disciples.

The writers mentioned in the last chapter, a very creditable company, remained active in this decade. A few new voices were heard. Georges Bernanos, who had first attracted attention in 1926 with *Sous le soleil de Satan,* became increasingly recognized as a strange and lonely power. He was a virulently unconventional Catholic, the scandal of timid souls, like Barbey d'Aurevilly, J. K. Huysmans, and his direct master, Léon Bloy. His art offers a unique blend of realism, abnormal psychology, and lyrical mysticism. He proved his independence by his radical opposition to Franco, in whom many French Catholics saw a new Clovis, a "man of God." Antoine de Saint-Exupéry wrote the epic of aviation not in terms of material progress but with a spiritual force which turned the diaries of his flights into noble poems. Jean Giono's Utopian return to nature, with its deceptive quasi-Homeric simplicity, was in fact a form of rebellion and escape. At times he attained a timeless purity of emotion and style; at times he recaptured the realistic irony of the old *fabliaux,* but without their cynicism (*The Baker's Wife*). His radical anarchism, his total indifference to political ideologies made him a lonely figure during the war. Although Jean-Paul Sartre had started his philosophical and literary work on the eve of the catastrophe (*Nausea,* a very symptomatic novel, appeared in 1938), his rise to world fame is a phenomenon, and perhaps a portent, of later days.

Whilst at the Palais-Bourbon dim figures were flitting across the pseudo-classical stage—commonplace like Paul-Boncour, Sarraut, Daladier, equivocal like Tardieu, Chautemps, Laval, pathetic like Léon Blum—France was experimenting in every realm and at times with results of surpassing interest. The Paris Exposition of "Technical Arts in Modern Life" in 1937 was in its successes and in its failures a good epitome of this troubled period. It was from the first a victim of political and social chaos. All expositions are late: this one was not even half ready when it opened, and certain buildings were not completed when it closed. Much of it was flimsy and gaudy, and there were many pathetic attempts at originality through eccentricity. But on the whole, the vitality that it revealed was magnificent. Those who had despaired of modern art and civilization, if not fully reassured, were given a new hope. But at the very center the two most ambitious buildings, those of Soviet Russia and Nazi Germany, were frowning defiantly at each other, both barbaric and both powerful.

More limited but more perfect achievements were the liner "Normandie," a masterpiece of technique, art, and comfort, which at once captured the imagination of the public, and the French building at the New York Fair in 1939–1940. Both were syntheses of a complex civilization, deeply rooted, proud and smiling, delicate and vigorous, still reaching for new forms of life. Such a France could not perish because a barbarian, Hitler, had got hold of deadly weapons, and because an old man, Pétain, had lost heart.

CHAPTER XXVII

World War II and Its Aftermath

It has been our purpose to present the biography of a nation; and by nation we mean a sovereign power, conscious of unity within and of differences without. If that definition be accepted in all its rigor, World War II marks the end of the national era. The story of France can no longer be told purely in terms of French interests and French ideals. She went into the struggle for a quarrel not her own. She fell because she was left alone at the crucial moment and in the most dangerous position. She rose again not exclusively through her own efforts but through her alliance with England, Russia, and the United States. The Rightists had said, "Rather Hitler than Blum!" But the Gaullists said no less decisively, "Rather Churchill and Roosevelt than Pétain and Laval!" The Resistance Movement was an uprising against the National Revolution, which was collaborating with Germany. The postwar world is torn between ideologies—there are far more than two—and all of them are represented in France. The national plane of reference has become wholly inadequate.

We need hardly insist upon the difficulty of translating current events into terms of history. In 1814 Napoleon had ceased to be popular: in 1830 his legend had reached its zenith. In 1840 Louis-Napoleon was a butt for the comic papers; so was Hitler in 1923. We cannot even forecast with any degree of security those slow anonymous processes which are the substance of history; this would imply faith in the future of our civilization, and, with Paul Valéry, Oswald Spengler, and Arnold Toynbee, we have come to the realization that civilizations are mortal. All that we can hope to do in these final chapters is to link contemporary happenings with the tradition of two thousand years. For this limited purpose the two world wars are not different, except in scale, from those of Francis I, Louis XIV, or Napoleon. We know how inadequate is this interpretation solely in terms of the national past. But this biography of France is no place for global and long-range anticipations.

✍ ARMY AND REGIME COLLAPSE. PÉTAIN AS RECEIVER

When the great struggle began on September 3, 1939, France and England were morally unprepared. The extreme Right, the Cliveden set and its French equivalent, was secretly, and in some cases openly, in agreement with Hitler, Mussolini, and Franco. The extreme Left had no sympathy with the reactionary Polish government which, after Munich, had acted as Hitler's jackal. What was Europe fighting for? Not a few "liberals" throughout the world had condemned the Polish Corridor as an absurdity; now the masses felt no imperious call to "die for Danzig." The Nazi-Soviet pact of nonaggression, the repeated professions of neutrality on the part of America were further causes of confusion.

It had been thought that the Polish army would offer a stubborn resistance: the blitzkrieg was over in three weeks. The campaign in the West was a stalemate from the beginning: once in a while, patrols scuffled between the Maginot and the Siegfried lines. For six months Europe knew the dreary *drôle de guerre,* the "phony war." Assured in the enormous preponderance of their material resources, the Allies proclaimed, and perhaps believed, that time was working in their favor. The exact reverse was true. The misgivings and divisions which weakened the Allies in September, 1939, were deepened, not allayed, during these months of dismal waiting.

The dull frustration of the French public forced the resignation of Daladier (March 19, 1940). Paul Reynaud became premier. He had a sharper, bolder mind than his predecessor; but he came too late. Suddenly Germany struck. Norway was occupied in a few days (April). The Allies' counterthrust at Narvik was a fiasco. On May 10 the great offensive began; Holland, Belgium were overrun.

Reynaud tried to strengthen his cabinet by calling Marshal Pétain as vice-president of the Council. Mandel, Clemenceau's right-hand man, became minister of the interior, and Charles de Gaulle, just promoted brigadier general, was made assistant secretary of war. But the battle was already lost.

In spite of a persistent legend it is not true that the Maginot Line proved ineffective. The brunt of the fighting was farther north. Out of consideration for Belgian susceptibilities, the French had been slow in extending their defenses as far as the North Sea. If they had, the Belgians, their allies until October, 1936, would have considered themselves as sacrificed in advance. On the other hand, the neutralists, King Leopold III at their head, would not allow the French to build fortifications in Belgian territory, for it would have attracted the wrath of Germany. For moral rather than strategic reasons the Allies marched into Belgium to meet the invaders. Thus they deprived themselves of whatever protection they had hastily prepared; and their advance was paralyzed by a vast stampede of refugees, perhaps the most effective weapon devised by the Nazis.

The front broke at Sedan. The region was thought too rugged for a full-size offensive. It was guarded by units which were not among the best in the French army. Corrap, their unfortunate general, was instantly bewildered. Gamelin, the generalissimo, Georges and Gort, the French and British commanders in the field, were neither fools nor traitors. They were the victims of a fossil strategy, taught and practiced for twenty years, still thinking in terms of a continuous and stable front, still blind to the lessons of the Polish campaign. It must be said that the break-through surprised the orthodox German generals almost as much as the British and the French. It was a daring stroke, and it paid splendidly. Swift armored German units, at times mere motorcycle detachments, dashed across and behind the sagging and tangled lines of the Allies. As in Belgium refugees cluttered every road. Dive bombers decimated and demoralized those fleeing hordes. The sedulous disciples of Foch and Pétain proved unable to cope with this unprecedented situation. Weygand, recalled from Syria, tried to reform an orthodox "front," first on the Somme, then on the Seine; but the Germans were already at Rennes in Brittany. They had entered Paris without a fight. The trapped northern armies, mostly British, made good their escape through Dunkirk; but they had lost their equipment. It was the time Mussolini chose for his stab in the back.

The military history of May and June, 1940, remains to be written. There undoubtedly were individual weaknesses on the Allied side. But, as in football, the decisive breaks seldom go consistently to the weaker team. Had the Belgians held out a few days longer, had certain bridges been destroyed in time, had there been better troops and a better commander in the Sedan sector, the story would have been different in details: the outcome would have been substantially the same. And for this military defeat of the Allies it was the military who were first of all responsible.

Of course, they pointed an accusing finger at the politicians; and until the Riom trials, at any rate, their bluff was successful at home and abroad. Politicians are the perfect scapegoats. We may believe in party politics as a necessary evil, but we are inclined to despise those who engage in that slimy and tortuous career. On the other hand, it is the very essence of patriotism to assert that the army can do no wrong. The army, by definition, is heroic and invincible. If it is defeated, it can only be through some "act of God," as when Napoleon discovered, with pained surprise, that a Russian winter was cold; or else it must be through the treachery of the civilians, which, according to Hitler, was the sole cause of the German collapse in 1918.

This is as fair as blaming an assembly of shareholders for a railway collision: the technicians were in full control. The Parliament had voted without stint all the billions that the fighting services chose to demand, including the fantastic cost of the Maginot Line. The French and the British had tanks equal in quality and in number to those of the Germans. They had at least one strategist, De Gaulle, who knew, theoretically and practically, how to handle them. Their aviation was inferior in strength, and at first in audacity, to that of the Nazis; but England was soon to show how her air force could beat off the German menace. Had she not withdrawn all her planes in order to protect her own cities, the disaster on the Continent might not have been so overwhelming; and the losses in the British Isles themselves would not have been greater in the end. The Battle of Britain is a great page in English history, but it ought to have been fought in France.

THE THREE FACES OF VICHY:
NATIONAL REVOLUTION, COLLABORATION, *Attentisme*

Pétain was summoned because at Verdun he had said, "They shall not pass"; Weygand, because in 1920 he was reputed to have saved Warsaw at the last hour. Both names symbolized the will of the nation to resist to the bitter end. But they were deceptive symbols. Both men hated democracy worse than Naziism. Their one thought was to surrender. In vain did Churchill offer a complete union of the French and British empires: an admirable proposal which came six months, perhaps six weeks, too late. The defeatists were not to be deprived of their defeat. In the government Reynaud, Mandel, De Gaulle urged that the fight be continued: they were outvoted, thanks to the prestige of Pétain and Weygand and to the intrigues of Baudouin and Chautemps. In the wings Laval exerted a hushed and insidious influence. After a despairing and futile appeal to President Roosevelt, Reynaud, weakened by a deplorable private servitude, felt compelled to resign.

Two lines of action remained open almost to the end: to establish a last bastion in Brittany, which could have been supplied from England and America, or to move the government from Bordeaux to North Africa. Marshal Pétain, now premier, rejected both. He proclaimed that the government would flee no farther and would not abandon the population: a noble veil thrown over the resolution to capitulate. In the storm President Lebrun was a derelict—ready to leave, resigned to stay, and at last swept from his nominal leadership without a gesture of protest. The steamer "Massilia," which was carrying a number of parliamentarians to Morocco, was ordered to return. Pétain openly offered to surrender eight days before the firing actually ceased. It was thanks to those eight days of utter confusion that over a million prisoners were rounded up by the Germans without a chance to strike an effective blow.

The Senate and the Chamber, assembled first at Bordeaux and then at Vichy, had to agree to the armistice: they could only bow to the judgment of the highest military authority. They practically abdicated in the hands of Pétain. Thus there were four steps in the rise of the Vichy men. The marshal was first called as the soul of resistance, and he proved the soul of defeatism. He was confirmed in power in order to secure the least disastrous terms, and the victor proved pitiless. He was granted emergency authority in order to preserve some order in the great debacle; and finally, in a veritable panic, the Chambers invested him with the right to frame a new constitution.

This panic was undoubtedly a confession of guilt; it was not, however, a condemnation of the Third Republic and all its works. The parliamentarians felt keenly enough that the curse of the last decade had been disunion, and now they rushed desperately into unity under the man who seemed a living flag. The extreme Left had been discouraged by Daladier's violent measures against them. The moderate Socialists and Radicals had had their morale sapped by the "Revisionist" campaign: for twenty years English and American "liberals" (Hitler could not have had more effective agents) had been repeating that Versailles was an iniquity, that every measure of defense was a provocation and a proof of imperialism. The Right Center was harking back to the days of appeasement: it had been unrealistic not to recognize that Poland, like Czechoslovakia, was within Germany's legitimate sphere of influence. The extreme Right believed that Hitler, in spite of his emergency pact with the Soviets, was the shield of Europe against communism. Thus, for a variety of causes, the French politicians had lost faith not merely in the power of France to resist but in the justice of her cause. All the doubts that had assailed them during the appeasement period and the demoralizing "phony war" were now focused into a resolution to quit. The ghost of Clemenceau might have frightened them away from their defeatism had they not been reassured by the living presence of Pétain: could one dare to pose as more patriotic than the hero of Verdun?

"Absolute power corrupts absolutely": Pétain, whose political attitude during his long career had been one of soldierly aloofness, now felt justified in imposing his personal beliefs. He thought of himself as the savior of society. He was too old to acknowledge the bankruptcy of his military conceptions, the inadequacy of the army he had guided so long, the timidity of his disciples: it was the Republic, and the whole modern spirit, that he made responsible for the disaster. He started a "national revolution" or counterrevolution. His aim was to create an autocratic paternal state with an old-world peasant economy. This fitted admirably with Hitler's plan for a New Order in Europe: a rural France could never again cross the path of an industrial Germany.

Many Frenchmen rallied to Pétain: probably a majority. France was stunned; the military acknowledged his authority; all opposition was silenced. No statistics will ever be available; no figures could ever discriminate between despairing acceptance for the sake of unity and order, and enthusiastic support. It was hard to realize that a national hero was more intent on chastising democracy than in resisting the invaders. Many preferred to believe that Pétain was playing a deep game, outwitting Hitler, saving what could be saved out of the wreck, biding his time. These were the *attentistes,* the "wait-and-see" people, and they found many sympathizers in America.

Their faith was sorely tried: they had to swallow Laval. Pierre Laval was a former Socialist, grown wealthy because he artfully combined his political career with a law practice. In 1914–1918 he had already been under suspicion as a defeatist. As premier he had sabotaged the sanctions against Italy and the alliance with Russia. Without his influence in the lobbies of the Chambers the Bordeaux-Vichy *coup d'état* could never have succeeded. Laval was not, any more than Pétain, a vulgar traitor bought over the counter; or like Quisling, a mediocrity eager to play a part, if only as a puppet. He had genuine convictions. Although a profiteer, he was still something of a socialist—of the Nazi persuasion. A sincere pacifist, he accepted Hitler's New Order as the most direct way of ending strife in Europe. Perhaps there was greater plausibility in his program of active collaboration than in Pétain's dream of a revived Ancient Regime. He never was respected; but he was obliging, a master "fixer," and his greasy good nature could be mistaken for friendliness. He was unscrupulous enough to be accounted a shrewd realist. The true Pétain clique, who claimed to be gentlemen of the old school, loathed him; but they had to accept him.

Thus began the long ambiguity of the Armistice Regime. France was divided into an Occupied Zone, the North including Paris, the whole Channel and Atlantic coast as far as the Spanish border,[1] and a Nonoccupied Zone, mostly the Central Mountains and the valley of the

Rhône. The French were not free to cross the boundary between the two. Theoretically, the Occupied Zone, although under direct German control, was still receiving orders from Pétain's capital, Vichy; practically, the Vichy government obeyed Nazi directives, turned political refugees and patriots over to the Germans, and applied the Nürnberg laws against the Jews. In both zones there were conflicts between resistance and acquiescence and, more subtly, between full collaboration and *attentisme*.

Laval won a decisive victory when he induced Pétain to meet Hitler at Montoire (October 24, 1940): this pledged France to a policy of collaboration with the victor. But on December 13 Laval was dismissed, and Pétain's popularity rose again. Laval's successor as actual head of the government, Admiral Darlan, was a figure of a totally different cast but hardly less equivocal. A patriot according to his lights, he had identified himself with the French navy. He was insanely anti-British, and the destruction of part of the French fleet at Mers-el-Kebir near Oran on July 3, 1940, had made his enmity more bitter still.[2] He may have hoped that Hitler, in his New Order would make him commander of the European naval forces. He went to Berchtesgaden to receive the instructions of his overlord. He was ready to turn Syria into an air base for the Axis. He gave the Japanese a free hand in Indochina. He was almost overtly helping Rommel in North Africa. Of all the collaborationists, none did the Allies more willful and more decisive harm.

On February 19, 1942, a special court, at Riom, opened the trial of Daladier, Blum, Generalissimo Gamelin, and a few others. To make doubly sure, Pétain, on his own authority, had already sentenced these men. The trial was first intended, by Hitler in particular, to condemn those who had opposed Germany: noncollaboration before 1939 was retrospectively made a crime against the state. But soon this was tacitly swept aside: the charge was not that the accused had started the war but that they had caused defeat. Gamelin was obstinately silent. Daladier, redeeming past weaknesses, and particularly Blum made a magnificent defense. They were able to hurl the accusation back at the men in power, the Pétain clique. The case, thus reversed, was so irrefutable that Vichy had to stop the proceedings (April 14).

Hitler was furious. He at once compelled Pétain to reinstate Laval as head of the government. Not only did the aged Marshal comply, but he went so far as to say, "Monsieur Laval and I are one," words which could never be forgotten. Laval did not betray Hitler's trust: he was a convinced and thoroughgoing collaborationist. He expressed his hope that Germany would be victorious. He would have liked France openly to declare war against the enemies of Germany and fight under her banners. French units were sent to the Russian front, and men received decorations for serving with the Nazis. He agreed to draft French labor for the benefit of Hitler's war industries and to herd free men into what amounted to penal servitude. In exchange, Hitler graciously liberated a few sick war prisoners. When Anglo-American troops landed in French North Africa (November 7, 1942), Pétain may have wavered, but Laval had the last word, and Laval went to Munich to take Hitler's orders. On November 11, 1942, the Germans occupied the whole of France without even a token resistance. Darlan might long before have ordered the French navy into African waters, but his attitude remained ambiguous. As a result the fleet, trapped at Toulon, had to commit suicide to escape capture by the Nazis. On November 18 Pétain empowered Laval to issue laws and decrees and restored him, instead of Darlan, as his successor.

With this complete capitulation the obstinate Pétain legend dissolved at last; the *attentiste* compromise, to which the American ambassador, Admiral Leahy, had given the fullest benefit of the doubt, was proved to be a delusion. It was the end of Vichy. For two years it continued to claim shadowy authority; but Laval, the "Head of the Government," was a soiled puppet; Pétain, the "Head of the State," was a senile ghost. In April, 1944, after an Allied air raid a visit of Pétain to Paris was staged; but no one was taken in, except perhaps Gertrude Stein.[3] When France was liberated, the Vichy men vanished altogether.

FIGHTING FRANCE: DE GAULLE AND THE FREE FRENCH. THE MAQUIS

This was not France. The French spirit had spoken when, even before the infamous armistice, General de Gaulle, from London, had issued his clarion call to all true Frenchmen. "A battle is lost, but not the war. France is not alone: she has her fleet, her empire, her great ally, America's inexhaustible resources. The mechanical power which has overwhelmed her will be crushed in its turn by a force immeasurably greater" (June 18, 1940).

Churchill lent his aid to De Gaulle. Thanks to the inflexible pride of the great Frenchman and to the farsighted generosity of the great Englishman, the followers of De Gaulle were accepted not as mere auxiliaries but as allies under their own flag. Volunteers flocked to the Lorraine Cross. Equatorial Africa, led by a colored governor, Eboué, rallied to the Free French. The whole empire would have followed De Gaulle if the prestige of Pétain and Weygand had not paralyzed the military mind. The Free French, later known as the Fighting French, organized in London and at Brazzaville, saved the honor of France.

They fought on every front. But many could not or would not leave the prison camp that was France. They formed secret groups of resistance. These sporadic units slowly managed to co-ordinate their efforts. Thanks chiefly to André Philip, the Underground within France and the Fighting French without united their forces. Jointly, they accepted De Gaulle as their sole leader. Many governments, including the U.S.S.R., recognized the Fighting French as the legitimate trustees of the Republic.[4]

Our landing in North Africa led to an incredibly kaleidoscopic situation. To the very last the Allies had appealed to Pétain as the acknowledged head of the French state. Pétain ordered his troops to resist ours. He thus frankly cast in his lot with Hitler, and so did his lieutenants in Morocco, Algeria, and Tunis: Darlan in particular, who happened to be in Algiers by the bedside of his sick son. Captured, Darlan nimbly changed sides and offered to help the victors. It was true that the North African army, long under the direction of Weygand, was an uncertain factor. The officers were all loyal to Pétain, but they were *attentistes* rather than out-and-out collaborationists. Darlan made his change of front in the name of Pétain, who, he claimed, was no longer a free agent; and he spoke as the marshal's confidential lieutenant. His move made it possible for us to take over Morocco and Algeria with a minimum of fighting. If Darlan had made up his mind a little earlier, Tunis would have been ours also, thus sparing us many weeks' delay and many grievous losses. But the admiral wanted to be absolutely sure that he was rallying to the stronger side. Had our landing forces been a little weaker, he would cheerfully have hurled them back into the sea. He was therefore an embarrassing ally. It remains doubtful whether the moral harm he did to the cause of the Western democracies was not greater than his material aid: "realism" exacts a heavy toll. He was mercifully removed by the accident of assassination.

The Allies then gave General Giraud supreme authority in civil, as well as in military, affairs. They were still fighting shy of De Gaulle who was reputed to be "difficult" and who had in France some embarrassing associates. Besides, the Vichy officers felt bitter against the Free French, who had given them a lesson in patriotism; and the hierarchical military mind rebelled at the thought of obeying a mere brigadier general. Giraud seemed an ideal solution. Captured with his staff at the very beginning of the 1940 campaign, he was not responsible for accepting armistice and collaboration. He had made a romantic escape from his prison. His position in Vichy France never was clearly defined. He was a five-star general, the highest ranking officer who could assume leadership against the common enemy, since Weygand had been unable to make up his mind.

There were grievous misunderstandings in the secret negotiations between the Allies and Giraud: he fully understood that the invasion would take place in France and that he would be in command. Patrioti- cally, he suppressed his personal disappointment and accepted a more modest assignment. But if his only thought was to defeat the Germans, he was still, both as a soldier and as a conservative, loyal to Marshal Pétain. The "Imperial Council" he formed was chiefly composed of colonial governors who had supported Vichy and fired on our troops. He called to Algeria, as his right-hand man in political affairs, a thor- ough Vichyite, Monsieur Peyrouton. It was impossible for the Fighting French to rally to such an ambiguous regime. It was not a question of two rival factions; it was a question of resistance *vs.* collaboration. The Allies were surprisingly slow in realizing the moral aspects of the problem and in gauging the competing forces. They finally imposed a compromise by which Giraud and De Gaulle became joint heads of a National Committee in Algiers. Everyone respected Giraud as a patriot and as a soldier; as a political factor, he had no definite policy, no skill, no prestige. He faded gradually away, a dignified and pathetic figure. Finally he resigned altogether. General de Gaulle gave him later the privilege of entering Metz as a victor. He was for a while an obscure member of the National Assembly. At his death France honored him with a state funeral and burial in the warriors' Pantheon, the Invalides.

The French Committee of National Liberation became the Provisional Government of the French Republic. It had unquestioned control over the whole empire except the French West Indies under Admiral Robert and Indochina ruled by Vichy under an ignominious Japanese pro- tectorate. It had armies with up-to-date American equipment and vigor- ous leaders like Catroux, De Lattre de Tassigny, Juin, Béthouart, Larminat; like Koenig, the hero of Bir-Hakeim; like young Leclerc, who roamed the Sahara destroying Italian fortresses. When Allied troops landed in Normandy and in Provence, it was found that the Under- ground army, now the French Forces of the Interior, at once obeyed Koenig, the general appointed by the Provisional Government and con- firmed by the Inter-Allied Commander-in-Chief, General Eisenhower. These forces greatly aided our troops. It was through their efficient sabotage of communications that the Germans could not bring suf- ficient forces to the Normandy beachheads. By their own efforts they freed one-third of France; the liberation of Paris was first of all their work (August 19, 1944).[5] Leclerc in a splendid dash recaptured Stras- bourg (November 23–24). Mulhouse also fell, and the French armies were the first of the Allies to reach the Rhine. By the end of 1944 the Germans controlled only a few coastal towns and a pocket round Colmar in Alsace.

The war was not yet over. Von Rundstedt had just lost the Battle of the Bulge, but in January (6–12) the Germans were still on the offensive in Alsace. They were converging on Strasbourg from the north and the south, and pushed within ten miles of the city. On the twentieth the First French Army counterattacked. By February 5 Strasbourg was safe, the Colmar pocket split, and the German road of escape cut. At the end of March the French troops crossed the Rhine and invaded Germany: they had a difficult task in the rugged wooded region of Baden and Württemberg. On May 7 the German High Command capitulated at Rheims, General F. Sevez present and signing. At the final act of unconditional surrender in Berlin General Jean de Lattre de Tassigny was the representative of France. A zone of occupation was assigned to the Republic (Saar, most of Baden, part of Württemberg), with a zone in Berlin and a place among the four powers which were to rule the Reich. At the San Francisco Conference which adopted the Charter of the United Nations (June 26, 1945), France was recognized as one of the five great powers with a permanent seat in the Security Council. The road back had been long and arduous. But France, stunned by defeat, betrayed into submission by the very men she had chosen to keep up the fight, had again, through the Fighting French and the Resistance, vindicated her indomitable spirit.

AFTER LIBERATION: THE PURGE

Now France had to address herself to a task far heavier than in 1919. In World War I if the casualties had been more grievous, the institutions of the country had not been shaken, the whole economy had not been shattered. In 1945 everything had to be rebuilt from the ground up: the morale, through a purge of those who had willingly served the invader; the whole transportation system, many cities, a great part of the industrial plant, the very soil, starved for five years, poisoned with mines; the political structure, through a new constitution; the colonial empire, which could be saved only by being transformed into a union of free and equal peoples; and above all, as an essential condition of prosperity and peace, a new Europe, a new world, liberated at last from fear and want. The work is woefully incomplete even as I write these lines. But if we are to judge by the achievements of the decade that followed the end of the fighting, there is no cause for despair.

The *Épuration* (literally "cleansing," or purge) was a tragic necessity, like the Nürnberg trials. The world still doubts the wisdom of letting criminals depart in peace, and in the eyes of the Resistance many of the Vichy men were not adversaries merely but criminals. They were not arraigned simply for having backed the wrong side: every one of them was accused of having aided and abetted the enemy in wartime. Every one had been responsible in some degree for the imprisonment, torture, and death of many innocent victims.

We must distinguish two moments in the *Épuration*. Before the Liberation and in the hectic weeks that followed drumhead courts-martial and summary executions could be considered as acts of war. The Maquisards, pardonably if not excusably, wreaked reprisals on those who had sought to annihilate them. That rough justice was undoubtedly stained with excessive haste, brutality, and at times sadism. There were cases of personal vindictiveness. It was the aftermath of a civil war, and civil wars invariably breed ferocity. But there were no wholesale massacres. The enormous figures vaguely hinted at by survivors of the Vichy spirit [6] have no foundation in reality.

The scene changed as soon as the Provisional Government of General de Gaulle established its authority. Great efforts were made to prevent any massacres or individual lynchings. Illegal "executions" were sternly discouraged: the FFI (French Forces of the Interior) who had taken part in such acts were rigorously punished. The French episcopate warned against the spirit of vengeance; and the minister of justice in charge of the purge, Monsieur François de Menthon, was a judge by profession, a Conservative, and a Catholic. On February 20, 1945, he reported that 7053 cases had been dealt with, and that there had been 574 death sentences. The Consultative Assembly urged greater speed but not greater severity. The judicial work proceeded in orderly fashion. Random denunciations were easily disposed of. Men who in good faith had served France in their official capacity while accepting the Vichy regime were not penalized. Women who had consorted too flagrantly with German soldiers had their heads shaved, but hair grows again. In proportion to the population there were fewer arrests in France than in Belgium, Holland, and Norway. Even at its height the purge was not marked by collective hysteria. Compared with the repression of the Commune in 1871, or with the massacres of September, 1792, it was remarkable for its restraint.

Among those who atoned for their misuse of power, three stand out as dramatic symbols: Maurras, Pétain, Laval. Had Maurras been guilty of mere paradoxes, however perverse, his high position in French literature would have made him immune. He had been the brains of the Vichy reaction: but addled brains might at worst lead to the lunatic asylum, as in the cases of the Marquis de Sade and the poet Ezra

Pound. But Maurras, with constant and concentrated ferocity, had advocated political murder and the ruthless repression of the Resistance. Lesser—and better—men like Robert Brasillach were shot: Maurras, an Immortal, was sentenced to life imprisonment.

The origin of Pétain's power may have been legitimate, and his defeatism in 1940 may have been a mere error of judgment. But as head of the French state he had said, "Monsieur Laval and I are one," at the time when Laval affirmed, "I wish for the victory of Germany." Pétain had condoned the atrocities committed in his name by Darnand's militiamen, including the murder of two former ministers, Georges Mandel and Jean Zay. Senility is no excuse. On August 15, 1947, Pétain, a marshal of France for twenty-eight years, was sentenced to death but commended to the clemency of the Chief Executive. General de Gaulle, as Provisional President, immediately commuted the penalty to life imprisonment. Both condemnation and commutation had been fully expected and caused no political commotion.[7]

Pierre Laval had been a much more thoroughgoing collaborationist than Pétain, and he had no such prestige to protect him from the people's hatred. He had banked to the full on Hitler's New Order and lost: his case was as clear as that of John Avery at Old Bailey in London and might have been as brief, a death sentence in eight minutes. With great dramatic skill he managed to turn his trial into a feverish political debate. His strategy was to infuriate his accusers so that his partisans could claim later that his condemnation had been sheer political murder. In his case there was no recommendation for mercy, and no appeal was permitted (October 9, 1945). He attempted to poison himself but could not cheat the firing squad. Had he dared to defend the doctrine that was already clear in his mind in 1914—pacifism and the necessity of Franco-German co-operation—there might have been a tinge of respect in the horror he inspired. But he attempted absurdly to pose as an *attentiste:* his sole aim had been to mitigate the rigors of German rule. He succeeded, at any rate, in creating not misgivings or compunction but a feeling of weariness and shame: his prosecutors lost something of their dignity. His trial was like his whole career: a grease spot in the history of France.

THE STAGGERING ECONOMIC PROBLEM

The return to a normal economy was bound to be protracted; by 1950 the recovery was still incomplete. The devastation everywhere in France had been appalling. Not one of the major ports, hardly any of the minor ones, had escaped destruction. One million, eight-hundred thousand buildings had been damaged, 442,000 of them beyond repairs.

Great cities such as Rouen, Le Hâvre, Brest, scores of smaller ones such as the lovely cathedral towns in Normandy were heaps of rubble. There was practically no main-line railroad bridge standing. Before the war France had 17,000 locomotives; at the time of her liberation only 2,900 were available. The Allies and the French Underground had outdone the Germans in crippling the industrial plant and the transportation system of the country. Agriculture had fared but little better. France in normal times could almost feed herself; now even the land was ruined. Vast areas had been turned into mine fields; fertilizer could be neither manufactured nor imported; farm labor was depleted; and there were few horses or tractors left to till the ground. The prewar wheat crop had averaged 80,000,000 quintaux (*quintal:* hundredweight): it was reduced to 40,000,000. Wine decreased from 60,000,-000 hectolitres (one hectolitre: 24 gallons) to 35,000,000; sugar beets from 11,700,000 quintaux to 4,000,000.

Food, coal, steel, cement, everything essential was wanting at the same time and everywhere. Nor could this extreme scarcity for many weary months be relieved by imports: no berths for ships to unload civilian goods, no trains to carry them; the fighting forces had first claim on supplies and transportation. North Africa, hit by a disastrous drought, had to be assisted from France's meager store: the hungry had to feed the famished. In that desperate situation, which the joy of liberation could mask only for a few hours, the French did not abandon themselves. Within a year main-line railroads were functioning; ports were reopened, even though with crippled facilities; the mines, under national management, were soon to top their prewar records. A fine body of architects and engineers, among them the great railroad manager Raoul Dautry, the veteran Perret, Prost of Moroccan fame, even Le Corbusier, the stormy petrel of "Functionalism," were drawing plans for the ruined cities. If the medieval center of Rouen is an irreparable loss, the modernization of Le Hâvre, Brest, Saint-Nazaire, the transformation of the Marseilles slums blasted by the Nazis could well be a clear gain. The National Planning Board, headed by Jean Monnet, without usurping the role of private enterprise, co-ordinated the efforts, provided a general framework—transportation, mining, key industries—for individual activities. Thirty-seven billion dollars were to be invested within five years in this total reconstruction. The present was dark; but it seemed, a year or so after the Liberation, as though the road ahead was clear.

We have seen France recuperating marvelously many times in the past: after the Hundred Years' War, after the forty years of religious and civil strife, after the great ordeal of the Revolution. But in the twentieth century, the economic structure had become infinitely more complex and, therefore, more sensitive. France in 1945, even more than in 1919, was faced with the fact that on the modern plane she could not live in isolation. England depends on foreign supplies for her food, but France needs to import coal, which is vital to her industries. Before the war she received that coal from Belgium, the Saar, the Ruhr, and particularly from England. After the war her share of the greatly reduced German output was inadequate; and England, before the nationalization of her mines, went through a coal crisis which made her once opulent resources barely sufficient for her own needs. France is working feverishly on hydroelectric developments. But the huge public works in the central mountains, the Pyrenees, the Rhône Valley cannot be improvised. In the meantime, she has had to import much of her coal all the way from America. A bad crop may darken the situation still further, a good crop relieve it; but the permanent fact remains that France, even if her industries were fully rehabilitated, cannot be economically sound until normal sources of supplies are again available, and normal markets reopened.

The country for the first five years after the war was remarkably active; yet there was a sense of insecurity, of anxiety, even of despair, because the financial situation seemed incurable. The enormous cost of reconstruction, which could not come out of savings or taxation, involved constant deficit, constant borrowing, constant inflation, constant increase in the cost of living, constant readjustment in the scale of wages. The simple and well-meant formula of Léon Blum, reducing all prices by 5 per cent, had a tonic effect for a few weeks only. The most ominous feature of the situation was that the gap between imports and exports could not be closed. Even if America had been willing to accept more French goods in exchange for equipment, food, and fuel, France with the most rigid austerity would have had but little to spare. A few luxury articles and the tourist trade are spectacular rather than essential items in the general economy. As the result of this imbalance, France, once second to England alone as a creditor nation, was now compelled to draw heavily from America, without any certainty of repayment: first through the lend-lease, then through UNRRA, after that through the Blum-Byrnes Agreement, and finally through the Marshall Plan. But foreign aid cannot be indefinitely extended, the standard of living cannot be drastically lowered; and if the franc were allowed to fall to zero, its successor would at once start on the same downward course. The situation was, and is, past any *léger-de-main*.

The remedy is not obvious; and the usual scapegoats—black market, profiteering, politics—are merely superficial symptoms. The government, with a great show of virtue and energy, once decreed the death penalty against those who find in the general confusion a splendid opportunity for gambling. But this Draconian rigor was a gesture not a cure. In this anxious and feverish age, any one who buys or sells, seeks or consents a loan, accepts wages, signs a contract is inevitably gambling. The old French virtue, thrift, was linked with a stable currency, the Germinal franc, which kept its value from 1795 to 1914. The present attitude is: hurry to spend your money while it still purchases anything.

Baron Louis said, "Give me good politics, and I'll give you good finances." The politics of the Fourth Republic, as we shall see, were none too good, and they looked even worse than they were. The difficulty, however, lay in the confusion of the majority rather than in the incompetence of the men in power. Ministerial instability also was an effect rather than a cause. The French changed their cabinets every six months because one combination after another failed to solve the irrepressible problem.

A European Union, heartily to be desired from the point of view of peace and culture, will not provide an economic panacea. For the whole of western Europe is suffering from the same ills, and pooling diseases does not relieve them. The leading Western nations, until World War I, were geared to a system in which they provided capital, services, and manufactured goods for vast agricultural areas, in eastern Europe, in Asia, in America. Now these areas are fast industrializing themselves. Some are practically closed to Western trade. In those which are still a market for industrial goods, Europe is undersold by American competition; for America, a more modern nation, has reached a higher degree of collectivism, that is to say of cheap and efficient mass production.

The methods which claim to go to the root of the matter stagger the imagination. Europe could adopt either of the two rival economic systems, *laissez faire,* or socialism, instead of attempting to combine them in ways which are unstable and may be explosive. But under present European conditions *laissez faire* would have nothing to offer except bankruptcy and starvation: economic laws, when they are given free play, are inexorable. Pure socialism—again under present European conditions—would mean the immediate loss of many liberties, and perhaps eventually of all liberty.

The frank recognition made by Dean Inge many years ago that western Europe, even France, is overpopulated by scores of millions is a diagnosis without a prescription.[8] There are no vast unoccupied or undeveloped areas fit for European colonization on the fantastic scale needed for prompt and effective relief. We may be on the eve of sensational developments in food production which would appease the hunger of two billion men. But this hypothesis takes us beyond the realm of national histories. It means a new departure in human destiny and if not a new heaven, at any rate a new earth.

It is well to realize that the present chaos is not due to self-indulgence, laziness, or stupidity on the part of the sufferers: scolding will do very little good. The tragic situation of the world demonstrates two elementary truths which only the wilfully blind refuse to see. The first is that politics, economics, thought, and ethics cannot be separated. The second is that, with the dubious exceptions of the United States and Tibet, no nation can live unto itself alone. As Arnold Toynbee prophesied, the age of separate *civilizations* is passing. The age of *civilization* is yet to come.

BOOK VI

SUMMARY AND CONCLUSION: THE FOURTH REPUBLIC IN THE PERSPECTIVE OF A THOUSAND YEARS

A DECADE OF THE FIFTH REPUBLIC

CHAPTER XXVIII

Home Politics

*Plus ça change, plus c'est
la même chose.*

✍ NO HAPPY ENDING

I wish I could close this biography of France with the Liberation. For
a few golden hours it seemed as though not the soil of France merely but
her very soul had been cleansed. From the abyss of material ruin France
could raise her eyes to greatness in the spirit.

There are few happy endings in history. Mighty Charlemagne, tradition avers, wept when in his old age he saw the Norsemen harrying his
empire. Louis IX, whose saintliness had exalted the prestige of his office
and of his nation, died frustrated in a senseless crusade. Joan of Arc's
career was but a flash in the murk: the king for whom she died was
unworthy. Pavia and Madrid, defeat and captivity, followed Marignano,
the fresh and joyous morning of the reign. Henry IV, the kindly and
wise, was assassinated. Versailles was as somber in 1715 as it had been
refulgent in 1680. The willing sacrifice of feudal rights on August 4,
1789, did not herald an era of good will. The fair dawn of the Consulate—peace, reconciliation, prosperity—was followed by tyranny,
eternal war, disaster. The fraternal Republic of February, 1848, stumbled in blood as early as June. The glory of Armistice Day in 1918
paled in a few weeks, obscured by squabbles and the mounting dread
of a worse ordeal. Historians think in headlines and revel in catastrophes, for these alone have the true epic quality. But catastrophes—
wars and revolutions—even when they culminate in apparent triumph,
are wasting diseases. Rudyard Kipling's *Recessional* should be the
anthem of all nations.

It is impossible to deal even with remote history in a strictly objective spirit. Facts will not speak for themselves: they have to be

selected, summoned, cross-examined. There is not a crisis in the annals of France, from the Roman conquest to World War II, that is not open to controversy. There is no final "verdict of history." In all cases, I must repeat, it might easily have been otherwise. What did actually happen seldom satisfies our sense of poetic justice and our cravings for spiritual health.

As late as May, 1958, it seemed as though this long story would have to close in an anxious twilight. In home politics, in world affairs, in the economic field, the position of France was precarious to the very brink of disaster. The sole comfort of the French, and of their well-wishers throughout the world, was a disenchanted shrug: *Bah! On en a vu bien d'autres!* We have seen worse, century after century.

Paradoxically, the foreign visitor in those troublous years received no impression of gloom. Outwardly, the country was orderly, prosperous, active, cheerful. Anguish wore a smiling mask: to all appearances, France was in a state of euphoria. Regimes in their last hours may have such moments of plenitude. The Second Empire never was so brilliant as in 1867, and even as late as the early summer of 1870 "there was not a cloud in the sky." Talleyrand could speak nostagically of "the sweetness of life" just before 1789.

Contemporary events in France offer a special difficulty for the historian who belongs to the English-speaking world. The politics of France are interwoven with our own. France is our friend, our ally; but she refuses to be our satellite. Now American opinion in all major issues is extremely cohesive. We believe 100 per cent in the eternal verities of the American tradition and in our leadership of the Free World. Whenever the French fail to agree with us, we are apt to accuse them of being confused, frivolous, disloyal, or perverse. We should realize that even our most cherished convictions, such as the Truman Doctrine, are not accepted as dogmas by the rest of mankind. For the French in particular some of these self-evident tenets fall far short of their own Cartesian conception of certitude. The French belong to the Free World, because they insist on being free according to their own lights.

It would be a caricature of history if I were to present the contemporary scene in France in the light of American orthodoxy: the American mind might well need more than one "agonizing reappraisal." But any attempt to explain the French point of view in terms of the French experience and in the light of the French tradition will inevitably be considered by many readers as arrant pro-French propaganda. I must take the risk or leave these last chapters unwritten. The most casual student of French affairs will realize that I am not, and cannot be, the retained advocate of that confused entity, the French government. I cannot even be accused of being the apologist of France. Under the Fourth Republic, there was no France as a definite entity, one and indivisible, with a lucid thought and a steady will of her own. And there was none in sight: paradoxically, salvation had to come from Algeria. There was no Richelieu at the helm, but a bewildered succession of Queuilles, Pinays, Laniels, and Mollets. There was openly a welter of aspirations and discontents, from raucous Poujade and aloof De Gaulle to the broken ranks of the Communists.

Even today, with the more obnoxious forms of chaos under a curb, there is discipline, but there is no unity. France is too much alive to be monolithic. Perhaps this pattern of teeming confusion—too familiar, alas! even under a royal, imperial, or Jacobin mask—is what we mean by *Eternal France*. Perhaps—a more comforting thought—the shadow of the Capetian dream, "one Faith, one Law, one King," is at last melting away. History is not a well-surveyed and smoothly paved highway, but a yearning, a wandering, a stumbling, toward a goal at best dimly discerned, which ever recedes, and which ever must be descried anew. That there is some sense in such a quest is the substance of our faith in France and in mankind.

FROM THE FOURTH REPUBLIC TO THE THIRD [1]

Even though constitutional jurists may quibble, public opinion in France and abroad accepted the capitulation of the Assemblies to Marshal Pétain in 1940 as the suicide of the Third Republic. The Vichy regime was legitimate enough from the legal point of view, but in 1944 its leaders and chief supporters fled with the German armies. After an expiring gasp at Sigmaringen it finally gave up the ghost. Everywhere the population rallied to General de Gaulle; the Underground and Maquis were exulting; even the *attentistes* could wait no longer. Albert Lebrun, last constitutional President of the Third Republic, refrained from creating the slightest difficulty. There are times when self-effacement is a high virtue and a necessity as well.

First known as the Free French, then as the Fighting French, later as the French Committee of National Liberation, the De Gaulle movement had been recognized *de facto* by all the Allies as the Provisional Government of the French Republic. On January 2, 1945, it had been admitted at last—not without reluctance on the part of America—to the San Francisco Conference and signed the Declaration of the United Nations. That government was undoubtedly of revolutionary origin, and it did not possess the organs of a well-established democracy. There was an Assembly, meeting at first at Algiers, then in Paris, in which the various Resistance groups were represented, as well as those parties which had not collaborated with Vichy. But the mode of election was complex and the apportionment of seats arbitrary. At best the Assembly was a blurred and uneven mirror of public opinion. Its functions were purely consultative.

Well aware of these ambiguities, De Gaulle had promised free elections at the earliest possible moment. He kept his word. Even though Frenchmen by the hundred thousands were still detained in Germany, as prisoners, deportees, or war workers, municipal elections were held on April 29 and May 13, 1945, and cantonal (district or county) elections on September 23–30. They confirmed what had been clear in everybody's mind: the Resistance elements, Catholics as well as Socialists and Communists, worked in close harmony and accepted the leadership of General de Gaulle. For the first time French women went to the polls: that sweeping reform was quietly taken for granted.

Finally the date was set (October 21) for the general elections. The mode of voting (proportional representation) and the very nature of the election itself were determined by the government, not without serious opposition within the Consultative Assembly. For General de Gaulle had decided to couple with the elections a referendum on two capital points. Now the referendum, a familiar institution in conservative Switzerland and in our Western states, is still anathema to the orthodox Radical mind. The politicians will have it that any direct consultation of the people is bound to be a farcical plebiscite of the Napoleon-Hitler-Mussolini type. But in spite of the misgivings of the *petits bourgeois* parties, General de Gaulle had his way.

The first question was: will the new Assembly be a Chamber of Deputies under the Constitution of 1875, *ipso facto* restored; or will it be a Constitutional Convention to establish a Fourth Republic? The people voted twenty to one in favor of an entirely new constitution. This quasi-unanimous verdict, as we shall see, was ultimately ignored; and André Siegfried, *facile princeps* among political observers, could define the evolution of the following decade as the return, or relapse, from the Fourth Republic to the Third. Hence the uneasy feeling among the people that "the politicians had been at their tricks again."

The second question, more delicate, was not presented with sufficient definiteness. In America constitutional conventions limit themselves to that single task; in France, in 1789, 1792, 1848, 1871, the body drafting the constitution also assumed sovereign power and governed the country. General de Gaulle proposed an intermediate solution. The Assembly would elect the head of the Provisional Government and could remove him, but only through a formal vote of censure. The Assembly, however, would be limited by a sort of rudimentary interim constitution outlined in the referendum. The aim of General de Gaulle was to postpone party politics at least until France had a permanent regime. This hybrid formula was endorsed by a two-to-one majority.

The vote was exceptionally heavy. There were no disturbances. The swing to the left was more pronounced than in the municipal and cantonal elections. The Communists won 152 seats, the Socialists 142, the M.R.P. (*Mouvement Républicain Populaire*) 141. The latter was a new party, born of the Resistance, predominantly Catholic, and supposed to be particularly close to General de Gaulle. The Radicals, who paradoxically defended the opportunist compromise of 1875, had only 25 seats.

These elections were a decisive vindication of the *Front Populaire* of 1936. Indeed, they were very much what might have been expected if there had been no world war at all and if the Blum experiment had proved successful. The Communists and Socialists between them had nearly a majority; and the M.R.P.'s, who took the place of the Radicals in the dominant coalition, were in social matters far less timorous than the prewar *petits bourgeois*. At the head of the Communists were the veteran Maurice Thorez and the more dynamic Jacques Duclos. In the Socialist party Léon Blum had now become a national elder statesman, admired even by such an advocate of the cautious middle course as André Maurois. Blum turned over the actual leadership of his group to Vincent Auriol. In the M.R.P. the chief men were Georges Bidault, particularly interested in foreign affairs, Pierre-Henri Teitgen, Maurice-Robert Schuman, and René Pleven.

On November 13, 1945, General de Gaulle, who had formally resigned his emergency powers, was duly elected Provisional President, the presidency and the premiership being merged, by 550 votes, one deputy abstaining, none dissenting. A glowing tribute to the Resistance and to General de Gaulle, moved by the heads of all the parties, was unanimously adopted.

Yet there were rifts from the very first. De Gaulle had Communists as well as Socialists and M.R.P.'s in his cabinet. He gave the Communists the economic departments, those which were of greatest interest to the workers: Industrial Production, Labor, National Economy, and even Armaments. But he would not entrust them with any of the key positions, Interior, National Defense, or Foreign Affairs. It was no secret that they were sworn to follow the directives of dogmatic leaders who knew very little of French conditions and cared not at all about French interests. But there was an even deeper difficulty. De Gaulle felt that the Assembly, disregarding the referendum, considered itself as wholly sovereign. It had elected him and could recall him. Such was not De Gaulle's conception of the relation between the executive power and the legislative. He decided to leave of his own accord and resigned "irrevocably," on January 20, 1946. The Socialist Gouin was chosen to succeed him.

The constitution elaborated by the Assembly under the inspiration of two men of keen intelligence, André Philip and Pierre Cot, was a bold departure from the Orleanist compromise of 1875. It reverted to the tradition of the old Radicals, so different from the trimmers and time-servers who had later adopted the name. The Senate was abolished outright. The President became an even more shadowy figure than under the Third Republic. The single and omnipotent Assembly elected and could remove the prime minister. It was a Jacobin constitution and paved the way for the autocracy of a majority party. It was passed by a coalition of the Communists and Socialists over the opposition of the M.R.P.'s. General de Gaulle, now a private citizen, pronounced against it. When on May 5, 1946, it was submitted to a referendum, it was rejected by 10,583,724 votes to 9,453,675.

A new Constitutional Assembly was elected on June 2, 1946. There was no sensational change; but since the M.R.P. was now the largest party, Bidault became president-premier with Gouin, Socialist, and Thorez, Communist, as vice-premiers. The second constitution diverged widely from the first but not, as De Gaulle had expected, in the direction of the American system, with a strong and independent executive. It was purely and simply a rehash of the Constitution of 1875, with a figurehead president, a senate renamed Council of the Republic, elected in a very complicated fashion, and a popular chamber or national assembly. Both constitutions were prefaced with elaborate declarations of rights. Both made provisions for a French Union or Commonwealth to supersede the colonial empire.

Again De Gaulle expressed his disapproval. On October 13, 1946, 9,120,576 Frenchmen endorsed the new regime, and 7,980,333 rejected it. But there were 25,379,917 registered voters: the nine million "yeas" represented only 36 per cent of the electorate. The constitution was evidently a compromise, unloved even by its sponsors. The M.R.P. in particular hastened to say that it was voted to end a provisional situation fraught with discomfort and dangers, but that it was in need of prompt and drastic amendment. So, with perverted logic, France progressed from the provisional to the precarious. It might have been wiser to do without a permanent constitution for a few years longer, or even, like the France of the Ancient Regime and like England to the present day, to dispense with a written constitution altogether.

As a matter of fact, the new instrument did not correct the most obvious evil of the Third Republic, ministerial instability. The dissolution of the Assembly—an essential feature in the British system—was indeed provided for, as it already was under the Constitution of 1875, but with such restrictions that it was not likely to prove a workable instrument. When on December 2, 1955, Prime Minister Edgar Faure dissolved the National Assembly and called for general elections, it was felt that he was not playing the game; and his sharp defeat at the polls on January 2, 1956, was a rebuke for what the politicians considered as almost a *coup d'état*. So, cabinets have been even shorter-lived than before 1939. Queuille and Guy Mollet are considered as veritable Methuselahs among premiers, because they managed to wobble and totter uneasily for a whole year. Vincent Auriol, elected President in January, 1947, served his whole term with faultless dignity and with the shrewdness of a parliamentary veteran. René Coty, who succeeded him after a protracted, and at times chaotic, election, kept up the safe and smiling tradition of Messrs. Loubet, Fallières, and Lebrun.[2]

THE THIRD FORCE

In the general elections which followed the adoption of the constitution (Nov. 11, 1946), the Communists regained their position as the most numerous party in France. But on May 5, 1947, they were eliminated from the triple alliance which hitherto had governed the country. This was the end of the "Sacred Union" which had given birth to the Fourth Republic.

Many causes contributed to this rupture. The Communists had long felt unhappy about the colonial policy of the French government. It seemed to them that the French authorities were not bold and generous enough in their negotiations with their fellow Communist Ho Chi Minh in Vietnam (Indochina). Ill-advised strikes, which they had not ordered but which they had not dared to condemn, greatly impaired their influence. Above all, the growing hostility between the U.S.A. and the U.S.S.R. made their presence in a coalition government increasingly difficult. They could not consider the Truman Doctrine as anything but a declaration of war against their own beliefs and activities; and so they were led into opposing both the Atlantic Pact and the Marshall Plan which the majority of Frenchmen accepted, albeit with misgivings. American leadership made itself heavily felt. It was rumored that when Édouard Herriot, now like Blum an elder statesman of the Republic, advocated a return to the *Front Populaire* including the Communists, Ambassador Jefferson Caffery broadly hinted that such a move would be frowned upon in Washington. *"Ah! Ne me brouillez pas avec la*

République!" ("Do not get me into trouble with my Roman protectors!") as King Prusias said in Corneille's *Nicomède.* "Liberty" and "independence" are not synonymous.

Co-operation between Communists, Socialists, Catholics, and democrats had been loyal and effective during the war. Such a merging of party differences in times of national peril occurred repeatedly under the Third Republic. It remained the ideal of many Frenchmen who did not believe that toughness ever was an intelligent method. The hope of preserving or renewing this liberal conception was now shattered. Doctrinaires on both sides insisted on drawing a sharp line; and a sharp line is in constant danger of becoming first a bristling frontier and then a battle front.

With the Communist eliminated from power, the position of the Socialists grew extremely insecure. Instead of being the center party, the arbiter of French politics, they became the left wing of the "Third Force" combination (neither Fascist nor Communist). Within that combination they were a minority, and their ideas were far from popular. No further socialization, no sweeping extension of social services had any chance of being carried through. Indeed the results already achieved, the nationalization of the main banks and of a few key industries, were vigorously challenged. Conservative financiers such as Paul Reynaud and René Mayer believed that, in the interests of general prosperity, salaries should be curbed and profits allowed to soar. The Socialist party was thus obliged to support a government frankly hostile to socialism. As a result its forces disintegrated. Those who took the old promise of a social revolution seriously went over to the Communists. The *petits bourgeois* who had flirted with socialism turned round when socialism seemed ready to reach for them. Their faith had constantly been: for big business, severe control, but for the little man, complete freedom. The Socialists, once a party of industrial workers with a sprinkling of intellectuals, has now become a league of *petits employés,* civil servants, and clerks in private concerns. There have been Socialist premiers, especially when France felt the need of adopting a more conservative policy. But their party label has become as meaningless as that of the old Radicals.

In the world of organized labor the situation was no less tangled. A number of Socialists under the veteran syndicalist Léon Jouhaux broke away from the Communist-controlled General Confederation of Labor (Confédération Générale du Travail, C.G.T.) and formed a new grouping called "Workers' Strength," *La Force Ouvrière.* There were, in addition, Catholic labor unions. But if many workers refused to serve the political aims of Moscow, they declined no less firmly to be the auxiliaries of social reaction. So, on a number of essential problems, the three branches of labor acted in harmony. They jointly forced the government to give up the policy of freezing wages in the name of economic liberty.

To increase the confusion, the deep sympathy of most Frenchmen for the United States was ruffled by America's complete ignoring of the French point of view. The press and our State Department vied in their blindness—the inevitable result of uncritical self-righteousness. The course of Washington was hesitant and contradictory enough, but on the whole, if half-consciously, it tended to the reconstitution of a united and independent Reich in sole control of the Ruhr and with a separate army of its own. Such a power, as soon as it had reached its full stature, would whittle down every restriction to its free development. It would receive bids from East and West and use them to reassert its supremacy over the Continent. The path was thus cleared for an even more ruthless Bismarck, a less histrionic William II, a less neurotic Hitler. France viewed the reconstitution of a militant Reich with all the deeper alarm because of the fact that England, willing enough to sign bilateral treaties, resolutely refused to consider herself as a fully committed member of western Europe. It would have taken at least another world war to penetrate the triple bronze, *aes triplex,* insulating the mind of Mr. Bevin.

The fumbling of the parties gave a new significance to the man who had always claimed that he stood above the party spirit, General Charles de Gaulle. His watchword was *grandeur,* by which he meant not bigness, not force in the brutal sense, but *grandeur d'âme,* loftiness of purpose and the rejection of whatever is mean. He was no mere Boulanger, although his immediate program might be summed up in the same words.[3] He had achievements, not merely music-hall ditties, to his credit. He was a hard-hitting, effective speaker, humorless, emphatic, seldom bombastic, never oversubtle. On Palm Sunday, March 30, 1947, he announced that he was returning to the political arena. On April 15 his organization—he still refused to consider it as a party—made its formal appearance. It was called *le Rassemblement de Peuple Français* (R.P.F.), "the Rally of the French People." Although a vigorous smear campaign was conducted against him and against his lieutenants, his R.P.F. scored a great success in the municipal elections of October 19–26, 1947. It became at once the first party in France, with 40 per cent of the voters. Many important cities were conquered, including Paris, where the general's brother, Pierre de Gaulle, became chairman of the Municipal Council. The government found it wise to postpone other local elections for fear they too would lead to Gaullist triumphs. In spite of an ingenious informal plebiscite (three million special stamps were purchased and mailed to De Gaulle), three full years passed without a decisive move. A gray, unassuming provincial politician, M. Queuille, sufficed to keep *le Grand Charlie* off the stage. In purest journalese: the politicians continued to fumble, the general to bumble, the French people to grumble.

We may wonder why the French did not eagerly seek, as early as 1947, the solution which they were to endorse in the triumphant referendum of September 28, 1958. The most obvious answer is that the inherent weaknesses of the constitution had not yet revealed themselves as irremediable. As a matter of fact, under fairly normal circumstances, they might have proved annoying rather than fatal: the Third Republic, with the same faults, had tottered for three quarters of a century. There may be a sort of stability in confusion. *Le gâchis,* which may best be translated "snafu," becomes a way of life. The most virulent critics of the regime added *sotto voce* the words ascribed to Louis XV: "Bah! The old machine will last my lifetime, at any rate!"

De Gaulle's immense prestige as the leader of the Free French had not vanished altogether, but it had passed into history. In the minds of many, he had served his turn and should now survive as his own monument. He stood for a glorious memory, not for a promise. No one, even among his most ardent followers, knew for certain what his bid for power would portend. For those who claimed to read "the lessons of history," the odds were against him: after all, there was an undeniable kinship between Gaullism and Bonapartism, which France had twice rejected. The "realists" affected to believe that there was a messianic tinge to his formidable self-confidence: "I, and I alone, am the Way." In secular history, messianism is hard to distinguish from the Führer principle, or from the faith of the Fascists: *"Il Duce ha sempre ragione."* What did he stand for, beside Gaullism pure and undefined?

For "the greatness of France," without a doubt; and dispassionate observers were willing to admit that he was not thinking in terms of crude power politics. Although a soldier by profession, he had transcended, like Galliéni and Lyautey, the obvious limitations of the military mind. The example of America was reassuring: the Republic had had many generals as presidents, from George Washington to Dwight Eisenhower, and had never been menaced by the autocracy of the sword. No one mistook De Gaulle for a Franco. It was taken for granted that he would accept no dictation from Germany, England, Russia, or America: his chosen role was to be "difficult"; but that he would be willing to co-operate with all nations on a basis of friendly equality. All this was clear enough. But on the disquieting colonial problem, on economic and social questions at home, he remained an eloquent sphinx. His adumbration of a commonwealth in which capital, labor, and the general public would have their share in the management remained a nebulous promise: unfortunately, the dictators, Mussolini, Hitler, Franco, Pétain himself, had stolen that thunder. He wished to stand above parties, and to call to the service of France the best men of all parties. But he felt compelled to rule out the Communists as "dissidents," and a government that excommunicates one-fourth of the electorate can hardly be called truly national. He had among his followers a man such as André Malraux, historian and philosopher of art, explorer, crusader in many lands, hero of the Resistance; but he had also Jacques Soustelle, highly educated, dynamic, but with a dangerous totalitarian streak. And he had others, denounced by Henri de Kérillis [4] who were plainly tainted with Fascism. So his impressive rock-hewn figure appeared in a dubious light; his indomitable will was steadily veiled in ambiguities.

In the light of later events, we can now offer a more definite interpretation of Gaullism between 1946 and 1958. It was not out of political cleverness, opportunism, and least of all timidity, that the General refused to commit himself to a concrete programme: it was out of genuine respect for the will of the people. He represented, not a set of reforms, but a spirit and a method. The spirit, we must constantly sound that key note, was *greatness,* the rejection of deliberate mediocrity, the scorn of short-sighted "realism," the curbing of petty interests. The method was, not the suppression of honest differences, but the abating of the partisan or factional spirit. This he proposed to achieve by destroying the chaotic omnipotence of Parliament, and strengthening the Executive. If such a spirit were affirmed, if such a method were followed, "trust God and the people!" De Gaulle thought of himself, not as a dictator, but as a liberator.

Meanwhile the Third Force maintained itself not through any inner strength of its own, but because it was pulled from two opposite directions. In their confused three-cornered fight, all sides had to resort to equivocal means. General de Gaulle transcended party by creating a new party, the Rally of the French People. The Third Force unblushingly resorted to trickery. The election law of 1951 was frankly intended to falsify the returns.[5]

The Rally of the French People showed a tendency to become openly a party, and a Rightist party. Several of its members voted with the Third Force in defense of social conservation, incarnated in Antoine Pinay. This was not De Gaulle's conception of his own role. So he purged his party of its "dissidents," and ultimately purged the party itself out of existence (May 6, 1953). Once more Gaullism was De

Gaulle: *"Moi seul, et c'est assez."* He stood alone, a great figure pointing neither to the right nor to the left, but heavenward. Cynics remarked that the force of gravity would make it difficult even for him to follow his own indication. Yet in the hopeless morass of Third Force politics, he remained for many a desperate hope. He, at any rate, possessed the grandeur that he had the right to preach. And once before, his refusal to compromise, his rejection of meanness in every form, had carried him to victory. There were persistent rumors of a possible conjunction between De Gaulle and Pierre Mendès-France[6] to form a national ministry in the grand tradition, with the Communists as friendly outsiders. Events took a different turn: in 1958, Mendès-France and the Communists were the only determined opponents of General de Gaulle.

When General de Gaulle retired a second time from active politics, many of his supporters reverted to the M.R.P. A few went to the extreme right. Malraux had returned magnificently to his old craft as art critic, and in his *Voices of Silence* (1951) gave a masterpiece of impressive *chiaroscuro*. Many had endorsed De Gaulle negatively, because he promised to "frustrate the knavish tricks" of the professional politicians. Repeatedly in history we find discontent reaching a high degree of intensity without a positive goal. Louis-Philippe had become extremely unpopular by 1847 ("France is bored!"); but very few people were deeply interested in the actual issue, a very moderate extension of the franchise. On the sixth of February, 1934, the masses which swirled angrily on the Place de la Concorde had no definite programme. A vast confused clamor is not a directive; but it is a warning.

Most Frenchmen were dismayed by the impotence of the Third Force. For a large minority this vague feeling turned into anguish and despair. They were "the little men," the small shopkeepers and manufacturers, squeezed to death by world competition and the growth of large concerns. It seemed to them an outrage that, when they were finding it so hard to make both ends meet, a callous government should actually call upon them to pay taxes. This rudimentary state of mind found its mouthpiece in Pierre Poujade. A small stationer in a small southern town, he defied the tax collectors (summer 1955) and started a movement of protest on a national scale. The vacuity of his eloquence was appalling: in comparison, Mussolini was a Cicero and Hitler a Hegel. Yet his meetings drew storms of applause, and in the general elections of January 2, 1956, Poujade's Union of French Fraternity (U.F.F.) secured fifty-two seats. "Secured" is too strong a term; for, with scant regard for political fair play, the Third Force majority quashed the elections of many Poujadistes. Their own antics disgusted the parties of the Right, which at first had welcomed these new allies. Yet Poujadism was a little more than a squalid nuisance: it was a portent.

✍ THE POLITICAL VOCATION OF THE MIDDLE CLASS

This arraignment of the Fourth Republic is not a *Vae Victis!* or a *post mortem*. Nor is it inspired by sheer partisanship. It was heard everywhere for the last decade, and at a time when there seemed no prospect of loosening the viscous hold of the Third Force. It was clearly voiced by members of the Third Force itself, like the veteran Paul Reynaud. Professor Maurice Duverger, in a masterly study of *The French Political System* [7] concludes without acrimony: "The new generation which is now taking over the reins of power rejects the habits, the style, and the myths of the earlier generation." Cosmopolitan observers such as Herbert Luethy and David Schoenbrunn reach the same verdict. Most weighty of all is the testimony of D. W. Brogan, who knows and loves France supremely well: "(A great nation—I am condensing in three words a long and well-deserved hymn of praise) had yet failed to find institutions that united the French people and gave them a political way of life worthy of their genius, their courage, their legitimate hopes." [8]

Institutions: Brogan is right. The fault lay with the system, not with the men in power. The drab Third Republic had found a few great leaders: Gambetta, Ferry, Waldeck-Rousseau, Jaurès, Clemenceau; and others whose intelligence and good will were of very high quality, such as Poincaré, Herriot, and Blum. The Fourth, in its briefer and more tormented career, offered no one, not even Mendès-France, a similar opportunity. Some of the men who were given the trappings of power were frankly mediocre: let them be mercifully forgotten. But, by and large, the ever-shifting teams of the Fourth Republic counted men who were honest, hard-working, well meaning, and highly educated: the personnel of the Fourth Republic could staff a large university of the highest rank. Some did, and I trust will continue to do, yeoman's service in the difficult creation of a United Europe. General de Gaulle acknowledged their integrity and their ability by including a number of them in his cabinet.

The roots of the evil go deeper. The Fourth Republic after 1946 represented the unqualified triumph of the *petit bourgeois* spirit; and it was that spirit that was weighed and found wanting.

The famous dictum of Abbé Sieyès: "What is the Third Estate? Everything. What has it been hitherto? Nothing," [9] is false on both counts. For centuries, the Third Estate, or middle class, or *bourgeoisie,* had held an important place in the political life of France. Its claim to be everything, to assume sole control of the state, was in 1789 and remained in 1958 a dangerous fallacy. Mesocracy, or the dictatorship of the middle class, is everywhere on the wane. But under the name of the Third Force, it still had power enough to keep French affairs in a state of unutterable confusion.

The alliance between the Capetian dynasty and the *bourgeoisie* goes back to Louis VI, the Fat and the Wide-Awake, who favored the newly arisen Communes—not, however, in his own domains. Bouvines (1214) is still celebrated as the triumph of the royal power, that of Philip Augustus, supported by the militia of the cities. Philip the Fair, Louis XI, both among the rulers who organized the national monarchy, put their chief reliance on commoners. This age-long process reached its climax under Louis XIV. He was the State by divine right, but he resolutely curbed the political activities of the nobility and exercised his authority through middle-class ministers. The nobles were but supers in the glamourous pageant of his court; and Saint-Simon, a passionate aristocrat, could with singular penetration denounce the rule of the Grand Monarch as "that reign of vile *bourgeoisie.*" Although there was a sharp nobiliary reaction at the very end of the Ancient Regime, Louis XVI could be served by such men as Turgot and Necker.

Nor did the class prove unworthy of its opportunity. The figure on the throne might be weak, capricious, or even demented, the nobles brutal or frivolous; but the *bourgeoisie* built up a long tradition of common sense and conscientious application. It provided the state not only with all its petty officials but with *Grands Commis* as well, able and devoted servants in posts of high responsibility: the model of these is Colbert. It was that class that kept France steady even during the wild adventure of the First Empire. While an uncontrolled genius piled up spectacular and fragile conquests, ministers, prefects, and councilors of state preserved administrative and financial order.

That great tradition survived, almost unimpaired, until the end of World War I. Then there was, if not a divorce, at least a rift between the higher *bourgeoisie* and the administration of the country. Impoverished by the inflation, the old bourgeois families could no longer afford to serve the state on meager salaries; they were driven to seek new careers in finance and industry. But their prolonged shadow is still with us. The sons of workers and peasants who assumed their heavy tasks became bourgeois at heart. There has been a gradual shift from the *grande bourgeoisie* to the *petite,* or petty, and the change was not a clear gain. But, grayer maybe than heretofore, the bourgeois spirit remained supreme. France has long ceased to be ruled, even nominally, by the aristocracy or by the Church; it is still governed not by and for "the people" but by and for the middle class.[10]

This predominance, amounting almost to a dictatorship, was not undeserved. We have seen that the class displayed, generation after generation, solid virtues which cannot be dismissed as narrow and stodgy. And it played an even greater part in French culture than in French politics. Almost up to our own time the roll of French writers is filled with bourgeois names. Great aristocrats like La Rochefoucauld, Madame de La Fayette, Madame de Sévigné, Fénelon are exceptions in the world of letters; and rarer still are the men arising straight out of the working masses. Among the men who ruled the Third Republic and its confused shadow the Fourth, many were notable for their intelligence, their integrity, their cultural interests. Raymond Poincaré, an extreme instance, bourgeois of the bourgeois, presented a rare combination of competence, energy, and devotion to his principles. If France should swing definitely to the Right or to the Left, we can only hope that she would find servants not unworthy of the bourgeois tradition.

Yes, the *bourgeoisie* has deserved well of France. But the major fallacy in Sieyès's dictum is the first: the Third Estate is (or should be) everything. That principle was elaborated into a doctrine by the great historian, political philosopher, and statesman, François Guizot: for him the course of civilization in Europe led to the unquestioned and permanent rule of the middle class. Guizot fell in 1848, but his spirit is still with us.

Guizot did say, and reiterated, *"Enrichissez-vous!"* ("Get rich!") However, the *bourgeoisie* in France is not committed to capitalism, and even less to plutocracy. Of course, a bourgeois, to deserve the name, must be tolerably well off, free from sordid care; else he could not preserve his independence and enjoy the delicate culture that demands spacious leisure. But wealth is the condition, not the goal. The bourgeois spurns manual labor, industrial or agricultural, as servile: a white-collar worker, even on a very scant salary, is closer to the *bourgeoisie* than is a rich peasant or a successful mechanic. Money counts for less than the way of life. And the true bourgeois distrusts the financier, the promoter, as tainted with the unbourgeois spirit of adventure. Incurably "safe and sane," moderate in his desires, he is eager to retire early on a substantial but modest competence. If plodding be virtue, gambling is sin. The bourgeois refused to understand the truly prophetic element in Law's bold schemes, and he shook his sensible head at the daring economy of the Second Empire.[11]

Whatever the collective and individual virtues of the bourgeois may be, his class as a class is excellently qualified to serve but unfit to rule. For the bourgeois spirit is negative. It does not possess the chivalric strain, the sense of *noblesse oblige,* the rejection of meanness, the readiness to face death with a smile in war or in single combat, which were the virtues—or perhaps the lovable faults—of the old aristocracy. It possesses even less the scorn of Mammon and the love for the poor which are the very essence of Christ's teaching. The bourgeois, without hypocrisy, can strike noble attitudes and profess high ideals. As the heir of the monarchy the middle class can speak in terms of national honor and be ready to draw the sword. It still mouths eloquently the great principles of 1789, once such an effective battering ram against the privileged orders. But chivalry, patriotism, democracy, Pauline charity are not rooted in the bourgeois mind. These lofty flights may be enjoyed as luxuries; when it comes to practical affairs, we must come down to earth and be "realistic."

Now realism, for the French *bourgeoisie,* implies the defense of vested interests. At one time this meant almost exclusively the protection of private property (an "inalienable and sacred right," on a par with life and liberty) and the quasi monopoly of high offices in the state. Now, with the diffusion of the bourgeois spirit, vested interests cover every dwelling, every shop, every job. French legislation has become a complicated mesh of regulations for maintaining the *status quo,* so aptly translated as "the mess we are in."

This defensive attitude is legitimate: security is not an unworthy goal. It becomes a peril, however, when it paralyzes every far-reaching and generous policy. Democracy should be the cautious yet fearless working out of great principles. Mesocracy is the ubiquitous scramble of lobbies, great and small, from home distillers and beet producers to the European minority in Algeria. Because it could not transcend mesocracy, the Third Force was a writhing mass of weaknesses.

On this point the peasant proprietors (there still are peasants in France, not ashamed of the name) work in close harmony with the bourgeois. In their ways of life the two classes are poles asunder. But they were long united in their opposition to feudal privileges. They were at one in their desire to stop the Revolution in 1789. What is more of a vested interest than a plot of land, especially one on which untold generations have toiled? Agriculture in France is the most powerful of defensive lobbies, and the most disastrous. For vested interests stubbornly refuse to recognize changing conditions. The tourist will justly praise the well-tended smiling fields of France: he does not recognize that French agriculture is anachronistic and a drag on the national economy. France has been tilled for twenty centuries. Marginal lands are under cultivation, and by methods which are still primitive. The result is that the rural classes would suffer heavily in a free market. They can maintain themselves only through hard work, parsimony—and rigorous protection. But protection, artificially raising the cost of living, is a fatal handicap to French industry, already suffering from the scarcity of certain raw materials. If French agriculture were to be rationalized so as to meet world competition, millions of peasants would be driven from their little farms; and it is doubtful whether industry could absorb them. On a purely traditional basis—and the Third Force is the desperate defense of tradition—the problem is insoluble.

It is not the part of the historian to preach or to prophesy. In the purest spirit of Ranke,[12] however, he may note "what is actually happening." A formidable revolution in technique—new sources of power, new materials, automation—is making the bourgeois mind obsolete. *Chacun chez soi, chacun pour soi:* let everybody stay at home and work for his own profit: this bourgeois and peasant creed, narrow as it may be, was not unworkable before the first Industrial Revolution, that of the later eighteenth century. It has become an absurdity with the second which is proceeding under our eyes with ever-increasing speed. The Village Blacksmith is a quaint survival, not an ideal. No rugged individualist can build an atomic pile in his own backyard and with his unaided hands. The *bourgeoisie* put in its great bid for power in 1789 at the very moment when the cautious bourgeois spirit had ceased to be adequate. Since that time it has been attempting to retard or even to stop the clock. If the *bourgeoisie* were indeed the core of France, then Herbert Luethy would be right, *"Frankreichs Uhren gehen anders,"* ("French clocks keep their own time")—which is behind the times.[13]

In the perspective of centuries, it is obvious that the *bourgeosie* has not been everything except under three regimes: the Directory, the monarchy of Louis-Philippe, the Third and Fourth Republics. They were not the sunlit peaks of French history. Indeed, to borrow terms from the Convention, they were rather the Plains, or even the Marshes. If by *bourgeoisie* we mean the rule of decency, honest work, and common sense, may the *bourgeoisie* continue forever! If by *bourgeoisie* we mean the sullen cult of small private interests, then it can lead us only into a morass and keep us there.

The test is De Gaulle's grandeur, which we are free not to interpret exactly as he does. Feudalism had grandeur; so had the absolute monarchy; so has Communism; so has capitalism of the American type.[14] The French *bourgeoisie* in precarious control until yesterday had nothing to offer but *"Chacun chez soi, chacun pour soi":* a faint and dubious star for a great nation to steer by.

CHAPTER XXIX

France Overseas

"France constitutes with the peoples
overseas a Union founded upon equality
of rights and duties, without any
distinction due to race or religion."
Preamble, Constitution of 1946.

⚔ EMPIRE, UNION, COMMONWEALTH?

World War I, fought in the name of democratic principles, had brought
hopes of emancipation to the peoples under colonial rule. Had these
promises been implemented with sufficient swiftness and vigor, the
transition from empire to free association would have been greatly
facilitated. Gandhi at that time was still in favor of the British connection, just as, a little earlier, the Ireland of John Redmond would have
been satisfied with Home Rule. It took tough men like Carson of Ulster
and General Dyer of Amritsar fame to destroy these peaceful prospects.
In 1919 the protagonists in world affairs were still England and France:
America had come in late, had not borne the brunt of the fighting, and
was soon to retire into isolation. Both England and France were colonial
powers and averse to liquidating their heritage. In World War II the
decisive factors were the Soviet Union and the United States; neither of
them was immune to the more insidious forms of imperialism, but both
were outspokenly hostile to the older and cruder methods. This time,
principles and force were on the same side. The Spanish, the German,
the Italian, the Japanese empires have ceased to be; the bulk of the
Dutch empire is gone; now the British and the French empires are in
process of transformation. It is a race between generous foresight and
catastrophe, and the issue is still uncertain.

The task would seem easy so far as France is concerned. No doubt,
her colonial history is long. It began in 1066 when the Normans, no
longer Norsemen, established their rule in England. For three hundred

years the dynasty, the higher nobility, the language of the court and of the tribunals were French. The crusades were to a large extent a French colonial expedition: the Assizes of the Kingdom of Jerusalem were drawn up in French. There are castles in Syria and a cathedral in Famagusta which would not be out of place in Île-de-France. The ill-fated Latin Empire in Constantinople was predominantly French in culture; and Villehardouin, who tells the somewhat disreputable story with such stark directness, ended his life as a French feudal lord somewhere in the Balkans. St. Louis encountered difficulties in Egypt and Tunis long before Guy Mollet. The French had an active, although not a leading, share in the great epic of discovery and conquest of the sixteenth century. Coligny, Richelieu, Colbert had ambitious plans for expansion overseas. In the eighteenth century France was England's strong rival in North America and in India. But these vast dominions were forfeited by Louis XV, and Napoleon gambled away their pitiful remnants. France lost interest in what seemed an enormous and insubstantial shadow. Louis-Philippe and Napoleon III managed to grab or extend some territories, but the heart and the imagination of France remained cool.

The bulk of France's huge empire was acquired recently under the Third Republic, almost by chance and not without reluctance. The great patriot Clemenceau was a determined anticolonialist, and Jules Ferry, who "gave" France Tunisia and Tonkin (North Vietnam), was rewarded with bitter unpopularity. The empire was not "discovered," i.e., appreciated by public opinion, until the very end of the nineteenth century, perhaps in reaction against the *fin-de-siècle* mood, the cult of sophisticated decadence, that had swept over the country; perhaps to alleviate the bitterness of having to give up the hope of military *revanche;* most definitely as a result of the Fashoda crisis. The French had known nothing of the Marchand expedition: but when it brought the two eternal rivals to the brink of war, France realized that she had an empire and that it must be defended. Great proconsuls, Galliéni in Madagascar, Paul Doumer in Indochina, Lyautey in Morocco, made the French conscious that they had not the territories merely but the resources, the men, the technique to create new French dominions.

Still, that feeling of confidence and pride never went very deep. The French had long been committed to the democratic principles of Woodrow Wilson and Franklin Roosevelt. The great declaration, "Perish the colonies rather than a principle!" could be derided but not expunged. The Radicals, the Socialists, the Communists had always been determined anticolonialists. The Catholics were more interested in missions than in conquests: and French Catholics have assumed their full share in that great work. Determined imperialists were found only among army and naval officers, and with a few business firms. Rare were the megalomaniacs who took seriously the boast of General Mangin, "France is a nation of a hundred million."

Yet the abolition of the colonial system is proving a delicate task. The principles of the French Union were formulated at the Brazzaville Conference in January, 1944, chiefly under the influence of the great Negro administrator, Governor-General Félix Eboué. Title VIII of the 1946 Constitution is the charter of the Union. It is extremely elaborate and yet hopelessly vague on some essential points. The Council of the Union has a prestigious president, the veteran Albert Sarraut, who many decades before had drawn up a great plan for the development of France overseas. It has been given a palatial home in Paris. Yet a complicated text, an elder statesman, a masterpiece in ferroconcrete fail to dispel an impression of unreality. Greater France, under the Fourth Republic was in the making, and in the unmaking. Even as we write these lines, we may be accused of excessive optimism if we admit that the balance is still in doubt.

This precarious situation, very dimly understood in America, is due not so much to the perversity of the imperial-minded as to the complexity of the problem. The simple words "empire" and "colonies" cover a great variety of conditions; and the subtler terms, "union," "association," "interdependence," "commonwealth," are even more elusive.

There are at least four main types of colonies. The only true colonies, in the original sense of the term, are those in which the bulk of the population came from the mother country. Such were the Thirteen Colonies at the time of their rebellion. Such are Canada, Australia, New Zealand today. Such are Argentina, Uruguay, and Chile. These grow naturally into daughter nations, to be fully emancipated, with or without a wrench, in due course of time. France can boast of no colonies of this type. Everywhere under the Tricolor, men of purely French origin are a minority. There are no natives in the Kerguelen Islands, but there are no Frenchmen either. Perhaps the Sahara might prove a brilliant exception. If the French with the aid of American capital and American technique were to develop the oil resources of the great desert; if they could harness the implacable rays of the sun, if they keep creating oases in that illimitable sea of sand, no one could accuse them of dispossessing the Tuaregs.

In the second kind a civilized nation—not invariably with pure missionary motives—undertakes the education of tribes whose cultures are hopelessly primitive or barbaric. The most scrupulous anthropologists will hardly countenance human sacrifices, pyramids of skulls, slavery, and cannibalism, even though they constitute the sacred way of life of the natives. This holds true of a great part of Africa, south of the Sahara and north of the Kalahari. It may apply to some of the South Sea Islands like the New Hebrides, or to the dimly known interior of Borneo and New Guinea. The case of Madagascar is more doubtful.

In the third type civilizations of different kinds and degrees, as a result of migration, infiltration, or conquest, happen to live side by side. The dominant element did not destroy, subdue, or assimilate the conquered. The Romans did create such a situation when they spread their empire, but so did the barbarians when they shattered the power of Rome. So did the Arabs and the Turks. There are traces of such a condition in Mexico where the pride of the Indians in their own past is being sedulously revived. In such cases symbiosis or pluralism is the ideal solution: no grinding conformity to a single pattern; coexistence, tolerance, co-operation in all matters of common interest with the hope of a richer synthesis as the result of "converging evolution." The French protectorate in Morocco, which may have strayed from Lyautey's ideal, was conceived and created in that spirit.

Finally, there are countries where a dense population, long rooted in the soil, is well aware of its cultural past. If such countries are held down by a handful of alien and remote overlords, that is "empire" in the literal sense of domination by force, the rule of Muscovy by the Golden Horde, of Hungary and the Balkans by the Turks, of India, Indochina, Indonesia by the British, the French, and the Dutch. Europe was not liberated from that kind of imperialism until 1918; it prevailed over a great part of Asia until yesterday. It was a brutal injustice even when European power was irresistible, European technique centuries ahead of native methods, European prestige undimmed. It became an absurdity when, in the two great civil wars of the West, European wealth, power, and prestige were ruined beyond repair. That type of "colonization" or imperialism has disappeared in its obvious forms. In the case of England the difficult operation was performed with singular success, for which both British statesmanship and the leadership of Gandhi and Nehru must share the credit. In an anxious hour Britain found wiser statesmen than Sir Winston Churchill, who had spurned the thought of "liquidating the British Empire." France's declared intentions were no less generous; but her experience, as we shall see, was far less fortunate.

At one time the French were accused of treating all their colonies alike with serene disregard of their exotic character. The five French settlements in India, for instance, elected a deputy to the Palais-Bourbon;

which would greatly have bewildered them had not very competent "bosses" like Chanemougane [1] relieved them of the embarrassment. Little Negroes on the banks of the Ubangi had to learn by heart, "Our ancestors the Gauls." This caricature of French methods has long ceased to bear any resemblance to the truth. On the contrary, the French administration for over half a century has been finely shaded, too finely shaded indeed to please certain local nationalists. The three countries in French North Africa, for instance, Tunis, Algeria, Morocco, although geographically, ethnically, and culturally closely similar, were divided into an extension of France (Algeria) and two very different protectorates. But even in Algeria uniformity did not prevail. The natives remained under their own Koranic law. Some districts where the European element was strong followed the French administrative pattern; others had a mixed system; the tribes on the confines of the Sahara preserved their autonomy with French officers to curb bloody feuds and brigandage. In the same way the five component parts of Indochina were under five separate regimes appropriate to their stages of development. The Jacobin or Napoleonic conception of centralized uniformity had been completely abandoned.

It is true that at least as late as 1848 the French ideal in dealing with alien races had been assimilation. All colored people were to be treated as Frenchmen and educated to French citizenship. The principle was crude but not ignoble. The French thought they were bringing to the natives not their own European pattern of life but universal truths, the Rights of Man, the rule of reason. All the traditions which were not in accord with these "eternal verities" were to be eradicated as superstitions. But anyone who accepted these basic truths was indeed treated as a man and a brother, irrespective of race, color, or previous condition of servitude. This method worked excellently (on a small scale and with a long period of preparation) in the old colonies, Martinique, Guadeloupe, Réunion, and even the four cities of Senegal. The French did not feel virtuous because Alexandre Dumas, the son of a mulatto general, was a great social favorite as well as a popular romancer; or because Negroes led French expeditions (Dodds, conqueror of Dahomey), reached cabinet rank (Diagne, Candace), won the Goncourt Prize (Mayran), taught French at Tours (Senghor), or governed large colonies (Eboué).[2] This local, limited, but undeniable success proves at least that the thing can be done. To speak of "liberating" the French West Indies, for instance, is pernicious nonsense. They are, because they feel themselves to be, French. Officially, they are now French departments, even that Cinderella of the French Union, woebegone Guiana, with a pestilential past (a convict settlement) and a hardly-less-pestilential climate. Left to their own devices, Martinique and Guadeloupe would have no thought of seceding any more than Meurthe-et-Moselle or Aveyron.

The same formula might very well be applied throughout Negro Africa, whose multifarious cultures are extremely primitive. Until recently, educated Africans refused to think of themselves as "blacks": in their own eyes they were French. The rise of race consciousness, and with it of race prejudice, among the natives is not altogether a happy development: mankind has taken many a backward step in the last two hundred years. The policy of assimilation on an enormously larger scale than in the old colonies would require sympathy and patience. Eboué very properly warned metropolitan Frenchmen against any hasty short cut. A naked savage does not become a Parisian overnight by being given the ballot: it was a grim jest when a West African constituency ate up its senator. But however gradual the evolution, its direction cannot be condemned as wholly evil. In the eyes of many Frenchmen it would be better for the A.O.F. and the A.E.F. (*Afrique Occidentale Française* and *Afrique Equatoriale Française*) to become vast French-speaking democracies, enjoying Pascal, Voltaire, and Jean-Paul Sartre, than to remain imprisoned in their fetishism and their village dialects. The proper task of cultural anthropology would be to guide, not to hamper, such a development.

It might be argued that at one time—barely a quarter of a century ago—the assimilationist ideal would have had a chance even in Algeria. The leaders of the natives then would have been satisfied with gradual accession to full French citizenship. We shall see that this opportunity was allowed to slip by. The situation is becoming increasingly difficult not exclusively because of the rise of North African nationalism but because of the loss of power and prestige suffered by France during the war. The heroic personality of De Gaulle, his genuine sense of grandeur might have retrieved such a loss to an appreciable extent: the utter confusion of the Third Force whittled away the last vestiges of France's moral authority. It is no longer a golden promise to become, in course of time, a second-class French citizen. French culture has not lost a subtle vitality second to none, but its appeal is not within the reach of minds which may be vigorous but are still primitive. The new situation is not desperate, but it demands a new approach; and, early in 1958 there was no sign that the parties in power were in the mood for such a thorough reappraisal.

✍ DEAD-END STREET: FRANCE IN ASIA

With countries which possess a mature culture of their own, assimilation is neither feasible nor desirable. All that can be hoped for is association. But fraternity between nations as well as between men cannot exist except on terms of freedom and equality. It must not be the partnership between horse and driver. The application of this principle, however, requires fine discrimination. France had four major problems of that kind on her hands, all complex, all different. Two, concerning Asian countries (Syria-Lebanon and Indochina), have been settled by the total elimination of the French. Two, Madagascar and the Maghreb (French North Africa: Algeria, Tunis, Morocco), are still pending.

Syria and Lebanon.—We have already expressed our conviction that the mandates over the Arab countries of the Levant were misbegotten. They were an example of the duality of purpose in the Western mind: the contrast between the ideal of liberty and justice, which many Englishmen and Frenchmen honestly desired to serve, and the old realistic game of power politics. It may be noted that power politics four decades after the end of World War I are still the curse of the Middle East.

As early as 1933 the French were eager to terminate their difficult connection with Syria and Lebanon, which was spoiling an ancient friendship. They proposed to end the mandate under the same terms that England had adopted with Iraq. In 1936 a new and even more liberal treaty was signed. Unfortunately, it had not yet been ratified when World War II broke out. The French troops massed in Syria, under the command of General Dentz after General Weygand had left for France, remained faithful to Vichy; and the country was being used as an Axis base. The British still believed that the Middle East was of vital importance to their survival: it was necessary for them to drive the Vichy French out. The Free French aided in that operation, not without misgivings, for they hated having to fight against their former comrades. With a fine display of disinterestedness the British turned Syria and Lebanon over to General de Gaulle. He at once reaffirmed the determination of France to recognize the full independence of the Levant states. But he cautioned them that no final settlement was possible so long as his own government was purely provisional. Iraq, however, had never given up King Faisal's dream of adding Syria to his dominions; an independent republic in Syria did not satisfy the Iraqi imperialists. The British commissioner, Major-General Spears, although he professed to be a fervent admirer of French culture, did not show himself invariably tactful or ingenuous. The situation in 1944 and early in 1945 was tense. The promise of De Gaulle, however, was clearly implemented when, with the full consent of France, Syria and Lebanon were invited to the San Francisco Conference (March 28, 1945).

On May 21 the Syrian and Lebanese governments broke with France under the pretext that she was reinforcing her garrison. The French claimed that the new troops were not additional forces but only replacements. Rioting occurred, and there was sharp fighting. For the third time in the course of their ill-fated mandate, the French shelled Damascus. They had apparently "restored order" (an ominous phrase) when an ultimatum came from Mr. Winston Churchill to cease firing. It was supported by a strongly worded note from the United States ambassador in Paris, Mr. Jefferson Caffery. British troops, far outnumbering the French, assumed control. France's request that the question be submitted to the Big Five was rejected by President Truman (June 7).

The secrets of this imbroglio may never come to light. Sectarian and economic interests played at least as great a part as Syrian nationalism in the whole crisis; there were oil contracts back of the political move; and this factor was not negligible in the repeated military *coups d'état* which have shaken the independent Syrian Republic. One thing was certain: the Syrians did not want the French as their masters or even as their mentors. The unpleasant chapter, no source of pride or profit to the French, is now closed. Lebanon, a creation of France, permeated with French culture, and almost evenly divided between Mohammedans and Christians, soon restored friendly relations. These, however, were endangered again when the conflict between France and Nasser's Egypt broke out in 1956. "Africa" and "Asia" are crude, artificial terms. There is an ill-defined, but undeniable, unity of sentiment among the peoples of Arabic speech. The problems of the Near East and those of the Maghreb remain entangled. They cannot be settled by force alone.

Indochina.—France had long been prepared for the complete independence of Syria and Lebanon. The way in which it was achieved left a bitter aftertaste, but relief was predominant. The loss of Indochina after a protracted and ruinous struggle was felt as a major disaster. The difficult problem has not yet been fully worked out. Perhaps it never was quite so simple as it appeared to President Franklin Roosevelt. The one thing certain is that the military and political power of the French in Indochina will never be restored.

The governor-general of French Indochina when Vichy assumed control, General Catroux, refused to accept the surrender. He was later to become General de Gaulle's right-hand man, and to play an important part in the affairs of the Fourth Republic. But Catroux was not supported by his staff. Military passive obedience won the day, as it did in most of the colonies, and Catroux was superseded by Decoux, who remained loyal to Marshal Pétain. Gaullist officers were carefully weeded out.

The situation of the colony, completely cut off from Vichy France, was precarious in the extreme. The difficulty did not come mainly from native unrest: Indochina had not been groaning under an intolerable yoke. The essential fact was the unquestioned supremacy of Japan in Southeast Asia. Decoux easily repelled an attack by Thailand (Siam); but he had to submit to a so-called Japanese mediation, which awarded to Thailand disputed provinces in Laos and Cambodia. Then he offered not even a show of resistance to Japanese "friendly" occupation, and Indochina was used as a springboard for the campaign against Singapore. With the collapse of Vichy in 1944 the position of the Vichy collaborationists became untenable: in March, 1945, the Japanese removed those useless puppets and proclaimed the "independence" of the colony.

The independence movement (Viet Minh Front) had first been encouraged by the Chinese as an anti-Japanese underground. Yet Chiang Kai-shek did not trust its leader, Ho Chi Minh, a Moscow-trained Communist, and kept him in prison for over a year. But it was the Japanese who created the Vietnam state as a satellite and part of their co-prosperity sphere. Their attitude did not endear them to the local population; it gave a sinister meaning to the slogan, Asia for the Asians!

The surrender of Japan seems to have taken the Allies by surprise. In spite of General de Gaulle's repeated requests, no provision had been made to have French troops in readiness. So, in September, 1945, the situation was confused. At times the Japanese were officially requested to keep order in Indochina, while it was well known that they were distributing their arms to the Communists. At the end of September the British landed in the south of Indochina, and the Chinese moved in from the north. Of the five regions in the union, Laos and Cambodia had not so far wavered in their loyalty to France, their old protector against Siamese aggression. In the other three states, Tonkin, Annam, Cochin China, which together form Vietnam, good observers claimed that if the colonial status was rejected, the vast majority favored some kind of association with France.

In spite of President Franklin Roosevelt's repeated assurances that France would be fully restored, his aversion to (French) colonialism was no secret. Woodrow Wilson admitted—or boasted—that he had a one-track mind; Franklin Roosevelt's had many tracks; they crossed and double-crossed at times in puzzling fashion. Not without reluctance, the occupying powers returned the country to France. By March, 1946, the French had peacefully reoccupied all the principal cities, although at Haïphong, the port of Hanoi, they were fired upon, "by mistake," by Chinese batteries. As soon as he landed, the new high commissioner or governor-general, Admiral Georges Thierry d'Argenlieu,[3] recognized Vietnam as a free and independent state within the Indochinese Federation and the French Union. Ho Chi Minh, who had assumed power as Vietnamese president, responded to this liberal attitude. Negotiations went on at Dalat, a health resort in Indochina, and at Fontainebleau in France. The discussions were laborious but not unfriendly; and on September 15, 1946, Ho Chi Minh signed in Paris an accord with France, establishing a workable *modus vivendi*. His messages on leaving France and on landing in Indochina were not merely correct but cordial.

In spite of fair if guarded words the situation, morally and materially, was obscure. It was hard, of course, for the Europeans to give up their privileged status; and Admiral Thierry d'Argenlieu was recalled because it was suspected that he leaned unduly in favor of the French colonists. Many Vietnamese must have felt this reluctance and doubted whether the French would or could learn wisdom. On the other hand, not a few were aware that Indochina, as a conscious entity, had been created by the French. Its culture, thanks to the use of *quôc ngu,* the Latin alphabet introduced by the missionaries, had been detached from Chinese tradition. The people, just because there were so many Chinese merchants in their midst, had no great taste for Chinese imperialism. It seems clear that many Vietnamese were not disposed to brook Viet Minh totalitarianism, since the local Communists were the open supporters of Moscow. The French Communists, of course, wholeheartedly supported Viet Minh, and so long as they were part of the coalition in power, some agreement with Ho Chi Minh could not be ruled out. Brave words, democracy, freedom, independence, were bandied by both parties. Ho Chi Minh continued to talk with two voices: a sign not of duplicity but of complexity. As a Vietnamese patriot he reiterated his willingness to come to an accord with the French and did not reject the idea of free membership in the French Union; and in this attitude he found many sympathizers in France. But as a Communist he wanted his party to have exclusive control over the whole country, and this the French were not willing to grant.

The tragic break, however, did not come from the official circles, either in France or in Vietnam. All they did, through timidity, loose thinking, and mottled sincerity, was to make the break almost inevitable. We do not know, and perhaps shall never know, the secret history of Viet Minh. It is quite possible that Ho Chi Minh was overruled by the extremists in his own party. When the deed was done, he could not very well turn against his old comrades and go over to the French: brutally, they had hastened an evolution which could hardly be reversed. Many heads of revolutionary movements could use the words ascribed to Ledru-Rollin in 1849, "I have to follow them, since I am their leader."

On December 19, 1946, a planned surprise attack was launched by Viet Minh elements in the fields and within the cities. There was sharp fighting even in the heart of Hanoi; European civilians, including many women, were removed as hostages. The coup fell far short of success. The French and their sympathizers managed to keep hold of the key positions. Indeed, the French were able to maintain themselves in northern Vietnam for another six years. The decisive factor in their defeat was the emergence of Communist China. A victorious Chiang Kai-shek would have preferred, as the lesser of two evils, a pro-French regime on his southern border to an ally of Moscow.

But even the blindest among the French knew that the era of direct colonial rule was over. Indochina must be given, at least, the trappings of independence. Ho Chi Minh was a national hero but also the leader of a fanatical party. He had now—perhaps not on his own initiative— become a declared enemy. No other native leader, however, had a similar hold on popular imagination. So the French sought one who, in default of stature, had at least the prestige of traditional position. It was not rank Machiavellism. They were earnestly looking for a compromise, a transition. And they thought they had found such a symbol of the middle course in the last emperor of Annam (Central Vietnam), Bao Dai.

So they dragged him back into nominal power, although he had no great desire to re-enter the dark jungles of Indochinese politics: he had quietly abdicated in August 25, 1945, and offered his services as a friendly adviser to the Vietnam government. An agreement was signed with him on Along Bay (June 5, 1948) and confirmed by a new treaty on March 8, 1949. Bao Dai returned to Indochina in April. He announced that, while he was provisionally retaining the title of emperor, the future constitution of Vietnam was to be framed by the people. Officially, he was only chief of state and president of the government. General Nguyen Van Xuan was made vice-president and minister of defense. The venture, now swept into the scrap heap of history, was not absurd. The Catholics, not a negligible quantity in Indochina, heartily supported the new regime; so did the very active followers of a new, and quaintly syncretic, religion, Cao Dai. So did many conservatives, who did not relish the prospect of a Communist dictatorship. So did many patriots, who preferred a nominal connection with France to Chinese overlordship—be China red, white, or simply yellow. Had the West unequivocally endorsed the Bao Dai government, events might have taken a different turn.

But the curse of ambiguity lay heavily on the Bao Dai regime. He could not hope to win even the qualified loyalty of his people unless he secured substantial concessions from the French. And the French did grant him more than they had offered Ho Chi Minh, at Dalat or Fontainebleau. But they could not give him everything, knowing all too well how precarious his power was. They were in constant fear that in the name of promised independence, he would demand independence, i.e., the right not to join the French Union. The French could not suppress their own die-hards; the Vietnamese their own now-or-nevers. Bao Dai found the situation inextricable and retired to his beloved Riviera, proving that a puppet and a playboy—if he deserved the terms —could at least show rudimentary political sense. When Southern Vietnam came into existence, Bao Dai was unceremoniously brushed aside.

So the inconclusive tussle went on not for months but for weary years. The French still ruled and even had their gay life, lurid on a background of tragedy, in the great cities, Hanoi, Saigon. The strength of the Viet Minh was in the fertile, densely populated delta of the Red River. The French controlled that area by day, the rebels by night, and the hapless peasants were impartially oppressed by both sides. In the sultry atmosphere of doomed Indochina corruption was rife—even in high military circles. This offered no final argument against the presence of the French: corruption when detected can be cured. But it created in France a feeling of unutterable nausea.

In 1950 the character of the war changed altogether. The Chinese Communists had finally defeated the Nationalist government of Chiang Kai-shek and reached the northern border of Vietnam. This immeasurably improved the moral and material position of the Viet Minh. It now had as a neighbor a powerful friend instead of a potential enemy, and its troops could be armed and trained by the Chinese, veterans of a long struggle. The rebels were no longer guerrillas, on the uncertain border between terrorism and brigandage: they could muster, organize, and supply modern armies. In October, 1950, they launched an offensive against the fortress of Caobang; the French suffered heavy casualties, and it looked as though Hanoi itself would be threatened. It would have been wisdom to heed the suggestions of General Revers, the French chief of staff, who, on his return from a mission in Vietnam, advocated a political approach to the problem; in plainer terms, negotiations with Ho Chi Minh. But the disastrous turn of events also opened favorable possibilities. With the recognition of Ho Chi Minh by Russia and China, the issue no longer was Nationalism *vs.* Colonialism but Communism *vs.* the Free World. The Truman Doctrine had been proclaimed, and the Korean War had begun. The position that France had lost as an imperial power could be retrieved in the name of liberty.

This new idealism offered a chance to settle the problem with true Bismarckian realism, through blood and iron. The task was entrusted to General de Lattre de Tassigny, with sole command both of political power and of the armed forces. He was one of the highest ranking officers in the French service. When southern France was taken over by the Nazis, he alone had attempted to resist. Then he had led his troops from the Mediterranean, up the Rhône, across the Rhine, to the very gates of Vienna: an impressive epic, although overshadowed by more massive movements. In 1951 he managed to stabilize the situation in the Red River Delta. Sickness compelled him to return to France where he died in the halo of his precarious victory. He was given a great state funeral and was rewarded posthumously with a marshal's bâton. An anachronism perhaps, but an impressive one.

De Lattre de Tassigny, however, was well aware that France alone was unequal to the task—and had no stomach for it. He came to Washington to urge upon the chiefs of staff the need of unstinted aid. Supplies and certain kinds of armaments were generously provided. But neither France nor America had a clear mind and a clear conscience about this equivocal contest. France knew that the Bao Dai regime would collapse without her support: she expected to remain in Vietnam as a disinterested friend but also literally as a protector for many years to come. America had not recanted the preconceptions of Franklin Roosevelt: the French must go. So, the French in 1951 were no longer fighting their own battle: they were hired to support an American policy. The United States called the tune, because they provided much of the steel and much of the gold. But France gave her blood and did not like the tune.[4]

Pierre Mendès-France then dared to suggest, as General Revers had hinted, that the war should be brought to an end by negotiations, not by force. He was a vigorous and unconventional statesman who, at thirty, had been undersecretary of finances under Léon Blum; during the war, an air-force officer; and minister of national economy in the cabinet of General de Gaulle. Nominated to the premiership, he failed in June, 1953, by a small margin to secure the endorsement of the Assembly. Washington was frowning on any kind of "appeasement." Once more, the great principle would be applied, "There is no substitute for victory." And General Navarre, the newly appointed commander in

Indochina, promised a "dynamic technique" that would break the deadlock.

On November 20, 1953, six battalions of paratroopers were dropped at Dien Bien Phu in the Thai region of North Vietnam, two hundred miles away from the beleaguered delta. It was hoped that the new base would divert large Viet Minh forces. A bold move, which, for a while, captured popular imagination. Isolated Dien Bien Phu was ignored at first by General Giap, the Viet Minh commander. But by February, 1954, it was already encircled. It had to depend entirely on air lift for supplies, the evacuation of the sick and wounded, and replacements; and the area on which the planes could land shrank inexorably day by day. The world stood breathless while Colonel de Castries was holding the fortress. But, unless drastic measures were taken, disaster was inescapable.

The fate of Dien Bien Phu depended on America's decision. Had the French been given adequate support, the symbolical stronghold might have been relieved—at the risk of turning the cold war into World War III. But America had given up, in doubt and weariness, the hope of a military decision in Korea: she was in no mood to unleash a major offensive in Indochina, where the moral case was not so clear and the military conditions even more unfavorable. Had the Viet Minh remained mere guerrilla fighters, Dien Bien Phu would have been impregnable: it came as a surprise to the French that their opponents had 105 mm. guns, which had come from the United States via Chiang Kai-shek and the Chinese Communists. After fifty-six days of almost continuous assaults, the fortress was swamped under and the remnant of its gallant garrison taken prisoners.[5]

On June 9, 1954, Pierre Mendès-France attacked vigorously and overthrew the fumbling cabinet of Laniel, incapable either of waging war or making peace. He thus became the logical candidate for the premiership. His program could be summed up in a threat and a promise. "If you want war, we shall have to send draftees, your own sons, to the battlefields of Indochina. If you want peace, I shall bring you a ceasefire agreement by July 20 [this was June 17] or resign."

The sharp realism of his attitude, after so many years of flabby grandiloquence, carried the day. At once the halting conference at Geneva was revitalized. Mendès-France did not capitulate: he defended the interests of France and her Vietnamese friends with great vigor. He overstepped his self-imposed deadline by only a few hours. An armistice line was drawn at the narrow waist of Vietnam, on the seventeenth parallel, the gradual and honorable withdrawal of the French forces was agreed upon.

The Viet Minh, which had the upper hand, gave up the hope of unifying the country at once, and by military means. It received in exchange the assurance that a referendum would be held in the whole of Vietnam within two years. This was understood to be a face-saving device and a period of grace granted to the French and their Indochinese collaborators. No one doubted then which way the elections would go. But a strongly anti-Communist and anti-French government was set up in Southern Vietnam under the leadership of Diem. It refused to be bound by the agreement, which had been signed in the name of the now defunct Bao Dai regime. So Vietnam joined the company of nations artifically divided—perhaps for many years to come: Ireland, Germany, India,[6] Korea.

The twilight of France in Indochina is not yet darkness absolute. The French are still trading actively with Vietnam. Their cultural institutions have not wholly disappeared. A large and brand-new pavilion in the Paris Cité Universitaire is ready to receive hordes of students from Cambodia. Saigon, although far more subdued than in its colonial past, is still the Paris of the Orient. The cross-fertilization of cultures, which is the one great hope of human culture, has not been completely ruled out by doctrinaires and fanatics.

The problem is: why did the French cling so desperately to a possession so remote and so alien? Over half a century ago, a very patriotic geographer, Onésime Reclus, had written a prophetic book: *Lâchons l'Asie, prenons l'Afrique* ("We must let Asia go, and stick to Africa"). And we cannot forget that Jules Ferry, perhaps the greatest statesman of the Third Republic, was called "the Tonkinese" in hatred and derision, for having given France a new empire she did not desire. If the French were pure rationalists, or pure *petits bourgeois,* the problem would not have arisen. Selfish interest is a poor explanation: the French had long realized that they were pouring gold into Vietnam at a rate which no profit-making could match. Blind pride, the Churchillian refusal to "liquidate" cannot be ruled out: many Americans who feel that the Truman Doctrine is not an eternal verity yet are reluctant to confess their error. Perhaps the French were suffering from a sense of injustice. They wanted the gradual transformation of empire into commonwealth as sincerely as England; they had no desire to retain more of a privileged position in Indochina than the United States has preserved in the Philippines; yet they were singled out for opprobrium. To some extent also—let the cynics smile—they were moved by a sense of moral responsibility. The definite secession of Vietnam began in terrorism— the coup of December 19, 1946, in Hanoi. Now yielding to brutal violence is not a wholesome attitude. The French felt themselves responsible for the many Vietnamese—at one time they may have been a majority—who openly or tacitly trusted them. All is not ignoble even in the most dismal failure. The essential fact was that the French had never quite made up their mind to grant—or rather to acknowledge— Vietnam's claims to liberty and equality. There always was a mental reserve: provided the paramount interests of France are not forfeited. The result was disaster. The lesson was costly, in treasure, blood, and pride. But the Fourth Republic failed to learn the lesson.

THE ARDUOUS PATH: FRANCE IN AFRICA

Africa, like Asia, is a delusive convention. The Maghreb (Tunisia, Algeria, Morocco) is manifestly part of the Mediterranean world. There are marked differences even between West Africa and Equatorial Africa. Madagascar is a curious little continent, geologically different from its huge neighbor, culturally linked with distant Malaya. The one thing these four regions have in common is that they offer the French a series of intricate problems, and that these problems are not yet beyond the hope of a reasonable solution.

Madagascar.—In Madagascar as in Syria the British, for reasons of global strategy, had been compelled to eliminate the Vichy authorities: if the great island had fallen within the sphere of Japan, the whole Indian Ocean would have been lost. Conquered after a brief campaign, Madagascar was correctly turned over to the Free French. But the years of isolation and uncertainty, the sharp struggle in which French forces had been defeated had naturally created a crisis: protectors cannot afford to lose face. When political life was restored, four main parties arose. The Party of the Disinherited comprised, among others, the descendants of the slaves liberated by the French. The Democratic Malagasy party and the Social Malagasy Movement were under the influence of the Protestant and Catholic missions respectively. The main force of the Democratic Movement of Malagasy Renovation was found among the Hovas, who were the ruling element in Madagascar under the native monarchy.

Here we have a clear example of the wide gap between "democratic freedom" and "independence." The Hovas represent not liberty but a local imperialism; they want to recover their lost overlordship. They are an oppressive minority posing as an oppressed nationality; but, better educated than the mass and more politically conscious, they are far more articulate. During the night of March 30, 1947, an uprising started simultaneously at four widely separated points. Documents seized by the French proved that the revolt had been engineered by the Renovation party with ignorant villagers as their tools. The rebellion was quelled, not without rigor; but it caused serious unrest in the island and angry debates in the French Parliament. The French Communists, following shibboleths rather than realities, stood for the upper-class Hovas against the Disinherited. But even liberal socialists were confused in their minds.[7] By 1957 it seemed as though the Malagasy would be satisfied with an increasing measure of self-government.

West Africa.—West Africa is in ferment, but in a fashion which is a sign of joyous vitality rather than a portent of despair. Both the British and the French sections of this subcontinent are now fully awake. Their development cannot proceed on the basis of tribal cultures: "independent" Ghana, for instance, definitely follows British patterns. The French more frankly proclaim their principle of ultimate assimilation, which is another word for full equality and the rejection of *Apartheid*. They feel that progress has to be rapid if it is to be safe. But they have learned—none too soon—that mere forms imposed from Paris will not promote their ideal. If their "union" eschews the dangers of mechanical standardization, if it is actually based on the spontaneous activities of the local population, it will in the end prove not very different from the commonwealth, and it may present definite advantages. At least this is ably argued by Félix Houphouet-Boigny, a Negro leader who became minister of state in charge of African affairs in several French cabinets.[8] Although Senghor has developed a race consciousness which may be considered regressive, he still believes that West Africa is deriving benefits from its participation in French culture. The face of West Africa is changing with startling rapidity. Dakar, a port of world importance with a new university and impressive modern buildings, is a striking example of this transformation. Abidjan, with its newly opened deep-sea harbor, is forging ahead. The natives are passing with surprising ease from prehistory into the later twentieth century. And their art—music, sculpture, even architecture—has won the respect of European connoisseurs. Indeed, there is a danger that sophisticated Paris might become Africanized.

Equatorial Africa.—French Equatorial Africa was long considered as hopelessly backward. Its coastal region was unhealthy, the interior difficult of access. Worst of all, it had been saddled with an imitation of the Congo Free State methods at the very moment when, thanks to the denunciations of Casement and Morel, the ruthless profiteering of the Leopoldian era was brought to an end. André Gide gave a damaging report of his journey through the Congo, a story almost as somber as Conrad's *Heart of Darkness*. French Equatorial Africa today is by no means idyllic, but it no longer is a blot on French civilization. The French like to remember that it was founded, without brutality, by

Savorgnan de Brazza, who in spirit stood closer to Livingstone than to the red-blooded and red-handed realist, Stanley.

The Mandates.—A very interesting and complex development is taking place in the former German colonies, Togoland and Cameroons, parts of which were placed under French mandate as a result of World War I. When the League of Nations was superseded by the United Nations, the term trusteeship was substituted for mandate, but the original ambiguity was not removed.

France has to report on her administration of the territories to the Trusteeship Council; and although acrimonious complaints have been lodged against her, the council invariably concluded that her methods were on the whole above reproach. But the correctness, indeed the courtesy, that prevailed in these discussions did not veil a conflict of ideals. For the doctrinaires of nationalism the goal of trusteeship should be complete independence: outright secession from the protecting power and cultural development on a purely native basis. The French do not conceal that their aim is to train their wards in the ways of liberty and culture; this does not preclude, it might even favor, closer union with France. It would not be colonialism in the old sense of domination and exploitation if the natives of their own accord should prefer French ways to their own tribal customs.

The inhabitants of the two territories are not French nationals; but, according to the Trusteeship Agreement of December 13, 1946, "The Administering Authority shall have full powers of legislation, administration, and jurisdiction in this territory, and shall administer it in accordance with French law as an integral part of French territory, subject to the provisions of the Charter, and of this agreement." Certain forces would emphasize divergent evolution; the French believe in convergent evolution. Both Togoland and Cameroons have become autonomous republics associated with the French Union. Both have an interesting method of implementing their interdependence with France: their citizens in France enjoy all the rights and privileges of French citizenship, and reciprocally. It is not inconceivable that the Togo-Cameroons formula, which has the great merit of flexibility, may gradually be extended to the former African colonies of France. Names do matter: a Republic of Senegal, for instance, within the West African Federation and the French Union would be far preferable to a Department of Senegal with prefect and subprefects.

Cameroons is perhaps best known because Lambarene is the home of Albert Schweitzer, theologian, musician, medical missionary; a man who, in the service of mankind, has transcended both French and German nationalism [9] and the deathly literalism of any sect.

The Maghreb (North Africa).—There is no resemblance between the Indochinese problem and the North African. Indochina was but an incident in French history: Algeria, in the course of a century and a quarter, has grown to be an essential part of French consciousness. Tunis and Morocco, on either flank, form with Algeria a single region, the Maghreb, which it would be unnatural to divide. The natives are in no sense an alien race. They are not pure-blooded Arabs but a historical mosaic of all the populations in the Mediterranean basin. Wave after wave of invaders—Cro-Magnons, Phoenicians, Romans, Vandals, Arabs, Turks, and, in the coast towns, Jews, Levantines, the descendants of slaves and renegades of all nations—have made the ethnic pattern so intricate that the various elements can be told apart by their costumes not by their features. I have met, particularly around Constantine, very handsome Berbers [10] who were blond, while some of the Europeans from southern Spain and Sicily were darker than the average Mohammedans. Saigon and Hanoi are at the other end of the world: Algiers is only five hundred miles from Marseilles, a thousand miles from Paris: a matter of a few hours' flight. The climate is perfectly healthy for northerners: in winter, it used to attract a large number of tourists. As a result well over a million and a half Europeans live in the Maghreb, the majority of them French citizens by birth or choice. Many of the natives, even without a formal education, speak excellent French with a pleasing slightly guttural intonation and are quicker at Parisian repartee than most people of the same class in the rural parts of France. There is no color line: in the best hotels and cafés Roumis and Mohammedans, some of the latter resplendent with impressive decorations, can be seen side by side. North Africa is an admirable field for the interpenetration and cross-fertilization of cultures.

We cannot, in such a study as this, give in full detail the tangled chronicle of events. Our task will be to present the essential conditions of the problem. The process of symbiosis, the friendly and fruitful cooperation of various elements, has been retarded, and at times actually endangered, by the idea of assimilation. That idea, as we have said, was neither absurd nor ignoble. But in North Africa it was hemmed in with mental restrictions. It embodied the conviction that ultimately all the inhabitants of French North Africa should enjoy full citizenship of the orthodox French pattern. In that form assimilation is a dream, and most decidedly not a beautiful dream. The privileged colonists were well aware of it and, indeed, rejoiced in the fact: Islam was there to stand guard.

When Bourmont landed near Algiers in 1830, he promised the natives that their religion, their institutions, their customs would be respected.

They constantly reminded the French of that promise: it was the palladium of their self-respect. Their special Koranic status emphasized the fact that they were free associates rather than a conquered people. To give it up would have offended their religious conscience, and it would also have destroyed their collective pride.

Pluralism, or peaceful coexistence, was, therefore, the essential condition in Algeria from the very first. But the French, in defiance of the plain facts, declared Algeria to be an extension of France under the minister of the interior; they divided it into French departments with their prefects and subprefects. Napoleon III, whose mind, hazy at times, was capable of generous and far-seeing intuition, reacted against this unnatural standardization. He refused to consider the natives as an alien and subject population in their own country. He referred to Algeria as "an Arab kingdom" and declared that he was the emperor of the Arabs as well as of the French. The Arabs responded to his appeal. But premature old age, disease, mounting difficulties at home and abroad prevented him from implementing this excellent policy.[11]

The colonists, with half-conscious duplicity, used the lofty assimilation ideal as a method of keeping the government in their own hands. Their argument sounded irrefutable: "Citizenship with all its privileges is freely open to all; but if you want to share in the making of French law, you first have to accept French law." Accepting French law meant giving up Koranic law; and this, the colonists knew very well, the natives would never consent to do. The number of naturalizations remained infinitesimal. The Mohammedans looked with contempt upon the "M'Tourni," or transfuges. The Catholic Europeans did not welcome them with open arms. As a result the Mohammedan masses were taxed and drafted into military service by political bodies in which they were not represented.[12]

In spite of the official doctrine that Algeria was made up of three departments "just like the others," the plain fact of a radical difference could not be altogether evaded. There was a governor-general as the symbol that Algeria possessed a separate identity. There was even the embryo of a local parliament, still very undemocratic in its mode of election and with purely consultative functions, called the Financial Delegations.

A breach in the wall was made when Mohammedans were allowed a minor place in municipal and departmental councils; but they were still kept out of general politics. A Socialist senator, governor-general, and minister, Maurice Viollette, proposed a gradual way out. A limited number of well-qualified Mohammedans would at once be given full French citizenship without having to renounce their Koranic status. The

Viollette Plan was the great issue in Algeria just before World War II. The European colonists, afraid of losing their political monopoly, fought it tooth and nail; the European officials and intellectuals, more disinterested, were inclined to favor it. It must be noted that at that time the native leaders expressed no desire for independence. They simply wanted equality of rights, including the right of preserving their religious traditions. The believers in "France One and Indivisible" found this coexistence of different laws hard to conceive. Léon Blum, leader of the *Front Populaire,* was, like ageing Napoleon III, well meaning but somewhat infirm of purpose. He too was absorbed in more pressing problems—the Spanish Civil War, the increasing aggressiveness of the Nazis, the sympathies that Hitler's spirit and method found among many Frenchmen. When the war broke out, nothing had been decided.

The history of French North Africa during the war was exceedingly tangled and would provide a fruitful field for a Phillips Oppenheim. The country remained under Vichy allegiance. It was not occupied, but there were German and Italian commissions to check up on the application of the armistice terms; and their action extended far beyond their official duties. On the other hand, American agents were watchfully waiting and carrying on secret negotiations with various French elements. In all the services there were Gaullists, Pétainistes of the strictest observance, *attentistes,* and even Royalists, all eyeing one another with deep suspicion. The shady Darlan episode, the landing of Allied troops, the tussle between Giraud and De Gaulle increased the fever: the French system appeared as a house divided. A disastrous drought was an added cause of discontent. In May, 1945, there were riots in the department of Constantine, and an uprising of Berber tribes. Three hundred Europeans were killed or wounded. The report, widely circulated in America, that ten thousand natives had been massacred in repressive operations proved a gross exaggeration.

The handling of the Algerian problem by the Fourth Republic was from the first a masterpiece of the middle course, that is to say, of hopeless confusion. The Algerian departments remained, in theory, departments of France: they were recognized as such under the Atlantic Pact. Any suggestion of an autonomous Algerian republic was frowned upon, and France felt legally justified in rejecting any interference on the part of the United Nations. Yet the manifest differences north and south of the Mediterranean were recognized with some approach to realism. Under the new regime everyone who belonged to the country enjoyed French citizenship, with equal rights, and without any distinction of religion. But citizens of European origin, Israelites, and a number of assimilated Mohammedans were to vote in one "college"; the rest, that is to say, the bulk of the Mohammedan population, in a second college. Both colleges were entitled to an equal number of seats, both in the French Parliament and in a local Assembly. This was a rough, but not wholly unfair, compromise. If the Mohammedan college was enormously superior in sheer numbers, the European college had a marked advantage in wealth, education, political experience. It was a case of weighted representation, not an ideal solution by any means; but if the Algerian problem had not been affected by conditions beyond the borders of Algeria, it might have proved a workable approach.

In the elections to the Algerian Assembly, which took place on April 4–11, 1948, the Gaullist R.P.F. (Rally of the French People) won a sweeping victory in the European college (39 seats out of 60). In the Mohammedan college the two parties advocating friendly co-operation with the French won 41 seats out of 60. It must be said that this all-too-auspicious result caused the raising of skeptical eyebrows. The only irreconcilable party, grandiloquently named Movement for the Triumph of Democratic Liberties, which was openly preaching secession, elected only nine representatives. The Democratic Union of the Algerian Manifesto, which demanded autonomy within the French Union, elected eight. The Communists had only one deputy in the first college; and although they had made great efforts to evangelize the native masses, they found no response among them. Inevitably, they claimed that the results had been tampered with.[13]

There was a lull in the Algerian crisis, but it did not prove lasting. For this worsening, many causes could be adduced. The most indefinite, yet probably the most effective, was the loss of prestige France was suffering from the irresolution and impotence of the Third Force. Tunis and Morocco, as we shall see, were agitating for the end of the protectorate regime. Their growing nationalism was bound to contaminate their Algerian neighbors, so closely akin to them and politically more advanced. But among the factors of unrest the most decisive was the flaring up of pan-Arabism. This in turn was due to the creation of the Jewish state in Palestine. The Arab nations considered Israel as the latest and most flagrant example of Western colonialism. And their sharp defeat at the hands of the intruder made the wound to their pride more grievous. Cairo became the center of a new faith. Arms were sent to the discontented in North Africa, and propagandists far more dangerous than arms. The bond of union between the Pan-Arab League and the Maghreb extremists was not racial, political, or cultural: the Mohammedan world has never been deeply moved by these ideologies. It was religious: Islamic lands must be freed from the yoke of the infidels. The rebellion might decorate itself with nationalistic and democratic trappings: in its essence it was a new Jehad, a Holy War.

Hence the fanaticism displayed by the terrorists. They, the men in the field, would not consider the possibility of a parley. The only alternatives they were offering the French were *"la valise ou le cercueil"* ("the suitcase or the coffin"), pack off or be killed. The Mohammedan élite, after agitating for political rights, was forced into an equivocal game. Educated natives who, twenty years before, would have been satisfied with the Viollette Plan, found it hard to condemn their coreligionists fighting in the name of "independence." Indeed, they were using the rebellion as a threat to secure concessions from the French. But they were well aware that if the fanatics were to triumph, their own hopes for a progressive Maghreb would be shattered. The terrorists killed far more Mohammedan moderates than they killed Frenchmen.

The same tense and tragic situation prevailed in the three countries of the Maghreb. But in Tunisia and Morocco there existed native governments: it was possible, if not easy, to increase their share of authority and responsibility. This possibility did not exist in Algeria, which had never formed a single state, and had actually been created by the French. Caught between the fanaticism of the European settlers, bent on maintaining their absolute supremacy, and the fanaticism of the Fellaghas, as the rebels were called, the moderates, both Christians and Moslems, were bewildered and powerless. They looked to Paris for guidance, and in Paris they found—the Third Force.

The French government could mask its confusion under an unimpeachable principle. There was an explosion of violence in Algeria, and no civilized government can yield to sheer lawlessness. As soon as order was restored, democratic elections would be held—if need be, under the supervision of foreign observers. Then Algeria could freely control her own destiny. But the ambiguity remained: the order to be restored was the pre-existing order, French order, maintained by 400,000 French soldiers. The moderates had no assurance that such an order would not mean the perpetuation of European power.

The last few years have shown the vanity of sheer force. There have been few engagements of any magnitude, only fierce sudden raids, ambushes, sporadic massacres, wanton destruction, followed by repressive measures which cannot be gentle, and are not invariably intelligent. Meanwhile, large elements among the French, not Communists merely, and friends of France throughout the world were growing uneasy. After exalting the heroism of the Resistance—Underground and Maquis—it was embarrassing to suppress men using the same slogan, freedom, and the same ruthless means. Police methods have failed; prosperity, if it could be revived and expanded, would not do the trick. There can be no reasonable solution without reasonable discussion; and by reasonable we mean a discussion in the light of justice, not from a position of strength.

In this arduous but not yet hopeless path the French have suffered three serious reverses. The first was at the beginning of the Guy Mollet administration. Guy Mollet, a Socialist, desired a peaceful settlement; and he appointed as minister resident—the new name for governor-general—one of the grand old men of the Fourth Republic, General Catroux, who in Syria and Morocco had shown his willingness to negotiate. His name was a program; and for that reason, he was anathema to the French colonists. Guy Mollet went to Algiers to investigate the situation: he was insulted and pelted with rotten vegetables by an angry mob (February 5, 1956). Before the threat of a *French* insurrection in Algeria, he capitulated at once, "accepted the resignation" of General Catroux and appointed Robert Lacoste in his stead. Lacoste, also a Socialist, was known to be a believer in firmness: order first of all, that is to say, the unconditional surrender of the opponents. Week after week, Robert Lacoste kept announcing that the situation was well in hand, and the end of the rebellion in sight; week after week, the cost was mounting and the returns diminishing.

The second blow to reasonable hopes came in October, 1956. Five Algerian leaders, offering some guarantee of responsibility, met Sultan (now King) Mohammed ben Youssef of Morocco. It was arranged that they would then confer with Premier (now President) Habib Bourguiba in Tunis, where Mohammed ben Youssef would join them. Both the Moroccan ruler and the Tunisian leader, against their own extremists, had struck acceptable bargains with the French. They were well qualified to secure somewhat similar terms for Algeria. A federation of the Maghreb countries in friendly co-operation with France would be an ideal way of breaking the deadlock. But by an all-too-clever trick the plane carrying the five Algerians was diverted to French territory where they were arrested. Documents in their possession proved their "guilt," i.e., their opposition to French rule. Mohammed ben Youssef and Bourguiba were incensed: they swore they could never trust the French again. Premier Guy Mollet was hardly less furious, for the plan for an all-Maghreb solution, it was rumored, had his secret blessing. He took again the safe middle course: he capitulated unconditionally.

The third defeat may prove the most irretrievable. Throughout the summer and early fall of 1957 the cabinet of M. Bourgès-Maunoury was preparing a *loi-cadre* for a new Algerian status. The definiteness and generosity of the plan were meant to impress the United Nations which, under pressure from the Asian Bloc and a notable part of American opinion, could not forever refrain from looking into that distressing problem. But the government was, in true Third Force fashion, hopelessly divided. The ministers could agree only on a program so vague and so dilatory that no one in France or in Algeria could consider it even as a basis for further discussion. There are moments of "normalcy" when it is safe enough to drift, ask no "iffy" question, cross no bridge until you come to it. But in a desperate crisis, masterly evasiveness will not suffice, and decisions cannot be shirked.

It was in Algeria, as we shall see, that the crisis broke out which led to the downfall of the Fourth Republic. We shall examine the paradoxical situation which arose from General de Gaulle's accession to power, and the curiously subtle diplomacy displayed by that man of inflexible will. He knew there was no single Gordian knot to cut, but, in all elements of the population, a tangle of passions, interests, and hopes. He brought into the conflict factors which had been woefully lacking and which may yet prove decisive: prestige, courage, and generosity. Difficulties will not suddenly dissolve before this Higher Realism. At any rate, the battle for sanity is not lost.

In Tunisia the Destour and Neo-Destour parties had long worked for a liberal constitutional regime: they felt that the nominal autocracy of the bey left too free a field to his French advisers. But that middle-class, middle-road movement, although it could claim the support of the masses, was in constant danger of being swamped by the extremists. These relied on the uneducated, semi-barbaric elements, on the ultraconservative Moslems, and on the Pan-Arabic agitators from Egypt: an unstable combination, but one which could become formidable because of its very irresponsibility. Even the trusted veteran Habib Bourguiba, who had been banned for years by the French, felt his leadership challenged by Salah ben Youssef, who stood for the straitest, most anti-Western Islamic tradition.

An effort was made in 1950 to liberalize the protectorate and give the natives a larger share in the administration of their country. But it was not far-reaching enough and soon ended in bickerings. Bourguiba, who had been allowed to re-enter active politics, was arrested again.

In June, 1954, when he assumed power, Pierre Mendès-France announced his intention to reopen friendly Franco-Tunisian discussions. On July 31 he dramatically flew to Tunis and had an interview with the bey. He declared himself ready to end the old protectorate regime and to recognize the right of Tunisia to complete self-government. This marked a new era in Franco-Tunisian relations. Bourguiba was recalled from exile; his party triumphed over the extremists in the elections for the Constitutional Assembly. In 1957 he felt himself strong enough to depose the bey, whose policy had been vacillating and less dignified than his stately appearance. Habib Bourguiba became the first President of the Tunisian Republic.

Again: there seldom are happy endings. Bourguiba is a thorough Westerner, perhaps more at home in French than in Arabic culture. He has defeated Salah ben Youssef. But he is aware that Moslem fanaticism and Pan-Arabic imperialism are forces which cannot be ignored. In a conflict between Islam and France, he cannot afford to hesitate. And two such conflicts have already occurred. The first arose out of the Algerian tragedy. Paradoxically, yet not unnaturally, the Algerian terrorists hated Bourguiba: he stood for the spirit of conciliation which, to them, means treason to their holy cause. It is probable that Bourguiba distrusts them in return. But in the eyes of the Tunisian people the fellaghas are fellow Moslems fighting for independence. The Algerian rebels have repeatedly organized and started raids from Tunisian soil, with the complicity of the local population. When the French attempted to break up their preparations, they were accused of violating Tunisia's sovereignty, all the more jealous for being so recent. In that atmosphere the presence of French troops, even in the large naval base of Bizerta-Ferryville, was resented as a trace of colonialism.

The second conflict in which Tunisia had to take sides was that of France with Nasser's Egypt. The French well knew that the center of North African agitation was in Cairo. The seizure of the Suez Canal was only the last straw. On October 29–30 Israel, England, and France started a concerted attack on Egypt. (The plea that the British and French forces were acting in the interest of peace, in order to separate the Egyptian and Israeli armies and impose a cease-fire agreement, was received with ironical smiles.) The operation began well from the military point of view. But, diplomatically, it was ill-prepared. It seems that England and France would not have engaged in such an enterprise unless they had expected a successful coup in Cairo. The aggressors must have counted also on the friendly neutrality of the United States, the great protector of Israel. But the wave of indignation that swept the world carried both America and Russia, somewhat embarrassed at finding themselves fellow travelers. This abortive act of force had a double effect in Tunisia. It made France appear as the enemy of the Arab world, and as an enemy of uncertain mettle.

Without French aid the economy of Tunisia would be precarious. But France, reasonably enough, is reluctant to pour money into the treasury of a dubious friend, an almost declared enemy. So Bourguiba is bargaining for credits, and even for arms, with the United States. The situation is extremely ambiguous. If France were to use financial pressure in order to restore her domination in Tunisia, Washington would be strongly tempted to come to the aid of President Bourguiba. But such an act would be considered inimical by France, whose co-operation is indispensable to America's European policy.

In Tunisia, as in so many other parts of the world, "one hand is cordially extended, the other holds a dagger." The battle for friendly co-operation is not lost, but it is wavering. If the French are to win the confidence of Tunisia again, the way will have to be through Cairo and Algiers. Tunisia is tame compared with Morocco, a land of dramatic contrasts and riotous picturesqueness. But with sharp differences in details the story of the two countries follows the same general lines.

Like Habib Bourguiba, Sultan Mohammed ben Youssef was no sworn enemy of the French. He realized all they had achieved not only in his country but for his country. He wanted his people to be Westernized at a faster rate than the French would allow. The French, very sincerely in the case of Marshal Lyautey, had a genuine respect for Moroccan culture. They liked it so well that they wanted it to remain traditional, that is to say, archaic. It rejoiced them that the caids and pashas in their mountain fortresses were purely medieval figures. This romantic love for the colorful past combined admirably with the shrewdest realism. Since everything modern had been brought into Morocco by the French, it should remain in the hands of the French.

In building a new country the French, leaving behind the timid spirit of the Third and Fourth Republics, showed themselves masters of the American spirit: the growth of Casablanca, a teeming mart of 700,000, is even more sensational than that of Houston, Texas. But in their government, they were relying on the most conservative elements: a theocratic sultan whose power they had restored, or rather created; the great feudal lords in the Atlas Mountains; the Berber tribes; and particularly the powerful chieftain of the South, El Glaoui, Pasha of Marrakesh. The pluralistic principle prevailed: the thirteenth century and the twentieth lived side by side. But no sufficient thought had been given to converging evolution. If, in the forty years of their predominance, the French had trained a sizable body of technicians—engineers, professional men, administrators—years of painful chaos could have been spared.

As in Syria, Indochina, Madagascar, Algeria, Tunis, it was World War II that ruined the prestige of the French: first the collapse of 1940, then the still more humiliating subserviency of the Vichy regime, finally the predominance inevitably assumed by England and America. In Morocco General Noguès, the very able resident general, had remained loyal to Vichy, opposed the landing of Allied troops, and, therefore, was counted among the defeated. America, the new leader, had never fully recognized the French Protectorate; and President Roosevelt, ignoring the French authorities, addressed the sultan as a wholly independent sovereign.

There arose in Morocco a party of independence (Istiqlal) which was anti-French only because the French would not relax their stranglehold of Moroccan economy. It comprised, of course, not a few extremists—fanatics, self-seekers, and genuine idealists—whose single article of faith was, "The French must go!" The sultan was not their leader, but he was their symbol. He, who had been educated in Western ideas, could not condemn their aspirations for a modern, self-governing Morocco. So the sultan, the pillar of France's Toryism for the natives, was inclining toward the more radical elements. The French, greatly chagrined, accused him of "flirting" with the subversive Istiqlal. Losing patience, they decided to keep Morocco true to the Moroccan way of life, and appealed to the conservative forces, the Berber tribes, El Glaoui. The sultan was condemned for his "modernism." Berber hordes advanced on Fez, Rabat, Meknès. The French felt they could not resist such a spontaneous uprising of native sentiment. Mohammed ben Youssef was smuggled out of the country and sent to comfortable exile in Madagascar (August, 1953); and the ulemas, or religious leaders, chose in his stead a member of the Sherifian family, Sidi Mohammed ben Moulay Arafa, noted for his piety. Just as the French had revitalized the Moroccan arts and crafts, they were now attempting to promote Mohammedan orthodoxy. So the Catholics and freethinkers of Paris gave Morocco an unimpeachable commander of the faithful. The Spirit Ironic plays strange tricks in history.

The new sultan was elderly, dignified, and perhaps even saintly. But Morocco refused to take him seriously. Mohammed ben Youssef in exile became more than ever the symbol of national consciousness. The result was an increase in terrorism. There were riots in the great cities; the sultan himself was wounded. Violence was not limited to the nationalists. A Frenchman, Jacques Lemaigre-Dubreuil, was murdered because he had advocated generous concessions to the Moroccans. The Berber tribes, the mainstay of the French system, proved that blind fanaticism is not a safe instrument: hordes swooped down from the Middle Atlas on a small town, Oued Zem, and proved the uprightness of their cause by mutilating women and children, sacking the hospital, and murdering patients in their beds.

Edgar Faure, then premier, recognized the hopelessness of the situation. He sent to Rabat an official of wide experience, Gilbert Grandval

(June 1, 1955). Grandval prepared the withdrawal of Sultan Arafa. Although Edgar Faure sacrificed Grandval to the clamor of the French die-hards in Morocco, events followed their course. General Catroux brought back Mohammed ben Youssef from Madagascar to France. El Glaoui prostrated himself at the feet of the sovereign he had betrayed, and the sultan (he now prefers the more Western title of king) returned to his country amid scenes of delirious enthusiasm.

He and the French agreed on a subtle formula which, while it elicited skeptical smiles, defines an ideal which may not be unworkable: independence with interdependence. The ruler, in the course of his checkered experience, has become aware of the many conflicting forces at work in Morocco. No country is less monolithic: races, creeds, and centuries jostle one another. The conservative pious *bourgeoisie* of Salé, the new intellectuals, the last feudal lords, the irresponsible primitives, the proletariat of the great cities, even the women on the eve of emancipation create a welter which might prove unmanageable. In this threatening chaos the presence of the French as economic promoters and managers, as educators, as political advisers would be a steadying factor. The sovereign is actually curbing the extremists of the Istiqlal. Like Bourguiba, his rival for Maghreb leadership, he finds the middle course full of hazards. He is known to be in favor of a North African Federation from which the French would not be excluded. 1958 was still a year of confusion: 1959 need not be an hour of despair.

One of the things that the three countries of the Maghreb have in common—alas!—is their appalling poverty. Their picturesqueness, the splendid urban development in Morocco, some spectacular public works, a few farms more modern than anything old France has to offer might easily create an illusion. The land is poor. Water is scarce for irrigation and for power. The mineral resources, so far, were not outstanding: nitrates and phosphates, iron in the Djebel Ouenza, coal—none of the best—at Kenadsa. Even a far-reaching plan, such as was proposed by Mendès-France, could not alter these conditions.

Even brilliant economic progress might fail to keep pace with the appalling increase in the native population. The sanitary measures introduced by the French, however crude they may seem by European standards, have proved effective. The death rate is falling much more rapidly than the birth rate.

But a new factor is coming into play, and it may not be a mirage. Oil resources have been discovered in the Sahara, and they are beginning to be exploited on an industrial scale. Government agencies, private capital, American participation, both financial and technical, are combining to make this promise a reality. We have expressed our belief that economic prosperity is no panacea for political troubles. Still, it might ease somewhat the difficult years of readjustment ahead of the Maghreb. It might offer an outlet for the intellectual proletarians who now devote themselves to political agitation. It might provide a compass for the converging evolution which alone can bring peace.

Who knows? The Sahara may be as fabulously wealthy as Saudi Arabia. We may live to see King Mohammed ben Youssef, President Bourguiba, and even President Ferhat Abbas drive proudly in gold-plated Cadillacs. But neither atomic weapons nor liquid gold can go to the root of human problems. *Erudimini, qui judicatis terram:* grandeur is found not in domination but in generosity.

CHAPTER XXX

France, Europe, Mankind

"Provided other countries reciprocate,
France accepts that her sovereignty
be limited, when such limitations are
necessary to the organization and
defense of peace."
Preamble, Constitution of 1946.

✍ GENEALOGY OF NATIONALISM

In the perspective of a thousand years we can discern two lines of evolution running through French history. On the political plane there was a constant effort to emerge out of feudal anarchy; for in its essence feudalism was the rule of the fighting caste, the sword as supreme argument. The Capetian monarchy was the center and symbol of that obscure and patient endeavor. Slowly, the monarchy made France, as a territory, as a government, as an ideal. But the France it created shaped the monarchy in return. The king, who fought the nobles in alliance with the commons, could no longer be solely the apex of the feudal pyramid; as his domains expanded, he had to rely more and more on officials who developed a tradition of their own. His power remained personal in theory but in fact was becoming national. In this barely conscious growth of two ideals, slowly blending, never completely merging, we may single out two moments, two persons, for their symbolical value. One is Joan of Arc, the woman of the people, who literally *made* a king out of her great pity for the distress of the realm. The other was Louis XIV, convinced that he, by grace divine, owned *and served* the whole people. Out of a welter of fiefs, provinces, cities, there arose the *kingdom,* striving for unity, "One faith, one law, one king." When the dynasty proved unequal to its mission, the royal trappings were discarded, and France appeared, a sovereign state, one and indivisible. The Convention, not Louis XVI, was the heir of the Capetians. Even though the Republic wore a crown, under the two Napoleons and under Louis-Philippe, Demos henceforth was the legitimate ruler; the realm had become a nation. Patriotism was dynastic loyalty with the personal fetishism purged away. *France d'abord!*, France first and last, is but a new version of "God save the king!"

The biography of France as an entity thus records the gradual formation, the increasing consciousness, the ultimate purification of nationalism. But the deeper history of the French people, how they lived and what they lived by, is not limited to the evolution of the dynastic state into the centralized republic. At all times and on all levels, the French have been, and felt themselves to be, part of a larger synthesis. It is obvious that from the material point of view—scientific, technical, economic—France was from the first and remains today a province of the Western world. Religiously, France never attained independence, or even autonomy. The hesitant efforts of the kings to assume religious authority ended in failure. No king dared to do what Henry VIII and Peter the Great had done, to make himself the supreme head of a national church. The Gallicans fought for minor privileges in questions of administration: they never challenged the spiritual supremacy of Rome, not even when a revolutionary assembly elaborated a Civil Constitution for the clergy. The bulk of the French people remained "Catholics," that is to say members of a universal church. Although Protestantism had vigorous roots in the soil of France, the Huguenots were conscious from the first of their kinship with their coreligionists across the border. And religious free thought—deeply religious and fearlessly free—perhaps the sturdiest among the spiritual families in France, has never been confined by political boundaries.

From the cultural point of view the great University of Paris was a center of light for the whole of Christendom, not for the Capetian domains alone. The learned literature of the Middle Ages was in Latin. Vernacular literature was European in its themes and forms, from the sophisticated romances of chivalry to the most uncouth folk songs, from the miracle plays to the down-to-earth, bawdy, realistic tales. The humanism of the sixteenth century discarded the purely local tradition to seek the common origin of our civilization, the art and philosophy of Greece and Rome. The classicism of the seventeenth century, the Enlightenment of the eighteenth asserted the sovereignty of universal reason against the unwisdom of parochial prejudice. French Romanticism turned against Boileau, the Lawgiver of Parnassue, and worshipped strange gods, Shakespeare, Ossian, Lord Byron, Walter Scott. In French literature yesterday Ibsen, Tolstoy, Nietzsche counted for far more than Octave Feuillet; today, Dostoevsky, Kafka, Joyce, Faulkner are presences, while Paul Bourget is a fossil. France has never been resigned to a literature "of the French, by the French, for the French." The field is the world.

This holds true even in the political field. It is the pregnant paradox of French history that while dynasty and people were creating France, a person, they were also transcending France, an idol. In that land of patriots [1] nationalism is a heresy. This goes back to the very adolescence of the French monarchy. No sooner had the Holy Roman Empire revealed its irremediable impotence than a demand arose for the more efficient organization of Christendom. The first definite plan for a United Europe was penned by Pierre Dubois in the early years of the fourteenth century. The task he proposed for the European Commonwealth —the recovery of the Holy Land—was also the goal of Joan of Arc: she invited the English, as brothers in the faith, to join in a crusade. Henry IV may not be responsible for the details of the "Grand Design" ascribed to him; but the plan was reported by his ablest lieutenant, Sully, a shrewd man of affairs. Abbé de Saint-Pierre, who witnessed the disastrous world wars of Louis XIV, declared that his project for perpetual peace (1711–1713) had been inspired by Henry the Great. Rousseau discussed Saint-Pierre's proposal with intelligent sympathy, and Kant acknowledged his indebtedness to his French predecessors. The French Revolution promulgated "the Rights of Man," not the immunities and privileges of French citizens. Napoleon attempted (by the wrong methods) to organize the Continent. He prophesied, in terms which find echoes in the American mind today, that "Europe must be either Jacobin [i.e., in the tradition of the French Revolution] or Cossack [i.e., under the Russian *knut*]." Henri de Saint-Simon offered the blueprints of a European polity. He thought its nucleus should be a close union between the truly liberal powers, England and France. He thus anticipated by 125 years the plan which was making headway in both countries just before World War II,[2] and which Winston Churchill endorsed dramatically, but a few weeks too late, in 1940.

The romantic "nationalism" of the mid-nineteenth century was fraternal and in truth supra-national. For Michelet, Quinet, Hugo, as later for Renan, Germany was a beloved Fatherland of the spirit; and the French felt the sufferings of the Italians and the Poles as if they were their own. The two antagonists, Hugo and Napoleon III, both filled with "the spirit of forty-eight," were at one on this point. Hugo, opening a peace congress on August 21, 1849, spoke prophetically of "the higher unity, the European brotherhood." Napoleon III was constantly striving to settle the problems of Europe through conferences, which in his mind were an inchoate Parliament. He won at least two minor successes: a commission to supervise the navigation of the Danube, and a monetary union between France, Belgium, Italy, Switzerland, and Greece.

✍ FRANCE AND THE UN

At the end of the nineteenth century there was a sharp conflict in the French mind caused by the Dreyfus Affair. Those who thought in terms of the past, the believers in "My country, right or wrong!", those for whom "the country" meant the flag, and the flag meant the army, and the army the General Staff, very properly called themselves Nationalists. They were defeated in that great contest by the "intellectuals," for whom patriotism was not enough, who placed justice and truth above the hoariest traditions, and whose leaders were Zola, Jaurès, Anatole France. Before World War I Léon Bourgeois, head of the Radical party, had given up home politics to devote himself to the organization of peace. It was he who promoted the idea and proposed the name of a Society of Nations—a much better term than League, which implies an enemy. In the debates, long kept secret, which led to Wilson's covenant Bourgeois defended a genuine union with actual power capable of enforcing sanctions.[3] In this he was in accord with Clemenceau: if the Tiger opposed Lloyd George and Wilson, it was because the halting scheme they proposed was meant to preserve the privileges of their own countries. We must not forget that Clemenceau told Pershing, "Above Paris, there is France; above France, there is civilization."

When Coudenhove-Kalergi started his long crusade for European integration, he found the coolest response among British statesmen— "A noble dream, but not in our time"—and the warmest among the French, Albert Thomas of the International Labor Bureau and the veteran Aristide Briand. Briand presented his plan for a European Federal Union before the League of Nations (September 5–9, 1929). Then came a chain of catastrophes: the Wall Street crash, the universal economic crisis, the resulting rise of the Nazis to power, World War II. They deferred the great hope of organized peace: they did not dispel it. They only proved how realistic it was. No peace without justice; no justice without a law; no law without a government.

Even before the guns were stilled, steps had been taken to end world anarchy. France should have been one of the leaders: it was a matter of deep regret that she took such a self-effacing part in the San Francisco Conference. She was invited, as an afterthought, to be one of the sponsors. She declined the honor, because the governments which had taken the initiative were already committed to the Dumbarton Oaks plan about which she had not been consulted. But although she thus preserved her freedom of action, she did not use it to oppose the essential flaw in the proposed scheme: the nefarious distinction between the privileged Big Five and the rest of mankind, thus placing power, and therefore power politics, at the very core of the new organization. France left it to Mr. William Evatt, of Australia, valiantly and unsuccessfully to fight that battle. It must be said that at the moment France had only a provisional government, and that in the military, economic, and colonial fields, she did not enjoy full independence. However, she has already expressed her willingness to give up her veto privilege, and she has constantly been in favor of a world force as a substitute for national armies.

✍ FRANCE AND FREE EUROPE

As early as 1945 the movement for a Federal European Union was already strong in France: the elder statesmen of the Republic, Herriot, Blum, the great technician Dautry, the acknowledged master of political science, Siegfried, Paul Reynaud, who, for all his failings, was dynamic, endorsed the supra-national idea. In May, 1948, there assembled at The Hague a nonofficial European Congress under the chairmanship of Mr. Winston Churchill. It was Paul Reynaud who proposed the creation of a veritable European Parliament: the sixteen eligible nations would be represented on the basis of one deputy for every million of their population. The representatives would be elected either directly by the people or by the popular assembly of each country; every member would vote as an individual, according to his conscience and judgment. Thus on every conceivable question Englishmen, Frenchmen, Germans, Italians might be found on either side. It would be the end of nations and the foundation of Europe.

In spite of English resistance the proposed organization got under way. A compromise was reached: the delegates would be appointed by their governments, but they would be free to vote as individuals. The first meeting of the new organization took place in the summer of 1949 at Strasbourg. It became at once evident that the people of Europe favored a closer union, a genuine federal state, not a mere confederacy; and the Consultative Assembly soon proved that it was not composed of yes-men. France was the first country officially on record in favor of the United States of Europe by a vote of its National Assembly on November 26, 1949.

But there is an insincerity inherent in all compromises, both sides tacitly cleaving to their own interpretation. France and England agreed that there should be a Council of Europe, but they did not agree about its powers. That confused conflict continues to the present day. England knows that she belongs to Europe, twenty miles away from her shores, but her tradition of splendid insularity will not yield. So while the council still exists and owns an impressive building at Strasbourg, it has not quite acquired substance.

The sharpest setback came in 1950: the British Labour party issued a manifesto precluding full co-operation. The Scandinavian countries followed England's lead. There is a caste feeling among nations. As compared with England, her glorious past and her world-embracing Commonwealth, with America and her enormous resources, with the sturdy and independent people of the North, the Continental powers are mere commoners. It must be admitted that too close an association with the Fourth Republic was not likely to rouse enthusiasm. This aristocratic pride is not invincible, but it will take a long process of education to wear it down.

Faced with this open defection, Paul Reynaud, André Philip, both excellent Europeans, and Coudenhove-Kalergi himself, the indefatigable apostle of European integration, were in favor of going ahead without England. They were resigned to a "Carolingian Europe," curiously coextensive with Charlemagne's empire. It was realized that such a Europe had no future. England would see to it that it remained weak and divided: an ancient game. Europe might assert herself by uniting against England, but this was neither feasible nor desirable. The safest policy was to keep the door open until England "saw the point" at last and muddled somehow into full partnership.

Nineteenth-century gradualism is still with us in spite of the breathtaking speeding up of contemporary events in every field. In the desperate race with catastrophe, we are still advised to "make haste with infinite slowness." Georges Duhamel tells of a native architect in Tunis who, requested by the French authorities to submit his plans, exclaimed, "How can I draw the plans? The house is not built yet!" If you want to construct a bridge, only radicals and daydreamers would think of starting with blueprints.

So, England remains present at Strasbourg, but as a check. Meanwhile, Europe is building herself up functionally, piecemeal, on a purely pragmatic basis. The first great step was the Schuman Plan, actually due to the great "technocrat" Jean Monnet. Proposed on May 9, 1950, it was embodied in a six-power treaty in April, 1951, and ratified by France in December, 1951. It organized a Coal and Steel Community, embracing "Carolingian" Europe, West Germany, Benelux, Italy, France. England declared in no uncertain voice that she could not make up her mind yet but that her ultimate participation, on her own terms, was not an impossibility. The plan is at work without insuperable difficulties and without sensational results. A purely economic agreement, it provides the rudiments of a constitution: a High Authority (not national), a Consultative Committee, a Common Assembly, a Council of Ministers, a Court of Justice.

The second step was the proposed creation of a Common Market and of Euratom, a consortium for the development of nuclear power. A treaty creating these two agencies was signed in Rome on March 25, 1957. The new fields of development will be closely co-ordinated with the existing Coal and Steel Community. Again, only the six countries of Carolingian Europe are directly concerned; but again England is stretching a cautious and reluctant toe. It is to be noted that the members of the Commonwealth have raised no radical objections to England's joining these various organizations, while France has proposed extending their fields to her African possessions. The walls of economic nationalism —jealousy, secrecy, protection—are thus crumbling down.

We are not on the eve but in the clear dawn of a tremendous technical transformation, and that transformation is bound to ignore the petty political boundaries of yesterday. In science and industry the nation-state is obsolete. The implications of these three developments—Coal and Steel Community, Common Market, Euratom—should be obvious. A region cannot be one from the economic point of view without a common social policy and without common financial institutions. All these make a political federation inevitable. Its advocates, who in France comprise all the protagonists of the Third Force, are not Utopians: they are facing realistically the problems of today. It is its opponents— General de Gaulle is not among them—who are fervently clutching ghosts.

✴ FRANCE AND THE EUROPEAN ARMY

The decline of nationalism is most marked at its very center, the field of national defense. In the old days a gentleman relied on his sword to maintain his honor. The king was a gentleman, and the nation which he personified inherited the same spirit: a country that cannot uphold her interests and her prestige by force of arms has lost caste. The Germans in 1919 found one-sided disarmament an intolerable humiliation. The Nationalists at the time of the Dreyfus Case were not wrong: the army is the very core of the nation.

Now France has fought many wars single-handed, and even against formidable coalitions: *nec pluribus impar*. But she realizes that the days of proud independence are over. In 1914, in 1939, she desperately needed assistance. In 1918 she might flatter herself that she was the leader among the victors; no such illusion was possible in 1945. France cannot say, "Myself alone!" And she has learned not to rely upon precarious, slow-moving, or improvised alliances. Both for her safety and for her dignity, she finds it better to join a permanent defense organization. Ever since 1918 she has been a consistent advocate of collective security. But if the feudal lord no longer depends on his castle and his sword to keep his honor unsullied, he turns into a law-abiding citizen. The glory has departed.

It was M. René Pleven, then prime minister, who, on October 24, 1950, formally proposed a European army. His plan was in full harmony with the Atlantic Pact and the defense of the Free World. Yet, in the many years of tangled, and at times snarling, controversies that followed, France and America seemed at times to follow antagonistic policies.

The irritating differences about details, which history will soon forget, proceeded from a fundamental difference in attitude. America at that time seemed committed to the cold war. France knew for certain that a cold war would inevitably lead to a shooting war. The rejection of peaceful coexistence is bellicose, even though we should indignantly reject the implication; and coexistence cannot remain peaceful unless it is prepared to become friendly. Reconciliation, mutual understanding cannot come overnight: we must be prepared for a long period of cool peace. But cool peace is incompatible with the spirit of the showdown and the threat of nuclear warfare.

Now war has a totally different meaning in the experience of France and in that of America. Until the age of intercontinental guided missiles, America was safe, and France was not. This feeling of insecurity was intensified by constant, if irresponsible, hints of "peripheral defense." The Free World was to be saved by using England, Spain, and Morocco as bases. It was admitted that France might be overrun by Soviet hordes; she would ultimately be "liberated" through a process of systematic devastation. No wonder this epic vision did not appeal to the French.

It is easy for America to be wholeheartedly opposed to communism: she has no Communists at home. In France 20 per cent of the voters are Communists; 30 per cent profess to be Marxians.[4] On the one hand, this makes the French more tolerant. They are not damning a horrific abstraction; they know that coexistence is not a hazy dream but a fact in their national life; they remember that Communists held ministerial positions under General de Gaulle. On the other hand, a war with Russia would open for France (and for Italy and Eastern Germany as well), the dread possibility, almost the certainty, of civil war. On this score again the French may be pardoned if they do not submit themselves unquestioningly to the spirited leadership of President Truman or Secretary Dulles.

America takes a bold—perhaps crude—view of the world situation: pure Manicheism, on the one hand the Free World of Light, on the other the Soviet Powers of Darkness. As a result, haunted by the fear of Communist aggression, America was bent on utilizing at once and to the full the enormous war potential of Germany in technical resources and manpower. In France the moral and spiritual wounds of two German aggressions within a quarter of a century are still imperfectly healed. Two wars have been fought to disarm Germany and keep her disarmed. It seemed as though as late as 1950 the German people had at last learned their lesson. They were extremely reluctant to rearm: *"Ohne mich!"* ("count me out") was the prevailing mood among them. The French knew, however, that the Germans would not be satisfied with the position of a pariah or of a paroled convict. *Gleichberechtigung,* equality of status, was the magic word which had been decisive in the rise of the Nazis to power. But France wanted Germany to participate in a European army, not to have an army of her own. With the reconstitution of the *Wehrmacht* before the building up of Europe, the old peril was revived. The French had to yield on this point under tremendous pressure and the threat of "an agonizing reappraisal." But they are not convinced to this day that it was the wiser course; and they resent, almost to a man, the methods by which the American solution was forced upon them.

The second difficulty in creating the European Defense Community was the part to be played by England. England is solemnly bound to France by a whole series of treaties, each implying that the preceding one was not quite good enough. She is bound yet not fully committed. She will do the right thing at the proper time: but the definition of "right" and "proper" rests entirely with her. France wants England not as a friendly outsider but as part and parcel of the European system of which England is the keystone. On this point France has secured a minor victory. After the French Parliament had rejected the European Defense Community treaty, Sir Anthony Eden at a conference in London (September 28, 1954) boldly reversed England's age-old policy of "no entanglements." A Western European Union was formed with England as a charter member. English divisions were to be permanently stationed across the Channel. This made German rearmament a little less unpalatable to the French. Even then, the agreement was ratified by the French Parliament only after a minor setback (December 24, 1954) and by a narrow majority.[5]

✍ FRANCE AND THE FREE WORLD

> No Free World without freedom. No
> freedom without equality of status.

This conflict within the Free World has been glossed over a number of
times, with commendable skill. It has not yet been fully resolved. No
doubt it will appear more sharply under the Fifth Republic than under
the Fourth. General de Gaulle is not a bewildered Third Force: he
knows his mind, and he speaks his mind. He will be found "difficult"
again, as Franklin D. Roosevelt and Winston Churchill found him difficult in the past. He will be accused of being a monadnock [6] a fossil of
obsolete chauvinism, an anachronistic believer in *grandeur* of the Riche-
lieu-Louis XIV pattern, a worshipper of glory with a Napoleonic tinge.
We may trust him to sharpen the issue: he scorns the petty cleverness
that "keeps 'em guessing." But we should realize that the issue is not
of his own making. His stand [7] was that of the whole French people,
bemused as they seemed, before he was called to power. That stand is
based on a sentiment which is permanent and unanimous, not in France
alone, but throughout the world. To ignore or misinterpret it would be
courting disaster. This leads us to a reappraisal of nationalism. Nationalism is at the same time a ghost and a spirit. The ghost cannot be exorcized unless the spirit is given its due.

In its literal and positive connotation, nationalism is the affirmation,
or rather the seeking, of absolute independence and absolute unity. It
can be formulated in many ways and in all languages: hundred-per-cent
loyalty, "My country right or wrong!" One Faith, one Law, one King,
*Ein Volk, ein Reich, ein Führer, Sacro egoismo, Deutschland über alles,
France d'abord!*, America first! one hundred and seventy-five million
minds with but a single thought. We need hardly point out that the
"nation" thus conceived is a monstrous idol without a shadow of practical reality. The United States is not a single entity, and has never been
one, either in its home policies or in its foreign policies. The American
way of life is freedom: that is to say not the obligation to conform, but
the right to differ in peace. The United States is not independent either.
At every turn we are driven by the necessity of frustrating our enemies
and by the more delicate task of placating our friends.

The real force of nationalistic sentiment is found in the quest for
equality. It is all too frequent for a narrow term to be confused with
a deeper feeling. When people are willing to inflict and suffer death for
their own peculiar sect, the motive power, however warped and dis-
guised, is none the less *religion*. People have been striving everywhere,
obscurely, for untold ages, for an increasing measure of liberty and

security, as the indispensable conditions of dignity. Men cannot breathe easily in an atmosphere of contempt. This rebellion in the name of self-respect is the one common element in all the manifestations of nationalism, otherwise so disparate.

There was no essential difference between the American colonists and their fellow subjects in the mother country. They might have remained a contented part of the English-speaking world: secession is not a prerequisite of democracy. But the forefathers of this country refused to be treated as second-class citizens, i.e., to be taxed without representation. It was a matter, not of dollars and cents, but of self-respect. The Spanish colonies rebelled because the *criollos* were reduced to a position of inferiority. At the other extreme, Hindu nationalism, without any foundation in race, religion, language, or interests, grew out of the privileged position assumed by the British. Chinese nationalism arose from the "unequal treaties" and from such deliberate insults as: "No dogs or Chinese allowed." It was because of France's claim to hegemony in polite culture that national sentiment first appeared in Germany. It was forged under the hammer blows of Napoleon. It reached its point of insane perfection with Hitler, in resentment against a peace which was not wholly unjust, but which was a *Diktat* and imposed a brand of guilt.

Arab nationalism, now such a burning problem for the French and for the whole world, had its inception in the efforts of the Young Turks to impose the supremacy of the Osmanlis. It was sharpened when, after fighting on the side of the Allies, the Arabs, and not the Turks, were placed under tutelage, as though they were a lesser breed. It was goaded into frenzy when the Zionist state was forced upon them, without any regard for their sentiments. It became more darkly fanatical when financial aid was proffered to Egypt, on the condition that the donors were to dictate its policy. The Arabs, in Cairo, in Iraq, in Algiers, will refuse to be bought. Prosperity may be a substitute for dignity, for a handful of profiteers: never for the depths of a people. I hold no brief for Sekou Touré, the Duce of French Guinea: but he was right when he proclaimed: "Rather starve as free men than thrive as slaves!"

Gleichberechtigung, equality of status, is the key word among races and classes as well as among nations. Every one is aware that equality is a delusion: but collective, irredeemable inequality imposed from above is a stigma that no group of men can indefinitely tolerate. For the assertion of inequality, even in its mildest form, means despising the inferiors. Ferhat Abbas, the President of the Algerian Republic in exile, a man of French culture and personally friendly to the French, said profoundly: "We are rebelling against a hundred and twenty-eight years of contempt."

For centuries, the smart of inequality was tempered by religious belief. Humiliations in this world were of little moment: what mattered was brotherhood in the faith, and the promise of a heaven where the first might be the last. But realists have long ago swept away the Christian ideal as starry-eyed. Jean Jaurès, the great socialist leader, warned the Voltairian *bourgeois:* "Beware! You have hushed the ancient cradle song that lulled mankind." Men are clamoring for justice here and now, and will not be denied.

This rejection of privilege takes the form of acute nationalism in the literal sense among the peoples subjected to alien rule. It is the obvious first step in liberation; but it is only a first step, not the final goal. The Chinese achieved nationalism under Chiang Kai-shek, and were not satisfied: democracy and the welfare state, also promised by Sun Yat-sen, had still to be conquered. Napoleon III's doctrine of nationalities, Woodrow Wilson's principle of self-determination, were well-meant, but did not go to the root of the matter. They were obsolete before they were formulated. The Four Freedoms are infinitely more precious than that will o' the wisp independence, or that dismal dream, monolithic unity.

This double aspect of nationalism is well exemplified in the career of Georges Clemenceau. His long political life was devoted to relentless war against nationalism in the literal sense,—enforced conformity, "My country, right or wrong!" and "My country" identified with the government, the army, the flag. In his young manhood, he had fought against the Second Empire, which claimed to be a *national* regime, upholding the honor and promoting the interests of France as a whole. After a fumbling start, he opposed the nationalistic sentiment represented by General Boulanger. In his advancing years, he was to wage a third battle against the Nationalists in the Dreyfus crisis; and as a consequence, he was branded as un-French. But, in the same spirit of liberty, he would rebel against foreign dictation. "The Germans," he said several years before the war, "are seeking to put their yoke upon us; it does not fit our necks." When the conflict broke out, he vowed to wage it to the bitter end and had to use dictatorial methods. But the peace he was striving for, as we have seen, was not nationalistic. We must never forget his great words to Pershing: "Above France, there is civilization," and his address to Parliament on the day of victory: "France, once the soldier of God, now the soldier of humanity." He was, like George Washington, a citizen of the Great Republic.

Hence the apparent paradox: France, more definitely perhaps than any of the great powers, has transcended the nationalistic ideal; yet France will react against any attempt at dictation with a virulence which, as in the case of Georges Clemenceau, may appear chauvinistic.

Our endeavor, in this study, is to understand France. But in order to understand France, we must first of all attempt to understand ourselves. For the first century and a quarter of our national existence, foreign affairs remained foreign to us. We had turned our backs on Europe; we rejected all entanglements. We took pride and comfort in an enormous *Sinn Fein:* ourselves alone. When with startling suddenness we became one of the major partners in the world commonwealth, we were ill prepared to deal with other nations on terms of scrupulous equality. In our eyes, they were either barbaric or effete. We jumped stiffly from isolation to leadership: both Woodrow Wilson and Franklin Roosevelt were grievous offenders in this respect. When our leadership is challenged, we call such resistance fractiousness, or treason against the Free World. We take it for granted, in a wider sphere than did Richard Olney, that our fiat is law. We affirm with Henry Luce that we must "exert upon the world the full impact of our influence, for such purposes as we see fit, and by such methods as we see fit." [8]

Now if this leadership is based on sheer power: "We've got the ships, we've got the men, we've got the money too," it is the realistic argument which justified Russia in imposing her will upon Finland and Hungary. The Free World will reject it, or cease to be free. Perhaps we desperately need France to be our conscience, and remind us of our own principles. Power politics, Might in its starkness and not in the service of Right, is but a gorgeous race to the abyss. If leadership should belong not to massive strength but to wisdom, are we sure of our pontifical infallibility? Are we wiser than Uruguay, Sweden, or Switzerland? The claim to leadership sounds a trifle hollow, when we hear what the Republicans have to say of Democratic guidance, and vice versa. Perhaps because of our very size, of the immunity to attack we have enjoyed so long, of our unchallenged and fossilized Eternal Verities, we are less clear of mind and less firm of purpose than a number of smaller nations. We are secretly conscious of our own bewilderment; our theme song might be: "I don't know where I'm going; but that's where I'm leading you."

One concrete instance, of yesterday and today, "in the light of a thousand years." The French believe very strongly not merely in curbing the race in nuclear armaments, but in outlawing such weapons altogether. If this is our sincere aim, we shall find them our steadfast supporters. What they will not admit, however, even under duress, is an invidious distinction between the Super-Powers, the United States, Great-Britain, and their "hyphen" Canada, in sole possession of such instruments of destruction, and, far below, the common herd destined to remain in subjection. If the Free World be one, let it act as one; let it pool the sources of supplies, the know-how, the stockpiles. "What! To place such power in the hands of some of our allies, who are not responsible?" If they are not responsible, they should not be our allies. We might elect to defend them against unprovoked aggression, in the name of general principles, for the sake of our own ultimate interests: but we should not be bound to them. It is obvious that France would spurn such an unequal protectorate. If it is not obvious, we have failed to read her long history aright. She can be associated with us only in the service of a common cause, and on a basis of ungrudging equality. This, I repeat, was clear to the French mind before May, 1958. The Free World has no place for satellite nations.

CHAPTER XXXI

The Dawn of
the Fifth Republic

"Confound their politics,
Frustrate their knavish tricks!
On him our hopes we fix . . ."

⚹ THE APPEAL TO DE GAULLE

While the politicians were wearily squabbling in Paris, a tough para-trooper, Brigadier General Massu, staged a coup in Algiers (May 13). The higher ranks of the army were tacitly with him, and the commander in chief, General Raoul Salan, played such a cautious game that it might be interpreted as complicity. The movement, a disquieting blend of militarism and demagogy, had but one slogan: "De Gaulle to power!"

This was actually the first pronunciamiento, of the Spanish and Latin-American type, in French history. The Eighteenth Brumaire, in 1799, had been an inside job, masterminded by one of the Directors, Siéyès; the intervention of the grenadiers at the last moment, to retrieve Bonaparte's fumbling, was but an accident. On the second of December, 1851, Prince Louis-Napoleon was the lawful civilian President of the Second Republic. The army was a willing instrument in his hands, but it had not taken the initiative. In our days, the brood of Cromwells has become innumerable. But France, so far, had been immune.

The bewildered Third Force attempted to react. After an interim of four weeks, Pierre Pflimlin, of the M.R.P., was at last confirmed in the premiership (May 14). But in Algiers, General Massu was forming what threatened to be a rival government, a Committee of Public Salvation, with a Mohammedan as his codirector. In reply, the Assembly gave Pflimlin emergency powers by an impressive majority (461 to 114). But on the seventeenth, Jacques Soustelle, supposed to be closely watched by the police, eluded their drowsy and perhaps winking vigilance and flew to Algiers. His arrival gave the local *Putsch* a new and ominous character. For Soustelle, once an eminent professor of anthropology, had been a trusted lieutenant of De Gaulle. As governor general of Algeria, his dynamic leadership had made him the idol of the die-hard colonists. As the impotence of the Paris government became more manifest, the Assembly granted still more powers to Pflimlin, and passed a unanimous vote of thanks to the army. The army, meanwhile, was unanimously shouting: "Vive De Gaulle!"

The peril was increasing every hour. Paratroopers were dropped in Corsica, which rallied at once and enthusiastically to the Algiers movement. The next step might be continental France. Admiral Auboyneau, whose squadron had been engaged in NATO maneuvres, rallied Algerian ports: a hint that the navy, the army, and the air force were in close accord. The sole remedy was to heap still more power upon the helpless Pflimlin. He was authorized to carry out a sweeping constitutional reform: wisdom *in extremis,* some twelve years too late. But the majority (408 to 105) included the 150 Communist deputies, whose support Pflimlin, as a good Catholic, rejected with horror. (So, by the way, had Mendès-France the Jew.) This gave him a justification for resigning. To fight for the survival of the Fourth Republic would have meant civil war. If Massu—or more probably Salan—had been forced into the position of a Franco, he could have relied upon the full sympathy of the Free World. Perish the Republic, rather than revive the *Front Populaire!*

The situation was inextricable. The M.R.P. themselves were hesitant. The Radicals were bitterly divided, and so were the Socialists. There were demonstrations and counterdemonstrations in the streets. The way out was provided, unexpectedly, by the President of the Republic, M. René Coty. In a cogent and dignified message to the assemblies, he urged them to trust the man who once before had saved the honor and the vital interests of the country. If his advice were not heeded, he himself would resign. Already unofficial negotiations were under way: Paris went to Colombey-les-deux Églises, and Colombey to Paris, in diaphanous secrecy.

De Gaulle had to be accepted on his own terms; but they were statesmanlike both in their firmness and in their moderation. No guilt clause was dictated to the politicians. There was no suggestion of a *coup d'état:* the constitution of the Fourth Republic committed suicide in a meticulously constitutional manner. De Gaulle did not countenance by a word the Algiers movement, which may have been started without his formal knowledge and consent. He was elected Premier on June 1, by a vote of 329 to 244. On June 3, the measures he considered indispensable were passed by both chambers: "plenary powers," the same powers that had been forced upon Pflimlin; Parliament adjourned for six months, and the Premier was entrusted with the framing of a new constitution. Openly, this was true to the form of both Napoleons and of Marshal Pétain. But precedents are not final arguments. The Republic had failed four times in France: this did not preclude the possibility that a fifth attempt might be successful. An authoritarian government had three times led to disaster: a fourth experiment might avoid the tragic blunders of the past. Trial and error.

General de Gaulle went at once to Algeria (June 4–6), where he was received with delirious enthusiasm. He neither snubbed nor endorsed the men who had used his name. He confirmed General Salan as commander in chief, and made him his special delegate. He did not dissolve the Committee of Public Salvation; but he made it clear that it was to be considered purely as a private organization, not as the nucleus of a government. Civil war was averted, without yielding an inch to the proto-fascist groups in Algiers.

In his cabinet, De Gaulle included former premiers and ministers of the Fourth Republic, Guy Mollet, Pierre Pflimlin, Antoine Pinay, and the West African Félix Houphouet-Boigny. But he also selected technicians who were not affiliated with party politics. He gave a post to André Malraux, his constant supporter, who, as a free man, had hovered on the very fringe of Communism. He gave none at first to Jacques Soustelle: the delay was to make it clear that no Warwick the Kingmaker had any claims upon him.

He addressed himself without bluster to his triple task: to curb factional anarchy, through a new constitution; to liquidate the empire; and, most delicate of all, to reconcile, in the spirit of liberty, equality, and fraternity, the warring elements in Algeria. He did not fritter away his time and his popularity in empty ceremonies; but he knew that great national demonstrations would help restore the sense of a common purpose and affirm a new spirit. The Eighteenth of June, anniversary of his assuming the leadership of the Free French, the Fourteenth of July, and the Fourth of September, when in the heart of a workingmen's district, he opened the campaign for the referendum, were days of national communion such as France had not lived since the Eleventh of November, 1918. He took a vast lightning tour of the French Union, as it was still called: Madagascar, Equatorial Africa, West Africa, Algeria again. At Dakar, the scene of his bitter failure in 1940, and at Cotonou, he faced opposition without flinching. The referendum took place on September 28. There were no disturbances and no coercion; no suspicious unanimity of the totalitarian type. There were substantial minorities in France herself, and Guinea felt free to vote overwhelmingly against De Gaulle. The result was a triumph of unexpected magnitude.[1]

There are no happy endings except in Nirvana: even doomsday does not qualify, for it will consign the vast majority of mankind to an eternity of torment. But there may be auspicious beginnings. England's revolution in 1688 and our own constitution in 1788 did not solve all problems for all time, but they provided a framework which made orderly progress possible. We repeat that Gaullism (a term which the General himself rejects) is not a rigid program of the Fascist-Nazi-Communist type. It seeks first of all to remove obstacles. Constructively, it is a spirit and a method, not a set of blueprints. The new French constitution, like the British, like our own, must remain constantly in the making if it is to have life. The new French community will have to be created with infinite patience and unremitting generosity. Violent antagonisms will not disappear overnight in Algeria. But in a country shackled by petty interests, torn by doubts, haunted with fears, the moral revolution led by De Gaulle has restored faith, the substance of things hoped for.

THE CONSTITUTION

The reader will remember the quip about the Consular constitution of 1799: "Complicated? There are but two words in it: Napoleon Bonaparte." Undoubtedly, in the eyes of the French people, the constitution was De Gaulle, and the referendum was a plebiscite. Yet the constitution is by no means a mere *Heil De Gaulle!* It embodies a very definite principle: a new balance between the executive power and the legislative.

In spite of the doctrinal affirmations of Locke and Montesquieu, these two powers have never been and can never be fully separated. In England, the cabinet is but the executive committee of Parliament. In America, we have alternately a presidential regime, when the President's position is strong, and a Congressional regime, when his position is weak—with vast zones of twilight. In France, radical differences in opinions, from royalist to communist, and the proliferation of ever-shifting parties have made both the American and the British methods unworkable. With no lack of good will, intelligence, and technical skill, the rule of assemblies had become confusion worse confounded.

De Gaulle's first care therefore was to curb the anarchistic omnipotence of Parliament, while reaffirming explicitly, in Lincoln's very words, the government of the people by the people. The field of legislation entrusted to the Chambers is generously defined: still, it is defined. Beyond that field, many problems of administration will be settled by executive orders. The Premier remains responsible to Parliament; but he cannot be overthrown except by a formal vote of censure. As in America, the members of the cabinet cannot belong to either house. If a congressman accepts a cabinet position, he must resign his seat. The appeal to the supreme arbiter, the people as a whole, remains constantly open. President and Premier can dissolve the houses and order new elections. On vital issues, they can also call for a referendum— that referendum which in 1920, divorced from party strife, would undoubtedly have endorsed the League of Nations.

The mode of electing the deputies is not provided for in the constitution. It will be the object of an "organic law." For the first elections at least, De Gaulle has adopted the single constituency system, with, if need be, a second ballot. Half a century ago, the present writer was converted by Charles Benoist and Aristide Briand to the merits of proportional representation; but he could never accept the clumsy version of it which prevailed until 1958. But the effect of proportional representation was to harden the parties without strengthening them. Now for De Gaulle, the party spirit is the enemy of honesty and efficiency. He wants a return to the original representative system, in which the electors choose a man they personally know and trust, and then allow him to use his own judgment. Party regularity is formally condemned in the new constitution under the name of *mandat impératif,* a categorical order for the deputy to vote according to the party line. De Gaulle wants men, ideas, and even interests, but not machines. Least of all a Gaullist machine: he has learnt his lesson from the failure of his Rally of the French People. A candidate may express his approval of De Gaulle's policy, but he will not be permitted to call himself a Gaullist. De Gaulle's only party line—in this he thoroughly agrees with our Founding Fathers—is that there should be no parties.

The organization of the executive branch is a new departure. De Gaulle has no use for King Log, a figurehead which in most cases was a doubtful ornament. But he rejects the Bonapartist and American method according to which the head of the state and the head of the government are one and the same. There is to be a Premier, to hold office as long as Parliament does not formally demand his resignation. The President, as under the constitution of 1875, is elected for seven years. Not by Congress alone, as under the Third and Fourth Republics, and not, as with us, by the whole people, but by an enormous electoral college of some sixty to eighty thousands, in which the representatives of the *communes* or townships will have the majority. All these people have been elected to some office, local or national, and therefore are presumed to enjoy the confidence of their fellow citizens; but they are not politicians first and last. The rural vote will probably be overweighted; but the presidency is expected to be a conservative force, a brake on the radicalism of the left or of the right that so often stirs the urban centers. The electoral college will be stolid, but it will be calm. As the delegates cannot meet in a single body, they cannot be swayed either by the collective hysteria of our circus conventions, or by the traditional "deals in smokefilled hotel rooms."

Some improvements on the constitution of 1875 have been taken over from that of 1946: a Superior Council of the Judiciary, to give that branch of the government the largest degree of autonomy and liberate it from political influences; and a rather shadowy Economic and Social Council. A High Court of Justice is to be created, to deal with cases of malfeasance in office, or of conspiracy against the safety of the state: hitherto this had been entrusted to the Senate as a whole. The most interesting creation is a Constitutional Council of Nine, to whom former presidents of the Republic will be added. This august body will assume the responsibility of our Supreme Court as the guardian of constitutional principles. The *Cour de Cassation* remains the highest resort for all cases not of a political or constitutional nature.

The constitution, chiefly credited to M. Michel Debré, Minister of Justice, offers curious zones of indeterminacy between its sharply defined features. The functions of the Senate, for instance, remain somewhat hazy: it seems that the second Chamber might become one of the organs of the still inchoate Community. These deliberate blurs are to be filled by "organic laws," which will rank above ordinary legislation, without attaining the full majesty and fixity of constitutional articles. There is a reason for this method. The British constitution is a loose mass of precedents saved from chaos by the tradition of seven hundred years. The process of amending the American constitution is perhaps unduly stiff. The De Gaulle system is meant as a *via media*.

The only constitution with which the new one offers a marked resemblance is that of the Second Empire in the very last months of its existence. Then there was a Premier, Emile Ollivier, responsible to Parliament in orthodox British fashion. But the Emperor considered himself as more than a figurehead. He held himself in reserve in cases of emergency. To the dismay of his bourgeois supporters, he could appeal directly to the people through plebiscite. It was a precarious blend of Orleanist parliamentarism and Caesarian democracy. We must remember that this constitution was endorsed by an overwhelming popu-

lar vote, and that a new springtime of good will and confidence seemed
to have come over France.

The regime failed through the accident of the Franco-Prussian War.
But this blow from without exposed its fatal inner weakness: too heavy
a responsibility had been entrusted to a personality enfeebled by age,
disease, and the weariness of bitter strife. The Empire fell, not because
Napoleon III made use of his reserve of power, but because he no
longer had the energy to curb the hysteria of Parliament, press, and
mob. To fulfill his function as supreme arbiter, the head of the state
must enjoy great moral authority, and he must also be in full possession
of his faculties. Of course De Gaulle in 1958 satisfies all the requirements: the constitution was tailored to fit him. But the situation and
the personality are both unique. Men prominent in politics, such as
Gambetta, Ferry, Waldeck-Rousseau, Clemenceau, Poincaré in their
fighting days, might be thought too controversial for a nonpartisan office. If we wait till they have reached the serene eminence of Elder
Statesmen, like Edouard Herriot and Léon Blum at the end of their
careers, their will power may have lost some of its firmness and of its
elasticity. The world is plagued today with stubborn old men. The
precedents of Napoleon III in 1870, of Hindenburg, of Pétain, are
ominous: even the strong and the wise are not free from the inroads
of senility. The selection of the first two presidents will be decisive.
In fourteen years, the people may have learnt the difficult art of choosing, not a wooden idol and not a demagogue, but a George Washington
every time. *Qui vivra verra.*

LIQUIDATING THE EMPIRE

The constitution of 1946, in its preamble, affirmed that "France forms
with the peoples overseas a Union founded on equality both of rights
and of duties, without any distinction due to race or religion"; and
the 13 articles of Title VIII provided a definite and elaborate framework for such a union. This implemented the policy outlined at the
Brazzaville conference under the leadership of the great Governor General Félix Eboué, himself a colored man.

The intentions of the Fourth Republic were therefore unimpeachable.
Yet, twelve years after these brave words, the problems of *France
Overseas* were still a cause of deep anxiety. An insurrection in Madagascar had to be sternly repressed. Indochina was entirely lost. The
hopes of a close and friendly association with the former protectorates,
Tunis and Morocco, were waning. Worst of all, Algeria had been torn
for five years by a campaign of wanton terrorism which barred the way
to any reasonable and orderly progress.

THE DAWN OF THE FIFTH REPUBLIC

For this prolonged and it would seem irremediable failure, no single explanation will suffice. Title VIII, the formal charter of the French Union, was not even a dead letter: it had never come alive. The institutions it prescribed were indeed created, but no one in France or overseas paid the slightest attention to them. The army, inevitably, had its share of blame. Its one duty is to maintain order, the existing order, not to promote drastic reforms. And every military man believes in his heart, like Napoleon and General MacArthur, that "there is no substitute for victory." The officials on the spot, particularly those who were humane and enlightened, thought it would be a betrayal of their civilizing mission if they were to turn over their authority to untrained and often fanatical natives. The influential colonists formed a class and almost a caste. They knew local conditions as the prattlers in Paris did not. Good realists, they were defending substantial privileges, economic and social, and they sneered at the vapid idealists who were ready to see "the colonies perish rather than a principle." The political tradition at home was still one of centralization, "France One and Indivisible." Anyone under the French flag who did not think and feel himself French was a traitor. And the politicians, in their congenital and cultivated confusion, were incapable of striking a bold course. They lived in deadly fear that their opponents would accuse them of giving away France's patrimony. Because of his rare courage, Mendès-France became "the lost statesman."

In spite of these obstacles, the record of the Fourth Republic was not altogether a failure. West Africa, in particular, was booming. An appreciable measure of autonomy was introduced, not merely in the territories under trusteeship, but throughout the vast African possessions of France. A *loi-cadre,* serving as a general framework for local government, was put into effect. Territorial assemblies were freely elected, and there were actual cabinets instead of governors' councils, composed almost entirely of natives. If the masses of French Africa could be consulted in the referendum of September 28, it was because they had been initiated into political life.

The problem was—and remains—a moral one. The French resented the accusations of ruthless imperialism, originating in Moscow, Washington, and Cairo—an unexpected Unholy Alliance. They knew they meant well and had achieved much. They were reluctant to yield to sheer terrorism. But they were dismayed at the enormous cost and the inevitable brutality entailed by the insurrections in Madagascar, Indochina, Algeria. The Empire as a nation of a hundred million Frenchmen, all with but a single soul, was not an ignoble dream, but it had melted away altogether. The Union was finding it hard to be born. The ideals, the sentiments, the interests of the French demanded a soul-searching reappraisal.

The rabid anticolonialism of the Moscow-Washington-Cairo axis might have exacerbated France's resolution to rule; more insidious and more effective in sapping it was the example of England and the Netherlands.

England, with marvelous skill, had managed to disengage herself, in peace and amity, from her Asian possessions. Spectacularly, she had given full independence to Ghana in West Africa, and set a definite date—1960—for the emancipation of Nigeria. Perhaps this willingness to part was due to the fact that the British had never entertained the possibility of associating with the natives on equal terms: this is well illustrated in the African novels of Joyce Cary, particularly in *Mister Johnson*. Great Britain had nothing to compare with the galaxy of French Negroes in high positions, Eboué, Monnerville, Houphouet-Boigny, or, in the realm of culture, Senghor. The French way might have been the better; but England's action left France off balance.

The Netherlands had fought hard and long to reconquer and preserve their vast, ancient, and well-administered Indonesian empire. Not with the good timing and the good grace manifested by England, they finally agreed to a Dutch Commonwealth, in which Indonesia and Holland would be associated on equal terms. Because it was belated and grudging, this move proved a failure: Indonesia won absolute independence, not from the Dutch, but against the Dutch. And the Dutch discovered with delight that instead of being beggared and humiliated by the catastrophe, they had been relieved of a material and moral incubus. In French colonial circles, people began whispering about "hollandism" as a contagious disease—or was it a hope? Before De Gaulle assumed power, French public opinion was obscurely being prepared for the radical solution: let the colonies go.

Had De Gaulle been merely a militarist and chauvinist, he might have said, in Churchillian phrase: "I have not become the leader of the French to liquidate the empire." The miracle he achieved was to climb down grandly, in an apotheosis. He gave up every thought of holding France's dominion through sheer force: such is not his conception of *grandeur*. Instead of yielding sullenly to native and foreign pressure, he assumed the initiative. He was realistic enough to believe that, in the long run, generosity is the safest policy. So he turned over the whole problem to the native populations themselves. They were free to vote themselves out of the proposed French community; and Guinea did so, by a quasi-unanimous vote, which is at least a tribute to the iron discipline imposed by its leader, Sekou Touré. The others no less freely voted to make the attempt. Even Madagascar, that remote little continent, which had traditions and a culture of its own, and which had had to be conquered, reconquered, and tamed into submission, gave De Gaulle an 82 per cent majority.

It must be distinctly understood that this response was not a vote for "the nation of a hundred million," standardized, centralized, and governed from Paris. The new states will determine their relations with metropolitan France. Even the most advanced federalists under the Fourth Republic took it for granted that defense and foreign policy would remain under the control of the Union: this is far less certain now. Some kind of an economic partnership is likely to prevail, but of a rather loose nature: for many of these territories already belong to the Conventional Basin of the Congo, a free trade area; and all have been invited to join the European Common Market. There will be technical assistance, provided it be sought, not imposed, and provided it does not claim a monopoly. There will be—and this might be the most substantial part of the Community—some form of educational and cultural co-operation: Senghor, for instance, is conscious that no African dialect can have the emancipating and the unifying power of French. Perhaps there will be the "interchangeable citizenship" adopted for the territories under trusteeship: Africans, while residing in France, would enjoy all the civic and political rights of Frenchmen, and vice versa.

The negotiations will be protracted and at times delicate; but if the generous spirit that conceived the referendum is not allowed to pale, there is an excellent chance that they may succeed. Guinea itself, under a *de facto* dictator in close sympathy with Moscow, seceded without rancor, and expressed the desire to retain certain close ties with France. Converging evolution may achieve wonders, if it is allowed to work itself out in peace and freedom. Our children may see Ouagadougou or Niamey as French as Fort-de-France or Pointe-à-Pitre, Castelnaudary or Romorantin: a voluntary association of equals, within the world community.

✍ THE ULTIMATE TEST: ALGERIA

Algeria had been the cause of the crisis; and Algeria remains the ultimate test of De Gaulle's success or failure. The situation is *sui generis:* if India had been an hour's flight from England, and the home of *fifty million* Englishmen rooted in the soil for generations, Great Britain would have found it much harder to disengage herself. Nationalism is the emptiest shibboleth in a divided country which had never been a nation; and we have no faith in the sacred rights of terrorism.

The attitude of the professional officers at the time of the crisis was natural enough. They were exasperated at being ordered to repress violence, and then reviled for using strong-arm methods. Although their action was parallel with that of the colonists, their point of view did not coincide with theirs. Yet they were pretty close together: both had the same enemies, the fellaghas, and both stood for French supremacy. Their common slogan was "integration": Algeria is French, Algeria is France. Let every trace of autonomy disappear, even the most superficial, like the issuing of special postage stamps. Algeria is merely three, four, twelve departments, governed from Paris by the Minister of the Interior. Let the natives have the vote: what does it matter? In the Palais-Bourbon, they will remain an uncomfortable but hopeless minority.

Army and colonists had united in clamoring for De Gaulle; and when De Gaulle, just elected Premier, came to Algiers, he was given a tremendous welcome. For a man who was believed to be single-minded and unyielding, De Gaulle displayed from the first a subtle but not tortuous diplomacy. He restored discipline in the army, and re-duced the Committee of Public Salvation to a mere political club. Above all, he silenced the colonists by agreeing with them better than they agreed with themselves, and giving a deeper meaning to their slogan, *integration*.

Integration? By all means. But this implies that every citizen in Algeria, without distinction of race or religion, must have exactly the same rights and opportunities. There must be no second-class citizen-ship. In the coming elections, De Gaulle expressed the hope that at least 60 per cent of the representatives would be Moslems.[2] Political equality would be immediate. Economic equality was to be achieved within five years. Within eight years, illiteracy would be stamped out. Not only would Moslems have their full share of public functions in Algeria, but—a bold and paradoxical engagement—ten per cent of all such positions in Metropolitan France would be reserved for them.

As Raymond Aron,[3] a fearless and keen-sighted critic, pointed out these glowing promises might seem unrealistic. To bring the natives' standard of living up to that of the Europeans would require untold billions, which the thrifty French might not unnaturally grudge. In a static *petit bourgeois* economy, Aron would undoubtedly be right. But miracles have become commonplace in our vertiginous age. The Arabs, of course, cannot be enriched overnight; but if they see a definite goal and a determined effort, "with all deliberate speed," they will eagerly work for their own betterment. The billions poured into Algeria need not be wasted: if the natives emerge from a bare subsistence level, they will be able, as they are only too eager, to buy French products. The newly discovered oil wealth of the Sahara came as a *Deus ex machina:* once again, a little late, *"Dieu protège la France."* It will not turn Algeria into another Saudi Arabia: wells, pipe lines, and desert. In combination with the known resources of the country in iron ore, it will make a vast industrial development possible.

This economic millennium is not a mirage: but neither is it a decisive argument. *Homo sapiens* (more or less) is not that dismal abstraction *Homo economicus.* We agree with Ferhat Abbas and Sekou Touré: free men cannot be bought. What De Gaulle offered Algeria was not mere wealth, but "the end of contempt." He treated the natives as fully integrated citizens. Here again, he was not unlike his distant predecessor Napoleon III, who proclaimed himself "the emperor of the Arabs as well as of the French." He did not call for abject surrender, but for the end of strife. He even referred to the rebels as brave men. He never precluded the possibility of negotiations.[4]

The solution De Gaulle had in mind, and which, through a patient process of education, he gradually brings into focus, is the permanent, but free and equal, association of two distinct personalities. He ended his speeches not with "Long live France, one and indivisible!," but with "Long live France! Long live Algeria!" He left the way open for the setting up of purely Algerian institutions: an Algerian assembly, an Algerian executive. He even envisages a more active partnership between the three parts of the Maghreb: Tunis, Algeria, Morocco. He is convinced that Habib Bourguiba, Ferhat Abbas, and Mohammed ben Youssef are closer to him in spirit than they are either to Ibn Saud or to Nasser. In such a spirit, the former protectorates, antagonized and almost alienated, might revert to the fruitful formula they once had freely accepted: pluralism, the peaceful coexistence of different communities; converging evolution in a swiftly changing world; independence within interdependence; in simpler terms, liberty, equality, fraternity.

Cynics might well raise their eyebrows: but De Gaulle's approach was put to the most realistic test. The rebels, who claimed to speak in the name of the Algerian masses, ordered a boycott of the referendum. But 4,402,250 Algerians registered; 3,505,719 voted; 3,356,969, as against 118,615 (96.5 per cent) expressed their faith in De Gaulle's promise. This massive victory came as a surprise, not only to the doctrinaires abroad who believed in "Nationalism right or wrong!" but to many Frenchmen, both of the right and of the left. It may have saved Algeria for France: more obviously, it saved the Algerians from the dictatorship of a fanatical minority. As for the Algerian dixiecrats, they have already expressed their disappointment in De Gaulle, whom they had so vociferously summoned as the supreme arbiter. He saved them from their own folly: thanks to him they will be spared the dilemma *la valise ou le cercueil:* pack your grip or fill your coffin. But they will be reduced to a dwindling knot of Die-hards.

It was of the utmost importance, in the eleventh hour, to choose the right road; but it is not sufficient. The road will be arduous; the effort must be sustained; the great hope must not be allowed to fade.

Because De Gaulle was a professional soldier, a born conservative, and an ardent patriot, many took it for granted that he was a chauvinist. Undoubtedly, there have been from the first and there still are many chauvinists among his supporters. Even his Minister of Justice, Michel Debré, is inclined to emphasize national consciousness as a primal reality, above the more shadowy loyalties to Europe and to mankind.[5] Many were afraid that De Gaulle's accession to power would impede the integration of Europe, of the Free World and of the Great Republic.

Those who entertained such fears had misread the rich and well-tempered mind of General de Gaulle. In a cordial meeting with Chancellor Adenauer, he affirmed that the co-operation, the ever more intimate union, of France and Germany were indispensable to the healthy development of both. In spite of many sharp conflicts in the past, he and Churchill could exchange deeply sincere tributes; and Sir Winston accepted from his *difficult* ally the Cross of Lorraine, no longer a heavy burden. De Gaulle has given his full approval to all the efforts which are shaping Europe, free and united at last: European army, Coal and Steel Community, Common Market, Euratom. He is far more definitely in favor of outlawing nuclear warfare than we are. And he has stated in unmistakable terms his faith in the necessity of a world state, a world law, and a world force.[6] When he seems *difficult,* to repeat a weary phrase, it is because he will not dwell in comfortable ambiguities, and because he believes that a fraternity of nations cannot exist except in liberty and equality. The unquestioned leadership of a single power and the faith of De Gaulle are incompatible.

He is therefore impatient of the wranglings which belong to the past, even though they are still cluttering the present. The experience of eighteen years has taught him that the new technical developments offer a clear alternative: One world or none. He knows that there are at present at least four Internationals: the Roman Catholic, the Capitalistic, the Communistic, the Humanistic.[7] He is aware that all four are represented in France. They clash and combine in many paradoxical ways. The French are convinced, realistically, that not one of these internationals can be eradicated by force: they must be harmonized through liberty and good will. In this immense and confused conflict, every Frenchman is conscious that he may be in full sympathy with men beyond the frontiers, while his next door neighbor may be an opponent. We have clearly reached the point—and no one sees it more clearly than De Gaulle himself—where *national* politics seem parochial, and *national* cultures provincial.

Thus, under our eyes, and with a leader whose supreme ambition is to integrate the French spirit, the long history of France as a material entity is approaching its close. Armaments, economic interests, political conflicts, as well as science, art, and religion have risen from the tribal plane to the national, and from the national to the continental, the intercontinental, the global. The myth that a soul is attached to a territory and a government is evaporating: unregretted, for that myth had become a Moloch. *France* no longer designates the estate of a family, even though that family should embrace the whole people: *France*—and that France is eternal—is a contribution to human culture.

This is not the dissolution, but the integration, of the French ideal. Sully-Prudhomme was right:

"My country gave me a heart that reaches beyond her boundaries,
    And the more French I am, the more human I feel." [8]

And the prophecy of Victor Hugo is fulfilled: "O France, adieu! Thou art too great to remain a nation." [9]

There arose in the darkness that foreshadowed the storm a school of thought quaintly or pedantically called existentialism. With the metaphysical profundities of Jean-Paul Sartre, with his indebtedness to Kierkegaard, Heidegger, Husserl, or Kafka, we are not here concerned. They are but the rationalization of an anguish which, under many names, is today universal. What stands out for us in existentialism, as represented by Sartre himself, and, quite independently, by Albert Camus, is first of all a moral attitude. This universe is "absurd"; it was not created according to the rules of man's reason, or for man's comfort. Its indifference is at times akin to malignity. Under the grid of scientific or logical consistency that we impose upon it, we feel that the reality, in human terms, is chaos.

But these men of France refuse to submit to chaos. They recognize it as such and thereby transcend it. If they call the universe "absurd," it is because they find within themselves a source of strength capable of conceiving and imposing some degree of order. In the world of current events these men took active part in the Resistance. In the world of the spirit they show themselves no less unyielding. We discover in them the pride and faith of Roland, overwhelmed but unsubdued; the steadfastness of Joan, betrayed, condemned by the men who claimed to be her spiritual masters, still true to her voices and to her mission; the sovereign will power of Corneille's heroes; the quiet daring of Descartes, brushing aside every authority except that of his own intimate and reasoned conviction; the stoicism of Vigny, spurning the indifference of Nature, facing undismayed the eternal silence of Fate. Above all, we find the supreme assurance of Pascal: "Man is but a reed, the weakest in nature; but he is a thinking reed." [10]

This, under the trappings of Gauls, Romans, and Franks, of kings and emperors, of philosophers and revolutionists, is the inner story I have been attempting to tell.

CHAPTER XXXII

A Decade of the Fifth Republic

Ten years ago, the late Albert Guérard said that the world was plagued with stubborn old men. He did not include President Charles de Gaulle among the old. Ten years later, the American press and State Department believed him more stubborn than ever. But even his enemies were not sure that he had yet aged in anything but years. The spring of 1968 saw him meet and overcome the worst political crisis of the Fifth Republic. The autumn found him leading a reluctant majority on the Right to his own version of social and educational reforms demanded by the Left, or some of the Left. Gaullism, Guérard said, was not a set of blueprints but a spirit and a method.

The spirit, called *grandeur* by De Gaulle himself, was caught in part by Guérard's other remark that the General was realistic enough to see that, in the long run, generosity was the safest policy. For most party politicians, generosity to opponents is not easy to exercise at any time. Here the General's method has so far served him well. He has always claimed to stand for France, above parties, for the national good, the popular will. He has again and again succeeded in casting his rivals, his enemies, even the recalcitrant among his own followers, as fractious, divisive men. He has, as many have observed, often carried out the policies of the Left (or, again, his own version of them) with majorities based on the Right.

One question inevitably arises in predicting the future of the Gaullist Republic. Who but De Gaulle could sustain either the spirit or the method? So much the patriot, so obviously the man of Order and of old-fashioned virtues, he has kept most conservative Frenchmen loyal to him in spite of certain policies they call radical. So often able to be, or to appear, generous to popular causes, he has stolen the thunder of the Left, forcing it to a vain search for political issues and a coherent alternative. What coherent alternative can there be to a nonprogram, without coherence, at least in political terms familiar to French parties? Gaullism is not a program but a performance, of statecraft and stagecraft, unique in modern history. Even less than Napoleon III is De Gaulle vulnerable to ordinary political campaigns. With the Second Empire in mind, one is left to watch the drama unroll, and to wait in suspense for the great accident, or physical decline, to bring the performance to an end—or, if one is sympathetic, to wish for an exit worthy of the hero's finer moments.

Modern historians are often ready to argue that politics is only a fraction of human, historical reality. A nation's life is affected little by political actors who at best can only express problems arising from forces deeper than politics can reach and broader than the nation itself, or at worst, can only obscure and tangle the questions men face in their daily lives. Good or bad politics are of little more significance than good or bad theatre. It is no accident that such a view of politics should flourish in our century. It is nonetheless a counsel of despair, and of evasion. In this, the present writer agrees with Albert Guérard that we cannot let ourselves or our leaders off so easily. We cannot retire into simplification. Politicians sometimes make a difference, as at other times they do not, to the hard problems of a people. Yet even when they do not achieve what we worship as practical results, they cannot but make a difference between a people's clarity and confusion of thought, between its hope and its despair, between its pride and its shame. These are not small things. Charles de Gaulle believes them to be, in the long run, the great things. In justice then, his performance must be weighed at least in part by his own view of what matters.

✦ THE ALGERIAN SETTLEMENT

Among De Gaulle's political acts, historians and political scientists most easily agree that he made a difference in the resolution of the Algerian dilemma. Without pursuing very far what might have been, many go on to say that he alone was capable of leading Frenchmen out of the Algerian war without provoking civil war or dictatorship. He was, of course, not lacking allies. Many Frenchmen wished an end of it. Fourth Republic politicians had sought escape. Alone, they had neither the prestige nor the force to succeed. Even had it been united, the Left would have had doubtful control over the police and soldiers by 1958. De Gaulle was a national hero, a monument to the Resistance, a General who had eschewed dictatorship in 1945. All this was important for his acceptance by the voters of the Left and Center, if not by their leaders. But in 1958 he also reaped the rewards of the dubious episode of the R.P.F. What many of his admirers regarded as a disappointing lapse into proto-Fascism now served to assure Frenchmen of the Right that he was, or could be, their man.

For nearly a year after his victorious referendum of 1958, he took no clear direction. His first cabinet (the last of the Fourth Republic) was a moderate coalition, excluding extremists at either side. The first parliamentary election of the Fifth Republic, in November 1958, gave his party (the U.N.R., Union for the New Republic) and its allies a majority of the Assembly. In December, he was chosen president by an overwhelming majority of the electoral college. Solidly established in constitutional power, it remained for him to bring the Algerian settlers and the army under his control.

Most of 1959 was taken to court the army while gradually removing extremist officers from posts of influence. General Salan was recalled to Paris; officers were forced to resign from the insurgent Committees of Public Safety; entire units were reassigned. By September 1959, De Gaulle was ready to pronounce the word: independence. He offered an Algerian referendum with three choices: integration with France, autonomous association, or independence. The vote would follow a cease-fire and the Algerians' decision would be submitted in turn to a French referendum. The settlers and their allies in France denounced De Gaulle as a traitor, but most of the U.N.R. and Right deputies had little choice but to approve the President's initiative. The Assembly approved in October an operation that only the Left could have supported had the name of the leader not been De Gaulle.

The settlers found themselves separated from France and, more decisively, from the army. In January 1960 an armed rebellion in Algiers killed twenty-one persons, but loyal troops ended the uprising after a dramatic television appeal by the President. The Algerian war continued for another year before a referendum of January 1961 on self-determination won overwhelmingly in both Algeria and France. De Gaulle and the Tunisian President Bourguiba arranged a start of negotiations with the Algerian rebels for April 1961. The European settlers were in despair, but it soon became clear that De Gaulle had not wholly succeeded in taming the military.

In April, a band of colonels and generals headed by Salan took over several army units, including legionnaires and paratroopers, to seize Algiers. For some hours, Paris itself appeared vulnerable to airborne invasion. But once more De Gaulle appealed to the nation and once more he won obedience from the bulk of the armed forces. The putsch collapsed. Negotiations began between the French government and the Algerian rebels a few weeks later, in May 1961. At this point the European extremists and rebellious soldiers in Algiers turned to terrorism in a final attempt to frustrate a settlement. The Secret Army Organization (OAS) bombed the shops, homes, and offices of liberal Frenchmen on both sides of the Mediterranean. Many innocent victims lost their lives in these attacks. Murdering Moslems wherever they could, the OAS hoped to provoke retaliation that would prevent a settlement. But the Moslem community limited its reprisals and the talks went on.

The long Algerian agony ended on March 19, 1962, with a cease-fire and agreements on free elections for Algerian self-determination, on amnesties, on French economic aid and military bases, and on joint control of Saharan oil fields. Now each side paid a last doleful price. The OAS went on a murderous rampage, slaughtering Moslem teachers, shopkeepers, workers, even hospital patients and women in the streets. Moslem leaders still held their people fiercely in check, but the dread of ultimate reprisal stirred hundreds of thousands of Europeans to flee to France, leaving behind their family homes of generations. In April, French voters approved the peace terms by seventeen million to two million. In July, Algerians voted for independence, and the first Algerian Republic was recognized by the Fifth French Republic as a sovereign nation.

✍ DE GAULLE AND THE WORLD

De Gaulle's statesmanship in Algeria won him new prestige in France and the world. He moved swiftly to take domestic political advantages. In October, he directly challenged the Assembly with his proposal for the revision of the constitution by referendum to make the president's election subject to universal suffrage. The Assembly overthrew his cabinet, headed by Georges Pompidou. But the referendum question was approved by more than six of ten French voters, and the general elections in November gave the Gaullists and their allies a comfortable margin in the new Assembly. Those who expected that the end of the Algerian war would result in a return to the ways of the Fourth Republic were deceived. The Gaullist Republic swept on. Automobiles poured from new works; the atom bomb was refined; André Malraux, minister of culture, pressed the cleaning of Paris' great buildings. In three years, the aging hero-President would be elected by universal suffrage to a second term.

The end of the Algerian war, French prosperity, and electoral victories allowed De Gaulle to pursue more directly his object of restoring France to leadership in world affairs. In so doing, his words and acts brought him more and more into opposition to the foreign policies and foreign preferences of the United States. Conflict was perhaps inevitable from his goal to win for France, and Europe, a measure of independence under the American protectorate. Conflict turned to bitterness as he saw, and described, the world as it was very differently from American leaders who were still caught in the attitudes of the Cold War and entangled in Vietnam.

It was thus to be expected that more nonsense about Charles de Gaulle was purveyed and believed by Americans in the 1960's than about any other public figure of the century. American commentators, in and out of government, wearied by problems close to home, found relief in displaying their wit on a subject they felt no need to understand. His "only passion is France," they said, as though this somehow set him apart from other national leaders, including their own. Rather than examining the kind of world he believed necessary to France's (and America's) well-being, it was easier to hurl imprecations: "antique nationalism," "disloyalty," "ingratitude," "obstructionism," "betrayal," "pathological hatred of Anglo-Saxons," all of which only confirmed De Gaulle's own view that "what it is customary to call opinion" in America was not to be taken seriously.

De Gaulle was not anti-American, but historical reflection and personal experience had taught him to doubt the quality and the consistency of American diplomacy, as well as the ability of Anglo-Saxons to understand the interests of France or Europe. Still, in spite of periodic misunderstandings between them, France and America were ancient allies, he repeated, bound by common devotion to the same human ideals. Toward America, Frenchmen should be grateful for her historical sympathy and massive aid in moments of common danger. Some form of the Atlantic alliance, De Gaulle said, was an "elemental necessity," and no one could doubt that American power alone was capable of balancing that of Soviet Russia. The balance between the super-powers made life possible for Europe. But the United States had its own interests and its own destiny, which were—as often demonstrated—not the same as France's or Europe's. No one expected them to be. The United States, after all, was normally nationalistic and did not dream of subordinating her interests to those of others (though she sometimes expected subordination of others). It was intolerable, then, and would some day imperil old friendships, perhaps even endanger world peace, for the United States to persist in dominating the foreign, the military, or the economic (which was also to say the cultural) affairs of Europe.

Under the weak and dependent governments of the Fourth Republic, De Gaulle repeated, France had had little voice in making Western policies critical to her future and Europe's. Without a strong lead from the

Fifth Republic, Europe would have little voice in the foreseeable future. Britain appeared content to remain a satellite to the United States; she also nourished imperial and Commonwealth interests. Of the other continental states, only West Germany could aspire to a leading role, but she too chose dependence on the United States, was distracted by the dream of unification, and was still suspect to other Europeans. France alone, then, could lead Europe to build her own strength, independent enough of the United States to shape her own future.

That future "European Europe" De Gaulle saw as a confederation of sovereign states, with close economic and military ties maintained not by a supranational authority, but by representatives of governments meeting together. His vision was contrary to John Kennedy's "Grand Design" for a united Western Europe within an Atlantic Community. The division of Europe, De Gaulle believed, was a temporary matter. To be herself, Europe must, and would, stretch "from the Atlantic to the Urals." Ideologies were fading, he believed, and the countries of East and West were becoming more like each other. The East-West conflict was fading also, as China rose to challenge Russia in Asia. Europeans should prepare for the détente, and do nothing that would delay or prevent its coming. The American concept of an Atlantic Community including a tightly-integrated Western Europe would pull Europe away from her natural future. Old Europe would emerge from the Cold War, as she had emerged from the ideological storms of the Reformation and the French Revolution.

Meanwhile, De Gaulle sought a leading role for France in differing ways according to the changing circumstances of the 1960's. Soon after returning to power in 1958, he sought an equal place for France in the Anglo-American directorate of Western global policy. His initiative followed the Lebanon crisis, in which Americans had taken direct military action in an old French sphere without consulting Paris. He was rebuffed by Washington, bringing back memories of Free France's humiliating experiences at the hands of Churchill and Roosevelt during World War II. His response was to withdraw the French Mediterranean fleet from NATO control and to remove American nuclear warheads and rocket-launching sites from French soil.

De Gaulle was also disappointed in his attempt to bring the Federal Republic of West Germany into partnership with France, to serve as a first step toward a "European Europe" increasingly independent of the United States. After an exchange of visits with Chancellor Adenauer, who greatly admired De Gaulle, the Franco-German treaty of cooperation was signed in January of 1963. But Adenauer's successor, Ludwig Erhard, was determined to put allegiance to America first and rendered

De Gaulle's attempt all but useless as an attempt to set Western Europe on a new course. That the Germans, and the English, were willing to take seriously the doubtful American proposal for a seaborne nuclear multilateral force under Washington's command proved to De Gaulle that building an independent Europe would be a long task indeed.

From this conviction sprang De Gaulle's insistence that any political integration of Western Europe should be postponed. France could not risk engagement with Great Britain, West Germany, Italy or the Benelux countries as long as they so obviously accepted subservience to the United States. On the other hand, France under De Gaulle adhered to the Common Market treaty in economic matters. Here, integration was vital to build Europe's economic strength, to protect her from the rapid advance of American investments and the political and cultural influences that would follow. De Gaulle pressed for European cooperation against American competition, calling for a European patent system, European-wide companies, and the pooling of scientific and technical research.

The two crises he forced on the Common Market followed logically from his wider goals. In early 1963, he caused negotiations for Britain's entry into the Common Market to be broken off. Other members of the Common Market were also worried about British membership, fearing that it would bring in its wake the other nations of the European Free Trade Association and a dilution of the Market itself. Some believed that President Kennedy's call for a worldwide reduction of tariffs was meant to open Europe to increased competition before the Common Market had solidified its economic union. But it was left to De Gaulle to deliver the famous No to London. To Frenchmen, De Gaulle was justified also by the Nassau agreement of late 1962 between Macmillan and Kennedy, which made Britain even more the special, and subservient, ally of Washington.

In 1965, De Gaulle boycotted the Common Market meetings on the grounds that the European Economic Commission was seeking to give itself a supranational political character, by seeking its own budget and a greater use of majority votes. Like the prospect of British membership, this appeared to De Gaulle to threaten France's leadership on the continent. The boycott was lifted in 1966 when the Commission largely abandoned its initiative. Meanwhile, the "Kennedy Round" of tariff-cutting was delayed again. Outside agreements, new members, and political accretions to the Common Market should wait until the economic integration of the six nations was further along, De Gaulle insisted. Indeed, it would be easier for the British and others to join later if membership did not entail political entanglements. That certain members of the Common Market agreed at each step was overlooked by those who accused the French of "wrecking" European integration. On the contrary, the Fifth Republic kept strictly to the original timetable of Common Market development, or ahead of it. The French economy was laid open to outside competition to an extent that might well have been impossible for the weaker Fourth Republic to risk.

As the 1960's wore on, General De Gaulle grew increasingly uneasy about America's global adventures. The world was changing. The entire Southern hemisphere was lagging behind in economic development, much of it in danger of starvation. In this, as in the emergence of China, the relaxations in Eastern Europe and in the Soviet Union, the questions of Berlin and German unification, and, most urgent, the escalation of the war in Vietnam, De Gaulle believed that it was Washington and not he that was anachronistic—and all the more dangerous and unpredictable for failing to see the world as it was. If public opinion polls, and the pronouncements of other French politicians across the party spectrum from Left to Right, were to be believed, De Gaulle carried most of his countrymen with him in his distrust of "what the United States calls its leadership" and in his movement toward a neutral position in world affairs.

The first French atomic bomb was exploded in the Sahara in February 1960. Thereafter, De Gaulle pressed the development of France's independent nuclear *force de frappe*. It was not, he admitted, a substitute for American power in a possible confrontation with the Soviet Union, but a means by which France could help determine where and when American nuclear force could be brought to bear. Given Russian nuclear capability, De Gaulle asserted that the Anglo-American deterrent might not be believable in the case of a threat to Europe unless a continental nation had the ability to trigger it. The obvious, though unstated, fact that the *force de frappe* gave France a lead on a possible revival of German militarism was overlooked by those who derided it as a useless extravagance. It was unlikely that any future French government would see the issue very differently.

In 1966, De Gaulle withdrew all French forces from the NATO command and forced NATO bases and headquarters out of France. While remaining a member of the Alliance and pledging that France would fight at the side of its allies in the event of European war, De Gaulle announced that France was no longer willing to risk the consequences of Washington's aggressive policy in Asia. In 1964, he had recognized Communist China. "No war, no peace" were conceivable in Asia without China's participation, he said, and no possibility of neutralizing Southeast Asia, where Cambodia offered the best example of what was possible. It was pointedly at Phnom Penh, Cambodia's capital, that in 1966 he denounced American military actions in Vietnam as a threat to world peace. Only a political settlement was possible, he said, followed by neutralization of Southeast Asia. Following his lifelong conviction that national feeling was stronger than ideology, he dismissed Washington's claim that the war was a fight against Communism. Instead, it was opening Southeast Asia to Chinese influence, much against the desires of the North Vietnamese themselves.

On the world scene, De Gaulle believed that Americans, for all their talk of reforms in backward nations, seriously misunderstood what was required. The "third world" of the poor nations demanded self-determination, but also a high degree of socialist economic organization. He prided himself on having encouraged such development in Algeria, on having avoided the American mistake in Cuba of pushing revolutionaries into the arms of foreign Communists. America, he said, decided too many issues on appearances rather than on realities, on short-run effects at home rather than on long-term developments abroad. She chose her allies and friends more on their professions of loyalty than on their real policies and actions. But such had been the habit of the United States for a generation, from its repudiation of the League of Nations in 1920, through its choice of Vichy and Darlan in World War II, to its errors in Cuba, the Dominican Republic, and Vietnam in the 1960's. To the large extent that De Gaulle's foreign policies reflected French views of American leadership and of the consequencs of American hegemony, it was not likely that his successors would alter them appreciably.

DOMESTIC POLITICS

Politics in France after the Algerian settlement followed a relatively serene course until the spring of 1968. The stresses of a dynamic economy breaking down old habits and endangering established interests created substantial opposition to the Gaullist regime. But the old parties were not able to exploit discontent effectively enough to return to power. As ever, the real wages of the working class, particularly in the nationalized industries, failed to keep pace with either the cost of living or the gains of the upper classes. Agricultural discontent frequently erupted into boycotts and demonstrations. Despite added expenditures in the social realm, France's needs for new housing and new schools, at all levels, were not met. Many Frenchmen believed that these deficiencies resulted from the expense of the *force de frappe* and foreign aid, or from De Gaulle's periodic difficulties with the Common Market. De Gaulle's narrow victory in the presidential election of December 1965 followed his boycott of the Market, but it is impossible to tell whether it was an important factor. Having failed to win a majority in the first round, he was elected in the second by only 55 percent of the votes cast.

The parliamentary elections of March 1967 resulted in an even narrower victory for the Gaullists. An election pact between the Communist Party, headed by Waldeck-Rochet, and the Leftist Federation led by François Mitterand, arranged for unity behind the more likely Leftist candidate in the second round of balloting. Continuing social and economic resentments brought out the voters of the Left. From 267 seats, the Gaullists and their allies fell to 245, only three more than a majority. The second-ballot alliance of the Left parties helped the Communists to rise from forty-one to seventy-three, and the Leftist Federation from ninety-one to 116. Former Premier Pierre Mendès-France was among many Fourth Republic deputies to return to the Assembly. The Gaullists nonetheless organized the new parliament; Pompidou remained as premier. On the surface, French political life returned to what so many observers called apathy, under the benevolent monarchy of Charles de Gaulle.

In the spring of 1968, apathy turned to violence, hope, and fear in the most dramatic political crisis of the Fifth Republic. What journalists called for a time the "French Revolution of 1968" began in March with student rebellion at the new, bleak, unfinished Nanterre campus of the University of Paris. The issues ranged from parietal rules, through the University's subservience to the "system," to the exploitation of man by neo-capitalism. In early May, the Latin Quarter students joined in. Buildings were occupied; the Sorbonne and Odéon flew the red flag and the black flag. Classes gave way to all-night discussion and hourly proclamations. Most students agreed that the French system of higher education was out of date, overcrowded and underdeveloped, that all French schools were authoritarian, over-centralized, and largely irrelevant to what they saw as the conditions of life in the late twentieth century. On such attacks, it was easy to unite those who decried the quality of education that Frenchmen would carry through their lives with those who merely resented the fact that the degree did not automatically produce a job, or with those who resented anything not leading directly to social action.

Despite innumerable, and strident, divisions among Maoists, Castroites, Trotskyists, anarchists, socialists, and moderates, an extraordinary mood of solidarity and exaltation suffused the great student demonstrations of May. As in the early hours of 1830, 1848, 1871, and 1936, the young could believe in reform, renewal, change in the very ordering of human life. For a time, public sympathy was with the students, at least on the Left bank. There then developed a wave of industrial strikes and sit-ins, many spontaneous, some against the orders of the unions, some finally at the call of the Communist CGT, anxious not to fall behind. Students and younger workers reinforced each other's efforts; the Left appeared to be on the march.

A general strike gripped Paris and much of France in mid-May. Closed were factories, stores, banks, schools, theatres, post offices, railways and the Metro. Frenchmen went without mail, newspapers, taxis, gasoline and garbage collection. Life and work came to a standstill. Paris was choked with trash and garbage; barricades rose in the Latin Quarter and, as police turned aggressive, trees were cut, autos burned, shops wrecked. Toughs and delinquents took advantage of the disorder, and their violence did much to discredit the student movement, as did the more revolutionary or nihilist proclamations of rival student leaders seeking to outbid each other in daring.

Fear of chaos, of possible civil war, spread from commentators who speculated on De Gaulle's resignation. With the state's authority in doubt, the seventy-eight-year-old President at first appeared to flounder in his response. As if by force of habit, he appeared on television to offer a national referendum on basic social reforms, to be carried out by himself. It was badly received. Observers doubted that striking printers would even consent to prepare the ballots. De Gaulle turned next to economic concessions, a threat of force, and a general election.

Over the objections of many workers and to the disgust of the students, the Communist and other labor leaders accepted the government's hasty offers: a 10 percent raise in wages and promises of a shorter work week and earlier retirement. Still the strikes went on, as militant workers refused their leaders' collaboration in the "system." They, like the students, demanded "participation," self-management, decentralization of decision-making. So seriously did De Gaulle take the situation that he turned to the army for support; to make sure of it—and of the voters of the Right—he released General Salan and other officers convicted during the Algerian crisis. With army units encamped near Paris, De Gaulle made a second television broadcast on May 30 (without live pictures; the technicians were on strike). He took a strong line: "I shall not withdraw, the Republic will not abdicate." He warned that he would use force against the state's enemies, and called for a new election. A strong majority, he said, would allow him to carry out reforms and insure "participation" in French institutions from schools to factories.

De Gaulle and his Premier, Pompidou, fought the elections of June as a choice between chaos, stirred by "totalitarian Communism," and

Gaullist progress. The results gave a stunning response to those, in France or abroad, who had hoped for, or feared, the demise of the Fifth Republic. For the first time in French parliamentary history, a single party, the UDR (the UNR renamed Union of Democrats for the Republic) won by itself an absolute majority in the Assembly. The old parties were routed. The month-long disruption of life had exasperated many Frenchmen; neither the students nor the Left parties were able to supplement their criticism with coherent alternative programs. Out of the 487-seat Assembly, the UDR won over 290 places, the often-allied Independent Republicans won sixty-three, for an overall "Gaullist" gain of over 100 seats from the previous Assembly. The Communists sank from seventy-three to thirty-three, the Left Federation from 119 to fifty-seven. Although the swing in the popular vote was not overwhelming, the Gaullists won nearly all the close contests they had lost the year before.

For all the drama of De Gaulle's victory, however, his success in making permanent a political system so dependent on his person is still in question. It has yet to be proved that the UDR is a party able to govern rather than merely follow a leader unique in prestige. As the events of May demonstrated, the pace and effects of French modernization raise problems that are new to all governments, and especially perhaps to the French, whose political rhetoric is still more traditional than innovative. Leaving aside the uneven quality of economic and social modernization in France, leaving aside the inequalities suffered by farmers and workers, the ultimate political question raised by modern mass industrial society concerns all men. The students and workers asked it in May, as Alexis de Tocqueville asked it over a century ago: whether a new despotism, more sweeping and less painful than any of the old, may not degrade men without torturing them. Nowhere is the question more likely to be debated, or to erupt at the expense of all political parties and regimes, than in France. Albert Guérard said that the men of France refuse to submit to chaos. The new chaos promises to be a kind of order, a physically comfortable order, but irrelevant and oppressive to certain deeper human desires that up to now have not often been the concern of politics. It has long been evident that many men cannot live by bread and circuses alone, that they will demand a certain quality of life, a measure of liberty and of honor, free access both to privacy and to community. Whether such desires can be met by any majoritarian political system, be its economic and social order neo-capitalist or neo-socialist, is very much in question. The "événements" of May 1968 in France, for all their confusions of aims and sentiments, may prove to be only the first of many such outbursts in the more affluent, more organized societies on earth. Albert Guérard would not have been surprised. Nor is Charles de Gaulle, whose "certain idea of France" has always led him to despise ordinary security, likely to be dismayed that the best among his adversaries despise it with him.

NOTES

NOTES TO INTRODUCTION

1. See Charles Seignobos' excellent epitome: *Histoire sincère de la nation française*, with the significant subtitle: *Essai d'une histoire de l'évolution du peuple français* (Paris, 1933).
2. See Appendix, note 1, France's Contribution to Western civilization.
3. Charles Maurras, Louis Dimier, Jacques Bainville.
4. Julien Benda, *Esquisse d'une histoire des Français dans leur volonté d'être une nation* (Paris, 1932).
5. "Tell your master that we are here by the will of the people. . . ." July 23, 1789.
6. Paradoxically, the monarchical ideal, "One faith, one law, one king," reached its formidable perfection not under Louis XIV, but under the "Republic, One and Indivisible," of the Jacobins. Even today, the heirs of the Jacobins are more averse than the Royalists to the autonomy of free associations and of provinces. King Demos is totalitarian: *Ein Volk, ein Reich, ein Führer.*
7. *Tous deux également nous portons des couronnes; Mais, roi, je la reçus; poète, tu la donnes.* (Date and authorship uncertain.)
8. Cf. "America's business is Business."

NOTES TO CHAPTER I

1. The French have been working for years on a great scheme to "civilize" the Rhône. The National Company entrusted with the project corresponds to our Tennessee Valley Authority.
2. *Canal du Midi ou des Deux Mers.* It had been repeatedly proposed to enlarge it so as to admit seagoing vessels. Although the project would not be profitable, it is perfectly feasible.
3. Onésime Reclus, a gifted but venturesome geographer, prophesied that Marseilles would become the capital of Greater France, African as well as European.
4. Great hopes are now set on oil developments in the southwest, as well as in the Sahara.
5. Names do not tell the whole story, for many patronymics were Frenchified: Herzog became Maurois; Kostrowitzky, Apollinaire; Papadiamantopoulos, Moréas. What could be more redolent of old France than Jean Malaquais? But that excellent novelist is, I believe, a Pole. Elsa Triolet and Henri Troyat are Russians.
6. I should be at a loss to name them; it certainly does not apply to England, Germany, or America.
7. *Oil* and *oc* mean "yes."
8. See Appendix, note 2.
9. This is confirmed by the experience of other countries. Italian en-

joyed great prestige for three centuries, although Italy was but "a geographical expression." That prestige grew dimmer when Italy became a united nation, and dimmest when she set up as a great power. Bismarckian—or Hitlerian—Germany ranked low compared with the Germany of Goethe, Schiller, Kant, and Beethoven.

NOTES TO CHAPTER II

1. Note that "prehistory," unbroken until the middle of the nineteenth century, is expiring under our eyes; immemorial customs and superstitions are melting before the radio and the cinema. If a new and perhaps less gracious folklore is arising, it is of an ever-shifting character. It would be bold to say that man has come of age: at any rate, he has entered upon another era.
2. Glacial ages: a series of age-long oscillations in temperature, with corresponding extension and recession of glaciers. There were several periods of glaciation, separated by milder interglacial stages. The range of variation need not have been very great. It seems that France never was wholly covered by the glaciers.
3. From Saint-Acheul, near Amiens (Somme), and Le Moustier, near Peyzac (Dordogne).
4. From a ravine in the region of Düsseldorf, Rhineland.
5. The use of French names for paleolithic stages of culture implies no French predominance, *à la* Louis XIV, in remotest antiquity. It is chiefly a tribute to the pioneering work of French anthropologists such as Boucher de Perthes and De Mortillet.
6. These Upper Paleolithic graphic documents show how varied the fauna of western Europe was at that time: animals of the tundra, the steppe, the mountain, the meadow, and the forest, now widely scattered, were all flourishing on the present territory of France.
7. Gros-Caillou: the Big Stone; Pierrefitte: the Standing Stone. The first is a central district in Paris at the foot of the Eiffel Tower, that nineteenth-century menhir of steel; the other is a residential suburb.

NOTES TO CHAPTER III

1. In the fifth century, Celts from Britain, fleeing from the Angles and Saxons, colonized Armorica, which became "Little Britain," or Brittany.
2. To make darkness more palpable, Homer's Cimmerians were brought in: "Later writers," says the Cambridge scholar Ellis Hovell Minns, "identified the Cimmerii with the Cimbri of Jutland, who were probably Teutonized Celts; but this is a mere guess due to the similarity of names."
3. Polybius in antiquity and Dr. Bang in our own century believed the Galatae to have been Germans. (Perhaps the Bastarnae, an eastern German tribe.)
4. The god of hot springs, "Borvo" or "Bormo," survives in the names of health resorts, the various Bourbons, Bourbonne, la Bourboule; he reached the throne with the Bourbon kings.

5. Diviciacus and Sacrovir, like Brennus and Vercingetorix, were probably titles rather than proper names.

NOTES TO CHAPTER IV

1. In the notable Preface to his *Life of Caesar,* Napoleon III expounded his doctrine of "Providential Men."
2. Roman colonies were as a rule composed of veterans from the legions, i.e., full citizens; Latin colonies, from the auxiliary troops; but in time even the legions were opened to noncitizens and even to freedmen of all races.
3. See Appendix, note 3.

NOTES TO CHAPTER V

1. Emperor 361–363. Julian has a special niche in French history, for he lived at Lutetia (Paris), where he was proclaimed emperor, wrote its praises, and adorned it with monuments, the ruins of which are still standing in the Latin Quarter.
2. At the end of the fourth century.
3. The exact location is in dispute; probably near Troyes in Champagne.
4. It was Bishop Hincmar in the ninth century who gave the story its definiteness, but it must have existed in vaguer form. Even if not literally authentic, it possesses deep symbolical truth.
5. Possibly a trace of Thor-worship.
6. In 778, as his armies were returning from one of these expeditions against the Saracens, the rear-guard was cut to pieces by the Christian Basques, and among the unavenged slain lay Roland, Prefect of the Breton March. Three centuries later, this obscure episode was to be magnified into *The Song of Roland.*
7. See Appendix, note 4.

NOTES TO CHAPTER VI

1. Died *ca.* 1050; wrote *World History* up to A.D. 1046.
2. See Henry Adams, *Mont-Saint-Michel and Chartres,* a study in thirteenth-century unity (Boston, 1912).
3. It has been surmised that Hugh derived his nickname *Capet* from wearing the cope (*Chape* or *cape*) of St. Martin's. Sheer guesswork: the exact significance of the word has long been lost. The Revolution affected to consider Capet as the family name of Louis XVI.
4. The Stuarts, as kings of France (*in partibus infidelium*), retained that gift to the end.
5. See Appendix, note 5.
6. In Part I (*St. Joan*) of his *Gott in Frankreich;* the title tamely translated as *Who Are These French?* (New York, 1932).
7. On the eve of the Renaissance an abbot of Cluny built in the Latin Quarter a charming town house, next to the Thermae of Julian; it has been turned into a museum of medieval art.
8. Also known as the Albigensians, from Albi (Tarn), one of their

centers. The "home mission" or crusade waged against them resulted in a great increase of royal power. Simon de Montfort (the elder), an Ile-de-France baron, led the expedition and was victorious at Muret (1213). The power of Toulouse was broken down by military defeat and savage persecution ("Kill them all! God will recognize His own!"), and the land, allotted to the conquering chief, ultimately passed under Capetian rule.

9. In Thomas Mann's *Dr. Faustus* (New York, 1948).

NOTES TO CHAPTER VII

1. See Jacques Barzun, *The French Race: Theories of Its Origins and their Political and Social Implications, prior to the Revolution* (New York, 1932).
2. See Appendix, note 6.
3. Its impressive ruins were shattered in World War I.
4. The fame of that village monarch was revived by a song of Béranger, a satire on imperial glory which Thackeray found worth translating. We are gravely assured that there is a legitimate heir to that toy crown, the marquis of Albon.
5. See C. S. Lewis, *The Allegory of Love* (Oxford, 1936); Denis de Rougemont, *Love in the Western World* (rev. ed.; New York, 1956).
6. In his classification of Victorian society, Matthew Arnold blandly called the aristocrats "the barbarians."
7. So named from *Jacques Bonhomme,* the typical French peasant.

NOTES TO CHAPTER VIII

1. At one time the peers were the archbishop duke of Rheims, the bishop dukes of Langres and Laon, the bishop counts of Beauvais, Noyon, Châlons, the dukes of Burgundy, Normandy, and Aquitaine, the counts of Flanders, Toulouse, and Champagne.
2. Villages such as Roissy and Mareil, some ten miles north of Notre Dame, are still known as Roissy-en-France, Mareil-en-France. Half a century ago people from such *pays* as Valois or Goëlle, a few miles farther, used to say, "I am going to France," when crossing the imaginary line.
3. The first began with Louis VI and ended with St. Louis; the second is the one generally known by that name, with Joan of Arc as the central character; there was a third one, which lasted from 1688 (William III *vs.* Louis XIV) to 1815 (Waterloo). All three were intermittent, with long, uneasy periods of truce.
4. Eleanor, who died in 1204, well over eighty, had a long, checkered, and at times tragic career in England under the reigns of her faithless husband and of her two unreliable sons, Richard and John. In her own domains of Aquitania she enjoyed great personal prestige, and her political vicissitudes did not prevent her from keeping an interest in the rich culture of her time. Bishop Stubbs said, "Few women have had less justice done them in history than Eleanor."

This injustice is now repaired, thanks to the thorough, sympathetic, and vivid studies of Curtis Howe Walker and Amy Kelly.

5. First stone laid 1163, under Louis VII; work completed under St. Louis, *ca.* 1260.

6. Market of the Holy Innocents. Site unchanged to this day—alas!

7. There were in French history five regencies by women: two, those of Blanche of Castile and Anne de Beaujeu, were successful; three, those of Catherine de Médicis, Marie de Médicis, and Anne of Austria, had very dubious records.

8. It is fitting that the memory of the Holy King should be associated with the most exquisite jewel of Gothic art, the Sainte-Chapelle in Paris. He had it erected (1245–1248) as a shrine for priceless relics obtained from the destitute Latin emperor of Constantinople.

NOTES TO CHAPTER IX

1. See Appendix, note 7.

2. The Sicilians had rebelled against the French and massacred them ("Sicilian Vespers," 1282); Don Pedro of Aragon was challenging Charles's title to the possession of the island. Charles died, defeated likewise, a few weeks before Philip.

3. Charles Seignobos, *Histoire sincère de la nation française* (Paris, 1933), Chapter XIV: "Formation de la monarchie absolue impersonnelle."

4. In 1302 the Parlement became finally settled in the Palace of the City, which remains to this day the Palace of Justice, or *le Palais, par excellence.*

5. There was nothing revolutionary in such a step: there had been regional and provincial States (or Estates) before. The sole purpose of these convocations was to raise revenue; no higher principle was involved. It was only half a century later (1355) that an attempt was made to turn the States-General into a parliament.

6. Avignon was in the county of Venasque (*Venaissin*), the possession of which had been confirmed to the Holy See by Philip III in 1274; it was to remain papal territory until 1791.

7. Guienne, in French Guyenne, a corrupt form of Aquitania (*l'Aquienne*), came into common use in the late thirteenth century. The count of Brittany had been made a duke by Philip the Fair.

8. According to a stipulation made when Dauphiné was acquired, the king's eldest son was to bear the title of dauphin, of mysterious origin.

NOTES TO CHAPTER X

1. I.e., grotesque little figures; perhaps connected with *marmot, marmaille,* urchins, brats.

2. Arthur, Earl of Richmond, brother of the duke of Brittany.

3. Easily available in English: *The Trial of Jeanne d'Arc,* translated by W. P. Barrett, with essays by Pierre Champion (New York, 1932).

4. Joan was known, at least since the days of Villon, as "the good Lorrainer"; but Lorraine did not finally become French until 1766.

5. These movements were called *Praguerie,* from Prague, as if they resembled the recent Hussite troubles in Bohemia.

6. Jean Dunois, proudly known as the Bastard of Orleans (1403–1468), was the ablest and the most loyal of Joan's companions. He was with her at Orleans and Patay.

7. The Hundred Years' War cannot be fully understood without the alliance—fitful, but constantly recurring—between France and Scotland. It was repeatedly important, although never decisive. At one time, the best fighters on the French side were Scots, and the king kept a Scottish bodyguard.

8. A Pragmatic Sanction in the same spirit had been ascribed to St. Louis, but it was proved to be a forgery.

9. Later known as Franche-Comté.

10. *Le Téméraire:* more accurately the Rash, or the Foolhardy.

11. Yet this is exactly what Prussia achieved in the nineteenth century.

12. Except for two decades, 1795–1814, under the Revolution and the Empire.

NOTES TO CHAPTER XI

1. His soldiers, to honor him, sang a naive dirge: "A quarter of an hour before his death, he was still alive." (They meant, fighting.) This served as a pattern for the kind of comic truisms later credited to Joseph Prudhomme and Marshal de Mac-Mahon.

2. The Sorbonne, a college endowed by Robert de Sorbon, confessor of St. Louis. Since the Doctors' examinations were held there, the name was used for the Divinity School, and for the whole university. At present, the Sorbonne is the main block of buildings of the University of Paris: chapel, assembly hall, library, administration, and a number of lecture rooms.

3. The practice was to be fully confirmed and legalized under Henry IV in 1604.

4. Jointly with his mother, Joanna, who was held to be insane and was not permitted to rule.

5. He held up Milan in true bandit fashion in order to pay his troops, marched on Rome with a motley army of Spanish and Lutheran mercenaries, and was killed in the assault by the skilled hand of Benvenuto Cellini (according to Cellini's report). His headless bands sacked the Holy City in thorough Gothic fashion (1527).

6. The alliance with the Turks was something of a scandal, but the fashion had been set by the Holy Father himself. Alexander VI commended Alfonso of Naples for seeking, against Charles VIII, the support of the Turks. Both Hitler and Winston Churchill made agreements with Stalin. Realism defies logic as well as morality.

7. Tradition has condensed his message to his mother in the lapidary form: *Tout est perdu, sauf l'honneur,* All is lost, honor is saved.

8. This curiously foreshadows the moving protest of the Alsace-Lorraine deputies at Bordeaux in 1871.

9. Known as the Ladies' Peace, because it was negotiated by Margaret of Austria, the emperor's aunt, and Louise of Savoy, the king's mother.
10. Rabelais, Book II, Chapter VIII, Urquhart's translation.
11. I am alluding to the *Pilgrimage of Charlemagne* of the early twelfth century, perhaps as old as the *Song of Roland,* so oddly blending epic and *fabliau.*

NOTES TO CHAPTER XII

1. The Huguenot, or at any rate the violent anti-Catholic, tone of Rabelais's Fifth Book, published posthumously, is usually accepted as evidence that the work is to a large extent apocryphal.
2. *In commendam:* commendatory abbots received the revenues, but did not perform the duties, of their office. Pierre de Bourdeille, Abbot of Brantôme (1540–1614), is chiefly known for his spicy *Lives of Illustrious and Gallant Ladies:* a Valois Suetonius.
3. Cf. the avowedly non-Christian Catholicism of Charles Maurras, for half a century the intellectual leader of the neo-Royalists, the brains of Pétain's National Revolution. (b. 1868; active 1895–1944.)
4. The son of Charles VIII's adviser, who, as a widower, entered the Church and became a bishop and a cardinal.
5. See Appendix, note 8.
6. From the German *Eidgenossen,* sworn companions, confederates; the spelling perhaps influenced by the name *Hugues.*
7. Henry III, Henry of Guise, Henry of Navarre.
8. The famous *panache,* which Edmond Rostand in *Cyrano de Bergerac* made the symbol of reckless bravery, with a touch of bravado.

NOTES TO CHAPTER XIII

1. Just as in 1830 Lafayette endorsed Louis-Philippe as "the best of Republics," and as Thiers in 1850 accepted the Republic as "the regime which least divides us."
2. His favorite oath was *Jarnidieu!,* I renounce God!—a trifle lurid for His Most Christian Majesty; so his confessor, Father Coton, suggested the softened version, which has remained popular, *Jarnicoton!*
3. Vive Henry Quatre!
    Vive ce roi vaillant!
        Ce diable à quatre
    A le triple talent
        De boire et de se battre,
    Et d'être un Vert-Galant.
4. A yearly payment equal to one sixtieth of the price they had paid for the office.
5. The present writer well remembers what unspeakable pride and comfort he found in the thought of "humbling the House of Austria," long before he knew where the House of Austria stood and what it stood for.
6. See Appendix, note 9.

NOTES TO CHAPTER XIV

1. Félix Gaiffe, *L'envers du grand siècle* (Paris, 1924). Partly a counter-blast to Louis Bertrand's unmeasured panegyric, *Louis XIV* (Paris, 1923).
2. Jean Chapelain, official head of French literature under Louis XIV, was well inspired when he selected *The Maid* (*La Pucelle*) as the subject of a national epic, a modern *Aeneid*. Unfortunately his inspiration did not carry him beyond the title.
3. At one time the Paris salons whispered the wicked lines of Bussy-Rabutin:

    > *On dit que Dieu nous l'a donné:*
    > *Ah! S'il pouvait nous le reprendre!*

    "They say God gave him to us: ah! if only He would take him back!"
4. See Appendix, note 10.
5. See Appendix, note 11.
6. See Appendix, note 12.
7. Turenne, a Protestant prince who was not formally converted until 1668, died in the field in 1675.
8. See Appendix, note 13.
9. The Lutherans of Alsace were not disturbed in their religion and have remained a great power in the province to the present day.
10. Blaise Pascal (1623–1662), physicist (the vacuum, atmospheric pressure), mathematician (epicycloid), practical inventor (wheelbarrow, computing machine, omnibus service), witty and profound controvertialist (*Provincials*, 1656), apologist (posthumous fragments known as *Thoughts*).

NOTES TO CHAPTER XV

1. Translation unprintable, as Ernest Hemingway would say.
2. See Appendix, note 14.
3. Maupeou was chancellor, i.e., head of the Judiciary; Abbé Terray was comptroller general of finances; the duke d'Aiguillon, minister of foreign affairs. They were dubbed the Triumvirate, and Terray in particular, *Vide-Gousset* (Pickpocket).
4. In 1768 Choiseul bought Corsica from the Genoese, who had failed to subdue the island. This real-estate deal (needless to say, the Corsicans were not consulted) made Napoleon Bonaparte a Frenchman by birth (1769).
5. The nobles resisted, but did not avoid, all taxes. One, however, they would never consent to pay, the principal one, *la taille,* which in their eyes was servile. Serfs had been *taillables* and *corvéables à merci:* liable to cash payments and forced labor at their lord's discretion.
6. *The Royal Tithe* was written in 1698 and published in 1707 when the situation had grown desperate. It was immediately suppressed by royal order. The marshal died heartbroken a few days later.
7. *Le mur murant Paris rend Paris murmurant.*
8. Rousseau, *Confessions* (1732), Part I, Book IV.

9. We have to use *philosophie* and *philosophe* in the French forms; for *philosophie* was not an abstract system nor an attitude of detachment, stoic or amused. G. B. Shaw and H. G. Wells were *philosophes* in the eighteenth-century meaning of the word.

10. Published as *Discourse on the Sciences and the Arts.*

NOTES TO CHAPTER XVI

1. Choiseul, who belonged to an illustrious family, also represented the new aristocracy of finance; he had married a daughter of Crozat and was the protégé of Madame de Pompadour.

2. De Sade (1740–1814) provides an admirable *reductio ad absurdum* of Rousseauism. According to the master natural instincts are good, it is society that creates vice. Therefore, says the disciple, an instinct which is both natural and antisocial is virtuous, for instance, the instinct to rape and kill.

3. These poems were not published until 1819.

4. Another English importation.

5. See Appendix, note 15.

6. Condorcet (1743–1794), who might be called the last of the Encyclopedists and who wrote a reverent biography of Voltaire, composed, when in hiding from the Terror, his noble *Essay on the Progress of the Human Mind.* He poisoned himself to cheat the guillotine: truly a spirit worthy of Pascal, rising superior to the brute force that crushes him.

7. See Appendix, note 16.

8. The physiocrats believed in nature, i.e., the soil, as the only source of riches and advocated long before Henry George a single tax on land. Dupont de Nemours, a friend of Jefferson, was to settle in America, where his son established the industrial dynasty which is still a power today.

9. The fascinating study has been told with scholarly care, lucidity, and charm by Georges Lemaître, *Beaumarchais* (New York, 1949).

10. In his noble farewell to Lafayette, after his visit to the States in 1825, President John Quincy Adams rightly refers to "that tie of love, stronger than death, which has linked your name for the endless ages with the name of Washington."

11. *Writings of George Washington* (1938), XXVIII, 250.

NOTES TO CHAPTER XVII

1. Franz Funk-Brentano, *L'Ancien régime* (Paris, 1927).

2. Taine, *Les origines de la France contemporaine* (6 vols.; Paris, 1876–1893), particularly Vols. II and III, *L'anarchie, La conquête jacobine.*

3. I fell on the ground: it was Voltaire's fault; my nose in the gutter: it was Rousseau's fault.

4. A number of theorists ascribe the Revolution, "so profoundly un-French and anti-French," to the nefarious activities of secret societies, particularly the Masonic Lodges, under the influence and even in the

pay of England. This thesis was defended by Nesta H. Webster and by a very able scholar—misguided and ill-fated—Bernard Faÿ.

5. On the site of a palace built by Richelieu, and known as Palais-Cardinal.

6. The duke, under legitimate suspicion, was kept out of mischief by being sent—diplomatically—on a mission to England. Later, he was to go to the extreme Left, called himself Philippe-Egalité, voted in the Convention for the death of his cousin Louis XVI, and was beheaded in his turn by his new friends.

7. This caution was morally justified: it was not their own property that the clergy were asked to renounce.

8. Jefferson was Franklin's successor in Paris until 1789; he refrained from interfering in French politics, although he was formally invited to sit on the Constitutional Committee; but he had many friends, and his influence was great.

9. See Appendix, note 17.

NOTES TO CHAPTER XVIII

1. A German from the Palatinate and, it is claimed, an ancestor of the Sea Devil, famous raider in World War I. Beheaded in 1794.

2. Once the seat of the Knights Templars suppressed by Philip IV, the Fair.

3. So called because they occupied the highest seats in the Assembly; the moderate center was the Plain, at times the Marsh (*Marais*).

4. It may seem absurd to challenge an expression accepted for one hundred and fifty years. Yet hoary misnomers have been corrected: the "Dark Ages," for instance, as applied to the glorious thirteenth century; or the pedantic "Revival of Learning" to denote the upsurge of energy we now call the Renaissance.

5. He was executed only two days before the downfall of Robespierre.

6. *Thermidor:* the Revolutionary calendar, finally discarded on January 1, 1806, had the following months: *Vendémiaire, Brumaire, Frimaire; Nivôse, Pluviôse, Ventôse; Germinal, Floréal, Prairial; Messidor, Thermidor, Fructidor.* These euphonious names, coined by the poetaster Fabre d'Eglantine, have left a long trace in French literature.

7. Fifty years later, Victor Hugo was still urging the Germans not to deny France what God Himself had given her, the left bank of the Rhine.

8. See Appendix, note 18.

NOTES TO CHAPTER XIX

1. A minor creation was the Legion of Honor (May 19, 1802). It resumed the tradition of the royal orders, particularly that of St. Louis, but on a democratic basis. Essentially military, it was somewhat grudgingly extended to civilians. Napoleon considered it as a good instrument of reign, one of those baubles for which men will die. The shrewd realist knew how to use idealism—with a spice of vanity.

2. Lucian declined a kingdom and kept the wife of his choice.

NOTES TO CHAPTER XX

1. Cambronne denied he ever uttered the grandiloquent phrase ascribed to him, "The Guard dies but does not surrender."
2. H. A. L. Fisher, *IF, or History Rewritten* (New York, 1931); Robert Aron, *Victoire à Waterloo* (Paris, 1937).
3. Talleyrand, who was responsible for the first Restoration, and Fouché, who had engineered the second, were the victims of this reaction. The first went into retirement; the second, as a regicide, was exiled.
4. A posthumous son was born to Berry and called "the Child of the Miracle." He was the duke of Bordeaux, later known as count of Chambord, the "Henry V" of the Legitimists (1820–1883).
5. He lived mostly at Holyrood in Scotland; died at Goritz, where he had gone for his health, November 6, 1836.
6. The name itself was a clever little touch: the new king was to be neither Louis XIX nor Philip VII; although linked with the past, he opened a new era.
7. Count Claude-Henri de Saint-Simon, born in 1760, had died in 1825; but his school was most active under Louis-Philippe and greatly influenced the Second Empire.
8. Among the minor socialist publicists was a disciple of Louis Blanc, Louis-Napoleon Bonaparte. His pamphlet *On the Extinction of Pauperism* (a proposal very similar to Upton Sinclair's *Epic,* End Poverty in California) had an enormous circulation.
9. See Théophile Gautier, *Les Vieux de la Vieille,* "The Veterans of the Old Guard," in *Emaux et camées;* the most perfect epitome of the legend.
10. The Orleanists, however, had a scare; the first news that reached Paris simply announced that the prince was marching through Strasbourg at the head of a regiment; then, melodramatically, the message over the "aerial telegraph" or semaphore was interrupted by the fog.

NOTES TO CHAPTER XXI

1. Taine, *Carnets de voyage* (Paris, 1896); covering the years 1863–1865.
2. Morny was the illegitimate son of Queen Hortense (the mother of Napoleon III) and General de Flahaut. Flahaut himself was the illegitimate son of Talleyrand.
3. She died in 1927 at the age of eighty-six.

NOTES TO CHAPTER XXII

1. Napoleon III was interned at Wilhelmshöhe near Cassel until March 19, 1871; liberated, he joined the empress and the prince imperial at Camden Place, Chislehurst, England. He died on January 9, 1873, as the result of a surgical operation. The prince imperial was killed in Zululand (1879). The empress survived until 1920.
2. Through an inconceivable oversight the army of the East was omitted in the armistice. The Germans pursued it relentlessly in the harsh

winter of eastern France; but, with its commander Bourbaki, it managed to escape into Switzerland, where it was admirably treated by the population.

3. In 1917 the Bolsheviks renamed one of their dreadnoughts "Paris Commune" and the other "Marat."

4. Dukes Decazes, de Broglie, d'Audiffred-Pasquier; the duke of Aumale, son of Louis-Philippe, held a high position in the army and was a member of the Academy. The president, Marshal de Mac-Mahon, was duke of Magenta.

5. The sayings of Mac-Mahon have passed into French folklore. Some are apocryphal, for it became a favorite game with the journalists to coin historic words *à la Mac-Mahon*. A few samples: to a Negro student in a military school, "You the Negro? Well, keep it up." To comfort the populations in a disastrous flood of the Garonne, *Que d'eau! Que d'eau!* ("What a lot of water!")

6. It was replaced in 1937 by the present twin Palaces of Chaillot.

NOTES TO CHAPTER XXIII

1. See Appendix, note 19.

2. President Carnot was named Sadi—the one romantic touch about him —after his uncle, the founder of thermodynamics (1796–1832).

3. This exposition, another brilliant success, was noted for two masterpieces of steel architecture, the Eiffel Tower and the Hall of Machinery: the promise of a revolution which was not fulfilled for many years.

4. Félix Faure: Sadi Carnot had been assassinated by an anarchist on June 24, 1894.

5. There were oddities in this division into camps. Arthur Meyer, editor of the Catholic-Royalist anti-Dreyfus paper *Le Gaulois*, was a Jew; *Le Figaro*, likewise Catholic-Royalist and fashionable, was pro-Dreyfus. Two survivors of the imperial era, the empress herself and General de Galliffet, were Dreyfusists.

6. On September 30, 1902, Zola had been asphyxiated by a faulty heating apparatus.

7. Prepared through friendly naval visits, 1891–1892; formally drawn, December 27, 1893–January 4, 1894.

NOTES TO CHAPTER XXIV

1. The Waldeck-Rousseau formula, so much more dynamic than the usual compromise coalition, was used three times again, each time with conspicuous success: Viviani's Cabinet of National Defense (Sacred Union) in 1914, Poincaré's Cabinet for the Defense of the Franc in 1926, and General de Gaulle's provisional administration, in which Socialists, Communists, and Catholics worked efficiently together.

2. Freemasonry, condemned by the Church ever since the eighteenth century, had become the backbone of the Radical party. Hence its suppression by the Vichy regime.

3. See Appendix, note 20.

4.   There was a touch of folklike humor, with no grandiloquence, in that nickname: it came from a popular song in the Boulanger era.

NOTES TO CHAPTER XXV

1.   Other treaties were signed in 1919–1920 in various western suburbs of Paris: Saint-Germain (with Austria), Neuilly (Bulgaria), Trianon (Hungary), Sèvres (Turkey).
2.   It would be more accurate to say the Covenant of the League of Nations failed, for the separate German-American treaty did not contradict or invalidate any of the Versailles stipulations.
3.   There is an abundant and fascinating literature on the Alsace-Lorraine problem. See particularly Erckmann-Chatrian, authors of the Alsatian theme song, *Dis moi, quel est ton pays?;* René Bazin *Les Oberlé;* Maurice Barrès *Les bastions de l'est: Au service de l'Allemagne, Colette Baudoche;* René Schickelé (*Das Erbe am Rhein,* trilogy). The outstanding representative of Alsace's hybrid culture is Albert Schweitzer, medical missionary, musician, and philosopher.
4.   *Sic.* This term belongs almost exclusively to the period 1919–1939. Before the war, it jarred on the ears of Radicals and Socialists, who were in principle anti-imperialists. The official term was *Colonies et Protectorats,* the literary equivalent—rather a delusive one—*France d'Outremer.* After 1939 the name *Union Française* was officially substituted; we trust it implied a change of heart.

NOTES TO CHAPTER XXVI

1.   We insist upon using the terms Bolsheviki, bolshevism, now antiquated, because they were current at the time, and because they do not establish a delusive identity between the government of Lenin and Trotsky on the one hand, and "Russia," "the Soviets," or "communism" on the other. Bolshevism is *sui generis,* the result of particular circumstances in one particular country; it deserves a name of its own.
2.   "Crosses won under fire": the usual rendering "Fiery Crosses" is misleading.
3.   Most Presidents are hardly part of French history and may be relegated to a footnote. When Doumergue's term expired in June, 1931, Paul Doumer was elected; he was then seventy-four years old and had missed the presidency a quarter of a century before. After less than a year in office he was assassinated by a crazy White Ukrainian. His successor was Albert Lebrun, an ideal President in the innocuous Loubet-Fallières tradition.
4.   *La pause:* technically, in the French army, the ten minutes of rest after fifty minutes of marching.
5.   In May, 1939, President Albert Lebrun's term of office expired. The logical candidate would have been the beloved veteran Edouard Herriot; but Daladier, who had shoved him out of the leadership of the Radical party, managed to secure the re-election of Monsieur Lebrun. The same honor had been granted to Jules Grévy: an ominous precedent. Herriot might have stood more firmly in 1940.

NOTES TO CHAPTER XXVII

1. Alsace-Lorraine had a special regime and, under a *Gauleiter,* was soon considered as part of the Reich; Pétain offered no public protest.
2. The British wanted to secure guarantees that the French navy would not be utilized by the Nazis. The French commander could only abide by the terms of the armistice and had to reject the ultimatum. The British gesture was brutal, ill-considered, and, as events were to prove, totally unnecessary. Admiralties, like individuals, have fits of ugly temper.
3. Gertrude Stein, *Wars I Have Seen* (New York, 1945), p. 174.
4. The Maquis was composed of those young men who had fled into the mountains chiefly in order to avoid being sent as laborers to Germany. The term is of Corsican origin: outlaws seek asylum in the *maquis,* i.e., the brush, after a vendetta. Zola, on trial during the Dreyfus Case, spoke of finding refuge in *le maquis de la procédure,* the wilderness of technicalities. Gradually, the Maquisards were formed into guerrilla units armed with weapons parachuted by the Allies.
5. Needless to say that the Parisian uprising would have been suicidal (even as the premature insurrection in Warsaw was) without the victories of the Allies.
6. "Monsieur de Menthon (the minister of justice) has 500,000 corpses on his conscience." This from *Aspects of France,* successor of Maurras's paper, *L'Action Française.*
7. Marshal Pétain was released on the plea of ill health shortly before his death in 1951 (July 23).
8. "Again, in 1919, Mr. Hoover, the American Food Controller, estimated that the population of Europe was at least one hundred million greater than could be supported without imports, and warned the world that unless productivity could be rapidly increased there could be nothing but 'political, moral, and economic chaos, finally interpreting itself in loss of life hitherto undreamed of.'" William Ralph Inge, *England* (New York, 1926), p. 205.

NOTES TO CHAPTER XXVIII

1. The phrase is borrowed from André Siegfried.
2. The election took six days (December 17–23, 1953) and thirteen ballots. The President was elected by the two houses in Congress assembled at Versailles. President Coty took office on January 17, 1954.
3. Boulanger's *Dissolution, Révision, Constituante.*
4. Henri de Kérillis: *I Accuse De Gaulle* (New York, 1946).
5. See Appendix, note 21.
6. The personality and achievements of Pierre Mendès-France, "the Lost Statesman," will be discussed under the colonial problem.
7. Maurice Duverger, *The French Political System* (Chicago: University of Chicago Press, 1958), p. 191.
8. D. W. Brogan, *The French Nation* (New York, 1957), pp. 302–3.
9. In his pamphlet: *What Is the Third Estate?* (January, 1789).

10. For the methods used, half consciously, to preserve such a privilege, see Albert Guérard, "Mesocracy: The Dictatorship of the Middle Class," *Beyond Hatred* (New York, 1925), pp. 19–38; or *The France of Tomorrow* (Cambridge, Mass., 1942), pp. 141–162.
11. See Appendix, note 22.
12. "The sole aim of history is to show how it actually happened." Leopold von Ranke, *Geschichte der römanischen und germanischen Völker* (Berlin, 1824).
13. A stimulating book, translated as *France Against Herself* (New York, 1955). The English title seems to me more adequate than the German: the France of Sieyès against the France of yesterday and the France of tomorrow.
14. See Appendix, note 23.

NOTES TO CHAPTER XXIX

1. In full: Madou-Chanemouganelayoudameliar.
2. The remains of Governor-General Eboué now rest in the national Pantheon.
3. A naval officer in both World Wars, he had retired as a monk in the interval.
4. France did "give her blood," especially that of young officers. But she did not dare to send draftees to die for Bao Dai, only volunteers, African troops, and the Foreign Legion, with a large contingent of Germans.
5. The nurse Geneviève de Galard won fame as the "Angel" of Dien Bien Phu.
6. See Appendix, note 24, on the five French settlements in India.
7. See Simone de Beauvoir's searching novel of the Leftist intelligentsia, *Les mandarins* (Paris, 1954).
8. Houphouet-Boigny, "Black Africa and the French Union," *Foreign Affairs,* July, 1957, pp. 596 ff.
9. Schweitzer is an Alsatian born and educated under the German regime.
10. The word "Berber" is extremely elastic and covers all the Mohammedans of the interior not fully assimilated by the Arabs, even when they have given up their own dialects. The very complex Mohammedan population of the towns is often referred to as Moorish.
11. See Appendix, note 25, on the Jews in Algeria.
12. See Appendix, note 26, on the polygamy argument.
13. See Appendix, note 27. The Abd el-Kader monument.

NOTES TO CHAPTER XXX

1. See Carlton J. H. Hayes, *France, a Nation of Patriots* (New York, 1930).
2. See Jean de Pange, *Mes prisons* (Paris, 1945), p. 34.
3. Stephen Bonsal, *Unfinished Business* (New York, 1944).
4. Including the Socialists, S.F.I.O., French Section of the Workers' International.
5. See Appendix, note 28, on the Saar controversy.

6. From Mt. Monadnock in New Hampshire. The term was applied, very appositely, to General Pershing. It denotes "isolated remnants of hard rock which remain distinctly above their surroundings in the last stages of an erosion cycle."

7. At a meeting with Secretary Dulles, and in a statement to the U.N. by his delegate Jules Moch.

8. Henry Luce, *The American Century* (New York, 1941), pp. 22–23.

NOTES TO CHAPTER XXXI

1. Figures of the referendum in the Appendix, note 29.

2. This may not be easy to achieve. To be a candidate would expose a Moslem to assassination, for the fellaghas believe in bullets (or throat slitting), not ballots.

3. *L'Algérie et la République,* 1958.

4. See Appendix, note 30, for excerpts from his speech at Constantine, October 3, 1958; and his Press Conference in Paris, October 23.

5. Michel Debré, *Ces Princes qui nous gouvernent* (Paris, 1957), pp. 145–49.

6. Addressing a delegation of the World Parliament Association, September 8, 1958.

7. The last includes arts, sciences, philosophy, and philanthropy. Its symbol is the Nobel prize.

8. "Je tiens de ma patrie un cœur qui la déborde,
   Et plus je suis Français, plus je me sens humain."
   Sully-Prudhomme, *Les vaines tendresses, La France,* IX (1875)

9. "France, adieu! Tu es trop grande pour n'être qu'une patrie." Victor Hugo, *Paris. in finem* (Paris, 1867).

10. See Appendix, note 31.

APPENDIX: SUPPLEMENTARY NOTES

1 Nationalist historians everywhere, while recognizing the larger group —the race, the civilization, or even the world—claim for their own country a position of leadership, a mission which sets her apart. These assertions were particularly vigorous in the Romantic era, let us say from Herder to Wagner. We have heard of Holy Russia, now reviving under a red mask; Gioberti wrote *Del Primato morale e civile degli Italiani,* which was to inspire Mussolini; the pretensions of the Germans, from Fichte to Hitler, are seared into our memory. If the English were less blatant, it was because their self-confidence was more absolute. Noble patriots such as Michelet and Hugo fell into the common snare: France to them was *la grande nation,* a Christ among the nations. If we were to assess the contributions of France to European civilization, we might jot down the following notes—and be aware of their crudeness.

France, still unformed, played a greater part in the crusades than any other group; but the crusades cannot be considered as a national movement. The predominance of the University of Paris in the thirteenth century was not due to its French character: its language was Latin, and it belonged to Christendom. Gothic art originated in the French royal domain and was known as *opus francigenum;* it was soon adopted and adapted by all countries. Perhaps the notion of courtly love was first and best focused in French poems, if we consider Provençal as southern French. Louis XIV offered the best example of the classical synthesis, the ideal of unity and measure. The French Revolution profoundly affected Europe, but the same principles had been proclaimed in America a decade earlier. Twice, in the thirteenth century and in the eighteenth, the French language enjoyed unique prestige.

On the other hand, the Renaissance obviously came from Italy; the Reformation reached England (Wyclif), Bohemia (Huss), and Germany (Luther) before it deeply stirred France. The French borrowed the Enlightenment from England. The rise of the modern commercial class was first manifest in Holland and England. The Industrial Revolution was first of all English. France "caught" Romanticism from England and Germany. The revival of great philosophical systems, from Kant to Hegel, is a German phenomenon.

In the social, physical, and natural sciences honors are fairly evenly divided, and claims of hegemony are puerile. Perhaps the contribution of Italy has been unduly slighted; the Soviet press is teaching a skeptical world that all great discoveries were first made by Russians. America a generation ago had an excessive belief in German supremacy. Germany is undoubtedly second to none, but all that can be safely affirmed is that in the nineteenth century she was more thoroughly organized for scientific research than France or England. With less elaborate instruments other countries brought out results of outstanding value. It is a striking fact that many countries had a share in the hypotheses and researches that led to the Atomic Revolution.

2   The situation is different in the United States: the immigrants came of their own accord, eager to learn the language of the majority. Preexisting languages (French in Louisiana, Spanish in New Mexico, the Indian dialects) were not forcibly suppressed. It is easy to see how France, extending the same principle of linguistic unity, attempted to Frenchify her colonial possessions and to make the natives of the Congo recite: *Nos ancêtres les Gaulois.* . . . She treated her wards in the same spirit as her own sons, Basques, Bretons, or Flemings. To nationalize in thought and speech was to emancipate not to enslave: "Thou shalt learn French, and the possession of French shall make thee free." The United States has followed to a large extent the same policy in the Philippines.

3   It may seem strange that in listing the contributions of Rome to the formation of France we should find no place for the greatest achievement of all, Roman law. The importance of that magnificent *Corpus,* "Reason in writing," is not in question. But in northern France, the France of Paris and the kings, Roman law was a late rediscovery, a slow reconquest, not a living tradition. Throughout the North custom law prevailed up to the end of the Ancient Regime; it had left some

traces even in Paris when I was a child. The Napoleonic Code is not pure Roman law brought up to date: it is a workable compromise between the edicts of the kings and the legislation of the Revolutionary Assemblies.

4 Here must be noted the striking and highly controversial hypothesis of the great Belgian historian Henri Pirenne. According to him the ancient world disappeared not in 476 with the end of the Western Empire but only with the rise of Mohammedanism. The Mediterranean was the highway of classical culture; so long as commerce was possible from the Nile and the Bosporus to the Columns of Hercules, there was some hope that the empire might recover. When control of the inland sea was lost, antique culture was shattered; it perished in the West and sickened in the East. Theodoric, the great king of the Ostrogoths, had inserted himself into the still unbroken Greco-Roman tradition; Charlemagne, on the contrary, in spite of his vigorous personality and of his high-sounding title, was the head of a purely Frankish and purely barbarian state. He represented not the continuation of the classical world but a new departure, a humble and difficult one.

5 When ascribing to the Church the great awakening of the eleventh century, we do not forget that a little earlier an even more brilliant development was taking place in Moslem Spain. Cordoba at the end of the tenth century, with perhaps half a million inhabitants, was a center of culture, industry, and trade without a peer in western Europe. Similar results may be due to different causes. Perhaps there was a hidden principle common to both movements. But that principle was not the rediscovery of Greek thought: in both cases the conscious reconquest of ancient wisdom came at the summit of the upward curve not at the beginning. The earlier and more brilliant Moslem Renaissance, while it did not create the Christian one, influenced it at many points. Already Gerbert of Aurillac, so learned that he was called *Stupor Mundi,* the world's amazement, and accused of having sold his soul to the devil, was a student of Arabic. It may be said that the two renaissances, Moslem and Christian, met in that incredible character, Frederick II, also called *Stupor Mundi* (d. 1250): a Holy Roman Emperor, crusader and king of Jerusalem, who fought savagely against the pope, was excommunicated, turned his crusade into a friendly and profitable tour, and in Sicily trusted mostly in his Saracenic guard: truly a striking example of what Henry Adams calls "thirteenth century unity"! The Arabs preserved ancient learning more faithfully than the Church had done and in certain fields added substantially to it. The debt of the Schoolmen to Mohammedan and Jewish scholars and thinkers, in particular to Averroes and Moses Maimonides, is not disputed.

6 Two processes starting from opposite ends and reaching the same stage. An illustration of that paradox is offered by Lord Bryce when he notes with stately, Gibbon-like irony that the American Senate "contains many men of great wealth. Some are senators because they are rich; a few are rich because they are senators." (Guizot's "confusion of

property and authority." James Bryce, *The American Commonwealth,* Part I, Chapter XII.

7   Compare the rich but severely functional beauty of thirteenth-century Gothic with the contorted fancies of the Flamboyant style. Carved keystones were made to pend incredibly from the vault, a triumph of the technician not of the artist. Some of these achievements were faked: hidden iron bars supported the stone. Compare also the robust simplicity of the *Song of Roland* with the trickiness of fifteenth-century versification. Decadence may have two forms, relapse into the crude but also excess of skill.

8   It is odd that this gentle, scholarly, and deeply religious princess should be chiefly remembered for her *Heptameron,* a pastiche of Boccaccio's *Decameron,* in which the themes and the treatment are as' risqué as in the original, while the brilliancy of the Italian writer is lacking. Clément Marot, the pretty court poet, belonged through mere accident to this twilit school; his elegant levity, his superficial sensuous grace hardly prepared him to be the translator of the Psalms and to suffer persecution and exile for a faith not deeply rooted in his soul.

9   Richelieu was at the height of his career when Descartes published his *Discourse on Method* (1637) and Corneille produced his major masterpieces, *Le Cid* (1636), *Horace* (1640), *Cinna* (1640), *Polyeucte* (1641). Richelieu's relations to literature reveal him as a singularly liberal dictator. He did impose his imperious protection on a society of gentlemen with literary tastes and turned that private body into the illustrious Académie Française (1634; finally chartered 1637). But he did not attempt to use it to force his own views. He could easily have suppressed *Le Cid*—and its author—since the play was a glowing apology for Spain and for dueling, which Richelieu was fiercely combating. He simply had *Le Cid* examined on literary grounds by the Academy, which returned a very cautious verdict (*Sentiments*).

10   This cult of measure explains why in French the term *baroque* still denotes a fault, not a period or a style: the baroque means wilful indulgence in melodramatic excess. There are traces of the baroque under Louis XIV, but they are of minor importance and are considered as blemishes. Racine, the most perfect representative of the age, is at the very antipodes of the baroque. When the great Cavaliere Bernini, supreme master of baroque architecture and sculpture, was brought to Paris to complete the Louvre, his work was praised, richly rewarded —and set aside: it was the severely classical colonnade of Claude Perrault that was carried out.

11   Fouquet's motto was *Quo non ascendam?:* What heights shall I not scale? In his château at Vaux he gave lavish entertainments which served as models for the festivities at Versailles. He died in the fortress of Pignerol (Pinerolo) after nearly twenty years of captivity. Madame de Sévigné and La Fontaine were among his friends. Another victim dear to historical romance was Lauzun, guilty of having attracted the favor of *La Grande Mademoiselle,* Mademoiselle de Montpensier, highest born and richest of the Bourbon connection. A third is the

Man with the Iron Mask. In spite of Voltaire, Vigny, Dumas, Hugo it does not seem that he was a royal twin but an obscure Italian diplomat, Mattioli, who had double-crossed the French. The evidence, however, is not conclusive.

12   There were high-born writers under Louis XIV, and of surpassing excellence: Cardinal de Retz, of the spirited *Memoirs;* La Roche-foucauld, of the disenchanted *Maxims;* Madame de La Fayette, his friend, who wrote the first and perhaps the most perfect of psychological novels, *The Princess of Clèves;* the Marquise de Sévigné, with her incomparable *Letters.* But they belonged to the generation of the *Fronde* and were among the defeated. Fénelon, Saint-Simon, on the contrary, were not active until the latter part of the reign.

13   Cornelius Jansen (Jansenius), Bishop of Ypres, expounded in his book *Augustinus* a doctrine similar to Calvinistic predestination. His thought influenced the religious of Port-Royal, a convent which had been re-formed early in the century by Mother Angélique Arnaud. The leader of the Jansenists was Angélique's brother Antoine, the "Great Arnaud," revered by Boileau. Pascal in his *Provincial Letters* brilliantly supported the Jansenists against the Jesuits. Racine was a pupil of the Jansenist school at Port-Royal.

The leading French Quietists were Madame Guyon and Fénelon (in his *Maxims of the Saints*). They were denounced by Bossuet and somewhat reluctantly condemned by Rome (1695–1699) "for excessive love of God." Even in that domain the classical rule was *Trop est trop.*

14   Pierre Gaxotte (*Le siècle de Louis XV* [Paris, 1933]; *Louis XV and His Times* [Philadelphia, 1934]) will have it that throughout his reign the king had been holding himself in readiness for such an emergency. Out of liberalism he had given his ministers a free rein, but in the hour of need he boldly assumed the responsibility of a royal dictator. So long as he was alive, the old machine would work; but after him the deluge might impend. Gaxotte is a brilliant publicist whose political record inspires very little confidence in his historical method.

15   In this coexistence—at times a combination—of antagonistic tendencies France, of course, was by no means alone. Romanticism and classicism alternate or blend in the works of Goethe and Schiller. Blake, Romanticism incarnate, copied the classical draftsmanship of Flaxman. A generation later, Keats could write his sonnet *On First Looking into Chapman's Homer,* his *Ode on a Grecian Urn,* and also his ballad *La Belle Dame sans Merci.*

16   The Diamond Necklace: that epic swindle was engineered by an adventuress, Jeanne, Countess de Lamotte-Valois, who claimed descent from the Valois kings. She pretended to act as an intermediary between the queen and the cardinal. One night in the gardens of Versailles, Rohan handed the priceless jewel to the queen—impersonated by a lady of easy virtue, Nicole d'Oliva (1784). The scandal soon broke out and grew in intensity for two years, leaving—most unjustly—the queen's name besmirched.

17   Charles-Maurice de Talleyrand-Périgord (1754–1838). Debarred from the army through an accident that lamed him in childhood, he was compelled to enter the Church. He was very successful as agent-general of the clergy (1780), and became bishop of Autun in 1789. By consecrating two new bishops he became the father of the Constitutional Church. He managed to escape from France in September, 1792, spent a few months in England and two years in America. He returned with the Thermidorian reaction (1794), served the Directory, the Consulate, the Empire (minister of foreign affairs, vice-grand elector, prince of Benevento). He swung over to the Bourbons and played a "masterly game" at the Congress of Vienna (1814–1815). Rejected by the Restoration in spite of his services, he lived to win a decisive diplomatic victory for Louis-Philippe as ambassador to England and died reconciled with the Church, if not with God.

18   When Louis XVI was beheaded, his son, the dauphin, became Louis XVII; and when the imprisoned "king" died in the tower of the Temple in 1795, the count of Provence, brother of Louis XVI, succeeded to the throne (*in partibus*) as Louis XVIII. There is reasonable suspicion that the dauphin had been sneaked out of jail and that an ailing and feeble-minded boy was substituted. However, none of the pretenders who claimed to be the lost dauphin could offer convincing proof, not even Naundorff, who found many supporters and even secured some kind of legal recognition in Holland and England.

19   In nineteenth-century France side whiskers denoted butlers, judges, and senior naval officers; a full beard, missionaries, doctors, and revolutionists (but both President Carnot and General Boulanger were bearded); a pointed beard, intellectuals (it almost demanded a steel pince-nez); the goatee, survivors or partisans of the Empire (including, unexpectedly, Anatole France); a smooth face, waiters, actors (excepted Mounet-Sully), and priests. (Renan was decidedly sacerdotal.) The moustache, with many varieties, was the standard style. These useful and picturesque distinctions have almost entirely disappeared.

20   According to the Treaty of Utrecht the French retained the right to catch *fishes* on the western shore (long known as the French Shore) of Newfoundland. When they started catching *lobsters,* the English objected and destroyed French fisheries—or lobsteries. It was finally established that at the time the treaty was signed the word *fish* covered all creatures of the sea. Diplomacy is not ruled by natural history.

21   Proportional representation was still the official doctrine. But it was was tampered with in two ways. If a "list" or ticket won even a bare majority of the votes, it would take all the seats. If various "lists" announced in advance that they were "associated" (*apparentées*), and if their pool secured a majority, they would take all the seats and divide them proportionally among themselves—the isolated minorities remaining unrepresented. Neither the Gaullists nor the Communists could join such combinations. The middle-course parties had a clear but narrow majority. But it was inflated in the apportionment of seats: Gaullists 117, Communists 101, Algerian Nationalists 12, Third Force 397.

22   The confusion between *bourgeoisie* and capitalism is one of the errors—
and perhaps the most ineradicable—committed by Karl Marx. More
venial was his belief that the Paris Commune in 1871 offered even
an adumbration of communism. It may be noted that the socialist
proletariat in its anthem "The International," blandly adopted the
Sieyès fallacy: *Nous ne sommes rien: soyons tout!* We are nothing: let
us be everything!

23   It is not the purpose of this French history to uphold the American
way of life. But comparisons are inevitable. Some very prominent
Americans have defended an ideology strikingly similar to that of the
French *bourgeoisie:* perhaps the greatest of them was Calvin Coolidge.
There are, however, profound differences. America has been in theory
from the very first, and has to a large extent become in practice, a
classless society, which France is not even today. So with us mesocracy
and democracy do merge. In the absence of privileged orders the
American elites have adopted something of the *noblesse oblige* spirit:
before he could do so, a French bourgeois would have to turn against
his class. In a new continent the cult of material wealth took the form
of pioneering, expansion, adventure. In an old, settled country of
limited resources like France the same spirit hardened into resistance
to change. The Second Empire with its Saint-Simonian ideal of service
and its bold "Captains of Industry" was far more "American" than
the Third Republic, or the Fourth.

24   The five French settlements in India, Pondichéry, Chandernagor,
Yanaon, Karikal, and Mahé, were the pathetic remnants of Dupleix's
immense dream. There was hardly anything French about them except
the blue and white plates bearing French street names. They were
not in the same category as Goa in India or Macao in China which
have been Portuguese for nearly four hundred years.

These harmless oddities might have been preserved, like Andorra,
Lichtenstein, Monaco, or San Marino, not to mention the Channel
Islands. But mighty India is still touchy about her independent status;
and Premier Nehru felt that, since the English had to leave, the French
had no right to remain. Logic is logic.

The first to go was Chandernagor, an inland enclave in the vicinity
of Calcutta. Threatened with suffocation, it voted in 1948 to unite
with India. The Indian flag was raised without protest on August 15,
1949, although the French authorities did not formally withdraw until
May, 1950.

At the same referendum the other four had voted 75 per cent in
favor of preserving their union with France. But events in Indochina
affected their confidence in the Fourth Republic. They shrewdly bar-
gained with both sides and secured from both the assurance of complete municipal autonomy.

India's interference with local politics, however, and an attempt to
force the issue through an economic blockade rather injured her cause.
When the blockade was lifted, the four cities engaged in a most
profitable contraband trade. This might have kept them loyal to the

spirit of Eternal France, if a local politician, E. Goubert, hitherto the mainstay of the French cause, had not swung to the support of India. He established in a detached district of Pondichéry a "Government of Liberation." The other three cities followed suit. Their municipal councilors met near Pondichéry on October 18, 1954, and voted for union with India, 170 to 8. The transfer of authority was peacefully effected on October 21.

Pondichéry's chief claim to distinction is the Ashram, or religious settlement, of a saint, Sri Aurobindo. The exotic names of the five cities still ring faintly in French ears, like sunken bells. Their loss caused a brief pang of melancholy but no lasting bitterness.

25   A triumph of the assimilation doctrine was the Crémieux Decree in 1870, which made all Algerian Israelites full French citizens, although they had by no means become French in speech, customs, and political maturity. This was resented by the Mohammedans and was among the causes of a serious insurrection in 1871. Anti-Semitism remained a latent force in Algeria, among the Catholics as well as among the Moslems. At the time of the Dreyfus Case, a declared anti-Semite, Max Régis, became mayor of Algiers; and the only two anti-Semitic deputies in the French Chamber came from Algeria. The problem of Israel is of course making the position of the Jews more precarious in all predominantly Mohammedan countries.

26   The colonists argued virtuously, "You would not grant French citizenship to a polygamist?" They failed to add that polygamy was but a vestigial exception in North Africa: long years of peace had brought the sexes to a fairly even balance. Polygamy is permitted under Koranic law, but it is not compulsory. Tunisia, which on achieving independence declared itself an Arabic and Mohammedan state, made polygamy unlawful.

27   On October 15, 1949, a monument to Abd el-Kader was unveiled in his city of Mascara in the presence of the governor-general, Mr. Naegelen. Abd el-Kader, who had fought bravely against Bugeaud, had become a cherished part of the French tradition in the same way that General Robert E. Lee is now a national hero even in the North. Retired in Syria, he had protected Christians against outbreaks of Moslem fanaticism. He was therefore an admirable symbol of reconciliation. Emir Sehel, a grandson of Abd el-Kader, delivered a speech in French; M. d'Ortes, a grand-nephew of Marshal Bugeaud, gave one in Arabic. On the monument can be read, in both languages, the words of Abd el-Kader, "If the Christians and the Moslems would listen to me, they would bury their differences and become brothers."

28   The Saar imbroglio was a cause of bitterness for nearly forty years. While Alsace-Lorraine was part of the Reich (1871–1918), the coal mines of the Saar and the iron mines of Lorraine formed a most profitable complex. The restoration of Alsace-Lorraine to France might endanger that co-operation. It was agreed that the property of the mines of the Saar—mostly owned by the Prussian state—would be turned over to France in compensation for the wanton destruction of the

French coal mines by the Germans. If the German state remained sovereign in the Saar, while the French state was economically dominant, an awkward situation might ensue. There was no thought of annexing the Saar outright to France: it would have created another Alsace-Lorraine. The treaty stopped short of creating an independent and neutral state like Luxembourg. The Saar formed an autonomous but not a sovereign state under the guardianship of the League of Nations. In order not to sever its natural connection with Lorraine, it became part of the French Customs Union. To satisfy the Wilsonian principle of self-determination, a referendum was to be taken after fifteen years.

The promised plebiscite was punctually held on January 13, 1935. Hitler had by that time revived German nationalism to fever heat, while France was in the throes of a perpetual political crisis. This contrast influenced, if it did not determine, the choice of the Saarlanders. By a 90 per cent majority they decided to be reunited with Germany.

After the victory of 1945 the question was reopened for two reasons. Then as before, the Saar and Lorraine formed an economic whole which should not be torn apart. Then it was thought desirable to reduce the enormous disparity between the industrial resources of the two eternal rivals. The French had proposed to make the Ruhr the nucleus of a new Europe. Their allies refused to endorse that policy. About the Saar they gave France ambiguous promises. Roughly, Saar and France together yielded 70,000,000 tons of coal to West Germany's 125,000,000, which was bad enough. But Saar and Germany together would have 140,000,000 against France's 54,000,000.

Again, there was an international regime with full autonomy for the inhabitants and economic union with France. Germany was in ruins, her prestige at the lowest ebb, and the Saarlanders accepted the new regime without demur. Their freely elected government, under Johannes Hoffmann, declared itself satisfied with the new status. Her allies supported France's claims but with evident tepidity. Chancellor Adenauer played a very shrewd game. France withdrew her objections to German rearmament and, as a token of good will, received the assurance that Germany would support the international status of the Saar (Agreement, October 23, 1954). The Saar was even slated to be the Federal District of the new Europe. Adenauer advised the Saarlanders to ratify the agreement—with his tongue in his cheek. The Saarlanders needed no hint. Europe was still nebulous, Germany was thriving, and evidently the great favorite of the United States. France was suffering from colonial disasters and the squabbles of the Third Force. So, on October 23, 1955, they voted for Germany, although not so unanimously as twenty years before.

If the Coal and Steel Community and the Common Market develop normally, the Saar problem will disappear without a trace. If they fail, the fate of the Saar will be decided, with that of western Europe, by the next war; and that fate will be destruction.

29   *The percentage voting "yes" in the referendum*

Territory	Per Cent	Territory	Per Cent
France	79.25	Tchad	98.7
Algeria	96.5	Madagascar	76.9
Senegal	97.2	French Somaliland	74.8
Guinea	2.6	Saint-Pierre	99.0
Ivory Coast	99.9	New Caledonia	99.8
Mauritania	93.6	New Hebrides	93.0
Sudan	97.3	Iles du Vent	64.3
Upper Volta	99.0	Iles Australes	63.7
Dahomey	96.9	Guadeloupe	78.9
Nigeria	76.1	Martinique	92.4
Middle Congo	99.1	Guiana	93.3
Gabon	97.7	Réunion	92.2
Ubangi-Shari	98.1		

30   Speech delivered at Constantine, Algeria, on October 3, 1958.

"Therefore, turning toward those who are prolonging a fratricidal conflict, who are organizing lamentable attacks in Metropolitan France, or who are spreading—through the chancelleries, through underground dens, by means of the radio and the newspapers of certain foreign capitals—vilifications of France, to those I say: Why kill? We must enable people to live. Why destroy? Our duty is to build. Why hate? We must co-operate.

". . . But in the present state of the world, where can these bitter incitements lead if not to a universal cataclysm? Only two paths lie open to the human race today: war or brotherhood. In Algeria as everywhere, France, for her part, has chosen brotherhood.

"Long live the Republic! Long live Algeria and long live France!"

(From Ambassade de France, Service de Presse et d'Information, Speeches and Press Conferences, No. 117, October 1958.)

Press Conference, Paris, October 23, 1958.

"Some say: but what would be the political conditions that the French Government would be willing to discuss? I reply: the political destiny of Algeria is Algeria itself. Opening fire does not give a man the right to determine that destiny. When the democratic way is open, when the citizens have an opportunity to express their will, then there is no other way that is acceptable. Now, this way is open in Algeria. The referendum has taken place. In November the legislative elections will be held; in March, the elections to the municipal councils; in April, the election of Senators. What will be the outcome? That is a matter of evolution. In any case, a vast physical and spiritual transformation is under way in Algeria. France, because it is her duty, and because she alone is capable of doing it—France is bringing about this transformation. As and when developments occur, political solutions will take shape. I believe, as I have already said, that future solutions

will be based—because that is the nature of things—upon the courageous personality of Algeria and upon its close association with Metropolitan France. I believe also that this ensemble, completed by the
Sahara, will link itself, for the common progress, with the free states
of Morocco and Tunisia. Sufficient unto the day is the burdensome evil
thereof. But who will win out in the end? You will see that it will be
the fraternal civilization that wins."
(From Ambassade de France, Service de Presse et d'Information,
Speeches and Press Conferences, No. 119, October 1958.)

31   *Elections to the National Assembly, November 23–30, 1958*

	Old Seats	New Seats	Per Cent of Vote, First Round
Communists and Allies	145	10	18.9
Socialists and assorted Left	88	42	15.5
Radicals	56	13	4.8
Left Center	18	22	6.7
Catholic, Mouvement Républicain Populaire (M.R.P.)	71	57	11.6
Right Wing Independents (Pinay)	94	132	19.9
Extreme Right (Poujadistes)	52	1	3.3
Union de la République Nouvelle (U.N.R.) and affiliated	16	188	17.6

i. The results prove that the elections were, technically and morally,
free. There was a sizeable opposition. Nothing like the 99.44 per cent
Communist vote behind the Iron Curtain, or the 100 per cent anti-
Communist vote in the United States. France is a pluralistic, not a
totalitarian country. Freedom still breathes.

ii. Proportional representation has its manifest drawbacks. But when
representation is too glaringly unproportional, the result is a distortion
of the democratic process. France has evidently not found the right
formula. But who has?

iii. For the conservatives, this is indeed another *Chambre Introuvable*,
an Assembly beyond their fondest dreams. Certain measures against the
Communist-controlled C.G.T. (Conféderation Générale du Travail),
and in favor of Catholic schools, are to be expected. But I do not believe there will be a sweeping fascist reaction. The Soustelle group
(U.N.R.), which is the core of the new majority, is heterogeneous and
and has no definite program. It owes its success solely to the prestige
of De Gaulle. But De Gaulle is not committed to it; it can achieve
nothing against or without De Gaulle. And the General, who is a
statesman and no *Caudillo*, has read the somewhat sybilline lessons of
history. He has no inclination to repeat the senile "National Revolution" of Marshal Pétain. At a time when Europe is in the making, it
may be auspicious that France should be moderately right of center,

like Italy and Germany. On the contrary, it would make integration more difficult, if British Labor should come into power.

iv. The Communist vote before 1958 was to a large extent a protest against the Third Force: its dazed colonial policy, its turning France into an American satellite, the morass which the politicians called the middle road. On all three counts, De Gaulle has stolen their thunder. On a lower plane, this was also true of the Poujade movement: the referendum on the Constitution and the election of a new Assembly fulfill the Poujadist demand for a "new deal" in the form of States General. The 19 per cent who voted Communist may be a hard core; but they may also include a number of non-Communist opponents of the New Republic.

SUGGESTED READINGS

A bibliography of French history would fill not an essay, not a volume, but a library. *Les sources de l'histoire de France,* by a host of noted scholars, is a mere introduction in some fifteen tomes. The extremely valuable *Clio* collection, although highly condensed, is impressive in bulk. F. M. Kircheisen barely scratched the surface when he collected a paltry hundred thousand titles in his bibliography of Napoleon. The purpose of this essay, as of the book itself, is not to be exhaustive but to point out the next step. Ultimately, with microscopes of increasing power, we may reach the atom of history, the plain, minute fact, and "how it actually happened": to find out, for instance, whether the young police officer Merda, or Méda, or Médal did or did not fire the shot that broke Robespierre's jaw.

In the following pages will be found, in the first place, the indispensable instruments for further study, the general presentation of the subject by specially qualified scholars with the proper critical apparatus and fairly complete bibliographies. In the second place are mentioned classics and monuments, works which inevitably have been superseded in many details but which cannot be ignored, because they present, with the authority of great talent, a definite if challengeable view of history. Extreme examples of these are Edmund Burke's *Reflections on the French Revolution* and Hippolyte Taine's *Origins of Contemporary France.* In the third place are listed a few books which, in the course of a long experience, I have found particularly appealing to myself, my students, and my friends. (For most valuable suggestions, which unfortunately could not all be embodied in this brief essay, I wish to thank my colleagues Georges Lemaitre, C. Langdon White, Gordon Wright, of Stanford; and Crane Brinton, of Harvard.) I wish I could have included a fourth section: *Warnings.* There is a brand of popular history—all too popular, alas!—which is an inexhaustible source of misinformation. I am a convinced feminist; yet this list would have had a somewhat ungallant slant, for many such books are written "of, by, and for," women. Brilliant exceptions are Amy Kelly's *Eleanor of Aquitaine and the Four Kings* (Cambridge, Mass., 1950) and Helen Waddell's *The Wandering Scholars* (New York, 1949).

This book is intended for the general reader and for the college student: even a cursory knowledge of foreign languages cannot be taken for granted. The works in English listed below will provide very extensive information from almost every possible approach. But I have included many titles in French. For among the readers sufficiently interested in the subject to reach beyond the present survey, it is not unreasonable to hope that not a few will be able to read French. French is one of the most difficult languages to speak and write correctly: its grammar has been aptly called in Bartonian terms "the grammar nobody knows." But for people of English speech it is one of the easiest to read.

Except when otherwise noted, books in English are available both in London and in New York; books in French, in Paris.

✑ INTRODUCTION

I.   GENERAL HISTORIES (WORLD AND EUROPEAN)

I agree with Arnold Toynbee that purely national histories give but a mutilated and deceptive view of their subject: "What should they know of England who only England know?" So, I recommend in the first place *general* histories, in which periods rather than territorial units are the centers of study. I found, for instance, that the best one-volume presentation of Napoleon's career is Georges Lefebvre's, in the series *Peuples et civilisations.*

The Cambridge Medieval History (8 vols.), ed. J. B. Bury *et al., The Cambridge Modern History* (13 vols.), inspired by Lord Acton, *L'histoire générale du quatrième siècle à nos jours* (12 vols.; 1896– 1901), ed. Ernest Lavisse and Alfred Rambaud, are monuments which have suffered at the hands of time yet remain imposing and useful. My objection to them is that they are a mosaic of detached chapters by different authors. This method, while it offers greater guarantees of competence, fails to provide the synthetic view that we seek. In the histories listed below a whole period, as a rule, is treated in a single volume by a single writer.

Gustave Glotz, *Histoire générale* (1925 *et seq.*); *Clio, Introduction aux études historiques* (1934 *et seq.*); Eugène Cavaignac, *Histoire du monde* (1926 *et seq.*); Louis Halphen and Philippe Sagnac (eds.), *Peuples et civilisations* (1926 *et seq.*); Maurice Crouzet, *Histoire générale des civilisations;* W. L. Langer, *The Rise of Modern Europe* (20 vols.; 1934 *et seq.*), one of the very best; excellent illustrations and bibliographies.

II.   GENERAL HISTORIES OF FRANCE BY SINGLE WRITERS

Louis-Pierre Anquetil (1723–1806), *Histoire de France* (1803 *et seq.*) is mentioned because in my childhood this venerable and perfectly insipid compilation, with proper supplements, was still in use. A curious case of undeserved longevity. Time will tell, but it may take a long time.

Henri Martin, *Histoire de France* (1836 *et seq.*); constantly revised and brought up to date, it was a bastion of *petit bourgeois* liberalism for three generations. Whoso wants to know the average Frenchman should glance at Henri Martin.

François Guizot (1787–1874), *Histoire de France* (5 vols.; 1870– 1875). This is an oddity. The great philosophical historian (*Histoire de la civilisation en Europe, Histoire de la civilisation en France*) in his extreme old age wrote his *Histoire de France racontée à mes petits-enfants,* which, because unpretentious narrative rather than doctrinaire, reached a much wider public than his more scholarly work.

It was long a standard work in America. The 1875 edition, which I have been using, is very pleasantly illustrated.

The one large-scale history of France by a single writer which deserves to survive is Jules Michelet (1798–1874), *Jusqu'au XVIe siècle* (12 vols.; 1833–1846); *Révolution française* (7 vols.; 1847–1853); *Temps modernes* (7 vols.; 1857–1867); *XIXe siècle* (3 vols.; 1875). Its unique value lies not in its information, but in its spirit and its style. In its pages bones gather flesh and blood, the past actually lives—at times a weird phantasmagoric life. The summits in that enormous epic are the chapters on Joan of Arc—the most touching, the most convincing in the vast literature on the subject; and those on the great popular "days" of the Revolution. It may not be sober history, but it is an evocation that historians cannot ignore. (This might be said also of Victor Hugo's romances, *Notre-Dame de Paris,* 1830, *Les Misérables,* 1862, *Quatre-vingt-treize,* 1873.) Perhaps the age of such titanic undertakings is over. We must note, however, that Arnold Toynbee and Will Durant have wrestled with even more impossible tasks.

The briefer one-man's histories—apart from textbooks, some of them of very high merit—are in fact pictures of the author's mind with the tapestry of French annals as a background. To this class belong: Jacques Bainville, *Histoire de France* (1924), a sensational best seller, committed to Royalism, yet judicious; Julien Benda, *Esquisse d'une histoire des Français dans leur volonté d'être une nation* (1932); Charles Seignobos, *Histoire sincère de la nation française: Esquisse d'une histoire de l'évolution du peuple français* (1933); Albert Bayet, *Histoire de France* (1938); Pierre Gaxotte, *Histoire de France* (2 vols.; 1951); André Maurois, *The Miracle of France* (1948), which apart from its literary charm, is truly miraculous because the author, constantly intelligent, succeeds in concealing his own mind. Many of his section heads are questions: "Why" and "How." The questions are clear; the answers are guarded. A revised edition appeared in 1957, under the title *A History of France.* His *Histoire de la France,* Paris 1957, is a brief survey of French culture, lavishly illustrated.

III.   GENERAL HISTORIES OF FRANCE: COLLECTIVE AUTHORSHIP

Ernest Lavisse (ed.), *Histoire de France depuis les origines jusqu'à la Révolution* (9 tomes, 18 vols.), *Histoire de France contemporaine* (to the Treaty of Versailles) (10 vols.). Each contributor, as a rule, discusses a period in a "half-tome," or volume. Very scholarly. Good working bibliographies. Moderate republican tendency, "just left of center." The work of Lavisse himself ("Louis XIV"; "General Conclusion") is outstanding.

Gabriel Hanotaux (ed.), *Histoire de la nation française, des origines préhistoriques jusqu'à nos jours* (15 vols.; 1920). Less conventional in material make-up than Lavisse's, a trifle on the showy side. Divided not into periods but into special histories (political, military, religious, economic, etc.). Definitely "right of center."

Frantz Funck-Brentano (ed.), *L'histoire de France racontée à tous,* translated as *The National History of France* (11 vols.). The first two volumes, by the editor, and the three volumes on the Revolution and Napoleon by Louis Madelin are the best known. For the educated general public. Very readable, but decidedly not free from bias. To the Treaty of Versailles.

G. Lefebvre, Ch. H. Pouthas, M. Baumont, *Histoire de France pour tous les Français* (2 vols.; 1950).

Histoire du peuple français. 4 vols.: Régine Pernoud, *Des origines au moyen age* (1951); Edmond Pognon, *De Jeanne d'Arc à Louis XIV* (1952); Pierre Lafue, *De la régence aux trois révolutions* (1952); Georges Duveau, *De 1848 à nos jours* (1953). Beautifully printed, and excellent writing.

Marcel Reinhard, and Norbert Dufourq (ed.), *Histoire de France,* Vol. I, to 1715; Vol. II, to 1945 (1954). Richly illustrated.

IV. GENERAL SURVEYS OF FRENCH CULTURE

a) *Factual*

Arthur Tilley (ed.), *Medieval France, a Companion to French Studies,* and *Modern France* (1922). An unsurpassed epitome. It is to some extent brought up to date by: Julian Park (ed.), *The Culture of France in our Time* (Ithaca, N.Y., 1954).

b) *Interpretations of French Culture*

A dangerous subject if you venture beyond the *Snakes in Iceland* brevity. The books I have found most stimulating were first written in German. Good reasons could be adduced for this apparent paradox. We are so familiar with the Anglo-American point of view that books presenting it are apt to be unprofitable. The Germans are less insular than we are, and their feelings toward France are both more intense and more ambivalent. Ernst Robert Curtius, *Die Französische Kultur* (1930); *The Civilization of France* (1932). Very sympathetic. Paul Cohen-Portheim, *The Spirit of France* (1933). Also very sympathetic. Friedrich Sieburg, *Gott in Frankreich* (*Dieu est-il français?,* lamely translated *Who Are These French?*) (1932). A great Nazi journalist with historical insight. Should be compared with: Karl Epting, *Die Französische Sendungbewusstein im 19. und 20. Jahrhundert* (*France's Consciousness of her Mission, 19th and 20th Centuries*) (Heidelberg, 1952). Unfortunately, not translated. Herbert Luethy, *Frankreichs Uhren gehen anders* (*The Clocks of France Keep Their Own Time*), misleadingly translated *France Against Herself* (1955). Sharply critical, but with a background of sympathy which the French appreciated. I disagree with the main thesis expressed in the German title; but the book is well informed, searching, and illuminating.

In the perilous middle road between information and interpretation will be found my four-volume *History of French Civilization: French Civilization from Its Origins to the Close of the Middle Ages* (1920);

The Life and Death of an Ideal: France in the Classical Age (1928–1956); *French Civilization in the Nineteenth Century* (1914); *The France of Tomorrow* (1942).

BOOK I: THE ORIGINS

I. THE LAND

Michelet was the first to follow Montesquieu's indication and present the geographic substratum of history. His *Tableau de la France* (Vol. II of his *History*) is captivating because frankly impressionistic; P. Vidal de la Blache, *Tableau de la géographie de la France* (Tome I, Vol. I, in Ernest Lavisse's *Histoire de France*); Jean Brunhes, *Géographie humaine de la France* (1920), and P. Deffontaines, *Géographie politique et economique de la France* (1926). These form Vols. I and II of Hanotaux's *Histoire de la nation française*. P. Vidal de la Blache, and L. Gallois (eds.), *Géographie universelle* (Tome VI, 3 vols.) *La France;* Emm. de Martonne, *France physique* (1942); Albert Demangeon, *France economique et humaine* (Vol. I, 1946; Vol. II, 1948); Ernest Granger, *La France, son visage, son peuple, ses ressources* (1932); P. Jousset, *La France, géographie illustrée* (2 vols.; 1920); Pierre Deffontaines, and Mariel Jean-Brunhes Delamarre, *Atlas aérien*, text, maps, and profuse aerial photographs. A new and most helpful survey of the country. In course of publication. Five volumes announced; two published by 1957.

There are innumerable richly illustrated books about France; as a collection I do not believe that *Sites et monuments,* published by Touring Club de France (33 parts in 6 vols., 1900–1906), has ever been surpassed.

In English: H. Ormsby, *France: A Regional and Economic Geography* (1931); Raoul Blanchard and Millicent Todd, *Geography of France.* And the chapters on France in the following: Raoul Blanchard and Raymond E. Crist, *A Geography of Europe* (1935); Jean Gottmann, *A Geography of Europe* (New York, 1954); George W. Hoffman, and others, *Geography of Europe* (New York, 1953).

II. THE RACE

W. Z. Ripley, *The Races of Europe* (1899), a richly informed and very intelligent book, has not been superseded; not because it could not be improved upon in the course of six decades, but because the study of race as a factor in European history has lost caste. Anthropology, which at first meant the study of stocks or breeds within the human race, is now chiefly concerned with cultural patterns. Among many others Jacques Barzun has done outstanding work in exposing the Boulainvilliers-Gobineau-Vacher de Lapouge-H. S. Chamberlain-Madison Grant-Adolf Hitler fallacy: Jacques Barzun, *The French Race* (New York, 1932), (history of the Idea before the Revolution) and *Race: A Study in Modern Superstition* (1937).

III.   THE LANGUAGE

Ferdinand Brunot, *Histoire de la langue française des origines à nos jours* (13 vols.; 1905–1953), completed by Alexis François and Charles Bruneau.

For a survey of the linguistic factor in modern history and politics, see Antoine Meillet, *Les langues dans l'Europe nouvelle* (1918); and Antoine Meillet (ed.), *Les langues du monde* (1924; new ed. 1952).

On the Celtic, Gallo-Roman, and Frankish periods the classics are: Henri d'Arbois de Jubainville, *Cours de littérature celtique* (12 vols.; 1883–1902), with a useful epitome: *Les Celtes depuis les temps les plus reculés* (jusqu') *à l'an 100 avant notre ère* (1904); Camille Jullian, *Histoire de la Gaule* (8 vols.; 1908–1926); N. M. Fustel de Coulanges, *Histoire des institutions politiques de l'ancienne France* (6 vols.; 1875–1892).

For special points see bibliographies of general histories. I mention four books only on account of their intrinsic excellence and their unusual point of view: Samuel Dill, *Roman Society in the Last Century of the Western Empire* (1910), a model of social history. Scholarly light turned on the Stygian murk of the period. Gaston Paris, *Histoire poétique de Charlemagne* (1865). I.e. the figure of Charlemagne in poetry: the disputed border between history and legend; cf. King Arthur, William Tell, Joan of Arc, Napoleon. Émile Mâle, *La fin du paganisme en Gaule et les plus anciennes basiliques chrétiennes* (1950), in the same spirit as his great series *L'art religieux en France, vide infra.* Henri Pirenne, *Mahomet et Charlemagne* (*Mohammed and Charlemagne*) (1939). In this posthumous work the great Belgian medieval scholar advances a startling hypothesis as to the end of the Roman world, its causes and its date.

BOOK II: MEDIEVAL FRANCE

I.   INTRODUCTIONS

Louis Halphen, *Introduction aux études d'histoire du moyen âge* (3d ed.; Rev. by Yves Renouard, 1951). Joseph Calmette, *Le monde féodal* (New ed. rev. with the assistance of Ch. Higounet [*Clio* Collection] 1951).

II.   TEXTS

France is fortunate in the possession of four great chroniclers, Villehardouin, Joinville, Froissart, and Commynes, radically different in spirit and style. These give the general reader direct contact with the life of the times. There are innumerable editions, both in English and in French. In French the latest and most convenient is: Albert Pauphilet, and Edmond Pognon, *Historiens et chroniqueurs du moyen âge: Robert de Clari, Villehardouin, Joinville, Commynes* (1952). Others are: Charles V. Langlois, *La vie française au moyen âge* (4 vols.; 1926–1928). Source books: well selected passages with scholarly introductions. A. Luchaire, *La societé française au temps de Philippe-*

Auguste (1909). A fascinating book, ably translated by E. B. Krehbiel.

As an example of the biographical approach at its best, free from any doctrinaire bias: Amy Kelly, *Eleanor of Aquitaine and the Four Kings* (Cambridge, Mass., 1950).

The following books I found stimulating, sound in the main, but not altogether safe: *Caveat Lector!* H. O. Taylor, *The Classical Heritage of the Middle Ages* (1911) and *The Mediaeval Mind: A History of the Development of Thought and Emotion in the Middle Ages* (2 vols.; Cambridge, Mass., 1949). Books of unusual breadth, insight, and charm, although somewhat puzzling in method and purpose. Henry Adams, *Mont-Saint-Michel and Chartres* (Boston, 1904–1913), a classic: rather as a satire on modern civilization than as an interpretation of the Middle Ages. With the main thesis, medieval unity, I thoroughly disagree.

The most luminous and the most nebulous episode in the Middle Ages is the career of Joan of Arc. *Roma locuta est:* Joan is a saint, yet mysteries and ambiguities survive. I believe that Jules Michelet gives the most credible version of that miraculous story. A new translation with introduction and notes appeared in 1957 (*Joan of Arc,* translated by Albert Guérard, Ann Arbor, Mich.). But the careful student should read it with, at his elbow, Gustave Rudler's *Michelet historien de Jeanne d'Arc* (2 vols.; 1926), and also—*Advocatus Diaboli,* an indispensable personage—Anatole France's *Vie de Jeanne d'Arc* (1908). Fortunately, the essential document is available to the general reader: W. P. Barrett's translation, *The Trial of Jeanne d'Arc,* with essay and copious notes by Pierre Champion, a noted specialist in the period (1932). (The minutes of the second trial [rehabilitation], which have also appeared in English, are of minor interest.)

Of commanding importance are the works of Émile Mâle on religious art in medieval France and the sources of its inspiration. The first remains the best: *L'art religieux en France au XIIIème siècle* (1898; many later editions). The thirteenth century was the apex of the Middle Ages and perhaps "the greatest of centuries." But the others, *Religious Art in the XIIth Century, Religious Art at the End of the Middle Ages,* are useful complements. The central thought goes back to Victor Hugo (*Lui! Toujours lui!*) in *Notre-Dame de Paris:* Hugo begat E. E. Viollet-le-Duc, *Dictionnaire raisonné de l'architecture française du XIe au XVIe siècles* (1854–1868). But John Ruskin arrived independently at the same conclusion: architecture is the Bible of the people (*The Seven Lamps of Architecture, The Stones of Venice, The Bible of Amiens*).

While there were many good books on commerce and industry in the Middle Ages, with E. Levasseur and G. Fagniez as pioneers, little had been done about agriculture. Hence the importance of Marc Bloch's great work, *Les caractères originaux de l'histoire rurale française* (1931; new edition with supplement, 1951–56).

Staid historians will frown at the inclusion of anything so unscholarly as love. Yet "a revolution in love," if it actually happened, would mean more to mankind than the democratic revolution or the industrial. Hence the importance of studies by two of the keenest minds in the present age: C. S. Lewis, *The Allegory of Love* (London, 1936), mostly about English literature but based on *The Romance of the Rose*, which, far more than *The Divine Comedy*, was the central classic of the Middle Ages; and Denis de Rougemont, *L'amour et l'occident* (1946; *Love in the Western World*, 1956).

BOOK III: CLASSICAL FRANCE

The political history of the period will be found in the standard works listed in the Introduction. Among the "monuments" should be mentioned Gabriel Hanotaux's *Histoire du cardinal de Richelieu* (1896). The work was interrupted for many years and was completed with the collaboration of Duc de la Force (new ed.; 6 vols.; 1932). Richelieu, far more than Louis XIV, was the central figure in the formation of the absolute monarchy.

The following I found stimulating (irritation being at times a legitimate and profitable form of stimulation): Maurice Andrieux, *Henri IV dans ses années pacifiques* (1954), by no means a debunking book, but not a hagiography either. It brings out the subtle shades, and the dark shadows, in Henry's attaching and perplexing personality. Louis Bertrand, *Louis XIV* (1923); this highly romantic hymn of praise, which would greatly have puzzled the Grand Monarch himself, started a lively controversy. Among the rebuttals: Félix Gaiffe, *L'Envers du grand siècle* (1924), the seamy side of the great century. Pierre Gaxotte, *Le siècle de Louis XV* (*Louis the Fifteenth and His Times*) (1934). A bold paradox: Louis XV, a truly great king, holding himself in reserve in case "the old machine" should break down and dying just at the moment he was assuming direct control.

The whole classical age was par excellence the age of Society, from the court of Francis I to the *salons* of Madame Geoffrin and Madame Necker. So, it is extremely difficult to separate political history from social history; or from the history of ideas, for Society, in those days, was intelligent; or even from the history of religion, for many of those aristocratic people, whose thought was surprisingly free, whose lives were frequently unedifying, were at the same time deeply concerned with their spiritual destiny.

As a model of cultural history: Paul Hazard, *La crise de la conscience européenne, 1680–1715* (3 vols.; 1935); conscience here is *consciousness*. Hazard had completed just before his death in 1944 a sequel, *Les origines intellectuelles de l'Europe contemporaine: le dix-huitième siècle de Montesquieu à Lessing*.

The same period is studied, mainly through literature, by: Arthur Tilley, *The Decline of the Age of Louis XIV, 1687–1715* (Cambridge, Eng., 1929), a very sound piece of work; W. H. Lewis, *The Splendid Century: Life in the France of Louis XIV* (New York, 1954), almost all aspects of life in that great period; the chapter on the Church longest and best; lucid and thoughtful as well as picturesque; excellent notes for further reading. V. du Bled, *La société française du XVIème siècle au XXème siècle* (9 series; 1903 *et seq.*), remains useful.

F. Bonnefon, *La société française du XVIIème siècle* (1907), and *La société française du XVIIIème siècle* (1914), *Lectures extraites des mémoires et correspondances*. Louis Ducros, *La société française au XVIIIème siècle d'après les mémoires et correspondances du temps* (1922), good selections; but the letters of Madame de Sévigné and Voltaire, the memoirs of Saint-Simon, deserve to be read if not *in extenso* at any rate in larger doses than in these meritorious books of extracts. M. Magendie, *La politesse mondaine au XVIIème siècle* (2 vols.; 1925), important bibliography, illustrated. Henri Carré, *La France sous Louis XV* (1891), solidly informed and very well presented.

I. RELIGION

Georges Goyau, *Histoire religieuse* (in Hanotaux's *Histoire de la nation française* (1922), Catholic. Henri Bremond, *Histoire littéraire du sentiment religieux en France depuis la fin des guerres de religion jusqu'à nos jours* (1916 et seq.), a masterpiece which unfortunately failed to conquer the American public. (*A Literary History of Religious Thought in France*. Vol. I, *Devout Humanism* [New York, 1928]). Abbé Bremond's orthodoxy had to be "cleared," but his keenness of thought never was under suspicion; neither was the charm of his style. André Ménabréa, *St. Vincent de Paul, le maître des hommes d'état* (1944), a good biography. But above all an interesting thesis: with Vincent, a peerless organizer, Christian charity assumed the form of great *services;* a Christian Socialist, he was almost a minister of public welfare. Had the nominally Christian state been more deeply influenced by St. Vincent's spirit, the rugged and realistic individualism of the next two centuries might have been mitigated.

II. THE ENLIGHTENMENT

A very convenient and almost too readable invitation to learning is George R. Havens' *The Age of Ideas* (1955).

For better acquaintance with Voltaire the ever-serviceable André Maurois has provided *Voltaire,* a brief biography (New York, 1932), and *The Living Thoughts of Voltaire,* introduction and extracts (1939). But nothing compares with Gustave Lanson's marvelous epitome, *Voltaire.* The nuclear works of Voltaire himself are his *Dictionnaire philosophique,* a breviary for inquiring minds, and the inevitable *Candide,* were it only to disprove the fallacy of modern conservatives that the Enlightenment was foolishly optimistic.

Diderot is at long last coming into his own: Lester G. Crocker, *The Embattled Philosopher* (Ann Arbor, 1954); Arthur M. Wilson, *Diderot: The Testing Years* (Oxford, 1957).

Irving Babbitt, *Rousseau and Romanticism* (Boston, 1919), one of those great and perverse works with which it is highly profitable to wrestle. Carl Becker, *The Heavenly City of the Eighteenth Century Philosophers* (New Haven, Conn., 1932), a searching mind applied to a great subject.

The division in 1750 in our text, like all chronological divisions, is highly artificial. The monarchy, Society, the Church remained ex-

ternally the same not merely until 1789 but far beyond. The Enlightenment survived in Condorcet and Beaumarchais and in the *Idéologues*
so hated (because dreaded) by Napoleon. To restore the sense of continuity, there is Alexis de Tocqueville's *L'ancien régime et la révolution* (1856): a masterpiece lesser in bulk and influence than his
Démocratie en Amérique but perhaps even more cogent in thought.
Louis XIV was already an equalitarian Jacobin; the Jacobins enthroned
a twelve-headed king, who continued the spirit and methods of Louis
XIV.

BOOK IV: THE BOURGEOIS-LIBERAL REVOLUTION (1750–1848)

On the twilight of the Ancient Regime: Frantz Funck-Brentano,
L'ancien régime (1926), an excellent survey of the whole field leading
to a sympathetic and perhaps too idyllic presentation of Louis XVI's
reign: Talleyrand's *"douceur de vivre."*

As a corrective H. Taine's powerful and somber *L'ancien régime*,
first volume of his *Origines de la France contemporaine* (1876).
Maurice Souriau, *Louis XVI et la révolution* (1893), in the same
series as H. Carré's *La France sous Louis XV;* this is not a narrative
but a total picture of the epoch, scholarly, well informed, well
illustrated. Georges Lemaître, *Beaumarchais* (1949), one of our half-
forgotten founding fathers; his *Mariage de Figaro* (1783), a symptomatic skirmish and a living classic.

J. Christopher Herold: *Mistress to an Age* (New York, 1958), a
searching and rewarding study of Mme de Staël's life, works, and influence.

Lafayette is as symbolical of liberalism as Richelieu of absolutism:
key figures both. A spate of works about Lafayette, not a few super-
cilious: he was honest and chivalrous, therefore naïve. Brand Whitlock's *La Fayette* (2 vols.; 1929), on the contrary, keeps true to the
tradition of Washington himself and is sympathetic to "the hero of
two worlds." A well-written book which, with some corrections, should
have become an American classic. Louis R. Gottschalk, a professional
historian, as Brand Whitlock was not, is engaged in a large scale
biography of Lafayette.

I. THE REVOLUTION

The official masters of Revolution scholarship, for several decades,
were F. A. Aulard and Albert Mathiez, both left of center but not
in agreement. Present-day students of the period are still arrayed as
disciples of either. Their essential works are available in English: F. A.
Aulard, *The French Revolution, a Political History* (4 vols.; 1910);
Albert Mathiez, *The French Revolution* (1928), *The Fall of Robespierre* (1927), *The Thermidorian Reaction* (1931), *Le Directoire*,
which he left incomplete, was published posthumously in 1934. Jean
Jaurès's *La révolution* (in *Histoire socialiste*, of which he was general
editor) has been republished by Albert Mathiez (8 vols.; 1922–1924):
a deserved tribute to the scholarly merits of the great orator.

II.   THE GREAT CONTROVERSY

The leading nineteenth-century historians of the Revolution were on the liberal, democratic, and even radical side: François Mignet, 1824; Adolphe Thiers, 1823–1827; Jules Michelet, 1847–1856; Alphonse de Lamartine (*Histoire des Girondins*), 1847; Louis Blanc, 1847–1862; Edgar Quinet, 1865. All had conspicuous merits; all, except Michelet's, are dust.

The antirevolutionary crusade began with Edmund Burke's *Reflections on the French Revolution* (1790) (organic growth, the wisdom of prejudice, the glamour of the storied past). Burke deeply influenced Carlyle (1837). In France, L. Mortimer-Ternaux, *Histoire de la terreur* (8 vols.; 1863–1881), a scholarly study, but fiercely biassed. Hippolyte Taine, in his *Origines de la France contemporaine*, Vol. II, *La révolution; l'anarchie* (1878); Vol. III, *La conquête jacobine* (1881); Vol. IV, *Le gouvernement révolutionnaire* (1884). Louis Madelin, *La révolution française* (1916), in Fr. Funck-Brentano's *National History of France: The French Revolution*.) Pierre Gaxotte, *La révolution française* (1928); *The French Revolution* (1932).

An essay of Goldwin Smith converted me to a third way, or *via media:* the liberals were right against the reactionaries; but, from the liberal point of view, the Revolution was a disaster for France and for the rest of the world.

III.   NAPOLEON

The monument, in this case, is Adolphe Thiers, *Histoire du consulat et de l'empire* (1845–1862). In many ways it is unsurpassable. A labor of love, but not uncritical (especially after the advent of Napoleon III). A limited but sharp and brilliant intelligence. An experienced statesman, extremely competent in matters of administration and finances. An amateur strategist, who thought he understood Napoleon's battles better than Napoleon himself. Personally acquainted with many survivors of the imperial era.

The Adolphe Thiers of our days is Louis Madelin with his *Histoire du consulat et de l'empire* (16 vols.). He had the advantage of a richer and better-sifted documentation, including Napoleon's enormous correspondence. Writes well for an academician, but cannot match either Thiers's lucidity or his occasional eloquence; more hopelessly tinged than Thiers with Napoleon-worship, although he could recognize his hero's fatal mistakes, his quarrel with the Papacy and his Spanish venture. Good bibliographies. Apart from his *magnum opus,* did excellent work on special points, *Fouché, La Rome de Napoléon,* etc.

Perhaps a more durable monument is Albert Sorel, *L'Europe et la révolution française* (8 vols.; 1885–1904). Sorel assumes that in the eyes of Europe the Revolution and the Empire formed a single whole. The masterpiece of diplomatic history; even though the writer compels admiration rather than conviction.

Out of the hundred thousand titles, *mas o menos,* I venture to select among single-volume histories: Georges Lefebvre (1935). In English:

F. M. Kircheisen, *Napoleon* (1932); Emil Ludwig's *Napoleon* based on good authorities, Kircheisen, Pariset, won exactly the kind of popularity that it deserved.

Napoleon in his own words: J. M. Thompson, *Napoleon Self-Revealed* (1934), an excellent selection of three hundred typical letters; R. M. Johnston, *The Corsican: A Diary of Napoleon's Life in His Own Words* (Boston, 1910); F. M. Kircheisen, *Memoirs of Napoleon* (English edition), *Napoleon's Autobiography* (American) (1931); Somerset de Chair (ed.), *Napoleon, Emperor of the French: Memoirs* (New York, 1950), sole originality: changes the Caesarian third person to the first; J. Christophe Herold, *The Mind of Napoleon* (1955), Napoleon's views rather than his autobiography; in analytical, not chronological, order; well edited.

As the weirdest books on Napoleon by authors of repute, I nominate: Dmitri Merezhkovsky, *Napoleon the Man,* and *The Life of Napoleon* (1929), both "funny without being vulgar." But Léon Bloy, Elie Faure, and Joseph Delteil are not far behind.

The legend of Napoleon (i.e., his epic and almost mystic impact on popular imagination) is of far greater importance in history than his personality. On this subject, at the same time familiar and neglected: Philippe Gonnard, *Les origines de la légende napoléonienne: L'oeuvre historique de Napoléon à Sainte-Hélène* (1906); *The Exile of St. Helena: The Last Phase in Fact and Fiction* (London and Philadelphia, 1909); Napoleon casting himself—a masterly paradox—as the apostle and martyr of democracy. Albert Guérard, *Reflections on the Napoleonic Legend* (1924). Napoleon, himself a great romantic poet, takes his place among the great romantic myths: Prometheus, Don Juan, Faust, the Wandering Jew. Neither of these books on the legend is "debunking"; both seek to understand and appraise a phenomenon which, even though detached from the material plane, had great material consequences. Pieter Geyl, *Napoleon: For and Against* (New Haven, Conn., 1949), a masterly critical survey of French historiography from Chateaubriand to Georges Lefebvre. Conclusion: "The argument goes on."

IV. THE CONSTITUTIONAL MONARCHY

On the Restoration the "monument" is Achille Tenaille de Vaulabelle, *Histoire des deux Restaurations jusqu'à l'avènement de Louis-Philippe* (8 vols.; 1844). The "monument" is somewhat faded, dusty, and deserted; but there is permanent merit in a record by a contemporary if he be intelligent and not too partisan.

On Louis-Philippe, Paul Thureau-Dangin, *Histoire de la monarchie de juillet* (7 vols.; 1884 *et seq.*), a fine example of bourgeois and academic history, in perfect harmony with the period described. Still illuminating, even though not dazzlingly.

The three men who had the greatest influence under the Constitutional Monarchy (1814–1848), Chateaubriand, Saint-Simon, Lamennais, are not so well known in the English-speaking world as they deserve. The never-failing André Maurois provided a good *Chateau-*

briand, Poet, Statesman, Lover (1938); and his biographies of George Sand (*Lelia*) and Victor Hugo (*Olympio*) throw a great deal of light on the period. On Saint-Simon we have F. E. Manuel, *The New World of Henri St. Simon* (1956). Of the greatest of the three, the master of religious and democratic thought whose primacy was felt even by more successful men, Lamennais, there is no adequate treatment. For the materialist, whether Marxian or Manchesterian, he is a dreamer; for the orthodox, a dangerous heretic; for the rationalist, merely a mystic. A great, strange, and somber flame.

Stendhal (Henri Beyle), at least in *Le rouge et le noir* (1830) and in his posthumous *Lucien Leuwen* (1894), and Balzac, throughout his teeming *Comédie humaine* (1833, planned; 1841, named), afford insights into the contemporary scene that no archives can provide. If history means resurrection, these two (and, in some of their works, Victor Hugo, George Sand, Alexandre Dumas, and even Eugène Sue) rank among the great historians.

BOOK V: MODERN FRANCE: 1848–1945

The "monuments": Pierre de la Gorce, *Histoire de la seconde république* (2 vols.; 1887), *Histoire du Second Empire* (7 vols.; 1894–1905), with a substantial postscript, *Napoléon III et sa politique* (1933). "Old-fashioned" history at its very best; a classic which Theodore Roosevelt—almost alone in America—knew and admired.

In comparison: Taxile Delord, *Histoire illustrée du second empire* (6 vols.; 1869–1876) is blatant journalism. However, its very partisanship makes it a document; and its abundant illustrations—cartoons and portraits—frankly popular, retain some value. Émile Ollivier, *L'empire libéral: Etudes, récits, souvenirs* (17 vols.; 1895–1915), a republican who rallied to the Empire—or to whom the Empire rallied. Like Alexander Kerensky he spent forty years demonstrating that his few months of rule, ending in catastrophe, deserved a better fate. But the work is more than an enormous *apologia pro vita sua*: it is an indispensable testimony. Émile Zola, *Les Rougon-Macquart: Histoire naturelle et sociale d'une famille sous le second empire* (20 vols.; 1871–1893). There was in Zola a conscientious observer, halfway between the reporter and the sociologist; most of his novels are valuable monographs (the Central Market, a department store, the mines, the railroads, prostitution). Among the most "historical," *La curée* (1871) (*The Kill, the Scramble, The Rush for the Spoils*); *Son excellence Eugène Rougon* (1876), i.e., Eugène Rouher, the Vice-Emperor; *Germinal* (1885), among the first proletarian novels, and still among the greatest; *La débâcle* (1892), the war of 1870–1871 and the Commune.

Briefer works: Octave Aubry, *Le Second Empire* (1938), *The Second Empire* (1940), encyclopedic, judicious, alert; the model of a substantial and readable introduction. Paul Guénot, *Napoléon III* (2 vols.; 1933–1934); an excellent epitome; not Bonapartist, but very favorable to Napoleon III. Philip Guedalla, *The Second Empire* (1922), a brilliant but vacuous essay in the early Aldous Huxley or Michael Arlen style. Extremely popular for a season, but nothing ages so fast as flippancy. I must add that Guedalla has done other work of much higher value, in particular *The Duke* (Wellington).

My own *Napoleon III* (Cambridge, Mass., 1943) is frankly an interpretation of the man, not a political or social history. I had been interested in the period for over thirty years: see *French Prophets of Yesterday: Religious Thought in French Literature under the Second Empire* (1913); condensed in *Napoleon III: A Great Life in Brief* (1955) more purely biographical.

There has been an abundant literature on the Second Empire in the last twenty years, mostly favorable. (The change may be due to the waning of the Bismarck legend.) Among the most useful: Franklin Charles Palm, *England and Napoleon III: A Study in the Rise of a Utopian Dictator* (Durham, N.C., 1948); Ivor Guest, *Napoleon III in England* (1952), an unpretentious, thorough, and illuminating monograph; Lynn M. Case, *French Opinion on War and Diplomacy during the Second Empire* (Philadelphia, 1954), how an authoritarian regime, which had—loosely—muzzled the press, attempted to keep in touch with public opinion.

I. THE THIRD REPUBLIC

An unfinished cathedral: Gabriel Hanotaux, *Histoire de la France contemporaine* (4 vols.; 1903–1908); *Contemporary France* (4 vols.; 1903–1909), intended to cover the period 1870–1900, but stopped with Gambetta's death, 1882. A trained historian, a diplomat, in close touch with the high personnel of the regime, and a very readable writer.

Jacques Chastenet, with equal qualifications—journalist, sociologist, historian—has undertaken a six-volume history of the Third Republic, 1870–1940. Published so far: *L'enfance de la troisième, 1870–1879* (1952); *La république des républicains, 1879–1893* (1954); *La république triomphante, 1893–1906* (1955).

Shorter works: Jacques Bainville, *La troisième république, 1870–1935* (1935); *The Third Republic* (1935). Monarchist, *"Action française,"* but without the hidebound doctrinairism of Charles Maurras or the truculence of Léon Daudet. D. W. Brogan, *The Development of Modern France* (English title); *France under the Republic 1870–1939* (American) (1940), a very fine achievement: full, sane, readable. Purely political, not cultural or social. Brogan shares with Siegfried the distinction of being an authority both on the United States and on France; he shares with no one the distinction of having a son named Vercingetorix. His recent *The French Nation: From Napoleon to Pétain, 1814–1940*, will be found a very valuable introduction. His *French Personalities and Problems* (New York, 1947) contains too many (27) brief, disconnected essays but is stimulating. A true friend of France: loyal, but critical and candid.

II. RELIGION

A. Debidour, *Histoire des rapports de l'église et de l'état en France. I. De 1789 à 1870; II. Sous la troisième république.* (2 vols.; 1898 *et seq.*), abundant and convenient collection of facts; useful bibliographies; marred by polemical tone. Adrien Dansette, *Histoire religieuse de la France contemporaine de la révolution à la troisième république* (2 vols.; 1952), from the point of view of a democrat and a Catholic. André Latreille and André Siegfried, *Les forces religieuses et la vie politique* (1951).

Two earlier studies, although no longer up to date, will be consulted with profit: G. Weill, "Le catholicisme français," *Revue de synthèse historique,* December, 1907; and Paul Sabbatier, *L'orientation religieuse de la France actuelle* (1911).

III. THE DREYFUS CASE

Of the innumerable books on the subject (Joseph Reinach's is the "monument"), I recommend Nicholas Halasz, *Captain Dreyfus: The Story of a Mass Hysteria* (1955), very good on the case itself, although surprisingly weak on the historical background: a thorough and convincing story fringed with manifest boners. In *Personal Equation* (1948) I offered my own testimony, and a convenient scenario. Maurice Paléologue, *An Intimate Journal of the Dreyfus Case* (1957) is extremely disappointing.

IV. THE EVE OF WORLD WAR II

Alexander Werth, *The Twilight of France, 1933–1940,* just the point where intelligent journalism merges with contemporary history. C. Micaud, *The French Right and Nazi Germany, 1933–1939,* a hard-to-refute implementation of the famous slogan (possibly apocryphal in that form), "Rather Hitler than Blum!" Pierre Cot, *Triumph of Treason* (1944), a plea *pro domo,* very able and well documented. Seeks to disprove the assertion that the *Front Populaire* was responsible for the downfall three years later. (André Géraud) Pertinax, *Les fossoyeurs.* I. *Gamelin, Daladier, Reynaud;* II. *Pétain* (1943), a famous journalist, conservative and patriotic, confirms by implication the thesis of Micaud and Cot: guilt of *Front Populaire* not proven.

V. WORLD WAR II. FOUR POINTS OF VIEW

Robert Aron, *Histoire de Vichy* (1954), provisional, but at present indispensable. The author, a brilliant mind, admirably qualified for his impossible task. The point where contemporary history is still immersed in journalism. William L. Langer, *Our Vichy Gamble* (1947), by a historian of high repute who was in close touch with out State Department. A very able plea for a very poor case. Raoul Aglion, *L'épopée de la France combattante* (1943); with a preface by Jacques Maritain, a respected sponsor. General Charles de Gaulle, *Memoires* (3 vols.), a truly noble document and, the personal equation of the author once discounted, convincing. But the *advocatus diaboli* should not be ignored: Henri de Kérillis, *I Accuse de Gaulle* (1946), like Pertinax a very able and patriotic journalist.

✍ BOOK VI: SUMMARY AND CONCLUSION

On France today, the best general handbook is Alexander Werth, *France, 1940–1955,* with Introduction by G. D. H. Cole and appendix to 1956 (1956). Werth has been called to a visiting professorship of contemporary history: a good definition of his part in journalism. Abundant bibliographies and other apparatus. Perhaps a little more confusing than his prewar works, and more polemical in tone. The present scene makes it difficult for a writer to preserve his equanimity. Alexander Werth: *Lost Statesman. The Strange Story of Pierre Mendès-France,* 1958. A confused but vital study of a "might-have-been" and of a "might-yet-be." André Siegfried, *De la troisième à la quatrième république* (1956), the indomitable veteran at his sanest, mellowest, and best. David Thompson, *Democracy in France* (1952); Gordon Wright, *The Reshaping of French Democracy* (New York, 1952); François Goguel, *France under the Fourth Republic* (Ithaca, N.Y., 1952), Philip Williams, *Politics in Post-War France: Parties and the Constitution of the 4th Republic* (New York, 1954), very thorough; singled out by André Siegfried as the most adequate treatment of the subject. Maurice Duverger: *The French Political System,* Chicago, 1958. Brief and thorough. Not purely of retrospective interest: the problems which the Fourth failed to solve will be plaguing the Fifth. André Maurois (*comme toujours*) *La France change de visage* (1956), recommended as an antidote to Luethy's *France Against Herself;* David Schoenbrun, *As France Goes* (1957), journalistic but intelligent.

I. COLONIZATION

H. Blet, *Histoire de la colonisation française* (3 vols.; 1947–1950); H. Deschamps, *Méthodes et doctrines coloniales de la France: du 16e siècle à nos jours* (1953); Gilbert Grandval, *Ma mission au Maroc* (1956), the book best illustrating the four-cornered fight between natives, colonists, administrators, and Paris politicians.

The attempt to clear up the problem in my own mind will be found in *Fossils and Presences* (Stanford, Calif., 1957), Chapters 13, 14, 15, pp. 212–258.

For the disconcerting and disheartening phenomenon known as Poujadism—the transient symptom of a deep-seated *dis-ease*—see Pierre Poujade, *J'ai choisi le combat* (St. Céré, 1955). Intellectually as far below Hitler as Hitler is below Spengler, and Spengler below Toynbee.

II. ON EUROPEAN INTEGRATION

Richard Coudenhove-Kalergi, *Aus meinem Leben: Kampf um Europa* (Zürich, 1949); *Eine Idee erobert Europa* (Wien-München-Basel, 1958); Hans Bauer and H. G. Ritzel, *Kampf um Europa Von der Schweiz aus gesehen* (Zürich, 1945); Albert Guérard, *Europe Free and United* (Stanford, Calif., 1945).

Progress has been confused and slow; but the historical background, the cultural conditions, the problems ahead have not changed. "In the perspective of a thousand years," the line of development is clear.

Books of a philosophical nature and personal impressions have a chance of surviving. They are not, in the strict sense of the term, *history*. It is infinitely difficult to write contemporary history apart from chronicles and ephemeral comments. The serious student of France today is advised to keep up with such magazines as *Foreign Affairs* and *Current History;* with the weekly editions of *The* (London) *Times, The Manchester Guardian, Le Monde;* with the world affairs section of the Sunday *New York Times* and *New York Herald Tribune;* with the various yearbooks, some of which are excellent. I have found, for instance, the reports by Georges Lemaitre in *Collier's* particularly fair and reliable.

The Cultural Division of the French Embassy publishes a very useful bibliographical digest. It gives the list of twenty-one periodicals and seven research centers devoted to French history. The division will supply any qualified investigator with documents on contemporary affairs: inevitably *ex parte,* but presenting the French case with definiteness and accuracy.

But what information will avail? All governments have large staffs of specialists—our State Department and our Office of Strategic Services are teeming encyclopediae. Arnold Toynbee is running an Institute of World Affairs. Yet the governments—and Toynbee himself—are more bewildered than the man in the street. Wisdom needs and commands knowledge, but knowledge alone cannot bring wisdom.

III. A DECADE OF THE FIFTH REPUBLIC

Among recent general histories of France in the modern era are Gordon Wright, *France in Modern Times: 1760 to the Present* (Chicago, 1960), Paul Gagnon, *France Since 1789* (New York, 1964), Donald Harvey, *France Since the Revolution* (New York, 1968). On the Fifth Republic, Alexander Werth continues his valuable "professorship of contemporary history" in *De Gaulle* (Baltimore, 1967). Raymond Aron, *France, Steadfast and Changing* (Cambridge, Massachusetts, 1960) and Stanley Hoffmann *et al., In Search of France* (Cambridge, Massachusetts, 1963) provide two very different kinds of spirited views of the early Fifth Republic, the latter a collection of superb essays. Useful handbooks are Dorothy Pickles, *The Fifth French Republic* (New York, 1962), Roy Macridis and Bernard Brown, *The De Gaulle Republic,* (Homewood, Illinois, 1960), Nicholas Wahl, *The Fifth Republic* (New York, 1959), Philip Williams and Martin Harrison, *De Gaulle's Republic* (London, 1960). On foreign policy, most balanced is Alfred Grosser, *French Foreign Policy Under De Gaulle* (Boston, 1967). On the Algerian settlement, see Dorothy Pickles, *Algeria and France* (New York, 1963). On French society, Edward R. Tannenbaum, *The New France* (Chicago, 1961) and John C. Cairns, *France* (Englewood Cliffs, New Jersey, 1965) are interpretative essays. Laurence Wylie *et al., Chanzeaux: A Village in Anjou* (Cambridge, Massachusetts, 1966) continues the close work of observation begun by Wylie in *Village in the Vaucluse* (Cambridge, Massachusetts, 1957). On De Gaulle himself, Robert Aron, *Charles de Gaulle* (Paris, 1964) and Paul-Marie de la Gorce, *De Gaulle entre Deux Mondes* (Paris, 1964) and the brilliant essay by Stanley and Inge Hoffmann, "The Will to Grandeur: de Gaulle as Political Artist" in *Daedalus,* Summer, 1968, pp. 829–87. Several of the works cited contain more detailed bibliographies.